american sociological association

the **contexts** reader

third edition

edited by SYED ALI, Long Island University–Brooklyn

and PHILIP N. COHEN, University of Maryland

with help from LETTA PAGE

 W. W. NORTON & COMPANY • NEW YORK LONDON

W. W. Norton & Company has been independent since its founding in 1923, when William Warder Norton and Mary D. Herter Norton first published lectures delivered at the People's Institute, the adult education division of New York City's Cooper Union. The firm soon expanded its program beyond the Institute, publishing books by celebrated academics from America and abroad. By mid-century, the two major pillars of Norton's publishing program—trade books and college texts—were firmly established. In the 1950s, the Norton family transferred control of the company to its employees, and today—with a staff of four hundred and a comparable number of trade, college, and professional titles published each year—W. W. Norton & Company stands as the largest and oldest publishing house owned wholly by its employees.

Copyright © 2017, 2012, 2008 by W. W. Norton & Company, Inc.

Editor: Sasha Levitt
Assistant editors: Miranda Schonbrun, Rachel Taylor
Associate project editor: Michael Fauver
Production manager: Eric Pier-Hocking
Copyeditor: Theresa Kay
Proofreader: Debra Nichols
Manufacturing by Maple Press
Book design by Joan Greenfield

Library of Congress Cataloging-in-Publication Data

Names: Ali, Syed, 1968– editor. | Cohen, Philip N., editor. |
American Sociological Association, issuing body.
Title: The contexts reader / edited by Syed Ali, Long Island
University, Brooklyn, and Philip N. Cohen, University of
Maryland ; with contributions by Letta Page.
Description: Third edition. | New York : W.W. Norton &
Company, 2018. | Includes bibliographical references.
Identifiers: LCCN 2017060278 | ISBN 9780393639650
(pbk. : alk. paper)
Subjects: LCSH: Social problems.
Classification: LCC HN16 .C674 2018 | DDC 361.10973—dc23
LC record available at https://lccn.loc.gov/2017060278

W. W. Norton & Company, Inc., 500 Fifth Avenue,
New York, NY 10110

www.wwnorton.com

W. W. Norton & Company, Ltd., 15 Carlisle Street,
London W1D 3BS

contents

preface   vii

acknowledgments   viii

part 1: how to do sociology

1   Sociologists as Outliers / Joel Best   3

2   Viewpoints: How to Do Ethnography Right / Dana R. Fisher; Stefanie DeLuca, Susan Clampet-Lundquist, and Kathryn Edin; Annette Lareau and Aliya Hamid Rao   8

3   Sense and Nonsense about Surveys / Howard Schuman   17

4   This Revolution Is Not Being Televised / Michael A. Messner, Margaret Carlisle Duncan, and Nicole Willms   26

5   From Summer Camps to Glass Ceilings: The Power of Experiments / Michael J. Lovaglia   33

part 2: culture

6   Babes in Bikeland / Bjorn Christianson   45

7   English Soccer's Mysterious Worldwide Popularity / James P. Curley and Oliver Roeder   54

8   Tiger Girls on the Soccer Field / Hilary Levey Friedman   60

9   Opera Thugs and Passionate Fandom / Claudio E. Benzecry   66

10   Our Hard Days' Night / Simon J. Williams   72

part 3: crime and punishment

11   Viewpoints: Rape and Rape Culture / Lisa Wade; Brian Sweeney; Amelia Seraphia Derr; Michael A. Messner; Carol Burke   81

12   Becoming a Stickup Kid / Randol Contreras   90

13   Explaining and Eliminating Racial Profiling / Donald Tomaskovic-Devey and Patricia Warren   98

14 Digital Punishment's Tangled Web / Sarah Esther Lageson 106

15 Six Lessons of Suicide Bombers / Robert J. Brym 113

16 Viewpoints: Trafficking in Humans / Sutapa Basu; Anne T. Gallagher; 122
Denise Brennan; Elena Shih; Ronald Weitzer

part 4: race and ethnicity

17 Viewpoints: Black and Blue / Shehzad Nadeem; Sudhir Venkatesh; 133
Laurence Ralph; Elliott Currie; Katherine Beckett

18 Covering the Three Missouri Michaels / Steven W. Thrasher 141

19 The Whiteness of Oscar Night / Matthew W. Hughey 144

20 Social Mobility among Second-Generation Latinos / Van C. Tran 148

21 Ask a Sociologist: Jennifer Lee on Naming Success / Jennifer Lee 155

part 5: gender and sexuality

22 Viewpoints: Boys / Niobe Way; C. J. Pascoe; Mark McCormack; Amy Schalet; 159
Freeden Oeur

23 What's So Cultural about Hookup Culture? / Lisa Wade 168

24 Hookups, Sex, and Relationships at College / Jessie Ford and 171
Paula England

25 Sexual Orientation versus Behavior—Different for Men 176
and Women? / Eliza Brown and Paula England

26 Women's Sexual Orientation and Sexual Behavior: How Well Do They 184
Match? / Mónica L. Caudillo and Paula England

27 Lesbian Geographies / Amin Ghaziani 191

28 #callmecaitlyn and Contemporary Trans* Visibility / D'Lane Compton 196
and Tristan Bridges

29 Bathroom Battlegrounds and Penis Panics / Kristen Schilt and 198
Laurel Westbrook

part 6: marriage and family

30 The Superstrong Black Mother / Sinikka Elliott and Megan Reid 207

31 The Joy of Cooking? / Sarah Bowen, Sinikka Elliott, and Joslyn Brenton 213

32 Working-Class Growing Pains / Jennifer M. Silva 219

33 Marrying across Class Lines / Jessi Streib 227

34 Viewpoints: After Gay Marriage Equality Forum / Andrew J. Cherlin;
Steven W. Thrasher; Joshua Gamson; Georgiann Davis   234

part 7: education

35 Oyler School against the Odds / Amy Scott   245

36 Academic Hack Heard Round the World / Philip N. Cohen and
Syed Ali   254

37 Friends with Academic Benefits / Janice McCabe   256

38 Whitewashing Academic Mediocrity / Tomás R. Jiménez and
Adam L. Horowitz   265

39 The Challenge of Diverse Public Schools / Toby L. Parcel,
Joshua A. Hendrix, and Andrew J. Taylor   271

40 Viewpoints: Affirmative Inaction / Richard D. Kahlenberg; Sigal Alon;
Jennifer Pierce; John D. Skrentny   278

part 8: health

41 Revisiting the Rationing of Medical Degrees in the United States /
Tania M. Jenkins and Shalini Reddy   289

42 Dealing with the Diagnosis / Gary C. David   296

43 Dropping the "Disorder" in PTSD / R. Tyson Smith and Owen Whooley   303

44 Getting the Most Out of the U.S. Health Care System /
Amanda M. Gengler   311

45 Breastfeed at Your Own Risk / Julie E. Artis   319

part 9: science

46 Not a Snowball's Chance for Science / Dana R. Fisher,
Joseph Waggle, and Lorien Jasny   331

47 Microscopic Hair Comparison and the Sociology of Science /
Simon A. Cole and Troy Duster   338

48 Learning from NASA's Robotic Planetary Missions / Janet Vertesi   345

49 What Gender Is Science? / Maria Charles   350

part 10: politics

50 Hiking the West Bank / Andy Clarno   363

51 Words Burn Lips / Silvia Pasquetti   368

52   Viewpoints: It's High Time / Shehzad Nadeem; Craig Reinarman;   373
Wendy Chapkis; Jake Browne

53   Community Organizing and Social Change / Randy Stoecker   382

54   Sacco and Vanzetti and the Immigrant Threat / Richard Alba   389

55   Viewpoints: Fifty Years of "New" Immigration / Shehzad Nadeem;   396
John D. Skrentny; Jennifer Lee; Jody Agius Vallejo; Zulema Valdez;
Donna R. Gabaccia

56   A Fracking Fracas Demonstrates Movement Potential / Brian K. Obach   406

part 11: work and inequality

57   Asian Americans, Bamboo Ceilings, and Affirmative Action / Margaret M. Chin   413

58   A Hand Up for Lower-Income Families / Sarah Halpern-Meekin, Laura Tach,   417
Jennifer Sykes, and Kathryn Edin

59   Falling Upward / Dalton Conley   423

60   Normal Unpredictability and the Chaos in Our Lives / Naomi Gerstel   425
and Dan Clawson

61   Viewpoints: On the Sharing Economy / Shehzad Nadeem; Juliet B. Schor;   429
Edward T. Walker; Caroline W. Lee; Paolo Parigi and Karen Cook

62   Same Trailer, Different Park / Esther Sullivan and Edna Ledesma   438

part 12: cities

63   Mumbai Sleeping / Dhruv Dhawan   449

64   Permanent Impermanence / Syed Ali   456

65   The King of Compton / Jooyoung Lee   462

66   Black Philly after the Philadelphia Negro / Marcus Anthony Hunter   469

67   I Gentrify Bed-Stuy / Syed Ali   474

editors and contributors   477

preface

Sociological writing is a kind of storytelling—empirical and theoretically driven storytelling. Or at least it should be. Most sociologists (and academics generally), however, do not tell stories; they report data. That's the bread-and-butter approach of academics, and it is required practice at journals.

Contexts is different, which is why we love *Contexts*. It is a place where sociologists, and non-sociologists, can come to tell their stories in a clear, concise, and simple way—remember, kids, simple is not simplistic!—but without sacrificing the scholarly rigor. Our articles teach readers new stuff, and they help us think differently about the world—they look at why the world is the way it is and how it came to be that way. Basically, *Contexts* articles make you go, "Huh. That's pretty cool. I never really thought of that." The magazine appeals to anyone who's interested in insightful social analysis but not so interested in wading through that most boring language of academese. That includes educated "lay" readers such as parents-in-law, policy professionals, activists, and the occasional academic. And you, the undergraduate student. Why should you have to suffer poor and turgid writing to get to someone's scholarly point? You shouldn't. So this book's for you. (You're welcome.)

The selections we've chosen for you for this Third Edition of *The Contexts Reader* reflect topics that are most often taught in intro sociology classes, but, because they're *Contexts* readings, they're far more interesting than things you're usually asked to read in such classes. (We refuse to apologize for this. And sociology instructors, you're welcome as well.)

And how do the articles here end up so well written if they're largely written by academics? Well, the two of us spend a lot of time editing. Seriously, a lot. We're pretty good at it, but we're not pros. The one to thank for the pretty prose is our senior managing editor, Letta Page. Letta goes through every word in every issue. A professional editor, she helps authors develop their ideas, then takes her red pen and cuts and crafts until that article reads something fantastic. While some of the articles here are from the early years of *Contexts*, the vast majority of articles we've chosen for *The Contexts Reader* have gone through her hands. And the articles are the better for it, and you, the reader, are happier for it. We hope you enjoy reading these articles as much as we enjoyed bringing them to you!

Syed Ali
Philip N. Cohen

acknowledgments

Making a magazine is a huge undertaking and there are lots of folks who have a hand in it. Members of our editorial board review a ton of articles for us, and many of them write a lot for the magazine. We're indebted to them. Margaret Austin Smith was our managing editor, and she did a great job of keeping us organized. Our section editors are the best and are responsible for most of the content in the magazine. Szonya Ivester brings us great book reviews, Andrew Lindner finds fantastic trends pieces, Shehzad Nadeem wins an award for organizing brilliant viewpoints forums every issue, and Nathan Palmer gets us lovely teaching and learning articles. Allison Pugh and Kristen Barber edited the culture section and brought us really great stuff. Our magazine is a work of art because of all the work our designers at ThinkDesign put into it.

We'd be remiss if we didn't acknowledge all the work Karen Edwards at the American Sociological Association has put in. The *Contexts* editors change every three to four years, but she's always there to help support the magazine and help the editors to make it better. And we're really happy that Sasha Levitt, our editor here at Norton, was just as excited as we were to put out a third edition of the reader. She's great and made the process go really smoothly.

And most of all, we thank our senior managing editor, Letta Page, for all the amazing work she does not only editing, but finding the images, dealing with layout, and making the magazine pretty, and pretty spectacular.

And, of course, we thank our families: Syed's wife, Eli Pollard (who did an interview for the magazine and helped get lots of articles), and kids, Sami and Noura; and Philip's wife, Judy Ruttenberg (who was really helpful in figuring a future direction for the magazine), and kids, Charlotte and Ruby.

Soon we'll no longer be the editors, but we're really excited to watch how *Contexts* grows and continues to be fantastic.

the **contexts** reader

part 1

How to Do Sociology

joel best

sociologists as outliers

1

spring 2009

when the american public wants to understand social behavior, they turn to economists instead of sociologists. to regain their place in the public consciousness, joel best argues sociologists could do worse than learn from author malcolm gladwell's popular books, which translate sociological knowledge and information.

Malcolm Gladwell's *Outliers: The Story of Success* (2008) was itself marketed to succeed. Gladwell appeared in numerous television interviews. *Outliers* was immediately reviewed by major newspapers in the United States, England, Canada, and Australia. Leading bookstore chains discounted the book and displayed it prominently. When I checked the day after it was released in November 2008, it was already fourth in Amazon.com's rankings.

Gladwell is the twenty-first century's preeminent popularizer of sociological research. He won the American Sociological Association's first Excellence in Reporting of Social Issues Award in 2007. Well-known for his earlier bestsellers *The Tipping Point* and *Blink*, he has been contributing articles (archived at www.gladwell.com) to *The New Yorker* since 1996. He specializes in provocative interpretations of work by social scientists, including psychologists, economists, anthropologists, and—yes—sociologists. *Outliers* is Gladwell's most sociological—and in my view his best—book. His theme is that success is socially patterned, often in subtle ways.

Why, for instance, do a disproportionate share of hockey players have birthdays in January, February, and March? Answer: Canadian youth hockey programs are organized by age cohorts, and each cohort contains kids born in the same calendar year. Thus, a boy born in January will be placed in the same program as a boy born in December of the same year—they are, for organizational purposes, considered to be the same age. But of course, just by virtue of being older, one boy is likely to be bigger, faster, stronger, and better coordinated.

Children start playing on hockey teams before entering elementary school—young enough that being a few months older can make a real difference. So, when the best players are picked for all-star teams, the kids born early in the year have an advantage. And, being on an all-star team means kids get more coaching, more practice, and more experience playing, so they become increasingly better players than those not selected for all-stars. So they begin to accumulate advantages.

The irony is clear: social arrangements designed to make youth hockey fair—by having kids compete with others of the same age—actually work to the advantage of those kids who have the earliest birthdays.

Americans tend to attribute success to the personal qualities of individuals. They think of

> Gladwell is the twenty-first century's preeminent popularizer of sociological research. *Outliers* is his most sociological—and in my view, best—book.

those who make it to the top as having worked especially hard, as having sacrificed, as being determined, dedicated, and therefore deserving. That is, they view success as a product of good character, of particular personality types—the result of psychological differences among people.

This makes intuitive sense. Ask successful people—and this certainly includes successful sociologists—what it takes to succeed and they will almost invariably talk about the importance of working hard. Success, whether in ice hockey or academia, rarely comes to those who don't work for it.

But, Gladwell argues, hard work isn't the whole story. Timing matters. It turns out that Bill Gates, Steve Jobs, and a large share of the other people who amassed vast fortunes when microcomputing began were all born around 1955. That meant they were about 20 years old in 1975 when microcomputers first emerged—old enough to have acquired considerable experience as teenage hobbyists working with computers, but not yet old enough to have completed college and taken jobs with IBM or other "real" computer companies. Being born in 1955 meant they were at the right age to take advantage of the historical moment when it became possible to build careers and make real money in microcomputing.

In other words, Gladwell argues, success isn't simply a product of individual character, it also depends on social context—the eligibility rules for youth hockey participation, technological developments in microcomputing, and so on. Reviews of *Outliers* often invoke the notion of luck (for example, the *Newsweek* review was titled "Maybe Geniuses Just Got Lucky"). But invoking luck, like emphasizing hard work, invites us to view success as a product of

individual differences. Just as some people work harder, some people have more luck.

However in Gladwell's universe, luck isn't some random outcome. Rather, luck takes the form of social arrangements—including cultural legacies and historical circumstances—that work to the advantage of some more than others. These may not seem advantageous on the surface. Gladwell shows, for example, how the anti-Semitism rampant in midcentury New York's leading law firms forced Jewish lawyers to join newer, far more marginal firms that practiced the sorts of law elite, white-shoe firms spurned, such as proxy fights. This turned into an advantage, though, when the business environment changed and hostile takeovers became commonplace. Those new firms and their partners, with their suddenly invaluable expertise, wound up making colossal fortunes.

In Gladwell's universe, luck isn't some random outcome. Rather, luck takes the form of social arrangements that work to the advantage of some more than others.

In the course of this well-written book, Gladwell frequently refers to sociologists. Robert Merton, C. Wright Mills, Pitirim Sorokin, Annette Lareau, Erwin Smigel, Stephen Steinberg, Louise Farkas, Charles Perrow, Karl Alexander, Orlando Patterson, and Fernando Henriques are all mentioned in *Outliers*, and not just in the endnotes. How often does a best-selling author invoke sociology, let alone name sociologists?

These days, when the public wants to understand social behavior, they seem to turn to economists. Consider the remarkable number of recent successful trade books extolling the value of economics for understanding the social order, books such as Steven D. Levitt's and Stephen J. Dubner's *Freakonomics*, Tim Harford's *The Undercover Economist*, Stephen E. Landsburg's *More Sex Is Safer Sex*, Nassim Nicholas Taleb's *Fooled by Randomness*, and James Surowiecki's *The Wisdom of Crowds*. Meanwhile, the sociology sections in many bookstores seem to be shrinking.

Explanations for sociology's low status often mention its fondness for jargon, for using an unnecessarily pompous vocabulary to describe the everyday world. And no doubt sociologists often commit the sin of jargon. But that hardly explains the vogue for economics. Does anyone believe the typical economist's prose is clearer, more readily comprehensible, or less jargon-ridden than most sociologists' work? Nor should we blame sociology's growing dependence on abstruse statistics. If anything, economics is far more quantitative, and less readily accessible, to nonspecialists.

Well, perhaps economics is seen as more practical, as linked to business and making money. Certainly Gladwell writes books considered relevant to business; *The Tipping Point* and *Blink* both seem to offer insights for marketing, while the examples chosen to illustrate success in *Outliers* often involve business careers. But *Freakonomics* and other economics-based best-sellers draw many of their examples from social behavior and public policy in order to show how rational choices and markets influence many aspects of our lives. The economists who write for the public certainly don't restrict their focus to moneymaking.

What both Gladwell and the pop-star economists share is a fondness for surprise, for the unexpected revelation. For example, economists favor a plot line that goes something like this: although at first glance some aspect of the world may seem confusing, even chaotic, once we understand that the people involved are making calculated choices in their own self-interest, we can recognize how their individual choices create consequential, often unexpected, patterns in behavior. Thus, the most notorious section in *Freakonomics* argues that the declining crime rates in the 1990s were an unanticipated by-product of liberalized abortion policies, which led to fewer unwanted children being born and going on to become delinquents. "Ahh," the reader is supposed to exclaim, "now I understand!"

Sociologists used to be in the surprise business, and we used to attract our fair share of public attention. Back in 1937, Robert and Helen Lynd made a splash with *Middletown in Transition*. *Life* covered the study with photos showing the distinctive lifestyles of different social classes expressed in, for example, living room decor. In the aftermath of World War II, David Riesman published *The Lonely Crowd* (the all-time best-seller by an American sociologist), which argued the United States had experienced a profound cultural change.

By the late 1950s, Vance Packard was preceding Gladwell as an author who translated sociology into the best-selling *The Status Seekers*. Just a few years later, Tom Wolfe was making frequent references to sociologists while showing the importance of status for everyone from car customizers to modern artists to astronauts. In each case, sociology seemed to shed new light on the everyday and, in the process, offer surprising revelations. Sociology was entertaining.

It's worth appreciating that sociology has had a noticeable effect on Americans' thinking. A remarkable number of sociological terms have crept into everyday speech: lifestyle; upper-, middle-, and lower-class; charisma; status symbol; gender; self-fulfilling prophecy; role model; even significant other. It isn't clear that economics has had such a favorable reception. Still, sociology doesn't get much credit for these contributions. Once its concepts enter common parlance, their sociological origins tend to be forgotten.

> Does anyone believe the typical economist's prose is clearer, more readily comprehensible, or less jargon-ridden than most sociologists' work?

Contemporary sociologists in particular seem to have trouble getting noticed, probably because they sound self-righteous. Economics may be the dismal science, but today's sociologists often describe a grim world governed by cruel, grinding inequalities of race, class, and gender. They portray a world of alienation, of lonely people living meaningless lives. Their idea of surprise is to expose the sexist imagery in advertisements and music videos. They seem to scold. The arguments seem familiar, predictable. Not surprisingly, they go over about as well as scolding usually does.

It isn't that inequality is unimportant, or that sociologists need to communicate via some sort of happy-talk. After all, much of *Outliers* concerns how social arrangements foster unequal outcomes. But Gladwell directs our focus toward success, rather than failure. The cover of the British hardcover edition of *Outliers* describes him as an "inspirational bestselling author." Rather than issuing blanket indictments of the social system, he identifies other non-utopian arrangements that might offer more equal opportunities: "We could set up two or even three hockey leagues, divided up by month of birth. Let the players develop on separate tracks and then pick all-star teams."

Later in the book he praises the KIPP schools, which give low-income middle-school children intensive training that boosts their math skills and opens doors to better high school and college opportunities. Success—even among those who seem predestined to fail—can, in Gladwell's view, be fostered by being alert to how social institutions work. In the chapter titled "The Ethnic Theory of Plane Crashes," he points to the once-alarming tendency of Korean Air jets to crash because their cultural obligations to be deferential kept Korean first officers and flight engineers from bluntly warning pilots about hazards. After Korean Air instituted a training program designed to change communication patterns among cockpit crews, the airline achieved an admirable safety record. Still, one can imagine some sociologists squirming at this example, explaining that we need to appreciate—not judge—diverse communication styles.

But of course it does matter if some cultures are ill-suited to producing the sorts of quick, appropriate decisions among cockpit crew members needed to keep airliners from crashing. And not all the patterns identified by Gladwell are subject to social engineering. Doubling or tripling the number of youth hockey leagues in Canada may give more kids with late-in-the-year birthdays a better shot at developing their skills, but it won't change the size of NHL rosters. Lest this example seem a little arcane, Gladwell reminds us that U.S. schools are also age-graded (so that school districts define one-year spans of birthdates that make students eligible to enter kindergarten), and those with earlier birthdays prove to have an advantage of maturity that carries right through college admissions. We might reduce the impact of age differences by placing students with similar birthdates in the same classroom. And perhaps schooling isn't a zero-sum game. Perhaps more students would excel if they learned alongside others of comparable maturity, so that more would take to school and seek higher education.

Social arrangements and historical processes shape individual's prospects for success, but they can't tell the whole story. Those born in big, baby-boomer birth cohorts find themselves in tougher competition than those born in birth-dearth years, just as those who enter the workforce in good economic times have better career prospects than those who look for work when jobs are scarce. We can't choose our birth cohort or our society's economic circumstances. Yet, within those larger arrangements, people do make consequential choices that also affect their prospects for succeeding.

Sociologists often call for appreciation of diversity, for recognition of the talent, skills, and resilience demanded to live in disadvantaged circumstances, and for understanding why some people make choices others condemn. They invite us to understand why some youths leave school, why some people act violently, and so on. They have a point. People have their reasons for doing things, and not everyone has the same reasons.

But sociology has to do more than endorse differences. Maybe we ought to appreciate different modes of communication, but also that all modes are not equally useful for, say, landing an airliner safely. Understanding the range of human behavior doesn't require that we endorse the full range.

In order to regain their place in the public consciousness, sociologists could do worse than learn from the remarkable resurgence of economics, and from Gladwell's ability to translate sociological findings into popular books. We can't expect to influence public debate if we can't get people to listen to us. Contemporary sociology has become all too predictable; successful bids for public attention require arguments that are themselves outliers—surprising, interesting, and compelling.

RECOMMENDED RESOURCE

Malcolm Gladwell. 2008. *Outliers: The Story of Success*. New York: Little, Brown and Company.

REVIEW QUESTIONS

1. The author says that we can't explain sociology's loss in popularity only by the discipline's fondness of jargon, use of statistics, and pompous vocabulary. Given this, how can we understand economics' popularity and higher status, despite its lower accessibility?
2. The author argues that sociologists need to make more efforts to regain the public consciousness. He provides some suggestions, for example, shifting gears toward "success" rather than "failure." Do you agree? Why or why not?
3. What are your suggestions for the revival of sociology?

how to do ethnography right

spring 2016

qualitative research offers rich insight and can illuminate processes. how can you make the most of qualitative data?

Ethnographies are works of deep research based on in-depth, open-ended interviews and keen observations of how people go about their lives in different contexts. Researchers often spend years in their research sites to get to know the people and places they study in a way that can't be done using other methods. Ethnographies are (arguably) the most visible and relatable research products that sociologists have to offer the general public. They tell stories about our social world backed up by rigorously gathered data. That's pretty cool.

While ethnographers are very much expert in their research domains, their work is increasingly subject to public scrutiny. It is important for sociologists to develop and maintain professional standards that allow them to conduct the best research without compromising quality in the face of potential criticism and controversy. Recent conversations about the practice of ethnography have been spurred by the responses––public and academic—to high-profile books in the past few years. But that is just the current manifestation of an evolving dialogue about the best way to do ethnographic work. A number of important issues have been featured in this conversation: data preservation and sharing, replicability and confidentiality, peer review, funding and research support, and others.

> Ethnographies tell stories about our social world backed up by rigorously gathered data. That's pretty cool.

At the suggestion of the American Sociological Association's Council, we organized this special forum with some of the top practitioners in the field. Here you'll find three papers that lay out "best practices" for ethnographers to follow.

We start with Dana R. Fisher's paper, "Doing Qualitative Research as if Counsel Is Hiding in the Closet." Whether you study elites or study the poor, Fisher says you should do your research as if the group you're working with has legal representation. It could save you headaches (and money, and even your reputation) down the road.

Ethnographers for the most part work alone, and they use convenience sampling, that is, they talk to people who are conveniently located for them to talk with. Stefanie DeLuca, Susan Clampet-Lundquist, and Kathryn Edin argue in their essay, "Want to Improve Your Qualitative Research? Try Using Representative Sampling and Working in Teams," that ethnographers can, and should, well, use representative sampling and work in teams. This will improve the depth and reliability of your data and your story.

The last paper here is by Annette Lareau and Aliya Hamid Rao, "It's about the Depth of Your Data." They remind us that ethnographers are not quantitative researchers, and that the small, nonrandom sample ethnographers usually have actually isn't a problem—in fact, that's a selling point for ethnography. The ethnographer is telling the reader a story, and Lareau and Rao tell us that detailed field notes, lengthy interviews with smaller numbers of people, smartly developed themes and analyses, and crisp writing are the key to good ethnographic storytelling. Sometimes ethnographers forget these things. It's good that Lareau and Rao are reminding us.

Taken together, we shouldn't consider these as a blueprint for criticism-free research or a set of "how to" papers. But it's close. So read, learn, enjoy—and if you're an ethnographer, go forth and do your thing!

dana r. fisher

doing qualitative research as if counsel is hiding in the closet

march 29, 2016

A lot of my research studies political elites. As such, I am frequently conducting participant observation and open-ended, semi-structured interviews in the halls of the U.S. Congress, offices of various federal agencies, political consultants, lobbying firms, and organizations that aim to represent the public's interest. In other words, my data are collected from a highly educated group of people, an overwhelming proportion of whom have law degrees. Moreover, most of these offices employ some sort of "corporate" counsel that monitors access—or what I think of as my field site and my research subjects. As a result, I have learned to be extremely careful since these lawyers have made it clear to me on a number of occasions that I can lose access and be booted from my field site at any point.

In the 15 years since I completed my PhD, I have been challenged by research subjects regarding my use of their names or the data I collected from them in two particularly anxiety-inducing cases. In the first, a subject of an interview who worked for a Congressional committee found a draft of a paper online that directly quoted him. While I was making the final edits on my first book, which named this subject and quoted him directly, I got a very aggressive e-mail from

him. In response, I passed on a copy of the transcript of the interview that included an exchange during which I asked if I could use the subject's name and he affirmed. His concerns were alleviated after receiving the transcript that included his consent. Nonetheless, I removed direct reference to this research subject in my book. I also adapted the way that I approach political elites whom I study.

Although these interviews are usually seen as exempt from IRB requirements because I am asking about subjects' political work and not anything personal, I have found I get better data (and avoid such interactions with JDs working in the political arena) if I grant all subjects confidentiality. When providing a description of my research before I begin an interview, I hand my subjects an IRB-approved information sheet about the research and tell them that nothing they say will be directly attributable to them. In journalists' parlance, the interview is "off the record." I state that I will e-mail them directly for approval if I find there is any segment that I would like to quote directly in my work. Because so many of my subjects have experience speaking with journalists, I find that following similar norms about attribution puts the subjects at ease. Although this process adds some work when I am writing, it tends to yield more interesting data. This process also gives me an electronic trail if I am approached by subjects *post hoc*, which can be very helpful if I am contacted by lawyers.

I have also faced challenges when studying political organizations. The most stressful experience so far took place during my research on the experiences of young activists who worked as canvassers, recruiting new members and renewing existing memberships for a number of progressive campaigns. The findings of this study went into my book *Activism, Inc.* Most of the data used for the book came from open-ended semi-structured interviews with one cohort of young people working on the summer canvass and the participant observations conducted in canvass offices during summer 2003.

Preparing to enter the field for this study involved gaining access to the largest canvassing organization in the United States—The Fund for Public Interest Research—which had never before been the subject of an academic study, and likely never will be again. (I created a pseudonym for the organization in *Activism, Inc.* because the findings from the research were not very complimentary. Since the organization came out in an article in the *Chronicle of Higher Education* after the book was published, I named it in subsequent publications.) After many rounds of discussions with the organization and positive support from well-known activists whom I knew from my life before I became a sociologist, the organization agreed to be the setting of my research project. Before going into the field to do participant observation in offices and interview canvassers, however, the organization required that we negotiate a memorandum of understanding

that would determine who and what I would gain access to and what I could ask about during my research. After some back-and-forth, the organization and I signed the agreement that stated, "The treatment of the data will be consistent with the protocol outlined by the Columbia University Institutional Review Board (IRB Protocol #02/03-998A)."

Although social scientists frequently complain that the requirements of our universities' IRBs put unnecessary limitations on social research—particularly for projects that collect little personal data about the research subjects—I found the IRB provided me with a welcome shield with which I could protect my research and my subjects from the organization. Throughout the duration of this project, people from the organization made multiple attempts to get my field notes and interview data. In fact early on in the project, a representative from the organization offered to hide in the closet or surreptitiously turn on the office's intercom so that she could listen in on my interviews.

Even though we had agreed from the beginning that my data would be kept confidential and both sides had signed the agreement that acknowledged that I would be following the regulations of the IRB, the organization persisted. Thanks to the university's human subjects requirements, however, I was able to respond to these requests by pointing out that my protocol, which is required by the university and was clearly outlined in our agreement, would not permit such activities.

In addition to protecting my subjects, the IRB protected me when the organization threatened to take legal action. Right before *Activism, Inc.* was published, the organization's legal team threatened to block the publication of the book (for which they had no legal grounds),

> I now conduct all of my research very carefully—basically doing it as if a corporate counsel is looking over my shoulder every step of the way.

stating that I had to turn over all of my data to them before they would approve any publication. Once again, the IRB and my human subjects protocol provided a welcome protection. It's worth noting that, even though my IRB Protocol was protected through Columbia University, I was still required to hire my own lawyer, which cost me thousands of dollars. After enduring hours of phone calls with lawyers from the University and Stanford University Press to go over the research and my methods, our "legal team" agreed that I had done nothing wrong and the book could be published.

Given these experiences, I now conduct all of my research very carefully—basically doing it as if a corporate counsel is looking over my shoulder every step of the way. Moving forward, qualitative sociologists who study less privileged communities should follow the lead of those of us who have been studying elites and do their work *as if* they're studying a group with their own legal representation. In other words, we all should treat our field sites as if they are populated by a privileged portion of the population who wield law degrees.

stefanie deluca, susan clampet-lundquist, and kathryn edin

want to improve your qualitative research? try using representative sampling and working in teams
march 19, 2016

In the mid-1990s, the federal government launched a high-profile social experiment in five cities to determine if escaping concentrated neighborhood poverty could change the lives of the nation's poorest families. The program—Moving to Opportunity (MTO)—would rely on housing vouchers as the policy tool to accomplish such change. In the Baltimore MTO site, over 600 families signed up, and they were randomly assigned to one of three groups. Those in the experimental group received modest housing counseling and a housing voucher that could only be used in a low-poverty neighborhood; another group received a voucher with no restrictions; and the control group received no voucher. Over the next ten years, researchers and policymakers would follow these families to determine whether the program worked to improve such outcomes as adult self-sufficiency and children's educational prospects.

Our team has primarily used qualitative methods to study the Baltimore site for more than ten years, beginning in 2003. Our original goal was to understand the mechanisms behind the experimental results from the MTO survey, as well as the role of family, school, and neighborhood in the lives of poor households. The focus in our book, *Coming of Age in the Other America*, and in this essay, stems from in-depth interviews we conducted in 2010. We drew a stratified random sample of 200 15–24-year-old youth from the final evaluation survey, which had occurred in the previous year. We interviewed 150 out of these 200 youth, for a response rate of 75 percent. Sampling from "shared origins"—the survey of all Baltimore MTO participants—meant that we knew the population our qualitative study applied to (poor African-American families living in Baltimore public housing in the 1990s). But because we did not sample on "shared outcomes," it also ensured heterogeneity in pathways into adulthood.

To ensure that we gathered consistent information from each youth, interview conversations covered a predetermined set of topics around the transition to adulthood (e.g., education, employment, family formation). However, while questions were phrased in ways that were broad and open-ended, details were revealed through skillful probing during the conversations, not usually via direct queries, such as those used in surveys. Right from the start, we needed to signal to these youth that our interaction would be very different from the MTO survey, which was still fresh in many participants' minds. To this end, we began each conversation with the question: "Tell me the story of your life." As each youth's narrative unfolded, we would follow their lead, probing as areas of interest emerged, rather than following a prescribed order.

Sampling and in-depth interviews allow for a way to get around the thorny problem for qualitative researchers that not all research participants are available and willing to be observed in the course of their daily routines. Given the frequency with which ethnographers have written about men hanging out at a particular street corner, diner, or takeaway (e.g., *Streetcorner Society, A Place on the Corner, Tally's Corner, Slim's Table*), it is probably the case that the method has underrepresented their peers who may prefer to spend their leisure time at home with their families or hanging out at the library reading books. By employing standard sampling techniques that allow one to calculate a response rate, and by comparing the demographic characteristics of those sampled to the larger population one is generalizing to, we can at least know something about who is *not* represented in our study.

Researchers who use qualitative methods usually do not attempt to get representative samples because the depth of the observations they employ often restrict their focus to a few individuals, or a narrow range of activities, or a single venue. Ethnographers often go into the field to study a particular group of people, thus they "sample on the dependent variable" by choosing the outcome they intend to portray. This is why Sudhir Venkatesh focused on the power brokers of the Robert Taylor Homes—the gang leader and tenant council head in *American Project*. Alice Goffman's meticulous recounting of the experiences of a few young men—whose lives she documented in her book *On the Run*—allowed limited time to focus on the women in their lives, or on the law-abiding members of the community. This is not a criticism; indeed, we applaud the rich portraits of the inner city from these accounts. But if the goal is to illustrate a wide range of a group of people in a community, sampling on the dependent variable is not the way to achieve it. A systematic, in-depth interview study that follows standard sampling procedures to ensure representativeness, or at the very least heterogeneity, can offer a wider lens on diverse individuals in the community. It should be said that some ethnographies at least partially accomplish this, such as Mary Pattillo's classic *Black Picket Fences*, and her more recent book, *Black on the Block*.

Such an approach can be even more effective if the sample is prospective. We were fortunate to be able to identify our sample in early childhood from a population of children whose parents' characteristics, collected in a baseline survey, were largely representative of those raising their children in public housing in the mid-1990s. Their shared origins, and not their outcomes, are what got them into our study. This allows us to observe diverse

> A systematic, in-depth interview study that follows standard sampling procedures to ensure representativeness, or at the very least heterogeneity, can offer a wider lens on diverse individuals in the community.

pathways and give equal voice to those youth who are seldom, if ever, to be found on the corner and who spend their time elsewhere—their homes, the library, or a job.

One hallmark of qualitative research—especially ethnography—is that it is often done by a lone researcher who conducts the fieldwork, analysis, and writeup. In contrast, our study was truly a group effort. Over the course of the ten years we were in the field, between 2003 and 2013, over forty individuals were involved—graduate students, undergraduates, postdoctoral researchers, professional staff, and faculty collaborators. Together, we: recruited participants, conducted interviews, and wrote field notes; logged, transcribed, de-identified, coded, and analyzed data; wrote, and edited papers. We also shared chapters of our book for feedback from others on the team, some who knew certain details better than we did.

Teamwork was woven into all aspects of the project. For example, we often interviewed in pairs. This was partly for safety, but also because it was easier for one person to drive while the other navigated, to call a youth to let him know we were on our way, or to begin writing the field notes on the return trip home. But the primary reason is that it improved the quality of the data. We have all watched each other conduct interviews and given feedback on how the other person could have done it better, or what was missed. We debriefed as a team on a weekly (sometimes daily) basis, talking about the day's interviews, what we noticed, what surprised us, and what patterns we were observing. Was there something in the interview guide that needed updating because of recent events? Did the team understand the terminology someone used when describing her sexual or romantic relationships?

An additional advantage to team research is that it's much harder to make a mistake when others who read and comment on your work have all been in the same neighborhoods, interviewed others from the same family, and have read the same transcripts. Often, during the course of analyzing and writing, we were challenged by colleagues who questioned whether a given conclusion is warranted. That kind of feedback sent us back to the drawing board more than a few times.

Certainly not every qualitative study warrants a representative sample, nor is random sampling feasible in each study. Exploring heterogeneity in a community does not always need to be the research goal. However, recognizing diverse pathways within a group of people broadens our understanding and translates into policy prescriptions that are a better fit for more people. Goffman's richly detailed focus on a small group of men and their immediate networks gives us invaluable information about the impact of mass incarceration on everyday life. But it doesn't offer insight for the majority of young adults in the same neighborhood who don't get "caught up." Employing a representative sampling frame makes it less likely that researchers mistake the exceptions for the norm. And while larger-scale team research is more expensive, it makes collecting data from a wider sample possible, as well as increasing the reliability of the findings.

annette lareau and aliya hamid rao

it's about the depth of your data

march 19, 2016

A key strength of in-depth interviews and ethnography is obtaining textured insights into social phenomenon. Yet, many qualitative researchers try to invoke the reliability of quantitative methods by shrouding themselves in numbers as a way to legitimize their work. They offer up the number of interviews, the number of hours, weeks, and years spent in the field and they propose bigger and bigger samples. Even as qualitative researchers assert that they have carried out in-depth qualitative research, they often revert to the language of quantitative research to justify the legitimacy of the work. The nod to numbers is a way of claiming trustworthiness and, importantly, scientific expertise, which is usually equated with quantitative methods. This dependence on large sample sizes for qualitative research as a form of legitimacy, however, is misplaced. Indeed, we see this seeking of legitimacy through quantification as a distortion of where the value of qualitative research truly lies.

Instead, it is the *depth* of qualitative data that determines the quality of the work. Qualitative methods have the capacity to illuminate meaning—particularly the micro-level nuances of attitudes and daily behaviors. Qualitative research can highlight the impact of large-scale social structural forces on the rituals of daily life as well as many other spheres of life. This depth may in fact be linked to a larger number of interviews, or to more time spent in the field, but it should not be seen as reducible to this. We want to point to three factors that we see as being indispensable to achieving depth in qualitative research: collecting high-quality data, trenchant data analysis, and vibrant writing.

Qualitative data has the advantage of making readers feel they are hearing the interview or seeing the scene unfold in their presence. Our trust of qualitative data should thus rely (more than it currently does) on how vividly the researcher captures the micro-level nuances. The point is to study *social interaction*—how people act and how others react to their actions, as well as how people react to the reactions. Descriptions in field notes need to be precise. Rather than using the word "said," for example (as in "She said"), we encourage sociologists to think more deeply about the way in which the communication unfolded. Did she seem angry, bored, thoughtful, unsure, frustrated, annoyed, or sad as she spoke? Was his tone of voice loud, boisterous, gentle, irritated, exasperated, discouraged, delighted, gleeful, cheery, or jovial? (A thesaurus is a crucial aid here.) The notes should be greatly detailed. Lareau's rule of thumb for the data collection for *Unequal Childhoods* was to spend five to twelve hours writing field notes after every two- or three-hour visit. At the very least, researchers want to take twice as long to write up their notes as they spent in the field.

These kinds of notes also can set the stage for description of interviewees. Although notes usually cannot be collected during the interview—since it breaks the flow and the connection between the respondent and the interviewer—they can be written immediately afterwards and must be done within 24 hours. As part of the creation of a high-quality data set, it is crucial to collect information on facial expressions, gestures, and tone of voice so as to better understand the social interactions being studied. It is also helpful to highlight the sounds, smell, and light in the setting researchers are trying to describe. Qualitative researchers want the reader to feel as if he or she is peering over the researcher's shoulder to watch the events which are unfolding. But this kind of depth traditionally comes at the cost of scope in the number of sites and also in the number of interviewees. (Many researchers have concluded that they can keep about fifty people in their heads during data analysis.) Extremely large studies are difficult for one researcher to carry out, are expensive to transcribe, and are hard to represent through words. Smaller studies may create difficult decisions on balancing groups to study, but all studies involve hard choices. The goal is to achieve deep knowledge in a particular research setting.

Data analysis is integral to data collection in qualitative research. As the first bits of data emerge, researchers should read over field notes and interview transcripts to search for emerging themes. Throughout the data collection process, researchers should consider the research question and try to figure out what interesting themes are surfacing. This analysis is almost always a pattern of discerning a focus (and letting go of other, interesting questions). But it is important to be skeptical as well. Researchers should search vigorously for disconfirming evidence to the emerging ideas. In the data analysis for *Unequal Childhoods*, for example, Lareau searched assiduously for middle-class, working-class, and poor families who had different behaviors than the general pattern for their social class. She found one White mother who was raised in an affluent home, but—as a former drug addict living below the poverty level—her parenting style followed the "accomplishment of natural growth," which was the cultural logic of child rearing in working-class and poor families. These and other examples increased Lareau's confidence in her findings. In other cases, if researchers find

disconfirming evidence, they need to investigate it thoroughly. Is it the exception that proves the rule? Or does it mean researchers should rethink their conclusions? Sociologists want to capture patterns that are decisively in the setting they are studying, and they want to be alert to variations on a theme. Writing memos, talking with others, giving "works-in-progress" talks all are helpful strategies to try to figure out what researchers are really doing in the field. Data analysis is ongoing and deeply entwined with data collection.

Our last point is that high-quality research is well written. Because doing qualitative research well is labor- and time-intensive, it can be frustrating for scholars that they cannot share all of the collected evidence with the reader. Instead, researchers only share an extremely small fraction of the data. But qualitative researchers know that they have more data to support their claims than what they are able to present. This conviction is important. Yet, the writing and the quotes need to be judicious. Readers enjoy being told a story, and readers like to "connect" with a person in the text. Researchers who collect and analyze these rich details of social interaction are able to create clearer, more sophisticated arguments. Hence, it is valuable for these details to appear in the analysis. Too many studies using interview data prioritize including numerous quotes on the same analytical point as evidence of the robustness of their data. We find it better to present fewer people in more depth by helping the reader get to know a person in the study. For example, rather than presenting disembodied quotes in a research report, we believe it is ideal to help the reader understand who is speaking. Even in a brief fashion, the author can bring the respondent to life. This can be done by delving into the relevant backstory of the participant, detailing facial expressions, gestures, and tone of voice. Then, the common themes can be illustrated more briefly with evidence from others. Tables also can be a succinct way of capturing patterns in the sample with very brief quotes—often less than ten words—which illuminate key themes.

In the end, qualitative research is about words. It is not about numbers. The "arms race" to have bigger and bigger samples is unfortunate, since many researchers spend valuable time and energy collecting data only to leave it on the "cutting room floor." Qualitative researchers need to evoke in readers the feeling of being there. But that knowledge of daily life comes from learning the details of a relatively small, nonrandom sample. It means systematically analyzing the experiences, looking for disconfirming evidence, and being sure that the patterns are solid. It also means bringing them to life through the written word. The value of qualitative research is not about brandishing the large number of cases in a study. Instead, qualitative researchers need to focus on the quality and the meaning of the data they have collected. This is the source of their legitimacy.

REVIEW QUESTIONS

1. DeLuca, Clampet-Lundquist, and Edin recommend conducting qualitative research in teams. What are the benefits and challenges of doing fieldwork in teams?
2. Fisher highlights some challenges of interviewing people with legal counsels. How does conducting research on groups with privilege differ from research about marginalized groups? What role does the IRB play in this process?
3. Think of a research project you would like to conduct. How could you use qualitative methods to answer your research questions? What lessons from these authors would you keep in mind when designing your study?

howard schuman

sense and nonsense about surveys

3

summer 2002

understanding surveys is critical to being an informed citizen, but popular media often report surveys without any guidance on how to interpret and evaluate the results. some basic guidelines can promote more-sophisticated readings of survey results and help teach when to trust the polls.

Surveys draw on two human propensities that have served us well from ancient times. One is to gather information by asking questions. The first use of language around 100,000 years ago may have been to utter commands such as "Come here!" or "Wait!" Questions must have followed soon after: "Why?" or "What for?" From that point, it would have been only a short step to the use of interrogatives to learn where a fellow hominid had seen potential food, a dangerous animal, or something else of importance. Asking questions continues to be an effective way of acquiring information of all kinds, assuming of course that the person answering is able and willing to respond accurately.

The other inclination, learning about one's environment by examining a small part of it, is the sampling aspect of surveys. A taste of something may or may not point to appetizing food. A first inquiry to a stranger, a first glance around a room, a first date—each is a sample of sorts, often used to decide whether it is wise to proceed further. As with questions, however, one must always be aware of the possibility that the sample may not prove adequate to the task.

> The percentage of people who refuse to take part in a survey is particularly important. In some federal surveys, the percentage is small, within the range of 5 to 10 percent. For even the best nongovernment surveys, the refusal rate can reach 25 percent or more, and it can be far larger in the case of poorly executed surveys.

sampling: how gallup achieved fame

Only within the past century—and especially in the 1930s and 1940s—were major improvements made in the sampling process that allowed the modern survey to develop and flourish. A crucial change involved recognition that the value of a sample comes not simply from its size but also from the way it is obtained. Every serious pursuit likes to have a morality tale that supports its basic beliefs: witness Eve and the apple in the Bible or Newton and his apple in legends about scientific discovery. Representative sampling has a marvelous morality tale also, with the additional advantage of its being true.

The story concerns the infamous *Literary Digest* poll prediction—based on 10 million questionnaires sent out and more than 2 million received back—that Roosevelt would lose decisively in the 1936 presidential election. At the same time, George Gallup, using many fewer cases but a much better method, made the more accurate prediction that FDR would win. Gallup used quotas in choosing respondents in order to represent different economic strata, whereas the *Literary Digest* had worked mainly from telephone and automobile ownership lists, which in 1936 were biased toward wealthy people apt to be opposed to Roosevelt. (There were other sources of bias as well.) As a result, the *Literary Digest* poll disappeared from the scene, and Gallup was on his way to becoming a household name.

Yet despite their intuitive grasp of the importance of representing the electorate accurately, Gallup and other commercial pollsters did not use the probability sampling methods that were being developed in the same decades and that are fundamental to social science surveys today. Probability sampling in its simplest form calls for each person in the population to have an equal chance of being selected. It can also be used in more complex applications where the chances are deliberately made to be unequal, for example, when oversampling a minority group in order to study it more closely; however, the chances of being selected must still be known so that they can later be equalized when considering the entire population.

intuitions and counterintuitions about sample size

Probability sampling theory reveals a crucial but counterintuitive point about sample size: the size of a sample needed to accurately estimate a value for a population depends very little on the size of the population. For example, almost the same size sample is needed to estimate, with a given degree of precision, the proportion of left-handed people in the United States as is needed to make the same estimate for, say, Peoria, Illinois. In both cases a reasonably accurate estimate can be obtained with a

sample size of around 1,000. (More cases are needed when extraordinary precision is called for, for example, in calculating unemployment rates, where even a tenth of a percent change may be regarded as important.)

The link between population size and sample size cuts both ways. Although huge samples are not needed for huge populations like those of the United States or China, a handful of cases is not sufficient simply because one's interest is limited to Peoria. This implication is often missed by those trying to save time and money when sampling a small community.

Moreover, all of these statements depend on restricting your interest to overall population values. If you are concerned about, say, left-handedness among African Americans, then African Americans become your population, and you need much the same sample size as for Peoria or the United States.

who is missing?

A good sample depends on more than probability sampling theory. Surveys vary greatly in their quality of implementation, and this variation is not captured by the "margin of error" plus/minus percentage figures that accompany most media reports of polls. Such percentages reflect the size of the final sample, but they do not reveal the sampling method or the extent to which the targeted individuals or households were actually included in the final sample. These details are at least as important as the sample size.

When targeted members of a population are not interviewed or do not respond to particular questions, the omissions are a serious problem if they are numerous and if those missed differ from those who are interviewed on the matters being studied. The latter difference can seldom be known with great confidence, so it is usually desirable to keep omissions to a minimum. For example, sampling from telephone directories is undesirable because it leaves out those with unlisted telephones, as well as those with no telephones at all. Many survey reports are based on such poor sampling procedures that they may not deserve to be taken seriously. This is especially true of reports based on "focus groups," which offer lots of human interest but are subject to vast amounts of error. Internet surveys also cannot represent the general population adequately at present, though this is an area where some serious attempts are being made to compensate for the inherent difficulties.

The percentage of people who refuse to take part in a survey is particularly important. In some federal surveys, the percentage is small, within the range of 5 to 10 percent. For even the best nongovernment surveys, the refusal rate can reach 25 percent or more, and it can be far larger in the case of poorly executed surveys. Refusals have risen substantially from earlier days, becoming a major cause for concern

calling spirits from the vasty deep

Two characters in Shakespeare's *Henry IV* illustrate a pressing problem facing surveys today:

Glendower: I can call spirits from the vasty deep.
Hotspur: Why, so can I, or so can any man; But will they come when you do call for them?

New impediments such as answering machines make contacting people more difficult, and annoyance with telemarketing and other intrusions discourages people from becoming respondents. The major academic survey organizations invest significant resources in repeatedly calling people and also in trying to persuade people to be interviewed. Thus far, response rates for leading surveys have suffered only a little, but other organizations more limited by time and costs have seen rates plummet.

Fortunately, research about the effect of nonresponse on findings has increased. Two recent articles in *Public Opinion Quarterly* report surprisingly small differences in results from surveys with substantial differences in response rates. One study focuses on the University of Michigan's Survey of Consumers and finds that the number of calls required to complete a single interview doubled from 1979 to 1996. However, controlling for major social background characteristics, the authors also report that stopping calls earlier and making fewer attempts to convert refusals would have had little effect on a key measure, the Index of Consumer Sentiments. In a second study researchers conducted two basically similar surveys: one accepted a 36 percent response rate to conserve time and money; the other invested additional time and resources to obtain a 61 percent response rate. On a wide range of attitude items, the researchers found few noteworthy differences in outcomes due to the large difference in response rates.

It is important to keep in mind that bias due to nonresponse will occur only if nonrespondents differ from respondents on the measures of interest and in ways that cannot be controlled statistically. Thus, while high response rates are always desirable in principle, the actual effects of nonresponse call for careful empirical research, not dogmatic pronouncements.

among serious survey practitioners. Fortunately, in recent years research has shown that moderate amounts of nonresponse in an otherwise careful survey seem in most cases not to have a major effect on results. Indeed, even the *Literary Digest*, with its abysmal sampling and massive nonresponse rate, did well predicting elections before the dramatic realignment of the electorate in 1936. The problem is that one can never be certain as to the effects of refusals and other forms of nonresponse, so obtaining a high response rate remains an important goal.

questions about questions

Since survey questions resemble the questions we ask in ordinary social interaction, they may seem less problematic than the counterintuitive and technical aspects of sampling. Yet survey results are every bit as dependent on the form, wording, and context of the questions asked as they are on the sample of people who answer them.

No classic morality tale like the *Literary Digest* fiasco highlights the question–answer process, but an example from the early days of surveys illustrates both the potential challenges of question writing and the practical solutions.

In 1940 Donald Rugg asked two slightly different questions to equivalent national samples about the general issue of freedom of speech:

- Do you think the United States should forbid public speeches against democracy?
- Do you think the United States should allow public speeches against democracy?

Taken literally, forbidding something and not allowing something have the same effect, but clearly the public did not view the questions as identical. Whereas 75 percent of the public would not allow such speeches, only 54 percent would forbid them, a difference of 21 percentage points. This finding was replicated several times in later years, not only in the United States but also (with appropriate translations) in Germany and the Netherlands. Such "survey-based experiments" call for administering different versions of a question to random subsamples of a larger sample. If the results between the subsamples differ by more than can be easily explained by chance, we infer that the difference is due to the variation in wording.

In addition, answers to survey questions always depend on the form in which a question is asked. If the interviewer presents a limited set of alternatives, most respondents will choose one, rather than offering a different alternative of their own. In one survey-based experiment, for example, we asked a national sample of Americans to name the most important problem facing the country. Then we asked a comparable sample a parallel question that provided a list of four problems from which to choose the most important; this list included none of the four problems mentioned most often by the first sample but instead provided four problems that had been mentioned by fewer than 3 percent of the earlier respondents. The list question also invited respondents to substitute a different problem if they wished (see table 1). Despite the invitation, the majority of respondents (60 percent) chose one of the rare problems offered, reflecting their reluctance to go outside the frame of reference provided by the question. The form of a question provides the "rules of the game" for respondents, and this must always be kept in mind when interpreting results.

Other difficulties occur with survey questions when issues are discussed quite generally, as though there is a single way of framing them and just two sides to the debate. For example, what is called "the abortion issue" really consists of different issues: the reasons for an abortion, the trimester involved, and so forth. In a recent General Social Survey, nearly 80 percent of the

table 1: experimental variation between open and closed questions	
A. Open question	B. Closed question

"What do you think is the most important problem facing this country today [1986]?"	"Which of the following do you think is the most important problem facing this country today [1986]—the energy shortage, the quality of public schools, legalized abortion, or pollution—or, if you prefer, you may name a different problem as most important."
	  1. Energy shortage
	  2. Quality of public schools
	  3. Legalized abortion
	  4. Pollution

Source: Adapted from H. Schuman and I. Scott, "Problems in the Use of Survey Questions to Measure Public Opinion," Science v. 236, pp. 957–59, May 22, 1987.

Note: In a survey experiment, less than 3 percent of the 171 respondents asked the question on the left volunteered one of the four problems listed on the right. Yet 60 percent of the 178 respondents asked the question on the right picked one of those four answers.

national sample supported legal abortion in the case of "a serious defect in the baby," but only 44 percent supported it "if the family has a low income and cannot afford any more children." Often what is thought to be a conflict in findings between two surveys is actually a difference in the aspects of the general issue that they queried. In still other cases, an inconsistency reflects a type of illogical wish fulfillment in the public itself, as when majorities favor both a decrease in taxes and an increase in government services if the questions are asked separately.

solutions to the question wording problem

All these and still other difficulties (including the order in which questions are asked) suggest that responses to single survey questions on complex issues should be viewed with considerable skepticism. What to do then, other than to reject all survey data as unusable for serious purposes? One answer can be found from the replications of the forbid/allow experiment

just given: Although there was a 21 percentage points difference based on question wording in 1940 and a slightly larger difference (24 percentage points) when the experiment was repeated some 35 years later, both the forbid and the allow wordings registered similar declines in Americans' intolerance of speeches against democracy (see figure 1). No matter which question was used—as long as it was the same one at both times—the conclusion about the increase in civil libertarian sentiments was the same.

More generally, what has been called the "principle of form-resistant correlations" holds in most cases: if question wording (and meaning) is kept constant, differences over time, differences across educational levels, and most other careful comparisons are not seriously affected by specific question wording. Indeed, the distinction between results for single questions and results based on comparisons or associations holds even for simple factual inquiries. Consider, for example, a study of the number of rooms in American houses. No God-given rule states what to include

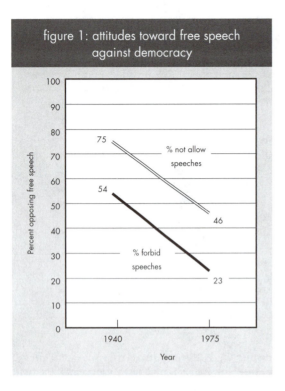

figure 1: attitudes toward free speech against democracy

% not allow speeches

% forbid speeches

Percent opposing free speech

Year

Survey researchers should also ask several different questions about any important issue. In addition to combining questions to increase reliability, the different answers can be synthesized rather than depending on the angle of vision provided by any single question. A further safeguard is to carry out frequent experiments like that on the forbid/allow wordings. By varying the form, wording, and context of questions, researchers can gain insight into both the questions and the relevant issues. Sometimes variations turn out to make no difference, and that is also useful to learn. For example, I once expected support for legalized abortion to increase when a question substituted *end pregnancy* for the word *abortion* in the phrasing. Yet no difference was found. Today, more and more researchers include survey-based experiments as part of their investigations, and readers should look for these sorts of safeguards when evaluating survey results.

the need for comparisons

To interpret surveys accurately, it's important to use a framework of comparative data in evaluating the results. For example, teachers know that course evaluations can be interpreted best against the backdrop of evaluations from other similar courses: a 75 percent rating of lectures as "excellent" takes on a quite different meaning depending on whether the average for other lecture courses is 50 percent or 90 percent. Such comparisons are fundamental for all survey results, yet they are easily overlooked when one feels the urge to speak definitively about public reactions to a unique event.

Comparative analysis over time, along with survey-based experiments, can also help us understand responses to questions about socially sensitive subjects. Experiments have shown that expressions of racial attitudes can change

when counting the rooms in a house (bathrooms? basements? hallways?); hence the average number reported for a particular place and time should not be treated as an absolute truth. What we can do, however, is try to apply the same definitions over time, across social divisions, even across nations. That way, we gain confidence in the comparisons we make—who has more rooms than who, for example.

We still face the task of interpreting the meaning of questions and of associations among questions, but that is true in all types of research. Even an index constructed from a large number of questions on the basis of a sophisticated statistical calculation called factor analysis inevitably requires the investigator to interpret what it is that he or she has measured. There is no escaping this theoretical challenge, fundamental to all research, whether using surveys or other methods such as field observations.

A2. We are interested in how people are getting along financially these days. Would you say that you (and your family living there) are *better off* or *worse off* financially than you were *a year ago*?

1. BETTER NOW   3. SAME   5. WORSE   8. DON'T KNOW

A3. Now looking ahead—do you think that *a year from now* you (and your family living there) will be *better off* financially, or *worse off*, or just about the same as now?

1. WILL BE BETTER OFF   3. SAME   5. WILL BE WORSE OFF   8. DON'T KNOW

A4. Now turning to business conditions in the country as a whole—do you think that during the next 12 months we'll have *good* times financially, or *bad* times, or what?

1. GOOD TIMES   2. GOOD WITH QUALIFICATIONS   3. PRO–CON

4. BAD WITH QUALIFICATIONS   5. BAD TIMES   8. DON'T KNOW

A8. Looking ahead, which would you say is more likely—that in the country as a whole we'll have continuous good times *during the next 5 years* or so, or that we will have periods of widespread *un*employment or depression, or what?

_____

_____

A18. About the big things people buy for their homes—such as furniture, a refrigerator, stove, television, and things like that. Generally speaking, do you think that now is a good or a bad time for people to buy major household items?

1. GOOD   3. PRO–CON   5. BAD   8. DON'T KNOW

Section of interview form used in the Survey of Consumers conducted by the Survey Research Center, University of Michigan. Courtesy of Survey Research Center, University of Michigan. Reprinted with permission.

substantially for both Black and White Americans depending on the interviewer's race. White respondents, for instance, are more likely to support racial intermarriage when speaking to a Black than to a White interviewer. Such self-censoring mirrors variations in cross-race conversations outside of surveys, reflecting not a methodological artifact of surveys but rather a fact of life about race relations in America. Still, if we consider time trends, with the race of interviewer kept constant, we can also see that White responses supporting intermarriage have clearly increased over the past half century (see table 2), that actual intermarriage rates have also risen (though from a much lower level) over recent years, and that the public visibility of cross-race marriage and dating has also increased. It would be foolish to assume that the survey data on

table 2: percent of white americans approving or disapproving of racial intermarriage, 1958–1997		
"Do you approve or disapprove of marriage between Blacks and Whites?"		
Year	Approve	Disapprove
1958	4	96
1978	34	66
1997	67	33
Source: Gallup Poll.		

racial attitudes reflect actions in any literal sense, but they do capture important *trends* in both norms and behavior.

Surveys remain our best tool for learning about large populations. One remarkable advantage surveys have over some other methods is the ability to identify their own limitations, as illustrated by the development of both probability theory in sampling and experiments in questioning. In the end, however, with surveys as with all research methods, there is no substitute for both care and intelligence in the way evidence is gathered and interpreted. What we learn about society is always mediated by the instruments we use, including our own eyes and ears. As Isaac Newton wrote long ago, error is not in the art but in the artificers.

___

RECOMMENDED RESOURCES

Philip E. Converse. 1964. "The Nature of Belief Systems in Mass Publics." In *Ideology and Discontent*, edited by D. E. Apter. London: The Free Press.

A profound and skeptical exploration of the nature of public attitudes.

Robert M. Groves. 1989. *Survey Errors and Survey Costs*. Hoboken: Wiley.

A sophisticated consideration of the sources of error in surveys.

Graham Kalton. 1983. *Introduction to Survey Sampling* (Sage Publications [Quantitative Applications in the Social Sciences]).

A brief and lucid introduction to sampling.

Benjamin I. Page and Robert Y. Shapiro. 1992. *The Rational Public: Fifty Years of Trends in Americans' Policy Preferences*. Chicago: University of Chicago Press.

In part, a persuasive reply to Converse's skepticism.

Howard Schuman and Stanley Presser. 1981. *Questions and Answers in Attitude Surveys: Experiments on Question Form, Wording, and Context*. San Diego: Academic Press. (Reprint edition with new preface, Sage Publications, 1996).

Several experiments discussed in the present article are drawn from this volume.

Samuel A. Stouffer. 2017. *Communism, Conformity, and Civil Liberties*, with introduction by James A. Davis. (Doubleday, 1955; Transaction Publishers, 1992).

Stouffer's keen awareness of both the possibilities and the limitations of survey data is reflected in this classic investigation. Also relevant to today's political climate.

Seymour Sudman, Norman Bradburn, and Norbert Schwarz. 1996. *Thinking About Answers: The Application of Cognitive Process to Survey Methodology*. San Francisco: Jossey-Bass.

A clear discussion of survey questioning by three well-known researchers.

Roger Tourangeau, Lance J. Rips, and Kenneth Rasinski. 2000. *The Psychology of Survey Response* Cambridge, UK: Cambridge University Press.

A comprehensive account of response effects, drawing especially on ideas from cognitive psychology.

REVIEW QUESTIONS

1. The author cites answering machines as a barrier to reaching potential survey respondents. The decline of landline telephones is another. With technological changes since telephone survey research began, who are the groups most likely to be excluded from surveys? What impact might their nonparticipation have on survey results?

2. News organizations often provide survey results with little background information or methodological detail. What questions should you ask when presented with statistics from surveys?

3. In describing survey sampling, the author uses the following words and phrases: *quota, economic strata*, and *bias*. What do each of these words mean in this context?

michael a. messner, margaret carlisle duncan, and nicole willms

this revolution is not being televised

4

summer 2006

american women have flooded into sports at all levels in the last several decades—but you would never know it from watching the evening news.

W ell, if you're like me, these are going to be three great days," gushed the news anchor on Los Angeles's KCBS evening news, as he introduced the sports report and passed the anchor to Jim Hill (who was reporting live, courtside from Staples Center before a Lakers game). "We got the Lakers tonight, we've got March Madness on Thursday and Friday. Jim, it doesn't get any better than this!" As predicted, that evening's sports news focused entirely on men's college and pro basketball, with a short interlude for men's ice hockey.

The sports news reports over the next few evenings offered plenty of men's NBA and men's NCAA basketball stories, and each included a token men's ice hockey story. All the reports ignored women's sports. Apparently, neither the women's professional golf (LPGA) tournament, women's NCAA basketball, nor any other women's sports taking place on those days were important enough to interrupt the excitement of "three great days" of men's basketball and hockey.

These three evenings in 2004 reflect a broader absence of women's sports from news and highlights shows. The news anchor's apparent throwaway opening comment, "If you're like me . . ." is especially telling. Nearly all the sports anchors and ancillary reporters, in the weeks of sports news and highlights shows that we studied, are just like him: they are men. And these men offer up a steady stream of verbal reports and visual images that focus on men's sports and largely ignore women's sports.

a wave of participation

Riding the cultural wave of feminism, and backed legally by Title IX (the 1972 statute intended to ensure sex equity in education), girls and women in the United States have enthusiastically increased their participation in sports over the past three decades. As a result, boys no longer totally dominate high school sports. In 1971, only 294,000 U.S. high school girls played interscholastic sports, compared with 3.7 million boys. In 1989, the first year of our sports media study, high school boys still outnumbered girls in sports, 3.4 million to 1.8 million. By 2004, the participation gap had closed further, 4.0 million boys to 2.9 million girls. College sports echo this trend. In 1972, when Title IX was enacted, the average college or university had two women's athletics teams. By 2004, the number had risen to more than eight teams per NCAA school. From 2000 to 2004, U.S. universities added 631 new women's teams. Women's participation rates in

> Amazingly, in these 15 years, we found almost no increase in the coverage of women's sports.

the Olympic Games have risen dramatically over the past three decades, and women's professional sports have also expanded.

Sports are no longer a "male preserve," to which boys and men enjoy exclusive or privileged access. Although men's sports still receive more than their share of community and school resources, and many girls and women still have to fight for full and equal access, the past three decades have seen a historic change in the gender dynamics of sports. But you would never know this if you got all your sports information from the network affiliates' evening and late-night news shows, or from the sports highlights shows on ESPN and Fox Sports. The media's continued marginalization of women's sports maintains the myth that sports are exclusively by, about, and for men. Women's sports are booming as never before. But if it is not in the news, it is, in a sense, simply "not happening."

a trickle of coverage

We analyzed 15 years of televised sports news and highlights shows to see how they cover women's and men's sports. In 1989, 1993, 1999, and again in 2004, we sampled two weeks in March, two weeks in July, and two weeks in November to study both the quantity and quality of news coverage of women's and men's sports by the three Los Angeles network affiliates. In 1999, we added ESPN's popular highlights show, *SportsCenter,* to our study. And in 2004, we added a regional highlights show, Fox Sports's *Southern California Sports Report.*

TV news and highlights shows cover men's college basketball and football, professional basketball and football, and professional baseball, peppered with generous doses of men's ice hockey, auto racing, golf, tennis, boxing, and occasional reports on other sports. Together, these reports make up a continuous stream of information, images, and commentary on male athletes and men's sports. Women's sports reports, by contrast, are occasional and seem to interrupt the steady flow of reporting on men's sports.

Amazingly, in these 15 years, we found almost no increase in the coverage of women's sports. In our 1989 study, the three network affiliates devoted only 5 percent of their airtime to women's sports. Ten years later, in 1999, there was a grudging increase to almost 9 percent. But in 2004, the proportion of coverage dropped back to 6 percent. The two sports highlights shows are even worse, with ESPN's *SportsCenter* devoting only 2 percent of its airtime to women's sports, and Fox Sports's *Southern California Sports Report* only 3 percent. In a full 30 or 60 minutes devoted to sports, there is still almost no time for women.

Reports on women's sports are not only less frequent, but less varied. When women's sports stories did appear in our sample, 42 percent of them were about tennis. Track and field stories were a distant second, accounting for 16 percent of all women's sports stories.

gags and sex appeal

On those rare occasions when women do appear on sports news and highlights shows, how are they portrayed? They are often part of gag features or stories on marginal but entertaining pseudosports, such as a women's nude bungee jump in 1999. Sports news and highlights shows are often peppered with humor in order to make the reports more entertaining. For instance, in a March report that included no coverage of women's sports, during a report on the Dodgers' spring training camp, KABC showed a few seconds of video about a middle-aged woman who had been invited to take batting practice at the camp. Ron Fukuzaki jokingly said to the news anchors, "Now we know the Dodgers are looking for a high-priced hitter, the way these ladies are hittin' the ball, hey, who

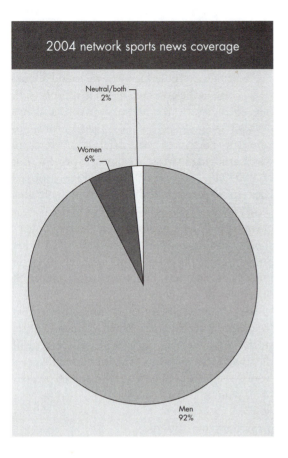

2004 network sports news coverage

Neutral/both
2%

Women
6%

Men
92%

sexual titillation. One news show, having run no coverage of conventional women's sports, reported on a promotional "football game" in which the female players competed in lingerie. Such shows commonly devote much of their scanty coverage of women's sports to individual athletes presented as icons of White, heterosexual, feminine attractiveness. In 1999 it was Anna Kournikova; in 2004, Maria Sharapova.

Several times that year, WTA stories focused on Sharapova (only coverage of Serena Williams came close to the amount devoted to Sharapova). This focus on Sharapova was legitimate: she had recently won Wimbledon and had become a highly ranked player. But commentators rarely seemed to report on Sharapova without also commenting (often jokingly) on her appearance. On November 11, 2004, KABC's Rob Fukuzaki introduced the day's only women's sports story—a 56-second feature on the WTA—with this teaser: "They slapped her on a billboard that read 'The closer you get, the hotter it gets.' Seventeen-year-old Maria Sharapova may have the same appeal as Anna Kournikova, but the young Russian can actually play tennis. Sharapova is a poster girl for the event." On one occasion, the Fox commentators were considerably less subtle. During their July 12 broadcast of a 33-second story on Sharapova, accompanied by footage of her win at Wimbledon, Barry LeBrock paused during his commentary as Van Earl Wright peppered the report with lusty howls: "In tennis news tonight . . . 17-year-old Wimbledon champ Maria Sharapova—[HOWL]—who has withdrawn from the tournament citing need for rest and recuperation—[HOWL]—now you know why—the Chase Open was to have been Sharapova's first tournament since beating Serena Williams in the Wimbledon final. Sharapova did add though that she plans to rejoin the tour on July 26—[both commentators together HOWL]."

knows, Marc and Michelle?" *SportsCenter* ran a 13-second story on a "weightlifting granny." Commenting on visuals of a woman lifting weights, Steve Berthiaume quipped, "We've been waiting forever for a sequel to the governor of California's hit, 'Pumping Iron.' We have it: here she is, the star of the show, the weight-lifting grandmama. Granny, you made us proud." We did not learn the woman's name or the location of the weight-lifting event. This was the only coverage of a "women's sport" during this broadcast of *SportsCenter*.

Women also appear in sexualized stories. Commentators seem endlessly amused by stories that combine gag features with opportunities for

Scantily clad women sometimes provide a visual backdrop for the reporting of men's sports. For instance, we noted the recurring use of shots of female cheerleaders during reports on various men's sports. On March 20, KNBC's report on NCAA men's basketball included a 2- or 3-second shot of Alabama's female cheerleaders shaking their pompons. Such shots were common in the visual imagery during March reports on men's college basketball on all three network affiliates, ESPN, and Fox. In fact, Fox Sports promoted its own programs using various shots of college cheerleaders (often wearing local USC and UCLA outfits) doing bump and grind dances, wearing short skirts, with exposed midriffs in tight-fitting cropped tops, accompanied by a voice-over saying, "The only sports network where Southern California fans come first. You're watching Fox Sports Network." Sexy female cheerleaders represent Fox Sports as a network, while female athletes are largely absent from its coverage.

the men's club

Sport may no longer be the exclusive preserve of men, but it still appears to be so in the realm of televised sports highlights shows. ESPN's *SportsCenter* and Fox's *Southern California Sports Report* offer an almost seamless vision of sport as an exclusive territory set up by and for men.

SportsCenter's ironic, often snidely humorous style has set the tone for other highlight shows like Fox Sports's *Southern California Sports Report*. This relatively new genre of televised sports entertainment meshes neatly with broader trends in contemporary popular culture that aim to entertain (and sell products to) young-to-middle-aged men. Television shows like *The Man Show*, magazines like *Maxim* and *FHM*, radio talk shows like the nationally syndicated *Tom Leykus Show*, and many radio and television sports talk shows share similar themes and target similar audiences of young men. These media typically present sports as a realm apart from women, where men can connect with each other "as men." This genre depicts and encourages a young, male lifestyle saturated with images of, and explicit talk about, sexy women as objects of consumption. Consumer products, including—often centrally, as in *The Man Show*—beer, create bonds among young men.

Strong, competent, decisive women (like most female athletes) have no place in this cultural field. Such women are either ignored or disparaged. *SportsCenter* and the *Southern California Sports Report* are "male spaces" (despite the occasional appearance of a female announcer). For the most part, they refrain from talking about or showing the athletic accomplishments of real female athletes. Women appear on these shows primarily as jokes, as sexual objects that prop up the men (Fox uses dancing cheerleaders in its ads), or as athletes, like Sharapova, who fit conventional stereotypes of heterosexual femininity.

mini-spikes

Sociologists often tell students in their introductory classes to walk into an elevator and face the other people, rather than the door. The resulting awkwardness signals the breaching of a social rule. Social conventions like facing the door in the elevator are often so well-ingrained that they are invisible to everyone until someone doesn't conform. The irregularity, the moment of resistance, or the deviant act tends to illustrate the rule. So too with moments in the mass media that contradict the dominant patterns.

More than half the news shows in our 2004 study had no coverage of women's sports. But we did notice two small surges in such coverage that, like facing the wrong way in an elevator, illuminate the larger patterns of (non)coverage of women's sports. The first mini-spike occurred on KNBC during July; the second (less dramatic) occurred during the November sample of the *Southern California Sports Report.*

In July of that year, KNBC devoted 15 percent of its sports news time to women's sports, far more than in the March sample (6 percent) or in the November sample (5 percent). In July, KNBC also devoted 21 percent of its ticker (the scrolling text at the bottom of the television screen) to women's sports. This was far more than the 5 percent and 2 percent of ticker time in March and November. Three times in July, the station led off a broadcast with a women's sports story. Twenty of KNBC's 36 women's sports stories in July focused on U.S. women's sports in the Olympics, and all three of the leads were on the Olympics. Neither of the other two network affiliate news shows, or the sports highlights shows in our sample, expanded its coverage of women's sports during the Olympics (KCBS had two women's Olympics stories during the March sample, KABC had six, ESPN three, and Fox three). How can we make sense of this single surge in coverage of women's Olympics sports? KNBC's expanded coverage of the Olympics on its news reports corresponded with the live and taped coverage of the Olympics by its parent network, NBC.

In the other surge, Fox devoted 7 percent of its *Southern California Sports Report* coverage to women's sports in November (compared to 1 percent in March and July). Five of Fox's six women's sports stories during the November sample were on tennis. This expanded coverage of women's tennis corresponded with a series of ads that Fox ran during the program, promoting a local WTA tournament, played at the Los Angeles Staples Center.

When asked why they don't cover more women's sports, producers, editors, and sports reporters often say they would like to, but they are just "giving the audience what they want."

The two mini-spikes suggest a more complicated story. Though our content analysis cannot show how producers decide what to show, we suspect that it was no coincidence that KNBC's March surge in the coverage of women's Olympic sports coincided with the parent NBC network's live and taped coverage of the Olympics. Similarly, Fox's small burst of coverage of women's tennis in November corresponded with the network's advertisements for a local WTA event.

KNBC's July surge in covering women's Olympic sports is especially noteworthy. When compared with other broadcasters, KNBC's surge in Olympics stories throws into relief the more general claim by producers that they choose their programming in response to audience demand for men's sports. Sometimes, it seems, when they perceive it to be in their interests, producers give us not what they think we want, but what they want us to want. The producers' party line asserts that the daily stream of stories and images of men's sports is simply a rational response to audience demand. This assertion obscures a more complicated reality: producers actively and consciously attempt to build audience demand for events in which they have a vested interest.

Audience-building, grounded in interlocking interests among television networks, news and highlight shows, commercial sponsors, and athletic organizations, is routine for men's sports. It appears to occur for women's sports only when a show's producers see a direct link between their interests and the promotion of a particular women's sporting event. The interlocking interests in women's sports appear to be simple and linear: when there is a direct interest in promoting a particular women's sports event (as KNBC did with the Olympics, and Fox did with the WTA), we see a surge in news or highlights coverage of that event. But this surge is both

> Producers actively and consciously attempt to build audience demand for events in which they have a vested interest.

temporary and local (confined to the particular network with the direct interest in promoting the women's event).

By contrast, the interlocking interests in the men's sports/media/commercial complex permeate the mass media in a seemingly organic, multi-nodal manner. These promotional efforts are more easily taken for granted and, ironically, may be less visible as promotion. News and highlights shows are two important links in the overall apparatus of audience-building for men's sports, but they rarely operate this way for women's sports. Like the student who faces the wrong direction in the elevator, the "mini-spikes" are exceptional moments of local or temporary promotion of women's sports events that serve to illustrate the rule.

what is to be done?

How can this "rule" be broken or changed? Clearly, our studies show that "evolutionary" growth in media coverage of women's sports does not simply happen automatically. Coverage of women's sports has remained the same for the past 15 years, and there is no reason to believe that this will change in the next 15 years unless producers decide that changing it serves their interests. Of course, producers want us to believe that they will give us more women's sports when we ask for them. For instance, on November 19, 2004, KNBC's Fred Roggin ended a broadcast of stories entirely about men with an 18-second report on women's golf that included game footage with this commentary: "And finally: got a call from a viewer last hour, [asking] why don't we show women's golf very often? Well, your wish is our command. Annika Sorenstam, the leader after two rounds of the ABT Championships. The Swedish superstar, who was seeking her eighth win of the year, fired a four-under 68 to grab a three-shot lead heading into the weekend. You call, we listen: there you go!"

Though viewers should phone television stations to protest sexism and ask for more-equitable coverage of women's sports, a few phone calls from viewers will not produce a shift toward fair and equitable coverage; this will require pressures from several directions. One source of change would involve the development and support of more female sports reporters and commentators. Sports organizations too can contribute by giving the sports media more and better information about female athletes. Indeed, a 2005 longitudinal study by Mary Jo Kane and Jo Ann Buysse shows that in recent years, university sports information departments have vastly improved the presentation of women's sports in their annual media guides.

But a dramatic change will require a critical examination of the ways that sports organizations and media cling to traditional masculine assumptions. Sport is one of the last bastions of men's traditional power and privilege. The women who have stormed the playing fields by the millions have contested this patriarchal institution. But televised sports continues to juxtapose images of powerful male bodies with sexualized images of women's bodies in ways that affirm conventional notions of male superiority and female frailty.

Sport is not a separate "world." It is intertwined with other aspects of social life in important ways. For the gender imagery of sports media to reflect and support this revolution in female athleticism, power relations and perceptions of gender must continue to change within sport organizations, among commercial sponsors who promote and advertise sports, within schools and universities, and within the mass media. This kind of social change may require a renewed feminist movement, both inside and outside sport.

RECOMMENDED RESOURCES

Amateur Athletic Foundation of Los Angeles. 2005. "Gender in Televised Sports News and Highlights Shows: 1989 through 2004." www.aafla.org/11pub/over_frmst.htm.

> The most recent addition to a longitudinal study that compares the quantity and quality of televised coverage of women's and men's sports.

Linda Jean Carpenter and Vivien R. Acosta. 2005. *Title IX.* Champaign: Human Kinetics Publishers.

> A vivid history of the role of Title IX in U.S. women's sports, written by two scholars who have studied and advocated for gender equity in sports for several decades.

Michael A. Messner and Jeffrey Montez de Oca. 2005. "The Male Consumer as Loser: Beer and Liquor Ads in Mega Sports Media Events." *Signs: Journal of Women in Culture and Society* 30: 1879–1909.

> An examination of gender symbolism in beer and liquor ads aimed at boys and men in *Sports Illustrated* and in televised coverage of the Super Bowl.

David Nylund. 2004. "When in Rome: Heterosexism, Homophobia and Sports Talk Radio." *Journal of Sport and Social Issues* 28: 136–68.

> A revealing study of one of the most popular sports-radio talk shows.

Sheila Scraton and Anne Flintoff, eds. 2002. *Gender and Sport: A Reader.* New York: Routledge.

> A collection of many of the most important scholarly articles on gender and sport.

REVIEW QUESTIONS

1. The author sampled television shows that aired during the months of March and July. What role does time of year play in the coverage that was analyzed? Do you think the findings would look different in other months or seasons?
2. The researchers note that when asked about the disproportionate coverage of men's sports, TV producers claim that they choose their programming in response to audience demand. Why might these assertions obscure a more complicated reality?
3. What are some important differences in the overall apparatus of audience-building for men's sports as compared to women's sports?
4. What do the authors suggest might contribute to an increase in coverage of women's sports?
5. This article was written more than ten years ago. What things have—or haven't—changed in the ways TV covers women's sports?

michael j. lovaglia

from summer camps to glass ceilings: the power of experiments

5

fall 2003

social science experiments on a few individuals from similar backgrounds can give rise to strategies for coping with social problems, ranging from intergroup conflict to women's inequality in the workplace. how does research on such narrow groups contribute to broad social understanding and insight?

A man in torn clothes sprawls across an urban sidewalk. He moans softly. Pedestrians hurry by with no more than a worried glance. No one stops to help. Someone watching from afar might wonder at such uncaring behavior; surely some conscientious person would stop. Moreover, these pedestrians are all young adults wearing clerical garb, seminarians studying for the ministry. They are hurrying to the church to deliver sermons on the Good Samaritan. Why did they not stop? Researchers who staged this test found that seminary students did not stop because they worried about being late. Their personal obligation to keeping an appointment outweighed their general commitment to helping others.

Experiments such as this one startle us into new ways of understanding people. Although we tend to explain why people do what they do—or, in this case, not do—as an expression of personal character, experiments show that the context of events determines behavior to a significant extent. Experimental studies carry great weight in the social sciences, gaining acceptance in prestigious journals and, in a high-profile example, last year's Nobel Prize in Economics. Some experiment results also get exposure in popular media, generating prime-time news coverage and Hollywood films.

Many people who hear about these experiments—and some social scientists, too—wonder how experiments achieve their power to convince, especially when their results often defy common sense. Experiments usually feature contrived conditions and record the behavior of at most a few hundred participants, many of whom are college students. Yet the results can tell us a lot about society.

the robbers cave experiment and summer camp movies

A sociological experiment in the 1950s demonstrated the effectiveness of a now-common strategy in which competing corporations form joint ventures that would appear to prevent one firm from gaining advantage over the other (much like the United States and Russia cooperating on the space station). In 1954, Muzafer Sherif, an early proponent of social science experiments, set up a summer camp near Robbers Cave State Park in Oklahoma to test theories about group conflict and how to avoid it. He believed that individuals develop a group identity when they work together toward a common goal. Groups become more cohesive and rigid when faced with competition from another group. This competition creates frustration, triggering hostility and conflict between the groups. Sherif thought a solution to the conflict might be found in the same process by which groups form: working toward a common goal. If hostile groups have to work together, then members might learn to see each other as part of a combined larger group, which would reduce their conflict.

A group of 22 boys—all White, middle class and close to their 12th birthdays—came to the Robbers Cave summer camp. Sherif and his colleagues divided them into two teams, the Eagles and the Rattlers. Each team completed projects requiring the cooperation of members, such as building a diving platform at a swimming hole. In the second phase of camp activities, the two teams competed against each other in various contests. The results are familiar. Rivalry between teams generated hostility and even a little mayhem (exaggerated in subsequent summer camp movies), and threatened to spin out of control. Hostility emerged during the first contest—a baseball game. Boys in each group cursed members of the opposing group and called them names. At dinner, Eagles refused to eat with Rattlers. Later, the Eagles tore down the Rattlers' flag and burned it. The Rattlers retaliated by vandalizing the Eagles' cabin. A food fight erupted in the mess hall.

The experiment showed that hostility between groups develops spontaneously when individuals within a group work together and then compete as a team against another group. The final phase of the experiment showed how to reduce conflict. On a hot summer day, researchers disabled the water supply and asked volunteers to find the problem. Boys from both groups stepped forward, located the problem, and worked together to solve it. Afterward, they all shared the water

in a friendly manner. Finding water was important enough that it neutralized the groups' mutual antipathy, fostering cooperation and the beginning of trust.

An overarching cooperative task that requires the contributions of both groups for success reduced intergroup conflict. This principle is widely applied today, in contexts as distant as international relations, even though the experiment had nothing directly to do with such serious settings.

describing the world or testing theories

The logic of social experiments differs from that of other social research. Survey researchers, for example, try to describe a population of people by selecting a large, representative sample and then asking questions to determine respondents' attitudes and other characteristics. In contrast, experiments test theories rather than describe a population. That is, they test for evidence of a specific social process in a small sample of people, chosen to be as similar as possible. If a theory predicts a particular result under certain conditions, experimenters then set up only those conditions. In this way, researchers can tell whether the predicted differences in behavior are produced by the conditions of the experiment instead of by individual differences among the participants.

Psychologist Philip Zimbardo's prison experiment at Stanford University is another famous example. He tested the theory that the brutal behavior of guards in prison camps (such as those in Nazi Germany) was a result of their being guards, rather than a result of their being individuals psychologically prone to act brutally. Zimbardo predicted that normal, mentally healthy, American men would become brutal or be brutalized simply because they became either prison guards or prisoners.

The hallmarks of good experimental research:
- A comparison between two groups as similar as possible but for one theoretically important difference (for example, undergraduate women assigned by coin flip to be team leaders or followers).
- Controlled conditions that allow the experiment to be repeated by other researchers.
- Follow-up studies that confirm the initial results and rule out competing explanations.
- A theory supported by experimental results that makes valid predictions in other contexts, spawning new research that reinforces the theory.

Pitfalls to avoid:
- Experimental results in one context cannot be simply exported to other contexts or cultures; they can support theories, which may then be used to make predictions for findings in other contexts.
- Ethical problems must be carefully considered. What effect might the research have on the lives of experiment participants?

In the early 1970s, Zimbardo created a "prison" in the basement of the psychology building at Stanford. He selected only male Stanford undergraduates to participate, ruling out those with any prior psychological problems. He then randomly assigned the participants to be either prisoners or prison guards. The procedure is like flipping a coin. Heads and the participant becomes a guard, tails and he gets arrested. Random assignment helped to ensure that the two groups in the experiment—guards and prisoners—would be similar in other ways. Within a day of the prisoners' arrival, guards began acting brutally and prisoners showed signs of anxiety. Conditions rapidly deteriorated until the experiment had to be stopped. (Because social experiments directly change people's lives, extraordinary care must be taken to avoid causing harm. Some social experiments have the potential to be as dangerous as a clinical trial testing a new drug. Today, universities' institutional review boards review proposed social experiments as stringently as they do medical and other scientific studies on people.)

The Stanford prison experiment helped shift thinking away from blaming German culture for the Holocaust and toward the social conditions that promote brutal behavior. The study received much media attention and was made into a popular German movie, *Das Experiment*. Ironically, the film version concluded that the solution to brutality is for individuals to take personal responsibility for their actions. But a solution that follows more consistently from the study itself is to construct social situations that discourage brutality.

Why was this experiment so influential? It said nothing directly about German behavior during the Holocaust. Rather, it tested a theoretical prediction that a coercive setting can induce brutal behavior. A good experiment subtly shifts the burden of scientific proof, challenging other researchers to show whether a social process demonstrated in the experiment operates differently in a complex, naturally occurring setting. Simple experiments are convincing in part because they demonstrate a difference in the behavior of people in contrasting situations. Simplicity helps build agreement; most people observing the results of the Stanford and Robbers Cave experiments would interpret their meanings similarly. Controlled conditions also allow other researchers to repeat the experiments to see if the same results occur, perhaps using slightly different procedures. Good experiments can in these ways extend theories and produce new knowledge.

Of course, no single study, theory, or method, no matter how good, establishes a scientific fact. Instead, science synthesizes different kinds of research from a variety of researchers to reach its conclusions. An experiment such as Zimbardo's Stanford prison makes a simple yet forceful statement that builds on earlier and inspires later research pointing to a conclusion. Eventually, we better understand the social processes underlying a problem and can attempt a practical intervention. Experiments also can be used to directly assess the effectiveness of alternative social policies.

arresting domestic violence: experimenting with social policy

In 1981, police in Minneapolis changed the way they responded to reports of domestic violence. Before 1981, police officers had the discretion to arrest the person who committed the assault, order him (or her) to leave the home for a short period, or provide on-site counseling. Advocates expressed concern that police were treating episodes of domestic violence too leniently, thereby failing to deter future assaults. Lawrence Sherman and Richard Berk designed an experiment to test whether making an arrest in a domestic violence case deterred future assaults better than the other two options of separating the couple and counseling.

The experiment had important implications for public policy, but it also addressed a long-standing dispute between two theoretical traditions in criminology. Deterrence theory holds that punishment discourages future criminal behavior. This school of thought maintains that suspects who are arrested will be less likely to commit another assault than those who are separated or counseled. A second theoretical tradition, known as labeling theory, suggests that when individuals are arrested, they become stigmatized as criminals by both society and in their own eyes. Their new self-image as a criminal then increases the likelihood of subsequent criminal behavior. (Labeling theory is the reason that names of juvenile offenders are kept out of the media except for serious offenses.) If labeling theory is valid, then those arrested for domestic violence actually would be more likely to commit another assault.

During the Sherman-Berk experiment, whenever Minneapolis police officers responded to a domestic violence call, they determined which procedure—arrest, separation, or counseling—to follow by random assignment. Researchers tracked the behavior of suspects in the study for six months following the domestic violence incident. Results showed a deterrent effect for arrest and no evidence for labeling theory. That is, suspects who had been arrested were slightly less likely to commit another assault during the subsequent six months than were those who had been separated or counseled.

Although the deterrence effect of arrest was small, the experiment had a large effect on public policy. Arrest in domestic violence cases became the preferred procedure in many police departments and 15 states passed mandatory arrest laws. Meanwhile, debate over implications for social theory continued. During the next decade, other researchers repeated the experiment in several other police jurisdictions. The new results were more complicated. Arrest deterred suspects who were employed, perhaps because arrest is more serious for those who have a lot to lose. For unemployed suspects, arrest had the opposite effect, as predicted by labeling theory. They were more likely to commit a subsequent assault than the unemployed men who had been separated or counseled. The theoretical advance was exciting, but it left policy implications unresolved. In practice, police officers are still uncertain whether making an arrest will be beneficial in a domestic violence case. More systematic research could better equip police and judges to make such critical, sometimes life-and-death decisions.

We may need a system that produces public policies in a way similar to the system of clinical trials that produces new medical drugs. None of the alternatives available to the police in the Minneapolis experiment was new. But we do not have an organized system to formulate new policies, test them, and then compare them to alternative policies in controlled experiments. Such a system is worth considering. It might lead to more-effective public policy the way that our system of developing new drugs has led to more-effective medicine.

why do some groups score low on standardized tests?

Low intelligence seems the obvious explanation for low scores on a mental ability test. But what if something besides intelligence determines test scores? In the 1990s, psychologist Claude Steele's experiments yielded the startling discovery that scores on standardized tests depend not only on students' ability to answer, but also on what they expect the consequences of their test scores to be. Students who are stereotyped as having low ability may underperform when they are apprehensive about getting a low score.

Steele and his colleagues conducted a simple experiment. They gave a difficult standardized test—like the college SAT but harder—to a group of Stanford students. Instructions for taking the test varied. Some students, selected at random, were told the test results could be used to compare their performance to that of other students. Some students were told the test was only to familiarize them with similar tests they would encounter at the university. When students were told the tests were just for familiarization, Black students scored about the same as White students of similar academic attainment. But when students thought they were going to be compared, Black students scored lower than did comparable White students—as is common on standardized tests.

My colleagues and I conducted subsequent experiments showing that Steele's theory was not limited to particular racial groups, but applied to any stigmatized group. We randomly assigned White university undergraduates to be treated as an advantaged "majority" or disadvantaged "minority," by telling some students that their left- or right-handedness made it unlikely that they would be able to contribute to a group project, and also that other group members might resent their inability to contribute. Then, we gave the students a standard test of mental ability, explaining that the results of the test would be used to assign them to group positions such as "supervisor," "analyst," or "menial" in the group project. We found that students' test scores were substantially lower if they were treated as a disadvantaged "minority" for as little as 20 minutes.

The line of research begun by Claude Steele now includes many studies by different researchers. They show that when Black and White students take the same standardized test, different expectations for the consequences of the test— not differences in mental ability—determine whether White students have an advantage.

That is, while the best mental ability tests do a fair job of determining differences in cognitive skills among otherwise similar individuals, differences in test scores between racial and ethnic groups are created by social conditions rather than by the groups' mental abilities.

Applied programs based on this research show promise for increasing the academic performance of disadvantaged students. One surprising detail is that the performances of the best Black students suffer the most. The threat of fulfilling a negative stereotype is felt most keenly by Black students with the potential to excel; it is they who worry most about the potential backlash from their competition with White students. This may explain why remedial programs to improve academic performance of weaker students have not closed the gap between Blacks and Whites generally. Honors programs that encourage Black students to undertake accelerated studies may have more effect, because promising Black students have more academic ability than their grades and test scores suggest. Claude Steele helped develop a successful program to improve the performance of incoming minority students at the University of Michigan that emphasizes high academic standards, affirming students' ability to achieve those standards, and building trust that successful minority students can be accepted in the academic community.

how can women attain status equal to men at work?

Social experiments can also suggest strategies individuals can use to improve their lives. Status Characteristics Theory explains how individuals attain influence in work groups: people who are expected to contribute more to the group gain more influence in the group and receive greater rewards from the group. That is, expected contributions often count more than actual contributions. Individuals expected to perform well are more often followed by the group and rewarded accordingly. For example, a woman may make a brilliant suggestion that guarantees a successful project, but her suggestion may be ignored until a respected male coworker endorses it. He then gets the credit.

Research using the theory confirms that people expect men to contribute more to group success than women and that men do have more influence in decision making. Men get more credit for the group's successes and less blame for the group's failures. And when group members are evaluated, men get higher performance ratings and bigger rewards. To achieve the same level of rewards, women must work harder and contribute more than men. Status Characteristics Theory can also explain the familiar strategies women have used to break through to positions of influence in the workplace. Traditionally, they have outcompeted men, following a masculine model that includes demonstrating competence through hard work and aggressive, even ruthless, competition. Successful women sometimes feel that they have sacrificed too much of themselves by following "male" strategies.

In the early 1980s, Cecilia Ridgeway conducted experiments using this theory that produced remarkable results for professional women struggling for career advancement under a glass ceiling. Ridgeway realized that people value not only the ability of a person to contribute, but also whether that person is motivated by a desire to help the group; they would not expect a person who is competent but selfish to contribute much of value. Ridgeway proposed that, because of gender stereotypes, however, people expect that even selfishly motivated men will contribute to the group, but expect contributions from women only when women demonstrate that they care about the group.

the hawthorne experiment

In the late 1920s and early 1930s, a Western Electric Company assembly plant near Chicago was the site of a series of studies aimed at developing scientifically based strategies for increasing worker productivity.

One experiment led to a concept called the "Hawthorne Effect." The researchers took a small group of female workers away from their peers and placed them in a separate room so the experimenters could study the effect of changes in lighting, work procedures, and break times on their productivity. It came as no surprise that improved lighting increased the workers' productivity, at least at first. But when the experimenters lowered the lighting to earlier levels, productivity continued to increase. Similar results after changing other aspects of the workers' environment led researchers to a conclusion that has since become known as the Hawthorne Effect: Workers increased their efforts because they were getting attention from the researchers, and because they bonded together as members of a prestigious "special" group.

Though legendary in its implications, the experiment has been criticized for design flaws and for confounding key variables, for example, two members of the study group were replaced mid-experiment with two new workers selected for their industriousness and cooperativeness. Simultaneous investigations by other sociologists revealed that workers who bonded strongly could unite to suppress work effort as well as speed it up.

Despite such shortcomings, reports of the Hawthorne experiment were used with enthusiasm by advocates of the human relations approach to workplace management. They felt that the results of the experiment challenged the scientific management perspectives that had shaped the Hawthorne studies in the first place. As a concept, the Hawthorne Effect—which posits that many interventions work, whatever they are, simply because people respond to being studied—also has been applied to a range of situations, such as student achievement in experimental schools, community organizing, and military campaigns. Such applications confirm the power of relatively small experiments to stimulate thinking about issues of great importance, both for sociologists and for the larger public.

Ridgeway conducted an experiment to test this theory. Four team members worked together to reach a decision. One of the team members—secretly collaborating with the experimenters—made comments that were either group-motivated ("It is important that we cooperate") or self-motivated ("I want to win points for myself"). As predicted, in the self-motivated condition, male collaborators had more influence over the groups' decisions than female collaborators.

In the group-motivated conditions, however, women collaborators' influence increased while the men's stayed at about the same high level as when they appeared selfish. Put another way, group-motivated women had as much influence as equally competent men regardless of the males' motivations.

The results suggest a strategy to succeed at work that women could use as an alternative to the competitive male one. Demonstrated competence is primary. Assertiveness also helps, but the focus on ruthless competition may be unnecessary for women's success. Instead, emphasizing a concern for other group members and the importance of working together to accomplish group goals can help competent women achieve recognition for their contributions. Future research in actual workplaces will help refine an effective strategy.

from theory to practice

The power of experiments flows from their use to test general theories. Sherif's Robbers Cave experiment tested a theory that explains how cooperation forms within groups and competition develops between them. Ridgeway tested her theory that influence in groups flows from the expectations people have about the ability and motivation of group members to contribute to group success.

Alone, a social experiment only demonstrates some phenomenon in one restricted context. But when experiments test theories, and their results lead to more tests in wider contexts, as well as other research with other methods, then we gain knowledge capable of transforming society. The experiments described have inspired lines of research with the potential to increase cooperation among competing organizations, decrease domestic violence, reduce the racial gap in academic success, and remove the glass ceiling limiting women in business. They successfully made the leap from small groups to helping us understand society at large.

RECOMMENDED RESOURCES

American Sociological Review. 1992. "Employment, Marriage, and the Deterrent Effect of Arrest for Domestic Violence: Replications and Re-Analyses." 57: 679–708.

Three research articles analyze follow-up studies to the original Sherman and Berk experiment on police responses to domestic violence.

Joseph Berger and Morris Zelditch Jr., eds. 1985. *Status, Rewards and Influence.* San Francisco: Jossey-Bass.

An overview of research on status processes in task groups.

Bernard P. Cohen. 1989. *Developing Sociological Knowledge: Theory and Method.* Chicago: Nelson Hall.

A classic text that describes social science as a reciprocal process in which research tests theory and theory develops through the interpretation of research.

Michael J. Lovaglia. 2000. *Knowing People: The Personal Use of Social Psychology.* New York: McGraw-Hill.

An accessible overview of social psychological research useful for individuals in their personal lives.

Michael J. Lovaglia, Jeffery W. Lucas, Jeffrey A. Houser, Shane R. Thye, and Barry Markovsky. 1998. "Status Processes and Mental Ability Test Scores." *American Journal of Sociology* 104: 195–228.

A research article demonstrating the adverse effect of a negative stereotype on the standardized test scores of White students.

Cecilia Ridgeway. 1982. "Status in Groups: The Importance of Motivation." *American Sociological Review* 47: 76–88.

An important research article that suggests a way for women to achieve equal status in the workplace.

Muzafer Sherif, O. J. Harvey, B. Jack White, William R. Hood, and Carolyn W. Sherif. 1988 [1961]. *The Robbers Cave Experiment: Intergroup Conflict and Cooperation.* Middleton: Wesleyan University Press.

The classic study on the origins of conflict between groups and a method for bringing together competing groups.

Claude M. Steele. 1999. "Thin Ice: 'Stereotype Threat' and Black College Students." *Atlantic,* August.

An accessible overview of research and applied programs for reducing the disadvantage of Black college students.

REVIEW QUESTIONS

1. The author writes, "Experimental results in one context cannot be simply exported to other contexts or cultures; they can support theories, which may then be used to make predictions for findings in other contexts." In what ways might differences in either context or culture yield different results from the same experiment?

2. Using experiments, a researcher can start from a theory and work toward understanding a social process. Choose one of the theories presented in this article and write a short paragraph on what it proposes.

3. Throughout the article, the author describes researchers using experiments to affect policy. What kinds of laws or policies do you think could be changed by results from experiments like these?

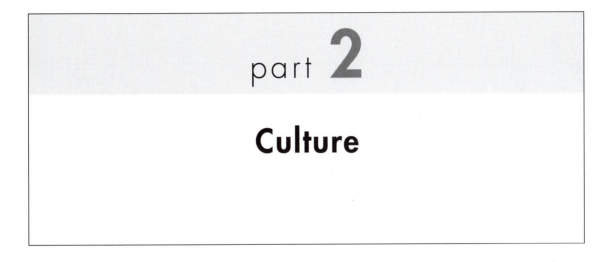

part **2**

Culture

bjorn christianson

babes in bikeland

6

winter 2016

in minneapolis, an annual "alleycat" bike race has become a powerful tool to educate and celebrate gender diversity in the cycling community.

One of urban cycling subculture's most interesting rituals is the alleycat: a bike race on open streets, where the riders choose their route between multiple checkpoints as outlined on a manifest. The competitions started as proof of skill among bicycle messengers, whose workday the events mimic. As bicycle messenger culture began to bleed into popular culture in the 1990s, leading to the new bicycle boom of the early 2000s, alleycat racing grew in popularity.

Babes in Bikeland was created in 2007 by Kayla Dotson and Chelsea Strate, with the aim of providing a safe place for women to compete in this unique, generally male-dominated format of bicycle racing. Nine years later, with hundreds of annual participants, the event is a celebration of the women/trans/femme (in the event's parlance, "WTF") cyclists—and is a powerful tool for educating the cycling community about gender issues.

Minneapolis, Minnesota, has long been a center of alleycat racing, playing host to one of the largest, longest-running of such events, the infamous Stupor Bowl, held each year since 1997 on the day before the American football event with a similar name. But alleycat racing and the culture surrounding it has been unwelcoming to WTF cyclists. From lack of prize equity to harassment, stories of WTFs being shut out of such events abound. Alcohol, ego, and a no-rules attitude often lead to uncomfortable or even dangerous situations for these riders.

At Babes in Bikeland, cisgendered males (men whose gender identity matches the gender they were assigned at birth) participate as volunteers at registration, running activities at checkpoints, or at the finish line. Each checkpoint has a captain, responsible for making sure that stop is a safe space. Riders, volunteers, and spectators are encouraged to know what a safe space is and feel empowered to enforce its boundaries, including no touching without both parties' "enthusiastic consent" and no questioning whether a racer "belongs" in the race. During the awards ceremony, men are encouraged to get to the back of the room: WTFs to the front.

The annual Babes in Bikeland race, now nearly a decade old, attracts a diverse range of cycling community members as riders and volunteers. Some 500 "WTF" racers competed in 2015. (© Bjorn Christianson)

The 2014 event started in Powderhorn Park in South Minneapolis, with a rousing crowd of riders and volunteers. (© Bjorn Christianson)

Planning an alleycat route often involves marking and consulting a map or writing a cue sheet. Riders receive their list of stops shortly before the race starts and have time to decide what they think is the best way to hit each location as quickly as possible. (© Bjorn Christianson)

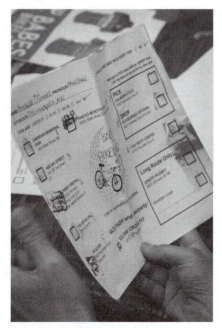

The list of places that each rider must go, a manifest, is stamped by a volunteer to prove the rider visited and completed any requisite task at the "stop." (© Bjorn Christianson)

A rider makes last-minute adjustments to their bicycle.
(© Bjorn Christianson)

Riders often participate in challenges at the various checkpoints. At this one, the racers compete in a game of "ring around the bike messenger." (© Bjorn Christianson)

Some participants celebrate the event with solo and group costumes, like this team inspired by the 1980 feminist revenge comedy film 9 to 5. (© Bjorn Christianson)

Competition, fun, and making a statement are all part of the event. (© Bjorn Christianson)

With the main event happening on open streets, riders travel to checkpoints around the city. (© Bjorn Christianson)

Riders are competing and the prizes at Babes in Bikeland are often impressive—including bicycle frames and equipment as well as other goods from many enthusiastic local businesses. That said, the ride is more event than race for many participants. (© Bjorn Christianson)

The traditional proof-of-participation for alleycat races, spoke cards are laminated art meant to be wedged between the spokes of a wheel. Riders often cherish their collections from past races. (© Bjorn Christianson)

Riders wait for a signal at a downtown intersection. They are riding with the normal flow of Minneapolis traffic. (© Bjorn Christianson)

A well-used street bike boasts a number of Babes in Bikeland and other spoke cards. (© Bjorn Christianson)

In addition to typical first, second, and third place prizes for the fastest racers, there are categories for new racers, riders from out of town, style, and others. All riders get a prize. (© Bjorn Christianson)

The top three veteran riders celebrate their win at the 2014 Babes in Bikeland after-party. (© Bjorn Christianson)

REVIEW QUESTIONS

1. According to the author, what is a safe space?
2. Think of some other places that are tradition-ally dominated by one gender or race. How do they operate to keep others out?
3. Like Babes in Bikeland, how can other institu-tions or organizations aim to be more inclusive?

james p. curley and oliver roeder

english soccer's mysterious worldwide popularity

7

winter 2016

what makes the english premiere league the most visually appealing broadcast spectacle in the world? data on the english premiere league disprove a few popular notions about its global popularity but ultimately can't tell us why it's so beloved.

The English Premier League recently signed an $8 billion contract with two cable channels, allowing them to broadcast games from 2016–2019. And this staggering sum is only for the domestic broadcasting rights. The league will generate another $5 billion over the same period from international TV deals. The EPL is carried by 80 broadcasters in 212 territories worldwide, and an average game is watched by over 12 million people. With these astonishing numbers, the EPL has every right to call itself the most popular league in the world. In comparison, its closest rival, Spain's La Liga, draws an average of just over 2 million fans per game. That league's top two teams, Real Madrid and Barcelona, negotiate their own TV contracts since they are able to get more money from the global TV audiences than selling La Liga as a whole. Other top European national leagues also languish in comparison to the English league. Italy's Serie A draws 4.5 million viewers for an average game and Germany's Bundesliga is roughly 2 million viewers.

Why is the EPL so popular worldwide? A number of theories have been floated but after close examination, we find that most prove to be no more than flimsy folk wisdom.

One theory is the passion of the players, commonly thought to be much higher than that of other European leagues. It is often remarked by commentators and pundits that English fans demand a higher intensity and work rate from their team's players. As the former Manchester United player, current England assistant coach and Sky TV commentator Gary Neville recently said, "When people talk about the DNA of English football, we've got one: we work hard, we're organized, structured, resilient, hard to beat, that never-say-die spirit."

English fans have come to expect a high tempo, blood-and-thunder style of soccer, compared to the slower more technical European style making the Premier League a quicker, more open, more physical and more attractive game for international viewers. Yet, the proportion of English players in the Premier League has been consistently falling from over 70 percent in the inaugural 1992–93 season to 36 percent in the 2014–15 season with many technically skilled foreign players now playing in England.

Another common refrain from English soccer personalities is that the English league's popularity is due to its highly competitive nature. It's often heard that the EPL is the only league where

> The English Premier League has every right to call itself the most popular football league in the world.

"bottom can beat top" and where upsets happen at a much higher frequency than in other top European leagues. For instance, the former Chelsea manager and agitator extraordinaire, José Mourinho recently compared the EPL to La Liga, the league where he managed Real Madrid:

To go to matches knowing that you are going to win for sure is not the best thing. In Spain everybody knows that two teams are top of the world. But after that there is a huge competitive difference and that's why the record is 100 points, 126 goals. In England, 100 points and 126 goals is impossible. If someone reaches 100 points and scores 126 goals, it's not the best competition for sure, they can be the best team, but not the best competition.

These comments regarding the supposed higher competitive balance in English soccer often go unchallenged. But just how true is this narrative? One top British soccer writer, Jonathan Wilson, is not convinced:

It's the most competitive league in the world. Anybody can beat anybody on their day. There are no easy games in this league. The mantra of the Premier League apologists is well known. . . . It's nonsense, of course.

We sought to test these claims by examining results and final standings data from six top European soccer leagues from 1995–96 and 2013–14. The leagues are England's EPL, Spain's La Liga, Italy's Serie A, Germany's Bundesliga, France's Ligue 1 and Holland's Eredivisie.

When looking at the number of unique winners of these European leagues, it appears that no one team has dominated. For instance, in these 20 complete seasons, Bayern Munich and Manchester United have won their domestic leagues 12 and 11 times respectively, and Juventus and Barcelona have won the Italian and Spanish leagues 10 times each. Further, England has only had four

unique winners during that time, Spain, Italy and Holland have had five, and Germany six. France's Ligue 1 is the only league with more diversity—it had 10 different winners in 20 seasons.

Examining winners may be too simplistic to come to any significant conclusion. Another way is to look at the diversity of teams in the top four places at the end of each season. From 1995–96 to 2014–15, the same four teams account for an astonishing 80 percent of EPL, 76 percent of Eredivisie, 68 percent of La Liga, 65 percent of Bundesliga, 65 percent of Serie A, and 58 percent of Ligue 1 top-four finishes. In terms of unique top-four finishers, 16 different teams have finished in the top four of Ligue 1 and 15 different teams in La Liga. Conversely, just 10 unique teams have finished in the top four of the EPL and Eredivisie. This analysis of the more successful sides in each league would actually suggest that the EPL is the least competitive league, while Ligue 1 is the most competitive.

But perhaps focusing on the top teams is a too restrictive view of "competitiveness." To get at the common refrain "anyone can beat anyone on their day," a more appropriate analysis might factor in the performances of the weaker teams. To do this, we examined the success of the bottom four teams in each season when playing against the top four teams. We asked how many points the bottom four teams were able to accrue in games against the top four. The results can be seen in figure 1.

In each season, the bottom four teams play a cumulative total of 32 games against top four opposition—a win is worth three points and a draw one, making 96 possible points available. In no year, in any league, did the bottom four achieve more than 28 points against the top four. Notably, in the EPL, Bundesliga and La Liga, the significant trend is toward the bottom four teams performing far worse against the top four. France is the league with the highest number of seasons where bottom four teams

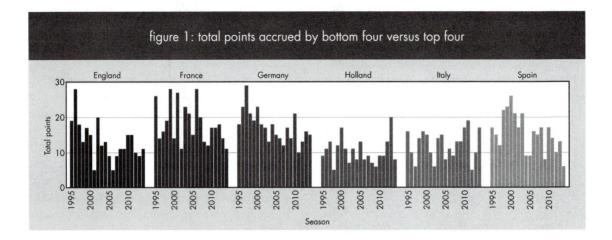

figure 1: total points accrued by bottom four versus top four

achieved more than 20 points against top four sides—but even this league hasn't had such a season since 2006. In Holland and Italy, the trend was fairly flat for a while, with the bottom four teams gaining on average only 10 points per season from their 32 games against top teams. Again, this shows there is actually some evidence that the EPL is becoming the least competitive in terms of these top–bottom matchups.

To get an even fuller picture of competitive balance, we can also look at the relative performance of all teams in a league in each season. To do this, we use a metric borrowed from the economics literature—the Gini coefficient. The Gini essentially describes the inequality in a group, and is often used to describe income inequality. If the relative difference between individuals of incremental ranks in some outcome measure (e.g., points gained in a season) is generally equal, then the Gini will be close to zero. But if this outcome measure is distributed highly *un*evenly then the Gini too will be higher. The Ginis of each

league from 1995–96 to 2014–15 are shown in figure 2.

In this figure, striking trends emerge. Since the mid-1990s, the Gini of three leagues (England, Spain and Germany) have been steadily increasing. This means that more points are ending up in the hands of relatively fewer teams—the leagues are becoming more unbalanced. Among these, the EPL has consistently been the most unbalanced. Ligue 1, for example, also shows a moderate tendency to becoming more unbalanced, but it is still much more equal in its points distribution than other leagues. The Dutch Eredivisie and Italian Serie A have historically been the most inequitable, though in the last few years they have been caught by other leagues—the EPL in particular.

The EPL may well be the most popular in terms of worldwide audience, but, from our analyses, this is not because of "competitive balance" or "upset likelihood." In actuality, a strong case could be made that all other leagues—with the possible exception of the Dutch Eredivisie—are far more balanced.

> In all sports, dominant dynasties are generally popular. However, if games and leagues become too predicatable, fans may lose interest.

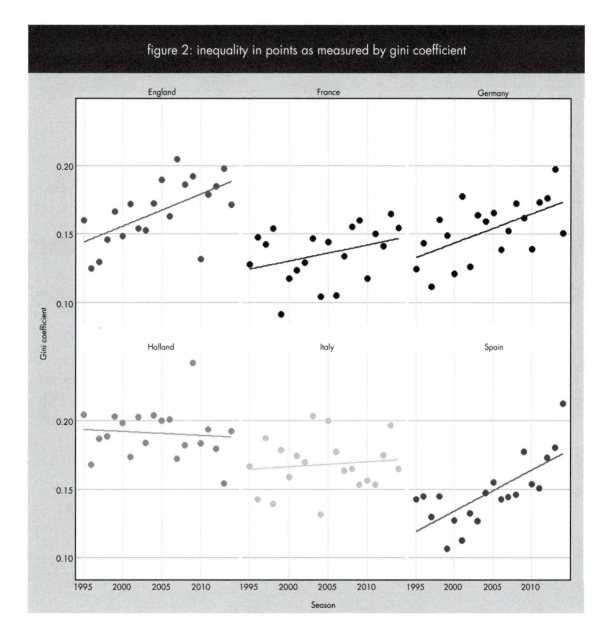

figure 2: inequality in points as measured by gini coefficient

After our analysis the question still remains: Why is the EPL so popular? Perhaps it could be as simple as the league's higher scoring. Fans love goals, after all.

While the EPL was historically a high-scoring league, it was never as high-scoring as the Spanish league. Over the last 20 or 30 years, the EPL is actually very similar in goals per game to La

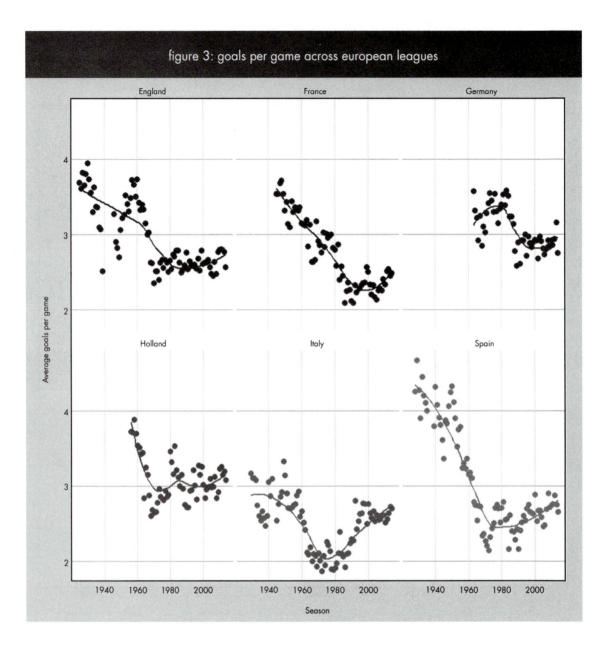

figure 3: goals per game across european leagues

Liga. During the same period, the more competitive French league has relatively low scoring, whereas the less competitive Dutch league has been relatively high scoring.

It appears that the disproportionate popularity of the EPL may not be due to competitive balance, upset likelihood or high scoring. What's more, the most competitive league—Ligue 1—is relatively unwatched outside of its own country. Equality certainly does not equal quality.

In fact, there must be a sweet spot of upsets and competitive balance. In all sports, dominant dynasties are generally popular. In the United States, look no further than the recent histories of the Yankees or the Bulls or the Patriots. Fans—particularly global fans—like to associate with winning teams. However, if games and leagues become too predictable it's possible that fans will lose interest.

In the end, perhaps the answer to English soccer's popularity lies beyond the database. Perhaps the key is in the aesthetics. The data disproves a few popular notions, but it can't ultimately prove that it is the tumultuous physical nature of English soccer combined with the English fans' vocal energies and fanatical loyalties to their clubs that makes the EPL the most visually appealing broadcast spectacle in the world.

REVIEW QUESTIONS

1. What do the data sets the authors review tell us about the English Premiere League?
2. In what ways do the authors argue that data are insufficient for showing why the English Premiere League is so popular worldwide?
3. How do certain sports leagues gain popularity in the United States, and are there factors at play outside of the popularity of the sport?

hilary levey friedman

tiger girls on the soccer field

8

fall 2013

scholar hilary levey friedman investigates how parental decisions result in different classed forms of femininity for girls who learn to be either "graceful girls" through dance, "aggressive girls" through soccer, or "pink warrior girls" through chess. she finds that parents higher up in the hierarchy of the middle class promote a more aggressive femininity, and we see this with both soccer and chess.

Charlotte, age 9, told me about her experiences playing competitive soccer:

At recess I'm like the only girl playing soccer. Everyone else is doing something else. So usually they call me a tomboy because I'm playing with the boys. But I'm NOT a tomboy. A tomboy is somebody who like wants to be a boy and is like always being with the boys and stuff. I have dolls and I like pink. I really like girl things, like I painted my nails.

To Charlotte, being a tomboy is a negative label. She is more eager to identify with her femininity, pointing out how she paints her nails and wears pink. She wants a strong femininity, the kind that lets her be an aggressive soccer player, too. "We play soccer against boys sometimes because it's better for the girls to learn to be more aggressive," she told me. While Charlotte thinks girls can be just as good as boys at soccer, she thinks they'll only improve if they become as tough as the boys.

Her mom Marie agrees. Looking ahead, she sees competitive sports as a way for her daughter to become aggressive—not just in the athletic arena, but also in life. Marie told me,

We have no illusions that our daughter is going to be a great athlete. But the team element [is important]. I worked for Morgan Stanley for ten years, and I interviewed applicants, and that ability to work on a team was a crucial part of our hiring process. So it's a skill that comes into play much later. It's not just about ball skills or hand-eye coordination.

"When I was interviewing job candidates at Morgan Stanley," Marie, a White woman with two Ivy League degrees, told me, "if I got a female candidate—because it's banking and you need to be aggressive, you need to be tough—if she played, like, ice hockey, *done*. My daughter's playing, and I'm just a big believer in kids learning to be confidently aggressive, and I think that plays out in life assertiveness."

> Many parents believe that being cutthroat and aggressive sets girls on a path to the corner office as a company executive.

Many parents like Marie believe that being cutthroat and aggressive sets girls on a path to the corner office as a company executive. The higher up you go in the class hierarchy, the more likely you will encounter parents like Marie, who believe in teaching their daughters what I call "aggressive femininity." They are taught to be both physically and competitively forceful, actively subsuming aspects of their femininity; many of their parents define their daughters in opposition to "girly girls."

As Sheryl Sandberg, COO of Facebook and author of the bestseller *Lean In*, declared, "Instead of calling our daughters bossy, let's say, 'My daughter has executive leadership skills!'" Girls today grow up in a world with an unprecedented set of educational and professional opportunities, and many look up to successful women like Sandberg. More girls will graduate from college and earn advanced degrees than ever before, and nearly all professions are open to them, even combat careers in the military.

Successful women want to raise daughters who share the qualities that have brought them success—qualities that some liken to bossiness.

nice girls competing

When I studied 95 families with elementary school-age children who were involved in competitive after-school activities—chess, dance, and soccer—I met parents like Marie who saw their kids' participation in competitive after-school activities as a way to develop certain values and skills: the importance of winning; the ability to bounce back from a loss to win in the future; to perform within time limits; to succeed in stressful situations; and to perform under the gaze of others—what I call "Competitive Kid Capital."

One of the most striking findings was that upper-middle-class parents of girls often perceive a link between aggression and success in athletics, and are more likely to enroll their daughters in soccer or chess, rather than dance—activities that are deemed more cooperative and less competitive. Like Sheryl Sandberg, they believe that executive leadership skills can be effectively developed and honed on soccer fields and basketball courts, even when the competitors are wearing pink shoes and jerseys.

Malcolm, an African-American lawyer with three Ivy League degrees, believes that sports don't just steer his seven-year-old daughter toward assertiveness, they actively drive her away from more traditionally feminine pursuits. "She's a cute little girl, but I don't like her to be a girly-girl," he explained. "You know, I don't want her to be a cheerleader—nothing against that—but I want her to prepare to have the option, if she wants to be an executive in a company, that she can play on that turf. And if she's kind of a girly-girl, maybe she'll be a secretary. There's nothing wrong with that, but let her have the option of doing something else if she wants."

Malcolm thinks being a "girly-girl" means less desirable, more traditionally feminine occupations. The images he evokes related to being an executive, such as "play on that turf," suggests the importance he places on athletics to help his daughter follow a historically male career path. And he identifies cheerleading—which was once a male-dominated area and still has an athletic and competitive component, even as the athletes are now expected to wear makeup, curl their hair, and often bare their midriffs—as being too much of a girly-girl activity.

sports make the girl

Today, sports are an important element of American upper-middle-class culture and child-rearing practices. But as recently as a century ago, organized team sports were limited to males. Women and girls were generally seen as physically inferior and mentally unable to handle competition. Even when they were allowed to participate, competition was off-limits, and seen as damaging.

When New York City's Public Schools Athletic Girls League was founded in 1905, for example, the director was opposed to keeping records, arguing that girls could easily injure themselves if they got too aggressive or tried to break a record. All-girls' elite schools were among the first to break with this view of women and competition, though they called competitive organizations "associations" instead of "leagues," lest people complain a league was too masculine.

Much of this changed, along with social attitudes, after the passage of Title IX 40 years ago. With time, young women who had once been focused on the arts came, in the twenty-first century, to see athletics as especially important tools for development. Two recent studies, one by the Women's Sports Foundation and the other by the Oppenheimer Foundation, have found that 82 percent of executive businesswomen played organized sports in middle school and high school. Of female *Fortune 500* executives, 80 percent said they were competitive tomboys during childhood. The Oppenheimer study also found that, while 16 percent of all American women describe themselves as athletic, among women who earn over $75,000 annually, the number rises to about 50 percent.

These conclusions are consistent with the studies like those of economist Betsey Stevenson, whose work on Title IX finds that par-

> While 16 percent of all American women describe themselves as athletic, among women who earn over $75,000 annually, the number rises to about 50 percent.

ticipation in high school sports increases the likelihood that a girl will attend college, enter the labor market, and enter previously male-dominated occupations. She suggests that sports develops such skills as learning how to compete and how to become a team member, which are both key as women navigate the traditionally male-dominated labor market.

But competition, athletic or otherwise, is still seen as a masculine attribute. In 2010, the journal *Sex Roles* published a study on high school boys and girls that found that even today, "boys are 'trained' from an early age to be competitive. . . . Research suggests that girls are less comfortable than boys in competitive

circumstances and that girls are socialized to mask overt competitiveness and aggressiveness more generally." David Hibbard and Duane Buhrmester, both psychologists, argue that a mentality of "competing to win" is at odds with the "nice girl" ideal. Girls who engage in head-to-head competition may have more social difficulties, even as they become prepared for a fast-tracked, upper-middle-class life.

pink girls and dancing queens

Parents of chess-playing girls also encourage their daughters to be assertive and competitive. As one chess mom explained to me, "We're raising her . . . to be feminist. And so she says she wants to be a grand master or the president [of the United States]. She doesn't have any ideas about gender limitations and I think that's a good thing."

Chess girls don't have to be as assertive as soccer girls like Charlotte. Partly because it is not a physical game, chess allows girls to be what one mother of two sons described to me as a "pink girl": "These girls have princess T-shirts on," she said. They have "rhinestones and bows in their hair—and they beat boys. And the boys come out completely deflated. That's the kind of thing I think is so funny. That girl Carolyn, I call her the killer chess player. She has bows in her hair, wears dresses, everything is pink, Barbie backpack, and she plays killer chess."

That a winning girl can look so feminine has an especially strong effect on boys, and sometimes their parents. Another chess mom told me how a father reacted negatively when his son lost to her daughter: "The father came out and was shocked. He said, 'You let a girl beat you!' "

In competitive dance, it's more common to see girls win, if only because the activity is dominated by girls. Dance is a physical activity that, like cheerleading, "no girly-girls" dad Malcolm would like his daughter to avoid. Competitive dancers are expected to wear makeup when they compete. While this has a practical purpose—to make sure the dancers' faces are not "washed out" by the stage lights—lipstick, blush, and mascara also accentuate feminine features; their practices are among those sociologist C. J. Pascoe would identify as part of "normative femininity."

As I sat in the audience at dance competitions, I often heard teachers and parents remark, "Wow, she looks beautiful up there," or, "They look very good." In addition to makeup, girls' dance costumes featured sequins, rhinestones, ribbons, and other decorative embellishments, and, at most competitions, costume and appearance are evaluated as part of the final score.

In contrast, in chess and soccer, appearance matters little to the outcome of the competition. Although soccer girls' appearances are regulated, it is done in a way that de-emphasizes femininity. Soccer girls must remove all jewelry (for safety reasons), and coaches direct girls to make sure all of their hair is out of their faces. To keep their view unimpeded, girls pull their hair back in ponytails, using headbands or elastic bands. This has become a fashion and identity statement itself—perhaps a way to assert femininity in a less-than-feminine environment, and to keep shorter hair and bangs off the face. And, of course, female soccer uniforms are not easily distinguishable from male uniforms. Many traditional markers of femininity are absent from the pitch.

It is not surprising, then, that although both soccer and dance parents mentioned lifelong fitness and health as a motivation for their young daughters' involvement with these activities, only dance moms linked their kids' participation to obesity and appearance. Dance mom Tiffany told me about her concerns about her daughter's future body: "My short-term goal for her is to keep, believe it or not, physically fit. Because, she's an eater, across the board. . . . [Dance] keeps her at a nice weight. You know what I mean? And she struggles with that [weight], that's going to be her struggle, I told her."

gender scripts and classed lessons

Another set of scripts—those about femininity—helps explain how parents (especially dance and soccer parents) choose among activities for their daughters. I call the dance script the "graceful girls," the soccer "aggressive girls," and the chess "pink warriors." When dance, soccer, and chess parents draw from different gender scripts, they are shaped by class, producing classed lessons in femininity for their girls.

Though nearly all of the families I met are part of the broadly defined middle class, parents higher up in the hierarchy of the middle class promote a more aggressive femininity, as seen in both soccer and chess families. Dance mothers, who generally have lower status than the chess and soccer parents, promote a femininity that is less competitively aggressive and prioritizes physical appearance. Lower-middle-class and working-class families place a greater emphasis on traditional femininity.

Among the 38 families I met who had competitive young girls, the vast majority of soccer families were upper-middle class. None of the dance families were upper-middle class, and over a third were lower-middle class; dance was the only activity of the three that had any working-class participants. Chess families with

Today, there are three times more female soccer players than Girl Scouts in the United States.

daughters who compete tend to look the most like soccer families, as the majority of families are upper-middle class.

These upper-middle-class families had at least one parent who has earned an advanced postgraduate degree and work in a professional or managerial occupation, and both parents had earned a four-year college degree. The lower-middle-class families have just one parent with a college degree; neither parent works in a professional or managerial occupation.

Recall Malcolm and Marie. The former is a lawyer, and the latter was an investment banker who recently stopped working to spend more time with her five children. Both attended elite universities and were representative of the rest of the parents. Most of the soccer parents had similar occupations, or they were professors or doctors.

It is not surprising that these highly credentialed, competitive parents have similar occupational aspirations for their children, including their daughters. They are trying to impart particular skills and lessons to their daughters at a young age to help them succeed in the long term. As Malcolm made clear, upper-middle-class parents do not want their daughters to end up as secretaries, so participation in competitive activities, where aggression is inculcated, becomes a priority so the girls can maintain their family's status in the future.

bossy is best?

Today, there are three times more female soccer players than Girl Scouts in the United States. This trend is due, in part, to the fact that upper-middle-class families are trying to strategically maintain their family's class position, preparing their daughters to enter what are traditionally male worlds. Parents are choosing after-school activities that will give these girls an advantage in college admissions and beyond; they are more likely to have the resources to enable their daughters to travel and compete.

But aggressive femininity can come at a cost. A recent study of the long-term effects of sports participation on adolescent girls by psychologists Campbell Leaper and Elizabeth Daniels found that many girls "struggle to reconcile their athleticism with traditional standards of hegemonic femininity that emphasize maintaining a thin body ideal and adhering to a rigid definition of beauty." Aggressive and pink warrior girls, along with graceful girls, face what psychologist Stephen Hinshaw calls the "triple bind" of being supportive, competitive and successful—and effortlessly beautiful.

In her work on female litigators, sociologist Jennifer Pierce similarly found that successful women had to become either "very male" or "very caring." She describes this binary: "Whereas men are praised for using intimidation and strategic friendliness, women who are aggressive are censured for being too difficult to get along with, and women who are nice are considered 'not tough enough' to be good litigators." Women need to be aggressive to succeed, but not *so* aggressive that they get labeled bitchy. It's a delicate balancing act for women in the workforce, and for parents who want to raise girls who can be the boss.

These classed gender ideals also have long-term implications for inequality. Girls from upper-middle-class families seem better equipped with the skills they need to succeed in more-lucrative careers, and in leadership roles as adults. Better understanding of socialization practices at the upper end of the class structure may open up real opportunities for others as well.

Sheryl Sandberg wasn't a soccer player. She wasn't even athletic, in an aggressive sense, at all. She was once an aerobics instructor who succeeded by leading others in a silver leotard. Her story suggests that soccer and contact sports aren't a direct path to the corner office, and that dance and cheerleading don't shut the door on success.

The future is not cast in stone: Tiffany's dancing daughter may yet become an executive, and Malcolm's daughter may become her assistant. That doesn't stop many affluent parents from being convinced that leaning in while wearing pink cleats produces girls with executive leadership skills.

RECOMMENDED RESOURCES

Elizabeth Daniels and Campbell Leaper. 2006. "A Longitudinal Investigation of Sport Participation, Peer Acceptance, and Self-esteem among Adolescent Girls and Boys." *Sex Roles* 55: 875–80.

One of the few longitudinal studies to look at competition and sports among young people.

David R. Hibbard and Duane Buhrmester. 2010. "Competitiveness, Gender, and Adjustment among Adolescents." *Sex Roles* 63(5–6): 412–24.

An example of how psychologists look at these questions, with provocative conclusions.

Stephan Hinshaw and Rachel Kranz. 2009. *The Triple Bind: Saving Our Teenagers from Today's Pressures.* New York: Ballantine Books.

Focused on the pressures girls face today, this book provides suggestions on how to help them navigate academic and social pressures.

C. J. Pascoe. 2007. *Dude, You're a Fag: Masculinity and Sexuality in High School.* Berkeley and Los Angeles: University of California Press.

An important book on how gender matters among young people today, with good discussions of athletics and appearance.

Betsey Stevenson. 2010. "Beyond the Classroom: Using Title IX to Measure the Return to High School Sports." *Review of Economics & Statistics* 92(2): 284–301.

The first study to look at the long-term impact of Title IX on women's achievement outside of sports.

REVIEW QUESTIONS

1. What does the author mean by aggressive femininity?
2. According to the author, what is the relationship between social class and the resources necessary for cultivating aggressive femininity?
3. Consider the three scripts defined in the article: the soccer "aggressive girls," the dance "graceful girls," and the chess "pink warriors." How do each of these scripts reify or disrupt traditional scripts of feminine performance?

claudio e. benzecry

opera thugs and passionate fandom

9

summer 2012

benzecry shows how passion for a cultural object develops, gets refined, and is sustained over time and the consequences of this for personal identity.

Franco calls himself an "opera thug." He is 41 years old and lives alone in a large apartment next to a traditional church in Buenos Aires, Argentina. He's tall and fit, easily approachable, and attends just about every opera performance in the city. There are many to choose from; opera exploded in Buenos Aires in the early 2000s, and a full secondary circuit boasts performances about every other night. The first time we met, in the standing-room area of the Colón, the nation's main opera house, Franco asked whether I was planning to attend a seldom-performed opera by Vivaldi. He had just returned from another performance at an off-circuit opera house, and got lost when he was detoured by a street protest along the way. "It's the risk you run if you want to attend everything!" he said.

Franco's family was never interested in classical music, and well into his teens he liked pop music. But during his fourth year of high school, a music teacher at his small, rural school suggested to students that if they wanted to listen to something that would never fall out of fashion, they should consider classical music, such as Vivaldi's *Four Seasons*. Franco told his mother, and she bought him some classical works. When Franco went away to study medicine, he saw that Mozart's *The Magic Flute* was playing and on a whim decided

to attend. Though he understood little about it, he remembered "Queen of the Night Aria." The next day he bought a version sung by Maria Callas. He was at the time "an absolute virgin" and "completely ignorant," as he put it. A month later, he saw his second opera *Lucia* and was hooked. He began attending multiple—and sometimes all—performances of each opera.

The first time he came to the Colón, for Wagner's *Tannhäuser*, Franco had already been living in Buenos Aires for four years. When I asked him what took him so long to get there, he said that he was scared. He had believed that opera was for the elite and that, if he did not have enough money or social status, he was going to feel out of place. But those days are long gone; the Colón is now his second home. And though he has met many people through opera, he does not socialize with them outside. They are, he says, like the "imaginary friends" he had when he was a child. Franco's family does not share his passion. "It's all mine. I didn't inherit anything from my parents," he says. They didn't have a stereo, and classical radio broadcasts did not reach all the way to their home. Plus, they never had much leisure time. His father was from a German farming family and his mother was a housewife. For a long time his family disapproved of his interest

> There was a time when Franco used to do other things, like go to the movies. But that is no longer the case.

66   culture

in opera because they considered it to be an inappropriate activity for a rugged, rural man.

Franco describes himself as "a professional opera fan," and spends about a quarter of his income on opera-related activities. He attends performance three times a week—five, if his schedule permits—regularly buys CDs, books, and DVDs, and constantly listens to opera on the radio. Although he has enough money to purchase subscription tickets, for him, opera is not about sitting quietly and properly; it is an activity that must be experienced standing. But key to being a "professional fan" is study. "After the show is over, I continue at home. I read, I listen to radio shows, pay attention to certain fragments of music in my records," he says. He dedicates at least two hours of every day to opera, in addition to the performances themselves, listening for one hour in the morning and one hour in the afternoon. He listens while cooking or ironing his shirts, or before going to work. Preshow preparation takes place on the weekends, when he has more time, is a bit more relaxed, and can focus intently. Like most opera fans, he tries to avoid reading reviews before attending an opera for the first time, so as not to cloud his critical judgment. There was a time when Franco used to do other things, like go to the movies. But that is no longer the case.

What makes someone like Franco an opera fan? Is it something that starts in one's home and upbringing, or is it something people pick up along the way? While class background and socialization are certainly part of the equation, the story of Franco—someone from a rural, working-class family who had no predisposition toward opera—suggests that such explanations can only be partial ones. While one's class position may influence the probability of being exposed to opera in the family, or at school, engaging and investing in opera works like a career in which individuals learn, day after day, to simultaneously enjoy opera

and become fans. The affective connection typically happens first—and often suddenly.

To love someone or something is to reorganize your life, navigate constraints and trials, rearrange activities, and even exclude others from entering or becoming close. These are often the terms fans used to speak of opera. In interviews, they talk of falling in love at first sight, working to maintain that love, being addicted to certain moments, and tragically falling out of love. Key to understanding what makes someone a fan, what pushes a person past an affection for a certain something into a real, genuine, overpowering love for it, requires us to look at how people come into fandom.

If loving opera happens suddenly for passionate fans, sustaining the love over time requires making an emotional commitment, dedicating oneself to learning, and informally socializing with other fans.

love at first sight

José Luis is 70 years old and works in the press department of the Catholic University. His Spanish parents were absolutely oblivious to opera. When he was eight years old, he discovered a Viennese waltz show that broadcasted on state radio. In 1950, one of his favorite conductors, Arthur Roshinski, came to Buenos Aires to conduct Rimsky-Korsakov's *The Golden Cockerel*. He thought that Roshinski would be conducting the symphonic suite drawn from the opera, which lasts 20 minutes. To his surprise, it was the whole opera—which lasted a bit over three hours. After attending with his mother, he was entranced by what he calls "the spectacle" of opera, and the next season he started going on his own to every performance. He still attends.

Fans often speak of their sense of surprise the first time they visited an opera house. They say they were ill-prepared to make sense of opera when they first encountered it, describing a kind of dissonance between what they were used to hearing, and what they experienced during that initial live performance. They describe the pleasing rush they felt, which they felt compelled to make sense of, and their passage from a regular, everyday state to an intensely frantic one in which they lost control and became a passive object moved by an outside force. "It drove me crazy," "It froze me," "It moved me," "It killed me," "It filled me up," "It made me stupid" is what they say. Their initial, passionate sense of surprise pushed fans to engage in activities designed to enable them both enjoy and control that initial sense of pleasure, and they made a career out of trying to reexperience that first rush.

Some fans were surprised by how powerful singers' voices were and by what they were able to do with their bodies. Those who had listened to opera in their homes were moved by live visual and sensorial experience. Others went crazy for the grandeur of the lush Beaux-Arts interiors of the halls. Later on, when they slowly become part of fan culture, they developed an understanding of "being an opera fan." Fan careers channel one's love for opera and solidify it in one's life trajectory. It is useful to think of this learning as an investment. In addition to bringing deeper aesthetic pleasures, it brings refinements to personal identity, and a distinctive sense of who they are as individuals.

Julio is a semiretired musical coach who is in his 60s. His parents, who lived in a working-class industrial area in the southern part of the city, took him to the opera for the first time when he was only eight, and he saw several children's operas, like *Hansel and Gretel*. When he was 17, he went to his first adult—or as he calls it "real"—opera, and then decided to attend the opera on a regular basis. It was a 1962 production of *Barbiere* with Victoria de los Angeles that

sparked his interest, and both the opera and the singer became his personal favorites. By 1977, he was following her all to the way to Montevideo, the capital of Uruguay. Julio can still vividly describe the timbre of her voice and the pastel pink and sepia-red dress she wore that first time.

By interacting with other fans, individuals learn to sustain the excitement of the initial encounter. They're "newbies" who want to learn more about what they've enjoyed, and how to enjoy it more. For them, passion becomes a career. The production of fandom tends to occur outside of the family, through informal channels such as bus trips, intermissions, and lines awaiting entry at the opera house door. Novices depend upon companions to experience opera with, with whom they learn to respond like seasoned opera lovers. They hang out with opera lovers, experience and observe events, and adopt words that more experienced opera fans use to describe and qualify particular shows and singers.

While waiting in line for Wagner's *Die Walküre* one evening, someone came to the secondary door of the Colón Opera House to distribute leaflets advertising a performance of *Un Ballo in Maschera*. It prompted the woman next to me to comment on how bad the first night of that performance was, which generated a conversation about who had already seen it, which in turn devolved into a discussion of the soprano in *Un Ballo*, whom many fans recognize, as they call her by her first name. An older gentleman mentioned the previous time he had heard the soprano. A younger guy reminisced about seeing her as the lead in Verdi's *Simone Boccanegra* and "being amazed." The woman and the older man disagreed about the quality of her performance, which led to a conversation about whether or not it was smart to stage

> If loving opera happens suddenly for passionate fans, sustaining the love over time requires emotional commitment.

an opera like *Un Ballo,* which had been performed so many times before, and by so many great singers. When the line finally moved, the small group became quiet as they prepared to bound up the hundreds of stairs that separated them from a complete and unobstructed view of the stage.

As new fans listen to opera live, they also take into account how others describe different shows and competing performances. They improve as fans as they attend more performances and as others react to their comments and gestures about what is being watched and listened to. Becoming a fan means getting to know opera and understanding what it means to be an opera lover. It entails making comparisons, associating and distinguishing one's private responses from that of others. This preparation increases the enjoyment, until the names of arias and references to music fragments spill out when an opera fan opens his or her mouth.

> Most of us have a difficult time making sense of fans' seemingly irrational relationships to opera, monster truck rallies, or *Twilight* movies.

coupling with opera

Older fans play a central role in getting novices excited about participating passionately in the world of opera. They discuss with them librettos and their staging, and share tales of their brushes with stars and their "treasure" hunts for new and talented singers and unheard before operas. Some spoke of traveling eight hours in a dilapidated bus to Cordoba, some 450 miles away, in order to explore undiscovered singers and musical pieces. Others waited for the artists as they exited the opera house or their hotels. Some become so well acquainted with them that they receive phone calls when the artists are in town, or they drive to pick them up to bring them to the hall and are rewarded by getting pictures and recordings

signed with special dedications, which they proudly display in their houses.

While fandom requires one to know recordings, as well as dates, casts, and personal histories of the performers, how that knowledge is acquired is important. This is the element that has newbies in awe of older audience members. While a person may know a lot about opera, she or he must experience it live. Showing one's sacrifice, enthusiasm and knowledge validates the claims of the most committed opera fans, which they assert through comparison with others. People tend to respect the elders and the experience they've acquired. Tito, an Italian-Argentinean in his 50s, deferred to Archimedes, an older man who witnessed Toscanini conduct in Buenos Aires in the early '40s, as someone "who actually has been going forever and really knows about it." I saw Tito at the opera house every time I attended. When I asked him how long he has been going, he said, "just 25 years."

From older fans, apprentices learn how to move, when to clap, when to stand, and how to act when their bodies are overwhelmed with emotion. Novices want to learn more about what they are listening to; older fans want to cultivate audiences for their war stories. They do so in isolated spaces, separated from other kinds of audience members. Much like baseball enthusiasts remembering the statistics of a forgotten player, they discuss whether an opera had ever been performed in Buenos Aires, whether it is the best version they've ever heard, who would be the best singer for a particular role, and how a singer might be judged in comparison to a big name from the past.

The compulsion to talk about, listen to, and learn about opera results in an intense relationship with the performance. While this entails numerous interactions, if asked, passionate opera fans would say they do not participate in the opera world because of the social aspects of the activity; on the contrary, they see their relationship to it as highly individualized. Together, they fall in love alone. They learn from and with others in order to enjoy the music in an intimate communion, surrounded by strangers in a full opera house. As Franco describes them, those around him on the top floors are his "his invisible friends."

Once they become a passionate fan, there's little going back. The pull of live music is too strong, and the love becomes an integral part of who they are. Though others might question their excessive love, fans care little about these opinions. Organizing one's life around operatic activities (going to the opera, music appreciation conferences, or small recitals) means that one cannot share this experience with very many other people. Therefore, many passionate fans choose to hide this part of their lives from others, and they develop long-term, albeit thin, relationships with those who can appreciate their degree of devotion. Other fans are really the only group of people they feel at home with, who truly understand them, who know they are "for real." They depend upon other passionate fans to share their experiences with, to discuss the music with, and to enact their love.

For these fans, cultural objects orient life and give it meaning. Most of us have a difficult time making sense of their seemingly irrational, or at least overly emotional, relationships to opera, monster truck rallies, or *Twilight* movies. This behavior is difficult to categorize and understand. We may see the objects of their fandom as "fluff" that is undeserving of such attention. Yet attachments, to cultural products help us define ourselves, shape how we present ourselves to others, and imagine who we wish to be.

> Attachments to cultural products help us define ourselves and imagine who we wish to be.

The types of people I've described are not simply found in opera houses. They are also found among fans of Manchester United football, who followed their team around Europe during the 1980s, sacrificing the rhythm of their daily lives, and wreaking havoc along the way. They are found among carnival goers in Brazil, who exploded with anger when their venue was moved into a strip exclusively dedicated to it, altering their love for the celebration, and among "deadheads," who followed the Grateful Dead on tour, went on pilgrimages to commemorate the death of band leader Jerry Garcia, and continue their dedication to innumerable Grateful Dead cover bands. In 2004, some nostalgic Red Sox baseball fans lamented that because their team had finally won the World Series they had become like fans of any other team.

Looking seriously at what people do with culture in a passionate way helps us better understand who participates in certain types of cultural events, but also how and why they do so. When I met him, José Luis was skeptical about what a sociologist could say about why people attend opera. "Why is it that you sociologists always ask if I go to the opera to be seen, to meet people, to see my friends, to achieve a better professional status?" he asked. "You always fail to ask me if I go because I like it or, better, because I love it?"

What José Luis did not realize was that loving opera, or any cultural object, is a socially produced experience in which one learns, with (and against) others, how to be a unique individual. Through this process, individuals develop a passionate commitment to the object of their love and to a way of being in the world. It's what being fanatical is all about.

RECOMMENDED RESOURCES

Howard Becker. 1953. "Becoming a Marihuana User." *American Journal of Sociology* 59(2): 235–42.

A classic article on how people learn to enjoy things.

Pierre Bourdieu. 1984. *Distinction.* Cambridge, MA: Harvard University Press.

This seminal book explores the relationship between taste, class, and status in France, using quantitative and qualitative indicators.

Tia DeNora. 2000. *Music in Everyday Life.* Cambridge, UK: Cambridge University Press.

A qualitative exploration of how people use music to make sense of themselves and their environments.

Antoine Hennion. 2001. "Music Lovers: Taste as Performance." *Theory, Culture and Society* 18(5): 1–22.

Describes how to understand taste as a series of activities.

Vera Zolberg. 1990. *Constructing a Sociology of the Arts.* Cambridge, UK: Cambridge University Press.

The first comprehensive book on what is sociological about producing, consuming, and distributing art. A wonderful introduction for anyone interested in studying the arts from a sociological perspective.

REVIEW QUESTIONS

1. What about Franco's roots made it difficult for him to become a "professional opera fan" at first?
2. Explain what Benzecry means when he states that "passion becomes a career."
3. Some novice opera fans view the more professional fans as a group they would like to become a part of. Explain how novice fans try to adopt the behaviors of professional fans in order to be able to identify more with the group.

simon j. williams

our hard days' night

10

winter 2011

sleep on this: sleep is a highly social endeavor, posing a puzzle and a prism through which to view life in the wired era.

We all sleep. But what does it have to do with society? Sleep seems like the most private and personal of things—a weird and wonderful place of "marvels and monsters" (recalling Goya), where we are not quite ourselves. So, for those of us interested in the things we do together, what is there to say about sleep? At best, from a social point of view, sleep would appear to be a sanctuary from the demands of social life, and at worst a downright antisocial act or even a waste of time that consumes a full third of our lives. But herein are points of entry.

At a very basic level, sleep is functional for society, a vital release from the grind of social life and an essential means of preparation for valued social roles. Recent sociological research amply demonstrates that sleep is not merely personal or private. The mysteries of sleep, though, cannot be fully unravelled in the modern sleep laboratory, despite its elaborate array of tools and technologies to monitor, manage, or even mend our "broken" sleep.

How we sleep, when we sleep, where we sleep, with whom with sleep, and the meanings we accord our sleep are all social, cultural, and historical matters that demand (and repay) our attention. Sleep is fast becoming a matter of public attention and concern, both a problem of and a prism onto life and living in the 24/7, wired-awake era.

Sleep, in other words, is both an important problem in its own right and a window onto the social world. It constitutes a prime example of how we might profitably link the private realm of "personal troubles" to broader public issues of "social structure," particularly at a time when the notion of a "well-slept" society appears to be an increasingly distant dream.

organizing rest

Sleep, like hunger and thirst, exerts a powerful call on a daily (or nightly) basis. It is a potent reminder that we all have bodies with needs, and sooner or later we must relinquish our involvements in the waking world and succumb to the will of our drowsy and subsequently dormant bodies. (Insomnia in this respect provides an interesting counterpoint: a sign or symptom of an overactive mind or incessant consciousness, in which the body fails to shut down when we wish or want it to. Even insomniacs, however, need to sleep, fitfully or otherwise.)

It is by virtue of this inescapable bodily need that all societies must organize the sleep of their members in some way or other. Important and necessary as sleep may be, no society can afford for all its members to sleep at once. Some citizens, recalling Shakespeare's memorable phrase, "must watch whilst others sleep." As sociologist Barry Schwartz argued long ago, sleep may be regarded not only as a socially sanctioned role but also as a socially scheduled one.

Like other social roles, sleep is often accompanied by a more or less elaborate series of transition routines or rituals to facilitate passage both into and out of the sleep role. On turning in for the night, for example, I lock up, wind down, go up stairs, brush my teeth, put my pajamas on, get into bed, read for a while, then turn the lights out and hit the sack. Similarly, on waking, I stretch a bit, go to the bathroom, shower, shave, brush my teeth again, comb my hair, get into my day clothes, have some breakfast, and read the paper (if I'm lucky). Presto! I'm ready again to face the workaday world.

Beyond one's own routine, there is a social series of rights and responsibilities on the part of both the sleeper and the waking world. These include respect for the sleeper (and their claim to freedom from undue noise or disturbance) and a host of other conventions regarding when, where, how, and with whom one can sleep. The conditions under which we sleep are, in fact, culturally and historically variable. This is particularly the case, as sleep researchers Lodewijk Brunt and Brigitte Steger have argued, when it comes to tolerance for public and private sleep or napping. Sleeping at an interview or lecture, for example, might not go down too well, in the Western world at least, while sleeping in the privacy and comfort of your home, at an appropriate time, is not only wholly acceptable, but normatively expected.

Citizens have sleep responsibilities as well, as illustrated by the societal dangers posed by individuals who do not get enough sleep. We are increasingly held accountable for our sleep these days—or at a minimum, for making sure we are not excessively drowsy given the deficits in performance and safety risks soporific states may engender. While doing without sleep is still all too frequently worn as a badge of honor or pride ("pulling an all-nighter" is seen as a sign

of self-discipline, self-mastery, or self-sacrifice in favor of other, supposedly higher, goals and greater values), this clearly can be taken too far. Drowsiness, as sociologists Steve Kroll-Smith and Valerie Gunter note, is increasingly regarded as the new drunkenness: a culpable state, since, for instance, we are every bit as dangerous behind the wheel when we are drowsy as when we are drunk. In states like New Jersey, *knowingly* driving whilst drowsy constitutes recklessness under a vehicular homicide charge. Public awareness campaigns such as Drowsy Driving Prevention Week, created by the National Sleep Foundation (that other NSF), add social urgency to our need for rest.

inequities among sleepers

Sleep—and the rights and responsibilities of sleeping—is unevenly distributed and closely bound up with power relations and social inequalities in the modern world. That is, we all have varying degrees of autonomy or discretion over when and where we sleep. Consider, by way of contrast to the normal round of everyday/night life roles and routines, the institutionalized sleeping patterns and practices evident in prisons, military barracks, boarding schools, and nursing homes, or, at the other end of the spectrum, the sporadic if not nomadic lives of those who "sleep rough" on city streets or in the slums and shanty towns of places such as Johannesburg and Mumbai. In a more extreme example, sleep rights may be deliberately withheld or denied in the name of torture or interrogation. Think of euphemistically termed "sleep restriction techniques" practiced on detainees at Abu Ghraib and Guantanamo Bay or, closer to home, imposed as one form of domestic abuse.

The matters of power, status, and control associated with sleep come further into focus through a life course perspective. Sleep, as we know, consumes a large proportion of children's time, particularly in the early years of life. Children who do not obtain sufficient night-time sleep are now constructed as at risk of social, health, or educational "problems." But the gradual "socialization" of children's sleeping patterns into the rhythms of family life provides a good indicator of the "sociocultural pliability" or plasticity of sleep, albeit within certain neuro/ chrono-biological parameters or limits.

And that babies and small children may, instead, wreak havoc with parents' sleep is merely one instance of the far broader sociological point; namely, that the so-called golden age of sleep in childhood is often marked by anxiety and conflict for parents and children alike. Romanticized images of children's bedtime conjure notions of bonding moments, but bedtime may actually become a source of struggle as kids grow older.

Bedrooms, sociologists Sue Venn and Sara Arber note, have become busy sites or bustling zones of increasing "networked" activity, housing televisions, computer games, mobile phones, and other forms of communication. Each of these poses risks of nighttime sleep disruption, which often remains missed or hidden from either parents' or teachers' view. Think also of the adolescent phase of "yawning youth" when sleep patterns shift to owl-like hours. These problems are compounded due to school start times. (The Minnesota experiments in the 1990s with later U.S. school start times may be a pointer for the future, if good school attendance and fewer sleepy pupils in the classroom are anything to go by.)

Parents' sleep, too, is linked with the sleep of children and young people living within the family home, reminding us of the relational nature and dynamics of sleeping throughout much of the life course, as child, parent, or partner. Parents, as recent sociological research shows, are often surprised by the way in which their older, seemingly more autonomous or independent children continue not simply to wake them up, but in some cases disturb their sleep even more than when they were younger. Venn and Arber reveal that worries about children's whereabouts and safety are frequently expressed sources of parental concern and sleep disturbance. Late-night noise, door slamming as teenagers come home, and the occasional late-night call for help are also commonly reported sources of parental sleep disturbance in recent sociological research.

After the child-bearing years, sleep continues to be marked by changes, transitions, and negotiations. These include what Arber and fellow sociologist Jenny Hislop have usefully identified as biological or physiological changes associated with aging; institutional changes in roles and statuses; relational changes associated with partners, children, parents, friends; and biographical transitions associated with life events and other transitions like marriage, parenthood, retirement, divorce, and widowhood—all of which impact sleep.

work and sleep

Work is another aspect of social life with complex relations to sleep. The obvious case is shift work (particularly rotating shifts or night shifts), and much of the research on sleep and work to date has concentrated on it. Sociological research is now beginning to explore the intersections among gender, paid employment, and rest. A 2009 analysis of the U.K. Time Use Survey by Arber and researcher Stella Chatzitheochari, for example, found an inverse relationship between length of working hours and short sleep duration (less than 6.5 hours) which was stronger for men than women. Arber and colleagues, however, have also shown, in other qualitative research, how women's sleep is

> Drowsiness is increasingly regarded as the new drunkenness.

typically disadvantaged due to family-care responsibilities.

Work and family responsibilities impinge not simply on sleep quantity but on sleep quality. In a study of retail food workers in the United States sociologist David Maume and colleagues found that women experience more sleep disruptions than men, and that more than half this gap was accounted for by "gendered reactions to work-family situations."

Other recent research highlights how employment significantly impacts the very meanings we attribute to sleep, including what medical anthropologist Douglas Henry and colleagues refer to as the "powerful internalizing role of labor" in experiences of sleep. Again, gender proves significant. While men, as sociologist Rob Meadows and his coauthors find, are inclined to link sleep "need" with ability to "function" (especially in paid labor), they are also inclined to identify paid work as one of the prime causes of "poor" sleep, both in terms of work constraints and work stressors.

And then there is the issue of workplace napping. Who hasn't snatched the odd forty winks on a lunch break, at a desk, or behind the office filing cabinets in a furtive act of desperation or defiance? In recent years, the idea of the office nap has undergone a transformation of its own, with napping literally being "put to work" with other (corporate) aims in mind (as the notion of "power napping" suggests). No longer simply the practice of Mediterranean siesta cultures or napping cultures such as Japan, China, or India, a midday rest is increasingly touted as an acceptable if not valued practice, particularly within certain sectors of the late capitalist economy. Sociologists Vern Baxter and Steve Kroll-Smith identify cognitive and information-rich sectors of the economy where mental rather than manual labor prevails and napping becomes a form of cognitive enhancement or performance upgrade. A cat or power nap gives these workers a creative boost or edge.

Workplace napping is not simply a case of the official sanctioning and spatial organization of sleep-friendly policies. Independent companies now specialize in "alertness management" and the art of napping both on and off the job. One corporation, Metronaps, bills itself on its website as a "leading provider of fatigue management solutions to public and private sector organisations." They count, among their diverse clients, PricewaterhouseCoopers, Procter and Gamble, Google, W Hotels, and the British Lawn Tennis Association, and their products range from the latest noise-cancelling headphones to the Zero chair ("based on NASA technology") and a gadget called the Pzizz, which not only "looks and feels amazing," but "allows you to nap any time, any place." This handheld miracle is, naturally, "recommended for frequent travellers, commercial drivers, mobile workforces, and in combination with purchases of the Zero chair."

Whether these moves are welcomed or instead regarded as the latest expression of the corporate management of our lives are still open questions. Nevertheless, these developments do signal, as Baxter and Kroll-Smith comment, the way in which sleep is neither a private matter nor an unproductive act. Sleep, as these researchers observe, has become a regulated, time-space behavior, both inside and outside the workplace.

sleep sick society?

Mention has already been made of the "problem" of sleep and sleep problems in contemporary society. There is still a vital piece of the story missing here: sleep science and sleep medicine. Experts play a big role in the framing of sleep as a "matter of concern" or "problem in the making." Developments in sleep science and sleep medicine in recent decades, coupled with the ongoing efforts of organizations such as the National Sleep Foundation (established in 1990 with the motto "Alerting the public, health care providers and policy-makers to the life-and-death importance of adequate sleep"), now serve to recast and reconfigure the ways we think about and manage our sleep problems.

Sleep "problems," of course, come in many forms, shapes, and sizes, some more serious than others, from bona fide sleep disorders to sleep disturbance, disruption, or deprivation in the absence of any underlying or identifiable disorder. Estimates of who's affected vary from study to study and country to country, depending on what precisely we're looking for. Overall, as science writer Paul Martin summarizes, it's probably safe to say that at least one in ten adults suffers from moderate or severe daytime sleepiness.

Some leading experts, like American sleep expert William Dement, claim these problems have reached epidemic proportions. As many as 70 million Americans, the U.S. National Commission on Sleep Disorders Research estimates, suffer from sleep problems of one kind or another. The annual cost of these problems adds about $16 billion to the national health bill. Dement concludes that we are a "sleep sick society," with many people suffering needlessly from undiagnosed and untreated sleep disorders, and most of us trading on dangerous levels of sleep debt. This has serious implications for public health and safety.

Whether or not we are all suffering from chronic sleep problems is a moot point. Consider A. Roger Ekirch's historical research on sleep in preindustrial times. Compared to the preindustrial past, when sleep was a more public and precarious if not perilous affair, our sleep quality may well indeed have improved, even if our sleep patterns have changed and our sleep quantity has declined.

Either way, sleep medicine is certainly big business. Over 1,000 officially accredited sleep clinics exist in North America. Sleep expert Jessica Alexander estimates that the "sleep aids" market in the United States, which includes everything from sleep clinics, sleep medications, and sleep devices like mattresses and pillows, was worth $23.7 billion in 2007, and will hit a staggering $32.1 billion by 2012. Even as an infant industry, sleep is another prime example of what sociologists call the medicalization of society.

sleep's (political) future

If the industrialization of light in the nineteenth century resulted in what historical scholar and researcher Wolfgang Shivelbusch memorably called the "disenchanted night," and if our modern-day sleep patterns have irrevocably changed courtesy of these developments, then what does the future of sleep hold? Will the mysteries of sleep for example be increasingly unravelled or unbundled in order to render it evermore optional or obsolete, like the banishing of darkness in our light-polluted skies?

The future of sleep looks pretty much assured, even if its quantity or quality continues to change. Who, after all, doesn't like a good sleep when they can get one—it's a sort of pleasure we surely wouldn't trade easily or lightly. On the other hand, our sleep time (if not our sleep rights) appears increasingly under threat in this restless, ravenous age.

And while we've always had the humble shot of caffeine to keep us going, developments in neuroscience and biomedicine hold out the prospect of not only breaking open the mysteries and mechanisms of sleep, but of opening up new options regarding both how well and how much we sleep.

Take, for example, Modafinil (brand name Provigil), a wakefulness-promoting drug officially

> Sleep is unevenly distributed and closely bound up with power relations and social inequities in the modern world.

licensed for the medical treatment of sleep disorders involving excessive daytime sleepiness such as narcolepsy, obstructive sleep apnea, and the intriguingly named "shift work sleep disorder." This is a medication with considerable appeal beyond the clinic—a "smart drug" with the potential to extend our days or prolong our nights for all manner of lifestyle or social purposes. The military is already well ahead of the game here, having long since used drugs (Modafinil included) and devices to help combat fatigue and turn sleep into a commodity of war, much like bombs and bullets. (Imagine for a moment the huge tactical advantage that troops wired awake would confer over their sleep-deprived enemies.)

In a Modafinil world, respect for peoples' sleep rights might also have to contend with respect for peoples' rights *not* to sleep, especially to the extent that "enhancements" of this kind actually reduce the risk of errors and accidents through sleep-related fatigue in occupations such as medicine, transportation, and other vital around-the-clock operations.

My final example reiterates the point that sleep is not simply a matter of growing concern or even a novel sociological lens on contemporary society and social change. Sleep is, once again, both a *problem* and a *prism* regarding life and living in the 24/7 era. It is for these reasons that I am beginning to think and work on the growing politicization of sleep today. It's what I would call the "politics of sleep."

So the next time you fall prey to the call of Morpheus, ponder briefly (lest it disturb your slumber) the circumstances under which you sleep. Remember, if you will, that the very places, spaces, schedules, and temporalities of sleep are themselves deeply social, cultural, historical, and political matters—and, potentially, subject to contestation and change. It's certainly something to sleep on.

RECOMMENDED RESOURCES

Sara Arber, Jenny Hislop, and Simon Williams. 2007. "Editor's Introduction: Gender, Sleep and the Life Course," *Sociological Research Online* 12(5).

Introduces a special issue exploring sociological dimensions of sleep and gender across the life course.

Vern Baxter and Steve Kroll-Smith. 2005. "Napping at Work: Shifting Boundaries between Public and Private Time." *Current Sociology* 53(1): 33–55.

An exploration of shifting boundaries between public and private time and the workplace nap.

Lodewijk Brunt and Brigitte Steger, eds. 2008. *Worlds of Sleep*. Berlin: Frank & Timee.

Anthropological, historical, and sociological essays on sleeping customs, patterns, and practices around the world.

A. Roger Ekirch. 2005. *At Day's Close: Night in Times Past*. New York: W. W. Norton.

An illuminating historical account of nighttime and sleep in the preindustrial past.

Simon J. Williams. 2011. *The Politics of Sleep: Governing (Un)Consciousness in the Late Modern Age*. Houndsmills, Basingstoke, UK: Palgrave Macmillan.

A systematic look at the parameters, problems, prospects, and possibilities of a politics of sleep in contemporary times.

REVIEW QUESTIONS

1. The author indicates that sleep inequities disadvantage groups who face other social inequities as well. Which groups face barriers to sleep and why?
2. What does the word *medicalization* mean, as the author used it?
3. What does the author say about the relationship of sleep to labor? Is it different from your ideas about work and rest?

part **3**

Crime and Punishment

viewpoints

rape and rape culture

spring 2014

social consciousness around putting the victims of rape on trial may be evolving, but are the environments that foster these assaults really changing? experts weigh in on the question of situational factors and institutional accountability for rape.

Sexual assault is epidemic in the United States. Recent media reports, public outrage, and activism have been focused on the institutional settings in which these assaults occur. Colleges and universities, as well as the military and athletic programs, have come under increasing scrutiny as settings that not only fail to deter, but possibly foster rape.

Vanderbilt, Notre Dame, Maryville, Steubenville, Florida State, and the University of Missouri, to name a few, are among the recent highly profiled institutions in which student athletes allegedly committed rapes that were ignored or downplayed by school administrators. The victims in these cases were treated with hostility by the schools, police, and even their peers, who considered the reports of rape to be exaggerated responses to a party culture where "everyone is just trying to have fun" and where "stuff happens." Some of these victims have committed or attempted suicide.

Social consciousness around putting the victims of rape on trial may be evolving, but are the environments that foster these assaults really changing? President Obama recently promised women who have been sexually assaulted in college: "I've got your back." Should we be guardedly optimistic that this message from the top signals change, or do policy trends indicate attempts to protect institutions at the continued expense of victims? In this *Viewpoints*, five experts weigh in on the question of situational factors and institutional accountability around rape.

Lisa Wade reviews what we know about who commits rape on college campuses and the conditions that support this behavioral profile. She asserts that campus officials need to understand the interplay of cultural, psychological, and situational causes for rape in order to make viable policy decisions. Brian Sweeney highlights the connection between alcohol consumption and sexual assault. He argues that campus policies that address binge drinking are doomed to fail unless they take into account that, for many young people, drinking and casual sex are rewarding. Amelia Seraphia Derr focuses on federal policies for reporting campus rape. She notes that colleges and universities are beginning to take these regulations more seriously, but raises concerns that they may trend in the direction of a "culture of compliance," where the fear of litigation that drives policy-making could be counterproductive for prevention and support programs.

Michael A. Messner turns the lens on rape culture among male college athletes and asks what can be done. He's not convinced that current reform programs that target individual men and men's sports teams will mitigate sexual violence. He suggests we need a deeper understanding of the link between sexual domination, and the ways we celebrate male athletes and their violent domination in sports. Writing about a different, though familiar context, Carol Burke examines recent rape scandals in the military.

She chronicles the mounting evidence for a high-level official blind eye on sexual assault and the resulting outrage among congresswomen who are calling for accountability. Is change in the offing? Read on and see what these experts have to say.

lisa wade

understanding and ending the campus sexual assault epidemic

College attendance is a risk factor for sexual assault. According to the U.S. Department of Justice, one in five women who attend college will be the victim of a completed or attempted sexual assault, compared to one in six women in the general population. Up to 90 percent of these women will know their attacker. Only about half will identify their experience as assault and fewer than 5 percent will report their experience to campus authorities or the police. Four percent of college men also report being sexually assaulted, overwhelmingly by other men.

> If institutions of higher education want to, they have the tools to reduce rates of sexual assault. And, even if they do not make this a priority, they face increasing pressure to do so.

Scholars have been working to gain a better understanding of the prevalence of rape on campuses, why it's infrequently reported to authorities, and what we can do about it. In a 2006 article, Elizabeth Armstrong and her collaborators point to cultural, psychological, and situational causes. In the effort to prevent sexual crimes, colleges and universities need to understand these interrelated causes and how they contribute to rates of sexual assault.

What are the psychological factors? A small number of men may be more predisposed to assault their peers than others. In a 2002 study by David Lisak and Paul Miller, 6 percent of male college students admitted to behavior that matched the legal definitions of sexual assault or rape. Of those men, two-thirds were serial rapists, with an average of six assaults each. Serial rapists plan their assaults, carefully choose their victim, use alcohol as a rape drug, and employ force, but only as a backup. Lisak and Miller find that these men are more likely than other men to engage in other forms of violence as well.

What about context? Some men may be inclined to harm others, but whether they do so is related to their opportunities. The right context can offer these men an opening to do so. Peggy Sanday first recognized the role that context plays in facilitating sexual assault. Studying fraternity parties, she found that some are generative of risk and others are less so. Parties that feature loud music, few places to sit, dancing, drinking, and compulsory flirting are, she explains, "rape prone." In these more dangerous places, rape culture camouflages the predatory behavior of serial rapists—like plying women with alcohol or pulling them into secluded areas—making it look normal and more difficult to interpret as criminal.

And then there's culture. Rape culture narratives—those that suggest that rape is simply a matter of miscommunication, that "date rape" isn't "real rape," that women frequently lie about being sexually assaulted for vengeance or out of shame—make it difficult for bystanders to justify intervening and for some victims to understand that their experience was a crime. Rape culture also gives rapists plausible excuses for their actions, making it difficult to hold them accountable, especially if members of the campus administration buy into these myths as well.

Armstrong and her colleagues show that all three of these causal factors interact together and with campus policy. Strict penalties for drinking alcohol in residence halls, for example, especially when strongly enforced, can push party-oriented students off campus to less safe places. Rape-friendly contexts offer a target-rich haven for the small percentage of individual men who are motivated to use force and coercion to attain sex. Rape culture contributes to concealing the predatory nature of their behavior to victims, their peers and, all too often, their advocates.

Currently, we're in the midst of a transformation in how colleges and universities handle sexual assault. While our understanding is far from complete, we know more than ever about the interaction of situational, cultural, and psychological causes. If institutions of higher education want to, they have the tools to reduce rates of sexual assault. And, even if they do not make this a priority, they face increasing pressure to do so. A strong national movement now aims to hold institutions accountable for ignoring, hiding, and mishandling sex crimes. Thanks largely to Know Your IX, 30 colleges submitted complaints to the U.S. Office for Civil Rights in 2013, nearly double the number from the year before. We should expect even higher numbers in 2014. Praising these activists, President Barack Obama announced that he was making the end of men's sexual violence against women a priority. The combination of "insider" and "outsider" politics, and a sympathetic media, is a promising recipe for change.

brian sweeney

drinking and sexual assault [kids just wanna have fun]

Getting wasted is fun, as is hooking up. In today's campus hookup culture, alcohol and sex often go together, and both can be rewarding experiences for young adults. Party culture glamorizes heavy drinking, making it seem less dangerous and, too often, causing students to dismiss the negative effects—whether getting puked on at a football game or being sexually assaulted—as "just stuff that happens." But sexual assault is a predictable result of party subcultures characterized by extreme drinking and sexual double standards. A majority of college rape victims are drunk when attacked, and rapists use alcohol as a weapon to incapacitate their victims. Men—and other women, for that matter—may see overly drunk women as fair game, giving up their right to feminine protection because they have failed to be respectable and ladylike. Given the connection between intoxication and sexual

> In today's campus hookup culture, alcohol and sex often go together, and both can be rewarding experiences for young adults.

assault, many ask, "Why not just tell women not to get so drunk?" But a mindset that places responsibility on women ignores the widespread attitudes and practices that encourage men's sexual predation and victimization of women in the first place.

To be clear, drinking, by itself, does not lead to sexual assault. Drinking heavily makes women more vulnerable, but it is overwhelmingly men who take advantage and rape. It is also men who stand by and watch their male friends ply women with drinks, block women from leaving rooms, and sometimes gang-rape women too drunk to walk home. Equipping women with "watch your drink, stay with your friends" strategies ignores both the fun of partying with abandon and the larger structures of domination that lead men to feel entitled to (drunk) women's bodies. Moreover, while rape-supportive beliefs are widespread, their influence over men's behavior is dependent on rape-supportive social and organizational arrangements—campus party culture and alcohol policy included.

Drinking subcultures have a long history on American college campuses, but since 1984 and the passage of the National Minimum Drinking Age Act, all 50 states have opted for billions in federal highway aid in exchange for passing Age-21 laws. As a result, many college campuses send mixed messages and endorse confused policies. Students are regularly fined and written up for drinking infractions but also educated about drinking responsibly. Students flock to so-called party schools and then spend most of their college years trying not to get caught—secretly "pre-gaming" with hard alcohol in dorm rooms, hiding out in fraternity basements during party inspections, and nervously sweating as the bouncer checks for fake IDs. Alcohol becomes a coveted commodity, with many students seeking access to it and fortunate others wielding control of it.

Problems related to drinking exist, in part, because we have constructed a firewall between students and the adults who run universities—a divide that surely undermines our mission of creating safe and rich learning environments. We are allowing young people, unsupervised, to initiate each other into adulthood, often through rituals built around drinking. The campus pub is long gone at most schools, a relic of a bygone in loco parentis era when many professors lived among students and mentored them academically and socially. We could perhaps learn valuable lessons from a time when drinking was less illicit and student social life more open and watched over. Bringing drinking "aboveground" would disrupt some of the party scenes that sociological research has shown to be productive of sexual danger for women, would remove some of the constraints college administrators face in crafting effective alcohol education and policy, and would embolden sexual assault victims to come forward, reducing their fears of being punished for drinking violations.

Many schools are trying to get students to drink more responsibly. Since 2008, over 125 college and university presidents and chancellors have signed on to the Amethyst Initiative, which calls for "informed and dispassionate public debate" on Age-21 drinking laws. The supporters of the initiative, while not explicitly endorsing a lowering of the drinking age, believe Age-21 laws drive drinking underground, leading to dangerous binge drinking and reckless behavior among students. Five years after its inception, it is unclear if anything will come of the Amethyst Initiative. Federal and state government officials seem stubbornly unwilling to open discussion on Age-21 laws. And yet, because the initiative focuses on moderate and responsible drinking among students rather than abstinence, its ideas should have traction in correcting party cultures that, as they are currently organized, produce both fun and sexual danger. What is fairly certain is that sexual assault policies that ignore the collective, rewarding nature of drunken, erotically charged revelry will likely fail among many young adults.

amelia seraphia derr

a culture of compliance versus prevention

The underreporting of campus sexual assaults has become a social problem. Students around the country are waging protests and demanding accountability from university administrators who have been accused of making light of alarming rates of sexual violence on college campuses. In 2011 the U.S. Department of Education Office of Civil Rights, in reaction to a Department of Justice report on the serious underreporting of campus sexual assaults, and with the encouragement of Vice President Joe Biden, issued a Dear Colleagues Letter (DCL) on the topic of sexual violence. Specifically, the DCL emphasized and reiterated the legally mandated expectations for systems of reporting and adjudicating cases of sexual violence, for training staff, and for developing prevention and support programs.

Legislated reporting of sexual assault is the fruit of efforts dating back to the 1972 issuance of Title IX of the Education Amendments, which included sexual violence along with a variety of other forms of gender discrimination. In 1986 the Clery Act clarified and expanded the reporting requirements that were part of Title IX by establishing clear expectations for support services for students who are victims of sexual violence, and for the types of sexual violence–related reports that colleges and universities must file annually.

This legislative action intensified in 2011 when Bob Casey (D-PA) learned of Title IX violation complaints against Swarthmore College, alleging underreporting cases of sexual misconduct, and took action. He introduced the Campus Sexual Violence Elimination Act (The SaVE Act), which became law with the passage of the Violence Against Women Reauthorization Act in August 2013. This act closes a serious gap in the existing law by requiring clearer and more-publicized policies, education on student's rights, "bystander education" for the purpose of prevention, expanded reporting requirements, mandated prevention programs, and procedural rights for the accuser and accused.

This federal-level attention has created a sense of urgency in higher education, prompting university administrators to revisit policies on sexual assault to ensure compliance. But does it actually help change an organizational environment that is highly conducive to assault?

> Federal-level attention has created a sense of urgency in higher education, prompting university administrators to revisit policies on sexual assault to ensure compliance.

Institutionalizing accountability is essential; policies are a sustainable tool for addressing sexual violence on campuses. Evidence of the effectiveness of such policies can be seen in the fact that since the 2011 DCL there has been a steep increase in the number of Title IX and Clery Act complaints filed. According to the U.S. Department of Education, 62 Title IX complaints dealing with issues of sexual violence and harassment were filed between October 1, 2012, and September 30, 2013, alone.

However, a heightened regulatory environment may create a culture of compliance where the fear of litigation—rather than expert knowledge on prevention—drives policy making. Institutional priorities and resources are directed differently depending on whether a university focuses on compliance-based reporting policies or prevention and support programs (which also include reporting policies, but within a framework of victim advocacy rather than institutional protection). For example, the DCL states that "if a school knows or reasonably should know about a potential sexual assault it is required to take immediate action." Ambiguity about what this means may prompt universities to adopt a mandated reporting policy for adult-aged students similar to those in place for minors or other vulnerable populations in order to avoid litigation.

Duke University (along with University of Montana, Swarthmore, and several others) has instituted such a policy, naming almost all of its 34,000 employees as mandated reporters. When staff or faculty members realize that students are about to share a concern with them, they must inform the student that the information they share will be reported to the designated administrator, with or without the student's permission. Duke University states that reports have increased since this policy

was adopted. However, some victim's advocates oppose the practice. They counter that campus policies that mandate reporting irrespective of the victim's desire perpetuate a campus environment of silence and isolation and limit victims' options for confiding in trusted sources. A student Resident Assistant (RA) at Swarthmore, where RAs are considered mandated reporters, was recently fired from her position because she refused to break confidentiality by identifying a victim. Critics warn that these policies could ultimately lead to decreased reporting from victims who feel there is no safe space for them to turn in confidence. This is especially likely to be the case at a campus with few or insufficient survivor support services.

The real issue is how to move beyond a culture of compliance to a culture of prevention. In response to the requirements of the Campus SaVE Act, university policies should foreground survivor self-determination, provide strong perpetrator-prevention programs, offer robust victim support services, and promote increased dialogue about sexual violence with all members of the university community. These efforts will take us beyond the high visibility that reporting requirements have had, and into the areas of support and education required for true change.

michael a. messner

can locker room rape culture be prevented?

Recipe for sexual assault: Assemble a group of young men. Promise them glory for violently dominating other groups of young men. Bond the group with aggressive joking about the sexual domination of women. Add public adulation that permeates the group with the scent

of entitlement. Provide mentors who thrived as young men in this same system. Allow to simmer.

What have we cooked up? Horrendous sexual assaults on unconscious girls by high school football players in Steubenville and Maryville as well as an ongoing parade of sexual assault accusations against college football players, most recently at Florida State, Vanderbilt, and the United States Naval Academy. Do we overemphasize cases of football player sexual misconduct because of their high profile? Perhaps. But research by sociologist Todd Crosset since the 1990s has shown that men who play intercollegiate sports are more likely than nonathletes to commit sexual assault—especially those in high-status sports that valorize violence.

Of course, most football or ice hockey athletes don't rape women. Recently, some male athletes have even formed organizations to stop violence against women. "Male Athletes Against Violence" has done peer education at the University of Maine for years. And since 1993, Northeastern University's Mentors in Violence Prevention program has created a template for a national proliferation of sports-based programs that deploy a "bystander" approach to violence prevention. These programs attempt to disrupt the ways that high-status male groups—like sports teams and fraternities—layer protective silence around members who perpetrate violence against women. A bystander approach teaches men to intervene to stop sexual assaults before they happen—for instance, stepping in when seeing one's teammates dragging an inebriated woman to a back room. A good man, the bystander approach teaches, steps forward not only to keep a woman safe, but also to keep the team safe from public trouble.

The years of silence surrounding Penn State University football coach Jerry Sandusky's serial sexual assaults of children is one example of the absolute failure by high-profile university coaches and administrators to model the responsible bystander behavior they say their young athletes should engage in. This case showed that, rather than resulting simply from the actions of one bad man, sexual assault is embedded in the routine values and culture of silence in organizations.

A number of years ago, I assisted psychologist Mark Stevens—a pioneer in working with athletes to prevent sexual violence—in an intervention with a college football program after members of the team were accused of sexually assaulting a woman at an off-campus party. Before the first of two workshops, I asked Stevens if he really thought that a few hours of talk could change the culture of sexual dominance that so commonly cements football team members' loyalties while simultaneously putting women and vulnerable men at risk. Stevens answered no. "But," he added, "if we can empower one or two guys who, down the road, might intervene in a situation to stop a sexual assault, then our work will have made the world safer for at least one woman."

I still worry that such interventions do less to prevent acts of violence than they do to contain the public relations nightmare that sexual assaults create for athletics departments. Confirming that fear, a man I recently interviewed told me that he had been hired by a big-time college sports program to institute a violence prevention program, only to find it "incredibly disappointing" when he learned his employers had hired him mostly to work with male athletes of color to keep them eligible to play sports. "I thought that they were genuinely ready to do something, you know, make some changes. . . . I got kind of duped. I had this particular background [in violence prevention] so that was really enticing for them, and they had no intention of actually letting me do any of that work."

> Sexual assault is embedded in the routine values and culture of silence in organizations.

While some schools have adopted sexual assault prevention programs for some of their men's sports teams, we just don't know how well they work. We need good research that points to how, or under what conditions prevention programs within institutions like football (or the military) can actually succeed in mitigating gender-based violence. To have such an impact, I believe these interventions will need to confront how sexism is routinely intertwined with male entitlement and celebratory violence. To be truly successful, I suspect, such a program would render the game itself to be no longer football as we know it.

carol burke

failure to serve and protect

Military scandals in the past two years have brought new attention to old problems: sexual harassment, sexual assault, and the potential for bias in the handling of these crimes. The general who commanded the 82nd Airborne was charged with forcible sodomy, indecent acts, and violating orders, and was issued a reprimand and ordered to pay a $20,000 fine. The commanders in charge of Lackland Air Force Base apparently didn't realize that, over a two-year period, 62 recruits were assaulted by 33 drill instructors. Even those tasked with preventing sexual assault were charged with the crimes they had pledged to thwart. A lieutenant colonel who headed the Sexual Harassment and Assault Response Prevention program at Fort Campbell, Kentucky, was arrested and charged with stalking an ex-wife and sending her threatening e-mails in violation of a restraining order. A lieutenant colonel in charge of the Air Force Sexual Assault Prevention and Response Program was charged with the sexual battery of a stranger in a parking lot. His alleged victim, according to witnesses, took justice into her own hands and after pushing away the drunken officer, ran after him and punched him in the face. At trial, the officer was acquitted.

> "Nowhere in America do we allow a boss to decide if an employee was sexually assaulted or not, except in the United States military."
>
> Kirsten Gillibrand

Ultimately, the scandal that ignited the outrage of several congresswomen was Lieutenant General Craig Franklin's decision to overturn Lieutenant Colonel James Wilkerson's court-martial conviction for sexual assault. To Franklin, it seemed incongruous that a man "who adored his wife and his 9-year-old son," a man who as a pilot had flown in the same unit as him, and a man who had been selected "for promotion to full colonel, a wing inspector general, a career officer" could be a sexual predator. So Franklin exercised the power granted him and other commanders under the Uniform Code of Military Justice (UCMJ) to reverse any verdict without explanation. Although this might have looked at the time like the decision of an out-of-touch commander from his lonely and lofty post, identifying more with the plight of the accused than of the victim, e-mails related to the case revealed that generals of even higher rank than Franklin's supported his decision.

According to the Defense Department's own survey, 26,000 anonymous respondents claimed that they had been sexually assaulted in 2012, yet only 3,374 complaints were officially reported in that year. The incendiary mix of the skyrocketing rates of assault and the apparent indifference of some commanders to the plight of victims captured the attention of many women in Congress, and they demanded reform. These congresswomen, joined by some of their male colleagues, took aim at the heart of military culture, the sacrosanct military justice system, which can only be as impartial as the commander who oversees it. Senator Kirsten Gillibrand (D-NY) proposed a two-part judicial system akin to those of many of our NATO Allies, a system that would take the most serious crimes like murder and sexual assault out of the chain of command and ensure that decisions to investigate, prosecute, and convict could not be arbitrarily reversed by a commander. In a statement issued December 20, 2013, Gillibrand said, "Nowhere in America do we allow a boss to decide if an employee was sexually assaulted or not, except in the United States military."

Senator Claire McCaskill (D-MO) fashioned a more moderate compromise that left the investigation and adjudication of crimes of sexual assault in the hands of commanders but that lifted the five-year statute of limitations on courts-martial for sex-related crimes, criminalized retaliation by commanders (but not by peers), provided counsel for victims, and did away with the "good soldier defense." The compromise carried the day, much to the chagrin of victims who regard the UCMJ as a system that often denies them justice.

For several years now the Department of Defense has required mandatory training intended to prevent sexual assault and sexual harassment, crafted public-service announcements for broadcast on military TV stations, established hotlines for victims, and posted pleas in bathrooms on bases here and abroad for bystanders to step in when they see abuse taking place. Unfortunately, these costly efforts have failed to build trust in a military judicial system. Victims see these public campaigns as the military's efforts to protect the institution and not them. As long as the investigation and adjudication of sexual assault cases remain within such a command-centric judicial system, the partiality of a single individual can easily trump justice.

REVIEW QUESTIONS

1. Compare and contrast the different perspectives of the authors. Are any of the authors' views complementary? Are any of them oppositional? Please explain.
2. What does Amelia Seraphia Derr mean by "culture of compliance"?
3. Lisa Wade notes the "cultural, psychological and situational causes for rape." How are these interconnected?

randol contreras

becoming a stickup kid

fall 2015

kids were not born criminals or torturers, so how do they become "stickup kids"? this article explores the ravages of the drug trade by exploring history, biography, social structure, and drug market forces. it offers a revelatory explanation for drug market violence by masterfully uncovering the hidden social forces that produce violent and self-destructive individuals.

The South Bronx summer night was warm and moist, with that mild glow we always felt after it rained. The neighborhood residents slowly resumed their places on the streets, first standing next to building entrances, then next to wet cars, and then sitting on the cars after they'd dried. The neighborhood bodega, or grocery store, revitalized the block, blasting the 1980s salsa classics that brought bolero lyrics to the dance floor: *Y me duele a pensar, que nunca mia seras, De mi enamorate-e-e-e* . . .

Dressed in large T-shirts, Nikes, and baggy shorts, some young Dominican men listened to the cool music alongside me. "Yo, that used to be the jam!"—we nodded our heads; "I used to dance to this shit!"—we tapped our feet; "*A si mi'mo!*"—one of us did a fancy salsa step; *Mira que e, e, e, e, e, e, e—el-l-l-l!*—some of us sang along, straining our voices with each rising octave. We were all in a good mood. Just chillin'. *Chilliando*, baby.

Then Jonah arrived. He pulled Gus aside for a furtive chat. Despite their low voices, we could hear them planning a drug robbery. After about ten minutes, they returned to the group, energized, and recounted stories of their past *tumbes* (drug robbery hits). Most of the young

> Just chillin'. *Chilliando*, baby. The young Dominican men recounted tales of drug robberies, of adventure and brutality.

Dominican men joined in with their own tales of brutality and adventure.

Jonah and Gus recounted a drug robbery when they'd targeted a Dominican drug courier who always delivered five kilos of cocaine to a certain dealer on a certain day. For a share of the take, the dealer told Jonah and Gus where to intercept the courier as he walked out of an apartment building. At gunpoint, they led him to the building's rooftop, beat him, and stole $100,000 worth of drugs.

Tukee and Pablo told the group about a drug robbery where they had pretended to be undercover officers. With fake badges and real guns, they stopped a pair of drug dealers on the street: "Freeze! Don't move, motherfucker!" they yelled out. They faced the dealers against a wall and grabbed their suitcase, stuffed with $40,000 in cash. "Keep facing the wall!" they commanded before trotting around the corner to their getaway car.

Neno and Gus told a third story, of a drug robbery that went wrong. They had tortured a drug dealer—punched and kicked him, choked and gagged him, mutilated and burned him—until he passed out. The victim, however, remained unconscious. Afraid, *se fueron*

The South Bronx neighborhood. (Courtesy Randol Contreras)

volando—they hurried out so if the victim died, they wouldn't be there.

Throughout my field research, I heard many of these robbery tales. In fact, I grew up with these stories and these men. As a young man, I had tried my hand at drug dealing. So I was used to seeing and hearing about drug market violence. Yet there were times when I questioned the humanity of the men next to me on front stoops and car hoods.

How could Pablo almost beat someone to death? How could Gus repeatedly burn someone with an iron? How could Tukee chop off someone's finger? How could Neno sodomize a dealer with an object? How could all of these men *torture*, a cruel and deplorable human act?

In trying to understand drug robbery violence, I realized how easy it was to fall into an individualistic, sociopathic-reasoning trap. Could one not argue that these men were sociopaths who enjoyed inflicting pain on others? Maybe they were evil and solely pursued the emotional thrills of crime?

As a sociologist, though, I took a step back to frame what seemed solely evil and sociopathic within larger historical and social forces, forces that sweep people in one direction or

A favorite hangout for the study participants. (Courtesy Randol Contreras)

another, that shape "why" some people do violence or crime.

Everyone respects Tukee for his tremendous violence during drug robberies. It seems like he could chop off fingers and pistol-whip someone to the brink of death with no hesitation or thought. Sometimes, he even seemed to enjoy torture:

"I remember one time, we put a[n] iron on this dude's back," Tukee recounts, laughing. "I had told him, 'Just tell me where the shit is [the drugs and cash]. If you don't tell us, I'ma do some things to you, B[ro]. Things you won't like.' He ain't tell us so, boom, [we] took off his shirt and made the iron real hot. I put that shit on his back and the dude started screaming, B, ha-ha-ha! Then he was like, 'Alright, take it! It's inside the mattress!' That shit was funny, B! Ha-ha-ha!"

Taken out of the proper sociohistorical context, the laughter and joy in Tukee's account make it seem like he's pure evil. Tukee, though, was born neither a drug robber nor torturer. His biography emerged within a particular social context: the rise and fall of crack cocaine in the abandoned and burned-out South Bronx.

tukee's story

Tukee was born to a Dominican father and a Puerto Rican mother in the South Bronx during the early 1970s. For reasons he never disclosed, his father abandoned the family, never to be seen or heard from again. His mother worked several informal jobs, mostly as a seamstress in a local sweatshop. Tukee went to underfunded public schools—when he went. A disengaged and unprepared student, he eventually dropped out of high school. He worked part-time, here and there, moving from one fast-food chain job to the next. But he wanted to make money, get rich.

Tukee's chances for upward mobility, though, were fading. Between 1947 and 1976, New York City lost about 500,000 factory jobs. That's half a million unionized jobs that, for about three-quarters of the twentieth century, had provided security and upward mobility for European immigrants and their children. By the time Blacks, Puerto Ricans, and, later, Dominicans, settled in the Bronx, the burgeoning service economy had taken hold. There were lower wages and less job security available to workers with little education, like Tukee.

Crack showed up right on time.

Crack had its origins in the powder cocaine craze of the 1970s. This was a time when professionals like doctors, Wall Street executives, and lawyers likened a line of cocaine to a sip of champagne. The federal government's hysteria over marijuana and its reduction of drug-treatment funds further widened the demand for and use of cocaine. Later, in the early 1980s, when cocaine users reduced their intake, desperate cocaine dealers then turned to crack, a smokable form of the drug, to maintain profits. Instead, their profits soared: crack yielded more quantity than cocaine after preparation. More importantly, crack invited binging. Soon many users were consuming the drug around the clock.

Crack quickly proliferated in inner cities across the United States. For marginal urban residents, who suffered because of both a declining manufacturing sector and Reaganomics but still hoped to take part in the grandest version of the American Dream—crack was a godsend. The start-up money for a crack business was low. And unlike the tightly knit heroin market, there was no need for pre-existing family or ethnic ties to edge your way in. Almost anyone could enter this market.

Tukee walked right in.

He and a friend started selling crack in his Highbridge neighborhood. He began earning between $300 and $500 per day, all profit. He purchased a salvaged luxury car and restored it to its former glory with stolen car parts. Along with his new expensive jewelry and clothes, the car made him a neighborhood celebrity. *Yo, here comes Tukee!* The sidewalk crowd flocked around. *What up Tuke'? Where you going?* The guys and gals wanted to cruise around in his ride.

Tukee also spent his *riquezas,* or riches, living the high life. He arrived at nightclubs *con estilo,* or in style, with an entourage-packed white limousine. Inside, he treated his broke neighborhood

> For marginal urban residents who still hoped to take part in the grandest version of the American Dream, crack cocaine was a godsend.

Hanging out at the local club. (Courtesy Randol Contreras)

friends to overpriced bottles of liquor and bought attractive women expensive drinks. Afterward, if he was still around, the weed was on him, too. Everyone loved Tukee. He was a drug market star.

Of course, Tukee was also feared. As crack use rose, more dealers tried to squeeze into the now-saturated market. Tukee pulled his gun on several newcomers, warning them to stay away from his "spot." He became a legend after he shot a dealer for dealing drugs without his permission. After coming out of hiding (the police investigation lasted a few weeks), everyone deferred to him, greeting him with open arms and a smile. *Tukee*—he's crazy!

Then, after about a year, it was over. Tukee's lucrative crack business slowed down. His night-clubbing and largesse took a hit, and he limited his outings to the affordable Dallas BBQ restaurant. "That was the only place I could take girls to," he remembers. "They served these big-ass glasses of margaritas for real cheap. Those shits looked like they came in Cheerio [cereal] bowls, so I could get bitches drunk for real cheap. I'm telling you, B[ro], times were real hard."

Tukee wasn't alone. During the mid-1990s, crack dealing across New York City took a mighty hit. Unbeknownst to dealers, many crack

users had reduced their intake because of the drug's stigma and frenetic, binging lifestyle. Also, the new generation of youth shunned crack because they had seen what it did to their family members, neighbors, and friends. Malt liquor beer and marijuana would become their recreational drugs of choice. The crack market shrank, bringing once-successful crack dealers to the lowest of the lows.

Riches and highlife—gone.

To maintain his dealing income, Tukee started transporting crack to Philadelphia, where he established a selling spot with a local. The money was decent, but it wasn't "Donald Trump" money. When he got word that the police were watching him, he returned to the South Bronx dejected and broke.

"I was sellin' all my guns, all my jewelry, everything B[ro], just to stay in the game," Tukee recounts. "I used that money to buy some dope [heroin] and sell that shit."

However, Tukee struggled to find an open dealing spot. The heroin dealers—who funded quasi-armies for protection—demanded a daily "rent" of $1,200 to $2,000 for the right to sell on their block. Tukee could not afford the rent. So he returned to Philadelphia to sell his heroin. No luck. Philly heroin users remained loyal to local brands. Defeated, Tukee again returned to the South Bronx.

Eventually, Tukee joined an auto-theft crew that catered to the Crack Era's big-time drug dealers (the same crew that had sold him the stolen car parts for his own ride). But the stolen car business was no longer lucrative—the shrinking crack market lessened its need, too. Tukee hardly earned any money. He was at a loss: "I was like, 'This is it,'" Tukee recalls. "Nothing's workin' out. This is the end of me."

Like Tukee, other displaced drug dealers felt a financial strain because of the crack market's decline. Several of them responded by creating a lucrative new niche in drug robberies. Now they beat, burned, choked, and mutilated their drug-dealing victims. Now they committed horrific acts that they had never done before. Now they were Stickup Kids, the perpetrators of the worst violence in the drug world. Tukee joined their ranks.

A former drug-dealing connection contacted Tukee for a drug robbery. They planned to rob a drug-dealer for about eight kilos of cocaine and $30,000 in cash. Tukee had never done a drug robbery before, not even a street robbery. But he was handy with a gun. "I didn't even think twice about it," Tukee recalls. "I was like, 'Fuck it. Show me where the money's at.'"

It was an inside job, where a drug dealer *wanted* to get himself and his partner robbed. The dealer, of course, would be absent. But he gave the Stickup crew the best time to storm the stash apartment, where his partner sometimes stayed alone. If all went well, the treacherous dealer would get half the proceeds just for providing the information. The crew would split the other half: $95,000 in drugs and cash.

For the robbery, they brought along "The Girl," a young, attractive female accomplice. "We needed her 'cause we can't just knock on the door and the dude just gonna open," Tukee explained. "He don't know us and he's fuckin' holding drugs. He's gonna be like, 'These motherfuckers are cops or trying to rob my ass.' So we got her to knock on the door and get the door open."

It worked. She knocked. The dealer peeped through the peephole. She smiled and flirted and asked for help. When he opened the door to get a better sense of her needs, the drug robbers, crouched on either side of the door, guns in hand, exploded into action. Tukee's crew rushed the dealer, rammed him back into the apartment, slammed him onto the floor, kicked him, punched

him, pistol-whipped him, threatened him to stay down, not to move, or they would stab him, shoot him, would do everything imaginable that would cause his death.

"The shit was crazy, son," Tukee recalls. "I was like watching at first. But then I had to make sure that niggas saw me do shit. Let niggas know that I ain't no slouch. [So] I started kickin' the dude—Bah! Bah! Then we tied him up with duct tape and I put my gun in his head [sic], I was like, 'Where's the shit at! You wanna die, nigga?'"

As Tukee and a partner terrified the dealer, the other two robbers frantically searched the apartment for the drugs and cash. After flipping mattresses, pulling out dresser drawers, and yanking out clothes from a closet, they found it. Everyone scrambled out of the apartment, leaving the dealer bloody, bruised, and bound on the living room floor.

There was no need for torture in this robbery. But the thrill energized Tukee. "I was amped up after that, like for awhile, B. I remember we was counting the money, weighing the drugs, splitting everything, giving this dude this much, me this much, him that much. . . . I was like, 'I'm ready to do this again.' Let's go, B!"

According to Tukee, the robbery netted him about $30,000 worth of drugs and cash. This was more than he had earned in a year of stealing cars and selling heroin. So, for him, the violence was worth the money. He wanted to be rich again. Soon, he became a violence expert. He knew how to overcome resistant victims.

"I started doing all types of shit," Tukee explains. "Like I would tie them [the dealers] up and ask them, 'Where the fuck the kilos at?' If they don't tell me, or be like, 'I don't sell drugs. I don't know why you doing this,' then I pistol-whipped them. If they still don't say nothin', I choked them. If they still don't

> Now these former dealers became Stickup Kids, the perpetrators of the worst violence in the drug world. They created a lucrative new niche: drug robberies.

say nothin', then you bring the iron out and burn them. Or you could go to the kitchen and get a kitchen knife, some butcher-type shit, and chop off one of their fingers. Then those dudes be like, 'Alright, alright, take it! It's over there!'"

Tukee, then, *learned* how to do one-on-one violence—fist-to-face, knife-to-neck, hands-to-throat violence—to someone vulnerable, tied up, who pled for mercy, to please, please leave them alone. Tukee felt he had to. *You gotta do what you gotta do,* he always said. Violence for money would become his way of life. *Tukee*—he's no joke.

> Tukee was born neither a drug robber nor torturer. His biography emerged within a particular social context.

social context and violence

Throughout his life, Tukee pursued meaning through the illegal drug market. And his words seem to support an evil and sociopathic understanding of his behavior. Did Tukee enjoy the emotional rush of a drug robbery—yes. Did Tukee enjoy doing violence—yes. But we must also ask: *Why* did he seek thrills as a drug robber rather than as a courtroom lawyer or a Wall Street executive? *Why* did he enjoy physically hurting people as a drug robber rather than as a hockey player, football player, or mixed-martial artist?

The answer lies in the social context, the South Bronx setting in which Tukee's life unfolded. He came of age during the Crack Era, which resulted from misguided drug policies, the decline of manufacturing, and the collapse of inner cities. If we add the daily cultural messages that try to make Americans pursue the ultimate, most gluttonous version of the American Dream, then we see marginal residents who not only used crack to exit poverty, but also to strike it rich. They wanted the material status symbols that Madison Avenue advertising agencies *taught* them to want and need.

Tukee was born into this world, a world not of his own creation, but one that influenced him first into crack dealing, then into drug robberies. If the Crack Era had not appeared, there is a great chance—though not absolute—that Tukee would have become neither a drug dealer nor drug robber. These lucrative criminal opportunities would have been unlikely, less abundant options. So to understand Tukee, we must understand how history and social structure intersects with his biography. Otherwise, the study of poverty-related brutality becomes a distorted enterprise in which Tukee and other marginal criminals are improperly portrayed.

RECOMMENDED RESOURCES

Timothy Black. 2009. *When a Heart Turns Rock Solid: The Lives of Three Puerto Rican Brothers on and off the Streets.* New York: Pantheon Books.

A long-term ethnography that economically and politically contextualizes the criminal and legal life course of three Puerto Rican brothers in Springfield, Massachusetts.

Philippe Bourgois. 2003 [1995]. *In Search of Respect: Selling Crack in El Barrio.* New York: Cambridge University Press.

A theoretically informed ethnography linking the declining manufacturing sector to the everyday lives of Puerto Rican crack dealers in New York City.

Randall Collins. 2008. *Violence: A Micro-Sociological Theory.* Princeton: Princeton University Press.

A theoretical examination of the emotional dynamics that produce violence during micro-interactions.

Jack Katz. 1988. *Seductions of Crime: Moral and Sensual Attractions of Doing Evil.* New York: Basic Books.

An examination of how emotional thrills and other foreground factors are linked to the commission of crimes.

REVIEW QUESTIONS

1. Why did the author argue that crimes are not driven mainly by individual-level reasons but rather sociohistorical reasons? Do you agree with this frame?

2. Do you believe social policies can ameliorate the vicious chain of social context and violence? What types of policies might work?

3. The author mainly dealt with brutality brought about by poverty. How do poverty and race intersect to create particularly problematic contexts for some racial groups?

donald tomaskovic-devey and patricia warren

explaining and eliminating racial profiling　13

spring 2009

racial profiling has fairly recent roots. the authors here show how racial profiling has become a widespread policing policy in the united states since 1984.

The emancipation of slaves is a century and a half in America's past. Many would consider it ancient history. Even the 1964 Civil Rights Act and the 1965 Voting Rights Act, which challenged the de facto racial apartheid of the post–Civil War period, are now well over 40 years old.

But even in the face of such well-established laws, racial inequalities in education, housing, employment, and law enforcement remain widespread in the United States.

Many Americans think these racial patterns stem primarily from individual prejudices or even racist attitudes. However, sociological research shows discrimination is more often the result of organizational practices that have unintentional racial effects or are based on cognitive biases linked to social stereotypes.

Racial profiling—stopping or searching cars and drivers based primarily on race, rather than any suspicion or observed violation of the law—is particularly problematic because it's a form of discrimination enacted and organized by federal and local governments.

In our research we've found that sometimes formal, institutionalized rules within law enforcement agencies encourage racial profiling. Routine patrol patterns and responses to calls for service, too, can produce racially biased policing. And, unconscious biases among individual police officers can encourage them to perceive some drivers as more threatening than others (of course, overt racism, although not widespread, among some police officers also contributes to racial profiling).

> The same politics and practices that produce racial profiling can be the tools communities use to confront and eliminate it.

Racially biased policing is particularly troubling for police–community relations, as it unintentionally contributes to the mistrust of police in minority neighborhoods. But the same politics and organizational practices that produce racial profiling can be the tools communities use to confront and eliminate it.

profiling and its problems

The modern story of racially biased policing begins with the Drug Enforcement Agency's (DEA) Operation Pipeline, which starting in 1984 trained 25,000 state and local police officers in 48 states to recognize, stop, and search potential drug couriers. Part of that training included considering the suspects' race.

Jurisdictions developed a variety of profiles in response to Operation Pipeline. For example, in Eagle County, Colorado, the sheriff's office profiled drug couriers as those who had fast-food wrappers strewn in their cars, out-of-state license plates, and dark skin, according to the book *Good Cop, Bad Cop* by Milton Heumann and Lance Cassak. As well, those authors wrote, Delaware's drug courier profile commonly targeted young minority men carrying pagers or wearing gold jewelry. And according to the American Civil Liberties Union (ACLU), the Florida Highway Patrol's profile included rental cars, scrupulous obedience to traffic laws, drivers wearing lots of gold or who don't "fit" the vehicle, and ethnic groups associated with the drug trade (meaning African Americans and Latinos).

In the 1990s, civil rights organizations challenged the use of racial profiles during routine traffic stops, calling them a form of discrimination. In response, the U.S. Department of Justice argued that using race as an explicit profile produced more efficient crime control than random stops. Over the past decade, however, basic social science research has called this claim into question.

> More stops and searches of minorities doesn't lead to more drug seizures than stops and searches of White drivers. In fact, the rates of contraband found in searches of minorities are typically lower.

The key indicator of efficiency in police searches is the percent that result in the discovery of something illegal. Recent research has shown repeatedly that increasing the number of stops and searches among minorities doesn't lead to more drug seizures than are found in routine traffic stops and searches among White drivers. In fact, the rates of contraband found in profiling-based drug searches of minorities are typically lower, suggesting racial profiling decreases police efficiency.

In addition to it being an inefficient police practice, Operation Pipeline violated the assumption of equal protection under the law guaranteed through civil rights laws as well as the Fourteenth Amendment to the U.S. Constitution. It meant, in other words, that just as police forces across the country were learning to curb the egregious civil rights violations of the twentieth century, the federal government began training state and local police to target Black and Brown drivers for minor traffic violations in hopes of finding more-severe criminal offending. The cruel irony is that it was exactly this type of flagrant, state-sanctioned racism the civil rights movement was so successful at outlawing barely a decade earlier.

Following notorious cases of violence against minorities perpetrated by police officers, such as the videotaped beating of Rodney King in Los Angeles in 1991 and the shooting of Amadou Diallo in New York in 1999, racially biased policing rose quickly on the national civil rights agenda. By the late 1990s, challenges to racial profiling became a key political goal in the more general movement for racial justice.

The National Association for the Advancement of Colored People (NAACP) and the ACLU brought lawsuits against law enforcement agencies across the United States for targeting minority drivers. As a result, many states passed legislation that banned the use of racial profiles and then required officers to record the race of drivers stopped in order to monitor and sanction those who were violating citizens' civil rights.

Today, many jurisdictions continue to collect information on the race composition of vehicle stops and searches to monitor and discourage racially biased policing. In places like New Jersey and North Carolina, where the national politics challenging racial profiling were reinforced by local efforts to monitor and sanction police, racial disparities in highway patrol stops and searches declined.

Our analysis of searches by the North Carolina Highway Patrol shows that these civil rights–based challenges, both national and local, quickly changed police behavior. In 1997, before racial profiling had come under attack, Black drivers were four times as likely as White drivers to be subjected to a search by the North Carolina Highway Patrol. Confirming that the high rate of searches represented racial profiling, Black drivers were 33 percent less likely to be found with contraband compared to White drivers. The next year, as the national and local politics of racial profiling accelerated, searches of Black drivers plummeted in North Carolina. By 2000, racial disparities in searches had been cut in half and the recovery of contraband no longer differed by race, suggesting officers were no longer racially biased in their decisions to search cars.

This isn't to suggest lawyers' and activists' complaints have stopped profiling everywhere. For example, Missouri, which has been collecting data since 2000, still has large race disparities in searching practices among its police officers. The most recent data (for 2007) shows Blacks were 78 percent more likely than Whites to be searched. Hispanics were 118 percent more likely than Whites to be searched. Compared to searches of White drivers, contraband was found 25 percent less often among Black drivers and 38 percent less often among Hispanic drivers.

how bias is produced

Many police–citizen encounters aren't discretionary, therefore even if an officer harbors racial prejudice it won't influence the decision to stop a car. For example, highway patrol officers, concerned with traffic flow and public safety, spend a good deal of their time stopping speeders based on radar readings—they often don't even know the race of the driver until after they pull over the car. Still, a number of other factors can produce high rates of racially biased stops. The first has to do with police patrol patterns, which tend to vary widely by neighborhood.

Not unreasonably, communities suffering from higher rates of crime are often patrolled more aggressively than others. Because minorities more often live in these neighborhoods, the routine deployment of police in an effort to increase public safety will produce more police–citizen contacts and thus a higher rate of stops in those neighborhoods.

A recent study in Charlotte, North Carolina, confirmed that much of the race disparity in vehicle stops there can be explained in terms of patrol patterns and calls for service. Another recent study of pedestrian stops in New York yielded similar conclusions—but further estimated that police patrol patterns alone lead to African-American pedestrians being stopped at three times the rate of Whites. (And similar to the study of racial profiling of North Carolina motorists, contraband was recovered from White New Yorkers at twice the rate of African Americans.)

Police patrol patterns are, in fact, sometimes more obviously racially motivated. Targeting Black bars, rather than White country clubs, for Saturday night random alcohol checks has this character. This also happens when police stop minority drivers for being in White neighborhoods. This "out-of-place policing" is often a routine police practice, but can also arise from calls for service from White households suspicious of minorities in their otherwise segregated neighborhoods. In our conversations with African-American drivers, many were quite conscious of the risk they took when walking or driving in White neighborhoods.

"My son . . . was working at the country club. . . . He missed the bus and he said he was walking out Queens Road. After a while all the lights came popping on in every house. He guessed they called and . . . the police came and

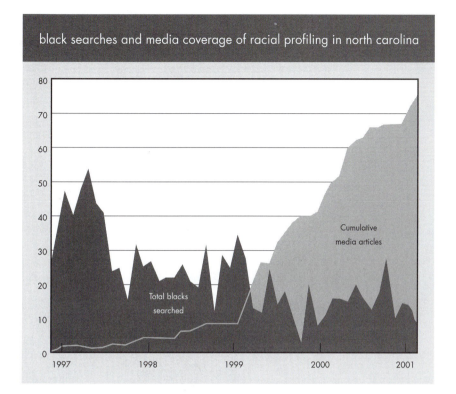

black searches and media coverage of racial profiling in north carolina

Cumulative media articles

Total blacks searched

they questioned him. They wanted to know why was he walking through Queens Road [at] that time of day," one Black respondent we talked to said.

The "wars" on drugs and crime of the 1980s and 1990s encouraged law enforcement to police minority neighborhoods aggressively and thus contributed significantly to these problematic patterns. In focus groups with African-American drivers in North Carolina, we heard that many were well aware of these patterns and their sources. "I think sometimes they target . . . depending on where you live. I think if you live in a side of town . . . with maybe a lot of crime or maybe break-ins or drugs, . . . I think you are a target there," one respondent noted.

These stories are mirrored in data on police stops in a midsize midwestern city reported in the figure "Blacks Stopped More in Neighborhoods with Few Black Drivers." Here, the fewer minorities there are in a neighborhood, the more often African Americans are stopped. In the Whitest neighborhoods, African-American drivers were stopped at three times the rate you'd expect given how many of them are on the road. In minority communities, minority drivers were still stopped disproportionally, but at rates much closer to their population as drivers in the neighborhood.

This isn't to say all racial inequities in policing originate with the rules organizations follow. Racial attitudes and biases among police officers are still a source of racial disparity in police vehicle stops. But even this is a more complicated story than personal prejudice and old-fashioned bigotry.

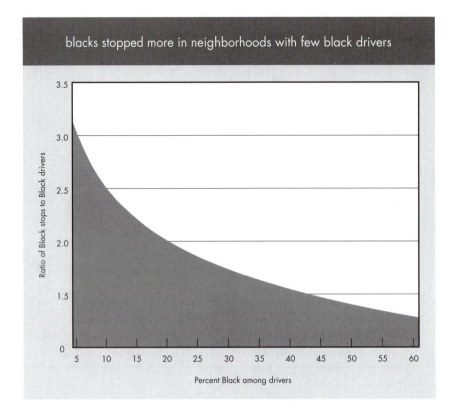

blacks stopped more in neighborhoods with few black drivers

Ratio of Black stops to Black drivers (vertical axis)

Percent Black among drivers (horizontal axis)

bias among individual officers

The two most common sources of individual bias are conscious prejudice and unconscious cognitive bias. Conscious prejudice is typically, but incorrectly, thought of as the most common source of individuals' racist behavior. While some individual police officers, just like some employers or real estate agents, may be old-fashioned bigots, this isn't a widespread source of racial bias in police stops. Not only is prejudice against African Americans on the decline in the United States, but most police forces prohibit this kind of racism and reprimand or punish such officers when it's discovered. In these cases, in fact,

organizational mechanisms prevent, or at least reduce, bigoted behavior.

Most social psychologists agree, however, that implicit biases against minorities are widespread in the population. While only about 10 percent of the White population will admit they have explicitly racist attitudes, more than three-quarters display implicit anti-Black bias.

Studies of social cognition (or, how people think) show that people simplify and manage information by organizing it into social categories. By focusing on obvious status characteristics such as sex, race, or age, all of us tend to categorize ourselves and others into groups. Once people are racially categorized, stereotypes automatically, and often unconsciously, become activated and influence behavior. Given pervasive media images of African-American men as dangerous and threatening, it shouldn't be surprising that when officers make decisions about whom to pull over or whom to search, unconscious bias may encourage them to focus more often on minorities.

These kinds of biases come into play especially for local police who, in contrast to highway patrol officers, do much more low-speed, routine patrolling of neighborhoods and business districts and thus have more discretion in making decisions about whom to stop.

In our research in North Carolina, for example, we found that while highway patrol officers weren't more likely to stop African-American drivers than White drivers, local police stopped African Americans 70 percent more often than White drivers, even after statistically adjusting for driving behavior. Local officers were also more likely to stop men, younger drivers, and drivers in older cars, confirming this process was largely about unconscious bias rather than explicit racial profiles. Race, gender, age, class biases, and stereotypes about perceived dangerousness seem to explain this pattern of local police vehicle stops.

strategies for change

Unconscious biases are particularly difficult for an organization to address because offending individuals are typically unaware of them, and when confronted, they may deny any racist intent.

There is increasing evidence that even deep-seated stereotypes and unconscious biases can be eroded through both education and exposure to minorities who don't fit common stereotypes, and that they can be contained when

> Unconscious biases can be eroded through education and exposure to minorities who don't fit common stereotypes. Biases can also be contained when people are held accountable for their decisions.

people are held accountable for their decisions. Indeed, it appears that acts of racial discrimination (as opposed to just prejudicial attitudes or beliefs) can be stopped through managerial authority, and prejudice itself seems to be reduced through both education and exposure to minorities.

For example, a 2006 study by sociologists Alexandra Kalev, Frank Dobbin, and Erin Kelly of race and gender employment bias in the private sector found that holding management accountable for equal employment opportunities is particularly efficient for reducing race and gender biases. Thus, the active monitoring and managing of police officers based on racial composition of their stops and searches holds much promise for mitigating this "invisible" prejudice.

Citizen and police review boards can play proactive and reactive roles in monitoring both individual police behavior as well as problematic organizational practices. Local police forces can use data they collect on racial disparity in police stops to identify problematic organizational behaviors such as intensively policing minority neighborhoods, targeting minorities in White neighborhoods, and racial profiling in searches.

Aggressive enforcement of civil rights laws will also play a key role in encouraging local police chiefs and employers to continue to monitor and address prejudice and discrimination inside their organizations. This is an area where the federal government has a clear role to play. Filing lawsuits against cities and states with persistent patterns of racially biased policing—whether based on the defense of segregated White neighborhoods or the routine patrolling of crime "hot spots"—would send a message to all police forces that the routine harassment of minority citizens is unacceptable in the United States.

justice in the obama era

Given the crucial role the federal justice department has played in both creating and confronting racial profiling, one may wonder whether the election of President Barack Obama will have any consequences for racially biased policing.

Obama certainly has personal reasons to challenge racist practices. And given the success of his presidential campaign, it would seem he has the political capital to address racial issues in a way and to an extent unlike any of his predecessors.

At the same time, the new president has vowed to continue to fight a war on terrorism, a war often understood and explicitly defined in religious and ethnic terms. In some ways, the threat of terrorism has replaced the threat of African Americans in the U.S. political lexicon. There's evidence as well that politicians, both Democrat [sic] and Republican, have increased their verbal attacks on illegal immigrants and in doing so may be providing a fertile ground for new rounds of profiling against Hispanics in this country. So, while the racial profiling of African Americans as explicit national policy is unlikely in the Obama Administration, other groups may not be so lucky.

Americans committed to racial justice and equality will likely take this as a cautionary tale. They will also likely hope the Obama Administration decides to take a national leadership role in ending racial profiling. But if it does, as sociologists we hope the administration won't make the all-too-common mistake of assuming racial profiling is primarily the result of racial prejudice or even the more widespread psychology of unconscious bias.

RECOMMENDED RESOURCES

American Civil Liberties Union. Campaign against Racial Profiling. www.aclu.org/racial-justice/racial-profiling/index.html

> The leading civil rights agency speaking out against racial profiling has actively challenged police departments across the United States on biased policing practices.

N. Dasgupta and Anthony Greenwald. 2001. "On the Malleability of Automatic Attitudes: Combating Automatic Prejudice with Images of Admired and Disliked Individuals." *Journal of Personality and Social Psychology* 81: 800–14.

> Shows unconscious cognitive biases can be countered by positive, stereotype-disrupting role models.

Alexandra Kalev, Frank Dobbin, and Erin Kelly. 2006. "Best Practices or Best Guesses? Assessing the Efficacy of Corporate Affirmative Action and Diversity Polices." *American Sociological Review* 71: 598–617.

> Shows that holding managers accountable for racial and gender bias leads to lower levels of discrimination.

Racial Profiling Data Collection Resource Center at Northeastern University. Legislation and Litigation. www.racialprofilinganalysis.neu.edu/legislation/

> Provides detailed information about racial profiling studies across the United States.

Patricia Warren, Donald Tomaskovic-Devey, William Smith, Matthew Zingraff, and Marcinda Mason. 2006. "Driving While Black: Bias Processes and Racial Disparity in Police Stops." *Criminology* 44: 709–38.

> Uses survey data to identify the mechanisms that give rise to racial disparity in traffic stops.

REVIEW QUESTIONS

1. What is the difference between conscious prejudice and implicit cognitive bias? Which is more common?
2. How is bias in policing produced?
3. How can racial bias in organizations be reduced?
4. Why has the claim that racial profiling in policing is more efficient than random stops been called into question?

sarah esther lageson

digital punishment's tangled web

14

winter 2016

online mugshots and crime reports comprise an emerging—and sticky—form of extralegal punishment. though widely available and broadly used, the predictive value of crime reports for public safety is questionable, at best. the very existence of an online mugshot or booking report communicates powerful signals of guilt by attaching a criminal label to millions of arrestees, with a host of social and psychological consequences.

Americans love crime. The criminal justice system is fetishized in popular culture and news media. We watch the news and scour the Internet to assess our own moral compass, take cues from others' digressions, and bear witness to justice and punishment. Historically, we learned about crime through news media and fiction. The Internet has dramatically changed this landscape: for the first time, mug shots and jailhouse rosters are available with a click.

I have studied the growth of what I call *digital punishment* by interviewing those who run criminal history and mug shot websites, by analyzing the content they produce, and by interviewing those working to clear their own criminal records through legal means even against the reality of an endless digital trail. Producers of these media (including bloggers, website publishers, and private background check companies) often have public safety-minded intentions, but online repositories of mug shots and arrest records haunt those whose criminal histories lurk online, even when charges are dismissed.

There are consequences to these practices. Websites can spread incorrect and dismissed records. While criminal-history data changes rapidly at the jurisdictional level, we don't have a good system in place to ensure corresponding updates are made online. Unregulated criminal history and crime reporting websites thus constitute a new form of punishment culminating in a searchable online history that its subjects often don't know exists, until they face real-world consequences because of these records. The very existence of an online mug shot or booking report communicates powerful signals of guilt by attaching a criminal label to millions of arrestees, with a host of social and psychological consequences.

public records

Digital crime reports are unique in their scope, breadth, availability, and permanence. Websites can post arrest records, full names, and booking photos before someone is charged with or convicted of a crime, and those records remain online indefinitely. Such sites appeal to consumers by providing access to real-time crime information, allowing them to feel they take an active role in crime prevention without directly interacting with the criminal justice system.

In the past, criminal records were on paper, stored in courthouses. To obtain someone's record, you had to physically ask for it, make a copy if you were allowed, and try to interpret what it all meant. Today, millions of digital criminal records are archived indefinitely and accessed anywhere there's an Internet connection. Online, these reports appear on Facebook crime watch pages, Twitter feeds, and on local newspaper websites. Once published, they are easily shared and reposted—leaving a digital trail that is nearly impossible to remedy.

Accessible, digital records have emerged from and within several important contexts. The first is the dramatic expansion of the criminal justice system, which has coincided with a push toward the open access of newly digitized and easy-to-transfer governmental data. Another context is the growing tendency to use criminal records in a variety of new settings as a way to assess morality and character. Potential employers, possible landlords—one Google search, and your job or housing might be jeopardized.

Criminal justice agencies maintain and work to update their own online databases, but these publicly available data have often already leaked onto unregulated, unofficial websites. A routine, informal Internet search might reveal a criminal history posted on a neighborhood crime watch blog or a background check company might reveal part of a criminal record, keeping the rest tantalizingly hidden behind a paywall. Again, your coworker, first date, or the parents of your kid's new friend at school can all stumble on this information, as a simple arrest—one that might not even lead to charges—appears online, accompanied by a booking photo. This photo and arrest record might be reposted to a Facebook page, a community blog, on a newspaper police blotter. These data are also purchased in bulk by private companies, whose sites are often paid top results in a Google search. We need to expand our definition of a "criminal record" to include all the different forms of documentation that result from any interaction with the justice system.

It is one thing to say that the whole system needs an overhaul, but wouldn't we all be curious if we saw our child's babysitter had a criminal record?

The look of many crime-related websites also makes it difficult for casual readers to distinguish between official governmental databases and private companies that offer background check services. The advent of citizen journalism on crime might also be unclear to online newsreaders. And while many reputable journalists report on crime online, bloggers and website publishers work without editors and fact checkers, sometimes just copying and pasting bulk data onto profit-seeking websites, as in the expansive mug shot industry.

For the well-meaning crime reporter, there are troves of data. This means editorial decisions must be made carefully and data sources scrutinized to a new degree. Quite simply, this public information is terrible data. It's been documented time and again by prominent criminologists at SUNY-Albany, the National Consumer Law Center, and the National Employment Law Project. Part of the issue is that there are no licensing requirements for criminal background agencies. Anyone with a computer and access to records can start a business, and the total number of companies is unknown. Unlike credit reporting agencies, there is no central system for registration for background checking companies. This means a consumer can't regularly order his or her own report to review for errors. Data are generally outdated and incorrect. The most common issues involve mismatching identities, divulging expunged or sealed records, and omitting case dispositions.

The problem isn't limited to the private sector or independently run websites. According to a 2013 National Employment Law Project study, about half of the FBI's criminal history records are incomplete and fail to include information on the final disposition of an arrest. While some

(© ThinkDesign Group for Contexts *magazine)*

states are working to regulate these industries, state-level interventions do not address websites with servers located in different jurisdictions or overseas.

It's important to consider the kinds of crimes that appear in Google searches. Most arrests are for low-level and nonviolent crimes. Of the 11.3 million arrests in 2013, only 4 percent were for violent crimes. The highest number of arrests that year were for drug abuse violations, theft, and driving under the influence. These rather typical encounters with police and other criminal justice actors constitute the bulk of criminal justice operations and mostly result in non-carceral sanctions, such as probation, parole, alternative programs or sentences, fines, or community service. Many arrests for non-felonious crimes—as many as half, depending on the location—are eventually dismissed. Increasingly, convictions are suspended after a period of time set by a judge, such as in a stay of adjudication (in which a case is dismissed after probation conditions are met), and the official record is supposedly cleared. Persistent online records undermine this judicial strategy,

creating a long-lasting and unregulated extralegal form of punishment.

Criminological studies show that past criminal behavior quickly loses its power to predict future offending. A landmark 2006 study by Megan Kurlychek, Robert Brame, and Shawn Bushway estimated that, after six or seven years, the risk of reoffense approaches the risk of *new* offenses among people with no criminal record. Though widely available and broadly used, the predictive value of crime reports for public safety is questionable, at best.

consequences

To understand the lingering effects of digital punishment, I spent several years doing fieldwork at criminal record expungement clinics. After interviewing dozens of people, it became clear that having your mug shot appear in online databases, social media, and blogs carries a broad set of consequences that span the social, psychological, and practical elements of life.

Expungement clinics are a unique research site because petitioners are people with low-level

records trying to seal their records from public view. Many expungement seekers came to the clinic after their record "popped up" online. This language was used repeatedly—nearly a third of respondents used the phrase specifically—and helped me see what a surprise the digital trail was to so many people.

Donna, an African-American woman in her 50s, told me, "When it pops up like that, it gives people the impression that you have this criminal record, and they don't know even what it's about. When they go on there, it doesn't tell them the whole truth." Another respondent, Daryl, an African-American man in his 40s, said, "I have looked myself up out of curiosity—my name anyway—and try to see what pops up. And it's not a pretty sight." Still, Daryl says the Google search "tells me that as long as I don't try for high-level jobs, that I should be okay. I should fly under the radar."

Sandra, a White mother, was able to obtain housing with her low-level drug record, "But it's not in a great neighborhood, not a great landlord." She wanted her records expunged so she could try for a better situation. And Tammy, a White woman in her 50s who was unemployed, had not actively searched for a job because she feared a potential employer would use a private background check company and find dismissed charges. Her fears were not irrational, of course: once these reports appear, they are easily sold and resold across online enterprises. Tammy recalled, "I applied for two jobs over Christmas, and then they said they 'We're gonna do a criminal background check,' and that means they hire a company to look up your record. Then they find it, and then it's permanently in databases, even if you get it expunged later. . . . It will go around the Internet. It could go anywhere."

Jaci, another expungement seeker, had a couple of drug offenses and had recently been arrested again, though the charges were dropped. Her online records were keeping her from volunteering and made her uncomfortable around people who might have seen her arrests online: "They seen me on this thing called 'Mug shots,' and I actually seen myself, and its pretty embarrassing. I got probably like five Facebook messages. They were like, 'Dude, you're on Mug shots.' I went and looked it up and seen myself. I was really pretty sure it has to do with like, online access, people exposing other people. Criminals. . . ."

She continued, "I would like to volunteer at my daughter's school, but I am not allowed to because of the background check. They give you a list of what you're not supposed to have on your background. So I'm like, 'Well, I can't do that.' And it's kinda hard telling that to your daughter. 'I can't volunteer today.' She knows I'm working a lot, so I just let her think that's why. I haven't talked to other parents. I kinda keep my background to myself, because I don't want people to know or to get into a conversation like, 'Oh, what happened?' "

Like those whose personal photos are shared on the Internet without their consent, people who appear on websites are responsible for getting their incorrect information removed or corrected. Proposed federal legislation would change this, but it hasn't passed yet. My interviews, meanwhile, revealed the near-impossibility of contacting website publishers to request these changes and a lack of official avenue to make these requests. At the expungement clinic, Roger seemed wary that anything could help him get a Google search clear of his history: "We are here today to try to clear our record. Let's just imagine that I am successful. There is like 3,000 services out there."

Roger actually works in technology and was better positioned than most to figure out how to contact the publisher of a website that persistently posted his dismissed arrest data. After many e-mails, he received a response: "A blank letter stating, 'We grabbed data from a public source and we are not responsible for data that we grabbed.' " Roger shook his head and laughed ruefully. "So, if you are grabbing the rotten data and then you are sharing with other people then yes, you are responsible for passing on the wrong data. . . . [But] there is just no legal recourse."

William felt defeated before even trying to contact a single website: "I haven't bothered. It's too much. It's too frustrating."

Online criminal records create a difficult landscape. Technology has expanded accessibility to records, and while this shift brings important opportunities to law enforcement investigations and local-level crime reporting, it exponentially increases the opportunity for erroneous, incorrect, outdated, and non-conviction records to exert their power.

My research has shown that, beyond economic effects, even minor justice-system contact also shapes relationships with family members, work, and social institutions. This ultimately leads to what sociologists Alice Goffman and Sarah Brayne refer to as "system avoidance" of medical, financial, labor market, and educational institutions. That is, people gradually avoid interacting with these institutions, and this has obvious social and individual consequences.

This isn't a small issue. Nearly 1 in 4 adults (an estimated 65 million people) in the United States has some kind of criminal record.

the public's right to know

Yet, there are Constitutional rights to freedom of speech and legal rights to obtain and disseminate governmental data, such as criminal records. To get at the other side of digital punishment, I interviewed crime website publishers.

In Europe, the courts have awarded the "right to be forgotten" on the Internet to those who have been exonerated or found not guilty.

I was amazed by the dedication the interviewees showed in their demand for open access to government information, as both a way to inform the public about criminals *and* as a way to keep an eye on the police and prosecutors by tracking who is getting arrested and charged in our communities, where, and for what.

One citizen journalist from rural North Carolina told me he ran his crime update Facebook page "To make citizens aware of the crimes going on and to ask for help to keep an eye out for these criminals. Citizens are the most valuable resource for the police in the war against crime."

Sheila ran a website that tracked sex offense cases as they worked their way through the system. She learned how to build a website after witnessing her stepdaughter's experience with the justice system as a survivor of abuse. She told me, "Because the national registry only lists those who have been convicted and served their time, I felt there was an obvious need to create an alert system that filled the gap between arrest and conviction."

Finally, a crime blogger named Bob told me his blog is "for people who want to revitalize the neighborhood versus the forces of crime and chaos."

The Internet is a powerful tool for protecting citizens from government, as newsrooms contract, and it provides a way to obtain hyper-local news about issues that directly impact livability and public safety in a community.

new forms of criminal punishment

In the end, though, online records raise questions of when criminal punishment should, or truly does, end. The permanent, public criminal record flies in the face of Constitutional guarantees to due process and the presumption of innocence.

I don't, however, think the situation is hopeless. First, we should better differentiate journalists and citizens who report on crime and deserve full First Amendment protection from those who obtain crime data en masse, reposting it without editorial oversight or curatorial responsibility.

We should also question allowing the sale of criminal records to private vendors that approach overburdened county sheriff's offices to offer their data management services or simply buy messy governmental data and repackage it without scrutiny, selling it to businesses and consumers. Federal oversight or licensing of background check companies and the creation of a process to remedy outdated or incorrect records—like the credit reporting industry—might be a step forward.

It would also be prudent to reconsider public distribution of arrest records and their use in noncriminal justice settings. Arrests are indicative of a discretionary point of contact with a police officer or prosecutor, but they are generally not helpful in identifying a dangerous or violent criminal. In Europe, the courts have awarded the "right to be forgotten" on Google search results to those who have been exonerated or found not guilty.

Online records are changing what we know about desistence from crime and recidivism, particularly the effects of labeling and stigma. Researchers must develop ways to measure the "effects" of these informal records across one's life, such as how their ready availability might change one's ability to be a good parent, create new relationships and friendships, volunteer in a

> People who appear on mug shot and crime-tracking websites are responsible for getting incorrect information removed or corrected.

community or church, or participate in other civic activities.

It's obvious this is a big and messy system, which undermines our ability to paint a clear picture of what should be done. And it's difficult to differentiate between journalists, citizen-journalists, website publishers, and open-data advocates when these roles overlap. Really considering online criminal records and their many uses asks us to differentiate between public and private data and public and private agencies at a time when partnerships between the two are increasingly complex and codependent. And it asks us to say "No, thanks" to information that is cheap, available, and overestimated in its value for improving public safety. It is one thing to say that the whole system needs an overhaul, but wouldn't we all be curious if we saw our child's babysitter had a criminal record, just a few clicks away?

There may be a shift toward regulation and governmental control of criminal justice data. Without it, it will be difficult to fix this leaky faucet. In the meantime, the deluge of online records should make us consider the social good of crime data if it's not *good* data.

RECOMMENDED RESOURCES

David Garland. 2001. *The Culture of Control.* Chicago: University of Chicago Press.

> An elegant theoretical look at the connection between crime and culture, especially in how crime is depicted in media accounts.

Chris Greer, ed. 2010. *Crime and Media: A Reader.* New York: Routledge.

> Provides rich history and context for the relationship between crime and media.

Sarah Lageson. 2014. "The Enduring Effects of Online Mug Shots." *The Society Pages.* thesocietypages.org/roundtables/mugshots/

> Sociologists share perspectives on the culture, politics, and effects of online mug shots.

Gary W. Potter and Victor E. Kappeler, eds. 2006. *Constructing Crime: Perspectives on Making News and Social Problems,* 2nd ed. Long Grove: Waveland Press, Inc.

> An edited volume, this book describes how publicizing crime through the news media feeds into public fear and stricter laws by developing crime as a social problem

David Segal. 2013. "Mugged by a Mug Shot Online." *New York Times,* October 5.

> A high-profile article on the harmful effects of mug shots for employment, housing, and relationships with several profiles of individuals impacted by their online trail.

REVIEW QUESTIONS

1. According to this article, the stigma that results from online criminal records is not only psychologically damaging but may also have significant social consequences. What are the social consequences the article describes?
2. What are some criteria the author lays out for determining whether available data are actually valuable for public safety?
3. Communities have always been self-policing, using whatever tools they have at their disposal. To what degree do you think this is an artifact of the Internet? Is this a new problem or a new twist on an old one?

robert j. brym

six lessons of suicide bombers

15

fall 2007

over the past quarter century, researchers have learned much about the motivations of suicide bombers, the rationales of the organizations that support them, their modus operandi, the precipitants of suicide attacks, and the effects of counterterrorism on insurgent behavior. much of what they have learned is at odds with conventional wisdom and the thinking of policy-makers who guide counterterrorist strategy. understanding the world from the assailant's point of view supports developing a workable strategy for minimizing suicide attacks.

In October 1983, Shi'a militants attacked the military barracks of American and French troops in Beirut, killing nearly 300 people. Today the number of suicide attacks worldwide has passed 1,000, with almost all the attacks concentrated in just nine countries: Lebanon, Sri Lanka, Israel, Turkey, India (Kashmir), Russia (Chechnya), Afghanistan, Iraq, and Pakistan. Israel, for example, experienced a wave of suicide attacks in the mid-1990s when Hamas and the Palestinian Islamic Jihad (PIJ) sought to undermine peace talks between Israel and the Palestinian Authority. A far deadlier wave of attacks began in Israel in October 2000 after all hope of a negotiated settlement collapsed. Altogether, between 1993 and 2005, 158 suicide attacks took place in Israel and the occupied Palestinian territories, killing more than 800 people and injuring more than 4,600.

Over the past quarter century, researchers have learned much about the motivations of suicide bombers, the rationales of the organizations that support them, their modus operandi, the precipitants of suicide attacks, and the effects of counterterrorism on insurgent behavior. Much of what they have learned is at odds with conventional wisdom and the thinking of policy-makers who guide counterterrorist strategy. This

paper draws on that research, but I focus mainly on the Israeli/Palestinian case to draw six lessons from the carnage wrought by suicide bombers. In brief, I argue that (1) suicide bombers are not crazy, (2) nor are they motivated principally by religious zeal. It is possible to discern (3) a strategic logic and (4) a social logic underlying their actions. Targeted states typically react by repressing organizations that mount suicide attacks, but (5) this repression often makes matters worse. (6) Only by first taking an imaginative leap and understanding the world from the assailant's point of view can we hope to develop a workable strategy for minimizing suicide attacks. Let us examine each of these lessons in turn.

lesson 1: suicide bombers are not crazy

Lance Corporal Eddie DiFranco was the only survivor of the 1983 suicide attack on the U.S. Marine barracks in Beirut who saw the face of the bomber. DiFranco was on watch when he noticed the attacker speeding his truck full of explosives toward the main building on the marine base. "He looked right at me [and] smiled," DiFranco later recalled.

Was the bomber insane? Some Western observers thought so. Several psychologists characterized the Beirut bombers as "unstable individuals with a death wish." Government and media sources made similar assertions in the immediate aftermath of the suicide attacks on the United States on September 11, 2001. Yet these claims were purely speculative. Subsequent interviews with prospective suicide bombers and reconstructions of the biographies of successful suicide attackers revealed few psychological abnormalities. In fact, after examining many hundreds of cases for evidence of depression, psychosis, past suicide attempts, and so on, Robert Pape discovered only a single person who could be classified as having a psychological problem (a Chechen woman who may have been mentally retarded).

On reflection, it is not difficult to understand why virtually all suicide bombers are psychologically stable. The organizers of suicide attacks do not want to jeopardize their missions by recruiting unreliable people. A research report prepared for the Danish government a few years ago noted, "Recruits who display signs of pathological behaviour are automatically weeded out for reasons of organizational security." It may be that some psychologically unstable people want to become suicide bombers, but insurgent organizations strongly prefer their cannons fixed.

lesson 2: it's mainly about politics, not religion

In May 1972, three Japanese men in business suits boarded a flight from Paris to Tel Aviv. They were members of the Japanese Red Army, an affiliate of the Popular Front for the Liberation of Palestine. Eager to help their Palestinian comrades liberate Israel from Jewish rule, they had packed their carry-on bags with machine guns and hand grenades. After disembarking at Lod Airport near Tel Aviv, they began an armed assault on everyone in sight. When the dust settled, 26 people lay dead, nearly half of them

Puerto Rican Catholics on a pilgrimage to the Holy Land.

Israeli guards killed one of the attackers. A second blew himself up, thus becoming the first suicide bomber in modern Middle Eastern history. The Israelis captured the third assailant, Kozo Okamoto.

Okamato languished in an Israeli prison until the mid-1980s, when he was handed over to Palestinian militants in Lebanon's Beka'a Valley in a prisoner exchange. Then, in 2000, something unexpected happened. Okamoto apparently abandoned or at least ignored his secular faith in the theories of Bakunin and Trotsky, and converted to Islam. For Okamoto, politics came first, then religion.

A similar evolution occurs in the lives of many people. Any political conflict makes people look for ways to explain the dispute and imagine a strategy for resolving it; they adopt or formulate an ideology. If the conflict is deep and the ideology proves inadequate, people modify the ideology or reject it for an alternative. Religious themes often tinge political ideologies, and the importance of the religious component may increase if analyses and strategies based on secular reasoning fail. When religious elements predominate, they may intensify the conflict.

For example, the Palestinians have turned to one ideology after another to explain their loss of land to Jewish settlers and military forces and to formulate a plan for regaining territorial control. Especially after 1952, when Gamal Abdel Nasser took office in Egypt, many Palestinians turned to Pan-Arabism, the belief that the Arab countries would unify and force Israel to cede territory. But wars failed to dislodge the Israelis. Particularly after the Six-Day War in 1967, many Palestinians turned to nationalism, which placed the responsibility for regaining control of lost territory on the Palestinians themselves. Others became Marxists, identifying wage-workers (and, in some cases, peasants) as the engines of national liberation. The Palestinians used plane hijackings to draw the world's attention to their cause, launched wave upon wave of guerilla attacks against Israel, and in the 1990s entered into negotiations to create a sovereign Palestinian homeland.

Yet Islamic fundamentalism had been growing in popularity among Palestinians since the late 1980s—ironically, without opposition from the Israeli authorities, who saw it as a conservative counterweight to Palestinian nationalism. When negotiations with Israel to establish a Palestinian state broke down in 2000, many Palestinians saw the secularist approach as bankrupt and turned to Islamic fundamentalism for political answers. In January 2006, the Islamic fundamentalist party, Hamas, was democratically elected to form the Palestinian government, winning 44 percent of the popular vote and 56 percent of the parliamentary seats. In this case, as in many others, secular politics came first. When secularism failed, notions of "martyrdom" and "holy war" gained in importance.

This does not mean that most modern suicide bombers are deeply religious, either among the Palestinians or other groups. Among the 83 percent of suicide attackers worldwide between 1980 and 2003 for whom Robert Pape found data on ideological background, only a minority—43 percent—were identifiably religious. In Lebanon, Israel, the West Bank, and Gaza between 1981 and 2003, fewer than half of suicide bombers had discernible religious inclinations. In its origins and at its core, the Israeli-Palestinian conflict is not religiously inspired, and suicide bombing, despite its frequent religious trappings, is fundamentally the expression of a territorial dispute. In this conflict, many members of the dominant group—Jewish Israelis—use religion as a central marker of identity. It is hardly surprising, therefore, that many Palestinian militants also view the struggle in starkly religious terms.

The same holds for contemporary Iraq. As Mohammed Hafez has recently shown, 443 suicide missions took place in Iraq between March 2003 and February 2006. Seventy-one percent of the identifiable attackers belonged to al-Qaeda in Iraq. To be sure, they justified their actions in religious terms. Members of al-Qaeda in Iraq view the Shi'a who control the Iraqi state as apostates. They want to establish fundamentalist, Sunni-controlled states in Iraq and other Middle Eastern countries. Suicide attacks against the Iraqi regime and its American and British supporters are seen as a means to that end.

But it is only within a particular political context that these ambitions first arose. After all, suicide attacks began with the American and British invasion of Iraq and the installation of a Shi'a-controlled regime. And it is only under certain political conditions that these ambitions are acted upon. Thus, Hafez's analysis shows that suicide bombings spike (1) in retaliation for big counterinsurgency operations and (2) as a strategic response to institutional developments which suggest that Shi'a-controlled Iraq is about to become more stable. So although communal identity has come to be religiously demarcated in Iraq, this does not mean that religion per se initiated suicide bombing or that it drives the outbreak of suicide bombing campaigns.

lesson 3: sometimes it's strategic

Suicide bombing often has a political logic. In many cases, it is used as a tactic of last resort undertaken by the weak to help them restore control over territory they perceive as theirs. This political logic is clear in statements routinely

> In Lebanon, Israel, the West Bank, and Gaza between 1981 and 2003, fewer than half of suicide bombers had discernible religious inclinations.

released by leaders of organizations that launch suicide attacks. Characteristically, the first communiqué issued by Hamas in 1987 stated that martyrdom is the appropriate response to occupation, and the 1988 Hamas charter says that jihad is the duty of every Muslim whose territory is invaded by an enemy.

The political logic of suicide bombing is also evident when suicide bombings occur in clusters as part of an organized campaign, often timed to maximize strategic gains. A classic example is the campaign launched by Hamas and the PIJ in the mid-1990s. Fearing that a settlement between Israel and the Palestinian Authority would prevent the Palestinians from gaining control over all of Israel, Hamas and the PIJ aimed to scuttle peace negotiations by unleashing a small army of suicide bombers.

Notwithstanding the strategic basis of many suicide attacks, we cannot conclude that strategic reasoning governs them all. More often than not, suicide bombing campaigns fail to achieve their territorial aims. Campaigns may occur without apparent strategic justification, as did the campaign that erupted in Israel after negotiations between Israel and the Palestinian Authority broke down in 2000. A social logic often overlays the political logic of suicide bombing.

lesson 4: sometimes it's retaliatory

On October 4, 2003, a 29-year-old lawyer entered Maxim restaurant in Haifa and detonated her belt of plastic explosives. In addition to taking her own life, Hanadi Jaradat killed 20 people and wounded dozens of others. When her relatives were later interviewed in the Arab press, they explained her motives as follows: "She carried out the attack in revenge for the killing of her brother and her cousin [to whom she had been engaged] by the Israeli security forces and in revenge for all the crimes Israel is perpetrating in the West Bank by killing Palestinians and expropriating their land." Strategic calculation did not inform Jaradat's attack. Research I conducted with Bader Araj shows that, like a majority of Palestinian suicide bombers between 2000 and 2005, Jaradat was motivated by the desire for revenge and retaliation.

Before people act, they sometimes weigh the costs and benefits of different courses of action and choose the one that appears to cost the least and offer the most benefits. But people are not calculating machines. Sometimes they just don't add up. Among other emotions, feelings of anger and humiliation can trump rational strategic calculation in human affairs. Economists have conducted experiments called "the ultimatum game," in which the experimenter places two people in a room, gives one of them $20, and tells the recipient that she must give some of the money—as much or as little as she wants—to the other person. If the other person refuses the offer, neither gets to keep any money. Significantly, in four out of five cases, the other person refuses to accept the money if she is offered less than $5. Although she will gain materially if she accepts any offer, she is highly likely to turn down a low offer so as to punish her partner for stinginess. This outcome suggests that emotions can easily override the rational desire for material gain. (Researchers at the University of Zürich have recently demonstrated the physiological basis of this override function by using MRI brain scans on people playing the ultimatum game.) At the political level, research I conducted with Bader Araj on the events precipitating suicide bombings, the motivations of suicide bombers, and the rationales of the organizations that support suicide bombings shows that Palestinian suicide missions are in most cases prompted less by strategic cost-benefit calculations than by such human emotions as revenge and retaliation. The existence of these deeply human emotions also helps to explain why attempts to suppress

insurgency, repression, and perceptions by party		
	HAMAS/PIJ	FATAH/other
Number of successful suicide attackers, 2000–2005	85	48
Number of attempted state assassinations, 2000–2005	124	82
Percentage of leaders never willing to recognize Israel	100%	10%
How has Israel's assassination policy affected the ability of your organization to conduct suicide bombing operations?	Increased 33% Not affected 42% Decreased 25%	Increased 9% Not affected 5% Decreased 86%
In comparison with other tactics used by your organization, how costly has suicide bombing been in terms of the human and material resources used, damage to your organization, etc.?	As or less costly 53% More costly 20% Don't know 27%	As or less costly 11% More costly 86% Don't know 4%

The first two rows of data in this table were calculated from a systematic analysis of newspapers the New York Times, ha-Areiz, al-Quds and ol-Arabij by Robert Brym and Bader Araj. The remainder of the data are based on a survey of 45 Palestinian insurgent leaders conducted by Bader Araj in the West Bank and Gaza during the spring and summer of 2006.

suicide bombing campaigns sometimes do not have the predicted results.

lesson 5: repression is a boomerang

Major General Doron Almog commanded the Israel Defense Forces Southern Command from 2000 to 2003. He tells the story of how, in early 2003, a wealthy Palestinian merchant in Gaza received a phone call from an Israeli agent. The caller said that the merchant's son was preparing a suicide mission, and that if he went through with it, the family home would be demolished, Israel would sever all commercial ties with the family, and its members would never be allowed to visit Israel again. The merchant prevailed upon his son to reconsider, and the attack was averted.

Exactly how many suicide bombers have been similarly deterred is unknown. We do know that of the nearly 600 suicide missions launched in Israel and its occupied territories between 2000 and 2005, fewer than 25 percent succeeded in reaching their targets. Israeli counterterrorist efforts thwarted three-quarters of them using violent means. In addition, Israel preempted an incalculable number of attacks by assassinating militants involved in planning them. More than 200 Israeli assassination attempts took place between 2000 and 2005, 80 percent of which succeeded in killing their main target, sometimes with considerable "collateral damage."

Common sense suggests that repression should dampen insurgency by increasing its cost. By this logic, when state organizations eliminate the people who plan suicide bombings, destroy their bomb-making facilities, intercept their agents, and punish the people who support them, they erode the insurgents' capabilities for mounting suicide attacks. But this commonsense approach to counterinsurgency overlooks two complicating factors. First, harsh repression may reinforce radical opposition and even intensify it. Second, insurgents may turn to alternative and perhaps more lethal methods to achieve their aims.

Consider the Palestinian case (see "insurgency, repression, and perceptions by party"). Bader Araj and I were able to identify the organizational affiliation of 133 Palestinian suicide bombers between September 2000 and July 2005. Eighty-five of them (64 percent) were affiliated with the Islamic fundamentalist groups Hamas and the PIJ, while the rest were affiliated with secular Palestinian groups such as Fatah. Not surprisingly, given this distribution, Israeli repression was harshest against the Islamic fundamentalists, who were the targets of 124 Israeli assassination attempts (more than 60 percent of the total).

Yet after nearly five years of harsh Israeli repression—involving not just the assassination of leaders but also numerous arrests, raids on bomb-making facilities, the demolition of houses belonging to family members of suicide bombers, and so on—Hamas and PIJ leaders remained adamant in their resolve and much more radical than Palestinian secularist leaders. When 45 insurgent leaders representing all major Palestinian factions were interviewed in depth in the summer of 2006, 100 percent of those associated with Hamas and PIJ (compared to just 10 percent of secularist leaders) said they would never be willing to recognize the legitimacy of the state of Israel. That is, the notion of Israel as a Jewish state was still entirely unacceptable to each and every one of them. When asked how Israel's

assassination policy had affected the ability of their organization to conduct suicide bombing operations, 42 percent of Hamas and PIJ respondents said that the policy had had no effect, while one-third said the policy had increased their organization's capabilities (the corresponding figures for secularist leaders were 5 percent and 9 percent, respectively).

And when asked how costly suicide bombing had been in terms of human and organizational resources, organizational damage, and so on, 53 percent of Hamas and PIJ leaders (compared to just 11 percent of secularist leaders) said that suicide bombing was less costly or at least no more costly than the alternatives. Responses to such questions probably tell us more about the persistent resolve of the Islamic fundamentalists than their actual capabilities. And that is just the point. Harsh Israeli repression over an extended period apparently reinforced the anti-Israel sentiments of Islamic fundamentalists.

Some counterterrorist experts say that motivations count for little if capabilities are destroyed. And they would be right if it were not for the substitutability of methods: increase the cost of one method of attack, and highly motivated insurgents typically substitute another. So, for example, Israel's late prime minister, Yitzhak Rabin, ordered troops to "break the bones" of Palestinians who engaged in mass demonstrations, rock throwing, and other nonlethal forms of protest in the late 1980s and early 1990s. The Palestinians responded with more-violent attacks, including suicide missions. Similarly, after Israel began to crack down ruthlessly on suicide bombing operations in 2002, rocket attacks against Israeli civilians sharply increased in frequency. In general, severe repression can work for a while, but a sufficiently determined mass opposition can

> Severe repression can work for a while, but a sufficiently determined mass opposition can always design new tactics to surmount new obstacles, especially if its existence as a group is visibly threatened.

always design new tactics to surmount new obstacles, especially if its existence as a group is visibly threatened (and unless, of course, the mass opposition is exterminated in its entirety). One kind of "success" usually breeds another kind of "failure" if the motivation of insurgents is high.

lesson 6: empathize with your enemy

In October 2003, Israeli Chief of Staff Moshe Ya'alon explicitly recognized this conundrum when he stated that Israel's tactics against the Palestinians had become too repressive and were stirring up potentially uncontrollable levels of hatred and terrorism. "In our tactical decisions, we are operating contrary to our strategic interests," he told reporters. Ya'alon went on to claim that the Israeli government was unwilling to make concessions that could bolster the authority of moderate Palestinian Prime Minister Mahmoud Abbas, and he expressed the fear that by continuing its policy of harsh repression, Israel would bring about the collapse of the Palestinian Authority, the silencing of Palestinian moderates, and the popularization of more radical voices like that of Hamas. The head of the General Security Service (Shabak), the defense minister, and Prime Minister Ariel Sharon opposed Ya'alon. Consequently, his term as chief of staff was not renewed, and his military career ended in 2005. A year later, all of Ya'alon's predictions proved accurate.

Ya'alon was no dove. From the time he became chief of staff in July 2002, he had been in charge of ruthlessly putting down the Palestinian uprising. He had authorized assassinations, house demolitions, and all the rest. But 15 months into the job, Ya'alon had learned much from his experience, and it seems that what he learned above all else was to empathize with the enemy—not to have warm and fuzzy feelings about the Palestinians, but to see things from their point of view in order to improve his ability to further Israel's chief strategic interest, namely, to live in peace with its neighbors.

As odd as it may sound at first, and as difficult as it may be to apply in practice, exercising empathy with one's enemy is the key to an effective counterterrorist strategy. Seeing the enemy's point of view increases one's understanding of the minimum conditions that would allow the enemy to put down arms. An empathic understanding of the enemy discourages counterproductive actions such as excessive repression, and it encourages tactical moves that further one's strategic aims. As Ya'alon suggested, in the Israeli case such tactical moves might include (1) offering meaningful rewards—for instance, releasing hundreds of millions of Palestinian tax dollars held in escrow by Israel, freeing selected Palestinians from Israeli prisons, and shutting down remote and costly Israeli settlements in the northern West Bank—in exchange for the renunciation of suicide bombing, and (2) attributing the deal to the intercession of moderate Palestinian forces so as to buttress their popularity and authority. (From this point of view, Israel framed its unilateral 2005 withdrawal from Gaza poorly because most Palestinians saw it as a concession foisted on Israel by Hamas.) Once higher levels of trust and stability are established by such counterterrorist tactics, they can serve as the foundation for negotiations leading to a permanent settlement. Radical elements would inevitably try to jeopardize negotiations, as they have in the past, but Israel resisted the temptation to shut down peace talks during the suicide bombing campaign of the mid-1990s, and it could do so again. Empathizing with the enemy would also help prevent the breakdown of negotiations, as happened in 2000; a clear sense of the minimally acceptable conditions for peace can come only from an empathic understanding of the enemy.

conclusion

Political conflict over territory is the main reason for suicide bombing, although religious justifications for suicide missions are likely to become more important when secular ideologies fail to bring about desired results. Suicide bombing may also occur for strategic or retaliatory reasons—to further insurgent aims or in response to repressive state actions.

Cases vary in the degree to which suicide bombers are motivated by (1) political or religious and (2) strategic or retaliatory aims. For example, research to date suggests that suicide bombing is more retaliatory in Israel than in Iraq, and more religiously motivated in Iraq than in Israel. But in any case, repression (short of a policy approaching genocide) cannot solve the territorial disputes that lie at the root of suicide bombing campaigns. As Zbigniew Brzezinski, President Jimmy Carter's national security advisor, wrote a few years ago in the *New York Times*, "To win the war on terrorism, one must . . . begin a political effort that focuses on the conditions that brought about [the terrorists'] emergence." These are wise words that Israel—and the United States in its own "war on terror"—would do well to heed.

RECOMMENDED RESOURCES

Hany Abu-Hassad. *Paradise Now.*

This movie sketches the circumstances that shape the lives of two Palestinian suicide bombers, showing that they are a lot like us and that if we found ourselves in similar circumstances, we might turn out to be a lot like them. (Nominated for the 2005 Oscar for best foreign-language film.)

Robert J. Brym and Bader Araj. 2006. "Suicide Bombing as Strategy and Interaction: The Case of the Second Intifada." *Social Forces* 84: 1965–82.

Explains suicide bombing as the outcome of structured interactions among conflicting and cooperating parties and organizations.

Mohammed M. Hafez. 2006. "Suicide Terrorism in Iraq: A Preliminary Assessment of the Quantitative Data and Documentary Evidence." *Studies in Conflict and Terrorism* 29: 591–619.

The first systematic analysis of suicide bombing in Iraq demonstrates the strategic and retaliatory aims of the assailants.

Errol Morris. *The Fog of War.*

Robert McNamaro's extraordinarily frank assessment of his career as secretary of defense in the Kennedy and Johnson administrations. This film is a profound introduction to strategic thinking and a valuable lesson on how to learn from one's mistakes. His first lesson: empathize with your enemy. (Winner of the 2003 Oscar for best documentary.)

Robert A. Pape. 2005. *Dying to Win: The Strategic Logic of Suicide Terrorism.* New York: Random House.

In support of the view that suicide bombing takes place mainly for rational, strategic reasons, Pape analyzes all suicide attacks worldwide from 1980 to 2003.

Christoph Reuter. 2004. *My Life Is a Weapon: A Modern History of Suicide Bombing.* Translated by H. Ragg-Kirkby. Princeton: Princeton University Press.

A succinct overview of the past 25 years of suicide attacks.

REVIEW QUESTIONS

1. How do the facts and findings reported in this article conflict with our usual cultural understanding of terrorists and suicide bombers?

2. Why don't terrorist organizations recruit "crazy" people for suicide attacks, according to this article?

3. Many countries refuse to negotiate with terrorists, stating that negotiation validates terrorism as a form of international relations. Based on this article, do you think policies like this reduce the "boomerang effect" or make matters worse? Explain your answer.

4. Activity: Pretend you are the head of an anti-terrorism advisory board for the United Nations. Using Brym's six lessons, devise a strategic action plan for combating and reducing instances of suicide bombing.

the essays here provide critical perspectives on human trafficking as a global social problem. topics covered include trafficking policy, causes and possible solutions to trafficking, and the backlash to the "savior ideology."

In the 2008 Luc Besson–directed thriller *Taken*, Liam Neeson is a former CIA operative whose daughter is kidnapped by an Albanian human trafficking ring in France. The Albanians sell his daughter, a virgin and thus quite valuable, to a French auctioneer, who then sells her through intermediaries to an Arab sheikh who is about to take her virginity when Neeson climbs aboard the yacht and shoots the sheikh in the head.

Taken is one of a growing number of movies and documentaries that examine and often sensationalize the story of human trafficking. Human trafficking, and its correlate human slavery, came into global consciousness with the U.S. Victims of Trafficking and Violence Protection Act of 2000, which established the U.S. Department of State's annual Trafficking in Persons Report, which ranks countries on their work to end human trafficking. Those that perform poorly—by the State Department's judgment— are subject to various sanctions. Around the same time, the United Nations established a trafficking protocol through the UN Transnational Organized Crime Convention in 2000, which presumed trafficking was a product of organized criminal activity, and that trafficking is a result of calculated and organized conduct. In other words, traffickers are evil and powerful, and

victims are unaware, innocent and weak, and need to be saved. Their saviors are sometimes police, sometimes NGOs like sociologist Kevin Bales's Free the Slaves, and sometimes journalists like Nicholas Kristof.

Recently, there has been a backlash to the savior ideology. Scholar-activist Laura Agustin coined the term "rescue industry" to describe and criticize people who want to rescue migrant sex workers from their plight, even though many sex workers neither want nor need to be rescued. This critical perspective has gained traction among a growing number of scholars.

Two of the articles here describe forms of human trafficking. Sutapa Basu writes that human trafficking, especially sex trafficking of women and girls, is a massive underground economy. She argues that poverty, structural inequalities between nations and men and women, and the cultural devaluation of women are at the root of sex trafficking. Anne Gallagher takes on the supposed urban myth of trafficking in human organs and provides evidence that it is actually increasing in frequency and global scope. She argues that as demand for organs has grown among the wealthy, organized syndicates have harvested the organs of poor people from poor countries through deception, extortion, and violence.

What happens to the former victims of trafficking? Denise Brennan suggests the plight of victims of labor exploitation in the United States remains precarious even after they escape. While they often get government assistance and some get visas that let them stay, they are commonly shunned by their ethnic communities and live in poverty. Elena Shih offers a critical examination of anti-trafficking NGOs that offer rescue, rehabilitation, and vocational training to former sex-trafficking victims. Shih questions who really profits in this endeavor.

The concluding essay provides a critical perspective on human trafficking as a global social problem. Ronald Weitzer claims that the evidence for the prevalence and scope of human trafficking, especially "sex slavery," is scant and has been overblown by anti-trafficking activists and governments. He suggests that sensationalizing sex trafficking detracts attention from other forms of labor trafficking and exploitation can be counter-productive in helping trafficking victims.

sutapa basu

sex, money, and brutality

The sale of human beings for profit, for both sexual and nonsexual labor, is the second-largest and fastest-growing underground industry in the world, valued by the International Labour Organization (ILO) at $32 billion yearly. The U.S. State Department estimates there are as many as 27 million trafficking victims at any given time. According to the ILO, of those trafficked into sex work, 98 percent are women and girls. In the last decade or so, government and nongovernmental organizations have poured resources into the eradication of human trafficking, particularly sex trafficking, yet the industry continues to thrive. This can be attributed to the intractable structural and social inequality between women and men, poor and rich nations, as well as the huge disparity between the poor and rich within nations.

Due in part to their cultural devaluation in many parts of the world, women and girls are especially vulnerable to a host of injustices and brutalities that are connected to human

trafficking. They are often mentally and physically abused and denied basic human rights of food, shelter, education, and health care. And unlike drugs, women and girls can be repeatedly sold. Often time victims are trafficked as preteens and used until they are deemed too old (approximately at 20–25 years old) or are dying of HIV/AIDS.

Globalization has created wealth and opportunities for some, but has widened already huge economic disparities and led to much social displacement for the poor majority. It has also exasperated the human trafficking problem. Women and girls are especially vulnerable to trafficking as a result of economic hardship that forces them to seek opportunities beyond home and family in the desperate search for income. Traffickers take advantage of this desperation by promising lucrative employment. Once these women are lured out of their homes and into the city, they are commonly tortured, abused, and sold to

> Women and girls are especially vulnerable to a host of injustices and brutalities that are connected to human trafficking.

brothel owners, and forced to engage in the sex trade.

In research trips to India I have collected the narratives of nearly 100 sex workers who averaged 20 clients per day. I've heard heart-wrenching stories about how abandonment by a husband or the need to feed their family led them to take up offers of travel to larger cities on tenuous promises of getting jobs as household workers. Each of these women ended up in the brothels of India's most notorious red-light districts including Kochi and Thiruvananthapuram in Kerala, Delhi, and Kolkata. Once there, they have no means of escape and are often too ashamed, and afraid of traffickers' threats of violent reprisal, to let their families know of their plight.

The young women I interviewed shared horrific stories of being forced into sex work and brutalized by their pimps and clients. One woman spoke about her pimp stuffing hot cayenne pepper into her vagina until she agreed to service any client of his choice—she was an 11-year-old girl at the time. Another woman shared how she became a sex worker when her parents gave her aunt custody of her when she was 13 years old, believing the aunt intended to find the daughter employment as a domestic servant. The hope was that their daughter would have the opportunity for some basic education, gainful employment, and the ability to secure enough money to pay off her family's debt to landowners and prevent them from dying of starvation. While her family was thankful for their daughter's newfound opportunity, this young woman's aunt forced her into sex work. Today, she is 26 years old and still works in the sex industry, where she also provides day care in the brothel during her spare time to protect children from witnessing the sex acts performed by their mothers.

The never-ending pipeline of issues that feed into poverty, especially for women, have resulted in hundreds of thousands of girls and women being sold in the sex-trafficking industry annually. I have seen the results of human trafficking with my own eyes and witnessed the inhuman condition and despair in which these girls and women work. It is imperative that we do everything in our power to eradicate sex trafficking and the selling of human beings in any form.

anne t. gallagher

trafficking for organ removal

In 2008 a young man with a large surgical scar collapsed at Pristina airport. His story led police to a group of migrants from Turkey, Moldova, and Russia, who had been lured to Kosovo to sell their kidneys and other organs to wealthy transplant recipients from Canada, Germany, Israel, and the United States. The victims, who included five children, were promised payments of up to $26,000—which never materialized—and were asked to sign false documents indicating they were engaging in altruistic donations to relatives. In April 2013, five Kosovars, including three medical practitioners, were convicted of involvement in the well-organized and highly profitable organ trafficking syndicate.

> Organ commercialization and transplant tourism constitute "trafficking in persons."

An acute shortage of organs for transplant is driving an international shadow market. Trafficking of persons for organ removal is not an urban myth, but an increasingly common means by which the global shortage in organs is being met. Recipients are generally independently wealthy or are supported by their governments or private insurance companies. Victims are inevitably poor and from poorer countries, often unemployed and with low education levels, which makes them vulnerable to deception about the nature of the transplant procedure and its potential impacts. Their passports are commonly withheld as a means of keeping control over their movement prior to the operation. If they try to back out of an agreement to sell an organ, they encounter violence or threats of violence, a practice that continues after the transplantation to ensure victims' silence. Victims are seldom provided adequate postoperative medical care and many suffer physical and psychological harm as well as social exclusion due to the stigma attached to being compelled to sell one's own organs.

Case studies from Bangladesh, Brazil, Egypt, Moldova, and other countries confirm that poor and desperate individuals are lured into selling their organs on the promise of considerable payment, which is rarely made in full. In 2010 South African courts convicted doctors and administrators for offenses relating to more than 100 illegal kidney transplants carried out in a single hospital. Most of the recipients came from Israel. The organs were sourced from persons brought to South Africa from Eastern Europe and Brazil on false or exaggerated promise of payment. Police investigations in Brazil and South Africa revealed the existence of an international organ trafficking syndicate, part of a long-standing and flourishing "transplant tourism" business that has been well known in South African medical circles for many years.

A recent study by the U.S.-based Coalition for Organ Failure Solutions documented the use of debt bondage and extortion as a means of coercing organ "donation." In this case, the victims are Sudanese asylum seekers making their way to Europe. Smugglers keep their victims in detention in Cairo and demand large sums of money for travel and other assistance. The victims are then offered the opportunity to sell a kidney to discharge their inflated debt.

Despite substantial gaps in our knowledge and understanding of trafficking in persons for organ removal, it is now well established that this form of exploitation occurs in all regions of the world and is not a rare event. My research has led me to conclude that the slick arguments of market-driven "realists"—for example, that a well-regulated market in organs is the only way to address global shortages and reduce exploitation—are ultimately unpersuasive. Put simply, the trade in organs is fundamentally unjust because the inherent imbalances of power are too great to prevent exploitation.

What can be done? Unfortunately, the international and national legal frameworks around the sale and purchase of organs are extremely weak. An exception can be found in the policies that have been developed to address trafficking in persons. It is not generally well known that international law recognizes "removal of organs" involving coercion, deception, or abuse of vulnerability as a form of trafficking-related exploitation. This means that that the brokered sale and purchase of organs, including through transplant tourism, effectively constitutes "trafficking in persons." As a form of trafficking in persons, the trade in organs *must* be criminalized by nations and subject to appropriate sanctions. International law

> The trade in organs is fundamentally unjust because the inherent imbalances of power are too great to prevent exploitation.

also requires that countries cooperate with each other in prosecuting such practices. Those who have been subject to exploitation for removal of organs are victims of trafficking and, as such, have specific and enforceable rights to assistance, protection, support, and remedy.

denise brennan

life beyond trafficking

Human trafficking is in the news nearly every day. These stories typically focus on the horrors endured and the drama of rescue or escape. Oddly, we hear little about life after trafficking. Splashy media coverage about trafficking, non-profit organizations' emotional fund-raising appeals, and celebrity public-service announcements tend to eclipse stories of formerly trafficked persons' actual day-to-day lives.

Trafficked people are men and women from all over the world whose plans to migrate for work went terribly wrong when they ended up severely exploited by their employers. Migrant exploitation is commonplace in low-wage workplaces. The individuals that the U.S. government designates as "trafficked" are just a small part of a much larger story of everyday exploitation of migrant laborers in the United States. The number of trafficking victims—the U.S. government has designated fewer than 4,000 people since 2000 as trafficked—pales against the millions of migrants who work in conditions that may not be considered abusive enough to fit the definition of trafficking. In short, trafficking into forced labor is on the extreme end of a continuum of commonplace abuse of undocumented migrants and workers with temporary visas.

For nearly 10 years I have been following how over 30 men and women who are survivors of human trafficking have resettled in small towns and large cities across the United States. Vulnerability characterizes their lives after trafficking. Despite the media fascination and fund-raising frenzy over trafficking, formerly trafficked persons are left largely on their own after modest government assistance and the granting of "T" visas (which allow trafficking victims to remain in the United States for up to four years and to apply for permanent residency). They must rebuild their lives from scratch—most do not even have a change of clothes. Typically they do not know a single person in the United States. Often they stay away from communities of co-ethnics if their abusers are still at large.

Beyond a fear of violence, feelings of stigma and shame also can steer these exploited migrant workers away from co-ethnic communities. A Mexican woman, who had been trafficked into Mexican-run brothels in New York City, was spotted by a former client while she was working in a restaurant frequented by Mexican clients. She quit after he told her coworkers about her past. Another woman was humiliated and shaken when the adult son of her abuser threatened her while she was working at a bar. Part of a tight-knit community of African migrants in the suburbs of Washington, D.C., she knew her fellow countrymen blamed her for "bringing shame" on their community by reporting her abuse (in domestic

> Formerly trafficked persons are left largely on their own with modest government assistance and "T" visas.

work) to the police. By relinquishing ties to these ready-made communities, formerly trafficked persons forgo the support, advice, and assistance they so desperately need.

Chronic financial insecurity characterizes formerly trafficked persons' lives, not only in the short term but also years into resettlement. They enter the U.S. economy in the ranks of the working poor, often working in the same low-wage and unprotected labor sectors as when they were in forced labor. They weather firings, divorce, and health emergencies. A single emergency can tip them further into debt and greater poverty. A $500 speeding ticket derailed a young woman's plans to take a full course load at a community college. Following a divorce, a woman with small children in Los Angeles could not afford to pay her car payments on time. She had no choice but to let the bills stack up: "It was either pay the rent or the car." Another woman, who could not

> Social, cultural, and economic vulnerabilities characterize formerly trafficked persons' lives.

travel overseas to visit her ill father while her green card was pending, summed up the shortcomings of the trafficking care regime: "The T visa does not really give you much."

Formerly trafficked persons resettle throughout the United States and recount similar stories from poverty's edge. They insist, however, that if they could endure their abuser, they can handle a few bills. "I have opportunities here others in my hometown will never have," Esperanza from Mexico explains. "And I have my son with me now. Just the other day was his birthday, and he was crying. He told me he hated his birthday since it reminded him of all the birthdays we were apart." Although their time in forced labor changed them, so too do their experiences afterward. Life after trafficking is a series of private daily struggles and successes, far from the media spotlight. As formerly trafficked persons like Esperanza quietly reclaim their lives, they make the United States their home.

elena shih

the anti-trafficking rehabilitation complex

Yan was a sex worker in Beijing for over five years. Sex work offered greater autonomy and better income relative to the typical low-wage service-sector jobs available to rural-to-urban migrants like her. After disagreeing with her manager over owed wages, Yan was recruited to work at a Christian vocational training and rehabilitation program for sex-trafficking victims in China. Yan and most of her coworkers don't consider themselves victims of trafficking, but the nongovernmental organization (NGO) that employs them does because they consider all sex work to be inherently exploitative,

and thus indistinguishable from human trafficking.

Anti-trafficking NGOs have created a cottage industry of "victim repair" through vocational training. In recent years, there has been a shift in how NGOs provide rehabilitation to victims of human trafficking. Many NGOs—both faith-based and secular—working in Thailand, Cambodia, Nepal, India, Mexico, Moldova, Uganda, and the United States now focus on selling wares made by trafficking victims to raise funds and awareness about human trafficking. Jewelry, tote bags, blankets, and placemats are among the many products sold by anti-trafficking NGOs at anti-trafficking fairs and conferences and by online vendors in the United States. The annual "Freedom and Fashion" show in Los Angeles attracts several thousand consumers yearly to view and purchase goods made by formerly trafficked persons.

Yan's NGO trains former sex workers to make jewelry, and sells this jewelry as fair trade and slave-free labor in the United States as part of the anti-trafficking movement. Employees earn 1,800 RMB (US$295) per month, similar to other low-wage jobs in Beijing, but a fraction of what they previously earned as sex workers. Yan discovered that the jewelry pieces she designed and produced for the NGO sell for up to US$70 apiece at anti-trafficking fairs in the United States. The "victim of trafficking" label adds tremendous market value to such products sold as slave-free goods, though it does nothing for her wages.

In addition to vocational training, NGOs rely heavily on moral rehabilitation to "repair the victim." At Yan's NGO, workers must sign a contract agreeing to no longer sell sex or patronize any entertainment establishments they once worked in. They are also required to live in mandatory shelter housing where they have a nightly curfew. There is also "optional" daily Bible study, but if they choose not to attend, they must work. So everyone goes to the Bible study and do not consider this to be much of a choice.

While some former sex workers consider the work these NGOs offer desirable and the social conditions at least bearable, many others leave the programs because of the social isolation and moral restrictions. After working as a jewelry maker for three years, Yan decided to leave the NGO because she saw limited opportunities for upward mobility relative to the daily social restrictions. When she returned to her hometown

in Fujian Province, she found herself once again facing limited opportunities in low-wage service-sector employment. She attempted to sell jewelry in local marketplaces, but quickly learned that she could not earn a living wage doing so. After three years of training, she still didn't have a financially viable vocation.

The niche market around the products of the labor of former human trafficking victims—"buying for freedom" as it is frequently marketed—is based on deceptively simple narratives of human trafficking that are created by the organizations that sell these products. In China, the branding of the slave-free product relies on the stereotype of an innocent young woman forced into sex work because of Chinese cultural pressures for women to support their families, and the cultural subordination of women to support their families, and the cultural subordination of women as seen with the government's one child policy. These narratives garner sympathy and support for the NGOs, but rarely do these stories reflect the complex decision-making processes of women who willingly, or unwillingly, enter sex work.

> Anti-trafficking NGOs have created a cottage industry of "victim repair" through vocational training.

The focus of anti-trafficking NGOs on moral reeducation, labor training, and selling their products does not favorably alter the long-term economic prospects of former sex workers. It does generate income for NGOs and privilege the perspective of First World rescuers. Rather than rescue, sex workers have long asked for enforcement of policies around employer accountability, measures for health and safety, and protection from police abuse. The focus on rehabilitation through labor, particularly when framed within the interests of human trafficking, has silenced these concerns and has resulted in increased surveillance, stigmatization, and unwarranted—and sometimes unwanted—focus on "rescue" from sex work.

ronald weitzer

macro claims versus micro evidence

Human trafficking is a hot topic. Over the past decade it has attracted substantial media coverage, generated growing anti-trafficking activism, and resulted in expensive government countermeasures. While no one doubts the existence and seriousness of the problem, much of the prevailing discourse and policy-making rests on four dubious macro-level claims. These claims sensationalize the problem and are counterproductive because they distract attention from what is actually happening in the lives of individuals.

First, human trafficking is depicted as a disproportionately huge problem. According to the U.S. government, the United Nations, the International Labor Organization, and many other state and international agencies and NGOs, *millions* of people are victimized every year. In 2005, the ILO asserted that 2.45 million people were engaged in forced labor as a result of trafficking, a figure that inexplicably jumped to 9.1 million in 2012. In 2010, the U.S. State Department's trafficking office somehow concluded that 0.18 percent of the world's population were trafficking victims. But the most outlandish claim is that 27 million people are enslaved today, many as a result of being trafficked into slavery. No sources, let alone convincing evidence, have been provided to document these figures.

The State Department's trafficking office recently declared that only 0.4 percent of the "estimated victims" worldwide had been officially "identified." Again, no source was given for the number of either estimated or identified

victims, nor was "identified" defined. Still, the number of confirmed victims (located and assisted by authorities) has been fairly small: a few thousand worldwide over the past decade. No one would expect the number of confirmed cases to be similar to the estimated number of victims (given the barriers to locating people in hidden operations), but the gulf between the two figures is enormous—raising serious questions about the alleged magnitude of the problem as well as the necessity of spending such a huge amount of money (in the billions) to combat trafficking.

> Because of its hidden nature and the lack of a reliable baseline from which to measure changes over time, global trends in human trafficking simply cannot be estimated.

Second, many commentators claim that human trafficking is a growing "epidemic." Human trafficking *may* have grown over time in certain regions, but this does not mean that the problem is steadily increasing worldwide, as it appears to have declined in other settings. Because of its hidden nature and the lack of a reliable baseline from which to measure changes over time, global trends in trafficking simply cannot be estimated.

Third, the UN and the U.S. government frequently assert that, in size and profitability, human trafficking is the second- or third-largest organized-crime enterprise in the world, with illegal drug trafficking being the biggest. No evidence has been offered to support this claim. Moreover, the estimated annual profits from trafficking ranges from a low of $5 billion to a high of $36 billion—an extremely broad range that should raise skepticism.

Fourth, most media reporting and policy-making center on the sensationalized issue of sex trafficking, rather than labor trafficking. The worst cases of abuse and exploitation and "sex slavery" are highlighted and depicted as representative, while the likely more typical cases of migrant labor exploitation are usually ignored. The most disturbing instances of trafficking clearly deserve priority by the authorities, but there is no evidence that sex slavery is typical of trafficking experiences. Moreover, the near-exclusive focus on sex trafficking may be criticized if—as the ILO and Obama Administration believe—trafficking in other labor sectors is far more pervasive.

It is not possible to satisfactorily count (or even estimate) the number of persons involved in, or the profitability of, an illicit, hidden economy at the macro level, nationally or internationally. So what is the alternative? Carefully conducted case studies—in a town, city, or small region of a country—are superior because they can yield more reliable numbers (in a measurable, limited setting) and also richer insights regarding participants' lived experiences. Recent case studies indicate that the experiences of individuals—both during the migration stage and subsequently at the work destination— range along a broad continuum. At one pole are individuals who have been forced into work or have been deceived about the kind of work and living conditions at the destination. At the other pole are those operating with full knowledge and agency. Most seem to fall in between the two extremes—for example, an individual who seeks work abroad because opportunities are unavailable at home and consents to some demands or conditions but not others. More in-depth localized research is also needed because it can pay policy dividends: the findings can be used for targeting specific trafficking "hot spots" and for better directing resources to assist victims in such locations.

> Case studies indicate that the experiences of individuals—both during the migration stage and subsequently at the work destination— range along a broad continuum.

REVIEW QUESTIONS

1. What are the root causes of sex trafficking, according to Basu?
2. Why does Gallagher argue against any trade in human organs, even a well-regulated one?
3. What are the long-term consequences of being a person who was previously the victim of sex trafficking?
3. What are Shih's criticisms of anti-trafficking organizations such as NGOs? Do you agree with these criticisms?
4. The essays address several debates about human trafficking: its causes, possible solutions, and its consequences. Choose one debate and outline two perspectives on the issue.

part **4**

Race and Ethnicity

viewpoints

black and blue

summer 2015

police violence is a grotesquely routine feature of american life, as one city after another is roiled by protests following the killing of yet another unarmed black citizen.

shehzad nadeem

Chicago, once pejoratively described as America's Second City, became the first city to offer monetary reparations to victims of police torture. The brutality, which took place between 1972 and 1991, was macabre: beatings, electric shocks, suffocation, mock executions, and other abuses. Under the direction of Jon Burge, a former detective, police officers exacted false confessions that resulted in long prison sentences, even placing some on death row. The hundred-plus victims were mainly African American, and the violence was baldly racial. A cranked device used to electrocute victims was painted black and called the "n——box." Nooses dangled from the South Side building's basement ceiling. The City Council's use of the word "reparations" thus held a particular meaning.

In announcing the agreement, Mayor Rahm Emmanuel spoke of righting wrongs and of bringing "a dark chapter of Chicago's history to a close." But it was a belated and reluctant reckoning, a poorly kept secret that the city had spent close to $100 million investigating and settling. "We are gratified, that after so many years of denial and cover-up by the prior administration, the city has acknowledged the harm inflicted by the torture and recognized the needs of the Burge torture survivors and their families by negotiating this historic reparations agreement," Joey Mogul, an attorney representing many of Burge's victims, told *USA Today.* "This legislation is the first of its kind in this country, and its passage and implementation will go a long way to remove the long-standing stain of police torture from the conscience of the city."

The reparations ordinance provides a fund of $5.5 million for torture victims as well as psychological counseling and job assistance. A memorial will be constructed, and the sordid episode will be included in the high school history curriculum.

Chicago is hardly alone in its struggles. Police violence is a grotesquely routine feature of American life, as one city after another is roiled by protests following the killing of yet another unarmed Black citizen. There is pressure on Cleveland and Ferguson to put their policing houses in order following the killings of 12-year-old Tamir Rice and 18-year-old Michael Brown. In New York City, the chokehold death of Eric Garner and the shooting of Akai Gurley revive memories of Amadou Diallo and Sean Bell, among others.

After killing Walter Scott, who fled a traffic stop in North Charleston, South Carolina, patrolman Michael Slager laughed about the adrenaline rush he felt.

Deaths are only the beginning. Each botched investigation, each farcical grand jury, each indictment not handed down is more than salt poured onto an already festering wound. It is to open a fresher, deeper gash. By comparison, Baltimore's decision to indict four officers over the death of 25-year-old Freddie Gray, who sustained fatal spinal injuries while in police custody, seems positively revolutionary.

The pieces that follow explore the tangled web of race, policing, and justice in America, with a view toward healing. Elliott Currie examines the societal devaluation of Black lives. This is revealed not only in the racial focus of police violence—Black men make up about 6.5 percent of the U.S. population but 29 percent of the police deaths so far this year—but also in the collective refusal to address long-standing patterns of discrimination and institutional racism. Katherine Beckett reports on commonsense reforms by the Seattle Police Department, itself under a Justice Department consent decree for the use of excessive force. Sudhir Venkatesh suggests we discard simple oppositions like "us and them" in understanding police–community interaction, foregrounding the role of community "brokers" who mediate relations between citizens and institutions of power. And lastly, Laurence Ralph considers Chicago's blue light system and its connection to other forms of police surveillance, violence, and control. He suggests the police's panoptic gaze be turned on itself as an initial step in repairing the broken contract between police and those they are sworn to protect and serve.

sudhir venkatesh

cops and brokers

I recently finished a two-year stint as a senior research advisor in the Department of Justice. I've also studied crime and policing for over a decade in Chicago, Los Angeles, and New York. An aspect of contemporary discourse on policing that always perplexes me is the strong dichotomy drawn between "cops" and the "community." The former typically refers to the institution of law enforcement, possessor of a monopoly on the use of force, on the other side are the civilians, whose role in enforcement is alert bystander. The dichotomy acquires particular poignancy when considering the harsh, sometimes abusive, often neglectful, treatment of Black Americans by police officers.

> A diverse group of people invested in maintaining the peace and addressing conflict, brokers are absolutely essential in keeping their communities intact.

Curiously, when we look at the sociology of policing and criminal justice, this polarity has very little empirical support. The institutional *field* of social order maintenance demonstrates a much more nuanced set of relations, among a diverse group of actors who are invested in maintaining the peace and addressing conflicts. A clergy member is as likely to respond to disputes as a cop; a school official or block club president may mete out justice rather than a judge; and a social worker or local conflict mediator, instead of a detective or police official, may investigate cause and circumstance. These brokers are absolutely essential in keeping their communities intact. And yet they are glaringly absent in discussions about community–police relations.

Why is it that we prefer the simplicity of such juxtapositions when the world out there is less neat? Consider Elijah Anderson's book *Code of the Street* and the more recent *On the Run*, by Alice Goffman. The power of these two excellent ethnographies lies in taking a messy world and disciplining it simply. Anderson follows the lead of inner-city residents who divide their social world into two—usually as a means of placating journalists and social scientists. "Street" and "decent" come to typify people, their values, and their actions. (You can probably guess which side of the divide the cops fall on.) The notion of a law-abiding population (and their cops) taking on a criminal element becomes the foundation for Anderson's eponymous analytic heuristic. Similarly, Goffman writes that there are two types of people in the ghetto: "clean" and "dirty." Her framework mimics Anderson's: "The designations of clean and dirty . . . attach to individuals or locations over time. . . . [They] become significant even when a police stop isn't imminent because they are linked to distinct kinds of behavior, attitudes and capabilities."

The beauty of these dichotomies comes with costs. It becomes difficult to reconcile this narrative with the evidence that suggests police are only one of several important agents of order maintenance. As Peter Moskos shows in his illuminating ethnography of policing in Baltimore, *Cop in the Hood*, an officer has much less agency than we might imagine. She is subject to the dynamics of local social structure, in which a wider range of actors holds power in matters of crime and justice. Of particular importance is the role of the broker in mediating the relationships of cops and residents. These persons typically do not have adversarial relationships with police. Instead, they help de-escalate conflict, often so that police can investigate effectively. They may work closely with police to broker truces and settle conflicts— thereby giving cops enough time to build up some legitimacy for their own presence. And, they may be the frontlines of communication so that future crime and delinquency can be effectively deterred.

The net effect is twofold. Police are assured that the interests of some members of the community are aligned with their highest priority: to control and contain the effects of criminal actions. Police also feel that some of their power is diminished by this shared authority. At times, the dynamic leads to heightened frustration for cops unable to influence behavior in ways that they desire.

Of course, this may not be a bad thing. As I've argued elsewhere, the uncompromising sanctimony of police often undermines the efforts of residents in low-income neighborhoods to keep their lives moving as best they can. Residents work off the books to make ends meet, and no amount of police preaching will stop either the need or the practice.

For better and worse, matters of policing are never black and white. A valuable contribution may be to bring the sociology of order maintenance into these shades of gray.

laurence ralph

the secret of the blue light

About every half mile, lampposts mounted with police cameras, encased in plastic domes, loom above the street. Atop the police cameras, a fluorescent blue light flashes—a siren that can be seen but not heard. In urban Chicago, it is said that the persistence of that silent blue light, its relentlessness, can transform a person.

Chicago's blue light system exemplifies a faith in policing that exposes just how misleading the notion of "objectivity" can be. Blue lights are technologies whose instrumental function is to collect evidence and deter crime. The irony is that there can never be irrefutable evidence to show that blue lights accurately gather evidence or are an effective crime deterrent. Many criminologists have lamented the reasons why this is true: (1) The blue light system has been implemented with no "control" neighborhoods. Thus, in high crime communities, there are few areas left without cameras to compare against areas that have them; (2) Many blue lights have malfunctioned, yet there is no system for identifying which cameras are working properly; and (3) there are not enough police staff to monitor the blue lights that actually _do_ work.

More than locating crime, then, blue lights serve another social function: to reaffirm, and preserve, the power of the law for the law's own sake. As the everyday embodiment of State authority, blue lights are indicative of the primary objective of policing—to minimize crime and capture dangerous subjects. Yet, in urban Chicago, residents often argue that blue lights are a pretext for a wider desire for social control

at the expense of particular populations. For them, the public secret that the blue light embodies is the larger history of police violence that still plagues them today.

In February 2015, for example, _The Guardian_ broke the story of a "domestic black site" in Chicago. In an abandoned warehouse on the South Side of the city, police officers kept criminal suspects out of the official booking database, beat them severely, and denied their access to lawyers for between 12 and 24 hours. At least one man was pronounced dead after he was found unresponsive inside an interrogation room. In the few months since the black site gained national attention, a number of attorneys have stepped forward, claiming that for years, the facility has been a public secret.

"Back when I first started working on torture cases and started representing criminal defendants in the early 1970s," said Flint Taylor, the attorney who has won millions of dollars on behalf of police torture victims in Chicago, "my clients often told me they'd been taken from one police station to another before [being] tortured. . . . That way, the police prevent their family and lawyers from seeing them until they could coerce, through torture or other means, confessions from them."

The longer history of police torture in Chicago connects blue lights, which reside on a seemingly harmless side of the continuum of force, to the opposite end, where torture resides. Both technologies betray a societal faith in policing that excuses and extends force beyond its legal domain.

> Blue lights serve a social function to reaffirm, and preserve, the power of the law for the law's own sake.

The implications for scholars interested in race and policing should be clear. We should abandon any uncritical faith in policing. It is due time that the glare of the blue light be redirected at law enforcement. Strapping police officers with body cameras is a start. But it will not solve the problem of police violence, since cultural ideas about who is a "criminal" always shape encounters and infiltrate the analysis of evidence.

What I am suggesting is that by linking itself to a broader history of protest against police violence, the cell phone camera that a protester points at a police brigade in the midst of occupying a burning city might be seen as one attempt to peel back the secrets that seldom gain public recognition. Such revelatory acts, one by one, aggregated, might just expose the cruelty a society allows itself.

elliott currie

shouldn't black lives matter all the time?

The country, indeed much of the world, has been transfixed by the recent spate of police killings of Black men in the United States. The names of those men—including Michael Brown, Walter Scott, and Freddie Gray—and the places where they died—Ferguson, North Charleston, and Baltimore, respectively—will surely resonate in our minds for a very long time. That's as it should be, but I've found myself increasingly troubled by the way we talk about these events. More precisely, by what we leave out when we talk about them.

The outrage over these killings is certainly justified, as is the sense that they reveal something both morally disturbing and deeply illuminating about the nature of race relations and of policing in the United States. But what troubles me is that we seem far less outraged by the much larger number of Black men who die quite predictably in America's cities year in and year out, mostly at the hands of people very much like them. Their deaths may or may not reach the media. But they are reflections of the larger social catastrophe of which police killings are only one part. And their lives and deaths should matter, too.

We can catch a glimpse of that catastrophe in the cold figures on race and homicide deaths supplied by the Centers for Disease Control and Prevention. Overall, in 2013, the Black homicide death rate in the United States was almost exactly seven times the rate for non-Hispanic Whites. If Black Americans had enjoyed the same homicide death rate as Whites, more than 6,900 of the roughly 8,000 Black homicide victims that year would have lived. Put the other way around, if non-Hispanic Whites suffered the same risk of homicide death as Blacks, there would have been about 35,000 White homicide victims instead of the roughly 5,000 who actually died in 2013.

For the group of Americans most at risk—young Black men—these differences are, of course, much starker. Between the ages of 15 and

> The American Black men who die quite predictably, year in and year out, at the hands of people much like them are reflections of the larger social catastrophe of which police killings are only one part. Their lives and deaths should matter, too.

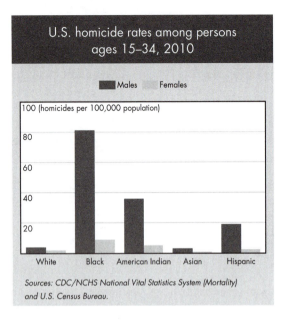

U.S. homicide rates among persons ages 15–34, 2010

Males Females

100 (homicides per 100,000 population)

80

60

40

20

White Black American Indian Asian Hispanic

Sources: CDC/NCHS National Vital Statistics System (Mortality) and U.S. Census Bureau.

29, Black men have 16 times the homicide death rate of their White counterparts. I think I can guarantee you that if 13,000 young White men had lost their lives to violence in 2013 (instead of 836), the outcry would have been deafening, and the demand for real solutions vocal and earnest.

It doesn't diminish the tragedy of Michael Brown's death in Ferguson to point out that over 100 young Black men died of homicide in the state of Missouri in 2013. But it does suggest that our concern about—even knowledge of—the loss of young African-American lives is troublingly selective. I doubt that, at least outside of Missouri, most of us could give a name to any of those young victims. But they are no less victims, and their deaths are no less a reflection of the devastating impact of the structural conditions that shape Black lives.

Why do the deaths of Black men at the hands of police stir a usually sleepy American conscience, while the far more common community violence mostly flies beneath the radar? Partly, I'm sure, because there is a special sting to killing when it's done by agents of the state: it symbolizes, in a particularly inescapable way, the reality of official complicity in maintaining the whole system of racial injustice. Killings by police are an especially harsh reminder of where things really stand in an ostensibly post-racial America. But I think there's more to it than that.

I suspect that it outrages Americans less when Black youth kill other Black youth because it is hard for us to grasp the idea that this kind of killing, too, has social roots—that it is part and parcel of the same system that gives us the callous brutality of police in Baltimore and North Charleston. When the hand that holds the gun is a White police officer's, the connection between the shooting and generations of structural racism is immediate and direct. When the hand belongs to a 19-year-old Black kid, the connection is complex and indirect. But our widespread failure to make that more demanding connection represents a failure of the moral as well as the sociological imagination. In a deeply individualistic culture, we "see" the social in killings by police in a way that eludes us when youth kill each other.

Let me be absolutely clear: I'm not suggesting that we should care less about the killings by police than we do, but that we should care about endemic youth violence more. And I'm also suggesting that we are unlikely to make much progress against either kind of killing until we clearly acknowledge that both result from the same stubbornly entrenched social forces that have made all too many Black lives seem expendable.

katherine beckett

toward harm-reduction policing

Across the country, urban governments face significant pressure to reduce outdoor drug market activity and visible homelessness. At the same time, critics increasingly urge police departments to avoid the heavy-handed and often racially charged tactics associated with "broken windows" policing, stop-and-frisk, and the failed drug war. Identifying a productive way forward in the context of these contradictory pressures is no easy task. But in Seattle, a new program shows how police discretion and resources can be mobilized to serve humanitarian ends and reduce reliance on our bloated criminal justice system.

Like most urban police agencies, the Seattle Police Department (SPD) relied heavily on racially disparate drug war tactics in recent decades. It also created and employed controversial new legal tools in an effort to restrict the spatial mobility of those deemed "disorderly." Yet these aggressive enforcement tactics did not eradicate the social ills associated with homelessness or open-air drug and sex markets.

> A recent evaluation indicates that Seattle's harm-reduction policing program represents a far more productive response to the human suffering that accompanies poverty and addiction than conventional drug war tactics.

The persistence of urban "disorder" triggered significant community pressure to do something to make the rapidly gentrifying and tourist-rich downtown area feel more hospitable to workers, residents, and visitors. At the same time, the racially disparate impact of the SPD's drug enforcement practices was the subject of lengthy, complex, and time-consuming litigation that exhausted all of those involved. By the late 2000s, no one was satisfied with the status quo, including the SPD itself. As Sergeant Sean Whitcomb, spokesman for the department, put it, "officers are frustrated arresting the same people over and over again. We know it's not working." Others agreed, including Racial Disparity Project staff who led the litigation.

Eventually, key leaders from affected institutions came together to identify a better way to address the problems associated with homelessness and outdoor drug market activity. The result—the Law Enforcement Assisted Diversion (LEAD) program—was launched in 2011. LEAD involves an unusually broad coalition of organizations including the Racial Disparity Project, the ACLU of Washington, the Department of Corrections, the SPD, the King County Sheriff, neighborhood organizations, and city and state prosecutors.

Under LEAD, eligible low-level drug and prostitution offenders are no longer subject to prosecution and incarceration, but are instead diverted to community-based treatment and support services. By diverting low-level drug and sex offenders into intensive, community-based social services that are guided by harm reduction principles, LEAD seeks to reduce the neighborhood and individual-level harm associated with Seattle's drug and sex markets. The incorporation of harm reduction principles means that client participation is entirely voluntary, and has been key to ensuring that LEAD does not represent yet another "diversion" program with net-widening effects. A recent evaluation indicates that LEAD significantly reduces recidivism—by up to 60 percent—and thus represents a far more productive response to the human suffering that accompanies poverty and addiction than conventional drug war tactics.

The success of LEAD in Seattle does not mean that implementing LEAD-like programs and ditching the drug war is a simple matter. For example, securing the support and involvement of line officers in LEAD has proven challenging. LEAD case managers continue to wrestle with structural problems such as the lack of appropriate treatment options and affordable housing for people with addiction histories and criminal records. And at the time of this writing, the SPD had recently worked with federal authorities to conduct a massive sweep of the downtown area, arresting over a hundred low-level dealers, many of whom are homeless and addicted.

Still, the slow but steady expansion of LEAD across the city, the increase in officer involvement in LEAD, and the steady uptick in clients served by LEAD—and diverted from the courts and jails—are encouraging. The unprecedented expansion of the criminal justice system in the United States has left critics of mass incarceration wondering how we can reduce our nation's reliance on police, jails, and prisons while more effectively addressing complex social problems such as poverty, mental illness, and addiction. LEAD suggests one plausible (if somewhat ironic) answer: use expanded police resources to divert people away from the criminal justice system, and use private and public monies to provide housing and desperately needed services, even when clients are unable to achieve abstinence. The future of our most vulnerable urban residents may depend on it.

REVIEW QUESTIONS

1. What are other agents of order maintenance aside from the police force? How are they involved in controlling crime or otherwise maintaining order?
2. What is Chicago's blue light system? What are the problems or benefits associated with this system? Do you support the system? Why or why not?
3. How do you think Trump's presidency will affect police violence?

steven w. thrasher

covering the three missouri michaels

18

winter 2015

a journalist and sociologist reflects on the three men who brought him to missouri and how their stories converged.

What did we learn about America as the media covered three young Black men in Missouri—an NFL recruit, an HIV-positive alleged sex offender, and a teenager killed by a cop?

In this country, Black bodies have long been commodified and controlled, and as I headed to Missouri for the second time in 2014, I realized not much had changed here. I was on assignment, first for BuzzFeed, then for the *Guardian*, to study three Missouri Michaels: Michael Johnson, Michael Sam, and Michael Brown. The first, better known as "Tiger Mandingo," was incarcerated; the second, Michael Sam, had the nation captivated as he entered the NFL draft as an openly gay man; the third, Michael Brown, was dead. He'd been shot, infamously, by the Ferguson police.

I was in a detention center in St. Charles, Missouri, last spring to interview detainee Michael Johnson, an HIV-positive 22-year-old former college student wrestler who had been arrested the previous October on charges that he had knowingly exposed five people to the virus. By the time he faces trial in 2015, he will have been waiting in jail for 18 months. Like everywhere in America, this jail was disproportionately full of African Americans, even though they are a small fraction of St. Charles' general population, a White flight suburb of St. Louis that is more lopsidedly White than its more famous suburban cousin, Ferguson, is Black.

The very next day in St. Louis I reported on Michael Sam, the 24-year-old gay college football player who had come out recently while playing for the University of Missouri, being recruited to the Rams. The differences between America's interest in these two Black, gay college athletes was immediate and obvious: there was lots of money to be made off of Michael Sam, and none to be made off Michael Johnson. Hence, celebration and tremendous interest in the former for being successful, handsome and on his way to being rich, and disgust lobbed at the latter for being "sick" with HIV, illiterate and just another "mandingo" behind bars.

But the Michael dialectic changed when I returned to Missouri for the *Guardian* just three months later to cover my third Michael, during the aftermath of the shooting of Michael Brown, the unarmed 18-year-old shot by Ferguson police officer Darren Wilson. Their stories overlapped in various ways. Michaels Sam and Johnson were both gay and athletes; Michaels Johnson and Brown both struggled to get into lowly regarded colleges; and while Michael Johnson the alleged sex predator was

> In this country, Black bodies have long been commodified and controlled.

largely forgotten once he was locked up, Michaels Sam and Brown have become symbols for the causes of gay visibility and police violence, respectively, which far supersede their individual stories.

A common trait all three Michaels shared: for a reporter, each was incredibly difficult to talk to. Even though Michael Johnson wanted to talk to me, I had to fly 1,000 miles, show up at his jail, and demand a meeting in person with his controllers, with no guarantee it would happen. (We were granted an hour to speak to each other, the last day of my trip.) Meanwhile, Michael Sam came out as gay through an incredibly scripted public relations campaign. The Rams would not let me talk to him, or even to a teammate who wanted to speak with me, when he was drafted.

And Michael Brown, of course, was dead—unavailable to speak to anyone. (Michael Johnson left an exhaustive social media archive to speak for him on the web, while Michael Brown did not.)

Each Michael's story was unique, of course. Michael Sam was the epitome of the success story that dominates narratives about lesbian, gay, bisexual, and transgender Americans in current media. These stories are embraced by LGBT groups, which champion people like Sam and make money off their tales. But as a reporter, Sam's story was frustrating and boring. It was sold, with the help of two agents, exclusively to one outlet. No other reporter was really able to talk to him after that, but his savvy was handsomely rewarded. Before he had even been drafted, Sam was offered an endorsement from Visa, Oprah wanted to make a series on him, and ESPN covered his draft on live TV. Kissing his White boyfriend raised only a blip of controversy, and Sam was "welcomed with open arms" by the mayor and people of St. Louis. (Though the Rams, welcoming at first, cut him. Then the Dallas Cowboys quickly signed him, only to release him a couple of months later. Sam later told *GQ*, "If I had it my way, I never would have done it the way I did, never would have told it the way I did.")

Michael Johnson's story was very different. He was a star wrestler, but there wasn't real money to be made off of him other than in college wrestling. He was arrested and charged with one count of recklessly infecting a sexual partner with HIV and four counts of attempting to recklessly infect others with HIV. (Lindenwood University admitted him even though he seems to be illiterate, then expelled him the day he was arrested and before he was even tried, let alone convicted, of anything.) Johnson's White sexual partners and "Tiger Mandingo" nickname branded him a sexual predator in both traditional and social media. Yet while Johnson's arrest went internationally viral, media interest peaked before the complicated story was understood. Reporters repeated prosecutor's talking points with no reporting, and untrue "facts" were repeated and retweeted. I was the only journalist to visit Johnson in jail and actually talk to him.

And, despite their stakes in HIV, not a single Black, civil liberties, or LGBT rights group took an interest in his case. The NAACP, the ACLU, and the Human Rights Campaign prefer heroes that kids (and, more importantly, donors) can relate to. They've little interest in defending an unsympathetic character like Michael Johnson.

Finally, as a dead person, Michael Brown fit a different role. He filled a major archetype we have become all too familiar with in American media (the gunned-down Black teenager) and a

> The respective bodies of Michaels Sam, Johnson, and Brown were controlled by corporation, incarceration, and extermination.

subcategory of it (the unarmed young Black man killed by a cop or "paracop," like Trayvon Martin, Jordan Davis, or John Crawford). But as a ghost, he is also *tabula rasa:* Brown can fill whatever archetype Americans and American media want to project onto him. To people like me, that meant seeing Brown as yet another dead Black child engaged with the "ultimate defense," where he had to prove his right to life from beyond the grave. To the *New York Times*, that meant Brown was "no angel." To Fox News, it meant that "race hustlers" prematurely decided "Officer Wilson is already guilty," with *habeas corpus* granted the shooter and not the shot, who must have done *something* to deserve it.

There is one last thing that binds all three of these Michaels: they did not control their own bodies. The respective bodies of Michaels Sam, Johnson, and Brown were controlled last year by corporation, incarceration, and state-sponsored extermination. Michael Sam's body was largely controlled by the NFL, a tax-exempt private corporation which takes in billions a year, which is subsidized by all Americans, and which profits greatly from athletic Black bodies. Michael Johnson's body was controlled by Lindenwood University, until the state took control of if it and Lindenwood walked away from its claim on the problematic Negro; Johnson's

bodily commodity now earns money for the Missouri Department of Corrections.

And with Brown, the state simply executed our third and final Michael, dispensing with a trial. Through Officer Wilson, now a free man facing no charges, the state of Missouri took control of Michael's body, shot it, saw no value in expending the cost of an ambulance to resuscitate it, and disposed of it.

REVIEW QUESTIONS

1. This piece was written in 2014. Think about the media coverage of Black men since then. Whose story would you add to this one? What do other Black men recently covered in the media have in common (or not) with the three "Missouri Michaels"?
2. Why is media coverage of men like these three Michaels important to how we understand race and gender in the United States?
3. Thrasher argues that the media covered the three Michaels differently. How so? Why?
4. The death of Michael Brown was one of the events that set the Black Lives Matter movement in action. Do you think there has been progress on the issue of police violence toward Black men since his death? Why or why not?

matthew w. hughey

the whiteness of oscar night

19

winter 2015

white actors have won 95 percent of the "big five" awards at the oscars to date. and among the black actors and directors who have won, they are predominantly rewarded for their work in films characterized by the "white savior" narrative.

In 2001, African-American actors Denzel Washington and Halle Berry took home Academy Awards for Best Actor (*Training Day*) and Best Actress (*Monster's Ball*), respectively. Many hailed the night as evidence of Hollywood's progressive politics and that the once stark and unbending color line had been irrevocably shattered. Actors of color were here to stay and their work would be evaluated and awarded—to appropriate Dr. King's famous words—not on the *color of their skin*, but by the *content of their character* performance.

Before the 74th annual Academy Awards in 2001, only six African-American actors had won one of the "big five" Oscars (actor, actress, supporting actor, supporting actress, and director). Since Washington and Berry's take-home night in 2001, there have been seven more "big five" Oscars awarded to African Americans (though not for best director).

To add, only two Hispanic Americans have ever won one of the big five Oscar categories, and Asians have only received six. Almost all other winners have been White; out of the 87 times that the Academy Awards have been held (1929–2015), White actors won 94.54 percent of the time (398 out of the 421 big five Oscars).

This year, nominees for the big five Oscars are all White—with the one exception of director Alejandro Iñárritu (for directing *Birdman*)—prompting the Twitter hashtag #OscarsSoWhite.

So much for color blindness and Hollywood progressivism.

This should come as little surprise to sociological students of the media. A recent *Los Angeles Times* study revealed that 94 percent of those who chose the nominees were White, 77 percent were male, and a median age of 62. Blacks represented 2 percent of the Academy, Latinos hovered around 1 percent, and Asians were nearly absent.

Many of these award-winning performances by African Americans were in films that follow the narrative structure of what I call a "White Savior" film. A White Savior film is often based on some supposedly true story. Second, it features a non-White group or person who experiences conflict and struggle with others that is particularly dangerous or threatening to their life and livelihood. Third, a White person (the savior) enters the milieu and through his or her sacrifices as a teacher, mentor, lawyer, military hero, aspiring writer, or wannabe Native American warrior, is able to physically save—or at least morally redeem—the person or community of folks of color by the film's end. Examples of this genre include films like *Glory* (1989), *Dangerous Minds* (1996), *Amistad* (1997),

(Illustration by Philip N. Cohen)

Finding Forrester (2000), *The Last Samurai* (2003), *Half-Nelson* (2006), *Freedom Writers* (2007), *Gran Torino* (2008), *Avatar* (2009), *The Blind Side* (2009), *The Help* (2011), and the list goes on.

When we look at the content of Oscar-winning roles by actors of color, especially African Americans, we see that many were awarded for performances that conform to racist views on what makes for an authentic and believable performance. Some roles emphasize Black servitude to Whites like Hattie McDaniel (*Gone with the Wind*), Octavia Spencer (*The Help*), and Lupita

Nyong'o (*12 Years a Slave*). Others show Blacks as little more than entertainers for the White gaze like Jamie Foxx (*Ray*) and Jennifer Hudson (*Dreamgirls*). Blacks are also awarded for playing dysfunctional welfare queens and pathological criminals, such as Halle Berry (*Monster's Ball*), Mo'Nique (*Precious*), and Denzel Washington (*Training Day*). Another critical favorite is the "Magical Negro" performance in which they present enchanted and folksy Black characters that exist only to assist disheveled and down-on-their-luck White characters get back on their feet, such as Whoopi Goldberg (*Ghost*),

Cuba Gooding Jr. (*Jerry Maguire*), and Morgan Freeman (*Million Dollar Baby*).

The recent film *Selma*—a film about Martin Luther King Jr.'s staging of the 1965 Selma-to-Montgomery march—did not follow the White Savior film script. While *Selma* quickly earned critical praise and predictions of Oscar glory, it was critiqued for its portrayal of former President Lyndon B. Johnson, who some felt was marginalized or misrepresented. For instance, Bill Moyers opined, "As for how the film portrays Lyndon B. Johnson: There's one egregious and outrageous portrayal that is the worst kind of creative license because it suggests the very opposite of the truth." LBJ biographer Julian E. Zelizer stated, "I think in some ways they went overboard in not wiping away, but downplaying how committed the top official, meaning the president of the United States, was to this," and the *New York Times* wrote that the film's portrayal of LBJ "raises hackles." In the end *Selma* did garner a nod for best picture but was omitted from the big five award categories.

In speaking to *Rolling Stone* about the criticism, director Ava DuVernay stated:

I wasn't interested in making a White Savior movie; I was interested in making a movie centered on the people of Selma. You have to bring in some context for what it was like to live in the racial terrorism that was going on in the Deep South at that time. The four little girls have to be there, and then you have to bring in the women. So I started adding women. This is a dramatization of the events. But what's important for me as a student of this time in history is to not deify what the president did. Johnson has been hailed as a hero of that time, and he was, but we're talking about a reluctant hero. He was cajoled and pushed, he was protective of a legacy—he was not doing things out of the goodness of his heart. Does it make it any worse or any better? I don't think so. History is history

and he did do it eventually. But there was some process to it that was important to show.

The relative snubbing of *Selma* and the ways actors and directors of color are awarded (if they are nominated) raises questions relative to DuVernay's comments. Does a film with either overt or subtle interracial relations and tensions need to follow the White Savior motif to gain Hollywood's approval?

I raised this question in my book *The White Savior Film: Content, Critics, and Consumption*, where I examined 50 recent movies over the past 25 years, analyzed nearly 2,800 reviews of those same movies, and examined interview and focus-group data with audience members of at least three of those recent White Savior films.

Nearly 40 percent of these films highlighted the claim that they are "based on a true story" or directly reference historical events of a highly racialized nature, such as the U.S. Civil War, Nazi Germany, South African Apartheid, Wounded Knee, or the U.S. civil rights movement. These films link the supposed authenticity of history with the standpoint of the White Savior, rather than from the points of view of the people of color who are supposedly being helped.

But when a film tells history from the point of view of the socially marginalized without the presence of a White Savior that saves the day, many may find those films somehow overly "political," "ideological," or simply "untrue."

For instance, when Melvin and Mario Van Peebles sought funds to produce the film *Panther* (1995), based on the formation of the Black Panther Party in Oakland, California, in 1966, they were urged repeatedly to create a White Savior in order to make the film more "mainstream." Mario Van Peebles stated:

We went around to Hollywood studios and we kept on getting the same message: "You really need to make this more mainstream." But when pressed to explain what they meant, it turned out that they meant that there had to be a White person as one of the main heroes of the movie. "People knew about the destruction of the Indians for years," we were told, "but no one really cared about it until they got Kevin Costner to star in *Dances with Wolves*. The civil rights movement might have been led by Stokely Carmichael and Martin Luther King Jr. but Americans didn't care to see a movie on that till *Mississippi Burning* tells the story from the standpoint of White FBI agents. So you've got to write this story in a way that gives focus to some big White stars, and then you can do your thing." One of the studio heads suggested that we make one of the leading Panthers a White man. Others suggested focusing on a Berkeley White person who would meet five young Black guys, teaches them to read and stand up for themselves, and then they become the Panthers!

And in 2008 African-American actor Danny Glover attempted to produce a Hollywood film on Haitian independence and the military hero Toussaint-Louverture. To back the project, he approached a host of financiers and hopeful co-producers, but few were interested. Glover stated,

Producers said, "It's a nice project, a great project . . . [but] where are the White heroes?" . . .

I couldn't get the money here. I couldn't get the money in Britain. I went to everybody. You wouldn't believe the number of producers based in Europe, and in the States, that I went to.

As these examples show, if one can abide by the White Savior script and convince others of the story's legitimacy, these tales will find production and resonance with many "mainstream" audiences. If not, they may be snubbed by the Academy—or not even made.

REVIEW QUESTIONS

1. What is the White Savior narrative, and why is it problematic?
2. Can you think of any examples beyond those Hughey mentioned in the article of movies that follow the White Savior narrative? How were people of color and Whites represented in this film?
3. Hughey argues that the movie *Selma* does not follow the White Savior narrative. Why not? Think of a movie that involves people of color. How could the plot have been changed to defy the White Savior narrative?

van c. tran

social mobility among second-generation latinos

20

spring 2016

using the current population survey (cps) 2007–2009, the author examined patterns of socioeconomic assimilation among latino youths (ages 25–40). educational and occupational outcomes of second-generation latinos were compared with native whites and blacks, and also with their proxy first-generation parents. the findings suggest a mostly optimistic story.

"They are bringing drugs. They are bringing crime. They are rapists." Donald Trump's June 2015 characterization of Mexican immigrants drew widespread criticism from the media for its racist undertone and from academics for its mischaracterization of the Latino community in the United States. And yet, as this issue of *Contexts* goes to press, Trump remains the front-runner with the highest level of support in what was once a crowded field of Republican presidential hopefuls. In a nutshell, Trump's statement underscores the perpetual myth among many well-meaning Americans on Latinos' potential failure to assimilate into American society. The good news is that Trump simply got it very, very wrong!

Over the last decade, four key trends have transformed the Latino experience in the United States. First, Latinos are the largest minority group in the country. In 2010 they comprised 16.3 percent of the U.S. population, or 50.5 million people, and they are projected to reach 132.8 million people or 30 percent of the U.S. population in 2050. Second, members of the Latino second generation (U.S.-born children of immigrant parents) are coming of age in sizable numbers and will transform patterns of ethnoracial inequality

in American society in the coming decades. Third, the replenishment of the Latino population with new immigrants has increased the heterogeneity among Latinos by ethnic origin, immigrant generation, social class, and legal status. Lastly, Latinos are increasingly settling in smaller cities and towns in new immigrant destinations outside of traditional immigrant gateways.

In light of these trends, I examine patterns of socioeconomic assimilation among Latinos using the most recent data from the Current Population Survey (CPS) following the Great Recession of 2007–2009. I address two key questions: How do second-generation Latinos fare in comparison to their native peers? And how do second-generation Latinos fare in comparison to their "proxy," first-generation parents? This new evidence tells a mostly optimistic story. Public and media discussions, such as Trump's statement, often conflate these two sets of comparisons, leading to confusion and slippage in discussions of upward and downward mobility among the second generation and in interpretations of the empirical evidence. Despite pervasive concerns about Latinos' potential failure to economically assimilate into American life, I find clear evidence of both intergenerational progress and rapid socioeconomic assimilation for many Latino ethnic groups.

socioeconomic assimilation

Two competing perspectives frame the discussion of Latino socioeconomic assimilation in the United States. On the one hand, the theory of "segmented assimilation" highlights the macro-structural sources of vulnerability that might lead to downward mobility among the Latino second generation: their racial minority status, segregated urban schools, concentration in disadvantaged neighborhoods, and the bifurcated economy that offers fewer good jobs. In their seminal study, Alejandro Portes and Rubén Rumbaut point out that Mexicans are most at risk of downward mobility into the "new rainbow underclass." On the other hand, proponents of "new assimilation" theory, Richard Alba and Victor Nee, argue that the Latino second generation will most likely follow the time-honored path of European immigrants and their descendants, who achieved parity with the White American mainstream over the course of three generations. Alba and Nee suggest that the barriers confronting Latinos are significant, but not insurmountable.

What accounts for such different predictions on Latino social mobility in prior research? Different studies have captured the Latino second generation in different life stages: from early adolescence to young adulthood. For example, the high aspirations for education that are nearly universal among many adolescents from an immigrant background might not be fully realized in young adulthood because of the reality of low-performing public schools and segregated neighborhoods that affect many Latinos. Further, different studies partially capture the anxiety and optimism that are not only emblematic of public sentiments toward immigration but are also reflections on the economic conditions of the period. For example, it is no coincidence that

Herbert Gans warned about second-generation decline in the 1990s during a severe recession whereas Philip Kasinitz, John Mollenkopf, Mary Waters, and Jennifer Holdaway reached a cautiously optimistic conclusion about second-generation progress, in part because their study was conducted during the Clinton era's economic boom. Similarly, Edward Telles and Vilma Ortiz documented race-based exclusion among second- and later-generation descendants of Mexicans who came of age during a specific historical period, whereas Douglas Massey's prediction about the racialization of Latinos recognized the role of punitive immigration policy and legal status in creating an increasingly negative context of reception toward Latinos.

In spite of these debates, I find no evidence of second-generation decline and clear evidence of intergenerational progress. To be clear, I only focus on two key measures of socioeconomic assimilation: educational and occupational outcomes. I do not address other indicators such as language assimilation, residential integration, and intermarriage. I focus on the children of immigrants between the ages of 25 and 40 from the ten-largest Latino ethnic groups, comparing their outcomes with their native-born counterparts and with their proxy first-generation parents. For clarity and parsimony, I present descriptive findings by ethnic group, but these results are consistent even after adjusting for group differences in demographic composition (such as gender and age) as well as in regional concentration in old and new immigrant destinations. (The technical details are in my article in the Recommended Resources.)

socioeconomic attainment in young adulthood

Are second-generation Latinos at a disadvantage compared to their native peers? Figure 1 presents two measures of educational and occupational attainment by ethnic group: the proportion of college graduates and the proportion in a professional occupation. With regard to education, second-generation Cubans, Colombians, Ecuadorians, Peruvians, and Central and South Americans report rates of college completion that are similar to those of native Whites and above those of native Blacks. For example, 39 percent of second-generation Cubans have a college degree or more, compared to 39 percent of native Whites and only 21 percent of native Blacks. This is striking given the widespread perception of Latinos as underachievers. Although second-generation Salvadorans, Guatemalans, Hondurans, and Dominicans report lower college completion rates than the native majority group, these groups still fare better than the native minority groups of native Blacks and Puerto Ricans. The one exception is second-generation Mexicans whose college completion rate is only 17 percent.

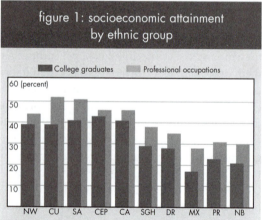

figure 1: socioeconomic attainment by ethnic group

Source: Pooled CPS 2008–2012.

Notes: Results are based on the sample of 25- to 40-year-old respondents in CPS. NW: native White; CU: Cuban; SA: South American; CEP: Colombian, Ecuadoran, and Peruvian; CA: Central American; SGH: Salvadoran, Guatemalan, and Honduran; DR: Dominican; PR: Puerto Rican; MX: Mexican; NB: native Black. The categories "SGH" and "CEP" are combined due to sample size. The residual categories of "CA" and "SA" include all the other ethnic groups from these two regions, excluding SGHs and CEPs.

The occupational data tell a similar story. Among those who report being employed, second-generation Cubans, Colombians, Ecuadorians and Peruvians, and Central and South Americans are as likely as native Whites to be in a professional occupation. For example, 52 percent of second-generation Cubans report being a professional compared to 44 percent of native Whites and only 30 percent of native Blacks. In addition, Salvadorans, Guatemalans, Hondurans, and Dominicans fare better than native Blacks, although these groups have yet to close the gaps with native Whites. Once again, Mexicans are the most disadvantaged, with only 28 percent (the lowest among all groups) reporting a professional occupation.

It is remarkable that the majority of second-generation Latino groups have achieved parity with native Whites. This suggests a rate of assimilation that compares favorably to the historical record among European groups, especially when one takes into account the many disadvantages Latinos face. The comparatively poor outcomes among Mexicans, and to a lesser extent Salvadorans, Guatemalans, and Hondurans, are likely due to their legal status and to the relatively low levels of human capital among the immigrant first generation, although the CPS data do not contain the information needed to directly test this hypothesis. The occupational disadvantages of Mexicans may also reflect the effects of the Great Recession because Mexicans are more concentrated in the service sector and construction work, industries severely affected by recent economic downturns.

social mobility across generations

Are second-generation Latinos at risk of downward mobility compared to their parents? Because the CPS does not contain data on the respondents' parents, I compare second-generation Latinos to their proxy first-generation immigrant parents using the lagged birth cohort method. This method essentially assumes that a 25-year period approximates one immigrant generation and renders the comparison across generations more accurate. Specifically, it compares a cohort of first-generation Latinos with a later cohort of second-generation Latinos 25 years younger. The data are arrayed so that I can meaningfully compare the average years of education and occupational status scores for first-generation Latinos in the 1945–1965 birth cohort with the same outcomes for second-generation Latinos in the 1970–1990 birth cohort. I focus on these two cohorts because they capture the post-1965 first generation in middle adulthood and the post-1965 second generation in young adulthood.

Figure 2 presents the average years of education and the average occupational status scores by immigrant generation, while also showing the gaps that have been closed between the first and the second generation. Here, the overall intergenerational progress is

clear. Among all Latino groups, the second generation reports significant gains in both educational and occupational outcomes compared to their proxy first-generation parents. For most Latino groups, the educational gain averages about one additional year between the first and second generation. For Mexicans, Salvadorans, Guatemalans, and Hondurans, the second generation significantly outpaces their proxy first-generation parents, reporting an impressive gain of about four years of education.

The occupational data tells a similarly optimistic story. For all Latino groups, the second generation reports working in better jobs with higher occupational status than their first-generation parents. Once again, the gains are largest among second-generation Mexicans, Salvadorans, Guatemalans, and Hondurans who report occupational scores about 2 points higher (on a 9-point scale) than to their parents. Overall, these analyses show clear evidence of second-generation progress and no evidence of a second-generation decline.

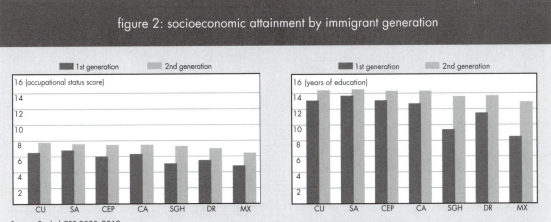

figure 2: socioeconomic attainment by immigrant generation

Source: Pooled CPS 2008–2012.

Notes: Combined samples are limited to those between the ages of 25 and 65. The data are arrayed so that the results represent the average years of education and occupational status score for the first generation in the 1945/1965 birth cohort, along with the second generation that were born 25 years later in the 1970/1990 birth cohort, essentially assuming that the latter group is the second-generation children of the first-generation cohort. Education is measured in years from 0 to 16, whereas occupational status score is measured on a scale from 0 to 9, with higher scores representing more prestigious occupations such as managers and professionals. Gap bars between two data points for each ethnic group illustrate the extent of intergenerational progress by each ethnic group.

assimilation into what?
progress compared to whom?

Questions about what it is people assimilate into and against whom their progress is measured are central to assessing the contention around outcomes among the children of Latino immigrants. What if the choice of different comparison groups leads to different conclusions about their progress, decline, or stagnation? Given the racially stratified nature of American society, these questions are not trivial ones.

In comparison to their proxy first-generation parents, there is no evidence of a second-generation decline or downward mobility, as none of the Latino groups report worse socioeconomic outcomes compared to their proxy first-generation parents. Quite the contrary, the evidence clearly points to both intergenerational progress and upward mobility among the second-generation Latinos. In comparison to their native-born peers in the same age group, the results point to significant diversity across Latino ethnic groups. Cubans, Colombians, Ecuadorians and Peruvians, and Central and South Americans have achieved parity with the native majority group, essentially closing the gaps within the course of two generations. This mobility pattern is best described as *long-distance mobility*. Salvadorans, Guatemalans, and Hondurans have outperformed the native minority groups, but have yet to achieve parity with the native majority group, so their mobility pattern is best described as *short-distance mobility*. Dominicans show outcomes on par with native minority groups, whereas there is a clear disadvantage among Mexicans even when compared to outcomes among the native minority groups.

How Latinos are assimilating into American life is not a new question, but prior studies were based on pre-Recession data, and the most recent evidence is now almost a decade old.

To be sure, the progress among Dominicans has been somewhat slow and the relative disadvantage among Mexicans provides some support for the concerns over their future trajectories. Still, the intergenerational progress in both groups suggests that they stand to make further gains by the third and fourth generation. Historical records also provide important lessons for our assessment of Latino progress: European ethnic groups closed gaps with the White Anglo-Saxon Protestant mainstream in the United States over the course of three generations. Therefore, it would be extremely unrealistic to expect Latinos to catch up with the American mainstream in two generations, given the economic, legal, and social barriers facing them. For example, ethnic groups with more human capital, legal status, and lighter skin tone (such as Cubans) should fare better than those with less education who lack legal status and face significant discrimination (such as Mexicans and Dominicans).

the future of latino socioeconomic assimilation

Given the sheer demographic presence of Latinos, evaluating their socioeconomic assimilation provides key insights into the continuing transformation of American society. Since the onset of the global economic recession in December 2007, there has been increasing evidence that Latinos and African Americans were hit the hardest, given their already tenuous position in the labor market and significant wealth gaps that left them with smaller safety nets than other U.S. racial groups. As a result, understanding social mobility among Latinos has become even more pressing in an era of growing inequality, economic recession, stagnation of wages, and increasing financial insecurity.

How Latinos are assimilating into American life is not a new question, but prior studies were based on pre-Recession data, and the most recent evidence is now almost a decade old. My post-Recession evaluation of outcomes among the Latino second generation with the most recent evidence is not only timely but also relevant because recent shifts in our politics and our economy have resulted in a rather negative context of reception for Latinos. First, the Great Recession disproportionately affected the Latino population. According to a report from the Pew Hispanic Center, the number of Latino children in poverty rose sharply from 4.4 million in 2007 to 6.1 million in 2010. This 36.3 percent increase compares to 17.6 percent among non-Latino Whites and 11.7 percent for non-Latino Blacks during the same period. Another direct consequence of the Great Recession was significant wealth loss, especially among Latinos due to the foreclosure crisis. According to one study from the Urban Institute, Latinos lost 44 percent of their overall wealth between 2007 and 2011, compared to only 11 percent among non-Hispanic Whites and 31 percent among non-Latino Blacks. Second, the debate around the undocumented population (estimated at 12.2 million in 2007 and 11.2 million in 2011) remains highly divisive, especially in a context in which millions of Americans have been out of work. As a result, Hispanics, especially Mexicans, have been stigmatized and have borne the brunt of a wave of anti-immigrant sentiment. The number of deportations reached a record high, rising from 359,795 in 2008 to 438,421 in 2013, an increase of 21.9 percent over five years. Debates about the undocumented unfolded alongside the DREAMers movement, which transformed the national conversation on immigrant rights and brought about significant immigrant education reforms.

At the same time, Latinos have yet to achieve full parity with native Whites and to secure a place in the highest echelons of the American mainstream. More importantly, the disadvantage among Mexicans highlights the profoundly negative impact of legal status on socioeconomic assimilation. Their situation deserves special attention because the Mexican-origin population accounts for two-thirds of the total Latino population in the United States.

Yes, these are some depressing trends. But the very good news is that Latinos are increasingly being integrated into American society. The second generation has made striking gains in education and escaped the dead-end jobs prevalent among the first generation. The clear intergenerational progress even among Mexicans suggests that they may close the current gaps with native Whites within the course of three to four generations, instead of two generations, as I have observed among many Latino groups. Although the future of Latinos as a group remains uncertain, we have reasons to be optimistic: they have weathered the economic downturn well and are poised to take advantage of the new opportunities that lie ahead.

RECOMMENDED RESOURCES

Jody Agius Vallejo. 2012. *Barrios to Burbs: The Making of the Mexican-American Middle Class.* Palo Alto: Stanford University Press.

Documents the extent of social mobility among Mexicans and examines the class origins, social trajectories, and identities of middle-class Mexican Americans.

Roberto Gonzales. 2015. *Lives in Limbo: Undocumented and Coming of Age in America.* Berkeley: University of California Press.

Examines the lives of undocumented youths and shows the negative impact of legal status on assimilation into American life.

Tomás R. Jiménez. 2010. *Replenished Ethnicity: Mexican Americans, Immigration, and Identity.* Berkeley: University of California Press.

Examines the ethnic identification process among later-generation Mexican Americans and their integration into American society.

Philip Kasinitz, John H. Mollenkopf, Mary C. Waters, and Jennifer Holdaway. 2008. *Inheriting the City: The Children of Immigrants Come of Age.* New York: Russell Sage Foundation.

Reports findings from a major study of the immigrant second generation from the New York Metropolitan area, including many Latino ethnic groups.

Edward E. Telles and Vilma Ortiz. 2008. *Generations of Exclusion: Mexican Americans, Assimilation and Race.* New York: Russell Sage Foundation.

Reports findings from a major longitudinal study on Mexican Americans across generations and cohorts.

Van C. Tran and Nicol M. Valdez. 2015. "Second-Generation Decline or Advantage? Latino Assimilation in the Aftermath of the Great Recession." *International Migration Review.* doi: 10.1111/imre.12192.

Presents postrecession results on the socioeconomic assimilation of Latinos, along with the technical details and model specifications for the findings in this article.

REVIEW QUESTIONS

1. The author compared the second-generation young people with the "proxy" first-generation parents (the lagged birth cohort method). What are the benefits and limitations of using this method?
2. Using postrecession data (2007–2009), the author found optimistic evidence for the mobility of second-generation Latino youths. How can we reconcile this finding with the evidence that Latinos and African Americans were hit hardest by the economic downturn?
3. What do you think will happen to undocumented immigrants and children of undocumented immigrants, given current political events?

jennifer lee

ask a sociologist: jennifer lee on naming success

winter 2016

a sociologist gives advice on how to name your children for success.

Editors' note: We asked friend-of-Contexts Jennifer Lee to do something that most sociologists are terrified of doing: give advice. Sociologists do a lot of research that help us understand how the world works, but too many are afraid of taking the short (if scary) step from "this is why the world is the way it is" to "and this is what you could do." We hope Lee's bravery will inspire other sociologists to apply their research to pressing questions!
— *Syed Ali and Philip N. Cohen*

Q: *I'm a second-generation Indian Muslim immigrant, married to a White woman. We both work in professional jobs. My kids, who look kind of nondescript tan and not Indian-looking at all, have my last name, Ali. To help the kids get into selective colleges and ultimately get great jobs, would it be better to change their last names to their mother's "American" name (Pollard), hyphenate (Pollard-Ali or Ali-Pollard), or just keep Ali?*

A: I understand your concern about wanting to provide the best educational and occupational opportunities for your children, and leveraging any advantages you may have to do that, including possibly changing your children's surname. People use surnames to gauge race, ethnicity, and national origin, even if they're not accurate identifiers. Despite the inaccuracy, you recognize that the surname you choose to give your children affects the assumptions that others make about them, so essentially you're asking what surname will accord them the greatest advantages in life.

Before I continue, allow me to state at the outset that sociological research consistently shows that the strongest predictor of a child's educational and occupational attainment is his or her parents' education and occupation. That you and your wife are college-educated professionals makes it highly likely that your children will reproduce your status. So the name you choose for your children will be less consequential than the class resources that they are fortunate to have.

This isn't to say that names don't matter. Research also shows that people make assumptions about others and also about themselves based on their surname. For example, having an Italian surname makes you more likely to identify as Italian, feel more Italian, and have an affinity toward other Italians, even if you aren't sure of your ethnic background. Sociologists Herbert Gans and Mary Waters refer to this as "symbolic ethnicity" because it is costless, voluntary, and fun for European Americans to consider themselves "ethnic" rather than just American.

Non-European surnames, however, are not costless. In audit studies, researchers show that employers are less likely to interview a job applicant with an African-American-sounding name (such as Malik or Jerome) even when he exhibits the same characteristics as an applicant with a White-sounding name (such as Thomas or David). Research also shows that professors are least likely to return e-mail messages when the sender has an Asian ethnic name, and professors with Asian ethnic names receive the poorest student teaching evaluations.

But what about college admissions specifically? There is a perception among some Asian-American parents that their children must pay an "Asian tax" when applying to the most selective universities, meaning that they have to have higher SAT scores and grades to be admitted at the same rate as their White, African-American, and Latino peers. In their study of the most selective schools in the United States, sociologists Thomas J. Espenshade and Alexandria Walton found that Asian-American applicants had higher SAT scores than other students, but they also stipulated that they could not conclude that Asian-American applicants experience racial bias in the admissions process because there are many variables that their study did not measure. College admissions officers consider more than just test scores and grades when making decisions, as they should.

Moreover, race and ethnicity are only one of a host of factors that universities consider when making decisions about admissions. They also consider whether you are the first in your family to attend college, whether you come from a state where few applicants apply, whether you have unique talents and skills, and whether you are a legacy (meaning that one of your parents is an alum), among many others. In fact, applicants get a much larger boost from their legacy status than their race or ethnicity. So while there may be rumors of an "Asian tax," there is no concrete evidence that it exists or that Asian-American applicants are disadvantaged in the college admissions process because of their racial status.

In sum, regardless of what name you give your children (Ali, Pollard, Ali-Pollard, or Pollard-Ali), your children will likely follow your and your wife's footsteps, attend a selective college, and become professionals—because you have given them the class resources to achieve this.

REVIEW QUESTIONS

1. Think about your surname. What does it say about you to others? How does it affect your identity?
2. According to Lee, why are the consequences of surnames different for Whites of European descent compared to other racial and ethnic groups?
3. What is the most important determinant of educational success, according to the article?

part **5**

Gender and Sexuality

viewpoints

boys

winter 2013

five experts shed light on the everyday lives of teenage boys and their relationships.

Boys are interesting creatures in the American public imagination. They start off all "slugs and snails and puppy-dogs' tails"—cute!—but then they hit puberty and become lazy, sexual, carefree, violent, detached, and irresponsible. They become scary. We fear teenage boys, in part because they are in-between—neither children, nor adults—and they seem to be beyond our control.

We're not only afraid of what they are now, we're also afraid of what they will become. Boys require special attention in school, many argue, because they're not performing as well as girls at all levels of schooling. What kind of a world will we have when these underperforming boys become underperforming men? Some, like journalist Hanna Rosin, have already passed judgment and declared "The End of Men." She finds that women now wear the pants in the American postindustrial, knowledge-based economy. While the trend is in that direction, it is not yet actually the case, as sociologist Philip Cohen has pointed out in the *Atlantic* and on his blog, *Family Inequality*. But facts have a way of getting lost in the face of interesting-sounding arguments, even when they're not true.

In this *Viewpoints*, we've gathered five experts who've spent a great deal of time interviewing and studying teenage boys' relationships, often with surprising results that debunk conventional wisdom. Niobe Way finds that boys, counter to stereotypes, want and need close friendships but may avoid shows of intimacy because of pressures not to be "girly" or "gay." C. J. Pascoe notes how similar pressures lead to bullying behavior. She argues that bullying that appears homophobic is actually targeted at not-masculine-enough boys and, interestingly, plays an important role in heterosexual boys' friendships. In contrast to Way and Pascoe, Mark McCormack finds British boys to be emotionally healthy and engaging in deep friendship ties. He attributes these expressions of intimacy to the relatively lower rates of homophobia in Britain, as compared with the United States, where similar behavior would earn boys the label of "fag." Amy Schalet offers a comparative focus on the sexual and romantic socialization of boys in the United States and the Netherlands. She finds that Dutch culture supports youthful romance and sex as healthy and something to be celebrated, whereas American culture treats sex among teens as inappropriate. Lastly, Freeden Oeur looks at relationships among poor Black teenage boys in an all-Black high school where Black adult administrators consciously cultivate a sense of manhood based on work and fatherhood.

boys as human

The popular stereotype is that boys are emotionally illiterate and shallow, they don't want intimate relationships or close friendships. In my research with boys over the past two decades, however, I have discovered that not only are these stereotypes false, they are actively hurting boys and leading them to engage in self destructive behaviors. The African-American, Latino, Asian-American and White teenage boys in my studies indicate that what they want and need most are close relationships—friendships, in particular—in which they can share their "deep secrets." These friendships, they tell us, are critical for their mental health. But, according to the boys, they live in a culture that considers such intimacy "girly" and "gay" and thus they are discouraged from having the very relationships that are critical for their well-being.

My longitudinal studies of hundreds of boys from early to late adolescence indicate that a central dilemma for boys growing up in the United States is how to get the intimacy they want while still maintaining their manliness. Boys want to be able to freely express their emotions, including their feelings of vulnerability; they want others to be sensitive to their feelings without being teased or harassed for having such desires. They want genuine friendships in which they are free to be themselves rather than conform to rigid masculine stereotypes. As Carlos said: "It might be nice to be a girl because then you wouldn't have to be emotionless."

During early and middle adolescence most boys, according to my research, do have close male friendships in which they can share their "deep secrets." It is only in late adolescence—a time when, according to national data, suicides and violence among boys soar—that boys disconnect from other boys. The boys in my studies begin, in late adolescence, to use the phrase "no homo" when discussing their male friendships, expressing the fear that if they seek out close friendships, they will be perceived as "gay" or "girly." As a consequence, they pull away from their male peers and experience sadness over the loss of their formerly close friends.

Michael, a participant in one of our studies, told his interviewer that friendships are important because, "if you don't have friends, you have no one to tell your secrets to. Then it's like, I always think bad stuff in my brain 'cause like no one's helping me and I just need to keep all the secrets to myself." Asked why friends are important, Danny said to his interviewer, "you need someone to talk to, like you have problems with something, you go talk to him. You know, if you keep it all to yourself, you will go crazy. Try to take it out on someone else." Kai implicitly concurred in his interview: "without friends you will go crazy or mad or you'll be lonely all of the time, be depressed. . . . You would go wacko." Asked by the interviewer why his friends are important, Justin said, " 'cause you need a friend or else, you would be depressed, you won't be happy, you would try to kill yourself, 'cause then you'll be all alone and no one to talk to." Faced with the prospect of having no close friends, Anthony said to his interviewer, "who you gonna talk

> A central dilemma for boys growing up in the United States is how to get the intimacy they want while still maintaining their manliness.

to? Might as well be dead or something. I don't mean to put it in a negative way, but I am just saying—it's like not a good feeling to be alone."

Over the past three decades, studies, such as those done by epidemiologists Wilkinson and Pickett, have found that adults without close friendships are more likely to experience poor mental and physical health and live shorter lives than those with close friendships. Despite the growing body of data that underscores the importance of close friendships for everyone, harmful stereotypes that ignore boys' social and emotional needs and capacities abound. According to the boys themselves, these stereotypes significantly contribute to their isolation, loneliness, and depression. As they get older, boys get stripped of their humanity. They learn that they are not supposed to have hearts, except in relation to a girl, and then it should be a stoic heart and not too vulnerable.

We must allow boys to be boys in the most human sense of the word, nurture their natural emotional and social capacities, and foster their close friendships. We need to make relational and emotional literacy an inherent part of being human, rather than only a "girl thing" or a "gay thing." The boys and young men in my studies know that what makes us human is our ability to deeply connect with each other. We must figure out how to help boys and young men strengthen rather than lose these critical life skills. Only then we will be able to address the psychological and sociological roots of this crisis of connection and the negative consequences associated with it.

c. j. pascoe

homophobia in boys' friendships

According to media reports, we are in the midst of a bullying epidemic whose primary victims are gay kids. But young people's homophobia is more complex than such popular views suggest. Much of it is perpetuated by and directed at straight-identified boys. As the school resource website Teach Safe Schools documents, 80 percent of those on the receiving end of homophobic epithets identify as heterosexual. While GLBQ youth are certainly harassed in school settings, these homophobic insults also play a complex role in heterosexual boys' friendships.

Researching teenage boys over the past decade, what I found is that boys' homophobia is not *only* about sexuality, or about pathological bullies going after gay boys; their homophobia is as much about making sure that boys act like "guys" as it is about fear of actual gay people. Through homophobic banter, jokes, and harassment, straight boys define their masculinity in ways that are hostile both to gay boys and to straight boys who don't measure up to a particular masculine ideal. Insulting each other for being un-masculine, even for a moment, reinforces expectations of masculinity and also provides space for straight boys to forge intimate ties with one another, while affirming to themselves, and to each other, that they are not gay.

Homophobic insults, talk, and jokes—or what I call "fag discourse"—permeates boys' relationships. Different behaviors or attitudes, such as being too touchy, too emotional,

> Boys' homophobia is as much about making sure that boys act like "guys" as it is about fear of actual gay people.

dancing, and caring too much about clothing, can trigger this "fag discourse." Boys try fervently to escape the label of "fag" by avoiding these behaviors or directing the epithet toward someone else. "Fag" is likely to be the most serious insult one boy can level at another. As Jeremy, a high school junior, remarked, "To call someone gay or fag is like the lowest thing you can call someone. Because that's like saying that you're nothing."

For many boys, calling someone a "fag" does not necessarily mean that they are gay. As J.L., a high school sophomore, explained, "Fag, seriously, it has nothing to do with sexual preference at all. You could just be calling somebody an idiot, you know?" Furthermore young men who engage in fag discourse often simultaneously support the civil rights of actual gay men, and condemn those who would harass them. Jabes, a senior, said, "I actually say fag quite a lot, except for when I'm in the company of an actual homosexual person. Then I try not to say it at all. But when I'm just hanging out with my friends, I'll be like, 'Shut up, I don't want to hear you anymore, you stupid fag.'" Simple homophobia is too crude a concept for characterizing what is going on here, because these insults seem to coexist with rising support for gay rights.

> What boys are doing as they lob these epithets is reminding one other that to be acceptably masculine is to be dominant, powerful, and unemotional.

If these epithets are simultaneously reducing boys to "nothing," and are not necessarily about homosexuality, what are these boys talking about? The answer lies in high school senior David's statement: "Being gay is just a lifestyle. It's someone you choose to sleep with. You can still throw a football around and be gay." In other words, a gay man can still be masculine. What boys are doing as they lob these epithets is reminding one other that to be acceptably masculine is to be dominant, powerful, and unemotional. Violating those expectations can trigger a round of "fag discourse."

Thus, homophobia in boys' friendships is not only about some global fear of same-sex desire (though certainly, for all of the protestations about equality, fear, disgust, or loathing of same-sex desire between men still exists), it is also a way in which boys define themselves and others as masculine. When we call these interactions between boys homophobic bullying and ignore the messages about masculinity in these insults, we risk divorcing these interactions from the way they perpetuate restrictive and sexist definitions of manhood. We also fail to appreciate how boys carve out moments of intimacy, and that complexity, beauty, and complicated ideas about masculinity lie at the heart of many of their friendships.

mark mccormack

embracing intimacy

When we think of boys' friendships, we tend to think of rough-and-tumble physical energy. But research conducted over the past three decades warns that rough-and-tumble play often leads to aggression and violence, and that shallow friendships have resulted in boys being emotionally stunted. Another pernicious element of boys' friendships has been virulent homophobia.

Given the cultural conflation of masculinity with heterosexuality, where acting feminine is perceived as being gay, boys go to great lengths to act "manly" and avoid homosexual suspicion. Homophobia prevents boys from expressing emotion, and makes them keep considerable physical distance from each other.

The centrality of homophobia to this damaging dynamic of friendship implies that as attitudes toward homosexuality change, so will the ways boys interact. I found this to be the case in ethnographic research that I conducted in high schools in England. Several studies indicate that homophobia has decreased at a greater rate in England than in the United States. For example, the most recent data from the British Social Attitudes survey show that only 29 percent of adults think same-sex relationships are wrong, down from 46 percent in the year 2000. Research from 2007 also finds that 86 percent of the population would be comfortable if a close friend was gay. Comparing BSA data with the American General Social Survey, in his book *Inclusive Masculinity*, Eric Anderson showed that American attitudes are approximately 20 percentage points less favorable than British ones, and that young people have the most progressive attitudes toward homosexuality.

Teenage boys are embracing once-feminized traits of emotional openness and physical intimacy.

In the three government-run schools I studied, heterosexual male students—ages 16 to 18—espoused pro-gay attitudes and condemned homophobia. They often had openly gay friends; some criticized their schools for their lack of openly gay role models. This inclusive culture has led teenage boys to redefine masculinity; as a result, their understanding of friendship is quite different than what one might expect.

The male students at these schools were proud of their close friendships and frequently demonstrated that publicly. For example, Jack had been away for the weekend and upon seeing his best friend Tim, he shouted, "Timmo, where were you all weekend, I missed ya!" and exuberantly kissed Tim on the top of his head. Then they talked about their weekend in a style best described as gossiping.

More frequent than this kind of boisterous demonstration of friendship, though, were the touching behaviors that occurred during quiet conversations. Here, boys used physical touch as a sign of friendship. Ben and Eli, for example, stood in a corner of the common room, casually holding hands as they spoke, their fingers gently touching one another. Halfway through the exchange, Ben changed his embrace, placing an arm around Eli's waist and a hand on his stomach. This kind of behavior was commonplace among the majority of boys; hugging was a routine form of greeting in these schools.

The boys also valued emotional support. Tim said, "I talk to my best friends about everything, if I've got girlfriend trouble, or when I'm upset or stressed. It's really important for me to be able to do that." Boys also openly recognized the closeness of their friendships, sometimes addressing each other as "boyfriend" or "lover" as a way of demonstrating emotional intimacy. Phil said, "Yeah, I call him boyfriend and stuff, but that's just a way of saying he's my best mate." Similarly, Dave commented, "I'll sometimes call my best mates 'lover' or something similar. It's just a way of saying, 'I love you,' really."

The friendships and social dynamics of the boys from my research are also evident in popular culture. Youth TV shows in the UK, such as *Skins* and *Hollyoaks,* show similar displays of physical and emotional intimacy between boys, and the latest boy band sensation, One Direction, models this new youth masculinity. While there are variations according to class, ethnicity, geography and other factors, the friendships

I documented signify that a profound social change is occurring. Teenage boys are embracing once-feminized traits of emotional openness and physical intimacy, rejecting the homophobia and violence that once characterized male friendship.

This is directly related to a decline in homophobia, and boys no longer caring if they are socially perceived as gay. This has enabled them to redefine masculinity and friendship for their generation. It is something we should celebrate.

amy schalet

love wanting

Michael, a high school senior, is not a fan of commitment. His ideal is "more than one girl, basically." Proud of his own sexual experience, he's excited that his current girlfriend is a virgin: "It's cool to be the first one. . . . It probably feels better too."

Tall, athletic and a "little rowdy," Michael would appear to epitomize the American teenage male.

Except that he doesn't. In my research on attitudes and experiences of sex and romance among high school–aged White middle-class American and Dutch boys, I found most American boys, like Dutch boys, want more than just sex; they want meaningful intimate relationships.

My findings are echoed in other studies that have surprised researchers. For instance, the *National Campaign to End Teen and Unplanned Pregnancies* found that when asked to choose between having a girlfriend and no sex, or sex but no girlfriend, two-thirds of American boys and young men surveyed choose the girlfriend over sex. A large-scale study published in the *American Sociological Review* in 2006 found that American boys are as likely as girls to be emotionally invested in romantic relationships—but feel less confident navigating them.

Boys in the United States and the Netherlands face very different cultural environments in which to make sense of their romantic feelings. For Dutch boys, falling in love is normal—something everyone experiences while growing up. In the Netherlands, the notion that everyone falls in love is so taken for granted that in a 2005 national survey on youth and sex, researchers thought nothing of asking boys, ages 12 to 14, whether they'd been in love—finding that 90 percent said yes.

But in the United States, even if most boys do want romantic relationships, their romantic stirrings are culturally coded as feminine. Boys are seen as motivated by "raging hormones," not by a desire for intimacy. As one American father puts it, "Teenage boys want to get laid at all times at any cost."

The popular stereotype of boys as acting only from hormones eclipses their desire for emotional intimacy as a normal part of maturation and masculinity. When boys do want or feel love, they think they're alone. Sixteen-year-old Jesse says his first priority in life is being in love with his girlfriend and "giving her everything I can." But he imagines these feelings make him very different from "most teenage boys" who "are pretty much in it for the sex."

To counteract stereotypes about them, American boys sometimes distance themselves not only from other boys but also from their own sexual desires. Patrick, for instance, says, "if you really care about someone, you don't really care if you have sex or not," echoing a theme from

American sex education curricula that teach youth to separate love from lust.

Unlike American culture and sex education, Dutch sex education curricula, with titles like "Long Live Love," encourage boys to view love and lust as intertwined. The Dutch boys I interviewed readily acknowledged being interested in sex, but they also connected physical pleasure closely to emotions and relationships. About the excitement he felt going through puberty, Gert-Jan says: "It also has to do with having feelings for someone. . . . You're really in love."

It's not just in school that cultures diverge, it's also at home. American boys are typically taught to view their sexuality as something symbolizing and threatening their freedom—for instance with an unintended pregnancy. While boys may receive tacit approval to pursue sexual interests away from home, most parents draw firm boundaries between the family and the exploration of sexuality, and rarely permit high school–aged boys to spend the night with their romantic partners at home.

Dutch culture, by contrast, places a premium on *"gezelligheid"* or "cozy togetherness," which validates their enjoyment of platonic and sexual relationships. In the Netherlands, teen boys and girls are typically allowed to have sleepovers in their parents' house. This interweaving of sexuality and domestic life teaches boys that physical pleasure and emotional intimacy—familial and romantic—are not at odds. As 18-year-old Ben says about his girlfriend sleeping over in his room, "if my mother thinks it's *gezellig*, then why not?"

Still, Dutch masculinity does constrain boys in some familiar respects. For instance, national surveys of youth show that Dutch boys face, and engage in, more strictures against same-sex sexual behavior than do Dutch girls. But Dutch boys receive more support at school and home to integrate different aspects of themselves that American boys are often encouraged to separate—love, lust, participation in family life, and sexual exploration.

> Most American boys, like Dutch boys, want more than just sex; they want meaningful intimate relationships.

Much of the debate around teenagers and sexuality in the United States focuses on what we should teach them about their bodies. Access to accurate information about anatomy, pleasure, and contraception—the usual hot-button topics—is critical. But just as important are the conversations about intimacy and emotions, and the question of how we can define and model manhood so those on its cusp might feel more empowered and equipped to love.

freeden oeur

time to bloom

In the United States today, single-sex classrooms and schools are increasingly making their way into public schools. Nationally, about 560 K–12 public schools offer some single-sex academic classrooms, and about 80 more are entirely separated by sex.

Debates over single-sex schooling usually center on questions of gender equity. Supporters claim that they accommodate boys' and girls' different learning styles; critics charge that they perpetuate gender stereotypes. My own ethnographic research shows that in schools that serve predominantly poor young Black men, the relationships boys have with one another, and with adult male staff members are key. A school I call Perry High—one of the schools in an East Coast city where I conducted my research—serves a predominantly poor and Black student population, grades 7 through 12. Led by an administration made up of nearly all Black men, the staff has made it a priority to cultivate more positive notions of manhood among the students.

Perry administrators believe that a school where Black men care for Black boys can be empowering. At Perry High, some of the boys assumed that being "put with other boys," as seventh grader Lenny told me, meant they were in trouble. Mass incarceration of African Americans led these boys to fear all-male institutions—prisons, along with the city's disciplinary schools, where boys who commit major offenses are sent. Administrators and teachers focused on earning the trust of their students, and on strengthening relationships among men and boys.

A common stereotype of young Black men is that they resist authority. But at Perry High, many boys were open to having close relationships with men, especially if the men first opened up to them. The boys believed they needed those relationships in order to thrive in school. Referring to the adults in the building, Dante, a twelfth grader, told me: "We need you. You don't need us." The youngest boys, from 12 to 14 years old, particularly doted on male teachers, shadowing them throughout the building and sticking around after school just to hang out. Groups of young boys were eager to connect with teachers who were willing to teach them a new hobby like playing the guitar, or spoken word poetry.

Mr. Westbrook, an administrator, remarked, "I see a lot of kids, especially the younger kids, who really cling onto certain adults for attention, and you become that surrogate father that so many of them are looking for." Male staff members used this as an opportunity to share visions of responsible adulthood. Gerald, an eighth grader, observed that what it meant to be a man was "to have a job and to be able to do important stuff like taking care of a family."

To instill a sense of responsible adulthood, a new mentoring program matched male adult professionals in the community with ninth graders. The organizers targeted this group because of the high dropout rates among Black boys after ninth grade. At a meeting of mentors and mentees, Raymond spoke eloquently about how the program had impacted him and his peers. Usually when male visitors came to the school, they aggressively relayed the message that the boys should avoid heading down a "dead-end street," he said. But Raymond appreciated that the mentors were not trying to scare the boys. Instead, they helped the boys to create positive visions of themselves: going to college or vocational school, contributing to the community instead of being a threat to it. Speaking directly to the male mentors in the room, he asked for their continued guidance and patience. "We're still learning how to be men and we need your help," he said. "Give us some time to bloom."

The mix of boys, encompassing six grades, meant that younger and older boys had opportunities to interact that they may not have had outside of school. The older boys felt the need to respond to seventh and eighth graders who were aching for male guidance. The younger boys tried to "play off," or imitate, older boys. Just as they did with male teachers, groups of young boys followed boys much older than them around the school. The older students took the younger students under their wing,

> At this unique all-boys public school, rather than forge relationships of fear, older boys and men took responsibility for and invested in the lives of the younger boys.

looking after them as though they were their own siblings.

At this unique all-boys public school, rather than forge relationships of fear, older boys and men took responsibility for and invested in the lives of the younger boys. In this environment, young Black boys are able to envision themselves, in turn, as responsible men who will one day hold steady jobs and care for boys who need them. Should more of these single-sex schools open, we're likely to find that it's for reasons that go beyond that of gender equity, reasons such as the opportunity to foster caring, mentoring relationships.

REVIEW QUESTIONS

1. Identify the American adolescent male stereotypes presented by the authors. Discuss how some teenage boys, and some institutions they belong to, are trying to deconstruct these stereotypes and "redefine masculinity."

2. Pascoe discusses fag discourse in "Homophobia in Boys' Friendships." What are some differing views of teenage boys on using the word *fag*? Do you think any use of the word is actually less harmful to boys than others?

3. Some authors discuss studies that compared adolescent males from different countries. What are some differences found among teenage boys, as well as the discourses on sexuality, in the United States, England, and the Netherlands?

4. Activity: Break into groups and discuss common stereotypes of teenage boys in America. Identify which of these stereotypes can be harmful, as well as some other characteristics of teenage boys that should be both encouraged and celebrated on a greater scale. (Hint: Think about the responses of boys who defied common stereotypes throughout the reading.)

lisa wade

what's so cultural about hookup culture?   **23**

winter 2017

hookup culture is ubiquitous on many U.S. college campuses. lisa wade explores how new students navigate the cultural landscape of hookup culture.

Arman was 7,000 miles from his family, one of the roughly million international students who were enrolled in U.S. colleges last year. Dropped into the raucous first week of freshman year, he discovered a way of life that seemed intensely foreign, frightening, and enticing. "It's been a major shock," he wrote.

The behavior of some of his fellow students unnerved him. He watched them drink to excess, tell explicit sexual stories, flirt on the quad and grind on the dance floor. He received assertive sexual signals from women. It was, Arman wrote, "beyond anything I have experienced back home."

By his second semester, Arman's religious beliefs had been shaken. He was deeply torn as to whether to participate in this new social scene. "Stuck," he wrote, "between a sexually conservative background and a relatively sexually open world." Should he "embrace, accept, and join in?" Or, he wondered, using the past tense like a Freudian slip, "remember who I was and deprive myself of the things I actually and truly want deep down inside?"

He struggled. "Always having to internally fight the desire to do sexual things with girls is not easy," he wrote. One night, he succumbed to temptation. He went to a party, drank, and kissed a girl on the dance floor. When the alcohol wore off, he was appalled at his behavior. "How

much shame I have brought onto myself," he recalled with anguish.

A few months later, he would lose his virginity to a girl he barely knew. His feelings about it were deeply ambivalent. "I felt more free and unbounded," he confessed, "but at the same time, guilt beyond imagination."

For my book *American Hookup: The New Culture of Sex on Campus,* I followed 101 college students through a semester of their first year. They submitted weekly journal entries, writing about sex and dating on campus however they wished. In total, the students wrote over 1,500 single-spaced pages and a million words. I dovetailed their stories with 21 follow-up interviews, quantitative data from the Online College Social Life Survey, academic literature, hundreds of essays written by students for college newspapers, and 24 visits to campuses around the country.

Arman was an outlier. Very few students are strongly motivated to abstain from sex altogether, but it's typical for students to report mixed feelings about the opportunity to have casual sex. Thirty-six of the 101 students I studied reported being simultaneously attracted to and repelled by hookup culture upon arrival at college, compared to 34 who opted out entirely, 23 who opted in with enthusiasm, and 8 who sustained monogamous relationships.

For students like Arman, who are unsure of whether they want to participate, hookup culture has a way of tipping the scales. Its logic makes both abstaining from sex and a preference for sex in committed relationships difficult to justify, and its integration into the workings of higher education makes hooking up hard to avoid.

When students arrive on campus, they don't just encounter the opportunity to hook up, they are also immersed in a culture that endorses and facilitates hookups.

the logic of hookup culture

Hooking up is immanently defensible in hookup culture. Students believe, or believe that their peers believe, that virginity is passé and monogamy prudish; that college is a time to go wild and have fun; that separating sex from emotions is sexually liberating; and that they're too young and career-focused for commitment. All of these ideas are widely circulated on campus—and all make reasonable sense— validating the choice to engage in casual sex while invalidating both monogamous relationships and the choice to have no sex at all.

For the students in my study who were enthusiastic about casual sex, this worked out well, but students who found casual sex unappealing often had difficulty explaining why, both to themselves or others. Many simply concluded that they were overly sensitive or insufficiently brave. "I honestly admire them," wrote one Latina student about her friends who enjoyed casual sex, "because I just cannot do that." A White middle-class student implored herself to not be so "uptight." "Sometimes I wish I could just loosen up," she wrote. A sexually sophisticated pansexual student wondered aloud if she was a "prude." "I'm so embarrassed by that," she confessed. "I feel as if by not voluntarily taking part in it, I am weird and abnormal."

If culture is a "tool kit" offering culturally competent actors a set of ideas and practices with which to explain their choices, to use Ann Swider's metaphor from her article "Culture in Action," then hookup culture offers students many tools useful for embracing casual sex, but few for articulating why they may prefer other kinds of sexual engagement, or none at all. Faced with these options, many students who are ambivalent decide to give it a try.

the new culture of college

In the colonial era, colleges were downright stodgy. Student activities were rigidly controlled, curricula were dry, and harsh punishments were meted out for misbehavior. The fraternity boys of the early 1800s can be credited with introducing the idea that college should be fun. Their lifestyle was then glamorized by the media of the 1920s and democratized by the alcohol industry in the 1980s after *Animal House*. Today, the reputation of higher education as a place for an outlandish good time is second only to its reputation as a place of learning.

Not just any good time, though. A particular kind of party dominates the social scene: drunken, wild, and visually titillating, throbbing with sexual potential. Such parties are built into the rhythm and architecture of higher education. They occur at designated times, such that they don't interfere with (most) classes, and are usually held at large, off-campus houses (often but not always fraternities) or on nearby streets populated by bars and clubs. This gives the institutions plausible deniability, but keeps the partying close enough to be part of colleges' appeal.

Almost all of the students in *American Hookup* were living in residence halls. On weekend nights, dorms buzzed with pre-partying, primping, and planning. Students who stayed in were keenly aware of what they weren't doing. Eventually residence halls would empty out, leaving eerie quiet; revelers returned drunker, louder. Students were sometimes kicked out of their own rooms to facilitate a roommate's hookup. A few had exhibitionistic roommates who didn't bother to kick them out at all.

The morning after, there would be a ritual retelling of the night before. And the morning after that, anticipation for the next weekend of partying began. Being immersed in hookup culture meant being surrounded by anticipation, innuendo, and braggadocio. As one of the African-American men in my study wrote: "Hookup culture is all over the place."

For students who went to parties, hookups felt, as several put it, "inevitable." Sooner or later, a student had one too many drinks, met someone especially cute, or felt like doing something a little wild. For young people still learning how to manage sexual desire, college parties combining sex with sensory overload and mind-altering substances can be overwhelming. Accordingly, anyone who regularly participates in the routine partying built into the rhythm of higher education will likely find themselves opting in to hooking up.

Sex on college campuses is something people do, but it's also a cultural phenomenon: a conversation of a particular kind and a set of routines built into the institution of higher education. When students arrive on campus, they don't just encounter the opportunity to hook up, they are also immersed in a culture that endorses and facilitates hookups. Ceding to or resisting that culture then becomes part of their everyday lives.

"Even if you aren't hooking up," said an African-American woman about her first year on campus, "there is no escaping hookup culture." Residential colleges are what sociologist Erving Goffman called "total institutions," planned entities that collect large numbers of like individuals, cut them off from the wider society, and provide for all their needs. And because hookup culture is totally institutionalized, when students move into a dorm room on a college campus, they become a part of it—whether they like it or not.

Students wish they had more options. Some pine for the going-steady lifestyle of the 1950s. Many mourn the utopia that the sexual revolution promised but never fully delivered. Quite a few would like things to be a lot more queer and gender fluid. Some want a hookup culture that is kinder—warm as well as hot. And there are still a handful who would prefer stodgy to sexy. Satisfying these diverse desires will require a shift to a more complex and rich cultural life on campus, not just a different one.

> Being immersed in hookup culture means being surrounded by anticipation, innuendo, and braggadocio.

REVIEW QUESTIONS

1. How does hookup culture provide a cultural "tool kit" for college students?
2. What does Wade mean when she calls hookup culture a "total institution"? Do you agree or disagree with the assertion that hookup culture is a total institution?
3. What do you think are the implications of hookup culture for gender equality (or inequality) on college campuses?

jessie ford and paula england

hookups, sex, and relationships at college   **24**

winter 2014

using data from an online survey of more than 20,000 students, ford and england look at hookup sex and exclusive relationships and how gender affects students' experiences.

What is going on in today's heterosexual college scene, which features both casual "hookups" and exclusive relationships? How does gender structure students' experiences? We'll give you an overview, using data from the Online College Social Life Survey (OCSLS) led by Paula England. This survey was taken online by more than 20,000 students from 21 four-year colleges and universities between 2005 and 2011. Since we're looking at heterosexual sex and relationships, we limit our analysis to those who said they are heterosexual.

Most students are involved in both exclusive relationships and hooking up at some point during their time in college. As students use the term "hookup," it generally means that there was no formal, prearranged date, but two people met at a party, or in the dorm, and something sexual happened. Hookups can entail anything from just making out to intercourse.

The survey asked students who said they had ever hooked up while at college to provide details about their *most recent* hookup. It provided a list of sexual behaviors; they checked all that applied. We found that 40 percent of hookups involved intercourse, and 35 percent involved no more than making out and some nongenital touching. The rest involved oral sex and/or hand-genital touching. Sometimes students hook up more than once with the same partner; if it was the first time hooking up with this partner, only 29 percent had intercourse. Students are seldom hooking up with strangers; only 13 percent said they didn't know the person at all. Often they knew the person "somewhat." Typically men had five and women four drinks the night of the hookup (these are medians).

By senior year, the typical student has had 7–8 dates and about the same number of hookups, and has been in 1–2 relationships that lasted 6 months (these are means).

who initiates dates, relationships, and sex?

Behavior in both hookups and relationships is structured by gender. For example, many women aim for male-traditional careers, but few ever ask a man on a date. Only 12 percent of students reporting on their most recent date said that the woman had asked the man out. (A large majority of both men and women report that they think it is okay for women to ask men out—it just doesn't happen much.) Relationships are often made "official" or "exclusive" by a talk, and it was twice as common for students to report that the man had initiated this talk as to say that the woman did. (Men and women's reports of who initiated the date or the talk defining the relationship match up quite closely.)

How about initiating sex in hookups? By either men or women's reports, male initiation is more common than female initiation. But the size of the gender difference in initiation is unclear because men and women report things differently. Consider cases where, on the most recent hookup, the two partners both attended the same school (this is typical), and intercourse occurred (as is true for 40 percent of hookups). When men were asked who initiated the sexual activity, 38 percent say they did and 30 percent said the woman did (the rest said both initiated equally). This shows that more men attribute initiation to themselves than to the woman, but not by a large margin. By contrast, only 13 percent of women reported that they initiated, and 56 percent said the man had initiated (the rest said both initiated); women are *much* more likely to attribute initiation to the man than to themselves. We suspect that women are reluctant to initiate or to claim doing so in hookups because of the double standard of sexuality, that is, because women are judged more harshly for engaging in casual sex than men are.

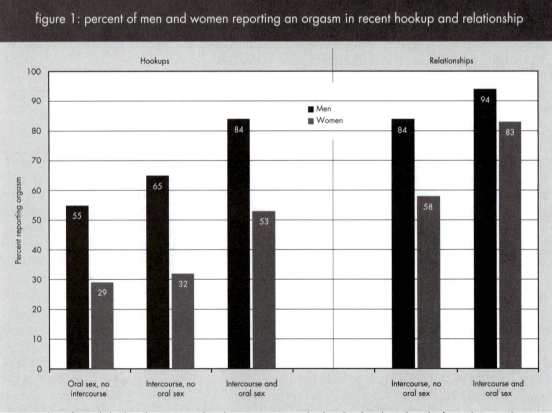

figure 1: percent of men and women reporting an orgasm in recent hookup and relationship

Note: Oral sex refers to whether the student reporting on his or her own orgasm received oral sex. Data limited to students identifying as heterosexual in male/female events.

who has orgasms in hookups and relationships?

When we analyze gender inequality in the workplace, we usually focus on the sex gap in pay. In the casual sex of hookups, we could see sexual pleasure as an analogous outcome measure. One available measure of pleasure is whether the student reported that she or he had an orgasm. Students were asked whether they had an orgasm on their last hookup, and also on the last time in their most recent relationship (of at least six months) when they did something sexual beyond just kissing with their partner. Figure 1 shows the orgasm gap in various types of hookups and in relationships.

We conclude several things from the graph:

1. There is a large gender gap in orgasms in hookups.
2. A gender gap in orgasms also occurs in relationship sex, but it is much smaller than in hookups.
3. Both women and men are more likely to have an orgasm in a relationship (given the same sexual behavior). This suggests that relationship-specific practice, caring for the

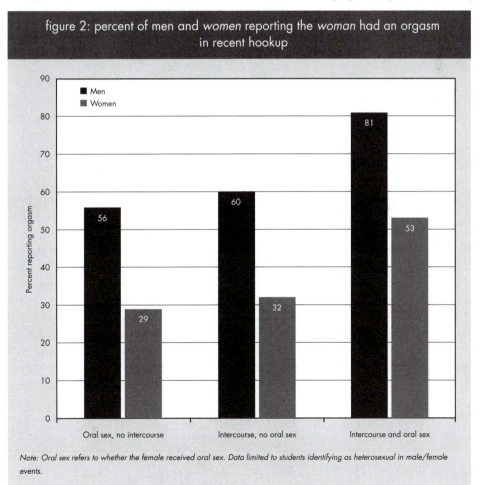

figure 2: percent of men and *women* reporting the *woman* had an orgasm in recent hookup

Note: Oral sex refers to whether the female received oral sex. Data limited to students identifying as heterosexual in male/female events.

partner, or both matter for both men's and women's pleasure.

4. When couples have intercourse, both men and women are more likely to orgasm if they received oral sex, and this is especially true for women.

In addition to being asked about whether they had an orgasm in hookups, students were asked if their partner orgasmed. Figure 2 shows women's reports of their own orgasm (the same numbers we saw in figure 1) compared to men's reports of their female partner's orgasm.

What is striking is how much men appear to overstate their partners' orgasms. This may be because women fake orgasms to make men feel better, and men are misled by this; we learned in qualitative interviews that some women do this, but don't know how prevalent it is. It is also possible that men simply don't know and make an exaggerated assessment. (Although we don't show it here, men's report of women's orgasm is closer to what women say in relationships than in hookups. Also, the percent of men that say they had an orgasm is matched almost exactly by women's report of their partners' orgasm, whether in hookups or relationships.)

If women had an orgasm, they are much more likely to report that they enjoyed the hookup. However, despite the gender inequality in orgasm, women report almost the same degree of overall enjoyment of their hookups as men report.

conclusions and speculations: gender in the college sexual scene

Our description of the college heterosexual relational and hookup scene shows it to be organized by gender in several ways. Men are more likely to initiate dates, sexual behavior, and exclusive relationships. Women may feel uncomfortable initiating or claiming initiation for sex in hookups because of the double standard of sexuality, under which they are judged more harshly than men for casual sex. Hookup sex leads to an orgasm much more often for men than women; this gender gap in orgasm is greater in casual than relational sex. We speculate that men's lack of concern for their partner's orgasm in hookups flows from holding the double standard that gives them permission for casual sex but leads them to look down on their partners for the same behavior.

A question people often ask about the hookup scene is whether it is good or bad for women and for gender equality. Does it represent sexual liberation for women, or intensified exploitation? While there is no simple answer, we suggest the following. First, other research shows that gender equality in careers is enhanced when marriage and childbearing are delayed until later ages. To the extent that hooking up rather than early involvement in relationships delays marriage and childbearing, it contributes to gender equality. Second, an alternative to a series of hookups in college could be a series of a few extended monogamous relationships. Because we find that women orgasm more and report more enjoyment in relationship sex than hookup sex, a change from hookups to relationships would improve gender equality in sexual pleasure. One question is whether this shift could occur without encouraging earlier marriage, which, as mentioned, is bad for gender equality in careers. Third, because we speculate that it is men's belief in the double standard that leads them to fail to prioritize their hookup partners' pleasure because they feel some disrespect for them, it follows that if the double standard could be changed, gender equality in sexual pleasure might be achieved within the hookup context.

RECOMMENDED RESOURCES

Armstrong, Elizabeth, Paula England, and Alison Fogarty. 2012. "Accounting for Women's Orgasm and Sexual Enjoyment in College Hookups and Relationships." *American Sociological Review* 77(3): 435–462.

Bearak, Jonathan Marc. 2014. "Casual Contraception in Casual Sex: Life-Cycle Change in Undergraduates' Sexual Behavior in Hookups." *Social Forces* 93: 483–513.

England, Paula, and Jonathan Marc Bearak. 2014. "The Sexual Double Standard and Gender Differences in Attitudes Toward Casual Sex among U.S. University Students." *Demographic Research* 30:1327–1338.

England, Paula, Emily Fitzgibbons Shafer, and Alison C. K. Fogarty. 2012. "Hooking Up and Forming Romantic Relationships on Today's College Campuses." In *The Gendered Society Reader*, 5th ed., edited by Michael Kimmel and Amy Aronson. New York: Oxford University Press.

REVIEW QUESTIONS

1. What are the broader implications for how society discusses women's pleasure of the information here on the orgasm gap in casual sex?
2. How do you see traditional gender roles exemplified in heterosexual hookup culture?
3. This paper used data collected through the Online College Social Life Survey (OCSLS). What are some benefits and drawbacks of getting students to answer intimate questions on an online questionnaire?

eliza brown and paula england

sexual orientation versus behavior— different for men and women?

25

winter 2016

using data from the national survey of family growth, this article shows how patterns of sexual identity and sexual behavior differ between men and women. according to the data, women, both lesbian and straight, are more flexible with either their identities or behavior than men.

If you know which sexual orientation people identify with, how much does that tell you about whether they have sex with women, men, or both? How similar or different are the links between identity and behavior for women and men? Building on our post from last June, "Women's Sexual Orientation and Sexual Behavior: How Well Do They Match?" we update the analysis of women to include more-recent data and add an analysis of data on men.

We're using data from the 2002, 2006–2010, and 2011–2013 National Survey of Family Growth for men and women 15 to 44 years of age. Detailed tables, along with how we generated our measures, are on pages 180–83. Here we focus on a few specific questions:

how common is it for heterosexual men and women to have sex with same-sex sexual partners?

Unsurprisingly, almost none of the men identifying as heterosexual have had only male sexual partners and only 2 percent say they have had even one male sexual partner (see table 1). For women, like men, almost none of those who identify as heterosexual have had only female partners, but 10 percent say they have had at least one same-sex partner, five times the rate reported by men. (We'll only mention differences

between men and women if they are statistically significant at the .05 level.) In sum, it is more common for heterosexual women than men to have had sex with members of their same sex.

We can get a little closer to assessing how common inconsistency between identity and behavior is by comparing men's and women's current identity with whether they've had same-sex sexual partners *in the last year*. Here we get a much smaller figure—only .4 percent of men and 2 percent of women who called themselves heterosexual on the survey report that they had sex with a same-sex partner in the last year (see table 2). Thus, behavior usually aligns with identity in any short (one-year) time range. But here too the percent of heterosexuals having same-sex partners is larger for women than men. Figure 1 shows the percent of each gender that identify as heterosexual but report having had a same-sex partner ever, and in the last year.

How should we interpret the finding that some men and women who identify as heterosexual have had sex with other-sex partners? It may mean that they had sex that doesn't match their stated sexual orientation at the time, perhaps because of the stigma associated with same-sex partnerships in some quarters. Another possibility is that, although they see themselves as straight now, they identified as gay/lesbian or bisexual at the time they had same-sex partners, so there was no inconsistency between identity and behavior. This is especially plausible regarding with whom one has had sex "ever." If that is the explanation, then women's higher rate may mean that they are more likely than men to change the sexual orientation they identify with. But we are speculating; we would need panel data following the same people over time and repeatedly asking about orientation and recent behavior to distinguish (a) changing sexual orientation where behavior and identity are almost always consistent from (b) inconsistency between current identity and current behavior. It is also possible that the way people see their own orientations don't fit neatly into the three categories provided in the survey in most years, so some respondents choose the best fit of not-well-fitting categories.

how common is it for gay men and lesbians to have sex with other-sex sexual partners?

As figure 2 (drawing from tables 1 and 2) shows, 39 percent (37 percent + 2 percent) of gay men have had a female sexual partner sometime in their lives, whereas a much higher 59 percent (5 percent + 54 percent) of lesbians have had a male sexual partner sometime. The proportion of either gay men or lesbians who have ever had sex with other-sex sexual partners is much larger than the proportion of heterosexual men and women who have had sex with same-sex sexual partners. And it is much larger than the proportion of gays/lesbians who have had sex with an other-sex partner in the last year, 5 percent

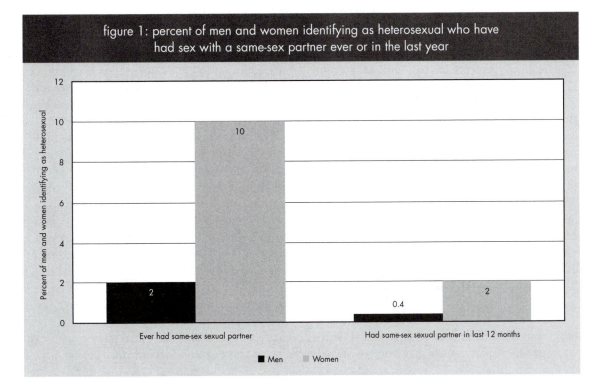

figure 1: percent of men and women identifying as heterosexual who have had sex with a same-sex partner ever or in the last year

Percent of men and women identifying as heterosexual

Ever had same-sex sexual partner — Men: 2, Women: 10

Had same-sex sexual partner in last 12 months — Men: 0.4, Women: 2

■ Men ■ Women

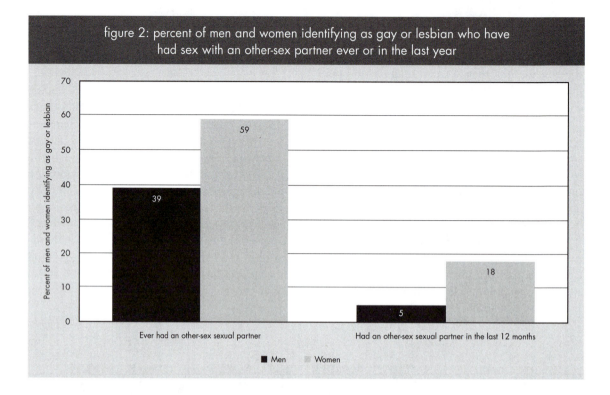

figure 2: percent of men and women identifying as gay or lesbian who have had sex with an other-sex partner ever or in the last year

■ Men   ▨ Women

(3 percent + 2 percent) for men and 18 percent (5 percent + 13 percent) for women.

As for how things differ by gender, it is clear that lesbians are more likely than gay men to have ever had sex with an other-sex sexual partner, whether in the last year (5 percent for men and 18 percent for women) or ever (39 percent for men and 59 percent for women). The larger share of lesbians than gay men who had other-sex partners in the past year comes both from lesbians being more likely than gay men to have partners of both sexes (13 percent of lesbians), as well as being more likely to have had sex with only other-sex partners (5 percent of lesbians).

Why would this be, that lesbians have sex with men more than gay men have sex with women? One explanation is that women's sexual

attractions don't fit the three categories allowed by the survey as well, or that women are more likely than men to change the sexual orientation with which they identify. Either can be seen as more fluidity in women's sexuality than men's, a topic taken up by Lisa Diamond and Leila Rupp and her coauthors. Another possibility is that either evolution or cultural conditioning make guys the initiators in sex. So it is probably a less likely scenario that a young man who thinks that he may be gay is approached by a woman for sex and acquiesces despite not wanting it, compared to an analogous scenario in which a young queer woman has sex with a man she doesn't want. Indeed, both lesbians and gay men are likely to have men as their first sexual partners, according to research conducted by Karin Martin and

Ritch C. Savin-Williams. In some cases these early partners may have raped them, as indicated by research on the prevalence of sexual assault among gay, lesbian, and bisexual individuals by Emily Rothman and her coauthors. We suspect, however, that greater sexual fluidity among women and the frequency of male initiation contribute more to the gender differences in partnership patterns than sexual assault.

how does the behavior of bisexual men and women differ from that of gay and heterosexual men and women?

Given that the commonsense meaning of the term *bisexual* is an interest in having sex and romantic relationships with men and women, we would expect more bisexual than heterosexual or lesbian/gay individuals to have

had sex with both men and women. Indeed, we find that 62 percent of bisexual men and 73 percent of bisexual women have (ever) had sex with both sexes, higher than the analogous figures for gay men and lesbians, and drastically higher than the figures for heterosexual men and heterosexual women.

Who have bisexual men and women had sex with *in the last year*? As figure 3 shows, drawing from table 2, the percent that have had sex with both women and men in the last year is 33 percent for bisexual men, 27 percent for bisexual women; 2 percent for gay men, 13 percent for lesbians; and 0.4 percent for heterosexual men, and 2 percent for heterosexual women. Thus, as we would expect, bisexuals are much more likely than either gays/lesbians or straight men or women to have had sex with both sexes. They are also more likely to have had sex only with other-sex partners in the last year

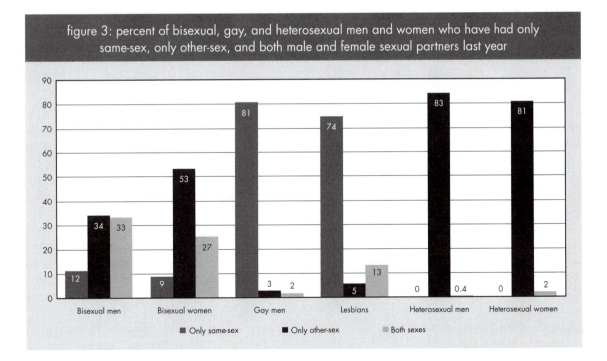

figure 3: percent of bisexual, gay, and heterosexual men and women who have had only same-sex, only other-sex, and both male and female sexual partners last year

than are gay men or lesbians, but are less likely to have done so than are heterosexuals.

All this suggests a tendency for behavior to conform to identity in any short time range, and that bisexual women and men in some respects are a middle point between straights and gays.

What about gender differences between bisexual men and bisexual women? The two groups have a similarly low percent who have ever had sex only with the other sex (14 percent for men and 12 percent for women), but it is much more likely for bisexual women than men to have had sex only with the other sex in the last year—34 percent for men but 53 percent for women (see table 2).

conclusion

We have shown that identity—the sexual orientation one identifies with—is strongly, but by no means perfectly, associated with whether men and women have had sex with women, men, or both. Heterosexual men and women are the most likely to have had sex only with other-sex partners, bisexual men and women are the most likely to have had sex with both women and men, and gay men and lesbians are the most likely to have had sex only with same-sex partners. In this sense, behavior is roughly consistent with sexual orientation. Unsurprisingly, this consistency between current identity and behavior is much stronger when the behavior being asked about is in the last year rather than over the whole lifetime.

However, the patterns differ between men and women. Women, both lesbian and straight, are more flexible with either their identities or behavior than men. Thus, they are more likely than men to have what could be seen as mismatches between identity and behavior. As an example of this, looking at behavior in the last year, heterosexual women are more likely than heterosexual men to have had sex with women,

and lesbians are more likely than gay men to have had sex with an other-sex partner.

As part of women's "flexibility," women are more likely to have partners of both sexes than men are. Taking people of all sexual orientations combined, 14 percent of women, but only 4 percent of men have ever had both male and female sexual partners, as table 1 shows. Similarly, in the past year, 3 percent of all women had both male and female sexual partners, compared with less than 1 percent of men. This is partly because more women than men identify as bisexual, but is also influenced by the higher proportion of women than men among those who identify as either heterosexual or gay having had *both* male and female sexual partners.

technical appendix

Our analysis uses data from the 2002, 2006–2010, and 2011–2013 National Survey of Family Growth (NSFG) on men and women 15 to 44 years of age.

To explore the relationship between sexual orientation and behavior, we began with the measure of sexual orientation in the survey. Men and women were asked whether they "think of themselves as" "heterosexual or straight," "bisexual," or "homosexual, gay, or lesbian." Actually, the wording of these options changed slightly between waves. In 2002 the "gay" option for both men and women was "homosexual," whereas in 2006 and later, it was "homosexual, gay, or lesbian" for women and "homosexual or gay" for men. Also, in some years of the survey (2002 to mid-2008), respondents were also given the option of calling their sexual orientation "something else." Because this response option was not consistent across years of the survey included in analysis, we excluded men and women who selected this response option.

We generated two different measures of sexual behavior from various questions in the survey.

1. **Have you ever had a male/female sexual partner?** For this measure, we relied on two questions. One question asked men and women the number of male (if male) or female (if female) sexual partners they have had during their lifetime, but did not specify what sexual behavior was meant for "sexual partners." Men were asked to answer this question if they reported that they had ever had oral or anal sex with a man, and women were asked to answer the question if they reported that they had ever had a sexual experience with a woman. If men and women said they had had one or more, we considered them to have had a same-sex sexual partner for this measure.

Regarding sex with other-sex sexual partners, men and women were asked how many women (if male) or men (if female) they had

	Sex with only other-sex partners	Sex with only same-sex partners	Sex with both women and men	Sex with neither women nor men	% of sample in identity category
Heterosexual					
Men	83%*	0%*	2%*	14%*	97%*
Women	77%*	.3%*	10%*	12%*	94%*
Gay					
Men	2%	55%*	37%*	6%	2%*
Women	5%	37%*	54%*	5%	1%*
Bisexual					
Men	14%	9%*	62%*	15%*	2%*
Women	12%	5%*	73%*	7%*	5%*
Total					
Men	81%*	1%	4%*	14%*	100%
Women	73%*	.9%	14%*	12%*	100%

table 1: percent of men and women of each sexual orientation who have ever had only other-sex partners, only same-sex partners, both female and male partners, or no sexual partners

Note: Men are asked their number of male sex partners if they report ever having had oral or anal sex with a man, and are asked their number of female sex partners if they have ever had intercourse with a woman. Women are asked their number of female partners if they report they have ever had a sexual experience with a woman, and are asked their number of male sex partners if they have ever had intercourse with a man. N = 14,732 men, weighted. N = 17,140 women, weighted. The asterisks indicate that men's and women's sexual activity are significantly different from one another, at p<0.05, two-tailed test.

ever had vaginal intercourse with; if this number was 1 or more we considered them to have had an other-sex sexual partner during their lifetime. These items were used to create a variable indicating whether each man had had no sexual partners of either sex, sex only with one or more men, sex only with one or more women, or sex with one or more women and one or more men.

2. **Did you have a male/female sexual partner last year?** This is constructed just like (1), but using questions about the number of female and male sexual partners one has had in the last 12 months.

One might worry that respondents would not be honest about same-sex sex or non-heterosexual identities, given the social bias

	Sex with only other-sex partners	Sex with only same-sex partners	Sex with both women and men	Sex with neither women nor men	% of sample in identity category
Heterosexual					
Men	83%*	0%	.4%	17%	97%*
Women	81%*	0%	2%*	17%	94%*
Gay					
Men	3%	81%	2%*	13%	2%*
Women	5%	74%	13%*	8%	1%*
Bisexual					
Men	34%	12%	33%	21%	2%*
Women	53%*	9%	27%	12%*	5%*
Total					
Men	81%*	2%	.9%*	17%	100%
Women	79%*	1%	3%*	16%	100%

table 2: percent of men and women of each sexual orientation who, in the last 12 months, have only other-sex, only same-sex, both female and male, or no sexual partners

Note: Men are asked if they have had male sex partners in the past 12 months if they have ever had oral or anal sex with a man, and are asked if they have had female sex partners in the past 12 months if they have ever had vaginal, oral, or anal intercourse with a woman. Women are asked if they have had female sex partners in the past 12 months if they report they have ever had a sexual experience with a female and are asked if they have had male sex partners in the past 12 months if they have ever had vaginal, oral, or anal sex with a male. N = 14,732 men, weighted. N = 17,140 women, weighted. The asterisks indicate that men's and women's sexual activity are significantly different from one another, at p < 0.05, two-tailed test.

against them. To try to avoid respondents saying what they thought the interviewer wanted to hear rather than the truth, the questions on sexual identity and sex with same-sex partners were asked through an Audio Computer-Assisted Self-Interview (ACASI) system in survey waves prior to 2011. The interviewer handed the respondent a computer and earphones and stepped away to provide privacy while the respondent keyed answers into the computer. This ACASI approach was used for questions on sexual orientation, as well as the questions on number of same-sex partners, and what specific sexual behaviors respondents had done with a man and with a woman. In the survey wave from 2011–2013, these questions were moved to the main male-respondent questionnaire.

One might also be concerned that there seems to have been a higher bar to saying a man than a woman had sex with a same-sex partner, since men were only asked the question of how many same-sex partners they had had if they reported they had ever had oral or anal sex with a man, whereas women were asked the question if they reported they had ever had any sexual experience with a woman. (Only in 2002, when an oral-sex screener question was used, would women have had to have oral sex to be counted as having had a same-sex partner.) However, we have ascertained that over 90 percent of those who report having had a female sexual partner (whether or not they have had any male partners) also report having had oral sex with a woman sometime. This convinces us that most women we are counting as having had female partners are not referring to experiences such as public kissing, but to sexual activity involving genitals.

REVIEW QUESTIONS

1. The authors use the term *sexual fluidity* throughout the article. How would you define sexual fluidity?
2. One of the possible limitations of the article, as discussed by the authors, might be the sexual-identity categories used in the survey. How might changing the categories alter the results?
3. Beyond sexual identity, what other identities do people hold that might align imperfectly with their behavior?

mónica l. caudillo and paula england

women's sexual orientation and sexual behavior: how well do they match?

summer 2015

if you know which sexual orientation a woman identifies with, how much does that tell you about whether she has sex with men, women, or both? both behavior and sexual orientation can change over time.

If you know which sexual orientation a woman identifies with, how much does that tell you about whether she has sex with men, women, or both? Here we answer this question for American women, using data from the 2006–2008 National Survey of Family Growth for women 15 to 44 years of age.

Detailed tables, along with how we generated our measures, are in the Technical Appendix on pages 189–90. Here we zero in on a few specific questions of interest:

how common is it for heterosexual women to have sex with women?

If we operationalize having had sex with a woman as having had oral sex with a woman, the answer is that 6 percent have ever done so. All of these have had sex with men as well (see table 1).

A second approach uses the question asking people how many male sexual partners they have had intercourse with, and how many female sexual partners they have had. One disadvantage of this approach is that we don't know what individual respondents think "counts" as having had sex with another woman. Nonetheless, on the question of how many heterosexual women have had sex with women, this strategy gives us a similar answer: Almost none of the women identifying as heterosexual have had *only* female partners (0.3 percent), and 9 percent say they have had at least one female sexual partner (see table 2).

The fact that 6–9 percent (depending on the measure) of women who identify as heterosexual have had sex with a woman doesn't necessarily mean that women's identity and behavior are inconsistent at any single point of time. It is possible these women identified as lesbian or bisexual at the time they had sex with women. Or it is possible that women engage in behavior inconsistent with their orientation. We would need panel data following the same people over time and repeatedly asking about orientation and recent behavior to distinguish (a) changing sexual orientation where behavior and identity are always consistent from (b) inconsistency between current identity and current behavior.

In the NSFG data, we can get a little closer to assessing how common inconsistency between identity and behavior is by comparing women's current identity with whether they've had men and women as sexual partners *in the last year*. Here we get a much smaller figure—only

2 percent of women who called themselves heterosexual on the survey have had sex with a woman in the last year (see table 3). This suggests that, at least for women who identify as heterosexual, behavior usually aligns fairly well with identity in any short (one-year) time range.

These results for heterosexual women—how many have ever or in the last year had sex with a woman—are shown in figure 1.

how common is it for lesbians to have sex with men?

As figure 2 (drawing from tables 1 and 2) shows, depending on the measure used, between two-thirds and four-fifths of lesbians have had sex with a man sometime in their lives. Eighty-one percent report having had either oral sex, vaginal intercourse, or anal sex with a man, while 67 percent report having had a male intercourse partner sometime in their life. By either measure, the proportion of lesbians who have ever had sex with a man is drastically larger that the proportion of heterosexual women who have ever had sex with a woman.

However, if, we restrict our focus to the year before the survey, we get a very different picture.

Only 22 percent of women who identify as lesbian have had sex with a man last year. If these are all women whose behavior is inconsistent with their identity, then it seems a sizable share—over a fifth; it is very different than the less than 2 percent of heterosexual women who had sex with a woman in the last year. However, it is also possible that some sizable share of the 22 percent may be cases where women changed their identity and behavior in the last year, but identity was consistent with behavior at all times. The data don't allow us to tell which it is.

how does the behavior of bisexual women differ from that of lesbians and heterosexual women?

Given that the commonsense meaning of the term *bisexual* is an interest in having sex and romantic relationships with either men or women, we would expect more bisexual than heterosexual or lesbian women to have had sex with both men and women. Indeed, depending on whether we use the measure in table 1 or 2, we find that 68–75 percent of bisexual women have had sex with men and women, higher

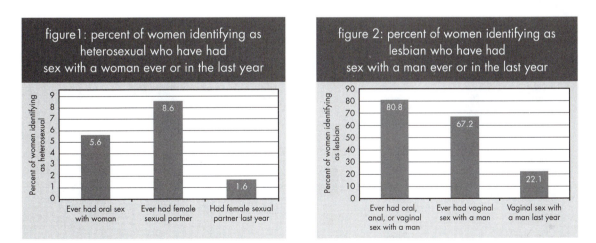

figure1: percent of women identifying as heterosexual who have had sex with a woman ever or in the last year

figure 2: percent of women identifying as lesbian who have had sex with a man ever or in the last year

than the analogous figures for lesbians of 67 percent and 55 percent, and drastically higher than the proportion of heterosexual women of 6–8 percent. In this regard, bisexual women look more like lesbians than like heterosexual women.

Also of interest is how many women in each group have only had sex with men, or only with women. The percent who have had sex only with men is 78–84 percent for heterosexuals, 12–14 percent for lesbians and 14–24 percent for bisexuals (see tables 1 and 2); in this regard also, bisexual women are more similar to lesbians than heterosexuals.

What about who has had sex only with women? Less than 1 percent of the heterosexual women reported having had sex with only women, compared to 16–31 percent for lesbians and 2–5 percent for bisexuals; in this regard

bisexual women are more similar to heterosexuals than to lesbians—almost none have had sex only with women. (See tables 1 and 2.)

Who have bisexual women had sex with in the last year? As figure 3 shows, drawing from table 3, the percent that have had sex with both men and women in the last year is 23 percent for bisexual women, almost 10 percent for lesbians, and only .2 percent for heterosexuals. Bisexuals are much more likely than lesbians to have had sex only with men in the last year—almost 57 percent compared to 12 percent for lesbians. But, not surprisingly, this figure is highest for heterosexuals—78 percent. The flip side of this is that bisexuals are much less likely than lesbians to have had only women partners in the previous year—almost 10 percent for bisexuals compared to 75 percent of lesbians (and less than 1 percent of heterosexuals).

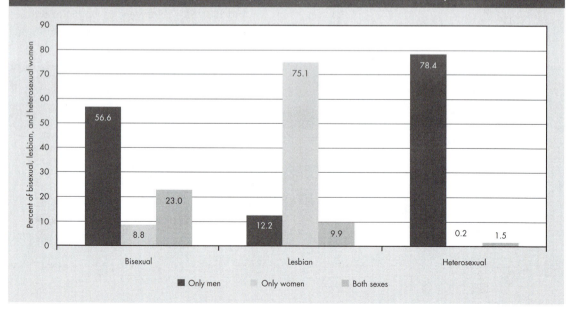

figure 3: percent of bisexual, lesbian, and heterosexual women who have had sex with only men, only women, and both sexes in the last year

table 1: percent of women of each sexual orientation who have ever had sexual contact with men, women, both, or neither							
	Sex only with men	Sex only with women	Sex with men and women	Sex with neither men nor women	Did not report	Total	% of sample in identity category
Heterosexual	83.8%	0.1%	5.6%	10.4%	0.2%	100.0%	92.2%
Lesbian	14.3%	15.9%	66.5%	3.3%	0.0%	100.0%	1.2%
Bisexual	24.3%	2.0%	67.5%	6.2%	0.0%	100.0%	4.0%
Something else	39.0%	0.0%	46.7%	14.3%	0.0%	100.0%	0.9%
Did not report	39.9%	0.0%	2.9%	8.1%	49.2%	100.0%	1.9%
Total	79.4%	0.3%	9.0%	10.2%	1.1%	100.0%	100.0%

Note: Women are considered to have had sex with a woman if they report ever having had oral sex with a woman. They are considered to have had sex with a man if they report ever having had oral sex or vaginal or anal intercourse with a man. N = 5,851.

table 2: percent of women of each sexual orientation who have ever had only male, only female, both male and female, or neither male nor female partners							
	Sex only with men	Sex only with women	Sex with men and women	Sex with neither men nor women	Did not report	Total	% of sample in identity category
Heterosexual	78.3%	0.3%	8.2%	12.9%	0.3%	100.0%	92.2%
Lesbian	12.2%	30.8%	54.9%	2.1%	0.0%	100.0%	1.2%
Bisexual	14.2%	4.8%	75.0%	5.3%	0.7%	100.0%	4.0%
Something else	32.5%	3.8%	49.9%	13.1%	0.7%	100.0%	0.9%
Did not report	39.6%	0.0%	2.9%	8.4%	49.2%	100.0%	1.9%
Total	73.9%	0.9%	11.7%	12.4%	1.2%	100.0%	100.0%

Note: Women are considered to have had sex with a woman if they report ever having had a female sexual partner (regardless of what behavior they report they have done with a woman). They are considered to have had sex with a man if they report ever having had vaginal intercourse with a man. N = 5,851.

	Sex only with men	Sex only with women	Sex with men and women	Sex with neither men nor women	Did not report	Total	% of sample in identity category
table 3: percent of women of each sexual orientation who, in the last 12 months, have only male, only female, both male and female, or neither male nor female partners							
Heterosexual	78.4%	0.2%	1.5%	19.8%	0.2%	100.0%	92.2%
Lesbian	12.2%	75.1%	9.9%	2.8%	0.0%	100.0%	1.2%
Bisexual	56.6%	8.8%	23.0%	11.5%	0.1%	100.0%	4.0%
Something else	53.2%	0.3%	21.8%	24.4%	0.3%	100.0%	0.9%
Did not report	32.7%	0.2%	2.7%	15.3%	49.2%	100.0%	1.9%
Total	75.7%	1.4%	2.6%	19.2%	1.1%	100.0%	100.0%

Note: Women are considered to have had sex with a woman if they report having had a female sexual partner in the last year. They are considered to have had sex with a man if they report having had vaginal intercourse with a man in the last year. N = 5,851.

We have shown that identity—the sexual orientation one identifies with—is strongly, but by no means perfectly, correlated with whether women have had sex with men, women, or both. Heterosexual women are the most likely to have had sex only with men, bisexual women are the most likely to have had sex with men and women, especially if we look only at the last year, and lesbians are the most likely to have had sex only with women, especially when we limit the scope to the last year.

If we make the assumption—undoubtedly unwarranted for some—that the women surveyed have had the sexual orientation they report all their lives, then there is substantial evidence of behavior inconsistent with identity. For example, a strong majority of lesbians have had sex with a man, 24 percent of bisexuals have had sex with a man but never had oral sex with a woman, and 9 percent of heterosexual women say they have had a female sexual partner. If sexual orientation doesn't change over the life course, all of these are evidence of inconsistency, with heterosexuals being the least likely to show inconsistency.

However, both behavior and sexual orientation can change over time, and if they do, then the patterns just discussed don't necessarily indicate inconsistency between orientation and behavior. Consider the hypothetical example of a woman who grew up assuming she was heterosexual—since virtually all the songs, stories, and movies suggested this was normal. Following custom, she dated and had sex with men, but later noticed she was attracted to women, which led to sex with women, and eventually to a stable lesbian identity. The data we've shown here, wherein most lesbians have had sex with men sometime, but the vast majority (about 80 percent) did not have sex with a man in the last year, would be consistent with this hypothetical woman's sequence, which would have entailed inconsistency only around the time of change. But the data are also consistent with some amount of recurrent mismatch between identity and behavior.

To distinguish mismatch between behavior and identity from changes in either sexual orientation or behavior, we need panel data that survey the same group of people repeatedly over time asking about both behavior and orientation near the time of the survey. Unfortunately, none of our national probability-sample panel data sets ask extensive questions about sexuality, and none of the studies, like the NSFG, that ask extensive questions on nonheterosexual behavior and identities also survey the same respondents repeatedly over time. We know of only one panel study, by Lisa Diamond (2008, 2009), following women for ten years and examining their change in identities and sexual behavior. Unfortunately, it did not include women who self-defined as heterosexual at the outset, and it is a relatively small sample (no more than 100).

technical appendix

Our analysis uses data from the 2006–2008 National Survey of Family Growth on women 15 to 44 years of age.

To explore the relationship between sexual orientation and behavior, we began with the measure of sexual orientation in the survey. Women were asked whether they "think of themselves as" "heterosexual or straight" (which we'll call "heterosexual" here), "bisexual," or "homosexual or lesbian" (which we'll call "lesbian" here). In some of the years of the survey that asked the following sexual-behavior questions, respondents were also given the option

to call their sexual orientation "something else." This option was only given in 2006–2008, then dropped because so few respondents chose it. Since the small proportion of women choosing "something else" might be different with respect to the link between their behavior and identity, we chose to use only the years where the option was given, and to put these women in a separate sexual orientation category so that the sexual-orientation categories available would be comparable for all these years.

We generated three different measures of sexual behavior from various questions in the survey.

1. **Have you ever done specific sexual behaviors with a man/woman?** For this measure, used in table 1, having ever had sex with a woman is defined as reporting that you have ever had oral sex with one or more women, and having ever had sex with a man is defined as reporting that you have had vaginal, anal, or oral sex with one or more males. Then we combined this information to create a variable indicating whether women had had neither oral sex with a woman nor oral, vaginal, or anal sex with a man; oral sex with a woman but none of the three types of sex with a man; one of the three types of sex with a man but never oral sex with a woman; or oral sex with a woman as well as one of the three types of sex with a man.

2. **Have you ever had a male/female sexual partner?** For this measure, we relied on two questions. One question asked women the number of female sexual partners they have had during their lifetime, but did not specify what sexual behavior was meant for "sexual partners." If women said they had had one or more, we considered them to have had a female partner for this measure. Regarding sex with men, women were asked

how many men they had ever had vaginal intercourse with; if this number was 1 or more we considered them to have had a male partner during their lifetime. These items were used to create a variable indicating whether each woman had had no sexual partners of either sex, sex only with one or more women, sex only with one or more men, or sex with one or more men and one or more women.

3. **Did you have a male/female sexual partner last year?** This is constructed just like (2), but using questions about the number of male and female sexual partners one has had in the last 12 months.

One might worry that respondents would not be honest about same-sex sex or nonheterosexual identities, given the social bias against them. To try to avoid respondents saying what they thought the interviewer wanted to hear rather than the truth, the questions on sexual identity and sex with same-sex partners were asked through an Audio Computer-Assisted Self-Interview (ACASI) system. The interviewer handed the respondent a computer and earphones and stepped away to provide privacy while the respondent keyed answers into the computer. This ACASI approach was used for questions on sexual orientation, as well as the questions on number of same-sex partners, and what specific sexual behaviors respondents had done with a man and with a woman. However, the question about number of male vaginal-intercourse partners women have had was taken from the main questionnaire, not the ACASI part.

RECOMMENDED RESOURCES

Lisa M. Diamond. 2008. "Female Bisexuality from Adolescence to Adulthood: Results from a 10-Year Longitudinal Study." *Developmental Psychology* 44(1): 5.

Lisa M. Diamond. 2009. *Sexual Fluidity.* John Wiley & Sons, Ltd. http://onlinelibrary.wiley.com/. doi: 10 .1002/9781118896877.wbiehs452/abstract.

REVIEW QUESTIONS

1. The authors make a distinction between sexual identity and sexual behavior. Provide a short definition for each.
2. Consider the following quote: "If we make the assumption—undoubtedly unwarranted for some—that the women surveyed have had the sexual orientation they report all their lives, then there is substantial evidence of behavior inconsistent with identity." What does it mean for behavior to be inconsistent with identity? Does your understanding of the terms *lesbian* and *heterosexual* allow for lesbians to have sex with men or heterosexual women to have sex with women?
3. What methodological suggestion does the author provide to obtain data that allow for a better understanding of women's sexual identity and sexual behavior?

amin ghaziani

lesbian geographies

winter 2015

just like gay men, lesbian women also have their own areas, cities, and neighborhoods that they are more likely to habitate. the process of, and reasons for, the establishment of lesbian communities are described.

When we think about gay neighborhoods, many of us are not immediately imagining lesbians. But like gay men, lesbians also have certain cities, neighborhoods, and small towns in which they are more likely to live. Back in 1992, for example, the *National Enquirer* cheekily declared the small town of Northampton, Massachusetts, "Lesbianville, USA." *Newsweek* piggybacked on the reference a year later and sealed the area's Sapphic reputation: "If you're looking for lesbians, they're everywhere," said Diane Morgan, who used to codirect an annual summer festival that drew thousands of women. "After living here for a couple years, you begin to forget what it's like in the real world." The bucolic town—"where the coffee is strong and so are the women"—had a lesbian mayor, Mary Clare Higgins, who held a near-record tenure of political office—six consecutive two-year terms.

If Northampton is the Lesbianville of the Northeast, then Portland, Oregon, and Oakland, California, are the lady-loving capitals of the West, while Atlanta, Georgia, and St. Petersburg, Florida, remain hot in the Southern imagination. And let us not forget about Park Slope in Brooklyn: "Being a dyke and living in the Slope is like being a gay man and living in the Village," one resident remarked to geographer Tamar Rothenberg. In recent years, New York City has also seen an influx of lesbians in Kensington, Red Hook, and Harlem.

There is an astonishing diversity of queer spaces for men and women alike, as Census data on zip codes show us (see table 1).

Sometimes lesbians live in the same areas as gay men, like Provincetown, Massachusetts; Rehoboth Beach, Delaware; and the Castro in San Francisco, California. But lesbian geographies are also quite distinct. Coupled women tend to live in less urban areas, while men opt for bigger cities (regrettably, the Census only asks about same-sex partner households, and so we cannot track single gays and lesbians). We do not have a good grasp on why this happens, but cultural cues regarding masculinity and femininity play a part. One rural, gay midwesterner confided to sociologist Emily Kazyak: "If you're a flaming gay queen, they're like, 'Oh, you're a freak. I'm scared of you.' But if you're a really butch woman and you're working at a factory, I think it's a little easier." Lesbians who perform masculinity in rural environments (by working hard labor or acting tough, for example) are not as stigmatized as effeminate gay men. This makes rural contexts safer and more inviting for women.

Concerns about family formation and child-rearing come into play as well. According to an analysis by the Williams Institute, a think tank

table 1: highest concentrations of gay and lesbian households								
Same-sex male couples				Same-sex female couples			
Zip code	Location	% of all house- holds	Median price per sq. foot	Zip code	Location	% of all house- holds	median price per sq. foot
94114	Castro, San Francisco, CA	14.2%	671	02657	Provincetown, Cape Cod, MA	5.1%	532
92264	Palm Springs, CA	12.4%	146	01062	Northampton, MA	3.3%	187
02657	Provincetown, Cape Cod, MA	11.5%	532	01060	Northampton, MA	2.6%	189
92262	Palm Springs, CA	11.3%	136	02130	Jamaica Plain, Boston, MA	2.4%	304
33305	Wilton Manors, Fort Lauderdale, FL	10.6%	206	19971	Rehoboth Beach, DE	2.4%	187
90069	West Hollywood, Los Angeles, CA	8.9%	481	95446	Guerneville, north of San Francisco, CA	2.2%	197
94131	Noe Valley/Glen Park/Diamond Heights, San Francisco, CA	7.4%	564	02667	Wellfleet, Cape Cop, MA	2.2%	340
75219	Oak Lawn, Dallas, TX	7.1%	160	94619	Redwood Heights/ Skyline, Oakland, CA	2.1%	230
19971	Rehoboth Beach, DE	7.0%	187	30002	Avondale Estates, Suburban Atlanta, GA	1.9%	97
48069	Pleasant Ridge, suburban Detroit, MI	6.8%	107	94114	Castro, San Francisco, CA	1.9%	671

Source: 2010 U.S. Census, analyzed by Jed Kolko, Trulla Trends.

at UCLA, more than 111,000 same-sex couples are raising 170,000 biological, step, or adopted children. There are some striking gender differences within this group. For instance, among those individuals who are younger than 50 and living alone or with a partner, nearly half of LGBT women (48 percent) and a fifth of LGBT men (20 percent) are raising a child under the age of 18. Among couple households, specifically, 27 percent of female and 11 percent of male couples are raising children. Finally, among lesbian, gay, and bisexual adults who report ever having given birth to or fathered a child, 80 percent are female. All these numbers tell us the same thing: lesbians are more likely than gay men to have and raise children.

Higher rates of parenting by lesbians create different housing needs for them. Traditional gay neighborhoods are more likely to offer single-occupancy apartments at relatively high rents, but lesbian households with children seek the reverse: lower-rent, more family-oriented units. This steers women either to different neighborhoods in the same city (Andersonville or Rogers Park rather than Boystown in Chicago, for example, or Oakland instead of the Castro in San Francisco), or to nonurban areas, as we can see in table 1 and the graphics on page 194.

Back in the city, lesbians exert a surprising influence on cycles of gentrification. The idea that gay people initiate renewal efforts is widely known but imprecise. Lesbians actually predate the arrival of gay men in developing areas. A 2010 *New York Observer* article put it this way: "[L]esbians are handy urban pioneers, dragging organic groceries and prenatal yoga to the 'frontier' neighborhoods they make hospitable for the rest of us. In three to five years." Lesbians move in first—they are "canaries in the urban coal mine"—and try to create a space for themselves. Gay men arrive next as they are priced out of previous enclaves. According to a 2013 Trulia report, "Neighborhoods where same-sex male couples account for more than 1 percent of all households (that's three times the national average) had price increases, on average, of 13.8 percent. In neighborhoods where same-sex female couples account for more than 1 percent of all households, prices increased by 16.5 percent—more than one-and-a-half times the national increase." As a point of comparison, the overall national increase for urban and suburban neighborhoods was 10.5 percent. Basically, the gayer the block, the faster its values will rise. Lesbian neighborhoods experience greater increases probably because they are in earlier stages of gentrification, further from a ceiling where prices eventually plateau, and because they had lower values from the start.

Gay men follow the trailblazing lesbians (awareness of where the women are circulates by word of mouth). As the numbers of men increase, the identity of the area gradually shifts from a lesbian enclave to a "gayborhood." During this transition, the composition of the district where the men previously lived becomes demographically straighter. Meanwhile, the texture of the new area becomes gayer and increasingly dominated by men. Many lesbians feel priced out at this point, and they migrate elsewhere, initiating another round of renewal.

Subcultural differences also help explain why it is harder to find lesbian lands. Gay men are more influenced by sexual transactions and building commercial institutions like bars, big night clubs, saunas, and trendy restaurants, while gay women are motivated by feminism and countercultures. This is why lesbian neighborhoods often consist of a cluster of homes near progressive, though not as flashy, organizations and businesses that were already based in the area—think artsy theaters and

Basically, the gayer the block, the faster its values will rise.

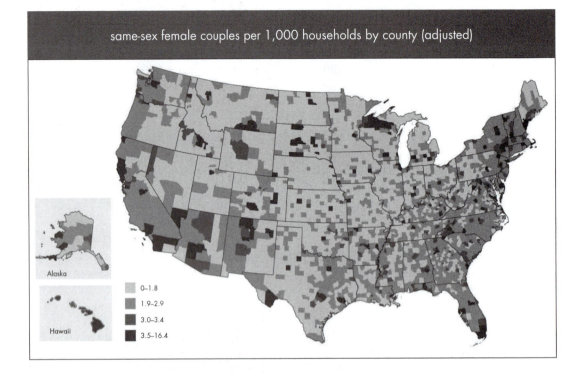

same-sex female couples per 1,000 households by county (adjusted)

Alaska

Hawaii

0–1.8
1.9–2.9
3.0–3.4
3.5–16.4

same-sex male couples per 1,000 households by county (adjusted)

Alaska

Hawaii

0
0.1–2.7
2.8–3.7
3.8–24.8

Source: 2010 U.S. Census, analyzed by Gary J. Gates and Abigail M. Cooke, The Williams Institute.

performance spaces, alternative or secondhand bookstores, cafes, community centers, bike shops, and organic or cooperative grocery stores. This gives lesbian districts a quasi-underground character, making them seem hidden for those who are not in the know.

But this begs us to ask another question: Why, after gay men arrive, do some lesbians leave? One reason pertains to women's relative lack of economic power. Real estate values and rents continue to increase as more gay men arrive. Although the gender wage gap (women's earnings as a percentage of men's) has narrowed, according to the U.S. Labor Department's Bureau of Labor Statistics, women still earn, on average, less than men—81 percent of what men earned in 2012. This persistent economic inequality explains why lesbian households are located in lower-income areas, and unfortunately, such material threats are always encroaching on them.

Finally, some lesbians move out because they perceive the area as unwelcoming after the male invasion. Gay men are still men, after all, and they are not exempt from the sexism that saturates our society. In reflecting on her experiences in the gay village of Manchester, England, one lesbian described gay men as "quite intimidating. They're not very welcoming towards women." Similarly, a lesbian from Chicago told me: "Boystown is a gay neighborhood. It's *boys'* town—it's all guys. Boystown is super, super male. Andersonville is definitely more lesbian. . . . It's very female-oriented. It's lesbian." Indeed, some women refer to Andersonville as "Girlstown," "the lesbian ghetto," or "Dykeville." Although gay men and straight newcomers often arrive at about the same time, some lesbians feel especially resentful toward the former. Another woman from Chicago vented, "The straight couples are guests in our community. The gay men are coming to pillage. Imperialism is coming up from Boystown."

What does all of this mean? Jim Owles of the New York Gay Activist Alliance said in 1971 that "one of society's favorite myths about gay people is that we are all alike." More than 40 years have passed, but the myth is still hard to shake. Our ideas about a gay neighborhood rely on a fairly unimaginative and singular understanding of queer life and culture, making it much harder for us to see and appreciate unique lesbian geographies.

REVIEW QUESTIONS

1. Ghaziani writes that lesbians are more likely to inhabit rural areas than urban areas. What are the reasons for this?
2. Explain the often inevitable transition of a lesbian community into a "gayborhood." What are the economic, financial, and interpersonal causes of this transition?
3. Jim Owles of the New York Gay Activist Alliance was quoted describing a common "myth" that all gay people are alike. Citing descriptions of gay men and lesbian women in this article, how can this myth be debunked?

d'lane compton and tristan bridges

#callmecaitlyn and contemporary trans* visibility

28

winter 2016

in 2015 the olympic gold medalist bruce jenner came out as a transgender woman, caitlyn jenner. compton and bridges explore what her celebrity status means for awareness of trans rights and the roles of celebrities in social justice.

It seems the media are discussing transgender people more than ever. This has the potential to promote social justice using celebrity faces as potent symbols for gender diversity, transgender rights, and more. They bring awareness and help expand the public's vocabulary regarding greater gender possibilities.

Although this is good news overall, public attention and support must extend and translate into legislation and rights. Paradoxically, trans* celebrities may be bringing attention to trans* issues *and* obscuring diversity within trans* communities. Simply put, not all transgender people are being celebrated. (We use trans* to denote the diversity of trans identities.)

In May 2014, *Time* put a transgender individual, Laverne Cox, on its cover. Just under a year later, Caitlyn Jenner came out as a transwoman, featured on the June 2015 cover of *Vanity Fair* alongside a story titled "Call Me Caitlyn." Quickly, the hashtag #CallMeCaitlyn took social media by storm, and Caitlyn Jenner broke the record for fastest accumulation of 1 million Twitter followers (four hours, beating out President Barack Obama's @POTUS record).

Jenner's case is interesting precisely because of her achievements and notoriety as Bruce.

As Bruce, she was a successful Olympic decathlete, a status cast as the pinnacle of human athleticism and masculinity. In fact, when Jenner won gold in 1976, there was no women's decathlon event. Now featured on the cover of *Vanity Fair*, Caitlyn has arguably been held up as a gold standard of femininity. One person has reached some of the greatest heights of gendered status as both a man and woman.

Jenner is also a cross-generation celebrity—known to previous age cohorts as a sports hero, and now popular as a member of one of the most visible and followed contemporary celebrity families in the United States. Jenner's celebrity invites gossip, but it might also prove a powerful way to start a discussion regarding gender and social justice issues related to gender, bodies, and civil liberties.

Through Jenner's transition, the American public is becoming familiar with transgender people, problems, and politics. For example, in her reality show, *I Am Cait,* she not only shares her experience but also gives attention to the experiences and knowledge of others, including transgender youth and longtime activists like Kate Bornstein and Jennifer Finney Boylan.

Yet existing research primarily paints a bleak picture of the experiences and lives of transgender people. Transgender youth suffer from depression at rates much higher than the general population, and they are at a much higher risk of suicide, homelessness, and homicide. The National Transgender Discrimination Survey found that about 1 in 4 trans* people have lost a job due to bias and discrimination, 1 in 2 experience harassment at work, and 1 in 5 were evicted from or denied housing as a result of their gender identity. Those transgender people who are least likely to experience the most damaging consequences are those best able to approximate heteronormative, cisgender ideals. This often means demonstrating feminine and masculine beauty and body standards associated with being "cis," or having a gender identity that is consistent with the one assigned to them at birth. The cultural standards the transgender people we most readily encounter in the media are less easily achieved—and not necessarily desired—by everyone identifying as trans*gender.

Moreover, while #CallMeCaitlyn was trending, #Occupotty and #TransLivesMatter received much less attention. #Occupotty began in reaction to proposed "bathroom bills" seeking to legally mandate that individuals use the public restroom facility associated with their assigned sex at birth. Bathroom bills are most often proposed and justified by playing on inaccurate stereotypes of transgender people as sexually deviant and potentially violent. Indeed, they are generally proposed as safety measures, though transgender women and men are much more likely to be the *victims* than the perpetrators of harassment and assault. The fears these bills play on are manufactured, but powerful. Fear of deviant men invading girls' bathrooms, for instance, led a Houston gay rights ordinance to fail—by a wide margin—in a public referendum last fall.

The public celebration and recognition of transgender people is a start, but it has not yet been matched by achievements in gender equality and diversity. There are limits to what celebration can do. Now we must work toward the legal and institutional changes required to turn ideals into policy.

REVIEW QUESTIONS

1. Why does the author use the term *trans** instead of *trans*?
2. What does the author identify as unique to Caitlyn Jenner's status as a trans* celebrity?
3. What do you believe should be the role of celebrities in standing up for social justice? Do you believe it's effective for raising awareness?

kristen schilt and laurel westbrook

bathroom battlegrounds and penis panics

29

summer 2015

transgender and gender-variant people face large-scale discrimination in areas such as employment, housing, and education. yet, while city and state policies to address such discrimination are rapidly expanding, each new transgender-supportive law or policy typically results in an outbreak of protest.

In January 2008, the city commission in Gainesville, Florida, passed an ordinance prohibiting discrimination on the basis of "gender identity and gender expression" in employment and public accommodations (such as public restrooms and locker rooms). Advocates argued that the legislation was a key step toward addressing discrimination against transgender and gender-variant people. However, 14 months later voters were considering a ballot initiative to overturn the law.

Even though there had been no reported problems, those that were pushing for the repeal of the new ordinance suggested that such protections had unanticipated, dangerous consequences for women and children. Citizens for Good Public Policy ran a TV ad that featured a young, White girl on a playground. She jumps off a merry-go-round, and, alone, enters a doorway clearly marked "Women's Restroom." A moment later, a White man with a scraggly beard, dark sunglasses, and baseball cap slung low on his forehead approaches the door, looks around furtively, and enters. As the door swings shut, the ad cuts to black and the message appears: "Your City Commission made this legal. Is this what you want for Gainesville?"

The question at the heart of the ballot initiative—the place of transgender people in society—has never been a more visible issue than it is today. Advocates for transgender rights have effectively demonstrated that transgender and gender-variant people face large-scale discrimination in areas such as employment, housing, and education. Yet, while city and state policies to address such discrimination are rapidly expanding, each new transgender-supportive law or policy typically results in an outbreak of protest.

As sociologists of gender, we were interested in accounting for the opposition to transgender rights in the face of greater societal acceptance of transgender people, as it presents a puzzling aspect of gender: Why are transgender people accepted in some spaces and not others? We did a content analysis of media articles about transgender-inclusive legislation from 2006 to 2010 and discovered that the Gainesville ad was not an anomaly. Opponents of transgender-recognition often brought up the specter of sexual predators in sex-segregated spaces as an argument against the passage of transgender-rights legislation. Interestingly, such fears centered exclusively on women's spaces, particularly restrooms.

What do sexual predators have to do with transgender rights? Moreover, why is the concern only about women's spaces? In our research, we find that opponents are making an argument against any bodies perceived as male having a legal right to enter a woman-only space because they imagine such bodies to present a sexual danger to women and children. Under this logic, they often conflate "sexual predators" (imagined to be deviant men) and transgender women (imagined to be always male). This exclusive focus on "males" suggests that it is genitals—not gender identity and expression—that are driving what we term "gender panics"—moments where people react to a challenge to the gender binary by frantically asserting its naturalness. Because most people are assumed by others to be heterosexual, sex-segregated bathrooms are imagined by many people to be "sexuality-free" zones. Opponents' focus on bathrooms centers on fears of sexual impropriety that could be introduced by allowing the "wrong bodies"—or, to be more precise, penises—into spaces deemed as "for women only." Gender panics, thus, could easily be relabeled "penis panics." The shift from gender panics to penis panics as a point of analysis accounts for critics' sole focus on the women's restroom—a location that, opponents argue, should be "penis-free."

While such arguments are not always politically effective—Gainesville, for instance, did not repeal its ordinance—they reinforce gender inequality in a number of ways. Opponents disseminate ideas that women are weak and in need of protection— what one of us (Laurel Westbrook) frames as creating a "vulnerable subjecthood"—and that men are inherent rapists. At the same time, they generate fear and misunderstanding around transgender people along with the suggestion that transgender people are less deserving of protection than cisgender women and children (cisgender people are those whose gender identity conforms to their biological sex). As such, the battle over transgender people's access to sex-segregated spaces is both about transgender rights and about either reproducing or challenging damaging beliefs about what it is to be a man and what it is to be a woman.

transgender-rights legislation to "bathroom bills"

The public response to transgender-supportive policies has varied across different social contexts. Within gender-integrated settings, such as college campuses and workplaces, the trend toward transgender-inclusive health care coverage and nondiscrimination policies in terms of hiring and promotion has become widely accepted as an important dimension of diversity. Yet, transgender inclusion in sex-segregated settings has proven to be more controversial. In particular, the part of inclusive policies that allows transgender people to use a bathroom that aligns with their gender identity and expression—rather than with their chromosomes or genital configurations—has generated a great deal of opposition.

Supportive politicians and advocates frame transgender rights policies as a way to alleviate discrimination against transgender and gender-variant people. Opponents, in contrast, reframe the debate as being about bathroom access. This concerted effort to focus on bathrooms was evident in the media accounts we analyzed. Critics did not discuss "transgender-rights legislation," but rather "bathroom bills." Reporters picked up on this aspect of the debate, creating pithy, attention-grabbing headlines such as "Critics: Flush Bathroom Bill" (*Boston Herald*) and "Bathroom Bill Goes Down the Drain" (*New Hampshire Business Review*).

Opponents repeatedly expressed their belief that public restrooms have to be segregated on

> In none of the media accounts we analyzed have opponents been able to cite an actual case of bathroom sexual assault after the passage of transgender-supportive policies.

the basis of gender and that people's genitals, not their gender identities, should determine bathroom access. Kris Mineau of the conservative Massachusetts Family Institute, quoted in the *Republican,* worried about the potential outcome of the proposed state transgender-rights bill. "This is a far-reaching piece of legislation that will disrupt the privacy of bathrooms, showers, and exercise facilities including those in public schools. . . . This bill opens the barn door to everybody. There is no way to know who of the opposite biological sex is using the facility for the right purpose." Evelyn Reilly, a spokesperson for the same institute, told the *Berkshire Eagle,* "Men and women bathrooms [sic] have been separated for ages for a reason. . . . Women need to feel private and safe when they're using those facilities."

In actuality, the segregation of public bathrooms on the basis of gender is a relatively recent phenomenon in the United States. Prior to the Victorian era, men and women used the same privies and outhouses. With the invention of indoor plumbing came water closets and later bathrooms, which were not segregated until Victorian ideals of feminine modesty—and the mixing of men and women in factory work—established a new precedent. By the 1920s, laws requiring segregated public facilities were *de rigueur* across the country. As sociologist Erving Goffman has pointed out, men and women share bathrooms in their homes. In public restrooms, by contrast, the sense that men and women are opposite is exacerbated by the placement of open urinals in men's rooms and the private stalls found in women's rooms. Such separation, then, is not biologically necessary but rather socially mandated. Highlighting this point, bathroom segregation is not universal, as some European countries, such as France, often have gender-integrated public restrooms.

> Such separation is not biologically necessary but rather socially mandated.

Transgender-supportive policies present a sharp challenge to this bathroom-segregation logic. Opponents struggle with the sense that their belief in a static gender binary determined by chromosomes and genitals is being undermined by institutional and governmental support for transgender people. The outcome of the resulting gender panics is often a call to socially reinforce what opponents position as a natural division of men and women. In a "Letter to the Editor" in the *Bangor Daily News,* a concerned author contests transgender bathroom access, arguing, "What makes an individual able to claim gender? As I always understood it growing up—and I know I am not alone in this—your anatomy dictates your sex." A follow-up response on the *Bangor Daily News* "ClickBack" page read, "The policy should be boys use the men's room and girls use the lady's room. Identification does not change physical plumbing."

These ideological collisions between those advocating transgender rights and those who insist on sex at birth determining gender, and the ensuing panics, put into high relief the often-invisible social criteria for "who counts" as a woman and a man in our society. Yet, in our study, such gender panics focused exclusively on the threat that transgender-supportive bills present to cisgender women and children. Highlighting this point, opponents to trans-inclusive policies proposed in Massachusetts and New Hampshire in 2009 and 2010 repeatedly discussed that these policies would, as the *Associated Press* reported, "put women and children at risk." It was in these fears of "risk" that the image of the sexual predator emerged.

enter the sexual predator

The conception of the "sexual predator" is deeply gendered. People often assume that they

(Jooyoung Lee)

2009, conservative activist Tony Dane told the *Las Vegas Review-Journal* that transgender-rights policies would allow men to legally enter women's restrooms "in drag," which would "make it easier for them to attack women and evade capture."

from gender panics to penis panics

Transgender people, along with gay men and lesbian women, have a long history of being conflated with pedophiles and other sexual predators. Within the articles we analyzed, opponents worried about what transgender women, who they assume have penises, might do if they were allowed access to women-only spaces. Demonstrating such concern, reporters frequently highlighted critics' fears about "male anatomies" or "male genitalia" in women's spaces. Transgender women in these narratives are always anchored to their imagined "male anatomies," and thus become categorized as potential sexual threats to those vested with vulnerable subjecthood, namely cisgender women and children.

In contrast, transgender men—assumed by critics to be "really women" because they do not possess a "natural" penis—are relatively invisible in these debates. Transgender men are mentioned directly by opponents only *once* in all of the articles we analyzed. After conservative opponent Tony Dane expressed his concern that the proposed Nevada policy would make women "uncomfortable" in the bathroom because they might have to see a transgender woman, a reporter for the *Las Vegas Review-Journal* asked about his position on transgender men. He stated, "they should use the women's bathroom, regardless of whom it makes uncomfortable, because that's where they're supposed to go." Transgender men are never referenced as potential sexual threats to women, men, or children. Instead, they are put into a category that sociologist Mimi

can establish whether someone is a potential sexual threat by simply determining if they are male (possible threat) or female (not a likely threat). Critics charge that transgender-rights laws will make such determination difficult and will, like "sheep's clothing" on a wolf, give predators open access to those seen as vulnerable. Reilly argued that a proposed state-level law protecting gender identity and gender expression would allow "a sexual predator using the guise of gender confusion to enter the restrooms." In Colorado, Bruce Hausknecht, a policy analyst for the evangelical organization Focus on the Family Action, fought against a proposed transgender rights bill in 2009, stating: "The fear . . . is that a sexual predator would attempt to enter the women's facilities, and the public accommodation owner would feel they had no ability to challenge that." In Nevada in

Schippers labels "pariah femininities." They are not dangerous to cisgender women and children, but they also do not warrant protection and rights because they fall outside of gender and sexual normativity.

As our research reveals, policies that would allow transgender people to access sex-segregated spaces and do not have specific requirements for genital surgeries generate a great deal of panic. These panics matter, as they frequently result in a reshaping of the language of such policies to require extensive bodily changes before transgender people have access to particular rights and locations. Such changes place severe limitations on transgender people who may not want or cannot afford genital surgeries. Further, while explicit bodily criteria for access to sex-segregated spaces can quell gender panics, these criteria force transgender people into restrictive and normative forms of gendered embodiment that perpetuate the belief that genitals and gender must be linked.

> Explicit bodily criteria for access to sex-segregated spaces can quell gender panics, but these criteria force transgender people into restrictive, normative forms of gendered embodiment that perpetuate the belief that genitals and gender must be linked.

transgender rights and the struggle for gender equality

In 2011, the National Center for Transgender Equality and the National Gay and Lesbian Task Force published "Injustice at Every Turn," a report that highlights the findings of the largest-ever survey of the experiences of transgender and gender-variant people. The report documents wide-ranging experiences of discrimination. For instance, respondents had double the rate of unemployment compared to the general population and 90 percent reported experiencing workplace discrimination, including being unable to access a bathroom at work that matched their gender identity.

Antidiscrimination legislation that offers protections for a person's gender identity and gender expression is an important strategy for addressing inequality in hiring and promotion. Additionally, these policies allow transgender people to use public accommodations, such as bathrooms, in line with their gender identity. In other words, a transgender man with a beard would not be legally required to use the women's restroom simply because he had been assigned female at birth. While the adoption of transgender-supportive policies has grown rapidly at the state, city, and corporate level in the last ten years, in 2015 there are limited federal protections—a situation that would be addressed by the passage of the Employment Non-Discrimination Act (also known as ENDA). The regional variation in protection for gender identity and gender expression—and the widespread violence and discrimination aimed at transgender people—makes this a key political issue for gender equality.

unmasking the real debate

Gender panics gain legitimacy in the realm of debate because many people believe that women and young children are inherently vulnerable and in need of protection from men. In dominant U.S. culture, men—or more specifically, people assumed to have penises—are both conceived of as the potential protectors of vulnerable people they have relational ties to, such as wives, sisters, daughters, and mothers, and a potential source of sexual threat to others. This idea emerges from a belief that men constantly seek out sexual interactions and will resort to violence to achieve these desires. As transgender women are placed into the category of persons with penises—making them, for many opponents, "really men"—they become an imagined source of threat to cisgender women and children. And, as there are no protective men present in women's restrooms, opponents to transgender rights imagine women (and often children, who are likely to accompany women to the restroom) as uniquely imperiled by these nondiscrimination policies.

Proponents of transgender-inclusive laws and policies can make strong arguments about the need for protections. The increasingly large body of empirical data on transgender people in the United States emphasizes that transgender people are much more likely to face violence in the restroom rather than to perpetrate such violence. In fact, in none of the media accounts we analyzed have opponents been able to cite an actual case of bathroom sexual assault after the passage of transgender-supportive policies. But deep-rooted cultural fears about the vulnerability of women and children are hard to counter.

It is not to be suggested that sexual assault is not a serious and troubling real issue; rather, such assaults rarely occur in public restrooms and no cities or states that have passed transgender-rights legislation have witnessed increases in sexual assaults in public restrooms after the laws have gone into effect. Raising the specter of the sexual predator in debates around transgender rights should be unmasked for the multiple ways it can perpetuate gender inequality. Under the guise of "protecting" women, critics reproduce ideas about their weakness, depict males as assailants, and work to deny rights to transgender people. Moreover, they suggest that there should be a hierarchy of rights in which cisgender women and children are more deserving of protections than transgender people.

> Raising the specter of the sexual predator in debates around transgender rights should be unmasked for the multiple ways it can perpetuate gender inequality.

Beliefs about gender difference form the scaffolding of structural gender inequality, as those that are "opposite" cannot be equal. Thus, bathroom sex-segregation must be reconsidered if we want to push gender equality forward. Many college campuses are moving toward gender-integrated bathrooms and widespread availability of gender-neutral bathrooms. And, in California, bill AB1266, passed in 2013, authorizes high school students to use bathrooms that fit their gender identity and gender expression. These examples demonstrate that the social order of the bathroom can change. While such changes may spark gender panics, these examples suggest that the battles fought over bathroom access can be won in favor of gender equality.

RECOMMENDED RESOURCES

Sheila Cavanagh. 2010. *Queering Bathrooms: Gender, Sexuality, and the Hygienic Imagination*. Toronto: University of Toronto Press.

> An instructive and exhaustive look at the cultural construction of bathrooms, including how they maintain binary understandings of gender and disadvantage queer and transgender people.

Erving Goffman. 1977. "The Arrangement Between the Sexes." *Theory and Society* 4(3): 301–331.

> This classic article theorizes the social construction of gender by exploring several venues, including bathrooms, which are designed to support the deeply held view that males are opposite and superior to females.

Jaime M. Grant, Lisa A. Mottet, Justin Tanis, Jack Harrison, Jody L. Herman, and Mara Keisling. 2011. *Injustice at Every Turn: A Report of the National Transgender Discrimination Survey.* Washington, DC: National Center for Transgender Equality and the National Gay and Lesbian Task Force.

> Summarizes the findings of the largest ever survey of transgender and gender-variant people, including experiences of unemployment, discrimination, and violence.

Harvey Molotoch and Laura Noren, eds. 2010. *Toilet: Public Restrooms and the Politics of Sharing.* New York: New York University Press.

> An interdisciplinary set of essays examining the history and implication of public restrooms.

REVIEW QUESTIONS

1. According to the authors, how is it that bathrooms came to be central in transgender-rights legislation?
2. How do the authors argue that the bathroom bills perpetuate gender inequality?
3. What is the authors' rationale for stating that gender panics could be easily relabeled as "penis panics"?
4. What are the differences between how transgender men and transgender women are referenced by opponents to transgender rights?

part **6**

Marriage and Family

sinikka elliott and megan reid

the superstrong black mother

30

winter 2016

when a baltimore mom hit her son to keep him away from protests, many applauded her—but the myth of the superstrong black mother does more harm than good.

altimore mother Toya Graham became a viral video sensation after being filmed yelling at and hitting her teen son. Graham, who is Black, was trying to stop her son from joining the protests following Freddie Gray's death in police custody in Baltimore in April 2015. Dubbed "mother of the year," news outlets applauded Graham for her fierce determination to keep her son out of harm's way by any means necessary. The media and ensuing public response to the video are illuminating for what they say about cultural notions of Black motherhood: the good Black mom should be superstrong to protect her children, but she is also responsible for controlling her children and preventing them from getting into trouble. In celebrating Graham, the media was implicitly condemning all the other mothers whose children participated in the protests—that is, the mothers who did not prevent their children from "senseless" rioting against institutional racism in policing.

According to the social theorist Patricia Hill Collins, the superstrong Black mom has long been a stereotypical image of Black mothers. Initially emerging from Black communities' valorization of Black mothers' intensive efforts to raise their children and shield them from the dangers of living with racism and poverty, the superstrong Black mother image now dictates the terms of good mothering for Black women: be strong and be solely responsible. The modern emphasis on individual responsibility as a solution to structural problems reinforces this idea. This context presents extraordinary challenges for Black mothers as they attempt to protect their children from the dangers of institutionalized racism. The nearly 50 low-income urban Black mothers of teenagers we interviewed in North Carolina and New York described the multiple strategies they use to insulate their children from danger—strategies that also bring stress and hardship to the mothers themselves. About half the mothers we spoke with are partnered but we focus exclusively on the mothers' parenting experiences here. Their stories reveal the staggering odds they are up against as they and their children confront the realities of historical and ongoing racial discrimination.

> The long-held superstrong Black mother image, Patricia Hill Collins argues, now dictates the terms of good mothering for Black women: be strong and be solely responsible.

mothers' common grief

Raising kids is hard, but raising children who face daily assaults on their very being is especially hard. In a study tracking a nationally representative group of mothers of children from kindergarten to third grade, researchers Kei Nomaguchi and Amanda House found that only Black mothers experienced heightened levels of parenting stress as their children grew older and mothers' concerns about their safety and survival increased. Recent analyses by statistician Nate Silver underscore how dangerous the United States is for Black Americans, who are almost eight times as likely as White Americans to be homicide victims.

Malaya, a New York mother of three, is a heartbreaking example of this reality. When asked in an interview about recent major events in her life, she said her 26-year-old son had been murdered three weeks ago while trying to break up a fight at a house party. "My son passed away at the same age as his father. He passed away two blocks from where his father got murdered," she somberly related. Malaya's son's death has made her even more worried about the safety of her two younger children.

The day before her son was murdered, Malaya joined a community gym with plans to lose weight because she was experiencing some health problems she wanted to manage: stress, diabetes, and high blood pressure. Since she received the late-night phone call about her son's death, she has not returned to the gym. Instead, she has been focused on getting justice for her dead son and insulating her two remaining children from danger. Especially since her son's death, Malaya tries to teach her 16-year-old daughter Nina to keep to herself and not to trust anyone. "I be just so afraid with my daughter outside now, even around friends. And she is like 'Ma, would you want me to be in the house forever?' No, I just, I don't even know how to even put it like. . . . Friends are friends, but your life is more important."

Malaya encourages Nina to avoid becoming too close to anyone. Her personal philosophy is "go to work, come home, take care of the house,

do what you've got to do. All that mingling in the streets is only going to cause trouble." She takes this approach in her own life: "I can't even trust my own friends. I don't have nothing against them, but I don't know what's their motive. I want Nina to understand it. Because when you came out of my womb, you came out alone. So there's always a boundary that you got to know." Malaya instructs Nina to avoid all unnecessary social contact and stay inside their apartment, hoping this will save her life.

Malaya's third child is a 3-year-old son. Even prior to her older son's murder, Malaya was concerned about the safety of her youngest son. To insulate him from danger, Malaya spoke of her interest in homeschooling: "I was really scared to let him out. I'm like that because I've seen what happens when someone gets out." A social worker convinced Malaya to enroll her son in public preschool, but she is strict about his socializing: "I don't have him with no friends. He goes to school on the bus, he comes home on it."

Malaya's story captures several aspects of the unfortunately common experiences of low-income Black mothers: losing a child, living in unsafe neighborhoods owing to subsidized housing policies that intensified poverty and racial segregation, deep social distrust and disenfranchisement, and profound efforts to insulate and protect their children. Her story also demonstrates the impact stress and self-sacrifice can have on mothers' health. Reflecting on how her son's murder affected her life, she said: "And me, all I just wanted is just to live a normal life and just be normal. I want to go to the gym."

safety from the streets, safety from the law

Not only do Black Americans have high homicide rates, they are also disproportionately arrested and incarcerated, leading legal scholar Michelle Alexander to argue that Black incarceration rates reflect a legacy of discriminatory laws and policies, such as racial profiling, the heavy police presence in low-income Black neighborhoods, and the war on drugs, which involved higher prison sentences for possession of crack cocaine (more common among Blacks) than cocaine (more commonly used by Whites) though there is no chemical difference between them.

With one in nine Black men behind bars, Black mothers worry about their children, especially their sons, ending up on the wrong side of the criminal justice system. Vivian, a New York mother of two boys, worried that her 17-year-old son Dixon would end up in jail or dead. Her fears led her to ask him: "Which one do you want to be, a name or a number? What I mean by that is, like, what do you want? A job or you want to go to jail?" Likening Dixon's social environment to crabs trapped in a bucket, Vivian said she had to pull him out and separate him from his friends: "You ever saw like a bucket of crabs, and you pull the crabs up, what is the other crab doing? Yeah, they are holding on. It's always going to be somebody that's going to try to pull you down, you know, but if you have a strong family behind you, they're going to break that arm. You know what I'm saying? And that's what the hell I did, I broke that arm. Yeah, and pushed those friends away from him. And look at him now, he's out there working." Vivian intervened to end her son's relationship with friends she worried would expose him to the long arm of the law, and Vivian's brother offered her son a job in his moving company, an option not available to many low-income urban Black youth who face bleak employment prospects.

Like Malaya, Vivian keeps to herself and encourages the same for her children, sending them away from the neighborhood as frequently as possible to "show my kids there's a different world out of this place. I know it's nothing but poverty up and down here, but if you can choose to walk outside of this, you will see a different world. I take my kids to 42nd Street, to do things upstate, somewhere out the house, things like that. To Virginia to go see my brothers." One in four Black Americans live in neighborhoods marked by extreme poverty thanks to a host of federal, state, and local housing policies that concentrate poverty in preexisting low-income areas. Moreover, these policies are racially based: Poor Blacks are much more likely than poor Whites to live in neighborhoods characterized by extreme poverty, crumbling infrastructure, and minimal job opportunities. When they are at home, Vivian tries to ensure her sons' safety by keeping them inside and occupied with video games. "If the [video] game keeps them from out of the street, they can play it all day, you know. Hey, if they keeps them under me, under my eye watch, go right ahead. I'm not saying all day, but it keeps them here, you know." Vivian's awareness that too much screen time is unhealthy for children is tempered by her fears for her sons' safety outside and away from her watchful eye.

Adrianna also worries about her children's safety outside their home. We interviewed Adrianna in North Carolina following her move from the northeast in the hopes of finding a safer place to raise her children. The

> Raising kids is hard, but raising children who face daily assaults on their very being is especially hard.

mother of three explained that even so, she is vigilant: "I keep very close eyes on my children. They can't be wandering the neighborhood. I need to know where my kids are at. If they're going somewhere with other children, I need to talk to the parents. Who's gonna be supervising them?" Only half-jokingly, Adrianna went on to say that she won't let her children leave the house without the "phone numbers, addresses, and social security numbers" of their friends' parents.

In addition to being vigilant to insulate their children from neighborhood dangers, Black mothers also find themselves advocating for their children in racist institutional contexts such as schools. Adrianna recounted the forms of racial discrimination her three children have faced in school since their move to North Carolina. A recent analysis of federal school data by researchers at the University of Pennsylvania found that, even as Black children represent less than a quarter of the student body in North Carolina and 12 other southern states, they make up about half of all expulsions and suspensions. At the time of her interview, Adrianna's 11-year-old son was facing a possible suspension for violating the dress code with his Mohawk hairstyle, which Adrianna defended as "a part of who we are as a people." In her frustration with the school system, Adrianna, like Malaya, is considering taking her children out of school to homeschool them. Their interest in homeschooling mirrors a larger trend of homeschooling becoming more popular among Black families as they try to insulate their children from discriminatory treatment.

Vivian's awareness that too much screen time is unhealthy for children is tempered by her fears for her sons' safety outdoors and away from her watchful eye.

blaming mothers

"I'm not one of those parents who is laxa-ditty," emphasized Adrianna, distancing herself from the stereotype of the bad mother. "I have always been a mother first. I don't put anything above my children's lives," she said. Black mothers across the income spectrum have to deal with the negative connotations of stereotypes about them as mothers and the stress of raising Black children in a racist society. In separate works, sociologists Dawn Dow and Karen McCormack found that the controlling images of Black women, such as the welfare queen and the strong Black woman, influence how both poor *and* middle-class Black mothers make parenting decisions, and create a sense of exclusion from White motherhood.

In her book on racial bias in the child welfare system, Dorothy Roberts, an eminent scholar of race, gender, and the law, argues that stereotypes of poor Black women as bad mothers mean that they are more heavily monitored by the state and their mothering is treated with suspicion. Racial bias can infuse even teachers' perceptions of Black mothers. A 2012 study by Susan Dumais and her colleagues found that elementary school teachers viewed Black parents' involvement in their children's schooling negatively, while interpreting White parents' involvement positively. Similarly, the Black mothers we spoke with whose children were involved with state institutions—including public schools and the criminal justice system—discussed the ways their mothering was assumed to be inadequate by institutional practices.

Several of the mothers spoke of their sons' entanglement with the court system in particular. As researchers Victor Rios, Nikki Jones, and others have observed, the institutions that surround Black children are eager to discipline and lock them up; when they do, their mothers also come under the authority of the criminal justice system. Tiana "felt like I was the one that committed the crime," when she recounted the things she had to do in order to meet the conditions of her 14-year-old son's probation for kicking a motorcycle, such as attending Saturday morning classes and advocating for him in the system. When a judge threatened to put her son on probation for another six months, Tiana said, "I was like, what? Uh-uh. I had to take him to all them little, you know, classes and it was cutting out time for my other kids." Tiana agreed to attend even more classes with her son, however, to demonstrate her commitment as a mother and to keep him from receiving an additional sentence.

When Mariah's 15-year-old son was caught trying to steal a moped, a condition of his probation was that Mariah had to take weekly parenting classes. She explained, "They send a guy over here to do a parenting class with us every Saturday. He shows us some videos of other parents and their children, going through probably the same things [and teaches us] maybe the different things that maybe I can do instead of yelling and screaming." Mariah described the classes as "sometimes" helpful but noted that they don't address what to do when she tells her son "don't go or you can't go outside today. Soon as you turn your back, he's out the door, like you didn't tell him nothing."

All too often the mothers' stories underscored how state institutions and policies positioned mothers as suspect parents *but also* solely responsible for their children's behavior. Tiffany's 16-year-old son Corey was in trouble for skipping school, for which the school blamed Tiffany. "I don't understand how they want to blame the parents for the kids when you send them out there to go to school," she said, explaining that both the school and the law punished her for Corey's truancy even though she made sure he was out the door with his school clothes and backpack every day. "I get like a phone call telling me that it is mandatory that I makes the school meeting. . . . Basically they were telling me [the principal] was going to call ACS (Administration for Child Services) on me because Corey is not coming to school. I was like, I have a seven-year-old and you can check, he has perfect attendance. So you cannot fault me for his mistakes."

Stereotypes of poor Black women as bad mothers mean that they are more heavily monitored by the state and their mothering is treated with suspicion, even by their kids' teachers.

They did, however, fault her, subjecting her to an embarrassing 30-day investigation involving multiple home visits by ACS workers.

praise and punishment

Highly publicized recent incidences of police brutality have highlighted persistent racism and the ongoing challenges of being Black in America. Black mothers not only fear for their children each time they step outside the door, they also encounter gender, class, and racial discrimination of their own, including stereotypes about them as mothers. The women we interviewed proudly spoke of their strength and the sacrifices they have made to insulate their children from the surrounding dangers, but as their stories demonstrate, these efforts stem from living in impossible conditions created by state policies and practices, and they are often not enough. Praising mothers for being superstrong also makes it easy to lay the blame for children's hardships at mothers' feet.

The U.S. welfare state is shrinking while an emphasis on small government grows, inspired and perpetuated by inaccurate understandings of the causes of poverty and by racist stereotypes about those who use social programs. State and institutional supports for poor families that do exist tend to focus on what mothers are doing wrong and how they could be better parents. This reflects a larger trend of shifting responsibility onto the individual, illustrated in the stories we presented earlier. The mothers we interviewed described how state involvement in their lives was at best neglectful and at worst exacerbated the parenting challenges and stress they faced. It's no surprise then that they see little choice but to be hypervigilant, separating their children from their peers, keeping them inside, and trying to get them away from the surrounding dangers, including discriminatory treatment.

Time and again sociological research has revealed that mothers like Malaya, Vivian, Adrianna, and others we spoke with face many challenges raising children, and that the vast majority do everything they can to protect and nurture their children. The adverse conditions these mothers and their children find themselves in are created by inadequate and racist past and current social policies, yet mothers are told it is up to them alone to remedy them, to be super-strong. This is a losing proposition that puts undue pressure on low-income Black mothers and blames them when their children falter.

As for Toya Graham, six months after she was filmed determinedly trying to keep her son from joining the Baltimore protests against police brutality, Graham described her life to a CBS reporter as a constant struggle. Speaking of her 16-year-old son, Graham said, "I know there's nothing out there but harm. But I'm going to protect him. . . . I know a lot of mothers out here understand where I'm coming from. We're struggling, we're just trying to make sure we keep food on our table for our children, keep them out of harm's way, keep them out of danger." On being dubbed a hero, Graham responded, "I just don't feel like a hero. This is a real struggle. When the cameras is gone, the reality of life is still there. It's still there."

RECOMMENDED RESOURCES

T. F. Charlton. 2013. "The Impossibility of the Good Black Mother," in *The Good Mother Myth*. New York: Seal Press.

> Explores the negative stereotypes that Black mothers face in their everyday lives through a combination of personal essay and gender and race theory.

Patricia Hill Collins. 2000. *Black Feminist Thought: Knowledge, Consciousness, and the Politics of Empowerment*. New York: Routledge.

> Explores the uniqueness of Black women's perspectives and develops an accessible critical social theory.

Ann Arnett Ferguson. 2000. *Bad Boys: Public Schools in the Making of Black Masculinity*. Ann Arbor: University of Michigan Press.

> Offers a rich account of students' and teachers' daily interactions to demonstrate the ways racialized gender stereotypes lead schools to disproportionately punish Black boys.

Judith Levine. 2013. *Ain't No Trust: How Bosses, Boyfriends, and Bureaucrats Fail Low-Income Mothers and Why It Matters*. Berkeley: University of California Press.

> Documents low-income women's interactions with untrustworthy actors and how they contribute to further lack of trust.

Dorothy Roberts. 2002. *Shattered Bonds: The Color of Child Welfare*. New York: Basic Civitas Books.

> Examines the racist underpinnings of the child welfare system and the consequences for Black families and communities.

REVIEW QUESTIONS

1. The stereotype about Black mothers that this article discusses is generally considered to be a positive stereotype. What are the unseen sides or consequences of that stereotype?
2. What role does the criminal justice system play in the experiences of some Black mothers?
3. Compare the experiences of White mothers and Black mothers, as described in the article.

sarah bowen, sinikka elliott, and joslyn brenton

the joy of cooking?

summer 2014

time pressures, trade-offs to save money, and the burden of pleasing others make it difficult for mothers to enact the idealized vision of home-cooked meals advocated by foodies and public health officials.

It's a hot, sticky Fourth of July in North Carolina, and Leanne, a married working-class Black mother of three, is in her cramped kitchen. She's been cooking for several hours, lovingly preparing potato salad, beef ribs, chicken legs, and collards for her family. Abruptly, her mother decides to leave before eating anything. "But you haven't eaten," Leanne says. "You know I prefer my own potato salad," says her mom. She takes a plateful to go anyway.

Her 7-year-old son takes medication for ADHD and often isn't hungry until it wears off, usually right before bedtime. Leanne's 1-year-old daughter gets fussy when her mom cooks, and looks for attention. Her husband doesn't offer much help; his contribution involves pouring barbecue sauce on the ribs, which Leanne calls "working his magic." Leanne wipes her brow and mutters to herself about the $80 she spent on ingredients. By the time she's finished cooking, she says, "I don't want to eat!"

In the fight to combat rising obesity rates, modern-day food gurus advocate a return to the kitchen. Michael Pollan, author of *Cooked*, and America's most influential "foodie-intellectual," tells us that the path to reforming the food system "passes right through the kitchen." *New York Times*' food columnist Mark Bittman

> Cooking is at times joyful, but it is also filled with time pressures, trade-offs designed to save money, and the burden of pleasing others.

agrees, saying the goal should be "to get people to see cooking as a joy rather than a burden." Magazines such as *Good Housekeeping* and television personalities like Rachael Ray offer practical cooking advice to get Americans into the kitchen, publishing recipes for 30-minute meals and meals that can be made in the slow cooker. First Lady Michelle Obama has also been influential in popularizing public health messages that emphasize the role that mothers play when it comes to helping children make healthy choices.

The message that good parents—and in particular, good mothers—cook for their families dovetails with increasingly intensive and unrealistic standards of "good" mothering. According to the sociologist Sharon Hays, to be a good mom today, a woman must demonstrate intense devotion to her children. One could say that home-cooked meals have become the hallmark of good mothering, stable families, and the ideal of the healthy, productive citizen.

Yet in reality, home-cooked meals rarely look this good. Leanne, for example, who held down a minimum-wage job while taking classes for an associate's degree, often spent her valuable time preparing meals, only to be rewarded with family members' complaints—or disinterest. Our extensive observations and interviews with mothers like Leanne reveal something that often gets overlooked: cooking is fraught.

feeding the family

Over the past year and a half, our research team conducted in-depth interviews with 150 Black, White, and Latina mothers from all walks of life. We also spent over 250 hours conducting ethnographic observations with 12 working-class and poor families. We observed them in their homes as they prepared and ate meals, and tagged along on trips to the grocery store and to their children's check-ups. Sitting around the kitchen table and getting a feel for these women's lives, we came to appreciate the complexities involved in feeding a family.

While Pollan and others wax nostalgic about a time when people grew their own food and sat around the dinner table eating it, they fail to see all of the invisible labor that goes into planning, making, and coordinating family meals. Cooking is at times joyful, but it is also filled with time pressures, trade-offs designed to save money, and the burden of pleasing others.

Wanda and her husband, Marquan, working-class Black parents of two young girls, were constantly pressed for time. Both were employed by the same fast-food chain, but in different rural locations 45 minutes apart. They depended on Wanda's mother, who lived 30 minutes away, for childcare. During the five weeks we spent with them, their car was broken down and since they did not have enough money to repair it, they relied on a complex network of friends and family members for rides. Their lives were further complicated by the fact that they didn't know their weekly schedules—what hours, shifts, or even days they would be working—until they were posted, sometimes only the night before. Once they learned their shifts, they scrambled to figure out transportation and childcare arrangements.

Wanda liked her job, but her unpredictable schedule made it difficult to cook regular meals the way she wanted to. This time dilemma was also hard for Leanne, who worked for the same fast-food corporation as Wanda and Marquan, but in an urban area that lacked reliable public transportation. Sometimes, Leanne would take a taxi to work only to find out that business was slow and she was not needed. At other times, she was asked to work late. Because of this, Leanne and her family had no set mealtime: cooking and eating were often catch-as-catch-can.

Wanda's and Leanne's situation is increasingly common. As real wages have stagnated, many households depend on every adult family member working, sometimes in multiple jobs and jobs with nonstandard and unpredictable hours, to make ends meet. Since the 1960s, working women have cut back on household tasks, including cooking and cleaning, according to sociologist Liana Sayer. Even so, balancing paid work and unpaid work at home, women today have less free time than they did a generation ago; and, in line with heightened expectations of motherhood, they now report spending more time engaged in childcare than did mothers in the 1960s. It's not surprising that they struggle to find time to cook.

And, of course, cooking isn't just about the time it takes to prepare the meal. It also involves planning ahead to be sure the ingredients are on hand, and it means cleaning up afterwards. Samantha, a single White mother of three, was blunt when we asked her if she liked cooking. "Not really," she said. "I just hate the kitchen . . . having to come up with a meal and put it together. I know I can cook but

> While some wax nostalgic about a time when people grew their own food and sat around the dinner table eating it, they fail to see the invisible labor that goes into family meals.

it's the planning of the meal, and seeing if they're going to like it, and the mess that you make. And then the mess afterwards. . . . If it was up to me, I wouldn't cook."

Though the mothers we met were squeezed for time, they were still expected to produce elaborate meals cooked from scratch. Even the middle-class women we talked with, who enjoyed regular work hours and typically shared the household work with a partner, said they lacked the time to cook the way they felt they should. Most got home from work around six o'clock, and then attempted to cook meals from scratch (as the experts advise) while their children clamored for their attention.

between time and money

Greely, a married middle-class White mother of one child, had recently started her own catering company. She was working long hours during the week to get her business off the ground, and reasoned that taking time on the weekend to prep vegetables and lunches would help her create ideal meals. She explained, "I feel [that] when I have the time, I enjoy cooking. And when it's so compressed and after a stressful day, it's kind of horrible. I feel like, because I'm not able to spend as much time with Adelle now, I don't want to spend an hour cooking after I pick her up from school every day. You know, like it's fine sometimes, but I want to be able to sit down and help her with her homework or help her finish her Valentines for her classmates or whatever that may be. I was supposed to soak black-eyed peas last night and I forgot."

The mothers we met who were barely paying the bills routinely cooked—contrary to the stereotype that poor families mainly eat fast food—because it was more economical. Isis, a poor single Black mother, told us that she got tired of cooking, but continued to do so to save money. "If I don't cook then they'll go get something out to eat," she said. "But then that's wasting money."

Yet being poor makes it nearly impossible to enact the foodie version of a home-cooked meal. The ingredients that go into meals considered to be healthy—fresh fruits and vegetables, whole grains, and lean meats—are expensive. A recent study of food prices around the globe found that it costs $1.50 more per day—or about $550 a year per person—to eat a healthier diet than a less healthy diet.

The cost of healthy ingredients is not the only barrier. Many of the poor mothers we met also lacked reliable transportation, and therefore typically shopped just once a month. As a result, they avoided buying fresh produce, which spoiled quickly. Mothers also struggled to prepare meals in small trailers or apartments with minimal space. We observed homes without kitchen tables or functional appliances, infested by bugs and rats, and lacking basic kitchen tools like sharp knives, cutting boards, pots, and pans.

The idea that home cooking is inherently ideal reflects an elite foodie standpoint. Romantic depictions of cooking assume that everyone has a home, that family members are home eating at the same time, and that kitchens and dining spaces are equipped and safe. This is not necessarily the case for the families we met.

During the month we spent with Flora, a poor Black mother who was currently separated from her husband, she was living with her daughter and two grandchildren in a cockroach- and flea-infested hotel room with two double beds. They prepared all of their food in a small microwave, rinsing their utensils in the bathroom sink. Many of the families we met lived in trailers or homes with thin

> Being poor makes it nearly impossible to enact the foodie version of a home-cooked meal.

walls that provided little protection from the outside elements. Some homes had holes in the floor or walls, making it nearly impossible to keep pests out. Claudia, a married Latina mother of four, was battling a serious ant invasion in her home. She watched in horror as the ant poison her 12-year-old son was scattering around the trailer's perimeter drifted through an open window and settled on the food she was preparing at the kitchen counter.

Still, mothers felt responsible for preparing healthy meals for their children and keenly experienced the gap between the romanticized version of cooking and the realities of their lives. When asked what an "ideal world" would look like for her, Ruth, a widowed Black mother of two, said she would like to have a bigger house that included a "bigger stove, and kitchen, and refrigerator so I can cook a little more and do what I need to do to cook healthier. Give me the money to provide for them a little healthier." With more money and space, Ruth could cook the elaborate meals she loves.

To our surprise, many of the middle-class mothers we met also told us that money was a barrier to preparing healthy meals. Even though they often had household incomes of more than $100,000 a year, their membership in the middle-class was costly. While they did not experience food shortages, they were forced to make trade-offs in order to save money—like buying less-healthy processed food, or fewer organic items than they would like. For low-income mothers, the trade-offs are starker: they skipped meals, or spent long hours in line at food pantries or applying for assistance, to make sure their children had enough to eat.

food fights

"I don't need it. I don't want it. I never had it," exclaimed 4-year-old Rashan when his mom served him an unfamiliar side dish. Rashan's reaction was not uncommon. We rarely observed a meal in which at least one family member didn't complain about the food they were served. Some mothers coaxed their children to eat by playing elaborate games or by hand-feeding them. One middle-class mother even set a timer, telling her son that he had to eat as much of what was on his plate as he could before the time ran out. Feeding others involves taking multiple preferences into consideration, and balancing time and money constraints.

Rather than risk trying new and expensive foods that might prove unpopular, many low-income mothers opted to cook the same foods again and again. They reasoned that it was better to stick with foods (often processed) that they knew their families would eat, rather than risk wasting money and food.

Giselle, a single Black mother of two, worked two part-time jobs to make ends meet. There was little room in the food budget to experiment with new or expensive foods. When it came time to decide what to make for supper, Giselle played it safe. She explained, "Because I don't want to cook something [they won't like] because I'll, like, waste the food. Right? Waste the food."

Low-income mothers tended to avoid using recipes, because the ingredients were expensive and they weren't sure if their families would like the new dishes. Instead, they continued to make what was tried and true, even if they didn't like the food themselves. Sandy, a White mother of two, tried hard to cook around her boyfriend's preferences. She liked fish, but her boyfriend didn't. So she ignored her food interests in order to "do something for my whole house." Sociologist Marjorie DeVault also found in her book *Feeding the Family* that women considered men's needs, sometimes above all others, when it came to preparing meals.

For middle-class mothers, cooking was about more than negotiating preferences for certain foods. They felt that offering new foods was crucial for developing their kids' palates—even if the process sometimes led to food fights. Their stories suggest that cooking like Pollan and other experts prescribe is time consuming and stressful. Some spent significant amounts of time reading the literature on the latest and best healthy foods, seeking out and trading new healthy recipes, and reworking the food budget to include more organic food—leading to greater anxiety about cooking and serving food.

For Elaine, a married White mother of one child, cooking involved high stakes. She and her husband worked full time, and Elaine's efforts to make meals from scratch rarely ended happily. She spent time prepping food on the weekends in order to cook ideal meals during the week. She explained, "When we get home, it's such a rush. I just don't know what happens to the time. I am so frustrated. That's why I get so angry! I get frustrated 'cause I'm like, I wanna make this good meal that's really healthy and I like to cook 'cause it's kind of my way to show them that I love them, 'This is my love for you guys!' And then I wind up at the end just, you know, grrr! Mad at the food because it takes me so long. It's like, how can it take an hour for me to do this when I've already cut up the carrots and the celery and all I'm doing is shoving it into a bowl?"

Even the extensive prep work that Elaine did on the weekends didn't translate into a relaxing meal during the weekday. Instead, like so many mothers, Elaine felt frustrated and inadequate about not living up to the ideal home-cooked meal. Their stories suggest that utopian family meals are nearly impossible to create, no matter how hard mothers try.

thinking outside the kitchen

The vision of the family meal that today's food experts are whipping up is alluring. Most people would agree that it would be nice to slow down, eat healthfully, and enjoy a home-cooked meal. However, our research leads us to question why the front line in reforming the food system has to be in someone's kitchen. The emphasis on home cooking ignores the time pressures, financial constraints, and feeding challenges that shape the family meal. Yet this is the widely promoted standard to which all mothers are held. Our conversations with mothers of young children show us that this emerging standard is a tasty illusion, one that is moralistic, and rather elitist, instead of a realistic vision of cooking today. Intentionally or not, it places the burden of a healthy home-cooked meal on women.

So let's move this conversation out of the kitchen, and brainstorm more creative solutions for sharing the work of feeding families. How about a revival of monthly town suppers, or healthy food trucks? Or perhaps we should rethink how we do meals in schools and workplaces, making lunch an opportunity for savoring and sharing food. Could schools offer to-go meals that families could easily heat up on busy weeknights? Without creative solutions like these, suggesting that we return to the kitchen en masse will do little more than increase the burden so many women already bear.

RECOMMENDED RESOURCES

Alison Alkon, Daniel Block, Kelly Moore, Catherine Gillis, Nicole DiNuccio, and Noel Chavez. 2013. "Foodways of the Urban Poor." *Geoforum* 48: 126–135.

> Argues that cost, not lack of knowledge or physical distance to food stores, is the primary barrier to healthy food access, and that low-income people employ a wide variety of strategies to obtain the foods they prefer at prices they can afford.

Kate Cairns, Josée Johnston, and Norah MacKendrick. 2013. "Feeding the 'Organic Child': Mothering through Ethical Consumption." *Journal of Consumer Culture* 13: 97–118.

> These authors coin the term "organic child," and find that middle-class mothers preserve the purity and safety of their children through the purchase of organic foods.

Marjorie DeVault. 1991. *Feeding the Family: The Social Organization of Caring as Gendered Work.* Chicago: University of Chicago Press.

> Argues that cooking (and "food work" more generally) is a form of care work that helps to maintain class and gender divisions.

Julie Guthman. 2007. "Can't Stomach It: How Michael Pollan et al. Made Me Want to Eat Cheetos." *Gastronomica* 7(2): 75–79.

> Critiques proponents of the local food movement for reinforcing apolitical and elite values, while offering no suggestions for how to change the food system in an inclusive way.

Sharon Hays. 1996. *The Cultural Contradictions of Motherhood.* New Haven: Yale University Press.

> An important book on the expectations modern mothers face to spend intensive amounts of time and energy raising their children.

Liana Sayer. 2005. "Gender, Time, and Inequality: Trends in Women's and Men's Paid Work, Unpaid Work, and Free Time." *Social Forces* 84: 285–303.

> Uses nationally representative time use data from 1965, 1975, and 1998 to analyze trends and gender differences in time use.

REVIEW QUESTIONS

1. Describe the ideal that this research is reacting to, and identify some of the ways that the reality falls short of the ideal.
2. Name and discuss some of the particular struggles that poor families face when trying to prepare home-cooked meals.
3. The last paragraph of the article suggests some ways to circumvent these problems. Using one of their suggestions (or coming up with one of your own), brainstorm and describe how that solution would work, or identify any problems you see with it.

jennifer m. silva

working-class growing pains

32

spring 2014

how do working-class men and women navigate the transition to adulthood amid economic insecurity and social isolation? research finds that young adults experience fear of intimate relationships, low expectations of work, and widespread distrust of institutions as they come of age.

In a working-class neighborhood in Lowell, Massachusetts, I sat across the kitchen table from a 24-year-old White woman named Diana. The daughter of a dry cleaner and a cashier, Diana graduated from high school and was accepted into a private university in Boston. She embarked on a criminal justice degree while working part-time at a local Dunkin' Donuts, taking out loans to pay for her tuition and room and board. But after two years, Diana began to doubt whether the benefits of college would ever outweigh the costs, so she dropped out of school to be a full-time cashier.

She explained, "When I work, I get paid at the end of the week. But in college, I would have had to wait five years to get a degree, and once I got that, who knows if I would be working or find something I wanted to be." Now, close to $100,000 in debt, Diana has forged new dreams of getting married, buying a home with a pool in a wealthy suburb of Boston, and having five children, a cat, and a dog—by the time she is 30.

But Diana admitted that she can't even find a man with a steady job to date, let alone marry, and that she will likely regret her decision to leave school: "Everyone says you can't really go anywhere unless you have a degree. I don't think I am going to make it anywhere past Dunkin' when I am older, and that scares

me to say. Like it's not enough to support me now."

Living with her mother and bringing home under $275 per week, Diana is stuck in an extended adolescence with no end in sight. Her yardsticks for adulthood—owning her own home, getting married, finishing her education, having children, and finding a job that pays her bills—remain spectacularly out of reach. "Your grandparents would get married out of high school, first go steady, then get married, like they had a house," she reflected. "Since I was 16, I have asked my mother when I would be an adult, and she recently started saying I'm an adult now that I'm working and paying rent, but I don't feel any different."

What does it mean to "grow up" today? Even just a few decades ago, the transition to adulthood would probably not have caused Diana so much confusion, anxiety, or uncertainty. In 1960, the vast majority of women married before they turned 21 and had their first child before 23. By 30, most men and women had moved out of their parents' homes, completed school, gotten married, and begun having children. As over a decade of scholarly and popular literature has revealed, however, in the latter half of the twentieth century traditional markers of adulthood have become increasingly delayed, disorderly, reversible—or have been entirely abandoned. Unlike their 1950s counterparts, who followed a well-worn path from school to work, and courtship to marriage to childbearing, men and women today are more likely to remain unmarried; to live at home and stay in school for longer periods of time; to switch from job to job; to have children out of wedlock; to divorce; or not have children at all.

> Working-class youth are growing up in a world without jobs, without community, and without trust.

long and winding journey

Growing up, in essence, has shifted from a clear-cut, stable, and normative set of transitions to a long and winding journey. This shift has been greeted with alarm, and the Millennial Generation has often been cast as entitled, self-absorbed, and lazy. In 2013, for example, *Time* magazine's cover story on "The Me Me Me Generation" headlined: "Millennials are lazy, entitled narcissists who still live with their parents." And a poll conducted in 2011 by the consulting firm Workplace Options found that the vast majority of Americans believe that Millennials don't work as hard as the generations before them. The overriding conclusion is that things have gotten worse—and that young people are to blame.

But this longing to return to the past obscures the restrictions—and inequalities—that characterized traditional adult milestones for many young people in generations past. As the historian Stephanie Coontz reminds us, in the 1950s and '60s women couldn't serve on juries or own property or take out lines of credit in their own names; alcoholism and physical and sexual abuse within families went ignored; factory workers, despite their rising wages and generous social benefits, reported feeling imprisoned by monotonous work and merciless supervision; and African Americans were denied access to voting, pensions, and health care.

The social movements for civil rights, feminism, and gay pride that emerged during subsequent decades erased many of these barriers, granting newfound freedoms to young adults in their wake. In many ways, young people today have a great deal more freedom and opportunity than their 1950s counterparts: women, especially, can pursue higher education, advance in professional careers, choose if and when to have children, and leave abusive marriages. And all young adults have more freedom to choose a partner regardless of sex or race.

As psychologist Jeffrey Arnett argues: "More than ever before, coming of age in the twenty-first century means learning to stand alone as a self-sufficient person, capable of making choices and decisions independently from among a wide range of possibilities." But that's not the whole story. Just as many social freedoms for young people have expanded, economic security—stable, well-paid jobs, access to health insurance and pensions, and affordable education—has contracted for the working class. Meanwhile, the growing fragility of American families and communities over the same time period has placed the responsibility for launching young adults into the future solely on the shoulders of themselves and their parents.

For the more affluent young adults of this "Peter Pan Generation"—those with a college fund, a parent-subsidized, unpaid internship, or an SAT coach—the freedom to delay marriage and childbearing, experiment with flexible career paths, and pursue higher education grants them the luxury to define adulthood in their own terms. But working-class men and women like Diana have to figure out what it means to be a worthy adult in a world of disappearing jobs, soaring education costs, shrinking social support networks, and fragile families.

From 2008 to 2010, I interviewed 100 working-class men and women between the ages of 24 and 34—people who have long ago reached the legal age of adulthood but still do not feel "grown up." I went from gas stations to fast-food chains, community colleges to temp agencies, tracking down working-class young people, African Americans and Whites, men and women, and documenting the myriad obstacles that stand in their way. And what I heard was profoundly alarming: caught in the throes of a merciless job market and lacking the social support, skills, and knowledge necessary for success, working-class young adults are relinquishing the hope for traditional markers of adulthood—a home, a job, a family—at the heart of the American Dream.

Coming of age means learning to depend only on yourself.

My conversations with these men and women uncovered the contours of a new definition of working-class adulthood: one characterized by low expectations of loyalty in work, wariness toward romantic commitment, widespread distrust of social institutions, and profound isolation from and hostility toward others who can't make it on their own. Simply put, growing up today means learning to depend on no one but yourself.

work and love amid inequality

Pervasive economic insecurity, fear of commitment, and confusion within institutions make the achievement of traditional markers of adulthood impossible and sometimes undesirable. The majority of the young people I spoke with bounce from one unstable service job to the next, racking up credit card debt to make ends meet and fearing the day when economic shocks—an illness, a school loan coming out of deferment—will erode what little stability they have.

Upon leaving high school, they quickly learned that they shouldn't expect loyalty or respect from their jobs. Jillian, a 26-year-old White woman, started out as a line cook, making $5.50 an hour the year she graduated from high school. Under the guidance of her manager, she worked her way up the line until she was his "right-hand man," running the line by herself and making sure everyone cleaned up their stations at the end of a long day. When Bill died suddenly from a heart attack, the owner waited to hire a new manager, causing a year of skeleton crews, chaos, and back-breaking 70-hour workweeks.

Jillian knew that she was lucky to have all those hours a week to work, especially in the recession, and she didn't complain: "you basically worshipped the ground they walked on because they gave you a job. You had to keep your mouth shut." But when Jillian pushed for changes and the owner snapped, "You won't get respect anywhere else, so why expect it here?" She quit. "I thought I had it going good for a while there. But everything really came to a screeching halt, and I bought a car, and now not having a job . . . I feel like I'm starting over."

Indeed, growing up means learning that trusting others, whether at school, home, or work, will only hurt them in the end. Rob is a 26-year-old White man whom I met while recruiting at a National Guard training weekend in Massachusetts. Rob told me his story in an empty office at the armory because he was currently "crashing" on his cousin's couch. When he graduated from his vocational high school, he planned to use his training in metals to build a career as a machinist: "Manufacturing technology, working with metal, I loved that stuff," he recalled longingly. As he attempted to enter the labor market, however, he quickly learned that his newly forged skills were obsolete.

"I was the last class at my school to learn to manufacture tools by hand," he explained. "Now they use CNC [computer numerical controlled] machine programs, so they just draw the part in the computer and plug it into the machine, and the machine cuts it. . . . I haven't learned to do that, because I was the last class before they implemented that in the program at school, and now if you want to get a job as a machinist without CNC, they want five years' experience. My skills are useless."

Over the last five years, Rob has stacked lumber, installed hardwood floors, landscaped, and poured steel at a motorcycle factory. His only steady source of income since high school graduation has been his National Guard pay, and although he recently returned from his second 18-month deployment in Afghanistan, he is already considering a third: "I am looking for a new place. I don't have a job. My car is broken. It's like, what exactly can you do when your car is broken and you have no job, no real source of income, and you are making four or five hundred dollars a month in [military] drills." He explains his economic predicament: "Where are you going to live, get your car fixed, on $500 a month? I can't save making 500 bucks a month. That just covers my bills. I have no savings to put down first and last on an apartment, no car to get a job. I find myself being like, oh what the hell? Can't it just be over? Can't I just go to Iraq right now? Send me two weeks ago so I got a paycheck already!"

Insecurity seeps into the institution of family, leaving respondents uncertain about both the feasibility and desirability of commitment. Deeply forged cultural connections between economic viability, manhood, and marriage prove devastating, as men's falling wages and rising job instability leave them uncertain about the meanings of masculinity in the twenty-first century. Brandon, a 34-year-old Black man who manages the night shift at a women's clothing chain,

explained matter-of-factly, "No woman wants to sit on the couch all the time and watch TV and eat at Burger King. I can only take care of myself now. I am missing out on life but making do with what I have."

For working-class women who have grown up shouldering immense social and economic burdens on their own, being responsible for another person who may ultimately let them down doesn't feel worth the risk. Lauren, a 24-year-old barista who was kicked out of her father's house when she came out as a lesbian, has weathered years of addiction, homelessness, and depression, finally emerging as a survivor, sober and able to pay her own rent. She has chosen to remain single because she fears having to take care of someone else.

"I mean, everybody's life sucks, get over it! My mom's an alcoholic, my dad kicked me out of the house. It's not a handicap; it has made me stronger. And I want someone who has, you know, similarly overcome their respective obstacle and learned and grown from them, rather than someone who is bogged down by it and is always the victim." As Lauren suggests, since intimacy carries with it the threat of self-destruction, young working-class men and women forgo the benefits of lasting commitment, including pooled material resources, mutual support, and love itself.

Children symbolize the one remaining source of trust, love, and commitment; while pregnancies are usually accidental, becoming a parent provides motivation, dignity, and self-worth. As Sherrie, whose pregnancy gave her the courage to break up with her abusive boyfriend, explained: "You have a baby to take care of! My daughter is the reason why I am the way I am today. If I didn't have her, I think I might be a crackhead or an alcoholic or in an abusive relationship!" Yet the social institutions in which young adults create families can work against their desire to nurture and protect their children.

Rachel, a young Black single mother, joined the National Guard in order to go to college for free through the GI Bill. However, working 40 hours a week at her customer service job, attending weekend army drills, and parenting has left her with little time for taking college classes. Hearing rumors that her National Guard unit may deploy to Iraq for a third time in January, she is tempted to put in for discharge so that she is not separated from her son again. However, her desire to give her son everything she possibly can—including the things she can buy with the higher, tax-free combat pay she receives when she deploys—keeps her from signing the papers: "I am kinda half and half with the deployment coming up. I could use it for the money. I could do more for my son. But I missed the first two years of my son's life and now I might have to leave again. It's just rough. You can't win."

Soaring education costs and shrinking support networks make it difficult to gain the skills and knowledge needed to build a secure adult life.

distrust and isolation

Common celebrations of adulthood—whether weddings, graduations, house-warmings, birthdays—are more than just parties; they are rituals for marking community membership and shared, public expressions of commitment, obligation, rights, and belonging. But for the young men and women I spoke with, there was little sense of shared joy or belonging in their accounts of coming of age. Instead, I heard story after story of isolation and distrust experienced within a vast array of social institutions, including higher education, the criminal justice system, the government, and the military. While we may think of the life course as a process of social integration, marked by public celebrations of transitions, young working-class men and women depend on others at their peril.

They believe that a college education will provide the tools for success. Jay, a 28-year-old Black man, struggled through seven years of college. He failed several classes after his mother suffered a severe mental breakdown. After being expelled from college and working for a year, helping his mom get back on her feet, he went before the college administration and petitioned to be reinstated. He described them as "a panel of five people who were not nice." As Jay saw it, "It's their job to hear all these sob stories, you know I understand that, but they just had this attitude, like you know what I mean, 'oh your mom had a breakdown and you couldn't turn to anyone?' I just wanted to be like, fuck you, but I wanted to go to college, so I didn't say fuck you." When he eventually graduated, when he was 25, he "was so disillusioned by the end of it, my attitude toward college was like, I just want to get out and get it over with, you know what I mean, and just like, put it behind me, really." He shrugged: "I felt like it wasn't anything to celebrate. I mean I graduated with a degree. Which ultimately I'm not even sure if that was what I wanted, but there was a point where I was like I have to pick some bullshit I can fly through and just get through. I didn't find it at all worthwhile."

Since graduating three years ago, with a communications major, Jay has worked in a series of food service and coffee-shop jobs. Reflecting on where his life has taken him, he fumed: "They were just blowing smoke up my ass—the world is at my fingertips, you can rule the world, be whatever you want, all this stuff. When I was 15, 16, I would not have envisioned the life I am living now. Whatever I imagined, I figured I would wear a suit every day, that I would own things. I don't own anything. I don't own a car. If I had a car, I wouldn't be able to afford my daily life. I'm coasting and cruising and not sure about what I should be doing."

Christopher, a 24-year-old who has been unemployed for nine months, further illustrates how distrust and isolation is intensified by bewildering interactions with institutions. As he put it, "I have this problem of being tricked. . . . Like I will get a phone call that says, you won a free supply of magazines. And they will start coming to my house. Then all of a sudden I am getting calls from bill collectors for the subscriptions to *Maxim* and *ESPN*. It's a run around: I can't figure out who to call. Now I don't even pick up the phone, like I almost didn't pick up when you called me."

Recently, Christopher was taxed $400 for not purchasing mandatory health insurance in Massachusetts, which he could not afford because he was unemployed, and did not know how to access for free. Like many of my respondents, he lacks the skills and know-how to navigate the institutions that frame the transition to adulthood. He tells his coming-of-age story as one incident of deception after another—each of which incurs a heavy emotional and financial cost. But while he acknowledges that he has not achieved the traditional markers of adulthood, he still believes that he is at least partially an adult because of the way he has learned to manage his feelings of betrayal: "I ended up the way I am because of my experiences. I have seen crazy shit. Like now if I see someone beating someone up in the street, I don't scream. I don't care. I have no emotions or feelings." Growing up hardened against and detached from the world, and dependent on no one, Christopher protects himself from the possibility of trickery and betrayal.

remaking working-class adulthood

The working-class men and women I spoke with lack the necessary knowledge, skills, credentials, and money to launch themselves into a secure adult future, as well as the social support and guidance to protect themselves from economic and social turmoil. But despite their profound anger, betrayal, and loss, they do not want pity—and they do not expect a handout. On the contrary, at a time when individual solutions to collective structural problems is a requirement for survival, they believe that adulthood means taking responsibility for one's own successes and failures. Emma, who works as a waitress, praised her grandfather who worked his way up digging ditches for a gas company; she says it is now up to her to "take what you are given and utilize it correctly." Similarly, Kelly, a line cook who has lived on and off in her car, explains, "Life doesn't owe me any favors. I can have a sense of my own specialness and individuality, but that doesn't mean that anybody else has to recognize that or help me accomplish my goals."

This bootstrap mentality, while highly praised in our culture, has a darker side: blaming those who can't make it on their own. Wanda, the daughter of a tow-truck driver who wants to go to college but can't afford the tuition, expresses anger at her parents' lack of economic support: "I feel like it's their fault they don't have nothing." Working-class youth have little trust even in those closest to them and—despite the social and economic forces that work against their efforts—they blame themselves for their shortcomings.

Julian, a young Black man, is a disabled vet who is unemployed, divorced, and living with his mother. Describing his inability to find a steady job and lasting relationship, he tells me: "Every day I look in the mirror, and I could bullshit you right now and tell you that race has something to do with it. But at the end of the day looking in the mirror, I know where all my shortcomings come from. From the things that I either did not do or I did and I just happen to fail at them." They believe that understanding their shortcomings in terms of structural barriers to mobility is a crutch; both Blacks and

Whites are hostile toward others who do not take sole responsibility for their own failures.

John, a 27-year-old Black man who sells shoes, explained: "Society lets it [race] affect me. It's not what I want to do, but society puts tags on everybody. You gotta be presentable, take care of yourself. It's about how a man looks at himself and how people look at him. Some people use it as a crutch, but it's not gonna be my crutch." That is, while Black men and women acknowledge that discrimination persists, they see navigating racism as an individual game of cunning. All make a virtue out of not asking for help, out of rejecting dependence and surviving completely on their own, mapping these traits onto their definitions of adulthood. Those who fail to "fix themselves" are met with disdain and disgust—they are not worthy adults.

This hardening against oneself and others could have profound personal and political consequences for the future of the American working class. Its youngest members embrace self-sufficiency, blame those who are unsuccessful in the labor market, and choose distrust and isolation as the only way to survive. Rather than target the vast social, economic, and cultural changes that have disrupted the transition to adulthood—the decline of good jobs, the weakening of unions, the shrinking of communities—they target themselves. In the end, if they have to go it alone, then everyone else should, too. And it is hard to find even a glimmer of hope for their futures.

Their coming-of-age stories are still unfolding, their futures not yet written. In order to tell a different kind of story—one that promises hope, dignity, and connection—they must begin their journeys to adulthood with a living wage and the skills and knowledge to confront the future. They need neighborhoods and communities that share responsibility for launching them into the future. And they need new definitions of dignity that do not make a virtue out of isolation, self-reliance, and distrust. The health and vibrancy of all our communities depend on the creation and nurturance of definitions of adulthood that foster connection and interdependence.

RECOMMENDED RESOURCES

Andrew Cherlin. 2009. *The Marriage Go-Round: The State of Marriage and the Family in America Today.* New York: Vintage Books.

> Traces the transformation of American families over the past century and points to alarming class-based differences in marriage patterns.

Kathryn Edin and Timothy J. Nelson. 2013. *Doing the Best I Can: Fatherhood in the Inner City.* Berkeley and Los Angeles: University of California Press.

> Sheds light on the experiences of low-income fathers and their struggles to care for their children despite their lack of jobs and rocky relationships with their children's mothers.

Frank F. Furstenberg, Sheela Kennedy, Vonnie C. McLoyd, Rubén G. Rumbaut, and Richard A. Settersten Jr. 2004. "Growing Up Is Harder to Do." *Contexts* 3: 33–41.

> Provides a comprehensive overview of the delayed transition to adulthood for working-class youth.

Jacob Hacker. 2006. "The Privatization of Risk and the Growing and Economic Insecurity of Americans." http://privatizationofrisk.ssrc.org.

> Documents the recent cultural and political shifts in the United States that have demolished social safety nets and promoted self-reliance, untrammeled individualism, and personal responsibility.

Arne L. Kalleberg. 2009. "Precarious Work, Insecure Workers." *American Sociological Review* 74: 1–22.

> Explains how and why working-class jobs have become increasingly scarce, insecure, and competitive.

REVIEW QUESTIONS

1. In what ways is the system working against working-class young adults?
2. The author uses qualitative interviews to look at the transition to adulthood. What kind of information do these interviews add that some quantitative work may miss?
3. How can policy-makers ensure that the policies they are creating to foster economic growth reach all members of the population?

jessi streib

marrying across class lines

33

spring 2015

even when married couples think childhood class differences are in the past, those factors shape how each spouse tackles tasks and allocates resources.

Christie, a cheerful social worker in her mid-40s, told me about the first time she met her husband, Mike. It was more than 30 years ago, when they were in junior high school. She used to watch Mike as he wiped off the tables before the next round of students entered the school cafeteria. She thought he was cute and smart. And she was not fooled by his job—she knew that it was people like her who usually cleaned tables, not people like Mike. In fact, her father worked on the maintenance crew at their school.

Mike's father, by contrast, was a productive professor who authored famous books and traveled the world attending conferences and giving lectures. As Christie knew, Mike washed tables in exchange for being allowed to go to the front of the line to collect his food, not because he needed the money.

When the couple began dating, their class differences became obvious. Her parents rarely bought new items; their cars were used and the ping pong table they gave her for Christmas was put together with items they found. Pop-Tarts were her favorite food, but one that they could rarely afford. Mike's family bought expensive new cars, went on annual vacations, had cable TV, and had enough money left over to tuck a good amount away in Mike's trust fund. But while they had grown up with different amounts of resources, by the time we talked, Christie did

not feel that their differences mattered. Over 25 years of marriage, they shared a house, a bank account, a level of educational attainment, and, later, three children. Their lives had merged, and so had their resources. To Christie, their class differences were part of their pasts, and, in any case, never mattered much: "I don't think that it was the actual economic part that made the tension for Mike and I. It was personality style more than class or money."

Christie was one of the 64 adults in 32 couples I interviewed about their marriages, their current families, and their pasts. In order to focus on how class background matters in a small sample, all respondents were White college-educated adults in heterosexual marriages. Half were like Christie—they had grown up in the working class. The other half were like Mike—they had grown up in the middle class. All were married to a partner whose class origin was different than their own. My goal was to discern how what most respondents, like Christie, did not think mattered—their class background—was related to their ways of attending to their own lives and to their marriages. Although respondents tended to think their class differences were behind them, irrelevant to their current lives, instead they left a deep imprint that their marriage, their shared resources, and their thousands of days together did not erase.

social class and family life

It is common knowledge that families located in different social classes develop different ways of going about daily life. Such differences were made famous in the 1970s by sociologist and psychologist Lillian Rubin in her classic book *Worlds of Pain*. Rubin interviewed couples and demonstrated that the texture of family life, as well as ideas of what it means to be a good parent, child, and spouse, are all shaped by the resources and jobs available to families. Later, sociologist Annette Lareau offered another in-depth look, observing that the daily interactions between parents and children, and, to some degree, between adult members of the family, differed by social class. Middle-class parents, she found, tended to manage their children's lives, while working-class parents more often let their children grow. French sociologist Pierre Bourdieu also observed wide class differences. He theorized that class not only shapes family life, but also individuals' ideas and instincts about how to use resources, spend time, and interact with others. Sociologists do not see each family as wholly unique, but shaped by the resources available to them in their class position.

Such work suggests that people like Christie and Mike, who grew up in different social classes, were likely to have different experiences of family and develop different ideas about a "good life." However, when scholars of social class and family life conduct research, they usually focus on the divide between college-educated couples and everyone else. This divide *is* critical for understanding inequality, but it is problematic to simply call couples like Christie and Mike a college-educated, middle-class couple. The label erases the fact that Christie and Mike spent two decades in a class apart, and that upwardly mobile people like Christie may carry their ideas of family and a good life with them into their marriage and the middle class.

Indeed, simply referring to Christie and Mike as a college-educated, middle-class couple ignores that Christie knew what it was like to grow up with limited savings, watch a parent go to a job that was consistently framed as a means to an end, and grow up in a family that expressed their emotions immediately and intensely. It ignores that Mike knew of none of these things. He knew, instead, of family safety nets, jobs that were enjoyed beyond their financial ends, and emotions that were rationalized and guarded.

When social scientists ignore these background differences, they present only differences *between* college-educated and high school–educated couples, overlooking differences *within* college-educated couples. And when married couples ignore these differences, they ignore that the class of each partner's past organizes and shapes the contours of their marriage.

> Although respondents tended to think their class differences were behind them, they left a deep imprint that their marriage, shared resources, and thousands of days together did not erase.

the organization of difference

Christie believed that her differences from Mike were driven by their personalities. She wasn't wrong. What she did not realize, however, was that what she called their personalities were, in turn, related to their class trajectory. People like Christie—born into the working class but now college educated—tended to prefer taking what I call a *laissez-faire* approach to their daily lives. They preferred to go with the flow, enjoy the moment, and live free from self-imposed constraints. They assumed things would work out without their intervention. People like Mike—those born into the middle class—instead tended to prefer to take what I call a *managerial* approach to their daily lives. They preferred to plan, monitor, organize, and oversee. They assumed that things would not work out without their active intervention.

The people I interviewed did not just apply laissez-faire and managerial tendencies to one aspect of their lives, but *seven*. When it came to how to attend to their money, paid work, housework, time, leisure, parenting, and emotions, middle-class-origin respondents tended to want to plan, organize, and oversee. Working-class-origin respondents more often preferred to let things take their own course without as much intervention.

Take, for example, how Christie and Mike thought about money. When I met them, they had shared a bank account for over two decades, but they did not share ideas of how to use the money in it. Referring to money, Christie repeatedly told Mike: "Live for the day!" Growing up, saving for long-range plans was not possible. Christie's family had to spend what they had to pay their bills today. A small amount in savings was also normal to her as a child, and continued to be normal to her as a college-educated adult. Christie said that she learned from her parents' experience that worrying about money was unnecessary: even without much money, things would work out. Now that she and Mike were both college-educated professionals who earned much more than her parents, this seemed especially true. Free from concerns over necessities, she now made a point to be free from worrying about money.

Mike, however, grew up in a family with more money and more options. His family could pay for their daily needs, then choose how to save for college tuition, retirement, rainy days, and leisure. For him, thinking about how to manage money was normal and he learned that management could make a difference. As an adult, Mike budgeted, monitored their current expenditures, forecasted their future expenses, and worried about whether he was earning enough. When Christie told him to "live for the day" and worry less, he reported responding: "I see that. But at the same time, we had three kids in college, and we're in our mid-forties. We have a lot of expenses." He felt that Christie's laissez-faire philosophy was reasonable, but he felt more comfortable with a managerial one.

Their differences also extended to work. Christie grew up observing her father work in a job as a maintenance worker at her public school while her mother did unpaid labor at home. There was no career ladder for her father to climb. Hours were circumscribed by a time clock and putting in more hours would not lead to more status or opportunities. Mike also saw his mother doing unpaid home labor, but observed his father, a professor, on a career ladder—from graduate student, to assistant, associate, and then full professor. More hours could lead to more books published, more prestige, and more opportunities to share his ideas.

Such differences likely shaped Christie's and Mike's ideas of work. Mike felt he had to prod Christie, a social worker, to not be "status quo"—to work longer hours and think about how moving to a new place might give them opportunities to get ahead. Christie, for her part, admired Mike's dedication to work, but did not understand it. Mike owned his own business. He worked long hours (despite not being paid by the hour) and he constantly felt pressure to achieve more. Christie asked him to work fewer hours and have more faith that his business would do fine without his planning, strategizing, and long

> Just as taking the person out of the class did not take the class out of the person, a marriage was not a new beginning that removed the imprints of each partner's class past.

hours. So, just as Mike asked Christie to take a more managerial approach to work—one where she organized and planned her career trajectory—Christie asked Mike to take a more laissez-faire approach—one where he put in less time, did less planning, and assumed his career would be okay. Though each understood the other's perspective, neither adopted it. Christie maintained her hands-off approach to work. Mike maintained his hands-on one.

This hands-on/hands-off, or managerial/laissez-faire divide organized many other aspects of their lives. Mike wanted to manage the division of housework by putting "more structure in the whole idea of who is going to do what" around the house. Christie wanted each to do the household tasks as they got around to them. Mike preferred to manage his feelings—to slowly process and weigh how to express them. Christie felt it was more genuine to express emotions as they were felt and in the way they were felt. Christie summarized their differences when she described Mike as Type A, driven, and organized—all things that she felt she was not.

Some of the differences that Christie and Mike expressed might sound like gender differences. Gender certainly shapes *how much* time each spouse spends on each task and *how much* power they have over decisions in different spheres. But with the exception of the highly gendered spheres of housework and parenting in which it was mainly women who followed the managerial/laissez-faire divide, class origin alone shaped how each partner wanted to tackle each task and use each resource. Take, for example, Leslie and Tom. They proudly proclaim that they are nerds: they met at a science fiction convention, continued their courtship through singing together in a science fiction–themed choir, and, as a married couple, engage in role-playing games together.

Their shared interests and college degrees, however, could not mask the lingering ways their class backgrounds shaped their lives and their marriage.

Leslie, a fit 40-year-old with short brown hair and glasses, was raised by a graduate school–educated middle-manager and a college-educated homemaker. She attended private school with the sons and daughters of celebrities, judges, and politicians—where, she said, "famous and rich people were the norm." Her husband, Tom, a shy, dark-haired 40-year-old, grew up as the son of a high school–educated security guard and a nurse. He attended public school. While their childhood class differences certainly could have been wider, they still mapped onto ways of organizing their lives. Leslie, like Mike, preferred a managerial approach to her life—scheduling, planning, organizing, and monitoring. Tom, like Christie, felt that a hands-off approach was a better way to live.

The differences that Leslie and Tom described about money mirrored those that Mike and Christie expressed. Leslie stated simply: "I'm the saver and he's the spender." But it was not just how much Tom spent that bothered Leslie, it was also that Tom did not actively think about managing their money. Leslie complained: "I do the lion's share of work. Beyond the lion's share of the work . . . balancing stuff, actually paying the bills, keeping track of things, saying we need to have some goals. Both big picture and small picture stuff." She said that Tom did not manage money; he spent without thinking.

Tom knew of Leslie's concern: "She worries a lot more about money than I do. About how we're doing . . . I think she would like it if I paid more attention to what our expenses are and how the money is going out." They had been having these debates for the past 20 years,

> Class origin shaped how each partner wanted to tackle each task and use each resource.

but their differences had not gone away. Leslie said she still couldn't get Tom to set financial goals or think about how each expense fit in with their overall plan. Their compromise was that Tom checked with Leslie before making big purchases. But this was not an optimal solution for Leslie, who called herself the "superego"—the one who still had to make the decisions about how to manage their money, about what they really needed and what they could forgo. Tom still assumed it would all work out, that a hands-off approach would do just fine.

Leslie also noted that she took a managerial approach to work, whereas Tom took a laissez-faire one. At the time of the interview, Leslie was a college-educated, part-time secretary at her children's school. Tom was a college-educated computer programmer. Though Leslie's job was less prestigious, she found much more satisfaction in it, talking about the sense of accomplishment she had at work, the meaning of doing good work, and her goals for the future. She was not sure what her next career move would be, but she knew one thing: "I want to get somewhere." Tom didn't want to get anywhere with work. Leslie cried as she explained: "He's been at the same job for quite awhile and only moves when forced to."

Leslie clarified that her concern was not about how much Tom earned, but about his approach to his career: "I can totally understand being content. It's more that sometimes I just don't know what he wants and I'm not sure he knows. And this may sound dumb, but the actual goals, what they are, worry me less than not having any." To Leslie, careers were to be managed. Goals were to be created and worked toward. Tom did not have the same sense.

Their differences also extended past what is directly related to class—money and work—to other parts of their lives. Like Mike, Leslie wanted to structure housework more than Tom

did, so she delegated tasks and monitored his work. Tom, like Christie, figured the housework could be done when he got to it, without as much of a schedule. Leslie and Mike liked to plan and organize in general. However, while Mike appreciated that Christie got him to pause his planning and "stop to smell the roses," Leslie was upset that Tom did not plan. She expressed it as a deficiency: "If you plan, if you're a planner, you do that mental projecting all the time. You're thinking ahead, saying, 'What's going to happen if I do this?' I really don't think he does that. I don't know if it's because he doesn't want to, it's too hard, he doesn't have the capacity, I don't know. But he just doesn't do that." Tom defended his approach: "She definitely wants more structure in things we do, more planning. I'm more of a 'Let's just do it' [person] and it will get done the best way we can get it done."

Leslie also insisted that their children's time be structured by adults, guided by routines, and directed at learning-related outcomes. But Tom, again, questioned this approach: "Leslie thinks they need more structure than they really do." As such, when he was in charge of parenting, he did not ask their daughters to have a regular reading time or strict bedtime. He did not view each of the kids' behaviors as in need of monitoring, assessing, or guiding. As sociologist Annette Lareau observed of people currently in the working class, Tom, who was born into the working class but no longer a member, felt that the kids would be fine without parents' constant management.

navigating difference

The laissez-faire/managerial differences that couples like Christie and Mike and Leslie and Tom navigated were common to the couples I interviewed—college-educated couples in which each partner grew up in a different class. The systematic differences that these couples faced meant that class infused their marriages, usually without their knowledge. These differences, however, were not experienced in a uniform way.

Most of the people I interviewed appreciated their spouse's differences, or at least found them understandable and valid. A minority of couples, however, found their differences to be more divisive. In these couples, middle-class-origin respondents disdained their spouse's attitudes and asked their spouse to change.

Christie and Mike were one of the couples who dealt with their differences with respect and even admiration. Mike did not always agree with Christie's laissez-faire approach, but he appreciated her sense that he sometimes needed to manage less and live in the moment more. Christie sometimes found Mike's managerial style frustrating, but she also admired how organized he was. She appreciated how well Mike had done in his career and respected that he needed more planning, organization, and monitoring to feel secure. They preferred different approaches, but they saw the benefits of the other's way and tried to accommodate their partner's differences.

Leslie and Tom did not navigate their differences with such ease. Leslie defined Tom's hands-off approach as deeply flawed. As such, her strategy was to get him to change—to get him to do things in a more managerial way. But her strategy left them both unhappy. Tom resented being asked to change; Leslie fumed that Tom would say he would change, but did not. She explained: "Mostly what happens is he says, 'You're right. That would be better.' But the implementation is just not always there." Leslie remained frustrated with what she saw as the inadequacy of Tom's style, and Tom remained frustrated that Leslie did not see the benefits of living a life that was less structured, scheduled, and planned. Asking for assimilation was a failed strategy, both in that it did not work and in that it

respondents said that it left them disappointed and dissatisfied.

Regardless of how they navigated their differences—with respect or demands for change—couples like Mike and Christie and Leslie and Tom had to navigate the subtle ways that the class of their pasts still shaped their lives and their marriages. The decades that each couple was together, their shared college degrees, and their shared resources did not erase the fact that the middle-class-origin partners preferred to take a managerial approach to their lives while working-class-origin partners favored a laissez-faire one. Just as taking the person out of the class did not take the class out of the person, a marriage was not a new beginning that removed the imprints of each partner's class past.

RECOMMENDED RESOURCES

Pierre Bourdieu. 1984. *Distinction*. Cambridge, MA: Harvard University Press.

> Offers a theoretically sophisticated examination of how social class is related to tastes, worldviews, and dispositions.

Marcia Carlson and Paula England, eds. 2011. *Social Class and Changing Families in an Unequal America*. Palo Alto: Stanford University Press.

> Charts demographic changes that have occurred between families in different social classes.

Annette Lareau. 2003. *Unequal Childhoods*. Berkeley: University of California Press.

> Explains how parenting styles differ by social class.

Lillian Rubin. 1976. *Worlds of Pain*. New York: Basic Books.

> Provides a detailed account of how marriage, parenting, and work are related to social class, especially for the working class.

REVIEW QUESTIONS

1. How do the laissez-faire and managerial approaches differ in terms of how people prefer to organize their daily lives? Do you think these distinctions make sense?

2. Think about your own life and class background. Do you think whether you grew up working class, middle class, or upper class has shaped how you approach your education and career plans?

3. Pretend you are a counselor working with couples who come from different class backgrounds. What advice might you give to couples to help them come to agreement about managing their finances?

viewpoints

after gay marriage equality forum

summer 2015

andrew j. cherlin, steven w. thrasher, joshua gamson, and georgiann davis discuss the implications of the legalization of gay marriage and what it says about what comes next.

Suddenly, the Supreme Court has declared marriage for same-sex couples a constitutional right. Now what? To help answer that, *Contexts* presents a symposium of short responses to the phrase "after marriage equality." The four writers featured are prominent researchers on the politics, demography, history, identity, law, and culture of where we are, how we got here, and what comes next. Together, this symposium offers a sociology of the moment.

—Philip N. Cohen and Syed Ali

(*Photo by Philip N. Cohen*)

andrew j. cherlin

the triumph of family diversity

Without doubt, liberal observers of American family life are delighted with the Supreme Court's decision in *Obergefell v. Hodges*. I am one of them. In 1996 I was one of five sociologists to sign a friend of the court brief in *Baehr v. Miike*, a case in which three same-sex couples sued the state of Hawaii for the right to marry. The brief, which supported the couples' position, was coordinated by Lawrence Wu, now at New York University. I soon moved on, but Wu and many other social scientists and historians took up the issue and have seen it through to its conclusion. The transformation of American law and public opinion in two decades is remarkable.

Yet most liberals would avoid the ringing rhetoric with which Justice Anthony Kennedy extoled "the transcendent importance of marriage" in writing the majority's opinion in *Obergefell*. I don't know many college professors who would be comfortable telling their students, as Kennedy told the nation, "No union is more profound than marriage, for it embodies the highest ideals of love, fidelity, devotion, sacrifice, and family." Instead, liberals are likely to celebrate the ruling not because it may strengthen marriage but rather because it establishes that families come in diverse forms and deserve equal rights and protections. In this sense, *Obergefell* represents the triumph of the idea of family diversity.

This irony of this triumph has not been lost on social conservatives. Ross Douthat wrote in his column in the *New York Times*:

Millennials may agree with Kennedy's ruling, but they're making his view of marriage as "a keystone of the nation's social order" look antique. In their views and (lack of) vows, they're taking a more relaxed perspective, in which wedlock is malleable and optional, one way among many to love, live, rear kids—or not.

Like Douthat, many of the defenders of heterosexual marriage over the past decade are wary of same-sex marriage. Their claim is that legitimizing alternatives to traditional marriage will serve to weaken marriage as an institution: diversity equals decline.

Will *Obergefell* weaken marriage? It is certainly possible that as alternative paths to adulthood are legitimized, the role of marriage in the American family system may lessen. In fact, that has already happened. It is simply less necessary to be married today, be it with a same- or different-sex partner, than it was for different-sex partners in the past. Attitudes toward having children outside of marriage are less negative than they used to be. Rates of marriage have declined; cohabitation has increased. The critics of the Court's decision argue essentially that the greater the number of acceptable ways of forming a partnership and having children, the less normative any one route is. *Obergefell* opens up another one.

And yet the opposite case—that *Obergefell* will strengthen marriage—can be made. On the level of social norms—on what's best for families, on what kind of family is preferred— marriage remains broadly popular among the American population, up and down the social-class ladder and across racial and ethnic groups. The legitimation of alternatives—what I have called the deinstitutionalization of marriage— does not seem to have altered Americans' preference for marriage. The announcement of the Supreme Court's decision and the attention paid to it in the media have sent a message to the American public: Marriage still matters. We shouldn't underestimate the influence of this message, which was issued by the most respected governmental institution in the nation. The public debate about the wisdom of *Obergefell* demonstrates how much Americans continue to value marriage. In contrast, the French or Swedish public would not care as much whether a court decision weakened or strengthened marriage.

Moreover gay men and lesbians in states that allowed same-sex marriage before *Obergefell* have been voting with their feet in favor of marriage. Demographer Gary Gates estimates that 34 percent of all same-sex couples in the Northeast—the region where same-sex marriage has been legal the longest—were married in 2013. That's a surprisingly large percentage, given the relatively short period during which more than a handful of states permitted same-sex marriages. To be sure, the high current levels of same-sex marriage may decline as the backlog

of committed couples in long-standing relationships decreases. Young gay men and lesbians in new partnerships are unlikely to marry with such fervor.

Nevertheless, some same-sex marriage advocates have joined with longtime proponents of heterosexual marriage to argue that we are at a "marriage opportunity" moment in which its advantages can be made plain to all. Liberals can now join conservatives in endorsing the benefits of marriage, they argue, without abandoning their commitment to inclusion and equality. "In short," they write, "for the first time in decades, Americans have an opportunity to think about marriage in a way that brings us together rather than drives us apart."

So the net effect of the legalization of same-sex marriage is hard to predict. It is by no means clear that it will weaken the institution of marriage. Meanwhile this highly valued and privileged status has been opened to all couples, regardless of sexual orientation—a major social advance.

steven w. thrasher

knowledge for the next generation's movement

In my career as a journalist, I have probably written more about the fight for marriage equality than on any other single topic, covering it nationally for ten publications over seven years (the *Ventura County Star*, the *New York Times*, *Out*, the *Advocate*, the *Village Voice*, *Newsweek*/the *Daily Beast*, *Gawker*, *BuzzFeed*, the *Guardian*, and, with this post, *Contexts*). In just two presidential administrations, gay and lesbian couples seeking the right to marry have gone from being wedge scapegoats used by President George W. Bush to whip up votes from his bigoted base, to being celebrated by

President Obama with a White House bathed in rainbow colors.

My interest in marriage equality was initially very personal: my parents' interracial marriage had once been illegal, I am gay, and when I started covering the movement, I was in a relationship with a foreign citizen. (He eventually left the United States, before marriage could have been an option to keep us together.)

Yet over the years, I've become increasingly critical of the ways the marriage equality movement was at odds with queerness, as it encouraged LGBT America to downplay sexuality and embrace a straight, Fordist notion of being "normal." I've never thought marriage equality was unimportant, but in my reporting I've become aware of its conservative nature and of the ways it overshadows challenges LGBT people face which can't be fixed by getting hitched. For example: No LGBT groups or even AIDS service organizations were part of Occupy Wall Street, not even its call for universal health care access—a goal which would greatly address HIV/AIDS and the disparate impact it has on LGBT people (especially gay men of color). Instead, gay rights groups pursued marriage as a vehicle to increase insurance access, a goal which leaves out all single uninsured people and those not able to marry someone with a job offering spousal health benefits.

Similarly, issues like HIV criminalization, LGBT youth homelessness, and LGBT immigration issues of the unmarried have been left largely ignored by the likes of the Human Rights Campaign, the largest LGBT organization (and a shamefully self-acknowledged "White Men's Club"). Black Lives Matter, though started by and filled with queer people of color, is also off the radar of most LGBT groups, who have found it easier to raise money off of smiling couples than to address the police brutality and systemic racism.

Sex has also been politely scrubbed from homo*sex*uality during the marriage movement. When I wrote about monogamy in same-sex couples for *Gawker* in 2013, I relied upon the work of the Gay Couples Study at the Center for Research and Education on Gender and Sexuality in San Francisco, which has found that about 50 percent of gay male couples are openly nonmonogamous. It occurred to me at the time that, as excellent as the research is (CREGS has been interviewing over 500 male couples for more than six years), the data could only tell us so much about the sexual practices of same-sex couples. The population was only from the San Francisco Bay Area, there's no data about women, and the participants' sex lives were shaped in an era where marriage equality was largely or entirely unavailable. The literature of the field is so scant, no literature review is yet possible.

To understand LGBT families as sociologists, journalists, or even simply as humans, we are going to need to study a full generation from June 26, 2015. The Williams Institute at UCLA School of Law has done excellent work on LGBT families across a broad spectrum of research, but until last month, it was all done in the context of an access to marriage that was largely unavailable in most of the country. Just as good research can now look at mixed-race families post 1967's *Loving v. Virginia*, a generation or two will be needed to see how LGBT families do or do not conform to American familial norms. (I'm especially curious, in the coming decades, to test a theory I've long had: that young heterosexual Millennials, close to their out queer peers, might decide to adopt the openly nonmonogamous sexuality that has been associated with gay male culture.)

It's going to take time even with marriage. Hopefully, government institutions like the Census, the Bureau of Labor Statistics, and the Centers for Disease Control will follow the excellent examples of CREGS and the Williams Institute and invest appropriate funds for the study of this newly legalized demographic. But as writers, scholars, and activists, this is a huge opportunity to broaden our scope of inquiry with one issue largely solved. It would behoove us now to actively study the many issues (homelessness, legal employment discrimination, violence against trans women, police profiling) not fulfilled by marriage, and to train our eyes on the systemic challenges LGBT people face which can remain invisible even when in plain sight—as marriage once was.

joshua gamson

the moment of maybe

In the days since *Obergefell v. Hodges* and its rainbow celebration, I spent way too much time on Facebook reading through the voluminous posts and commentaries about how wonderful, awful, incomplete, conservative, progressive, lame, and historic the Supreme Court's decision is. Setting aside the more strident, ungenerous, overstated, patronizing, and self-serving of these—frankly, that eliminates a lot of them—these stocktaking discussions highlight several important, basic points. First, marriage equality symbolically and legally marks the end of outsider status for many within gay movements, and that is both an uneasy and vexed transition. Second, there's a whole lot more work to be done, both in terms of completing the equalization of rights and the broader work of social justice and institutional change; beware of what Michelangelo Signorile has called "victory blindness." Third, the fact that the Supreme Court ruled favorably toward marriage equality, and that public opinion, pop culture, and big business have shifted so favorably toward gay rights in recent years, stands in stark, telling juxtaposition to the heightened attacks on Black Americans and the rollback of reproductive rights.

Clearly, the Supreme Court's marriage equality decision marks a turning point for the LGBT movement—or rather, for the diverse, messy array of efforts and organizations that fall under that rubric. The question now is what that movement will do in this moment of possibility. A lot of smart people have been thinking, writing, talking, and acting on that question, and the best I can do is to cull from them the intertwined principles that might guide the next stages in this vibrant, ass-kicking movement.

Formal equality is not enough. Activists such as Urvashi Vaid have for decades been pointing to the limits of pursuing a "state of virtual equality that would grant legal and formal equal rights to LGBT people but would not transform the institutions of society that repress sexual, racial, and gender difference." If you needed a devastating reminder of legal equality's insufficiency, you could get that by flipping from the breathless SCOTUS celebrations to Rev. Pinckney's dead body being carried past the Confederate flag. Now that gay and lesbian virtual equality is well within reach—legal scholar Nan Hunter predicts that the LGBT-rights movement "will seem banal in 20 years if not sooner"—LGBT movements can return to a more ambitious social-justice agenda.

Do not close the doors. A few years ago, Vaid suggested the guiding movement principle of "Leave No Queer Behind," and it's a crucial one at this moment. One of the risks when some beneficiaries of a movement are invited into social institutions is that they will abandon those who remain by necessity or choice on the margins. Refusing to do so—refusing to betray or abandon those who aren't easily assimilated or who don't want to assimilate—may involve the movement, as historian Timothy Stewart-Winter points out, in challenging the institutions that have just invited some of us in.

Intersectionality is not just a theory. That sexuality is intertwined with race, class, gender, physical ability, age, and the like is often noted but has not deeply informed much of mainstream LGBT rights organizing. It should be impossible to see the attacks on Black and Brown bodies, for instance, as an issue separate from LGBT concerns, if only for the obvious reason that some of us *are* LGBT people of color. The fight for gay rights has advanced in part by deploying economic and racial privilege, and over time, Vaid asserts, LGBT organizations have moved away from their earlier intersectional roots; the movement has been "oddly complacent in its acceptance of racial, gender, and economic inequalities, and vocal only in its challenge to the conditions facing a White, middle-class conception of the 'status queer.'" At this turning point moment, she has advocated, a "re-formed LGBT movement focused on social justice [must] commit itself to one truth: that not all LGBT people are White or well-off."

Coalitions, coalitions, coalitions. All of these linked principles—seeing formal equality as a starting rather than end point, refusing to leave anyone behind, making intersectionality a core organizing principle—promote a renewed focus on building and strengthening coalitions. The movement itself has always been a coalition, of course, and a fragile one; this transitional moment offers an opportunity to recommit to a coalition of lesbian *and* gay *and* bisexual *and* transgender coalition. It's also an opportunity to imagine and enact new progressive coalitions; some are already working on these coalitions, and others have long ties that can be renewed.

Until last week, these principles seemed right but like a bit of a lost cause. As sociologist Suzanna Danuta Walters puts it, the gay marriage fight, for all its practical and symbolic value, took up a lot of "bandwidth and sucked the air out of the potentially more capacious room of queer world-making." Now, at this turning point, when energy can be redirected and different voices emboldened, they seem instead like hopeful possibilities. Whether the LGBT movement manages to, as Walters says, "pivot and recalibrate," I can't predict, but the principles for recalibration are certainly well articulated. We are in a big moment of maybe.

georgiann davis

what's marriage equality got to do with intersex?

Intersex people have, consciously or not, been queering marriage long before U.S. activists were fighting for marriage equality. Intersex people, that is, people whose bodies defy arbitrary markers of sex, including genital, chromosomal, and gonadal characteristics, didn't have to wait for the U.S. Supreme Court's historical decision to legally say "I do!" to a romantic partner with the same sex chromosomes, a key, albeit arbitrary, marker of biological sex.

I vividly remember queering my own marriage in 2001. On a rainy October Saturday in a suburb of Chicago, I walked down the aisle in a traditional white wedding dress and married a cisgender man who, like me, has XY chromosomes. We were legally married surrounded by our families and friends (and later amicably divorced, but that's for another blog post).

I was diagnosed with complete androgen insensitivity syndrome (CAIS) when I was a young teenager, but I didn't know this until years after my parents received the diagnosis and I underwent "normalization" surgery, the removal of my internal and undescended testes. Like many intersex people with CAIS, I had no idea that I had testes and XY chromosomes because doctors lied to me and told me I was born with precancerous ovaries, not healthy testes that were removed because medical providers didn't think it was acceptable for a girl to have testes. Encouraged by the health professionals who "fixed" me, my parents went along with the medical lies in order to protect the development of my gender identity.

I uncovered the medical lies I was told when I obtained my medical records and read through the redacted text to learn I had testicular feminization syndrome (what my intersex trait was called when I was initially diagnosed). I didn't discuss my diagnosis with anyone, as I was too ashamed and was worried others would see me for the freak that I felt I was. I remember questioning whether or not I was really a man. Why else would providers and my parents lie to me? I also remember making a conscious decision to keep my medical history from my then soon-to-be husband. I was convinced he would call off our wedding if he knew what I had just found out about my body.

When the time came to sign the marriage license, I felt my gender as a woman legally validated. Marriage, a state-sponsored institution, was the powerful vehicle that disentangled my sex (biological, albeit arbitrary, markers of "male" or "female" characteristics) from my gender (socially agreed upon, and also arbitrary, markers of "masculinity" and "femininity" characteristics). Marriage, to a man, was a big step in making me a woman.

In 2008 I found myself in a sociology doctoral program studying the complexities of sex, gender, and sexuality. It was then that I decided to embrace my intersex trait and question my gender identity, although this time in a liberating, rather than stigmatizing, manner. As I learned about the arbitrary markers of biological sex, the complexities of gender, and fluidity of sexuality, I felt like a unique variation, not a freak of nature. It was then that I started to refuse to keep my medical past a secret, and instead wanted to bridge my personal experience with intersex and professional passion in sociology in an in-depth analysis of the ways intersex

people, their parents, and medical experts define, experience, and contest intersex in contemporary U.S. society. That project has evolved into my book, *Contesting Intersex: The Dubious Diagnosis*, where I tell the complicated story of how *intersex* was reinvented as *disorders of sex development* in order for medical providers to escape critiques from intersex activists over medically unnecessary and irreversible surgeries providers force intersex people to endure.

My research also reveals that some intersex people, encouraged by medical providers who wanted to make sure our gender identity aligned with the sex they surgically constructed, looked to heterosexual partnering to validate their gender identity. This was especially the case for those who were not exposed to feminist ideas about sex, gender, and sexuality, and more specifically, bodies and embodiments.

As it was in my case, marriage was a path by which intersex people learned to accept themselves as "real" women, or in some cases "real" men, while also pleasing their parents, medical providers, and others in their lives by assuring them they made the correct medically unnecessary and irreversible surgical decisions.

On June 26, when the U.S. Supreme Court ruled same-sex marriage was a constitutional right, my social media exploded with rainbows and excitement. Many of my intersex friends from around the world also shared these celebrations. But marriage has historically functioned as a heteronormative institution, and one of the primary ways intersex people have validated their gender assignment and normalized their selves. So I wasn't surprised that the marriage equality ruling also seemed to cause some discontent or uneasiness among a few, albeit a minority, of intersex people and parents of intersex children. For decades now, many medical providers viewed their medically unnecessary and irreversible interventions as successful when those they "fixed" enacted or engaged in heterosexual relationships, which was formally achieved with marriage.

This theme even came up in my own medical records. After a routine exam soon after my marriage, the doctor who removed my testes wrote in my chart: "She has recovered well from surgery and is married and doing well."

The marriage equality decision leaves me, as both an intersex person and as a feminist sociologist, with a number of questions. What will happen, I wonder, to intersex people who would have or do seek gender validation through the institution of marriage? Because marriage is now more inclusive than it once was, will it no longer serve as a viable path to gender validation? What other state-sponsored institutions will rise to become mechanisms of gender validation? What new markers of successful gender assignment will medical providers rely on as they seek to (problematically) categorize intersex people?

REVIEW QUESTIONS

1. Cherlin discusses the institution of marriage in his response. What does he argue has changed about marriage? In the future, what are different ways the institution of marriage may (or may not) be affected by the legalization of gay marriage?
2. All of the author's reactions to the legalization of gay marriage mention that the fight is not over. What other important issues are mentioned in terms of policy?
3. Which response stuck out the most for you? Why?

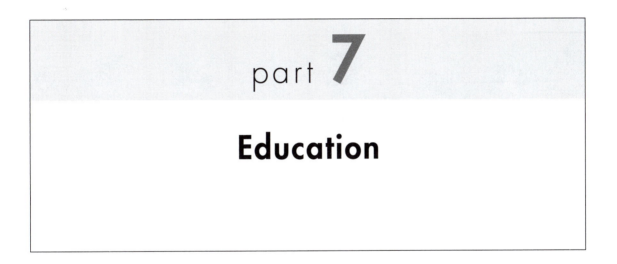

part **7**

Education

oyler school against the odds

spring 2015

oyler community learning center in ohio has become a national model for integrating education with social and health services. in a neighborhood where many children don't finish high school, partnerships with outside organizations bring in necessary services to help support their success.

Drive west from downtown Cincinnati, over the railroad tracks that snake beneath the 8th Street Viaduct, and you'll find a little slice of Appalachia, nestled between the Ohio River and the steep slopes of Price Hill. When coal mining jobs in Kentucky and West Virginia declined after World War II, hundreds of families came to Cincinnati for factory work. Many eventually settled in a small neighborhood of brick row houses now known as Lower Price Hill.

I first visited the neighborhood on assignment for *Marketplace*, public radio's daily business and economics program. I was reporting on Cincinnati's efforts to close the achievement gap between poor children and more advantaged students by fighting the effects of poverty. Lower Price Hill's Oyler School is part of a growing national movement to help poor children succeed by meeting their basic health, social, and nutritional needs at school.

From the moment I saw the stately 1930 brick and terra-cotta building, against its backdrop of boarded-up buildings and vacant lots, I knew there was much more than I could tell in a four-minute radio piece. Today, Lower Price Hill is a diverse mix of White families, many with Appalachian roots, and growing numbers of African Americans and Latinos. Many of the factories in the area have long since closed, and

half of families live below the federal poverty line. After a $21 million renovation, the new Oyler seemed like an oasis in a neighborhood devastated by neglect and crime.

"I could walk you outside the door, not even 15 steps away, and I could probably get just about any drug that I want," then-principal Craig Hockenberry told me. "I could walk you another 15 feet down and there are our parents that are prostituting and hooked on heroin and crack cocaine."

My initial story turned into a series for *Marketplace*, then a newly completed documentary film, *Oyler*. The documentary follows long-serving principal Hockenberry and senior Raven Gribbins through a year of school, focusing on Hockenberry's mission to transform the neighborhood and on Raven's quest to be the first in her troubled family to finish high school. When Hockenberry's job is threatened, it becomes clear it's a make-or-break year for both.

The story was compelling to me because, as I learned, until about ten years ago, very few children from the neighborhood graduated from high school, let alone went to college. Oyler was an elementary and middle school. After eighth grade, most students eventually dropped out, rather than attend a high school outside the neighborhood.

Then, after an Ohio Supreme Court ruling that found the state's school finance system unconstitutional, Cincinnati received an influx of funding to rebuild its schools. City leaders not only decided to rebuild their rundown school buildings, but to transform them into "community learning centers" that would be neighborhood hubs, providing health and social services as well as traditional instruction.

When it came time to plan for Oyler's renovation, organizers got an earful from parents and community members. Why bring in all of this money for a new building when what they really wanted was a high school?

So they got both. Today Oyler Community Learning Center serves children from six weeks old to twelfth grade. Inside the school you'll find a health clinic staffed by a nurse practitioner, a vision center where children can get free eye exams and glasses, a dental clinic, and mental health counselors. Kids can eat breakfast, lunch, and dinner at school, and bring home food for the weekends. Enrichment programs include college advising, after-school activities, and a large network of volunteer tutors and mentors. All these partnerships are self-sustaining. The school provides the space; the organizations tap their own budgets or bill Medicaid for their services.

Oyler's results have been mixed. While performance on state tests climbed for five years, scores have lagged in the past two years. The school has been identified as a "priority school" by the state of Ohio, meaning it ranks in the bottom 5 percent of schools for its academic performance. Yet each year, 40 or 50 students graduate. Many go to college. Oyler has become a model for similar efforts around the country, including an initiative in New York City to create dozens of new community schools with health services and other resources.

According to an analysis by the Southern Education Foundation, more than *half* of children in U.S. public schools now qualify for free and reduced-price lunch. It's an imperfect measure of poverty, in that it relies on families to apply for the federal program, but it reflects the deepening inequality in our country. Our schools are struggling to raise achievement against growing odds. Helping more children overcome the obstacles of poverty so they can learn and succeed has never been more urgent.

The documentary film Oyler *follows long-serving principal Craig Hockenberry through a year of school as he faces what could be his last shot at transforming a neighborhood by reinventing its school. Though Hockenberry and his staff have made significant progress, he comes up against an accountability system focused on standardized test scores and the official graduation rate. Here, Hockenberry is pictured making his regular rounds of the neighborhood, talking with parents and making sure students come to school. (Photo by Glenn Hartong. © 2013, Amy Scott. Used by permission of Broken Top Productions, LLC. All rights reserved.)*

Raven Gribbins, age 17 when the documentary begins, grew up in Cincinnati's Lower Price Hill and has been a student at Oyler since kindergarten. Her father and grandparents all attended Oyler, but none had finished. Raven is determined to be the first in her family to graduate from high school and go to college. "Everybody used to tell me . . . 'you're not going to make it through high school, you're going to have a baby by 16,'" she said. "I'm glad to prove all them wrong." (Photo by Glenn Hartong. © 2013, Amy Scott. Used by permission of Broken Top Productions, LLC. All rights reserved.)

Oyler School, with its gargoyles and ornate terra-cotta trim, looms large in Lower Price Hill. It's named for a popular former principal, George W. Oyler. The current building was built in 1931. After a two-year, $21 million renovation, the new Oyler Community Learning Center reopened in 2012. (Photo by Glenn Hartong. © 2013, Amy Scott. Used by permission of Broken Top Productions, LLC. All rights reserved.)

Today, Oyler Community Learning Center serves children from six weeks old through the twelfth grade, with additional classes and services for adults. Like many of the services at Oyler, the preschool is run by a nonprofit group that provides its own funding in exchange for the rent-free space. (Photo by Amy Scott. © 2013, Amy Scott. Used by permission of Broken Top Productions, LLC. All rights reserved.)

Oyler School sits near the Ohio River, just a few miles—but a world away—from downtown Cincinnati. Once home to many factories and retail businesses, the neighborhood became an "economic desert," says Hockenberry, plagued by industrial pollution. Recent efforts to improve riverfront access and replace a noisy viaduct that bordered the neighborhood are expected to improve the quality of life. (Photo by Amy Scott. © 2013, Amy Scott. Used by permission of Broken Top Productions, LLC. All rights reserved.)

A memorial of Styrofoam cups pays tribute to Brian Thompson, age 27, who was murdered across the street from the school in the summer of 2012. Thompson was an Oyler parent who had attended the school as a child. When the new Oyler School reopened later that summer, Hockenberry hoped its presence would help slow the crime in the neighborhood. (Photo by Glenn Hartong. © 2013, Amy Scott. Used by permission of Broken Top Productions, LLC. All rights reserved.)

The Lower Price Hill Historic District is characterized by its Italianate-style brick buildings, some dating to the 1850s. The area surrounding Oyler School was added to the National Register of Historic Places in 1988. Many residents still call their neighborhood "Eighth and State," a reference to the major intersection. (Photo by Stacy Doose. © 2013, Amy Scott. Used by permission of Broken Top Productions, LLC. All rights reserved.)

During much of her childhood, Raven lived with her grandmother, Darlene Gribbins. Raven's mother and father both struggled with alcohol and drug addiction and spent time in jail. "They learned not to do drugs," Darlene says of her grandchildren. "You lose everything you got. You even lose your own children." (Photo by Stacy Doose. © 2013, Amy Scott. Used by permission of Broken Top Productions, LLC. All rights reserved.)

Before her senior year in high school, Raven moved back in with her father, Michael Gribbins. A recovering cocaine addict and alcoholic, he had been sober for several years and became more involved in Raven's life. "This is probably the only year that I'm going to have to spend it with my daughter," he says, "so I feel lucky that I got this opportunity." Though he made it through the eleventh grade, Michael never learned to read and write, and he works as a maintenance man. "Not having an education, sometimes work's hard to find," he says. "You struggle." (Photo by Stacy Doose. © 2013, Amy Scott. Used by permission of Broken Top Productions, LLC. All rights reserved.)

Timothy Drifmeyer, age 13, tries on glasses at the OneSight Vision Center inside Oyler School. Opened in 2012, the center provides free eye exams and glasses to children throughout the school district. Established through philanthropy, the clinic sustains itself by billing Medicaid or, if a family has it, private insurance. Before the clinic opened, around 140 kids at Oyler failed a routine eye screening each year, but many went untreated. "Poverty interferes with children getting health care," says Marilyn Crumpton with the Cincinnati Health Department. (Photo by Stacy Doose. © 2013, Amy Scott. Used by permission of Broken Top Productions, LLC. All rights reserved.)

Friends Joe Saylor (left) and Gary Thomas talk in front of Thomas's house in Lower Price Hill. Thomas has lived in the neighborhood for more than 50 years and volunteers at Oyler School. "You always seem to find somebody who you can lean on and talk to," he says of the close-knit community. Saylor grew up a block away from Oyler and was a student there. Now he teaches at the school. (Photo by Glenn Hartong. © 2013, Amy Scott. Used by permission of Broken Top Productions, LLC. All rights reserved.)

Oyler is a documentary produced and directed by Amy Scott, in association with American Public Media's Marketplace. (Photo by Glenn Hartong. © 2013, Amy Scott. Used by permission of Broken Top Productions, LLC. All rights reserved.)

REVIEW QUESTIONS

1. The Oyler Community Learning Center combines public and private efforts to meet the needs of the community it serves. What are the benefits of public/private partnerships like this? Are there any downsides?
2. The article uses eligibility for free or reduced-price lunch as a measure of poverty. How is eligibility determined?
3. Oyler offers medical services and provides food resources and enrichment programs for students. What other community services might help to support students' learning?

philip n. cohen and syed ali

academic hack heard round the world

36

winter 2016

publishers invest in new technology to prevent access to what they're selling, while the reading public is increasingly frustrated that it appears their money—through individual sales, or private or institutional subscription fees, as well as government research support—is being spent as much to keep knowledge away from people as to make it available for public benefit.

A researcher from Kazakhstan, Alexandra Elbakyan, in 2011 created a system known as Sci-Hub that has since unlocked almost 50 million paywalled academic articles. Elbakyan claims, "We have already downloaded most paywalled articles to the library. . . . We have almost everything!" According to *Science Alert*, rather than attempting to steal and store everything at once, her system waits for someone to request an article, then (if it's not already pirated somewhere) pretends to be a university with a subscription to the journal. As Sci-Hub returns the paper, it keeps a copy (or leaves it on another site), allowing the system to answer the next request faster. That means the archive keeps growing as new material is published.

Of course, Elbakyan was working from an earlier generation of code, which built off earlier work, and so on. That's the way the giant underworld of pirated information works. Now, for more or less the same reason that drug deals and child pornography are so hard to stop, the corporate masters of the academic universe are coping with a major breach.

The technical aspect is one story; another is why are people illegally downloading copyrighted materials in the first place? Well, one obvious reason is—as journalists, librarians,

academics, and anyone else looking for scholarly material is well aware—academic journals and individual articles have become prohibitively expensive. Elbaykan, who studied at Kazakhstan University, explained, "Prices are very high, and that made it impossible to obtain papers by purchasing. You need to read many papers for research, and when each paper costs about 30 dollars, that is impossible."

Another part of the story is that for-profit publishers, like the world's largest one, Elsevier, are hugely profitable while relying on unpaid labor of academic writers, reviewers, and editors (whose salaries are paid by the same institutions that also pay institutional subscriptions—to get their knowledge back).

Sci-Hub was found to be in violation of copyright laws and was shut down by a court order in October of last year—in the United States. But it moved to a new domain in Russia, and if that gets shut down too it could move to a "dark net" space. Elbakyan says it could survive even harsher attacks, although using it would become more inconvenient. (The American Sociological Association journals, published under contract with Sage, are among the content Sci-Hub serves up in apparent violation of U.S. law.)

It's not that information does or doesn't *want* to be free, but it is certainly the case that information travels very light. It's hard to keep knowledge pinned down. As the legal battle goes on, and publishers invest in new technology to prevent access to what they're selling, the reading public is increasingly frustrated that it appears their money—through individual sales, or private or institutional subscription fees, as well as government research support—is being spent as much to keep knowledge away from people as to make it available for public benefit.

REVIEW QUESTIONS

1. What kind of structural obstacles made Sci-Hub desirable and popular for researchers?
2. How would you argue against this service? How did scientific research become so difficult to obtain?
3. What other work-arounds might scholars and journalists use to obtain good scholarly information without access to established (and expensive) databases?

janice mccabe

friends with academic benefits

summer 2016

friendship networks in college have different academic and social benefits. this article analyzes the friendship networks of 67 university students, finding that friendships people form are also shaped by their experiences within specific contexts, such as race- and class-based isolation on a predominantly white campus. the analysis reveals how friendships have the potential to ameliorate inequalities, as well as the potential to reproduce them.

"Sometimes it's a good thing to be like your friends, and sometimes it *isn't*. . . . If they're getting all As, of course I want to be like them," said Valerie, an 18-year-old college student during her first year at "MU," a large, public, four-year university in the midwestern United States. Like Valerie, many college students use their friends as academic motivation, finding support among a close-knit group surrounding them. Other students view only *certain* groups of friends as academically helpful. Betsy explained that the friends on her dorm floor constantly help each other with schoolwork, but her friends from home do not. Still others desired more support and encouragement than they received from friends. Steve told me, "I'm doing it myself. . . . I want [help], but at the same time I don't really need it." All three students graduated from MU within four years, yet reflect some of the wide array of experiences students have with their friend networks.

The new or interesting story isn't just that Valerie, Betsy, and Steve's friends had different social and academic impacts, but that they had various types of friendship networks. My research points to the importance of network structure—that is, the relationships among their friends—for college students' success. Different network structures result from students' experiences—such as

race- and class-based marginalization on this predominantly White campus—and shape students' experiences by helping or hindering them academically and socially.

I used social network techniques to analyze the friendship networks of 67 MU students and found they clumped into three distinctive types— tight-knitters, compartmentalizers, and samplers. *Tight-knitters* have one densely woven friendship group in which nearly all their friends are friends with one another. *Compartmentalizers'* friends form two to four clusters, where friends know each other within clusters but rarely across them. And *samplers* make a friend or two from a variety of places, but the friends remain unconnected to each other. As shown in the figures, tight-knitters' networks resemble a ball of yarn, compartmentalizers' a bow-tie, and samplers' a daisy. In these network maps, the person I interviewed is at the center and every other dot represents a friend, with lines representing connections among friends (that is, whether the person I interviewed believed that the two people knew each other). During the interviews, participants defined what friendship meant to them and listed as many friends as they liked (ranging from 3 to 45).

The students' friendship network types influenced how friends matter for their academic and social successes and failures. Like Valerie, most Black and Latina/o students were tight-knitters. Their dense friendship networks provided a sense of home as a minority on a predominantly White campus. Tight-knit networks could provide academic support and motivation (as they did for Valerie) or pull students down academically if their friends lacked academic skills and motivation. Most White students were compartmentalizers like Betsy, and they succeeded with moderate levels of social support from friends and with social support and academic support from different clusters. Samplers came from a range of class and race backgrounds. Like Steve, samplers typically succeeded academically without relying on their friends. Friends were fun people who neither help nor hurt them academically. Socially, however, samplers reported feeling lonely and lacking social support.

I followed the experiences of Valerie, Betsy, and Steve during and after college to examine how friendship networks matter. These students are typical of those in my broader sample. Their experiences show how students' race and class, more than other individual characteristics, shaped the networks they formed and the benefits they gained through these networks. The students I interviewed were racially (half were Black or Latina/o, the other half were White) and class diverse (half were the first in their family to attend college). I recruited MU undergraduates as widely as possible through 12 different campus clubs and organizations, flyers posted in coffee shops and stores, and asking participants for suggestions of students unlike themselves with whom I should speak. Certainly, I could not capture all views or generalize my findings across all U.S. college students, but I am able to provide important insights into the processes through which friends provide social and academic benefits in the critical college years.

> Tight-knitters' networks resemble a ball of yarn, compartmentalizers' a bow-tie, and samplers' a daisy.

the power of peers

Scholars who study education have long acknowledged the importance of peers for students' well-being and academic achievement. For example, in 1961, James Coleman argued that peer culture within high schools shapes students' social and academic aspirations and successes. More recently, Judith Rich Harris has drawn on research in a range of areas—from sociological studies of preschool children to primatologists' studies of chimpanzees and criminologists' studies of neighborhoods—to argue that peers matter much more than parents in how children "turn out." Researchers have explored students' social lives in rich detail, as in Murray Milner's book about high school students, *Freaks, Geeks, and Cool Kids*, and Elizabeth Armstrong and Laura Hamilton's look at college students, *Paying for the Party*. These works consistently show that peers play a very important role in most students' lives. They tend, however, to prioritize social over academic influence and to use a fuzzy conception of peers rather than focusing directly on friends—the relationships that should matter most for student success.

Social scientists have also studied the power of peers through network analysis, which is based on uncovering the web of connections between people. Network analysis involves visually mapping networks and mathematically comparing their structures (such as the density of ties) and the positions of individuals within them (such as how central a given person is within the network). As Nicholas Christakis and James Fowler point out in their book *Connected*, network structure influences a range of outcomes, including health, happiness, wealth, weight, and emotions. Given that sociologists have long considered network explanations for social phenomena, it's surprising that we know little about how college students' friends impact their experiences.

In line with this network tradition, I focus on the structure of friendship networks, constructing network maps so that the differences we see across participants are due to the underlying structure, including each participant's centrality in their friendship group and the density of ties among their friends.

tight-knitters

I first spoke with Valerie at the end of her first year at MU. She is a Black student whose parents both had college degrees and professional jobs. During her first year, Valerie made friends in campus clubs and maintained ties to many friends from home who attended other colleges

or joined the army. She described having a tight-knit network of 20 friends.

When you map her tight-knit network, it looks like a ball of yarn. Being surrounded by a group where friends all know each other provided tight-knitters with multiple friends to whom they could turn. This cultivated a sense of belonging. Tight-knit networks typically provide tremendous social support, and I found students who experienced these tight-knit friendship networks often referred to them as a "family" or their "home." Most tight-knitters were students of color who found the social support of their network helpful in navigating a predominantly White campus. Valerie put it this way: "Being a minority, it's kind of hard coming here and finding people who [have] the same interests as you. . . . This [friendship group] is like being at home again. It's like when you come

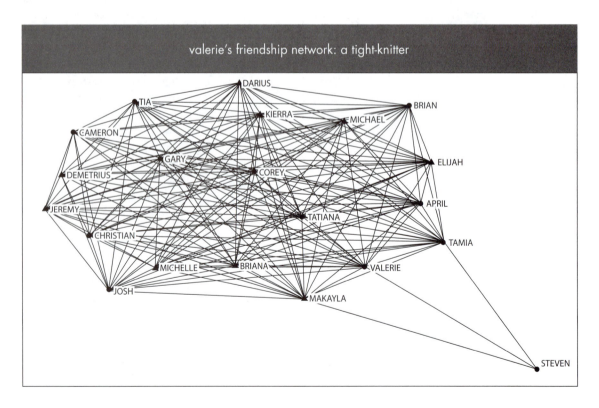

valerie's friendship network: a tight-knitter

to college, you don't need the whole home but you want to feel somewhat of being at home." Students who felt race- or class-based isolation were often consciously bringing people together to form a friendship network (for others, the process seemed less intentional).

Tight-knit networks varied considerably in terms of friends' level and types of academic involvement. Some tight-knitters had friendship networks that helped them academically in multiple ways. Valerie said her friends' emotional support and successes motivated her to "want to succeed." Her friends studied together, quizzed each other before exams, proofread each other's papers, and occasionally engaged in intellectual discussions. For Valerie, friendship was an academic boon.

Tight-knit networks, however, did not always pull students up academically. They pulled some tight-knitters down, helping to reproduce race- and class-based inequalities. Valerie contrasts the positive peer effects she experiences with what she sees among some other students: "If you're around your friends a lot and they didn't care about books and stuff like that, I have potential to not care about books and stuff like that." About half of the 22 tight-knitters in my sample were in this situation, surrounded by friends who pulled them away from academics. Nearly all students discussed friends distracting them from academics, but for lower-achieving tight-knitters who did not graduate from MU or who graduated but with low GPAs and in more than four years, friends were a *constant* distraction. Lower-achieving tight-knitters, like Madison, were often aware of this impact. When asked about her biggest academic obstacle, Madison admitted, "I hate to say [it, but] I can't help but think about my friends." She went on to describe how her friends distracted her from attending class,

> Tight-knit friendships among students from disadvantaged backgrounds can help reduce racial and socioeconomic class gaps in grades and graduation rates.

studying by herself, and even while studying together. This distraction was not counterbalanced by other academic involvement, as lower-achieving tight-knitters' friends often lacked academic skills and provided, at most, limited emotional support and intellectual engagement for each other. All behaviors—negative and positive—were quite contagious within tight-knit networks. Consequently, all tight-knitters who described their friends as providing academic support and motivation graduated; only half of the tight-knitters who felt they lacked this support graduated.

Tight-knit networks provided tremendous social support, while also posing social challenges for some students. Tight-knitters were more likely than others to tell me that they both felt different from their friends and that they kept these feelings from their friends. When uniformity was valued, it seemed harder to deviate in these dense networks. Still, while tight-knit networks are not always positive for students' social lives, they generally provide important social support for students from disadvantaged backgrounds dealing with race- and class-based isolation on campus. In this way, friendships among students from disadvantaged backgrounds can help reduce racial and socioeconomic class gaps in grades and graduation rates.

compartmentalizers

Betsy named a similar number of friends as Valerie, but described different relationships among those friends as well as different benefits accrued from these relationships. Betsy's 17 friends were divided into two clusters: those she met at MU, mostly on her dorm floor, and those from home, most of whom are students at other colleges.

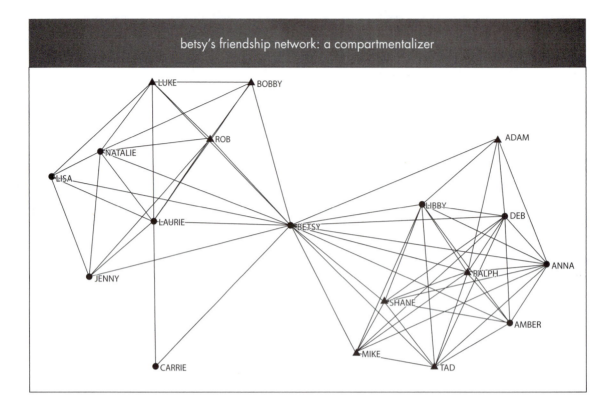

Compartmentalized networks look like a bow-tie, with distinct clusters of friends. Students' friends within each of the 2–4 clusters were connected to each other, but friends were not connected across clusters. Like Betsy, most compartmentalizers were White and middle class. They typically had one socially oriented cluster and one academically oriented cluster. Betsy explained her friends' closeness primarily as a result of their shared interests—"having fun," going to parties, and watching movies. When I asked about her friends from home, she sheepishly explained that those friends did not discuss schoolwork or intellectual ideas. Her MU friends, however, were involved academically in several ways. They bounced ideas for papers off of one another, quizzed each other before exams, and watched TV together while they studied. Although her friends' academic involvement was more modest than Valerie's, it was adequate to support Betsy, who felt she could "easily" navigate academic and social life. Betsy explained, "I will study and I will get good grades, but I will also go out almost every night. It's funny because my friends . . . they're like, 'Blah blah blah. Are you going out tonight? Of course you are! I don't know how you do it.' But I think some people can be both [academic and social]. Easily." Betsy also noted that her friends could be an academic distraction, "but sometimes you can afford to get distracted." She felt her two clusters of friends enabled her to balance schoolwork and friendly fun, and she graduated in four years. Students with more than two clusters of friends felt pressure—on their time and identity—in keeping up with multiple friendship groups. The clusters provided a sense of belonging, but maintaining ties can be demanding, and these demands escalated with each additional cluster.

All compartmentalizers had separate academic and social clusters of friends. To be academically and socially successful, Black and Latino compartmentalizers and those from lower-class backgrounds had two other features in their networks: they found multiple types of academic involvement within one cluster of friends (similar to the tight-knitters, such as Valerie) and they had a cluster of friends who helped them deal with race- or class-based marginality. Regarding the latter, Wendy, a Black compartmentalizer, pointed to the "support systems" within a cluster of Black friends in her major as most helpful for her social success at MU. These additional network features helped compartmentalizers from disadvantaged backgrounds achieve social and academic success; those compartmentalizers whose networks lacked such social and academic support clusters typically had low GPAs. In general, compartmentalizers came from more-advantaged backgrounds (like Betsy), experienced greater ease on campus, and succeeded in college with less support from friends as compared to those with other network types. Friendships among students from more-advantaged backgrounds helped to reproduce their advantages.

samplers

When I interviewed Steve, he was in his third year at MU. As we talked about his friends, it quickly became clear that his friendship choices were not what he had hoped for. He had not made the intense friendships he expected among other Black males at MU, and he found it challenging to maintain close friendships with his hometown friends a four-hour drive away. Steve had four Black male friends from home, one Black female friend from home, and twelve Black female friends from MU. His MU friendships were not clustered, but separated, since Steve would meet one person at a specific place, club, or event. His strategy was to constantly search for new opportunities, describing how he "came [to college] to meet new people." This strategy resulted in a friendship network that resembled a daisy. Steve's total number of friends was similar to Valerie and Betsy's, but fewer of his friends knew each other—thus the shape and support of his network were quite different.

Like Steve, other samplers had friends, but generally did not describe them as socially supportive. Steve admitted: "I haven't really found a best male friend here yet. And I don't think I will." Students of color frequently described experiencing race-based isolation on campus regardless of their network type; samplers, however, *remained* isolated. They rarely discussed isolating experiences with friends, and samplers were ambivalent at best about whether their friends provided social support or whether they needed social support. For example, Matthew's eyes became gloomy when he described feeling "slightly distant" from his friends, whereas Jocelyn firmly characterized her friendships as "disappointing." Compartmentalized and tight-knit networks, in contrast, facilitated a sense of support and belonging on campus.

Samplers are academically successful in spite of their friends. Their friends provide little academic help or engagement, but they don't pull the samplers down academically either. Negative behaviors that were contagious within

> While samplers demonstrate that friends are not necessary for academic success, one can't help but wonder if they might be even more successful if they allowed or encouraged their friends to become friends with academic benefits.

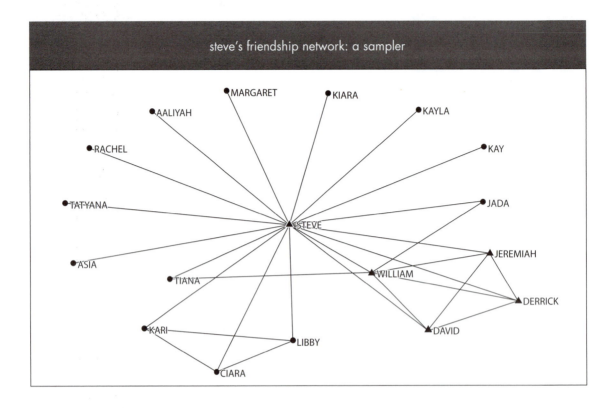

steve's friendship network: a sampler

tight-knitters' networks did not spread within samplers' networks due to lack of ties among friends. In other words, their network structure shielded samplers from friends' negative influences.

Many samplers, such as Steve, described their main source of academic support as their family, but often desired more intellectual conversations with friends. Similar to how he gave up on the possibility of finding a best male friend at MU, Steve seemed to give up on the possibility of finding academically engaged friends, groaning that, "some people don't think that deep." Many samplers described one friend with whom they could discuss intellectual ideas, but they wanted more of these relationships and more of these discussions. With only one friend involved academically in a limited way, samplers lacked the tremendous breadth and depth provided by tight-knitters' full

network and the adequate support provided by compartmentalizers' clusters. Samplers frequently described themselves as "academically self-sufficient" or independent. Amanda said outright that academics, for her, were "more of a personal journey. I've never really learned anything with somebody." While samplers demonstrate that friends are not necessary for academic success, one can't help but wonder if they might be even more successful if they allowed or encouraged their friends to become friends with academic benefits.

the lasting effects of college friendship network types

The networks students build during college are part of a pathway of friendships that informs their social and work lives after college. When I interviewed these youth five years later when many but not all of them had graduated, I found less variation in young adults' post-college networks than during college. Yet there remained differences across network types. Compartmentalizers remained compartmentalizers, and tight-knitters generally stayed tight-knitters, but the samplers mostly became tight-knitters too. After college, Betsy still had two groups of friends while Valerie and Steve both had one large, tight-knit group with a few pairs of friends and disconnected friends. Further, the network types appear more durable than the specific friends within them: there was much turnover in networks, with only about 25 percent of friends remaining over this five-year period.

Young adults were more likely to maintain friendships with socially and academically supportive friends than other types of college friends. This was true for young adults from each of the network types, and it helps explain why tight-knitters maintained more of their prior friendships (almost one-third) over time than did the samplers and compartmentalizers (with about a quarter retention among their college friends five years later). Not only do supportive and academically engaged friendships help students academically and socially during college, these are relationships that are more likely to last beyond graduation (I rarely saw friends help each other in terms of career advancement in the period right after graduation).

Samplers experienced the largest change, not only in terms of network structure but also in terms of social support. While samplers' college networks left them feeling isolated, after college, most samplers had networks that provided meaningful social support. For example, Steve did not maintain contact with his MU friends after college, though he kept some ties to childhood friends from home and formed new friendships after college. Steve described these post-college friends as "like family" and noted

how they are "learning more about each other in a deeper way instead of just surface, like what you like to do for fun." Although Steve reported slightly fewer friends after college (12 compared to 17), he described his post-college friendships as more meaningful and supportive. Sampler networks facilitate self-sufficiency, rather than a sense of belonging. Only one of the samplers (Jocelyn) remained isolated after college, which suggests that a mismatch with MU rather than some constant personality trait or friendship preference distinguishes samplers from the other network types.

When I talk about these findings, people are often excited to figure out which of the three network types they had during college and have now. Most people have no problem placing themselves into a type. As the examples of Valerie, Betsy, and Steve show, each network type comes with particular academic and social benefits as well as drawbacks. Tight-knitters benefit from social support, but need to watch out for friends who can distract them or drag them down academically. Compartmentalizers find balance in social and academic involvement from different clusters, and samplers appear academically successful, but often feel socially isolated.

Individual characteristics certainly shape the friendships people form, though my findings show that friendships are also shaped by one's experiences within specific contexts, such as race- and class-based isolation on a predominantly White campus. Tight-knit, compartmentalized, and sampler networks are a response to specific contexts, and they are associated with specific social and academic benefits. Friendships thus have the potential to ameliorate or reproduce inequalities. It is important, therefore, that students, their parents, professors, and college administrators recognize that students' friends can be incredible resources as well as liabilities. At a time when only 40 percent of students graduate from four-year colleges within four years, we need to better understand how friends can either pull students up academically or bring them down.

RECOMMENDED RESOURCES

Elizabeth A. Armstrong and Laura T. Hamilton. 2013. *Paying for the Party: How College Maintains Inequality.* Cambridge, MA: Harvard University Press.

An examination of how a large public university aligns with the expectations and backgrounds of some students but not others.

Daniel F. Chambliss and Christopher G. Takacs. 2014. *How College Works.* Cambridge, MA: Harvard University Press.

Based on research at a liberal arts college, this book offers suggestions to colleges and students for improving higher education through personal relationships.

Nicholas A. Christakis and James H. Fowler. 2009. *Connected: The Surprising Power of Our Social Networks and How They Shape Our Lives.* New York: Little, Brown and Company.

A comprehensive look at how social networks, including those to which we are only distantly connected, impact many aspects of people's behavior and attitudes.

Elizabeth M. Lee and Chaise LaDousa, editors. 2015. *College Students' Experiences of Power and Marginality: Sharing Spaces and Negotiating Differences.* New York: Routledge.

A collection of research studies investigating how students navigate differences on campus.

Murray Milner Jr. 2016. *Freaks, Geeks, and Cool Kids: American Teenagers, Schools, and the Culture of Consumption,* 2nd ed. New York: Routledge.

An examination of status hierarchies in high schools that identifies factors that separate or bring teens together.

Mario Luis Small. 2009. *Unanticipated Gains: Origins of Network Inequality in Everyday Life.* New York: Oxford University Press.

An impressive mixed-methods study of childcare centers and mothers' social networks in these centers.

REVIEW QUESTIONS

1. What are the three types of friendship networks the author identifies?
2. What are the different academic and social consequences the author links to each type of friendship network?
3. In what ways do the author's data reveal how race and class identities shape friendship networks?
4. Why is it important for colleges and universities to pay attention to the kinds of friendship networks the school environment facilitates?

tomás r. jiménez and adam l. horowitz

whitewashing academic mediocrity

38

summer 2015

in a silicon valley city, whiteness has become the new code for academic mediocrity and laziness.

Angelica is a typical teenager in the Silicon Valley town of Cupertino. She is poised, well-spoken, involved in lots of extracurricular activities, and connected to her friends 24/7 through various social networking platforms. She works extremely hard in school, and it's mostly paying off. She earns nearly straight As, and has even been admitted to a program at a local community college that allows her to take classes for college credit.

In spite of all of her academic success, Angelica feels like she has something to prove. As Angelica tells it, she frequently has to fend off assumptions by classmates and teachers that she is probably academically mediocre because of her race: Angelica is White.

Such assumptions about the inferior academic performance associated with Whiteness reflects what we heard over and over again when we interviewed residents of Cupertino as part of a research project aimed at understanding how the "third-plus generation" (those who were born in the United States to also U.S.-born parents) make sense of immigration-driven change. Angelica and her peers do not live in the Northern California suburbs her parents knew as kids. Back then, Whiteness was synonymous with doing well in school; the overwhelming success of Whites relative to a handful of minority students affirmed Whiteness

was the model of achievement. That picture largely represents what many think of as the norm throughout the United States. Angelica's Silicon Valley is different, having undergone massive immigration-driven change. It is characterized by upheaval in how people think about the connection between race and academic success. Compared to her parents' experience, what it means to be White has been turned on its head. Whiteness, to Cupertino residents of Angelica's generation, represents academic mediocrity and laziness.

That notion is the product of how people in the city associate Asianness with academic excellence and hard work. It is not that Angelica and other White teens in Cupertino, as a whole, are doing—or have ever done—badly. Quite the opposite. Cupertino has bred academic success for a long time. In the late 1960s and early '70s, a burgeoning technology industry transformed Santa Clara Valley into "Silicon Valley," and White engineers and other professionals began buying homes in Cupertino. The children of these highly educated

> In spite of all of her academic success, Angelica feels like she has something to prove. Angelica is White.

Cupertino residents were as driven as their parents, and Cupertino's public schools quickly earned a reputation for excellence. When Silicon Valley was in full bloom, it was that very reputation that made Cupertino an attractive landing spot for high-skilled Chinese and Indian tech workers, who began arriving in the region in large numbers in the 1990s. Cupertino's changing demographics, then, tell part of the story: between 1990 and 2010, the immigrant population grew from 22 percent of residents to 49 percent. Most were from Asia, with Chinese and Indian immigrants driving an increase in the overall proportion of Asian residents from 23 percent in 1990 to 64 percent today. Whites have become a numerical minority, shrinking from 74 percent of the population in 1990 to 29 percent two decades later.

If Cupertino is a major immigrant destination, it is hardly home of the "poor, huddled masses" commonly associated with American immigration lore. The largely Chinese- and Indian-immigrant populations that have settled there are highly educated, and their settlement has only bolstered the city's upper-middle-class status profile. Three-quarters of the adult population holds a college degree or more, and an equal proportion works in managerial or professional careers, many in the technology sector. The median household income is around $125,000 a year, and purchasing a typical home in the city will set a buyer back more than $1 million.

Cupertino is just the kind of place designed for kids to do well in school and beyond. And, by most standards, White and Asian kids alike generally succeed. But most standards don't apply here. In Cupertino, status is tied to performance on the SAT, sleeping less to study more is the basis of informal competition among high school students, and football and cheerleading don't make anyone terribly relevant. The settlement of the high-skilled Asian immigrant population, according to residents, has elevated the meaning of academic success. In the process, Asianness has replaced Whiteness as the racial emblem of academic achievement, and third-plus-generation parents and kids are undergoing a challenging adjustment.

shifting terrain of race and achievement

Most observers would agree that there is a crisis in education defined by race. Regular reports of the "achievement gap" highlight how Whites continue to outpace Blacks and Latinos on just about every measure of academic attainment. The larger concern is that the achievement gap produces racially defined income and wealth disparities later in life. If the most glaring and problematic gaps are those between Whites on one end and Latinos and/or Blacks on the other, there is a less noted gap at the "top": the one between Asians and everyone else, including Whites. Asian students outpace Whites on just about every standardized test, a fact that has led the State Boards of Education in Virginia and Florida to set group-specific academic achievement standards that are higher for Asians than for Whites, and well above those set for Blacks and Latinos.

This depiction is hardly abstract to the people we studied. Achievement gaps reflect in their experience of racial identity, especially when it comes to academic success. Third-plus-generation kids in Cupertino are pushed by their parents in many of the same ways that upper-middle-class kids are pushed to succeed anywhere else. But as the people we interviewed see it, high-skilled Asian immigration has introduced a new set of achievement standards that requires more than typical upper-middle-class striving. People working closely with students for a long period, like teachers and coaches, were quick to note the changes resulting from the settlement of large numbers of Asian immigrants: less emphasis among students on athletics and more emphasis on all things

Whiteness, to Cupertino residents of Angelica's generation, represents academic mediocrity and laziness.

academic. Everyday residents reported much the same. What is clear is that this influx also introduced an atypical racial inflection of academic achievement.

Social scientists have observed that students and teachers typically connect notions of race to academic ability, seeing Whiteness as emblematic of scholastic aptitude and success. Survey researchers implicitly share that view, regularly treating Whites as the reference group against which to judge the progress of racial minorities. But that ordering of the academic racial hierarchy is almost unrecognizable to Cupertino residents. Marcus, a White, 22-year-old recent college graduate, echoed what other respondents told us about the stereotypes that existed at his Cupertino high school: "The Asian kids and the Indian kids were really smart and they were really good at math and they were always going to do really well in the AP classes, whereas the White kids were less academically oriented. And they did okay, but they didn't put in as much effort."

It is not necessarily surprising that Asians are stereotyped as smart. Popular culture, the news media, and teachers have touted Asians as a "model minority" that stands apart because the group's high levels of success comes in spite of minority status. Yet the very idea that the minority group is a "model" implies a comparison between Asian success and the supposed failure of other minorities—Blacks and Latinos, in particular. But Blacks and Latinos make up an incredibly small share of Cupertino residents, and so the city's demographics do not provide for multigroup comparison. Instead of Asian achievement highlighting Blacks' or Latinos' underperformance, then, it places Whites at the bottom of the academic heap. To be sure, the bottom of that heap finds third-plus-generation Whites well above the achievement levels that most other American teens will ever know. The people we interviewed are likely on their way to replicating their parents' class standing. Still, that likelihood is rendered almost irrelevant to the daily lives of our third-plus-generation respondents who are very much regarded as academically inferior in the context they navigate daily.

Seemingly everyone we interviewed—everyday residents, teachers, and students—acknowledged that hierarchy without our prompting. One high school teacher's acknowledgment of the unconventional position of Whites in Cupertino's academic hierarchy only seemed to make their inferior place clearer: "As the teacher, I try not to stereotype, of course, but after a while, I guess I just assume . . . the White kids probably aren't going to be my very, very best students. . . . If I were to go back and look at the grades I've given . . . I'm sure that the GPA for the White kids I've had would be lower than the GPA for the Asian kids I've had. I'm sure of it."

As we interviewed more individuals, we were surprised by how uniformly people talked about the academic hierarchy in explicitly racial terms. Students, in particular, repeatedly used "White" and "Asian" as shorthand for how students approach school, with the former indicating a lax approach and the latter suggesting a more intense approach. One teacher reported an instance in which two students discussed their course schedule, with one asking, "Well, are you taking AP?" According to the teacher, the other student replied: "Oh no, I'm White."

These stereotypes can have a biting edge. Social psychological experiments by Joshua Aronson and his colleagues show that Whites fare worse on standardized tests when they are primed to think about Asians' intellectual ability. The perceptions of the people we interviewed

> The view of Asians as smart and driven might be a more positive stereotype, but it is an unwelcome one to Asian-American interviewees.

support those findings. Whites—especially the more academically oriented among them—have a sense that they need to constantly fight against stereotypes that tag them as dumb. Teens like Angelica and their parents often explained the situation with a tone of exhaustion. Angelica told us, "I've gotten a lot of feeling like I'm not taken seriously because I'm a preppy White girl." An instance capturing that feeling took place after she got a test back in a chemistry class: "We were all comparing answers that we got on the test afterwards. . . . I said, 'Oh. I know how to do that one.' And they were like, 'Oh, okay,' and then asked their other friend, anyway. It was two Indian guys, and I was like, 'Do you not think that I know the answer?' . . . And I was like, 'Is it because I'm White that you don't think that I know?' And he's like, 'Well, I don't know if you know or not.' 'Could I just give it a shot?' I guess I constantly feel like I have to prove people wrong."

Students like Angelica generally push through, even when confronted with these stereotypes. But less academically inclined Whites said that they more or less give up on trying to excel in school, opting out of what they characterize as an achievement rat race that places them as slow runners because of their Whiteness. These students coasted in school, and either made it to a four-year college via community college or wound up at one of the California State University campuses (which lack prestige in Cupertino as compared to the University of California heavyweights). These are hardly disastrous outcomes. Perhaps that's why the parents of these students condoned their child's opting out, seeing what it would take to swim against a tide of stereotypes as too big a price to pay for the chance to compete.

> Regular reports of the "achievement gap" highlight how Whites continue to outpace Blacks and Latinos on just about every measure of academic attainment. The larger concern is that the achievement gap produces racially defined income and wealth disparities later in life.

the stereotype promise bind

If "acting Asian" means taking school very seriously, the Asian category is bound up with being an immigrant or the child of an immigrant. These categories involve a nuance that becomes clear from our interviews with young, third-plus-generation Asian Americans, whose families have been in the United States for multiple generations. They frequently described themselves as "whitewashed"—a reference not only to a weak connection to a Japanese or Chinese ancestry and culture, but also to a less intense approach to academic pursuits (one that's one more akin to Whites'). Melanie, a high school junior we spoke to, said that her household is more similar to White households and less like the stereotypical Asian ones because, as she put it, "We want to have fun. But when it does come down to academics, we can do our work, but still have fun at the same time. And sometimes the academics get put on the back burner and the fun takes control first. My household is definitely not focused on studying at all."

These respondents are also subject to the consequences of stereotypes, albeit with some differences from their White, third-plus-generation peers. While high-achieving Whites feel like they have to counter prevailing stereotypes, third-plus-generation Asian-American respondents said that they feel a stress-inducing pressure to live up to them. Tiffany, an Asian-American high school sophomore whose great-great-grandparents came to the United States from China and Japan, does fairly well in school. But her Asian ancestry, combined with a more relaxed approach to school, put her at odds with prevailing stereotypes. Tiffany described the result: "All the teachers expect all the Asians to do really well. When one Asian doesn't do well, they're looked down upon in a way, because they're Asian and they're smart, automatically. I think it's tough. . . . If I didn't do that well, I'd be a little bit ashamed because [the other Asian students] probably did really well and I'm kind of lagging on that one test or something."

Sociologists Jennifer Lee and Min Zhou argue that these "positive" stereotypes can give a boost to Asian Americans who are not doing so well in school, a phenomenon that they call "stereotype promise." Yet as psychologists John Siy and Sapna Cheryan conclude from their research, even positive stereotypes "fail to flatter" precisely because they take away the ability to be seen as an individual. Thus, the view of Asians as smart and driven might be a more positive stereotype, but it is an unwelcome one to Asian-American interviewees.

Even if the Asian Americans whose families "have been here forever" (i.e., for multiple generations) have a much more dialed-back approach to school, they continue to face heightened expectations that indicate a conflation of racial origin and immigrant generation driven by Cupertino's racially encoded notions of achievement.

a bizarro world of race and achievement?

Is Cupertino to race and education what Bizarro World is to Earth in the Superman comics—a place where things work in opposition to widely regarded norms? Yes and no. Cupertino's large, concentrated, relatively wealthy, and highly educated Asian-origin immigrant population gives Asians a certain power to set the standards for academic success. And there are other U.S. towns with traits similar to those found in Cupertino: large, highly educated White and Asian populations and a near absence of other racial groups. These include San Marino, California; Skokie, Illinois; and Princeton, New Jersey. Anecdotal evidence further suggests that similar achievement processes occur in high schools in places like Sugar Land, Texas; Irvine, California; and Oakland County, Michigan, though it would certainly require more systematic research to be certain.

The fact that Cupertino is a White/Asian city with no substantial representation of other racial groups means that Whites—not Blacks or Latinos—are the only comparison group against which stereotypes about Asians make "sense." Interviews we did in another Silicon Valley neighborhood with a different history of immigration and demographic composition—a middle-class subsection of San Jose called Berryessa—affirms that the presence of Latinos and Blacks prevents the fall of Whites to the bottom of the academic hierarchy. Just as the people we interviewed in Cupertino easily articulated a racially inflected academic hierarchy, so too did interviewees in Berryessa. The difference is that, in Berryessa, interviewees repeatedly told us that Asians were at the top, Whites were below Asians, and Mexicans and Blacks were at the bottom. Whites don't necessarily excel according to Berryessa residents, but they don't perform as badly as Blacks and Latinos. Still, the large presence of high-achieving Asians (mostly of Vietnamese descent) in Berryessa means that Whites do not wind up on top either. Among the highest achieving students, the experience of Whites in Berryessa and Cupertino are more similar than different.

It's important to note that what might seem like benefits for those with Asian ancestry in high school may not necessarily pay off in equal proportion in college and beyond. As sociologist Thomas Espenshade and his colleagues have shown, there may even be an Asian-American penalty in college admissions, where colleges require more of students with Asian ancestry in order to gain admission.

Nonetheless, the situation in Cupertino is illustrative of a larger—though little recognized—phenomenon unfolding in the United States: native-born populations are adjusting to new linguistic, religious, culinary, political, and job-market-related changes resulting from immigration. Our work suggests that the very strategies that immigrants use to find their way in places that are new and strange to them can make those very places new and strange to the people who have been living there for a long time. That is, it is not just immigrants and their children who are adjusting to the new contexts in which they settle. The people with family roots extending back generations are also adjusting to contexts that immigrants and their children are changing.

Racial dynamics are central to that change. The intersection of immigration, race, and achievement in Cupertino show that immigrants and their children are not "becoming" White, Asian, Latino, or Black. Instead, immigration is changing what is becoming of Whiteness, Asianness, Latinoness, and Blackness. In Cupertino, that means the third-plus generation is adjusting to a new notion of what it means to be "White" in schools. But more generally, in places across the United States where immigrants have settled in large numbers, everyone is undergoing a new and sometimes bumpy adjustment.

RECOMMENDED RESOURCES

Richard Alba and Victor Nee. 2003. *Remaking the American Mainstream: Assimilation and Contemporary Immigration.* Cambridge, MA: Harvard University Press.

> Offers a theory of assimilation that accounts for the possibility that immigrants change the very mainstream into which they assimilate.

Tomás R. Jiménez and Adam L. Horowitz. 2013. "When White Is Just Alright: How Immigrants Redefine Achievement and Reconfigure the Ethnoracial Hierarchy." *American Sociological Review* 78(5):849–71.

> The academic article in which we first reported the full results of the study discussed here.

Phillip Kasinitz, John H. Mollenkopf, Mary C. Waters, and Jennifer Holdaway. 2008. *Inheriting the City: The Second Generation Comes of Age.* Cambridge, MA and New York: Harvard University Press and Russell Sage Foundation.

> Examines the experiences of the immigrant second generation in New York City, offering a fresh take on why some excel and some do not.

Jennifer Lee and Min Zhou. 2015. *The Asian American Achievement Paradox.* New York: Russell Sage Foundation.

> Examines the institutional factors that explain the success and failure of Chinese and Vietnamese second-generation youth.

Vivian S. Louie. 2004. *Compelled to Excel: Immigration, Education, and Opportunity among Chinese Americans.* Stanford: Stanford University Press.

> Examines the relative role that ethnoracial origin and class play in the academic experiences of Chinese Americans.

REVIEW QUESTIONS

1. What does this article suggest about the process by which social norms and stereotypes are formed? How global are norms and stereotypes in the United States?
2. Asian Americans constitute a very diverse population, one that is growing quickly in the United States. How do you think this type of stereotyping affects the lives of Asians who are exposed to it? Does the stereotype apply to all Asians living in the United States?
3. Does this article change how you see the connection between race and education? How?

toby l. parcel, joshua a. hendrix, and andrew j. taylor

the challenge of diverse public schools

39

winter 2016

decades of successful integration efforts are at stake when one school district fights over school proximity and school "balancing."

Wake County, North Carolina, citizens are divided. Some believe that school integration—by race and social class—is important for the well-being of all children. One citizen told us of the dangers of the opposite: "It is not OK to segregate our schools. It is not OK to deliberately create high-poverty schools and claim that you are going to have all these fixes, whether it is funding or innovative programs, etc. It is just wrong, and that is why I am in this debate."

Another parent's concerns reflected the costs of implementing a "diversity" policy: "I see young children standing out there in the cold and dark at 6:30 in the morning, and it is totally obnoxious that any polite society would do this to the children. It is not safe, it is not fair, and it certainly is not fostering any good educational system; people generally want good schools close to home."

Heated debates around these issues culminated in a watershed Wake County school board election in October 2009 that switched the board from majority Democratic and liberal to majority Republican and conservative, which resulted in consequences. By early 2010, this new board voted to discard the district's diversity policy in favor of one that placed more emphasis on neighborhood schools.

These events garnered attention because they threatened to roll back decades of successful school integration, a policy vehicle for promoting positive race relations and facilitating upward mobility. Integration had also been associated with county growth and prosperity. Would these trends now be reversed and mean the end of Wake County's economic and social progress? Would Wake become more like other large school districts characterized by strong school re-segregation, with negative educational and social consequences?

consensus and its dissolution

Wake's history shows that a large southern county comprised of urban, suburban, and rural populations could sustain successful school desegregation over many years. In 1976, after federal pressure, Wake County and the city of Raleigh merged their school districts to create one countywide system of 55,000 students. Innovative superintendents used magnet schools located in central Raleigh to entice White and middle-class families to enroll their children, thus promoting voluntary school integration through school choice. This worked: there were rising test scores, decreased racial gaps in student achievement, and strong satisfaction with schools among parents. Wake County's population rose, but the county was able to educate this growing number of students, many of them from families migrating to Raleigh from other parts of the country.

To promote desegregation in the early 1990s, up to 1,000 African-American and White children were bused across the county each year, with minority children more likely to be bused than Whites. This strategy meant that some children were transferred to new schools for reasons beyond graduating to middle or high school. Children were often re-assigned in groups, which preserved social ties but parental relationships with schools and teachers were inevitably disrupted. Still, at this time, complaints were few, especially compared to other communities in the South.

Heated debates around integration in Wake County's October 2009 school board election threatened to roll back decades of successful policy promoting positive race relations and facilitating upward mobility.

The county prospered both socially and economically, but prosperity had its price. By 2000, suburban communities such as Cary and Apex had acquired the reputation of some of the "best places" to live. Population growth in these areas exceeded school capacity, while parts of central Raleigh were decreasing in population. The county was now responsible for educating close to 100,000 children. By 2000, court rulings had largely disallowed race as a basis for school assignments, so Wake began using social class and achievement data instead. Estimates varied regarding how many children were bused for purposes of achieving diversity along economic and achievement lines, with the board arguing it was always less than 5 percent of children each year. But county growth appeared to increase this proportion and board reliance on reassignment increased over time. By 2008, the board proposed that more than 25,000 children be reassigned over the next three years. Some children from kindergarten through high school had already been moved multiple times. Younger children could not be assured they would attend the same schools as older siblings. Parents could

not be guaranteed that relationships they formed with teachers, administrators, and other parents would pay off in the future. Population growth was also increasing commute times for both parents and children, who might be traveling many miles from home. Complaints about annual reassignments increased.

A second school board strategy proved even more controversial. To make good use of fixed resources, the board created year-round schools, which had some elementary and middle school children on three out of four nine-week tracks, but rotated one group of students out at all times. Although year-round schools required more personnel, this strategy cut costs by slowing down the need for school construction. Some parents liked year-round schools and sought them out. Board policy eventually mandated large groups of families to enter the year-round system or face unattractive alternatives. For example, opting out of a year-round school could saddle some kids with a longer bus ride and earlier pickup times. Families with a child in a year-round magnet school who also had a child in a public high school automatically had kids on two different school calendars, because all county high schools remained on traditional calendars. By 2009, these conditions were politically unsustainable. We wondered, what is the price of diverse schools? Had adherence to the diversity policy come at too high a cost?

We began our study by reviewing media reports, and continued by interviewing 24 locals who were either pro-diversity or favored neighborhood schools. We conducted two focus groups, and used those discussions to help us develop a telephone survey for more than 1,700 Wake County adults. We asked questions about learning benefits for children when they experience economic and racial diversity in schools and in classrooms; learning benefits from neighborhood schools; opinions on the length of bus rides; implementation of student assignment policy; general thoughts about the school board; and a variety of social and background characteristics.

diversity versus neighborhood schools

Wake's debate seemed to originate with two different views of how children should be assigned to public schools. One promoted a countywide perspective in which the school board would assign children so that no schools were disproportionately poor or low-achieving.

This would disrupt any connection between residential segregation and school segregation. Proponents of this policy feared the county's economic future would be threatened if public schools were viewed unfavorably by firms and middle-class employees considering relocating to Raleigh. Since the county's assignment policy was associated with rising test scores and decreased achievement gaps, they viewed diverse schools as an investment in county well-being.

The other side championed proximity of home and school so that children's school attendance reinforced neighborhood social ties and vice versa. Under these conditions, however,

Year-round schools, similar to this one in West Virginia, offer Wake County a good cost-cutting option that would slow new school construction. (USDA)

schools would replicate residential segregation, a familiar condition in many American communities. Such realities would intensify inequality across generations, a situation that diversity advocates disliked.

Media reports, interviews, and focus groups reflect either pro-diversity sentiments or worries about the disadvantages of diversity policy implementation. However, our findings showed other sentiments as well. First, disrupting the proximity of home and school was clearly a challenge for families. As a former superintendent noted in an interview, "I was having a forum over at Moore Square Middle School and it was about 200 . . . predominantly African-American parents . . . and I will not forget the parent who stood up and said, 'Well, we do not understand why we have to put our 5-year-old on that bus and ride for an hour and twenty minutes to a school that is a [significant] distance from the house.' "

Others suggested that having children attend school far from home affected their capacity to meet parental responsibilities. It meant challenges for parents who were often juggling the demands of multiple jobs and commuting to work, as well as managing children's school assignments and their changes. One African-American interviewee recalled a storm when half an inch of snow accumulated, causing icy roads, early dismissals, and long traffic delays. Some students ended up spending the night at their schools. She said, "But that assignment [plan], how far is [too far]? For the parent, how quickly can I get to my child? That was exhibited when we had that freak storm. How quickly can I get to my child in an emergency, from [my] workplace or home?"

Second, citizens worried that children's academic well-being would be harmed by reassignments to distant schools. As one interviewee stated: "Really, if you think about elementary school, you know a lot of it is creating a love for school and so if you are putting a heavy burden on a child and . . . they are having to get up extra early . . . you would think (this situation) would potentially, in some students, create more of a negative taste for education and send them down the wrong road."

Similarly, one African-American community leader suggested: "I just don't think diversity, shipping kids around, really matters as much as them getting a good education, and at the end of the day, there is a job." Nor was this concern confined to those skeptical of diversity's benefits. An African-American, pro-diversity parent at a focus group said: "I will use the word 'repulsive,' and the reason I say it is repulsive is because I am tired of all of this sitting on the backs of the children. . . . It is the children that you are busing, it is the children that you are manipulating. . . . It is not on their back to take the long bus ride or be pulled out of your class."

Third, the process of changing student assignments created uncertainty for families and for children. Each winter the school board identified groups of children they were proposing to move to keep up with uneven population growth and to avoid schools becoming disproportionately low income. Hearings with the board followed. Sometimes parents were granted exemptions from proposed moves. Others applied for magnet schools, preferring those placements, and their certainty, to the possibility of future reassignments. Board decisions came out in May, which meant that

> Wake's debate had two camps: one that viewed diverse schools as an investment in county well-being and favored school "balancing," the other that championed proximity of home and school.

some families were unsure about school placement for several months during each year. Emotions of both parents and children ran high.

One involved parent stated, "The discontent that I was hearing was the unbelievable inconsistency in feeder patterns. People would not know from one year to the next where their kid was going to school, and not only would they not know where they were going to go this year, they did not even have a sense of, OK, well, you will go to this elementary school, this middle school, and then this high school. It switched with no rhyme or reason." This uncertainty meant parents felt unsure about how to protect child well-being, clearly at the heart of the conflict, but seemingly beyond the debate between preferences for diversity and neighborhood schools.

From our survey we also learned that preferences for diversity and neighborhood schools were not even diametrically opposed. Citizens who favored diversity were less likely to favor neighborhood schools and vice versa, but the relationship was far from perfect. We found that nearly everyone favors neighborhood schools. They are well ingrained in American life and likely reflect the type of school arrangement many of today's adults experienced when they were young. However, a significant subset of Wake County citizens who favor neighborhood schools also strongly support diversity as a basis for children's school assignments.

Finally, our survey also showed that attitudes among African Americans in Raleigh were complex. They were more supportive of diversity-based school assignments than Whites, and less supportive of neighborhood schools. But social class also mattered. Affluent African Americans favored diversity more than their lower-income counterparts, who were managing both work and family with fewer resources.

For them, having children assigned to schools far from their homes, even in the name of diversity, was less attractive. More highly educated African Americans worried less about the challenges, dangers, and uncertainties inherent in assignment policy implementation than those with less education.

is wake typical?

We wondered how unique Raleigh was. Wake's history lacked examples of "massive resistance" to desegregation characteristic of other southern communities during the 1960s and 1970s. The district was never under a court order to desegregate; it had done so voluntarily (although within the context of federal pressure). Wake's public education system had improved for more than 30 years after its creation in 1976. These factors, we reasoned, made it at least somewhat unique, and had created a social and political climate supportive of diverse schools. In addition, the county began creating diverse schools before significant amounts of White flight and "bright flight" occurred. While the diversity policy was in effect, middle-class residents had less incentive to locate in just a few neighborhoods because street address did not strictly dictate which schools children would attend, thus discouraging residential segregation.

We concluded that compared to other large school districts, Wake is relatively unique in the longevity of its school diversity policy, which we see as based both on the demographic capacity to create diverse schools as well as the collective political will to make that happen. For example, it sustained diverse school assignments longer than Charlotte, and it avoided the substantial segregation of schools experienced in places like Richmond. Despite the challenges involved in implementing economically diverse schools, Wake persevered longer than many other school districts. This means Wake was an exemplar for other large school districts that had the demographic capacity and political will to create diverse schools.

what does the future hold?

The 2011 and 2013 elections returned the school board to firm Democratic majorities, likely because of citizen concerns with a lack of transparency by the Republican board. However, this new board chose to maintain past reassignments, not initiate new ones. This approach responded to concerns regarding the challenges, dangers, and uncertainties previously associated with mandatory reassignments and year-round school attendance. This also meant that school resegregation based on socioeconomic status increased. Magnet schools remain popular, while parents now also have an increased number of charter-school options. The impact of greater school choice on the traditionally strong middle-class character of Wake public schools is still unclear.

Demographics remain important. Currently the district enrolls more than 155,000 students, making it the 16th largest school district in the country, and managing district growth continues to be challenging. Wake's public-school-aged population has now become majority–minority, largely because of Latino immigration. Given the association between race and family income, in the future Wake will find creating schools mixed by family income to be more complicated. More than ever, it will need to rely on its strong traditions of maintaining diverse schools to promote both equal opportunity and encourage county prosperity.

RECOMMENDED RESOURCES

Annette Lareau and Kimberly A. Goyette, eds. 2014. *Choosing Homes, Choosing Schools.* Thousand Oaks: Russell Sage Foundation.

Explores the reality that for many families, choosing homes and choosing schools happens simultaneously.

Toby L. Parcel, Joshua A. Hendrix, and Andrew J. Taylor. 2015. "Race, Politics, and School Assignment Policies in Charlotte Mecklenburg and Wake County, North Carolina." In *Yesterday, Today, and Tomorrow: School Desegregation and Resegregation in Charlotte,* edited by R. A. Mickelson, S. S. Smith, and A. Hawn Nelson. Cambridge, MA: Harvard Education Press.

A comparison of Charlotte and Raleigh history, demographics, and school characteristics suggests why Raleigh sustained school desegregation longer than Charlotte.

Toby L. Parcel and Andrew J. Taylor. 2015. *The End of Consensus: Diversity, Neighborhoods, and the Politics of Public Schools Assignments.* Chapel Hill: The University of North Carolina Press.

A mixed-methods study of the creation of the Wake County Public School System, the evolution of consensus surrounding diverse schools, and why this consensus dissolved, with comparisons to other school districts.

James E. Ryan. 2010. *Five Miles Away, A World Apart: One City, Two Schools, and the Story of Educational Opportunity in Modern America.* New York: Oxford University Press.

The story of two racially segregated high schools, one in urban Richmond and the other in Henrico County, Virginia.

REVIEW QUESTIONS

1. What are the advantages of "integration" or "diversity" in school? What are the disadvantages?

2. Will Wake's achievements be possible in other counties? If poor, disadvantaged counties apply school policies enforcing integration, what will be the expected results? State possible scenarios.

3. One of the key debates discussed in this article is whether it is preferable for schools to be close to home or have high levels of integration but be farther from a child's home. If you were the parent of a child in this county, which would you choose? Why?

viewpoints
affirmative inaction
fall 2013

four experts explore what the fisher v. university of texas *supreme court decision means for the future of race preferences in higher education.*

isher v. University of Texas is one of the most important cases on higher education to be heard by the Supreme Court. Given its conservative bent, many observers expected the Court to end affirmative action with this case. But instead of issuing a landmark decision, it remanded the case back to the Fifth Circuit Court of Appeals.

Abigail Fisher, the Caucasian plaintiff (as described by the Supreme Court), sued the University of Texas for denying her admission. She alleged that the consideration of race in admissions violated the Equal Protection Clause. Her argument was framed in meritocratic language; considering race to help Blacks and Latinos would harm more-deserving White students.

Fisher's perspective reflects an ideal of meritocracy that runs deep in U.S. culture. We say things like "work hard and you'll get ahead" and "pull yourself up by your bootstraps." White people are big proponents of the idea of meritocracy, likely because they do well in meritocratic systems due to sociohistorical advantages of income, wealth, parents' education, better schools and neighborhoods, and so forth. But University of Miami sociologist Frank Samson found an interesting twist on White support for meritocratic admissions. As he expected, the Whites he surveyed in California were great cheerleaders of basing admissions on test scores. But when they were told that the proportion of

Asians in the University of California is twice their proportion of the state's population, Whites decided that using criteria other than just tests was a good idea. So being judged on their merits is a great system for Whites, until they think it might stop working for them. Then some kind of affirmative action program becomes desirable.

The authors in this *Viewpoints* approach the topic of affirmative action from very distinct angles. Richard D. Kahlenberg argues that instead of race-based affirmative action, we'd all be better off using class as a proxy for race, as it would greatly increase class diversity, sorely lacking at top universities. Also, it would short-circuit political objections to the use of race as a criterion for affirmative action and achieve the same goal of diversity in the end. Writing from Israel, Sigal Alon tells us that when class-based affirmative action programs were adopted, geographic and socioeconomic diversity increased at elite universities, and half of all students admitted under the programs were ethnic minorities at the bottom of Israel's social hierarchy. Still, she says that under race-based policies, the overall level of ethnic diversity would have been much higher.

Two other articles discuss why the fact of continued discrimination belies the idea that we are becoming a color-blind country. Jennifer Pierce examines how in one large company she studied, White lawyers keep Black lawyers out of the loop by leaving them out of social events and not mentoring them. And finally, John D. Skrentny argues that racial preferences, reviled by Republicans, are widely practiced outside of formal affirmative action programs in a great number of settings, including within the Republican Party.

richard d. kahlenberg

in defense of proxies

The Supreme Court's decision in *Fisher v. University of Texas* was a victory for racial diversity and a defeat for racial preferences. The Supreme Court, by a 7–1 margin, affirmed that achieving the educational benefits of diversity is compelling, but made it much harder for universities to employ race per se in admissions. The Court ruled universities have "the ultimate burden of demonstrating, before turning to racial classifications, that available, workable race-neutral alternatives do not suffice." Moreover, as the Court noted, "the University receives no deference" on this question.

The sole dissenter in the case, Justice Ruth Bader Ginsburg, suggested it was silly to require universities to camouflage their true intent by employing proxies for race. Even where proxies produce the same level of racial diversity as using race in admissions, there is no reason to force universities to engage in subterfuge, she said. The Texas Top Ten Percent Law, she noted, was specifically designed with the intent of indirectly producing racial diversity, capitalizing on widespread racial segregation in the state's high schools. If universities are authorized to seek racial diversity, why not just allow them to be honest and use race in admissions? Pointedly, not a single justice—liberal or conservative—joined Justice Ginsburg's dissenting opinion.

When proxies produce a similar degree of racial diversity, they are superior to racial preferences. Proxies avoid the disadvantages associated with policies that directly use race, as there are costs and dangers to policies that legitimize grouping people by racial characteristics—even when statistically valid. If there is another way of getting to the same valued goal—racial diversity—without legitimizing race-based decision making, the alternative is to be favored. For instance, Black and Latino students who are admitted by achieving at the top 10 percent of their high school class or having overcome economic obstacles are likely to face less stigma than those admitted through direct racial preference. And for those advocating progressive social policies, there is also a political danger of race-specific policies that signal to working-class Whites that they have less in common with working-class Blacks than they do with wealthy Whites.

Even more importantly, legal rulings that push universities to employ proxies for race may spur officials to address abiding issues of class inequality that institutions would otherwise rather avoid. Research finds that today, socioeconomic obstacles to a student's success

> Research finds that today, socioeconomic obstacles to a student's success are far greater than racial obstacles.

are far greater than racial obstacles. While the Black/White test-score gap used to be twice as large as the income gap, today the achievement gap between rich and poor is twice as large as the racial gap. Policies that provide a leg up to students who have overcome hurdles, therefore, should give more consideration to class than race.

Yet selective universities, according to a number of studies, give large weight to race but virtually no consideration to class. One exception is public universities in states where race has been banned from consideration, often because of voter referendum. In many of these states, university administrators turn to socioeconomic status as an indirect way of achieving racial and ethnic diversity. Bans on race have also led universities to eliminate legacy preferences for the children of alumni (for example, at UCLA and University of Georgia), form new partnerships with disadvantaged high schools, and boost financial aid. A December 2011 report from UT–Austin finds that students admitted to the institution under the Texas Top Ten Percent Law are more socioeconomically diverse than students admitted under discretionary programs, including race-conscious affirmative action. Moreover, in 1996 in Texas, as the Supreme Court noted, the use of race produced a class that was 4.1 percent Black and 14.5 percent Hispanic, but in 2004, race-neutral strategies produced a class that was 4.5 percent Black and 16.9 percent Hispanic. Likewise, in 7 of 10 leading universities Halley Potter and I studied in which race was dropped from admissions (usually because of voter initiative), race-neutral strategies produced as much, or greater, levels of Black and Hispanic representation as the use of race had in the past.

In this way, proxies for race can address large class inequalities that currently result in selective colleges having roughly 25 times as many students from rich families as poor families. Given the growing economic divide in this country, policies that look solely at race might be considered a poor proxy for what matters most.

sigal alon

insights from israel's class-based affirmative action

In the United States, the term "affirmative action" has been synonymous with preference policies based on race and ethnicity. Today, however, due to the growing controversy around these policies and to recent Supreme Court rulings, affirmative action policy in U.S. higher education may be embarking on a new path. In *Fisher v. University of Texas,* the Supreme Court affirmed the importance of diversity on college campuses, but instructed that universities may take race and ethnicity into account during admissions only after race-neutral solutions have been thoroughly exhausted. In light of the strict scrutiny imposed by the court, elite universities that employ affirmative action will, in the coming years, likely seek new and creative ways to achieve campus diversity.

The obvious alternative to affirmative action policies based on race are those based on class—that is, policies that give an edge in college admissions to the socioeconomically disadvantaged. The problem, however, is that we know very little about class-based affirmative action—mostly because, with the exception of sporadic experiments, it has never been implemented in the United States. Statistical simulations performed using U.S. data sets suggest that affirmative action policies based only on income will not be able to generate the racial and ethnic diversity of race-sensitive policies. But these simulations are limited in their ability to replicate many of the factors that are likely to be significant in fostering broad diversity. With few actual educational programs to observe, we are left wondering about the implications of class-based policy for disadvantaged populations and for campus diversity.

The Israel program focuses on structural determinants of disadvantage, in particular on neighborhood socioeconomic status and high school rigor.

There is one country that does offer a large-scale, race-neutral, class-based affirmative action policy for scrutiny—the first of its kind, in fact, to ever be implemented in university admissions worldwide: Israel. The program, adopted in the mid-2000s by four of the country's most selective universities, targets disadvantaged applicants, and it is completely race-neutral and also need-blind. That is, in evaluating the eligibility of applicants, neither their financial status nor their ethnic origins are considered. The emphasis, rather, is on structural determinants of disadvantage, in particular on locality/neighborhood socioeconomic status and high school rigor (certain individual hardships are also weighed, such as being an orphan or having a parent with a disability or chronic illness). The program's distinctive—and theoretically attractive—design is rooted in the long tradition of sociological research on the effect of social structures, such as neighborhoods and schools, on education outcomes.

I have been studying this policy for several years now and have found that it has increased geographic, socioeconomic, and demographic diversity at the elite universities in Israel. This class-based model of affirmative action enhanced, for example, the level of sociogeographical diversity at elite institutions. In the student bodies of Israeli universities, youth from deprived localities are underrepresented. Only a quarter of university admits come from poor localities, and in the most selective majors, only 15 percent do. Yet, more than one of two applicants admitted under the class-based affirmative action policy were from such weak localities.

The class-based—yet strictly need-blind—plan also taps into students with economic constraints: 22 percent of affirmative action admits had an unemployed father while this was the case for only 7 percent of admits from the general pool. Moreover, given the color-blind nature of the class-based policy, it is quite remarkable that about half of all affirmative action admits are ethnic minorities, Jews of Asian and African origin and Arabs, groups at the bottom of Israel's stratification system. Clearly, a policy that spotlights geographical and school inequality stretches the diversity dividends to include national and ethnic origin. Even so, if a race-based affirmative action policy had been implemented instead of this policy, the level of ethnic diversity would have been much higher.

In our search for effective class-based preference policies in U.S. higher education, we can learn from the design and outcomes of Israel's innovative affirmative action policy. For instance, because of the overlap between geographical boundaries and economic and racial–ethnic inequality, this neighborhood- and school-based policy has enhanced the access of wide-ranging disadvantaged populations to even the most selective university majors and departments, successfully generating broad diversity dividends. Nonetheless, such a policy cannot match the level of ethnic diversity generated by race-conscious tools. In examining the suitability of this approach for the U.S. context, a key question is whether race-neutral admission plans can yield sufficient racial and ethnic diversity at elite schools in the United States, or whether race should continue to be at least one of the factors considered.

jennifer pierce

still racing for innocence

What is especially insidious about racism in our post–civil rights era is its stealth. The visibly racist Jim Crow formulation of "Whites only" has come to be replaced by a newer form of racism in our post–civil rights era, one that has been described alternately as "color mute" and "color blind." In turning the *Fisher v. University of Texas* case back to the lower court, the U.S. Supreme Court failed to consider the fact that race continues to be a fundamental basis of structural inequality in the United States. Race affects where we live, what schools our children attend, how much education we attain, whom we hire and promote at work, how much money we earn, how much wealth we accumulate, and whom we might marry.

In my research with attorneys who worked in the legal department of a large California corporation, I found that White lawyers were often "color mute." They noticed race, but were reluctant to use racial designations. In doing so, they could avoid being labeled racist. While most of the White men in my study espoused color blindness and seldom used racially specific terms, they practiced racial exclusion. They seldom included African-American men in informal socializing events that are often crucial to career development and success. And they systematically failed to mentor the few Black male lawyers in their workplace or to take them seriously in professional conversations.

Black men were aware that they were treated differently than their White counterparts, and when they complained, White male attorneys professed their innocence—"I'm not a racist!" Rather, they dismissed men of color's remarks and blamed them for "not fitting into" this professional milieu and for lacking "qualifications." In fact, as I found, "not qualified" became a code word used again and again to denigrate Black men. White male attorneys never actually said that Blacks as a group were unqualified, but in informal conversations, they systematically referred to individuals who were Black as not qualified. In this way, they justified their exclusionary practices with color-blind meritocratic language. Similarly, in their opposition to affirmative action, they did not mention race, but complained about government regulations interfering in their hiring decisions.

One of the Black male attorneys I interviewed called this practice "racing for innocence." As he put it, "It's like they're just working like crazy to convince me that they aren't racist when they know they've done something wrong. But they won't admit they've done anything wrong. . . . So, they're racing to be the most liberal, most hip, non-racist White guy."

The kind of simultaneous disavowal and practice of racial exclusion these White attorneys performed is a historically specific practice drawing from the broader American discourse of liberal individualism. Liberal individualism recasts long-standing systematic racist practices, such as discrimination against African Americans in employment, into seemingly individual isolated incidents of personal prejudice. Because the White lawyers in my study regarded each interaction with African-American lawyers as individual, they were unable to see how their collective practices excluded people of color. Further, because they refrained from using racially loaded language to describe Blacks, they saw themselves as "innocent" of racism. As my ethnographic research demonstrates, liberal individualism not only contributed to White lawyers' understandings of success and failure in their professional world, but also enabled them to overlook how their collective practices maintain and reproduce Whiteness as a structure of inequality.

The White lawyers systematically failed to mentor the few Black male lawyers in their workplace or to take them seriously in professional conversations.

Paying attention to what Americans *do* is why affirmative action is such an important policy. It compels employers and college admissions officers to monitor their practices whether in hiring and promotion or in college admissions.

Are hiring practices resulting in job searches with predominantly White pools of applicants? If so, why? Have recruitment efforts gone beyond the conventional networks of White professional organizations, colleagues, and friends? Have the credentials of an applicant been undermined or dismissed because s/he has an ethno-racial sounding name? Once hired, are Blacks and Latinos mentored in the same ways as White men are? Are workplaces adapting to people of color? Or are they treated as "tokens"? Affirmative action compels us to keep asking these questions in a social and historical context where discrimination continues to affect the life chances of people of color. If we don't keep asking these questions and attending to these practices, like the Supreme Court, we continue to be racing for innocence.

john d. skrentny

our national delusion about race

The Supreme Court's recent decision in *Fisher v. University of Texas* continued the Republican-appointed majority's record of skepticism toward the use of race in the allocation of opportunities. The majority presented its usual lofty language about how racial preferences are always wrong, no matter which groups they benefit.

But *Fisher* ignores the obvious: political elites across the U.S. ideological spectrum regularly give racial preferences when allocating opportunities. Regardless of what the law says, Americans routinely use race as a basis of admission, appointment, and opportunity. Racial preferences are deeply woven into the

nation's DNA. The national dialogue on this issue will not be advanced until the Court and political elites acknowledge these realities.

Let's start with the Republican Party, which consistently opposes racial preferences. The irony is Republican leaders regularly practice racial and ethnic preference. Minorities in the party can expect a meteoric rise. Most recently, first-term Senator Marco Rubio followed first-term New Mexico governor Susan Martinez in addressing the 2012 Republican National Convention. Rubio had been in the Senate a little more than a year when many Republican leaders openly acknowledged that the freshman senator's appeal to Latino voters made him especially qualified to be Mitt Romney's vice presidential pick. The party continually telling us it is wrong to allocate opportunities based on ancestry was doing just that.

Adamantly anti-preference Republicans elevating inexperienced or relatively unknown conservative minorities to positions of prominence is not new. After President Barack Obama's first State of the Union address, Republicans chose untested Indian-American Governor Bobby Jindal of Louisiana to give the GOP response. They chose African-American Congressman J.C. Watts, in office barely two years, to give the response to President Bill Clinton's 1997 State of the Union address. Before that, we saw President George H. W. Bush's appointment of Clarence Thomas to the Supreme Court in 1991. Staunchly anti-affirmative action, Thomas replaced the retiring pro-affirmative action African-American justice, Thurgood Marshall.

For Democratic Party leaders, just as for their GOP peers, race can pay political dividends: having non-Whites in positions of high visibility can attract non-White voters, make all Americans feel included in government, and at the least, offer a shield from charges of racism or xenophobia. President Clinton boasted of his cabinet that it "looked like America." President Obama may have angered Latino voters with his aggressive campaign of deporting undocumented immigrants or not passing comprehensive immigration reform, but at least he gave them something to be proud of with the appointment of the first Latina to the Supreme Court.

Outside the realm of politics, appointments and opportunities based on race are no less prominent. Medical experts point to the benefits of non-White doctors treating non-White patients, offering cultural understanding and a trusting environment—and at the end of the day, better health care. News organizations add minorities to their ranks under the assumption they can ask the right questions and better find answers on issues regarding their communities. Police departments strategically manage the placement of officers while considering race—a practice some federal courts have approved. Educational institutions regularly

> *Fisher v. University of Texas* ignores the obvious: political elites across the U.S. ideological spectrum regularly give racial preferences when allocating opportunities.

extol the benefits of racial role models on their staffs, as well as the culturally compatible teaching styles they may offer diverse students. And corporations boast about the bottom-line benefits of their racially diverse workforces.

Of course, most racial preferences benefit Whites. Political party leadership remains overwhelmingly White, especially in the Republican Party. Even as corporations diversify, the top positions of the Fortune 500 remain bastions of Whiteness. Preferences for Whites may be most obvious in Hollywood, where casting calls still specify race, and when African-American stars do get top billing, they typically have to share it with a White buddy.

The point here is not that the allocation of opportunities based on race is right. It is that it is reality. The Court majority opinion's deep skepticism regarding the use of race in admissions at the University of Texas ignores practices that are ubiquitous in America. Focusing on what the law says ignores what lawmakers do. Despite proclamations on the virtues of color blindness, both major political parties practice race-consciousness. The first step to a sound debate on university admission policies is acknowledging that Americans, both red and blue, still pay attention to skin color.

REVIEW QUESTIONS

1. In "Still Racing for Innocence," Pierce introduces the idea of tokenism. Does this idea fit with Skrentny's discussion of the elevation of minorities, or are there differences between the two?
2. What is the argument for and against employing proxies for race to increase racial diversity in college admissions instead of policies that directly use race?
3. What is "liberal individualism"? How does the ideology of liberal individualism overlook how collective practices maintain and reproduce race as a basis of structural inequality?

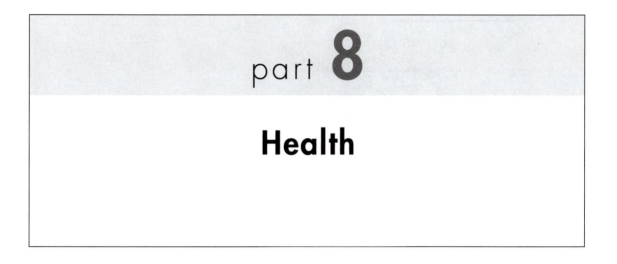

part **8**

Health

tania m. jenkins and shalini reddy

revisiting the rationing of medical degrees in the united states

41

fall 2016

degree rationing is good for U.S. medical school graduates, even as it exacerbates physician shortages.

The first time Spencer applied to medical school, he sent applications to 28 colleges across the country. As a well-rounded graduate of an Ivy League university with extensive biomedical research experience, he felt confident that he would get accepted somewhere. When he was unsuccessful, he retook the MCAT, got a higher score, and narrowed his search to a few state schools with high acceptance rates for in-state applicants. Still nothing. By the third time around, Spencer felt resigned to apply out of the country. "I decided to go to the Caribbean. I knew [medical school] was something I was capable of, and I thought I wasn't given an opportunity," Spencer explained.

Since 2000, 24 new offshore for-profit medical schools have opened in the Caribbean, with over 20,000 graduates like Spencer currently practicing in the United States (Spencer eventually became a general internist). Acceptance to stateside postgraduate residency positions from these schools is only around 50 percent though. This means half of the graduates are left to either retry next year or abandon medicine altogether. At the same time, the United States is facing a serious shortage of physicians. Revised estimates place the overall deficit anywhere between 61,700 and 94,700 doctors by 2025, especially in primary care, where the projected shortfall ranges between 14,900 and 35,600.

As the country debates how to fix this shortage, one factor that has garnered relatively little attention is why there are so few MDs graduating from U.S. medical schools (USMDs). In 2016, less than two-thirds of residency positions nationwide were filled by USMDs, with nearly 94 percent of them successfully "matching" to a residency program. In other words, after almost every graduating USMD got a residency position, there were still nearly 11,000 residency spots left over. They would be filled by non-USMDs, specifically osteopathic and international medical graduates. (U.S. osteopathic doctors, or DOs, are trained under a parallel medical curriculum that is nearly identical to MDs', but with additional emphasis on whole-person care and disease prevention.) For the past ten years, there have been 29–35 percent more residency positions than U.S. seniors applying for them—an average of 1.47 positions per USMD applicant.

These "extra" positions should not be mistaken for an overabundance of physicians, however, as the nationwide shortage of doctors persists *despite* the fact that DOs, U.S.-citizen international medical graduates (USIMGs), and non-U.S.-citizen international medical graduates (IMGs) respectively fill approximately 8.6 percent, 10.3 percent, and 13.5 percent of residency positions each year. Hospitals, which benefit tremendously from inexpensive resident labor, have pushed Congress to increase the funding allocated to graduate medical education and expand residency programs, with only limited success. Yet despite the impending shortage of doctors, the proportion of USMDs to residency positions has remained relatively unchanged since the early days of modern medical training. Since 1950, the United States has consistently graduated anywhere between 20 percent and 45 percent *fewer* USMDs than are needed to fill residency positions nationwide.

This gap is not for lack of interest in medical careers; in 2014, for example, only 43 percent of all medical school applicants in the United States were admitted to traditional medical schools, suggesting that far more people are interested in medicine than there are spots available. Although it is costly to open new medical schools or expand existing ones, medical schools in the United States have responded to the predicted shortage by increasing enrollment by almost 20 percent. Even so, the number of USMDs remains far from sufficient to fill all residency positions, despite the profession having had ample opportunity to ramp up its production of doctors since the 1950s. The question is, why?

degree rationing increases usmds' status

The answer may have to do with increasing professional status. One of us (Jenkins) spent 23 months from 2011 to 2014 observing and interviewing USMD and non-USMD residents and hospital administrators at two different northeastern internal medicine programs, as part of a broader study on the medical profession. The fieldwork revealed status distinctions between USMDs and non-USMDs—even within the same specialty—and sought to identify some of the mechanisms contributing to these distinctions.

One reason USMDs enjoy higher status is because they are relatively scarce. As one American-trained resident noted, USMDs' exclusivity "makes us something special. Costly and rare." This phenomenon, known as degree rationing, may or may not be a conscious

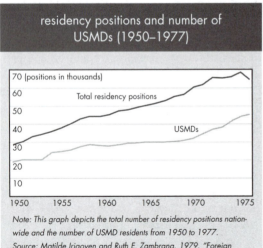

residency positions and number of USMDs (1950–1977)

Note: This graph depicts the total number of residency positions nationwide and the number of USMD residents from 1950 to 1977.
Source: Matilde Irigoyen and Ruth E. Zambrana. 1979. "Foreign Medical Graduates (FMGs): Determining Their Role in the United States Health Care System." Social Science & Medicine 13A(6A): 775–783.

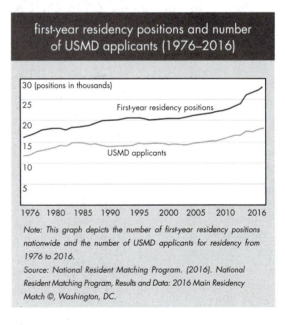

first-year residency positions and number of USMD applicants (1976–2016)

Note: This graph depicts the number of first-year residency positions nationwide and the number of USMD applicants for residency from 1976 to 2016.
Source: National Resident Matching Program. (2016). National Resident Matching Program, Results and Data: 2016 Main Residency Match ©, Washington, DC.

intention of the profession, but by underproducing doctors, USMDs remain in high demand by residency directors. That demand increases their value and prestige compared to non-USMDs. This is important because thousands of international and osteopathic graduates fill residency positions every year, and by importing what some have described as the "world's best and brightest," the U.S. medical profession risks competition from highly skilled non-USMDs.

To help stave off this competition, state licensing boards, staffed primarily by USMDs, require all internationally trained physicians to complete at least three years of residency before practicing independently in the United States. Requiring non-USMDs to apply alongside USMDs for residency positions, regardless of their level of previous training, levels the playing field considerably. (A fully trained dermatologist from another country, for example, must apply to redo a dermatology residency alongside a USMD senior applicant.) Because USMDs are generally considered higher status than non-USMDs, in part due to degree rationing, they more often match to desirable and prestigious specialties. In 2016, for example, nearly 76 percent of residency positions in surgery were filled by USMDs, even though they comprised only 55 percent of applicants. In contrast, non-USMDs generally occupy positions in less competitive fields like family medicine, where they comprise nearly 55 percent of new residents.

Importantly, there are no formal regulations requiring residency programs to prioritize USMDs, so prestige becomes an important, albeit informal, mechanism for ensuring their access to top positions. Programs benefit from USMDs' high status, too. A hospital administrator explained: "One way that you increase the prestige of the training program is to eliminate international medical grads." Elite programs therefore attract elite applicants (USMDs), who, in turn, help reinforce the program's prestige.

Professions have long been described by sociologists as cartels that monopolize the provision of certain services to protect against competition from other occupations. Doctors, for example, have the exclusive permission to perform surgery, a service that makes them highly valuable in society. If physical therapists could also perform surgery, surgeons would likely lose status and income, because patients could go to alternative professionals for the same service. Professions therefore try to delineate "jurisdictions" to keep other professions from competing for their clients—something medicine has been exceptionally good at, despite incursions into its technical core by other professionals, such as nurse practitioners and physicians' assistants.

An important dimension of this dominance is controlling the supply of doctors. This keeps the value of membership high and enhances the profession's contention that only a select group of people can do the highly technical work that distinguishes the profession from its competitors (a process known as "external social closure"). Our findings, however, suggest that scarcity may also be useful for *internal* social closure—staving off competition from the inside. As the number of international and osteopathic graduates vying for residency positions increases every year, American MDs must remain valuable—and scarce enough—to successfully fend off the additional competition. This is especially true if hospitals prefer recruiting top-notch international or osteopathic graduates who may have better test scores or interpersonal skills than "bottom of the barrel" USMDs. Match statistics reveal that, in specialties like internal medicine, IMGs have to score up to three standard deviations *higher* on their licensing exams to have the same probability of matching to residency as USMDs, which suggests that the elite core of the profession has been remarkably successful at protecting its insiders, despite fierce competition from those trained outside the usual channels.

a history of titrating supply

Importantly, the United States has a long history of using top-down approaches to control the nation's supply of doctors. Since the beginning of modern residency training, the country has relied particularly on IMGs, whose influx has been regulated through centralized governmental policies such as visa restrictions and licensing laws. Depending on the perceived supply of USMDs at any given moment, policies have either increased or decreased the number of IMGs allowed into the United States to practice medicine, with the aim of protecting the elite USMD core of the medical profession.

The Smith-Mundt Act of 1948 extended exchange visitor (J) visas to IMGs for the first time, allowing them to pursue residency training in the United States on the condition that they leave the country for at least two years prior to applying for permanent residency. This meant, however, that while the United States was attracting more foreign doctors, those doctors were not staying in the country after their training, thereby doing little in the long-term to add to the nation's medical workforce.

By the early 1960s, the Department of Labor determined that a doctor shortage was looming, so laws were passed to facilitate an influx of IMGs. In 1961, the Mutual Educational and Cultural Exchange Act (also known as the Fulbright-Hays Act) waived the two-year foreign residency requirement for IMGs. By 1962 doctors were exempted from national quotas that limited the number of migrants from certain countries. Preference categories for skilled workers were created in the 1965 Immigration Act, encouraging the immigration of professionals who could help fill gaps in the U.S. economy. And by 1970, IMGs could simply exchange their J-visas for regular work (H-1B) visas to facilitate their application for permanent residency. Unsurprisingly, the supply of IMGs increased considerably.

> The current social contract in medicine hinges on being able to offer U.S. medical students gainful and satisfying employment upon graduation.

Concerns about the shortage of doctors were replaced with fears of an oversupply from the 1970s until the 1990s. These fears stemmed from a perceived abundance of international medical graduates. Around this time, offshore medical schools began emerging in the Caribbean, offering an outlet for U.S. citizens wanting to become doctors but unable to gain entry to mainland universities. Numbers were also rising domestically: between 1965 and 1985, the number of U.S. medical schools increased from 88 to 127, with an increase in the total number of yearly graduates from 7,574 to 16,191. Ten new osteopathic schools opened in the United States between 1968 and 1988, further crowding the workforce.

The result was an estimated *surplus* of doctors ranging anywhere between 35,000 to 70,000 doctors. Panic ensued. Scholars wrote about the threat of unemployment for junior doctors and how the outlook was grim for USMDs applying to residency. The government passed the Health Professions Educational Assistance Act of 1976 and the Health Services Extension Act of 1977, which reinstated the two-year foreign residency requirement for J-visa holders and required new IMGs to apply to the Department of Labor for approval of their visa. In the mid-1990s, the American Medical Association, the Pew Health Professions Committee, the Institute of Medicine, and other professional bodies called for the contraction of residency positions and a reduction in the number of IMGs to protect USMDs from the impending physician surplus. Based on policy directions from the late 1970s to the mid-1990s, many expected the nation to become less dependent on IMGs, eventually preferring to hire American-trained personnel over foreign doctors.

Yet, self-sufficiency has not come to pass. The country remains as dependent on non-USMDs as in the 1950s and '60s. Even the laws have relaxed again to allow non-U.S. citizens to practice and ultimately stay in the country long-term. (Depending on the residency program, IMGs can be sponsored for either H1-B or J-visas, with the option of waiving the two-year home residency requirement by working in an underserved area upon graduation.) Why not simply graduate enough USMDs so that the country no longer has to rely on international and osteopathic doctors, thereby eliminating competition altogether? After all, Medicare pays for residency training—yet another reason to invest in American talent.

the social contract

Findings suggest that this gap persists to buffer USMDs from having to take residency positions in less attractive locations, specialties, or hospitals, relying instead on non-USMDs to fill these spots. As long as doctors are in sufficiently high demand, there is little incentive for USMDs to dramatically increase their supply; non-USMDs fill the positions that few want to fill. As one medical school administrator put it, "The whole system is set up to basically reward [USMD] students." Self-sufficiency could therefore threaten the livelihoods that American medical students have come to expect.

Many USMDs undergo medical training with the understanding that in exchange for hard work, debt, and deferred gratification, they will be able to pursue the career of their choice in the specialty of their choosing—representing a kind of social contract between trainees and the profession. As one USMD resident described: "There are a lot of people that want to go into this field [medicine] and not everyone is going to make it, so the ones that are able to make it [into a U.S. medical school]—I'm going to sound very awful—but I think we deserve something. . . . I feel like, if I can get to that next step, I should be entitled to the things that come along with that," referring to getting priority for top residency spots. In the words of another USMD resident, "It's maybe fair for U.S. medical students to be prioritized [for] U.S. residency positions. . . . We're kind of paying our dues to get these spots, in some sense." Indeed, as sociologists Caroline Hodges Persell and Peter W. Cookson have found, going to an elite school is often associated with a perceived set of "rights" or guarantees—in this case, admission to their preferred residency.

Other USMD residents described the contract more explicitly as a return on their investment: "I think you have to accommodate the people that have put money into their education here before you train outside physicians to do the job." Another USMD intern said pragmatically, "I'm $130,000 in debt, right? I'm not willing to put that on a degree that I don't know is going to get me a job afterwards." Thus, U.S. medical trainees go through schooling with the expectation that their considerable investment

> Should the terms of the contract change, however, fewer medical graduates may want to enter a profession that does not guarantee job security or fulfillment of aspirations, an outcome that would undoubtedly worsen the current shortage of physicians.

of time, money, and effort will be rewarded with lucrative positions in favored specialties and locations. If the United States achieved self-sufficiency in terms of staffing its residency programs, USMDs would undoubtedly have to fill positions in undesirable geographic and professional areas, and potentially embark upon careers they did not sign up for—or worse, be left with no medical career at all.

The legal profession provides a powerful cautionary tale in this regard. The Great Recession of 2008 prompted many individuals to turn to law school as a "safe" route toward near guaranteed employment. It resulted in a massive surplus of lawyers. Today, lawyers are facing unemployment, layoffs, and significant student debt, in part because the relative demand for lawyers is closely linked to the vagaries of financial markets. (Demand for doctors, in contrast, is far more stable and relatively impervious to market forces, so the rationing of supply leads to more-predictable outcomes.) As the markets struggle to bounce back, the legal profession can no longer guarantee that it can fulfill law students' expectations of gainful employment and a degree of social prestige. As you might expect, interest in the profession has declined. In 2015, only 41,000 individuals applied to law school nationwide, compared to 90,000 in 2004 and 77,000 in 2010. Getting a job as a lawyer is no longer a sure thing, and as a result, law schools have been described as being in a "death spiral," with some schools laying off faculty due to decreased enrollment.

This is precisely the kind of situation that medicine has managed to avoid by ensuring that the number of USMDs is lower than the number of training positions available. The current social contract in medicine hinges on being able to offer U.S. medical students gainful and satisfying employment upon graduation. As one USMD resident explained, "With the number of spots, anyone can get into law school, but not everybody can get a job. But we can. We have good job security." Should the terms of the contract change, however, fewer medical graduates may want to enter a profession that does not guarantee job security or fulfillment of aspirations, an outcome that would undoubtedly worsen the current shortage of physicians.

questions remain

As the country struggles to address a nationwide shortage of doctors, we should not overlook the profession's inner dynamics. In addition to helping professions control the service market (a long-standing contention of the literature on social closure), we find that rationing may also help professionals control competition in a globalizing market for medical education.

These results leave us perhaps with more questions than answers. What are the material and symbolic barriers to increasing the supply of USMDs? How would self-sufficiency in residency positions impact the profession's social contract with its trainees? Should USMDs get priority above all other candidates for residency positions? Should fully trained IMGs be required to redo residency? And what are the impacts of rationing on doctors' well-being and burnout, given that there are fewer doctors to address demand? To address the physician shortage, policy-makers will have to consider how the profession's social contract with its own ranks may be perpetuating an underproduction of doctors.

RECOMMENDED RESOURCES

David Grusky. 2011. "Occupy the Future: Rationing Education Protects the Rich." *Boston Review.*

An account of degree rationing in elite institutions by a leading sociologist of stratification.

HS Inc. 2016. The Complexities of Physician Supply and Demand 2016 Update: Projections from 2014 to 2025. Washington, DC: Prepared for the Association of American Medical Colleges.

> A look at current projections of supply and demand within medicine for the next ten years.

Matilde Irigoyen and Ruth E. Zambrana. 1979. "Foreign Medical Graduates (FMGs): Determining Their Role in the United States Health Care System." *Social Science & Medicine* 13A(6A): 775–83.

> A historical look at how the United States has controlled the external influx of doctors.

National Resident Matching Program. 2016. Results and Data: 2016 Main Residency Match©. Washington, DC.

> A yearly report on the Residency Match results, including information about the placement of USMDs and non-USMDs.

Caroline Hodges Persell and Peter W. Cookson Jr. 1985. "Chartering and Bartering: Elite Education and Social Reproduction." *Social Problems* 33(2): 114–29.

> A classic article about the special "status rights" that accompany an elite education.

REVIEW QUESTIONS

1. What is degree rationing, and how is it happening with medical degrees in the United States?
2. In your opinion, what are the ethical implications of rationing medical degrees?
3. How did policies contribute to the current scarcity of U.S. doctors?

gary c. david

dealing with the diagnosis

spring 2015

naming a medical malady can be both horrifying for new parents and a key to unlocking resources and care.

Following an ambulance down Route 2 toward Boston was not the way I envisioned my day would go. That morning I pictured my wife and me bringing home our second daughter. Now, our newborn lay strapped in an ambulance as we tailed behind, her new car seat empty. Our destination was not home, but the NICU at Massachusetts General Hospital (MGH). In the span of two days, we had gone from being "parents of two children" to members of another club: parents whose newborn is suffering from an unidentified condition.

You do your time in the NICU waiting for something to happen, passing the hours in rooms intended to be as comfortable and comforting as possible, but are never really either. Tests are conducted, monitors go off, nurses weigh diapers, residents come through on rounds, parents eat meals in shifts. You wait for pieces of the medical puzzle to become a finished picture, still cautious about what that clarity might reveal. Sometimes not knowing is better, but knowing is the reason you are there. A diagnosis is needed, the puzzle needs to be solved. Uncertainty percolates. You anticipate a sense of the future that will arrive in the form of a diagnosis. For better or worse, it will define your child, your family, and your life.

> Being simultaneously the parent of a child in the NICU *and* a sociologist created a field experience that I did not seek out, a research project I didn't sign up for.

the sociology

Diagnosis is the instrument through which questions of medical condition are answered. Mildred Blaxter, in her key 1978 piece "Diagnosis as Category and Process," succinctly noted that, even though "The activity known as 'diagnosis' is central to the practice of medicine," researchers have not given it adequate attention. A sociology of diagnosis has emerged to fill this gap, exploring the importance that diagnosis has in medicine and among people and society.

Sometimes the presence of a condition is projected by a change in a person's physical state. A lump might appear, something starts to hurt, a feeling of being "not quite right" results in the decision to seek clinical analysis and guidance. Other times, the diagnosis is a blindside attack. There was no indication of a condition to be discovered. A narrative report titled "The Road to Diagnosis: Stories from Patients with Rare Diseases," from the website Inspire, relates the experience of getting a diagnosis Most of the stories describe the impact the moment of diagnosis had on the authors' lives. Perhaps the most unfortunate, though, are those without a diagnosis. Problems exist in the absence of identification, a kind of

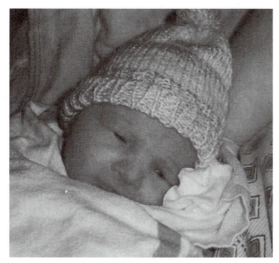

Hailey, the author's daughter, at birth. (Courtesy Gary David)

The three David sisters: Cailin, Hailey, and Amelia (from left). (Courtesy Gary David)

conditional anonymity. You know you are no longer yourself, but don't know who you now are.

Annemarie Jutel describes her own experience in *Putting a Name to It: Diagnosis in Contemporary Society.* "Receiving a diagnosis is like being handed a road map in the middle of a forest. It shows the way—but not necessarily the way out."

Sometimes there is no way out. Rather than showing you how to get back to where you came, the map simply shows where you now reside, what the neighborhood is like, who your new neighbors are going to be, and maybe how long you are going to live there. There is no way out. Nothing to be conquered, nothing to be cured, nothing that can be "fixed."

Harold Garfinkel, the founder of ethnomethodology, calls for direct observation of social action, in some instances going so far as enacting the practices of those being studied. Essentially, Garfinkel sought to understand how activity is coordinated through interaction and out of which meaning and context

are achieved. The goal of the researcher, then, is meeting the *unique adequacy requirement,* a level of competence such that s/he could be recognizable as a member of the group being studied. I quickly fulfilled this requirement, but not by choice.

Being simultaneously the parent of a child in the NICU and a sociologist created a field experience that I did not seek out, a research project I didn't sign up for. Achieving an analytic sociological orientation can be challenging when you are also the parent talking to the specialists, whose child is attached to monitors and whose questions need answering.

developing the diagnosis

Under "Chief Complaint" and "Principal Diagnosis," my daughter's medical record listed the reason for her admission as "multiple congenital anomalies." This included difficulty feeding, low oxygen saturation, polydactyly (the presence of extra digits), and other morphological features that came together as an unrecognized pattern of symptoms. These anomalies by themselves might not be cause for alarm. Upon finding polydactyly on a prenatal ultrasound, the technician joked that such a feature used to be evidence of special powers and was prized among royalty. Nothing to worry about. Now this feature was perhaps a clue of something more significant.

As our NICU stay lengthened, so did the list of specialists. We would get visits from the radiologist (giving our daughter the top-to-bottom once-over), nephrologist (hydro-nephrosis), cardiologist (ASD and bicuspid aortic valve), orthopedist (polydactyly and syndactyly on hands and feet), nutritionists and lactation consultants (low tone and difficulty feeding), and social workers (to help manage it all).

While each dealt with issues related to their separate areas of expertise, one specialist loomed large: the geneticist. The geneticist was the central figure, hoped to unify all of the "multiple congenital anomalies" into a coherent theme. The separate medical issues that had been uncovered could be treated, but genetics would answer the overarching question of a diagnosis at the root of all the disparate problems. Other specialists might be able to describe what was happening in parts of our child, but the geneticist would attempt to describe what she "was." In many ways, this might lead to answering what, if anything, could and should be done.

When seeing someone's new baby, it's customary to coo "how cute," "isn't she adorable," and "she looks just like you." This was not the case when the geneticist entered the room. When Foucault wrote of "the clinical gaze," this must be the look he meant. The process of dissection began as the geneticist walked in and viewed my daughter in my wife's arms. After a long pause and with a tilt of the head, her assessment started:

"Her ears are a little low. Her eyes are somewhat far apart. Her palette is high. She has epicanthal folds."

No congratulations were given. The geneticist did not smile or comment on how cute our daughter was. Instead, the placid listing of atypical morphological features conveyed what we had come to learn over three days: our baby was not like other babies. In other words, "Your child is not 'normal,' and it is written all over her face."

The geneticist believed she knew what was wrong, but it would not be confirmed until the FISH test (flourescence *in situ* hybridization) and karyotype results, used to see into our daughter's chromosomes, came back. She warned, "I'm going to tell you what I think it is, and I'm going to tell you not to look it up online. You're going to do it anyway, so keep in mind that what you see online are the extreme cases." The geneticist was clearly familiar with the parental freak-out that ensues from even a casual WebMD or Google Image search. This warning was our first indication that our daughter's condition was potentially severe.

The genetic specialist's initial thoughts would be confirmed: Trisomy 13 Mosaicism. "Hard" findings tend to have a quantitative nature. In this case it was: "8 of 20 cells with three copies of chromosome 13." This simply means that some of our daughter's cells had an extra 13th chromosome. Full Trisomy 13 (or Patau Syndrome) is the presence of an extra 13th chromosome in all cells (just as Down's syndrome is the presence of an extra 21st chromosome). Trisomy 13 is reported to occur in 1 in 10,000 births, with mosaicism accounting for 5 percent of those births. Other than a random error during mitosis (the dividing of the embryonic cells), there's no

Looking back, our daughter's diagnosis was actually one of the first baby gifts we received.

known cause, and the prognosis for children with full Trisomy 13 is bad. First-year mortality rates are over 90 percent. Though Patau is often considered "incompatible with life," it is clearly not true—children with Trisomy 13 do live, even if for a short time. What *kind* of life is entirely another question, depending on individual circumstances and who is asked to judge.

Mosaicism is different. We were told our daughter would live, "somewhere in between normal functioning and severely disabled." As the diagnosis became clearer, our future, ironically, became less knowable. Our initial uncertainty was amplified. Sure, all new parents wonder what their child's future will be. The difference is most parents start with the expectation that things will be normal. We started on the opposite end of the spectrum. We needed to expect the worst while trying to find normal.

Before leaving the hospital, a doctor told us he was sorry. He encouraged us to enjoy the time that we had with our daughter. With that, we were finally able to take that car ride home from the hospital.

the good and the bad news

It is strange to think of diagnosis as a gift. Typically, a diagnosis of illness or condition is unwelcome information. No parents want to hear their child has a condition that will impact his or her quality of life (let alone their own). On the other hand, the diagnosis makes other things possible. Medical treatment might be available, and children with qualifying diagnoses can get educational and therapeutic services more readily than those without. Looking back, our daughter's diagnosis was actually one of the first baby gifts we received.

Oddly enough, as I have found in my own research on medical records, it is not uncommon for doctors to *not* provide a diagnosis. The symptom(s) and treatment(s) are seen as enough

Hailey David. (Courtesy Gary David)

clinical information that any competent practitioner will know what the diagnosis is. For doctors, this may be understandable. If you document that "Patient complains of a pain in his head" and that "Aspirin were prescribed which resolved the problem," the next doctor will likely infer that that the person was suffering from a headache. However, because that diagnosis was not written down, it cannot be coded, may not be submitted for billing, and might not be counted in other metrics. As medical professionals say, "If it isn't written down, it didn't happen." We might add that, "if it isn't diagnosed, the condition isn't there."

A diagnosis can thus be treasured for parents seeking services for their child. Our child's genetic testing provided institutionally valid confirmation of a condition that would qualify us for services, a kind of "key to the treatment kingdom" presented through the karyotype. For parents whose child has no diagnosis, but needs extra assistance, the absence of a confirmed, scientific label is frustrating, to say the least. It can also lead to conflict with various local, state, and even federal agencies. One parent reports that an application for respite care was rejected with the phrase, "No diagnosis of intellectual disability." The parent noted, "No one had ever officially stated the obvious." No parents want to hear that their child is "developmentally disabled," except when it officially confirms what the parents already know, in order to get the help they need.

When we have told other parents of developmentally disabled children that we received our diagnosis three days postpartum, we have been told, "Oh, you're so lucky!" Clearly not in terms of drawing the cosmic short-straw in having a child with a syndrome whose frequency is over 1 in 10,000 births, the luck refers to the institutional recognition that a condition exists, which then makes you eligible for services and care. There will not be questions about qualification or arguments over criteria. We can walk into a meeting, slap down our daughter's test results—"Trisomy 13 Mosaicism"—and we are eligible. The key works.

I also have been told by parents that they were glad not to have a diagnosis right away, especially when the eventual diagnosis was a terminal one. These parents fondly recall the time when they could enjoy their newborn without any diagnostic cloud. My wife and I had no such time. Looking back, it is hard to say which situation is preferable. My wife and I would also wonder why our daughter's condition wasn't found in all of the prenatal testing. What we would have done if it *was* found? What would we have done if we knew, if we had a diagnosis with no definite prognosis? What if we'd known the syndrome before we got to know our daughter? We never answered these questions. The answers were unknowable.

dealing with the diagnosis

In the end, everyone has to deal with a diagnosis. While traditionally thought of as the identification of a disease or disorder, every person gets assessed in the sense that they are or are not diagnosed. They either have a condition or are free from one. A healthy person, in essence, has a treatment plan: routine checkups. As one health care professional put it, "Everyone gets an ICD-9 code," every instance of medical examination is an assessment.

Still, diagnoses differ in the degree to which they put us on a new life trajectory, whether they shake our foundations or future expectations, call us to question the certainty we once had before symptoms appeared and the diagnosis was delivered. Armand Marie Leroi, in his book *Mutants*, writes, "Mutation is a game of chance, one we must all play, and at which we all lose. But some of us lose more heavily than others." Within us all is some alteration as yet unnamed, unidentified.

Parenting a child with a disability is a constant battle between thinking "what might have been"

> Parenting a child with a disability is a constant battle between thinking "what might have been" in the face of what is.

in the face of what is. It can be hard to appreciate what you have when you are preoccupied with "it was not supposed to be like this." Relatively minor developmental milestones are less expected and more joyous, given the uncertainty about whether they would ever be reached. One parent described it as dealing with "what if" moments, where a routine observation of other "normal" children playing can hit you with the feelings of loss. Your "sick" child will never be able to do what the other kids are doing. It can be difficult not to let the diagnosis define the child and, instead, see the child in terms of deficits rather than abilities. The diagnosis becomes the shorthand for those limitations, and as a parent, your instinct is to fight against it. At the same time, you need the diagnosis. Parenting is always uncertain, but dealing with the diagnosis is unsettling at every level.

My child may belong to a certain syndrome, but she is so much more than that. Today, she is an active 8-year-old who goes to school, fights and plays with her two sisters, attends birthday parties and inclusive summer camps, has the ability to remember anyone's name, memorizes song lyrics, and forms friendships. The diagnosis doesn't *begin* to say anything about her as a person. It never will. What the diagnosis has done is make much of her development possible through the services received, the dedication of her teachers and aides, and programs aimed at children with special needs. From Early Intervention before she was 3 years old to the one-on-one assistance when she started school, the diagnosis on her medical records gave us access.

I'd rather not have to deal with my daughter's diagnosis at all. I'd rather a situation in which my knowledge of genetics was limited to ninth-grade biology class. I'd rather not know that 23 pairs of chromosomes is the optimal number, and more or less than 23 is

trouble. But this is the world we have, in which we continue to have challenges and triumphs, in which humor and irreverence are required to make the days manageable. We, like many parents, have a diagnosis. The moment of our daughter's diagnosis is that life-changing moment that we will never forget. We were fortunate enough to have it.

RECOMMENDED RESOURCES

Mildred Blaxter. 1978. "Diagnosis as Category and Process: The Case of Alcoholism." *Social Sciences and Medicine* 12: 9–17.

> Recognized as one of the foundational pieces establishing the area of sociology of diagnosis.

Phil Brown. 1990. "The Name Game: Toward a Sociology of Diagnosis." *The Journal of Mind and Behavior* 11: 385–406.

> An early call for the establishment of a sociology of diagnosis, this article looks at how diagnosis is used in psychiatric professions and provides a recommendation for examining diagnosis in historical and social contexts.

David Goode. 1994. *A World Without Words: The Social Construction of Children Born Deaf and Blind.* Philadelphia: Temple University Press.

> The book chronicles Goode's work with children who were born during the Rubella Syndrome epidemic (German Measles) during the 1960s, as well as their families, to understand the ways in which they were able to communicate and create meaning.

Annemarie Jutel. 2011. *Putting a Name to It: Diagnosis in Contemporary Society.* Baltimore: The Johns Hopkins University Press.

> An excellent examination of diagnosis as a medical, social, and personal object and experience. Explores all aspects of diagnosis from

multiple perspectives, with examples drawn from different medical conditions.

PJ McGann and David J. Hutson, eds. 2011. *Sociology of Diagnosis.* Bradford: Emerald Group Publishing.

> An edited collection that contains a wide-ranging examination of the field and its applications.

REVIEW QUESTIONS

1. In terms of self-identification as well as identification with others, what are some implications behind receiving, or not receiving, a diagnosis for a medical condition?

2. David also discusses some institutional advantages that come with receiving a diagnosis versus not receiving one. What are they? In what ways does not having an official diagnosis make interaction with institutions more difficult for some?

3. What is Foucault's "clinical gaze"? How did David's interaction with his daughter's geneticist differ from other common conversations about a newborn?

r. tyson smith and owen whooley

dropping the "disorder" in PTSD

43

fall 2015

a new movement to drop the word disorder *from PTSD focuses on stigma.*

Retired U.S. Army General Peter Chiarelli, director of the organization *One Mind,* wants to redefine post-traumatic stress disorder (PTSD). While a main priority of *One Mind* is to accelerate "the research-to-cure time frame exponentially," a core element of its "paradigm-changing" program is advocating for changing PTSD to the lesser classification of "post-traumatic stress," or "PTS." Dropping "disorder" in favor of "injury," Chiarelli's organization hopes to reduce the stigma associated with PTSD. "Injury" can be overcome, "disorder" implies something permanent. As Chiarelli puts it, "No 19-year-old kid wants to be told he's got a disorder."

Thanks to Chiarelli's campaign, "PTS" is increasingly accepted terminology in many military and policy settings. Indeed, former President George W. Bush has said publicly he would no longer use the word "disorder" when discussing veterans' "post-traumatic stress" and earlier this year, Obama twice spoke about "post-traumatic stress." Additionally, there are efforts being made to recognize June as "National Post-Traumatic Stress Awareness Month" and June 27, 2015, as "National Post-Traumatic Stress Awareness Day." "Disorder" seems to be falling out of military lexicon.

But the change is fraught. In the wake of two large-scale wars involving more than 2.5 million U.S. soldiers, how we define and conceive of war-related mental distress is significant.

Why, in this day of headline-grabbing veteran suicides and deadly shootings on military bases, would a decorated military veteran like General Chiarelli want to redefine a diagnosis that has served an indispensable role in securing the mental health treatment of veterans?

Thirty-five years ago, Vietnam veterans, along with allies in the mental health field, won a hard-fought campaign for the recognition of psychological wounds from war, establishing PTSD as a mental disorder. However, once a diagnosis is recognized and institutionalized, it can take on a life of its own. PTSD in 2015 is different than PTSD in 1980. In response, several advocacy groups—most with ties to the Pentagon and affiliated nonprofit organizations—are now attempting to *de*medicalize PTSD. This marked shift in the diagnostic politics of PTSD highlights the vicissitudes of medicalization—the process by which social problems become defined and treated as medical in nature.

Diagnoses provide the interpretive framework by which amorphous symptoms and experiences are transformed and reified into disease categories subject to the intervention of medicine. As such, diagnoses can become, in the words of sociologist Phil Brown, "an arena of struggle" in which medical professionals and lay patient groups fight to secure diagnostic understandings that promote their particular interests. PTSD has long represented an exemplary case of successful, lay-initiated medicalization.

PTSD affects millions, yet is experienced as profoundly isolating. (U.S. Air Force/Staff Sgt. Shawn Weismiller)

We join our separate research—Whooley's archival work on the history of psychiatric classification and Smith's ethnography on veterans' returning from Iraq and Afghanistan—to explain the emergence of the movement to "drop the D."

medicalizing the trauma of war

The process of defining a disorder does not necessarily end with its official recognition. It can continue in unanticipated ways that sometimes run contrary to the spirit of the original impetus. Instead, PTSD has undergone a series of changes since its official recognition by the American Psychiatric Association (APA) in 1980.

For the overwhelming majority of mental disorders, the underlying neurological and biological mechanisms are still not well understood. For this reason, the construction of diagnostic categories proceeds by expert consensus. Every decade or so, the APA meets to discuss and revise the *Diagnostic and Statistical Manual of Mental Disorders* (*DSM*), the "Bible of American psychiatry," which defines criteria for every mental disorder. When constructing diagnostic categories, psychiatrists fall back on defining mental disorders by the presentation of manifest symptoms. This process is vulnerable to subjective interpretations and political influences. Thus, behind the *DSM*'s neat lists of symptoms are complicated histories; the final diagnostic categories often represent negotiated accommodations to competing interests. The history of PTSD, in fact, reflects these tensions. The diagnosis was cocreated by psychiatrists and veterans' advocacy groups.

Lay advocates seek a medical diagnosis for three primary reasons. First, a medical diagnosis legitimizes the experience of distress, as a diagnosis is thought to reduce stigma and alleviate personal responsibility. Second, it provides an interpretive schema to make sense of what can be diffuse and ambiguous problems. A diagnosis can explain the distressing symptoms a sufferer has been experiencing in silence, be it PTSD or fibromyalgia, and in turn, can serve as a basis for an identity. Finally, having a personal problem defined as "medical" is a means to secure resources like treatment, reimbursement, and disability support.

While mental distress from the trauma of war has been sporadically recognized under different monikers—among them, "shell shock," "combat neuroses," "soldier's heart," and "operational fatigue"—PTSD did not exist prior to 1980. As sociologist Wilbur Scott recounts, in the mid-1970s, Vietnam veterans, led by the group Vietnam Veterans Against the War (VVAW), sought to change the military culture around war trauma by medicalizing it. Along with sympathetic allies in the mental health field, notably Sarah Haley, Robert Jay Lifton, and Chaim Shatan, veterans fought for official diagnostic recognition for what was first termed "Post-Vietnam Syndrome Disorder" and later "Post-Combat Disorder." This early diagnosis originated from what Scott referred to as "street-corner psychiatry" through "rap groups" run by VA outreach centers, and the diagnosis was consciously tied to the anti-war effort.

After a decade of lobbying the APA, contesting the skepticism among psychiatrists who were ambivalent about a specific diagnosis for combat stress (*DSM-I* contained a "gross-stress reaction" diagnosis but it was dropped from *DSM-II*), veterans' advocates secured the diagnosis of "Post Traumatic Stress Disorder." With

> Why would a decorated military veteran want to redefine a diagnosis that has served an indispensable role in securing the mental health treatment of veterans?

its inclusion in the 1980 *DSM-III*, the psychic consequences of war were acknowledged. Traumatized combat soldiers could be treated as psychiatric patients.

the expansion of ptsd

From its inception, PTSD fit awkwardly in the *DSM-III*. As a disorder caused by a traumatic event, PTSD was always understood as emanating from *social* factors. This departed from the *DSM-III*'s biomedical model of mental disorders, which treats disorders as analogous to physical diseases. Changes to PTSD in subsequent editions of the *DSM* have sought to bring it into alignment with the prevailing model of mental disorders.

Like the *DSM* itself, PTSD has been expanded over the decades to include more and more cases under its purview. In this process, the distinct social nature of the precipitating trauma has been de-emphasized. First, the *DSM-IV* (1994) broadened the notion of what is considered a traumatic event. The *DSM-III* instructed psychiatrists to interpret trauma *objectively* as a recognizable stressor "generally outside the range of usual human experience" that would "evoke significant symptoms of distress in almost everyone." The revisions for *DSM-IV* reoriented the diagnostic focus toward the *subjective* reactions of individuals; trauma became defined not by the inherent qualities of the event but by an individual's response to it. The loss of a loved one (a sad, but normal stressor) is made equivalent with combat (a recognizably extraordinary experience) if the subjective reactions (avoidance, numbing, hyperarousal, etc.) to these events are similar.

Second, *DSM-IV* extended what it meant to "experience" trauma to include witnessing an event or receiving information about it. PTSD

Army Col. Michael J. Roy, left, who oversees exposure therapy at Walter Reed Army Medical Center, conducts a demonstration of a lifelike simulator meant to help treat PTSD. (John J. Kruzel, U.S. Dept. of Defense)

could occur in individuals that did not directly undergo the trauma. As anthropologist Allan Young observes, *DSM-IV* signaled "the repatriation of the traumatic memory . . . back home from the jungles and highlands of Vietnam." Embracing this expansion, some psychiatrists argue that PTSD should be extended to non-life-threatening events (for example, divorce) and that PTSD can develop from indirect witnessing of traumatic events, even on television. These changes have increased the number of potential traumas eligible for a PTSD diagnosis far beyond the bounds of the extreme violence of war.

Diagnostic patterns clearly demonstrate that shift. PTSD now includes more civilians,

women, and children. To win inclusion in *DSM-III*, veteran advocates extended the notion of trauma beyond combat to include victims of other types of physical trauma (like burn victims). Feminist groups long recognized the overlap between PTSD and the symptoms experienced by women suffering from what they referred to as "rape trauma syndrome" and embraced the disorder as a way to recognize the mental distress of rape victims. With *DSM-IV*'s explicit inclusion of sexual assault as a traumatic event, diagnostic practices changed, and PTSD is now twice as common in women as in men. Built on two different models of trauma—combat and rape—the concept has split along gendered lines, with veterans stressing geopolitical violence and feminists, interpersonal violence. Interestingly, even sexual trauma taking place *within* the U.S. military has come to be called "military sexual trauma"—not PTSD—thereby maintaining a gendered distinction.

reassessing ptsd

PTSD has morphed into something broader, more civilian, and increasingly a part of international contexts (as journalist Ethan Watters has documented in his book *Crazy Like Us*). At the same time, the United States has fought its first large-scale wars since the diagnosis was established. With these developments, the "drop the D" movement is reassessing the benefits—and pitfalls—of medicalization. Returning to the initial goals of PTSD's medicalization—to decrease stigma, increase self-understanding, and open access to resources—we see that the evolving diagnosis fails to serve these ends for veterans, and, to a significant extent, the institution of the military as well.

First, medicalization has not necessarily alleviated the long-standing stigmatization of soldiers experiencing mental distress from war. Dozens of military health studies show that stigma remains a significant impediment to receiving PTSD treatment; roughly 60 percent of soldiers report that seeking mental health help would be perceived as weakness. Of the American soldiers in Iraq and Afghanistan who had a "serious mental health disorder," only 40 percent stated that they were interested in receiving help, according to Charles Hoge, doctor and retired Army colonel. A 2008 Rand study concluded that "just 53 percent of service members with PTSD or depression sought help from a provider over the past year, and of those who sought care, roughly half got minimally adequate treatment." Self-stigma, the internalization of prevailing prejudices against mental illness, continues to undermine treatment among soldiers; those who met the criteria for a mental disorder were *more* likely than those who did not to associate the diagnosis with embarrassment and weakness. There is also a growing concern that the public awareness of PTSD has hurt veterans, particularly when seeking employment.

Our interviews with veterans confirm that "toughing it out" remains an essential part of military life. Given the associations between military masculinity and invulnerability, many soldiers suffer from mental and moral anguish, but their suffering is dismissed or disrespected by fellow service members and military superiors. As Nathan, an Iraq and Afghanistan veteran explained, "Usually the guys with PTSD won't admit [to], you know, crying. They don't have an issue. They can handle it fine. So they don't look into things. And it's seen as a weakness." Another veteran admitted his reluctance to take seriously the post-deployment health assessment, worrying that if he provided accurate responses about his mental health, his fellow soldiers might wonder, "Is this guy a pussy or what?"

Second, the changing face of PTSD has diluted its fit for soldiers trying to make sense of their particular experiences in war and their subsequent reactions. If one benefit of the medicalization of PTSD was to provide veterans with an understanding of their war trauma and a basis for shared identity, what happens when the dominant, cultural associations of the diagnosis shift? Of particular importance here is the mismatch between the masculine culture of the

> While mental distress from the trauma of war has been sporadically recognized under different monikers—"shell shock," "combat neuroses," "soldier's heart," "operational fatigue"—PTSD did not exist prior to 1980.

military and the increasing prevalence of the diagnosis among women and civilians. As a result, some veterans advocating the name change claim that soldiers "prefer the old terms such as 'battle fatigue' because *anyone* can get PTSD" and have petitioned the Defense Secretary that "any new name be unique to combat and utilize terms such as 'war' or 'battle.' "

The concern around the expansive definition of PTSD joins a long-held criticism of medicalization within some anti-war veterans' circles: conceiving of war trauma as mental illness is wrong because the behaviors that manifest themselves as PTSD are actually *normal* reactions to abnormal circumstances. PTSD pathologizes individuals instead of pathologizing the *true* toxin, war itself. Some activists therefore advocate jettisoning the diagnosis altogether and focusing their energies on combating the seemingly endless growth in militarism.

But what of the final goal of PTSD's early advocates, that of securing resources? To be sure, the recognition of PTSD has opened access to resources that veterans would not otherwise have. The Iraq and Afghanistan wars are the first major wars since the institutionalization of PTSD, and PTSD has become the most common military service–related mental health diagnosis. Whereas access to resources undoubtedly benefits veterans, concerns over the cost have driven select members of the military and political leaders to advocate "dropping the D." Former Defense Secretary Leon Panetta said that "post-traumatic stress will remain a critical issue for decades to come." (Note the missing "disorder.") On the other side of the political aisle, former President George W. Bush, the person most responsible for today's soldiers' psychological distress, has stated that PTSD is mislabeled

> Mental health in the military—the paradoxical context in which health and routine violence coexist—is hardly straightforward. Dropping the word "disorder" is possibly as thorny as getting the PTSD diagnosis recognized in the first place.

as a disorder and that calling it "post-traumatic stress" would go a long way in erasing its stigma.

While military leaders do not publicly state that the diagnosis strains military resources, the treatment costs are at odds with their overall mission; high rates of PTSD mean more expenditures, fewer boots on the ground, and more bad headlines. And these costs continue to swell; a 2012 study of six years of data from the Veterans Health Administration (VHA) by the Congressional Budget Office found the cost of treating a typical patient with PTSD in the first year of treatment averaged $8,300. From 2004 to 2009, the VHA spent $3.7 billion on the first four years of care for all the veterans tracked by the study. This is to say nothing of the tremendous VA backlog plaguing veterans' care and compensation, which deflates the true costs. The costs are particularly glaring given the mixed efficacy of PTSD treatments, which pale in comparison to the incredible advances in other domains of military medicine.

If "disorder"—a term suggesting chronicity—were dropped, perhaps soldiers might be more willing to seek treatment. "Injury," a term more suggestive of something people can heal from, could change perspectives. Perhaps the VA would then be less strapped with providing indefinite care. And perhaps PTS would better reflect the unique experience of war trauma. . . . So goes the thinking of those who would rename this multifaceted distress.

resistance

Mental health in the military—the paradoxical context in which health and routine violence coexist—is hardly straightforward. Dropping the word "disorder" is possibly as thorny as getting the PTSD diagnosis recognized in the first place. General Chiarelli and *One Mind*'s efforts have rekindled long-standing debates over how to publicly appraise and evaluate "invisible injuries."

Resistance to the movement is vigorous. Matthew Friedman, director of the National Center for PTSD at the Department of Veterans Affairs, has campaigned against a change to "PTS" or "PTSI," stating that "injury" suggests a short-term recovery process, whereas disorder better honors a condition that can last for decades. Dropping "disorder" may also jeopardize disability payments. Some wonder whether a change could be an attempt by the VA and Pentagon to eschew their accountability for long-term care. After all, the traditional diagnostic category has been instrumental in helping veterans secure long-term disability coverage and treatment. Other critics of the change note that dropping one word will not result in any difference, since the cultural associations are already there. "Schizophrenia," for example, does not have the word disorder in it, yet it remains very much stigmatized.

For other critics, dropping "disorder" represents a mere nominal change further obscuring the reality that *war* is what psychologically harms people. Here the limits of medicalization may be seen. Does the transformation of war trauma into a medical diagnosis sufficiently capture the moral valence of the issue of war in the first place? Perhaps attention and effort could be focused less on helping those who cannot cope with the trauma of battle and more on the collective mobilization to avert such trauma from happening? If PTSD were considered a serious, *dangerous* public health threat, wouldn't we want to prevent it in the way we do other public health threats, like cancer, cardiovascular disease, and obesity?

For now, the status quo has been upheld; the recently published *DSM-V* maintains the *DSM-IV*'s PTSD diagnosis. The D remains. The work group charged with reviewing the diagnosis rejected a proposal to include a subtype of PTSD for wartime trauma exclusively. In fact, by adding a dissociative subtype and a subtype for children six years and younger, the revision expanded the diagnosis.

Nevertheless, the history of the PTSD diagnosis reveals the extent to which medicalization can go awry for the lay groups who fought for the establishment of its classification in the first place. Once recognized, PTSD, like other diagnoses, is shaped by an array of interests and transformed into something no longer strictly moored to the original definitions. In the case of PTSD, members of the military brass—worried about stigma, high rates of prevalence, and rising costs—have allied with soldiers and veterans who are concerned with stigma, help-seeking, and identity to demedicalize PTSD and bring it back into the military fold. Given the vagaries of PTSD to this point, the movement might want to heed the experiences of their medicalizing precursors and consider the potential unintended consequences of such a campaign.

RECOMMENDED RESOURCES

Erin P. Finley. 2012. *Fields of Combat: Understanding PTSD among Veterans of Iraq and Afghanistan.* Ithaca: Cornell University Press.

> An ethnographic illustration of PTSD's devastating effects on veterans and their families.

Allan V. Horwitz. 2002. *Creating Mental Illness.* Chicago: University of Chicago Press.

> A thorough study of how most mental illnesses are forms of deviant behavior, normal reactions to stressful circumstances, or cultural constructions.

Ken MacLeish. 2013. *Making War at Fort Hood: Life and Uncertainty in a Military Community.* Princeton: Princeton University Press.

An ethnography of post-9/11 American soldiers and their understandings and experiences of the U.S. military's routine violence.

Wilbur J. Scott. 1990. "PTSD in *DSM-III*: A Case in the Politics of Diagnosis and Disease." *Social Problems* 37(3): 294–310.

An early sociological analysis of the politics involved in securing the diagnosis of PTSD in *DSM-III*.

R. Tyson Smith and Gala True. 2014. "Warring Identities: Identity Conflict and the Mental Distress of American Veterans of the Wars in Iraq and Afghanistan." *Society and Mental Health* 4(2):147–161.

Examines veterans' postwar psychological distress as the result of strains from conflicting understandings of self.

Allan Young. 1997. *The Harmony of Illusions: Inventing Post-Traumatic Stress Disorder.* Princeton: Princeton University Press.

An in-depth history of how PTSD came into being and evolved through *DSM-IV*.

REVIEW QUESTIONS

1. List one example from the article of the connection between language and policy. Why do the words we choose matter in this case?
2. What do the authors mean by medicalization?
3. What do the authors mean when they use the term *self-stigma*?

amanda m. gengler

getting the most out of the U.S. health care system

44

winter 2016

kids with life-threatening illnesses need cutting-edge technology and medical expertise, but families face uneven access and paths to such care.

When their six-month-old son, Jacob, was diagnosed with Tay-Sachs—a fatal degenerative neurological disease—Todd and Savannah Marin, White, first-time parents in their early 30s, were devastated. The only option the diagnosing physician offered them was palliative hospice care. But the Marins were not willing to accept this outcome. They began scouring FDA databases for new clinical trials and contacted the founder of a Tay-Sachs research foundation. They flew Jacob across the country for assessment by national Tay-Sachs experts, and ultimately identified an experimental treatment option: an umbilical cord blood-derived stem cell transplant at Kelly-Reed (a pseudonym), a top-10-ranked university research hospital. Savannah, a registered nurse, successfully lobbied her insurance company to cover the million-dollar treatment. Todd, a contractor, quit his job, and Savannah requested a medical leave of absence. They put their house up for sale, placed their belongings in storage, and moved from one coast to the other, hoping to save their son.

In Buenos Aires, Argentina, 10-year-old Ignacio Maldonado—Iggy for short—was also diagnosed with a fatal degenerative neurological disease: Metachromatic Leukodystrophy (MLD). Because international patients must pay the full amount of anticipated treatment costs at Kelly-Reed upfront, Iggy's parents—Eva Campos, a public school principal, and Miguel Maldonado, who works in corporate sales—launched a national fund-raising campaign to raise the money to cover Iggy's bone marrow transplant at Kelly-Reed. Though bone marrow transplants are available in Argentina, local doctors had never transplanted a child with MLD. Doctors Eva contacted through a clinical trial in Italy referred her to Dr. Vogel, the head of the pediatric transplant unit at Kelly-Reed. Eva sent videos of Iggy's symptoms to Dr. Vogel, who responded personally. When I asked Eva if the decision to travel so far for such a long and risky treatment had been difficult, she told me plainly; "No. *Me hubiera ido a la luna*." To save Iggy, "I would have gone to the moon."

The Marins and Campos-Maldonados are two of the 18 case-study families I interviewed and observed at Kelly-Reed. About half of the families were also there for stem cell transplants. Others came for enzyme replacement therapy, cancer immunotherapy, standard cancer treatments or organ transplants, and, in one case, a curative treatment for an immunodeficiency disorder available at no other hospital in the world.

Some of these families, like the Marins and the Campos-Maldonados, had an array of

A physical therapist provides cognitive stimulation to Jacob Marin at 18 months. (© Amanda Gengler)

resources to leverage on behalf of their children to obtain the best possible medical care. Without their social networks, medical vocabularies, financial reserves, and savvy research skills, these families would likely not have obtained the specialized care and treatment they got for their critically ill children.

Janet Shim calls this bundle of knowledge and skills that can help people effectively interact with health care providers and navigate the health care system "cultural health capital." The ability to communicate efficiently with doctors or accurately read a prescription label—much less medical journals or clinical trial protocols—can net people key health advantages.

This is especially important within the unequal landscape of health care. A study at the University of Alabama–Birmingham found that major teaching hospitals offered higher quality care and a survival benefit over minor teaching and nonteaching hospitals, even for elderly heart attack patients. Sociologists Karen Lutfey and Jeremy Freese found similar inequalities between two diabetes clinics. More complex—and effective—treatment regimens were prescribed by the clinic serving primarily middle-class patients, while those treated by the clinic serving primarily poor and working-class patients received less patient education, were prescribed simpler (less beneficial) regimens, and were less

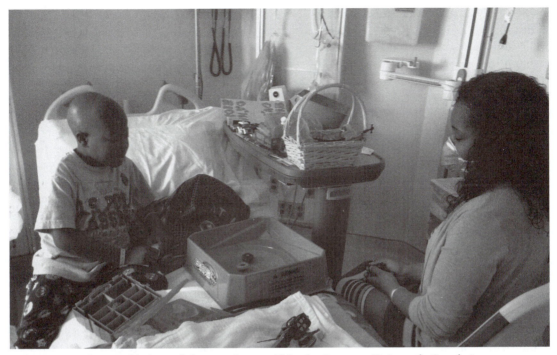

Lakira Harris plays Beyblades with her son, 8-year-old Jayden Lacoste. (© Amanda Gengler)

likely to see the same doctor from one visit to the next.

Among the families I met at Kelly-Reed, cultural health capital was often a critical factor that allowed them to strategically negotiate the stratified U.S. health care system to access better care. Families with less cultural health capital might eventually be referred to Kelly-Reed, but often after being shuffled around lower levels of the health care system.

Connie and Nicholas Henderson, a poor White couple in their early 40s, brought their son to the emergency room of the rural county hospital in their hometown on multiple occasions. They were repeatedly sent home with instructions to give 4-year-old Elijah high doses of over-the-counter Tylenol and Miralax for his extreme abdominal pain. The Hendersons saw two different pediatricians at their family practice clinic before one doctor suggested possible appendicitis and ordered a CT scan. The scan revealed a massive tumor on Elijah's liver. The Hendersons were then sent to a nearby regional hospital for surgery and standard treatment involving radiation and chemotherapy, but, Nicholas reported, the initial dose of radiation "burned him up real bad." The dose was subsequently cut in half, but had no effect on the tumor. Unlike another family I met, which had been advised by a neurosurgeon they had

> Without their social networks, medical vocabularies, financial reserves, and savvy research skills, these families would likely not have obtained the specialized care and treatment they got for their critically ill children.

seen previously to take their son to a highly regarded surgeon at a more distant hospital who specialized in their son's particular type of pediatric brain tumor, the Hendersons simply went to the nearest-equipped hospital and were treated by the doctors they were assigned. Only after it became clear a liver transplant was needed were they directed to Kelly-Reed.

Without the same skills to confidently assess treatments and providers, Nicholas still worried about the quality of his son's care. "You're kind of wondering," he told me. "'Well, did I make the right decision? Or *could I have done something different?*'"

care-captaining

Even after accessing care at Kelly-Reed, families with lots of cultural health capital remained deeply involved in the provision of their child's medical care. They poured over detailed information on daily lab reports, negotiated with doctors, and requested treatment interventions and medication changes. Savannah Marin, for instance, lobbied doctors to decrease her son's steroid dose to minimize his exposure to its damaging effects. Before Jacob's treatment even began, she had requested therapies (physical therapy, occupational therapy, and even swim therapy) that "nobody at that point was recommending." She hypothesized, "if he has a neurological disease, that's going to affect the neural connections. Let's make more neural connections . . . so then maybe he would have more places that the [metabolic] waste would have to build up . . . so he has even *further* to have to deteriorate."

Nora Bialy, a White, middle-class mother of four in her early 40s, also requested additional medical interventions after her 16-year-old son,

Benjamin, accessed elite care. When radiation for a brain tumor caused burning on the back of Ben's esophagus (making swallowing painful), Nora asked doctors to place a gastric feeding tube to allow food to be delivered directly to her son's stomach. She believed that this would allow Benjamin to maintain his strength and nutritional status, and reported that, once the doctors placed the tube, "he did great on it."

Parents like the Marins and Bialys often engaged in nearly constant surveillance of their childrens' medical care. They asked questions, made suggestions, and offered providers detailed information about their child's responses to prior treatments beyond what might be recorded in their charts. For instance, Todd Marin told me that he had prevented a respiratory therapist from administering a breathing treatment that Jacob had responded poorly to in the past. "If I hadn't been there," he recalled, "it would have just been done. And then we could have had more of a negative thing." The Marins and other very medically involved parents also caught and prevented medication errors. When mistakes were made, parents with lots of cultural health capital were able to intervene or hold providers accountable for mistakes and keep them from happening again. These small advantages could accrue to keep a sick child a bit more comfortable, a bit stronger, and a bit less likely to experience additional pain and suffering. This gave parents some sense of control over an otherwise terrifying experience.

> Small advantages can accrue to keep a sick child a bit more comfortable, a bit stronger, and a bit less likely to experience additional pain and suffering.

care-entrusting

Families with less cultural health capital did not get as deeply involved in medical decision-making. These parents instead usually deferred to their child's doctors, who they hoped would make the best medical decisions for their children. Mary Shaw, a White, retired, working-class custodial grandmother in her late 50s, followed a series of in-state referrals to Kelly-Reed for treatment for her 7-year-old grandson's rare genetic metabolic disorder. When I asked how she made decisions about treatments and medications, Mary told me, "I always leave it [up to them]. I say, 'What you think [we should do] is the way I want to go.'" Pauline Donnoly, another White, retired, working-class custodial grandmother, pointed directly to her lack of knowledge about the medical system to explain why she had followed local doctors' referrals to Kelly-Reed rather than seeking out treatment options and hospitals herself, telling me: "If I had had time to have sought out different hospitals, I still wouldn't have known what I was looking for, or what would have been right."

Lakira Harris, a Black, working-class, single mother of four in her early 30s, traveled hundreds of miles to bring her 8-year-old son, Jayden Lacoste, to Kelly-Reed for a stem cell transplant. But she did so not as a result of her own independent research, but because local doctors struggled to keep Jayden's sickle-cell disease under control and eventually sent them to Kelly-Reed. This endeavor was far more logistically challenging for Lakira than for the Marins, who could rely on salary and a leave of absence, or the Campos-Maldonados, who, with a similar leave and two participating parents, could more easily care for Iggy's older siblings back in Argentina (Eva stayed in the United States with Ignacio full-time, while Miguel and the other children visited regularly). Lakira, in contrast, had already had to quit her job as a security guard because of Jayden's frequent hospitalizations, and now had to recruit relatives to care for her three younger children (separated from one another under this arrangement) whom she did not see during the seven months she and Jayden were away.

Though Lakira did not regularly intervene in decision making about Jayden's medical care (beyond providing consent as needed), her devotion to her son was apparent. A warm and affectionate mother, she played games with Jayden during long days in the hospital, made special trips to the cafeteria for his favorite curly fries, and wrote notes on the whiteboard in his room to keep track of the "Beads of Courage" Jayden earned for daily accomplishments like walking laps around the unit or enduring a difficult procedure. Lakira saved all the paperwork she was given about his medications and treatments, which she kept neatly organized in a plastic file tub. But she struggled to understand the medical complexities involved in his treatment protocol and, though she occasionally tried to get clarification from doctors, communication difficulties meant she sometimes found their answers unclear and remained uncertain after these interactions. When Jayden's body began rejecting his donor cells and he was

The whiteboard in Jayden Lacoste's hospital room, on which his mother keeps track of the "Beads of Courage" he earns each day. (© Amanda Gengler)

getting the most out of the U.S. health care system   315

placed in the pediatric intensive care unit (PICU), Lakira found it too painful to watch him suffer. She returned to the nearby Ronald McDonald House and spent most of her time there, making short, once or twice daily visits to see her son and speak a few words of love and encouragement to him. Though her less consistent presence may have made her seem disinterested to hospital staff and other parents, she told me it was just too hard for her to "stay positive" for Jayden if she watched him sedated and suffering helplessly for long. She, too, felt helpless.

staying "positive"

Parents' efforts to "stay positive" or otherwise cope with the emotional turmoil of a child's life-threatening illness played a big role in how involved they became in directly influencing their child's care. For parents like Lakira Harris, less cultural health capital made it nearly impossible to become deeply involved in the medical arena. Without the knowledge base and medical vocabulary that might encourage doctors to take their input seriously, their occasional attempts to intervene were not likely to succeed. But even parents with loads of cultural health capital sometimes felt emotionally compelled to pull back. Nora Bialy told me that she had decided not to look at Benjamin's most recent MRI because "I don't need to make myself crazy with seeing a spot that I know has something, but it's going away. That's just, 'punch me.'"

Pauline told me, "If I had had time to have sought out different hospitals, I still wouldn't have known what I was looking for, or what would have been right."

Parents who could feel confident deciding when to take control of their child's care and when to relinquish that control to medical experts had more coping strategies available to them than parents who could only "hope" that doctors were making the best possible decisions for their children. After their five-month-old son, Noah, died following complications from an unsuccessful stem cell transplant, Edward Rivera and Juliana Cruz, middle-class Puerto Rican parents in their early 30s who had actively participated in Noah's care and negotiated with his physicians through his final days, told me their greatest comfort was that they had "tried everything that was in our hands." That knowledge, at least, provided some solace.

Other parents could not feel as certain that they couldn't or shouldn't be doing something more. Nicholas Henderson worried that he didn't know if Kelly-Reed was the best hospital for his son's organ transplant. He recalled seeing commercials for St. Jude's, and wondered aloud whether he should have taken Elijah there. But Nicholas's knowledge about hospitals came from television rather than medical research, hospital rankings, or social network expertise. This sense of doubt and uncertainty could make an already nerve-wracking crisis in family life even more harrowing. Families who understood university and hospital rankings could verify their selection of doctors and physicians with medical experts in their own trusted social network. Those who were reading the latest medical journal articles about their child's illness—sometimes those written by their child's own medical team—could use these medical hierarchies and status symbols to feel good about their child's care and hopeful about their prognosis.

Those poor and working-class parents who stayed on the sidelines of their child's medical care could appear less engaged to health care providers, but believed they were doing the best they could for their children by letting the medical experts lead the way and directing their own efforts toward the nurturing and loving care they could bestow. These parents often

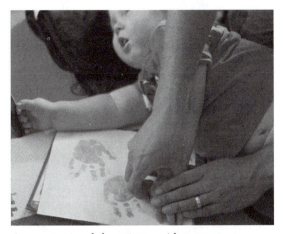

An occupational therapist provides sensory stimulation to 2.5-year-old Jacob Marin. (© Amanda Gengler)

assured me it was best for them not to get medically involved because, as the mother of another teen brain-tumor patient explained while we baked cupcakes at the Ronald McDonald House, "the doctors and nurses know better than I do anyway."

On the flip side, parents with solid working medical knowledge who intervened regularly to direct their child's care could potentially risk intervening too much. The Marins once spent enough time getting multiple opinions about whether Jacob should be intubated and placed on ventilation (life support) that they nearly prevented doctors from providing what may have been critical treatment soon enough. Yet even though parental intervention could at times become a challenge, the physicians I interviewed on the transplant unit at Kelly-Reed told me that they preferred parents who could be their "partner" in the treatment process. One senior physician lamented that, "some parents micromanage things and negotiate medication doses to an absurd point where they don't know what they're doing," but admitted that parents often suggested treatment options, caught medication

errors, or identified side effects providers sometimes missed. "Sometimes the parent's right . . . sometimes we're right . . . sometimes nobody's right," she told me. In this context of uncertainty, parents tried to find ways to get the best possible care for their children while managing the often overwhelming angst they felt about the treatment process and their children's futures.

It may come as little surprise that well-to-do families accessed high-quality medical care more swiftly than poor and working-class families, but the families I met in my research help us begin to see the nuts and bolts of how this happens—what people *do* that leads to differences in illness experiences. Getting the best possible medical care wasn't just about insurance coverage, an ability to pay out-of-pocket, or differences between institutions in quality of care—though these issues are vital. But even after basic economic hurdles had been cleared, a tightly interwoven web of cultural health capital, differing care strategies, and efforts to meet powerful emotional needs combined to produce advantages and disadvantages during an already grueling journey for any parent or child.

leveling the playing field

Many of the inequalities I found between the experiences of the families in this study can be traced not only to inequalities in health care provision, but to core structures of inequality that, as medical sociologist Jo Phelan and her colleagues have suggested, are "fundamental causes" of health disparities. Some people have many more resources to protect and defend their own and their families' health than others. Inequalities in education, wealth, and social networks are particularly intractable problems that require large-scale social change.

No matter how many resources the families I came to know at Kelly-Reed had, the hoops they had to jump through to navigate the mazes of the U.S. health care system and the time, energy, and perseverance required to access needed care took a significant toll. Those with fewer resources to seek out clinical trials, evaluate providers, and negotiate for the best possible care might benefit from assistance in doing so. Disease-specific advocacy organizations might usefully reach out to newly diagnosed families to help them strategically seek options beyond their local hospitals and physicians and provide direct assistance in negotiating the bureaucratic hurdles of seeking new technologies farther away from home. Separating access to cutting-edge care from a family's ability to pay and universal paid family leave to care for seriously ill children would also go a long way toward smoothing the rocky road all of these families faced and reducing the inequities between them. Contentious as such policies may be, it's hard to justify why they should be any more elusive than the medical miracles these families and their physicians are fighting for.

RECOMMENDED RESOURCES

Jeroan Allison, Catarina Kiefe, Norman Weissman, Sharina Person, Matthew Rousculp, John Canto, Sejong Bae, O. Dale Williams, Robert Farmer, and Robert Centor. 2000. "Relationship of Hospital Teaching Status With Quality of Care and Mortality for Medicare Patients With Acute MI." *Journal of the American Medical Association* 284 (10): 1256–62.

> A large-scale study of quality of care and survival outcomes for heart attack patients treated across different types of hospital systems.

Amanda M. Gengler. 2014. "'I Want You to Save My Kid!' Illness Management Strategies, Access, and Inequality at an Elite University Research Hospital." *Journal of Health and Social Behavior* 55(3): 342–59.

A deeper examination of the care-captaining and care-entrusting strategies discussed here, and the advantages they confer throughout the care-seeking and treatment process.

Karen Lutfey and Jeremy Freese. 2004. "Toward Some Fundamentals of Fundamental Causality: Socioeconomic Status and Health in the Routine Clinic Visit for Diabetes." *American Journal of Sociology* 110(5): 1326–72.

> Describes how diabetes treatments differed across clinics serving primarily middle-class or primarily poor and working-class patients. The authors also consider how patient's daily lives made adherence to complex treatment regimens more or less practical.

Jo C. Phelan, Bruce G. Link, and Parisa Tehranifa. 2010. "Social Conditions as Fundamental Causes of Health Inequalities." *Journal of Health and Social Behavior* 51(S): S28–S40.

> An overview of the connections between our health and our position in structures of inequality.

Janet K. Shim 2010. "Cultural Health Capital: A Theoretical Approach to Understanding Health Care Interactions and the Dynamics of Unequal Treatment." *Journal of Health and Social Behavior* 51(1): 1–15.

> Proposes that one's medical vocabulary, interactional skills, self-presentation, attitudes about health, and other subtle and not-so-subtle skills and resources influence relationships with health care providers.

REVIEW QUESTIONS

1. What is "cultural health capital"?
2. How do differences in cultural health capital contribute to inequality in the type and quality of heath care provided to poor and working-class families as compared to well-to-do families? What measures might help address disparities in cultural health capital?

julie e. artis

breastfeed at your own risk

45

fall 2009

the author explores how science, ad campaigns, and legislation have influenced breastfeeding trends around the world. while some mothers view breastfeeding as a "cultural imperative," others do not believe it is so emphatically essential or necessary.

For nearly two years, the U.S. Department of Health and Human Services spent $2 million on an ad campaign to promote breastfeeding by educating mothers about the risks of not doing so. Those risks were often communicated in provocative ways. One television ad, for example, showed a pregnant African-American woman riding a mechanical bull, and then the message appears on the screen, "You wouldn't take risks before your baby is born. Why start after?"

This campaign was the culmination of three decades of increasing consensus among medical and public health professionals that, as the saying goes, "breast is best"— that there is no better nutrition for the first year of an infant's life than breast milk. The endorsement of the medical establishment is echoed in advice books and parenting magazines that overwhelmingly recommend breastfeeding over formula. Communities have passed laws to support breastfeeding mothers in the workplace and to ensure public breastfeeding isn't legally categorized as indecency.

And rates of breastfeeding in the United States have increased dramatically—nearly 75 percent of mothers now breastfeed newborns, up from 24 percent in 1971. Rates of breastfeeding are even higher among middle-class, educated mothers. For these mothers, breastfeeding has become less of a choice and more of an imperative—a way to protect their infant's health and boost their IQ. Breastfeeding is a way to achieve so-called good mothering, the idealized notion of mothers as selfless and child-centered.

Taking a sociological look at the cultural imperative to breastfeed illustrates how mothering is shaped by discussions among scientists, doctors, and other experts, as well as policy recommendations that grow out of scientific findings. It also reveals that breastfeeding and infant feeding practices differ by culture, race, class, and ethnicity, and that the "breast is best" conventional wisdom doesn't take these differences into account. Thus, this campaign leaves many mothers feeling inadequate—and perhaps unnecessarily so because the scientific evidence about the benefits of breastfeeding are less clear cut than mothers have been led to believe.

> Mothering is shaped by discussions among scientists, doctors, and other experts, as well as policy recommendations that grow out of scientific findings.

historical trends in breastfeeding

Cultural ideas about motherhood and family in the United States have changed significantly over time, thanks in part to science and technology.

Religious authorities, midwives, and physicians encouraged mothers in the seventeenth and eighteenth centuries to breastfeed their infants. The practice through the mid-1800s, in a primarily farm-based society, was to nurse infants through their "second summer" to avoid unrefrigerated and possibly spoiled food and milk.

Wet nursing—breastfeeding a child who is not a woman's own—became necessary when a mother was severely ill or died during childbirth. Breast milk was widely thought superior to "hand-feeding"—providing milk, tea, or "pap" (a mixture of flour, sugar, water, and milk)—in promoting infant health, but even so, according to historian Janet Golden in her study *A Social History of Wet Nursing*, families worried about having a wet nurse of "questionable" moral fitness, and these fears were exacerbated by race and class divisions. In the North, wet nurses were typically poor immigrant mothers; in the South, they tended to be African Americans, and it was common for female slaves to be wet nurses in the antebellum South. However, by the turn of the twentieth century, the use of wet nurses had declined, in part because pasteurization made bottle-feeding a safe alternative to breast milk. This was also the era in which children came to be seen as priceless, in need of protection, and worth extraordinary investment, sociologist Viviana Zelizer explained in *Pricing the Priceless Child*.

Technological advancements led to the development of mass-marketed infant formula in the 1950s. Doctors then began to recommend formula, saying a scientifically developed substance was at least equivalent to, and possibly better than, breast milk. By the early 1970s, breastfeeding rates in hospitals were at a low of approximately 24 percent, with only 5 percent of mothers nursing for several months following birth.

It was in this era that some feminist women's health groups and Christian women's groups such as La Leche League began challenging the medical model by promoting "natural" childbirth and breastfeeding. These groups promoted the benefits of breastfeeding and also raised public awareness about the activities of formula companies.

For example, some feminist health groups helped organize a boycott of Nestle in the late 1970s for promoting formula in developing countries. These groups claimed that Nestle's formula marketing tactics in Africa had led to 1 million infant deaths (from mixing powered formula with contaminated water, or feeding infants diluted formula because of the expense). The success of these small groups in challenging the corporate marketing of formula led to increasing consensus that breastfeeding was better than bottle-feeding. Soon, the medical establishment was embracing breastfeeding, based on scientific studies that confirmed the benefits La Leche League and other feminist health groups had been talking about for years. In 1978 the American Academy of Pediatricians (AAP) recommended breastfeeding over formula, marking the beginning of the shift in mainstream medical advice to mothers. Since then, scientific evidence and the medical establishment have continued to reaffirm the benefits of breast milk.

Trends over the last 40 years gathered from a survey of mothers show how experts' recommendations and public discussions about breastfeeding have influenced breastfeeding rates. Figure 1 shows the sharp increase in breastfeeding in the 1970s. In the 1980s, there is a slight decrease and plateau in breastfeeding initiation rates, and then, in the 1990s, the rate steadily rises to nearly 70 percent. The rates of

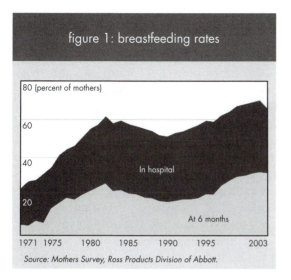

figure 1: breastfeeding rates

80 (percent of mothers)

60

40

In hospital

20

At 6 months

1971 1975   1980   1985   1990   1995   2003

Source: Mothers Survey, Ross Products Division of Abbott.

breastfeeding until six months of age follow a very similar pattern, although overall the rates are quite lower than breastfeeding initiation; currently, only about one-third of mothers report breastfeeding at six months. This recent rise in breastfeeding rates can be explained, at least in part, by the ideology of intensive mothering.

breastfeeding as intensive mothering

Child-rearing advice books, pediatricians, parenting magazines, and even formula companies themselves now universally recommend breast milk over formula. The consensus that "breast is best" is embedded in cultural ideals of motherhood.

In her book *The Cultural Contradictions of Motherhood,* sociologist Sharon Hays identifies an ideology of intensive mothering and describes how it's at work in the United States: Mothers—not fathers—serve as the primary caregivers of children; mothering practices are time-intensive, expensive, supported by expert advice, child-centered, and emotionally absorbing; and children are viewed as priceless, and the work that must be done to raise them can't

be compared to paid work because it's infinitely more important.

The ideology of intensive mothering helps explain why we hear so much playground chatter and read so many magazine articles about getting children into the "best" school, the idea that natural childbirth is better than one assisted by medication or other medical interventions, and the recent discussion of "opt-out" mothers who leave high-powered jobs to stay home with their children. Hays contends the strength of the intensive mothering ideology is the result of an "ambivalence about a society based solely on the competitive pursuit of self-interest."

This may be one reason, for example, journalist Judith Warner, in her book *Perfect Madness: Motherhood in the Age of Anxiety,* felt such a difference when she was mothering in France compared to when she returned with her children to the United States. In France the state offers practical support to mothers, including subsidized childcare, universal health care, and excellent public education beginning at age 3. Furthermore, Warner explained that, as a new mother there, she found herself in the middle of an extensive and sympathetic support network that attended to her needs as a mother as much as they attended to the needs of her child. "It was a bad thing [for mothers] to go it alone," she wrote. In contrast, upon her return to the United States Warner felt isolated and anxious. She linked this directly to what she called the "American culture of rugged individualism." Mothers in the United States were under extraordinary pressure to be a "good mother"—otherwise, who else would protect their child from an individualistic, self-interested society?

The cultural imperative to breastfeed is part of the ideology of intensive mothering—it requires the mother be the central caregiver, because only she produces milk; breastfeeding is in line with expert advice and takes a great deal of time and commitment; and finally, the act of breastfeeding is a way to demonstrate that the child is priceless, and that whatever the cost, be it a loss of productivity at work or staying at home, children come first.

Since Hays links the intensive motherhood ideology to American individualistic sensibilities, it would seem to suggest that breastfeeding rates in the United States would be higher than other countries. To return to the example of France, only 50 percent of French mothers breastfeed their newborns, compared to 75 percent of American mothers. However, upon closer examination of statistics compiled by Le Leche League International, U.S. breastfeeding rates lag far behind many other countries, including European countries other than France (Germany, Italy, Spain, and the Scandinavian countries all have breastfeeding initiation rates around 90 percent). Most countries in Asia, Africa, and South America report breastfeeding initiation rates higher than the United States, as do New Zealand and Australia.

Clearly the cultural imperative to breastfeed in the United States has met some resistance. This resistance may be reflected in public debates about breastfeeding, which quickly dissolve into mudslinging, judgmental arguments that pit mothers against mothers. Not "the mommy wars" in the traditional sense—working moms versus stay-at-home moms—but instead bottle-feeding versus breastfeeding moms.

Breastfeeding mothers, and a subset of those mothers who are deeply committed to breastfeeding promotion (sometimes referred to as "lactivists"), point to a continuing undercurrent of resistance to breastfeeding. Despite the fact that scientists and doctors recommend breastfeeding, and that these recommendations have been disseminated through a public-health ad campaign and parenting magazines, breastfeeding remains controversial. While society wants mothers to breastfeed to protect and promote infant health, it wants them to do so behind closed doors. Indeed mothers are often asked to cover themselves while nursing in restaurants.

For example, in 2007 a nursing mother was asked by an Applebee's employee to cover herself while nursing or leave the restaurant. After repeated calls by enraged nursing mothers to the corporate headquarters, executives there insisted it was reasonable to ask the nursing mother to leave, despite a state law that extended mothers the right to nurse in public spaces. This incident resulted in "nurse-ins" at Applebee's locations all over the United States in protest. The social networking site Facebook found itself in a similar firestorm of controversy at the beginning of 2009 when it removed photos of breastfeeding mothers because they violated the site's decency standards. The resistance to nursing-in-public arises from the link between breasts and sexuality, including the idea that breasts are indecent.

Note that these public debates about breastfeeding and mothering in the United States emerge primarily from discussions by and about middle-class mothers. The ideal of intensive mothering is much easier for these women to achieve. Even so, studies have explored the extensive labor middle-class mothers must engage in just to meet current breastfeeding recommendations.

Sociologist Orit Avishai demonstrates through interviews of White, middle-class mothers that they treat breastfeeding not as a natural, pleasurable, connective act with their infant but instead as a disembodied project to be researched and managed. They take classes about breastfeeding, have home visits from lactation consultants postpartum, and view their bodies as feeding machines. When returning to work, they set up elaborate systems to pump breast milk and store it. These middle-class women were accustomed to setting goals and achieving them—so when they decided to breastfeed for the one year the

AAP recommends, they set out to do just that despite the physical and mental drawbacks. Although it's easier for middle-class mothers to meet the recommended breastfeeding standards than it is for less privileged mothers, they're at the same time controlled by a culture that equates good mothering with breastfeeding.

variations in class and culture

In *At the Breast*, sociologist Linda Blum examined how mothers of different classes aspired to or rejected the intensive mothering ideology and mainstream cultural imperative to breastfeed. Through interviews with White middle-class mothers who were members of La Leche League, as well as with a sample of both White and Black working-class mothers, Blum's study was the first (and is also the most extensive) to expose how the meaning of breastfeeding varies by class and race.

Her interviews with the La Leche mothers revealed the organization's emphasis on an intimate, relational bond between mother and child created through breastfeeding. They rejected medical, scheduled, and mechanized infant feeding and emphasized how important it is for mothers to read their babies' cues and be near them all the time. As such, a mother's care is seen as irreplaceable. One mother told Blum, "Only a mother can give what a child needs, nobody else can, not even a father. A father can give almost as close, but only a mother can give what they really need." Some of these mothers were also very critical of working mothers. "I'm pretty negative to people who just want to dump their kids off and go to work eight hours a day," one said. Ultimately, Blum contends La Leche League is a self-help group largely created by and for White, middle-class women.

In contrast, interviews with White working-class mothers revealed they understood the health benefits of breastfeeding and embraced the ideal of intensive mothering, but that they often didn't breastfeed because of constraints with jobs, lack of social support, inadequate nutrition, and limited access to medical advice. Working-class mothers were less likely to have jobs that allowed time and privacy to pump breast milk and were less likely to have access to (paid or unpaid) maternity leave. Some felt it was embarrassing or restrictive. Yet, they still aspired to the middle-class ideal of intensive mothering, so they were left feeling guilty and inadequate. Many reported feeling like their bodies had failed them. One mother, for example, said, "At first [breastfeeding] was great. I can't explain the feeling, but at first it was really great. [But then,] I felt . . . useless. If I couldn't nurse my baby, I was a flop as a mother."

Ethnic and racial differences were even more unique and revealing. Black working-class mothers in Blum's study were similar to White working-class mothers in understanding the health benefits of breast milk. However, their discussions about not breastfeeding were, for the most part, remarkably free of guilt. In short, Black mothers rejected the dominant cultural ideal of intensive mothering, and had a more broadly construed definition of what it meant to be a good mother. Many African-American women, for example, talked about the importance of involving older children and extended family in caring for the child, and insisted one way this could be accomplished was through bottle-feeding. Some Black mothers reacted negatively to breastfeeding because they believed it reinforced long-standing racist stereotypes about the Black female body as threatening or even animalistic. By rejecting medical advice about breastfeeding, Black mothers asserted some control over their own bodies. "The doctors said that breast milk was the best, but I told them I didn't want to. They tried to talk me into it, but they couldn't," one interviewee told Blum.

These cultural differences in the meaning of breastfeeding to White and African-American mothers are reflected in breastfeeding initiation statistics. White, Asian, and Hispanic mothers have roughly similar rates of breastfeeding initiation, while African-American and American-Indian mothers have lower rates (see figure 2).

The importance of cultural differences and how they play out in breastfeeding practices has also been explored in studies of immigration. A study by public policy professor Christina Gibson-Davis and Jeanne Brooks-Gunn, codirector of the Columbia University Institute on Child and Family Policy, found that breastfeeding rates among Hispanics were related to the mother's country of birth. If the mother was born outside the United States and immigrated, she was more likely to breastfeed. Furthermore, for each additional year the mother had lived in the United States, her odds of breastfeeding decreased by 4 percent. These patterns suggest that the more acculturated the mother is in U.S. society, the less likely she is to breastfeed.

However, another study examining Vietnamese immigrant mothers in Quebec contradicts that model. Medical anthropologist Danielle Groleau and colleagues interviewed 19 Vietnamese mothers who immigrated to Quebec. They argue that geography and culture combine to create a context in which mothers decide not to breastfeed. In the Vietnamese traditional understanding of postpartum medicine and breastfeeding, women are said to suffer from excessive cold, which leads to fatigue, and the production of breast milk that isn't fresh. In Vietnam, new mothers are cared for by extended family for several months postpartum in order to balance their health and allow them to produce "fresh" breast milk. However, Vietnamese immigrants in Quebec had low rates of breastfeeding primarily because the lack of social support and caregiving that would have been offered in Vietnam wasn't available in Canada. They saw bottle-feeding as optimal for their babies because their breast milk wasn't fresh. These mothers weren't adopting the dominant Canadian cultural model and had retained their own cultural ideals about breastfeeding.

problematic science

The understanding that "breast is best" is based on scientific studies linking breastfeeding to a variety of health benefits. The breastfeeding recommendations issued by AAP, the World Health Organization, and other public health organizations state that breastfeeding increases IQ and lowers the likelihood of ear infections, diabetes, respiratory and gastrointestinal illnesses, and obesity. These benefits are transmitted to the public as unambiguous scientific findings. But upon closer examination, the science behind these claims is problematic.

Political scientist Joan Wolf, in the *Journal of Health Politics, Policy, and Law,* argues that the benefits of breastfeeding have been vastly

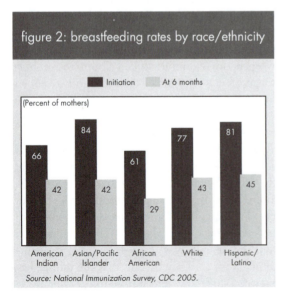

figure 2: breastfeeding rates by race/ethnicity

■ Initiation   ▢ At 6 months

(Percent of mothers)

American Indian: 66, 42
Asian/Pacific Islander: 84, 42
African American: 61, 29
White: 77, 43
Hispanic/Latino: 81, 45

Source: National Immunization Survey, CDC 2005.

overstated. Perhaps the largest problem is that it's impossible to conduct a controlled experiment—by asking some mothers to breastfeed and others to formula-feed—so all studies are observational. In other words, researchers have to tease out the characteristics of those who decide to breastfeed from the benefits of breast milk itself. Mothers who choose to breastfeed may also promote a host of other health-protective and IQ-promoting behaviors in their children that go unmeasured in observational studies. The problem becomes even more pronounced when trying to examine the long-term health benefits of breastfeeding because there are even more potential unmeasured factors between infancy and adolescence that contribute to overall health.

Some researchers have attempted to control for potential unmeasured factors by studying the health of siblings who were fed differently as infants. Although these studies can't discern why the mother breastfed one child but not the other, they do control for parenting factors that go unmeasured in other studies. For example, a recent sibling study by economists Eirik Evenhouse and Siobhan Reilly, based on data from the National Longitudinal Study of Adolescent Health, suggests correlations between breastfeeding and a variety of health benefits, including diabetes, asthma, allergies, and obesity, disappear when studying siblings within families. Only one outcome remains significant—that the breastfed sibling had a slightly higher IQ score (siblings who were ever breastfed scored 1.68 percentile points higher than siblings who were never breastfed).

Most of these studies can be critiqued for exaggerating the importance of small and weak associations, however, although these correlations are weak, they are consistently

Trends over the last 40 years show how experts' recommendations and public discussions about breastfeeding have influenced breastfeeding rates.

found. Furthermore, despite weak correlations, biomedical researchers have in some cases been able to identify the biological mechanisms that offer infants health protection. For example, one very consistent finding seems to be that breast milk lowers the incidence, length, and severity of gastrointestinal illness because gut-protective antibodies, including IgA and lactoferrin, are passed from mother to child through breast milk.

To be sure, not all biomedical research on breast milk identifies beneficial biological mechanisms. Medical researchers have found breast milk to contain HIV, alcohol, drugs, and environmental toxins. How these findings are used by public health officials varies. To take the case of HIV, in parts of the world with high rates of infection, public health officials debate whether to recommend breastfeeding or not. Even if the mother is HIV positive, some argue the infant may gain other protective health benefits from breast milk, especially in resource-poor countries plagued by inadequate water supply, limited refrigeration, and poor sanitary conditions. In the United States, however, mothers are now routinely advised to bottle-feed if they have HIV. Mothers in the United States are also advised to stop nursing if, for medical reasons, they have to take medication that passes through breastmilk and may be harmful to the baby. Nevertheless, the overwhelming public health message continues to be "breast is best."

breastfeeding for public health

The "Babies Were Born to Be Breastfed" public-health ad campaign was designed to educate the public about the benefits of breastfeeding and the risks of not doing so. The campaign hoped to achieve goals established by the Department of Health and Human Services "Blueprint for Action on Breastfeeding"—75 percent of mothers initiating breastfeeding and 50 percent breastfeeding their babies until five months by 2010.

But the campaign, along with doctors' advice and parenting publications, treat the decision to breastfeed as an individual choice without attending to the social and cultural situations in which this choice is made. The decision to breastfeed is shaped by a variety of social and cultural factors, including doctor–patient interaction, social support networks, labor force participation, childcare arrangements, race and ethnicity, class, income, and education. Treating breastfeeding and other parenting practices as individual, decontextualized choices holds mothers solely responsible for their children's health.

In an analysis of discussions about mothering, bioethics professor Rebecca Kukla argues that we hold mothers accountable for all kinds of childhood health problems, including obesity, malnutrition, birth defects, and behavioral disorders. The fact that many of these health problems are disproportionately overrepresented among the lower class further demonizes poor, working-class mothers. Furthermore, by focusing on mothers' individual responsibility for child health and well-being, we aren't attending to other, more egregious societal issues that negatively affect children, such as pollution or lack of adequate health care.

Scientific research on infant health is incredibly important. However, as these findings are reported to the public, shaped into recommendations, and developed into public policy, it's important to view them with a critical eye. We need to consider the unintended consequences of breastfeeding promotion and other recommended parenting practices. These recommendations and policy based upon this science may inspire stress and guilt in mothers, especially poor and non-White mothers, when they don't measure up.

RECOMMENDED RESOURCES

Orit Avishai. 2007. "Managing the Lactating Body: The Breast-Feeding Project and Privileged Motherhood." *Qualitative Sociology* 30: 135–152.

Challenges the notion that breastfeeding is empowering and pleasurable through interviews with middle-class mothers.

Linda M. Blum. 1999. *At the Breast: Ideologies of Breastfeeding and Motherhood in the Contemporary United States.* Boston: Beacon Press.

Uses in-depth interviews with mothers and analyses of popular advice literature to explore how mothering and breastfeeding vary by race and class.

Eirik Evenhouse and Siobhan Reilly. 2005. "Improved Estimates of the Benefits of Breastfeeding Using Sibling Comparisons to Reduce Selection Bias." *Health Sciences Research* 40: 1781–1802.

This quantitative analysis of sibling pairs suggests observational studies may have overstated the long-term benefits of breastfeeding.

La Leche League International. 2003. Breastfeeding Statistics (La Leche League International Center for Breastfeeding Information).

Summary of cross-national breastfeeding initiation and duration rates.

Joan B. Wolf. 2007. "Is Breast Really Best? Risk and Total Motherhood in the National Breastfeeding Awareness Campaign." *Journal of Health Politics, Policy, and Law* 32: 595–636.

A forceful critique of the public health campaign to promote breastfeeding, as well as the science behind it.

REVIEW QUESTIONS

1. Artis writes that sometimes it is a "cultural imperative" for a mother to breastfeed her child. Explain some features of the public discussion on breastfeeding that might lead it to being characterized in such a way.

2. Trends in breastfeeding have been influenced by "expert opinions" based on scientific findings over the past several hundred years. Does this speak to how some societies might rely heavily on expert opinions to make health and lifestyle choices, or do you think easily influenced trends are exclusive to the discussion of breastfeeding?

3. According to Linda Blum's *At the Breast*, how do opinions on breastfeeding differ based on race, class, and ethnicity?

4. Think about Artis's discussion on "problematic science." What should we make of correlations that might be "small and weak," yet are consistently found in several scientific studies? In other words, how heavily should we allow such findings to influence our choices and opinions?

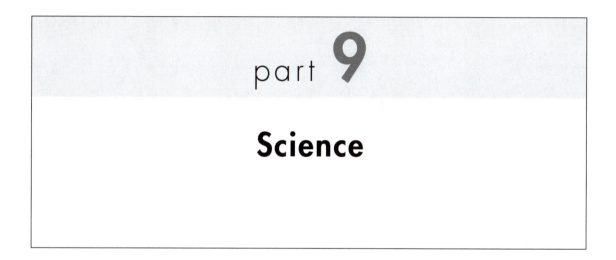

part **9**

Science

dana r. fisher, joseph waggle, and lorien jasny

not a snowball's chance for science

46

fall 2015

using climate change denial as a case, the authors demonstrate how echo chambers are formed and reinscribed to limit information within bounded networks.

Senator James Inhofe of Oklahoma wrote the book on climate science denial, literally. He titled it *The Greatest Hoax,* and in it he slaps the label "alarmist" onto the thousands of geologists, hydrologists, and atmospheric scientists worldwide who argue that climate change is a human-driven phenomenon with dire consequences for the health and habitability of this planet. At the same time, he uses the book to laud the "bravery" of the handful of contrarian scientists who support his perspective that a changing climate is neither caused by human action, nor especially threatening to human life. So it isn't surprising that, in February of 2015, Senator Inhofe—newly named chairman of the Senate Committee on Environment and Public Works—brought a snowball to the floor of the U.S. Congress. That snowball, Inhofe argued, was all he needed to demonstrate that climate change is a fraud.

"In case we have forgotten," he said with a flourish, "because we keep hearing that 2014 has been the warmest year on record, I ask the chair, you know what this is? It's a snowball. And that's just from outside here. So it's very, very cold out."

Such antics stand in stark contrast to the findings of the Intergovernmental Panel for Climate Change in its 2014 Fifth Assessment Report, which synthesized 30,000 peer-reviewed studies to show a "clear link" between long-term climate change and human activity. But how "clear" can the scientific evidence really be if the debate continues to rage at the highest levels of policy-making? How does misinformation persist in the face of vast amounts of expert testimony, extensive media attention, and international activism? When political actors debate climate "science," what is it exactly that they're debating?

To answer these questions, we have used social network analysis to dissect what we call the "elite climate-policy network" in the United States. Using data collected from a survey of the politicians, federal agency workers, business leaders, activists, and scientists most engaged in American climate politics, we demonstrate that it is the unique shape of the relationships among these "policy actors" that has distorted the message of consensus science. This shape—an echo chamber—has intensified debate by amplifying marginal opinions and keeping misinformation in circulation.

In the summer of 2010, our research team approached the top 100 policy actors engaged in climate-change politics and asked them to participate in our study—to be surveyed and interviewed. This time was exceptionally active

> Political actors do not cross ideological or party lines until they are ready to argue.

and contentious for U.S. climate politics. A bill to regulate carbon dioxide emissions had passed in the House of Representatives for the first time and a companion bill was being considered in the Senate. That summer remains the closest the United States has come to passing climate legislation at the federal level. The 64 policy actors who agreed to participate in our study had all been highly active in the climate-policy arena: They had participated in numerous Congressional hearings related to climate science and policy, and many had attended the international climate negotiations in Copenhagen in 2009, which had been expected to yield an updated international climate treaty. From these data, we saw the emergence of an echo chamber (technical details and more background are in our paper just published in *Nature Climate Change*).

who you know (and who they know)

Social network analysis enables us to look at how people are connected. We asked respondents whom they saw as their sources of "expert scientific information," providing each with a list of the 100 policy actors and asking them to check off every office, institution, business, or individual they considered one of their expert sources of scientific information. By using a method called Exponential Random Graph modeling, or ERGM, we were able to look at how information flows within and throughout this climate-policy network. We were also able to isolate the influence of specific relationships, such as the echo chamber, within the entire network.

the echo and the chamber

We define echo chambers by their constituent parts: the "echo" and the "chamber." We are particularly interested in who lists whom as a source of information and how these people are

similar and different. Although one might expect these policy actors to list scientists in the network as their sources of "expert scientific information," our results show that this isn't always true. Instead, members of the policy network tend to list other policy actors who are ideologically similar as sources of scientific information. We assessed this similarity—known in the social networks literature as *homophily*—by looking at responses to attitudinal questions important to climate politics. Although scientists and political actors from the Executive Branch of the government were most likely to be cited as sources of information, it turned out that respondents overwhelmingly referenced policy actors who held the same opinions as themselves.

This belief agreement is what we call the *echo*. Figure 1 shows the individual networks of two respondents in our sample—the Nature Conservancy and a scientist at the University of Alabama–Huntsville who has frequently testified in Congressional hearings about climate science. These "ego networks" represent the specific part of the network made up of a single actor, or ego, and everyone tied to that individual. An ego network is like the ego's neighborhood: it contains everyone who sends information to or receives information from the ego, as well as all the ties among those actors. The arrows point in the direction of information flow.

Nodes in each network are shaded based on how they responded to the statement, "There should be an international binding commitment on all nations to reduce greenhouse gas emissions." This statement represents an issue of contention in American climate politics since the mid-1990s (that's when the Senate unanimously passed the Byrd-Hagel Resolution, limiting the Clinton Administration's ability to negotiate for an international climate treaty). Black indicates strong disagreement, and light gray indicates strong agreement (the grayed markers indicate a

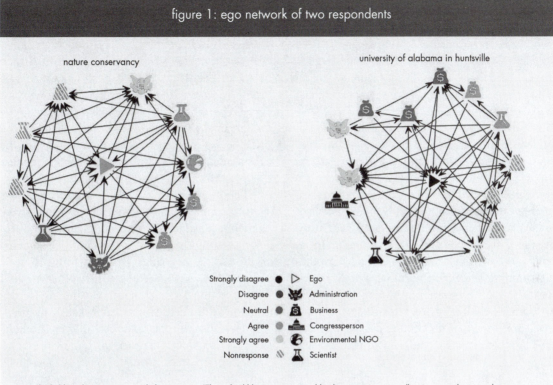

figure 1: ego network of two respondents

nature conservancy

university of alabama in huntsville

Strongly disagree ● ▷ Ego
Disagree ● 🦅 Administration
Neutral ● 💲 Business
Agree ● 🏛 Congressperson
Strongly agree ● 🌎 Environmental NGO
Nonresponse ◌ ⚗ Scientist

Note: Shaded based on agreement with the statement: "There should be an international binding commitment on all nations to reduce greenhouse gas emissions."

Full-color, high-resolution graphics available at https://contexts.org/articles/snowball.

nonresponse to the question about an international binding agreement).

The ego networks for both actors illustrate that they have a diversity of political actors in their networks—they listed many sources of information, and they were, in turn, listed as sources by many others. We also see strong patterns in issue agreement and information flow. For example, the Nature Conservancy is an environmentally focused nongovernmental organization that regularly lobbies for environmental protections at the federal level. Most of their contacts agreed with the statement, and none disagreed. These findings are consistent among all of our respondents: policy actors

reliably cited sources who held the same ideological position as they did.

In addition to these actors getting their information from those who already share the same opinions, the information is also amplified when it is transmitted through multiple pathways. These pathways describe our metaphorical *chamber mechanism*. In social network analysis, this mechanism is also known as the "transitive triad." A transitive triad is a group of three actors in which one individual is the source of information and transmits information to a second person both directly and indirectly through the third person. In other words, the same information gets diffused directly and

not a snowball's chance for science   333

indirectly through intermediary actors repeating that same information. Note that, from the perspective of the person receiving the information, this information appears to be coming from multiple sources, though, in fact, it is coming from a single source.

> Echo chambers provide the perfect environment for such a selective discussion of scientific facts.

When three people hold similar levels of agreement about a subject and pass information among themselves via multiple pathways, we call it an *echo chamber*. Echo chambers are active in a network if the network has more transitive triads that form around a shared attribute or belief. In other words, echo chambers of information sharing about "expert scientific information" on climate change exist when political elites who hold the same opinion about whether there should be an international binding agreement on climate change share information. In this case, any information that is passed through the chamber echoes the agreement they already share.

The scientist from the University of Alabama, who strongly disagrees that there should be a binding commitment to reduce carbon dioxide, has one echo chamber in his network: he transmits information to a scientist and to the office of Senator Inhofe (the Congressperson in his network). The other scientist also transmits information to Inhofe, and because they all disagree with a binding greenhouse gas commitment, they form an echo chamber. We can see a number of echo chambers within the Nature Conservancy's ego network as well, as this group passes on information directly and indirectly to other actors that agree that there *should* be a binding commitment to reduce greenhouse gas emissions.

The network graph (see figure 2) presents the entire network of respondents. The nodes are again shaded based on their responses to the question about whether there should be a binding agreement on climate change. The size of the nodes is reflective of the number of echo chambers—transitive triads among actors with the same ideological position—in which each actor is engaged. The possible number of echo chambers for each ideological category is, of course, related to the number of respondents in each category; the respondents with the most echo chambers also display the most popular viewpoint.

Echo chambers can occur randomly in a network. Imagine an alternative network where we randomly assign the same number of connections among the policy actors and the same distribution of attitudes that we found in our survey. In such an alternative network, we could observe some echo chambers due to chance alone. We use ERGM to test our results and see if the presence of echo chambers in these findings can be explained by random chance or a combination of other possible network structures and attributes. ERGM enables us to simulate hundreds of thousands of alternate networks to estimate how important the echo chambers are in modeling our data.

politics in the echo chamber

The results of our analysis show that echo chambers occur in our network more often than random chance or the other characteristics of the network would predict. Furthermore, the ERGM shows that chambers of agreement among political elites—the transitive triads—do not exist significantly outside those who agree to the attitudinal questions about climate politics. Together, these findings confirm that echo chambers have formed in the U.S. climate-policy network.

Our analysis also found that scientific actors and those from the Executive Branch of the government were more frequently cited as

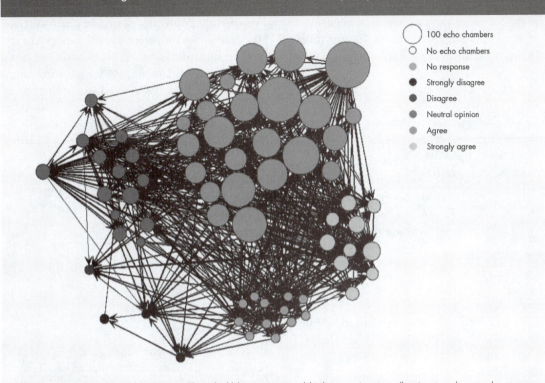

figure 2: echo chambers in the full climate-policy elite network

○ 100 echo chambers
○ No echo chambers
● No response
● Strongly disagree
● Disagree
● Neutral opinion
● Agree
● Strongly agree

Note: Based on agreement with the statement: "There should be an international binding commitment on all nations to reduce greenhouse gas emissions."

Full-color, high-resolution graphics available at https://contexts.org/articles/snowball.

sources of information than business organizations. Although it is encouraging that science is widely cited as a source of information on climate change in our network, we return now to the question of how scientific consensus can be so hotly contested in the political sphere.

When James Inhofe brought a snowball to the floor of the U.S. Senate, he was expressing more than the temperature of Washington, D.C., in February. He was *demonstrating* politics in an echo chamber: the particular networks in which Inhofe—and all political elites—operate make it not only possible to assert that snow equals

science, but it also makes such claims plausible. The combination of ideological homophily and closed communication structures make arguments like this compelling for those who already agree with the position, but baffling for everyone outside the echo chamber.

Our results also demonstrate that while the debate about climate change engages many different sides of the argument, the critical information-gathering stage is strikingly homogenous. In other words, although climate politics—and the political process in general—ought to be bipartisan and open, our research shows that the debates are the *only* "mixed" component of the process. Political actors do not cross ideological or party lines until they are ready to argue. A true bipartisan approach to climate change policy-making means breaking open these echo chambers at both the information-gathering and information-sharing stages.

the future of science and politics

These findings are telling for the science communication process. It seems that climate science is more beholden to politics than politics is to the actual science. In the political arena, echo chambers structure how climate science is discussed, perceived, accepted, or dismissed by different political actors. Rather than discussing a single scientific consensus position, political actors can cherry-pick exactly which parts of the science they wish to amplify or undermine. Echo chambers provide the perfect environment for such a selective discussion of scientific facts.

The onus of breaking the echo chamber, then, is borne by those who advocate for greater scientific literacy in policy-making. Climate activists, and even scientists themselves, must be prepared to facilitate discussion among policy actors with diverging ideological views on climate change in order to break apart these echo chambers. Furthermore, these opportunities for discussion should come as early as possible in the political process, perhaps even preceding the information-gathering stage. For issues as long-fought as climate change, it may be too late. But avoiding the persistent effects of echo chambers in other political issues may still be possible where the debate is young.

This research also shows that responsible citizens must be careful with our own sources of scientific information if we want to ensure that our perception on any issue is accurate. Although the data here are gathered from political elites, echo chambers have important implications for information transmission in our own lives. We face the same potential problems of cherry-picked information in our day-to-day routines as we turn to specific sources for information. As other researchers have noted, the online social media environment accentuates such echo chambers as we are able to create increasingly personalized media profiles. Such "narrow-casting" can lead to echo chambers that distort our own perception of the risks, responsibilities, and opportunities present in political and policy issues.

> For issues as long-fought as climate change, it may be too late. But avoiding the persistent effects of echo chambers in other political issues may still be possible.

RECOMMENDED RESOURCES

Dana R. Fisher, Joseph Waggle, and Philip Leifeld. 2013. "Where Does Political Polarization Come From? Locating Polarization with the U.S. Climate Change Debate." *American Behavioral Scientist* 57(1): 70–92.

> An empirical demonstration that political polarization around climate change does not stem from disagreements about science, but from disagreements on the policy instruments proposed to address the issue.

Linton Freeman. 2004. *The Development of Social Network Analysis: A Study in the Sociology of Science.* North Charleston: Book Surge LLC.

> An accessible and concise history of network analysis and its applications in the social sciences.

Intergovernmental Panel on Climate Change (IPCC). 2014. Fifth Assessment Report. Available at www.ipcc.ch/report/ar5/.

An overview of the current state of peer-reviewed climate change science.

Lorien Jasny, Joseph Waggle, and Dana R. Fisher. 2015. "An Empirical Examination of Echo Chambers in US Climate Policy Networks." *Nature Climate Change* 5: 782–86.

Employs social network analysis to show that echo chambers are present in U.S. climate politics and they transmit distorted scientific information throughout the policy-making process.

Naomi Oreskes and Erik M. Conway. 2010. *Merchants of Doubt: How a Handful of Scientists Obscured the Truth on Issues from Tobacco Smoke to Global Warming.* New York: Bloomsbury Press.

Uses politically and scientifically charged case studies to demonstrate how scientific expertise and the political process can help and hinder one another.

REVIEW QUESTIONS

1. How do the authors define the term *echo chamber*?
2. What role do echo chambers play in debates about global climate change at the highest levels of policy-making in the United States?
3. Why might James Inhofe's use of a snowball to make his point about global climate change be compelling for those who already agree with his position, but baffling for everyone outside the echo chamber?
4. Has this article made you reconsider where you will go for information about scientific debates and current events in the future? Why or why not?

simon a. cole and troy duster

microscopic hair comparison and the sociology of science

winter 2016

47

flawed forensics and overstated claims make scientific evidence tricky at trial.

Nearly a year ago, an FBI press release generated a great deal of media attention. The release reports initial results from a joint project of the Department of Justice (DOJ), the Federal Bureau of Investigation (FBI), the Innocence Project (IP), and the National Association of Criminal Defense Lawyers (NACDL) created to review cases in which a forensic technique known as microscopic hair comparison was used. This alliance of at least somewhat strange bedfellows—the IP and NACDL are often critical of the forensic science practiced by the FBI and used in court by the DOJ—was convened after the *Washington Post* reported on three cases of wrongful conviction in the District of Columbia, each of which relied heavily on microscopic hair comparison. The groups then agreed to undertake a comprehensive, joint review of the FBI's deployment of microscopic hair comparison.

The press release reports the results of this panel's initial analysis of almost 500 cases. Most startlingly, it reports that FBI examiners gave inaccurate testimony in 96 percent of those cases. The DOJ is now working to notify all the defendants affected. The NACDL is trying to ensure that those defendants have counsel. For their part, the FBI has agreed to provide free DNA testing, and the DOJ has agreed not to invoke statutes of limitations. However, that will not necessarily apply to the majority of cases, which originated in state, not federal, courts.

That staggering 96 percent stat is likely behind some of the rather sensational headlines that accompanied blog posts about the report, including "The FBI faked an entire field of forensic science" and "CSI Is a Lie." One might read such reports and wonder how it is even possible to be wrong at a rate so much higher than chance. As it turns out, knowing a little more, well, *context*, makes the story a little more understandable—if no less damning.

The popular view still has it that jury trials are the way criminal prosecutions are decided, but well over 90 percent of all convictions come from plea bargains that are never subject to public scrutiny. Instead, behind closed doors, the prosecution typically confronts the accused with what is claimed to be overwhelming and incontrovertible evidence (not just forensic evidence—DNA matches, blood samples,

> An interagency press release from 2015 reports the results of its initial analysis of almost 500 cases that relied heavily on microscopic hair comparison. Most startlingly, it reports that FBI examiners gave inaccurate testimony in 96 percent of those cases.

bitemarks, fingerprints, bullet casings, and so forth—but also incriminating statements by the defendant and others, eyewitness and informant testimony, and so on), then "bargains" with the accused to get him or her to plead guilty to a lesser charge. A guilty plea garnered in this fashion avoids a costly and time-consuming jury trial, but it also means that the evidence-claims rarely make it into broad daylight. High-profile cases may get jury trials, such as O. J. Simpson's, or media coverage, such as that surrounding the Grand Jury decision to not pursue an indictment in Ferguson, Missouri, after Michael Brown's death, but such saturated media coverage only serves to reinforce the impression that juries review evidence. Moreover, the extraordinary popularity of *Law and Order*–type television series, from *Perry Mason* to the full panoply of *CSI* spinoff productions to *Bones* all reinforce the completely false impression that juries typically review evidence in criminal cases. In one of the only empirical studies done on this topic, the ironic finding is that those convicted are more convinced of the invincibility of scientific evidence against them than are the prosecutors. That is, even if the evidence is flawed (or nonexistent), the claim to that evidence is a powerful weapon in the hands of prosecutors in their leveraging of a guilty plea.

And, of course, the race and class dimensions of both criminal trials and plea bargains are well known. For example, the ACLU published a 2013 report using massive national data to document the extent to which the war on drugs targeted African Americans, at four times that of Whites. For example, although Whites consume either the same or more marijuana in the relevant age groups (17–29) than do African Americans, in major urban areas, the latter are seven times more likely to be arrested for possession. With the dominance of the plea bargain as a weapon in the hands of prosecutors, the accused typically plead guilty to a lesser charge rather than mount a challenge against a looming mandatory-minimum prison sentence. No other factor explains the huge race differential in the nation's incarceration rates.

Microscopic hair comparison is basically what it sounds like: a forensic analyst compares one or more hairs relevant to a crime. One or more of the hairs is unknown, and one or more are known to come from a specific person. For example, the analyst might be asked to compare pubic hairs from a rape kit (that appear not to come from the victim) to pubic hairs plucked (by court order, if necessary) from a suspect. Human hair varies in a number of characteristics, such as color, treatment, pigment aggregation, and shaft form. Although all hairs from a single anatomical site on a single individual are certainly not identical, they tend to be "consistent" in some of these characteristics. Thus, the analyst seeks to determine whether the suspect's sample hairs are consistent in these characteristics with the unknown hairs.

These characteristics, however, are certainly not uniquely possessed. Millions of people may have hairs of a certain color or thickness. Even combining a number of characteristics does not reduce the potential pool of donors of the hair to a single person. Faced with a finding of "consistency," then, we must ask what "weight" (as forensic statisticians would call it) or "probative value" (as lawyers would call it) should we assign to this finding? Answering this question requires information about the rarity of the various characteristics being considered. As a

> With the dominance of the plea bargain as a weapon in the hands of prosecutors, the accused typically plead guilty to a lesser charge rather than mount a challenge against a looming mandatory-minimum prison sentence.

simple example, we already have intuitive, experience-based information that a finding of consistency of the color red should be assigned greater weight than a finding of consistency of the color black. There are fewer natural red-heads in the world than there are people with naturally black hair.

Here is where the story takes its first odd turn: As a 2009 review of forensic science by the National Research Council (NRC) put it, "No scientifically accepted statistics exist about the frequency with which particular characteristics of hair are distributed in the population." Without such information, the weight of microscopic hair comparison cannot be estimated. Did FBI hair analysts write reports and give testimony stating that the weight of microscopic hair comparison cannot be calculated? No. In most cases, they devised verbal characterizations of the weight of the evidence, including verbal characterizations of *probability* ("I would say there is a high degree of probability that the hair comes from the defendant"), invoking *professional experience* ("based on my experience in the laboratory and having done 16,000 hair examinations, my opinion is that those hairs came from the defendant"), or characterizing *rarity* by reference to professional experience ("In 12 years as a hair analyst, I have looked at hairs from around 10,000 people, and only on two occasions have I seen hairs from two different people that I could not distinguish"). As late as 2004, forensic hair analysts, including FBI hair analysts, defended the practice of testifying "that the likelihood of finding someone else with indistinguishable hair is remote, a rare event." They attributed criticism of this practice to "confusion and misunderstanding ... and an incomplete knowledge about forensic hair comparisons by the non-scientific members of the legal system and non-forensic scientists."

Here, of course, is how the whole episode illustrates a systemic failure of the criminal justice system that transcends the specifics of microscopic hair comparison. FBI analysts without sufficient data to estimate the weight of their evidence resorted to vague but overstated verbal formulations of certainty. These analysts trained local analysts all over the United States to do the same thing. Some prosecutors, in their summations, interpreted these overstated verbal formulations to sound like powerful statements of guilt. Defense attorneys often failed to understand or expose the limitations of the testimony. And, perhaps most importantly, the courts often failed to act as effective gatekeepers to ensure that expert witnesses could support their claims.

Although legal standards for allowing expert testimony differ from state to state, almost all such standards impose at least some "gatekeeping" responsibility on the judge to ensure that potentially misleading evidence is not put before a jury. Many states require "general acceptance in the field" in which the evidence belongs (the "*Frye* standard"), and still more require evidence of reliability (the "*Daubert/Kumho* standard"). Still, while microscopic hair comparison might have problems under either standard, most courts have allowed expert testimony by FBI examiners and the examiners they trained. Further, both standards tend to distract courts from the key issue of whether the weight of the evidence is being properly stated, regardless of the technique's general acceptance or reliability.

By 2012, however, the FBI had become convinced that it was improper to try to characterize the weight of hair comparison evidence

> Almost all state standards regarding expert testimony impose some "gatekeeping" responsibility on the judge to ensure that potentially misleading evidence is not put before a jury.

without studies or data, and that reports or testimony that did so were improper.

In other words, the FBI's belief about what constituted proper scientific interpretation of microscopic hair comparison evidence changed sometime between 2000 and 2012. The FBI found itself in a consensus position with its erstwhile adversaries, the Innocence Project and NACDL.

This, then, is what accounts for the seemingly startling 96 percent figure. By changing its mind about what counted as "accurate," the FBI caused thousands of scientific reports to seemingly magically transform from "accurate" (in its view) to "inaccurate." Essentially *all* microscopic hair comparison evidence was considered inaccurate, because no one has enough information to properly estimate the weight of microscopic hair comparison evidence.

In a way, this story is perhaps a particularly stark example of what is by now a rather garden-variety finding in sociology of science: that scientific knowledge changes through the social consensus of its practitioners. By deliberately forming an organized consensus group and charging themselves with issuing a report, the four institutions (DOJ, FBI, IP, NACDL) whose cooperation, as Norman Reimer, executive director of NACDL, put it, was "once an almost inconceivable concept," were able to transform thousands of scientific results from "accurate" to "inaccurate." Now the view that the ordinary way of testifying was inappropriate was no longer a product of "confusion and misunderstanding" and "incomplete knowledge," but, rather, the correct "scientific" view.

The science didn't "shift." In fact, no scientific research was performed at all—that, after all, is the point. What happened was that relevant actors became convinced that it was not scientifically acceptable to report about a hair comparison without making a reliable estimate of the potential donor population. In essence, the relevant social actors agreed it was necessary to think about hair evidence in a probabilistic fashion. This formation of agreement could reasonably be called both a scientific act and a social one.

Sociologists might also want to answer what is perhaps a more interesting question: why the FBI would have entered into this consensus in the first place. The FBI is not exactly known for its receptiveness to criticism of its forensic practices. And yet, the 2015 hair comparison press release is notable for its self-flagellating tone. The FBI's own press release quotes IP Co-Director Peter Neufeld saying, "These findings confirm that FBI microscopic hair analysts committed widespread, systematic error, grossly exaggerating the significance of their data under oath with the consequence of unfairly bolstering the prosecutions' case," and "this epic miscarriage of justice calls for a rigorous review to determine how this started almost four decades ago and why it took so long to come to light." It quotes Reimer saying, "It seems certain that there will be many whose liberty was deprived and lives destroyed by prosecutorial reliance on this flawed, albeit highly persuasive evidence." Compare that tone with the more characteristically stonewalling tone of the FBI's 2005 press release announcing its discontinuation of comparative bullet lead analysis (CBLA): "While the FBI Laboratory still firmly supports the scientific foundation of bullet lead analysis, given the costs of maintaining the equipment, the resources necessary to do the examination, and its relative probative value, the

FBI analysts without sufficient data to estimate the weight of their hair comparison evidence resorted to vague but overstated verbal formulations of certainty. These analysts trained local analysts all over the United States to do the same thing.

FBI laboratory has decided that it will no longer conduct this exam."

What explains the FBI's willingness to throw the "science" of microscopic hair comparison under the bus? A number of possible explanations present themselves. Certainly, we should not discount the agency and hard work of the actors who created this consensus group with the FBI and insisted on moving it forward: the IP and NACDL, the *Post* (which continued to press the story), and, of course, progressive forces within the DOJ and the FBI. Nor should we discount genuine motivation to do right. The results of this report may cause enormous amounts of work for law enforcement and attorneys as they try to sort through thousands of closed cases to determine whether erroneous forensic evidence made a difference in those cases. Changes in leadership at the level of president of the United States, attorney general, or FBI director could have had an impact. The bipartisan turn against overpunitiveness in the United States is another possible reason for turning against microscopic hair comparison.

There is another obvious explanation: microscopic hair comparison is almost obsolete. As the NRC report noted:

> The availability of DNA analysis has lessened the reliance on hair examination. In a very high proportion of cases involving hair evidence, DNA can be extracted, even years after the crime has been committed. Although the DNA extraction may consist of only mitochondrial DNA (mtDNA) [nuclear DNA, preferable for forensic analysis, is not always retrievable from hair; mitochondrial DNA usually is], such analyses are likely to be much more specific than those conducted on the physical features of hair. For this reason, cases that might have relied heavily on hair examinations have been subjected more recently to additional analyses using DNA. Because of the inherent limitations of hair comparisons and the availability of higher-quality and higher-accuracy analyses based on mtDNA, traditional hair examinations may be presented less often as evidence in the future, although microscopic comparison of physical features will continue to be useful for determining which hairs are sufficiently similar to merit comparisons with DNA analysis and for excluding suspects and assisting in criminal investigations.

We certainly don't mean to valorize DNA analysis or claim that it is devoid of social issues. As social scientists (ourselves included) have pointed out, there are a host of concerns raised by DNA profiling, including contamination, planting, errors of interpretation, categorization of databases by racial groups, familial searching, phenotypic profiling, as well as privacy, surveillance, discrimination, and civil liberties concerns raised by the expansion of genetic databases.

Most important, even if microscopic hair comparison continues to be used for the sorts of coarse screening purposes described by the NRC (such as distinguishing hairs from fibers and human from animal hair), with the spread of DNA analysis, hair analysts are now less likely to be called upon to give evidence of identity than they were prior to 2000. That is, even if hair comparison is used as an investigation tool, testimony about identity—the kind of testimony that is the target of the joint report—is much less likely to find its way into trials.

> Long before issues of bias, accuracy, and validity in forensic science get to the laboratories or are subject to challenge, the overreliance on plea bargains guarantees very little science will ever go before a jury.

Under these circumstances, it is difficult not to suspect the FBI gave up hair comparison when it no longer needed it for criminal prosecutions and trials.

Indeed, we would argue that the CBLA story also supports this hypothesis. CBLA was not obsolete in the same sense as microscopic hair comparison; it has not been replaced by a superior technology. But CBLA was an exotic forensic technique used by only one laboratory (the FBI) in the United States and in only a small number of criminal cases. Discarding it would affect those cases but do little to change the overall landscape of crime investigation. Since data were not available to estimate the weight of the evidence for CBLA either, discontinuing the technique was easier than undertaking the difficult work of putting CBLA on a firm foundation of data and statistical inference.

The fall of a contested forensic discipline may seem like progress to criminal justice reformers who have been trying to improve American forensic science for years. But which disciplines fall may have as much to do with their perceived utility in the crime investigations of the future as with the inherent weaknesses of the disciplines themselves.

The 2009 NRC report was very critical of the state of forensic science, and it recommended Congress establish a National Institute of Forensic Science. However, after the 2010 elections shifted control of the House of Representatives to the Republicans, it became clear that any request for funding for such an institute would be blocked. So President Obama and his attorney general, Eric Holder, decided to pursue a compromise or interim solution: the appointment of a National Commission on Forensic Science. This commission held its first meeting in early 2014 and was comprised mainly of criminal justice career professionals, including judges, attorneys, and laboratory scientists. Among the appointed members, only one was a social scientist (another *ex officio* member is a physical anthropologist).

At the outset, the commission faces two huge hurdles that could thwart its ability to effect meaningful reform. First, it will be challenging for those who work inside the institutional and organizational framework of criminal justice to effect reform from within. Second, as noted, long before issues of bias, accuracy, and validity in forensic science get to the laboratories or are subject to challenge, the overwhelming reliance on plea bargains means that more than 90 percent of those incarcerated got there through plea bargains rather than trials. The forensics never even came before a jury.

RECOMMENDED RESOURCES

Spencer S. Hsu. 2012. "Convicted Defendants Left Uninformed of Forensic Flaws Found by Justice Department." *Washington Post*, April 16.

> The first in the *Post*'s series about wrongful convictions that prompted the historic review of microscopic hair comparison.

Helena Machado and Barbara Prainsack. 2012. *Tracing Technologies: Prisoners' Views in the Era of CSI*. Farnham: Ashgate.

> An innovative comparative study of Austrian and Portuguese prisoners that finds a high degree of belief in the power of DNA profiling and other forensic technologies.

National Research Council. 2009. *Strengthening Forensic Science in the United States: A Path Forward*. Washington, DC: National Research Council.

> The landmark report finding much forensic science poorly validated and critiquing the judiciary's failure to ensure validation.

Daniel Nohrstedt and Christopher M. Weible. 2010. "The Logic of Policy Change after Crisis: Proximity and Subsystem Interaction." *Risk, Hazards & Crisis in Public Policy* 1(2):1–32.

> A helpful work from the policy process tradition that argues "most policies . . . cannot be changed from within."

Jed S. Rakoff. 2014. "Why Innocent People Plead Guilty." *New York Review of Books,* November 14.

> A critique of the U.S. criminal justice system's reliance on plea bargaining by a federal judge and member of the National Commission on Forensic Science.

Clive A. Stafford Smith and Patrick D. Goodman. 1996. "Forensic Hair Comparison Analysis: Nineteenth Century Science or Twentieth Century Snake Oil?" *Columbia Human Rights Law Review* 27: 227–91.

> One of the earliest critiques of the validity of microscopic hair comparison.

REVIEW QUESTIONS

1. Explain the significance of decision-making by "relevant social actors" brought up by Cole and Duster. What kinds of power do these actors potentially wield by being able to deem a forensic science technique "accurate" or "inaccurate"?
2. Why did the FBI respond so strongly to criticisms of this particular technique of forensic science?
3. Do you believe this press release warrants the reopening of those cases in which there were potentially inaccurate testimonies? Why or why not?
4. Cole and Duster discuss two potential obstacles for the National Commission on Forensic Science at the conclusion of the article. What are these obstacles? How can the commission try to overcome them?

janet vertesi

learning from NASA's robotic planetary missions

48

summer 2015

an ethnographer learns that the line between human and robot is blurred for some scientists at NASA and considers how the human–robot relationship reflects social context and structure.

The scientist at the front of the room hunched over and splayed his arms out to his sides. Waddling a bit like a penguin, he shuffled his feet over to one side, then the other as he described how the Mars Exploration Rover *Opportunity* had recently explored a part of the planet Mars. Suddenly he looked up, his eyes searching for the ethnographer in the back of the room. "Janet, get your camera!" he exclaimed, "I'm doing the Rover dance!"

Most scientists who work on NASA's robotic space exploration missions can tell you how their spacecraft works and what their instrument of choice can measure on other planets. But in my eight years as an ethnographer with the scientists and engineers who explore our solar system, I never saw anyone foster the same interplanetary connection with their robots that the Mars Exploration Rover team members did.

It started with the little things: stories about what the robot was doing on Mars that day that used anthropomorphic language to tell the tale. *Spirit* and *Opportunity* needed time in their day to take a nap, wake up, or go to sleep at night. Sometimes people talked about the robots like their children or their aging grandparents, with a language of care filled with emotion. We celebrated Martian birthdays with cake and ice cream on Earth. Like other ethnographers on the team before me, I got used to the fact that whenever someone on the team said "we," they were usually talking about the robot.

It got stranger. Team members explained how they used the thousands of images that the robots returned from Mars to "see like a Rover": peering into the infrared to detect minerals in Martian rocks that would be invisible to the human eye, getting used to 3-D projections, fisheye lenses, and false colors that lit up like a Warhol print. There were images for press releases too—the ones painted in red, butterscotch, and brown that were supposed to imitate what it would look like if you were standing on Mars—but these were mainly for the public. Behind the scenes, I got used to seeing the world from a perspective taken at five feet off the ground, with eyes set 30 centimeters apart, a planet brilliant in pink, green, and turquoise blue.

It wasn't long before "seeing like a Rover" turned into feeling and *being* like a Rover. People used their bodies to imitate the Rovers' own physical form and range of motion. They splayed

> "Janet, get your camera! I'm doing the Rover dance," exclaimed the scientist at the front of the room.

Mars Exploration Rover. (Courtesy NASA/JPL)

their arms out to embody the solar panels, reached an arm over their heads to imitate the cameras atop the robotic mast, maneuvered their wheelie chairs to approximate the roll of robot wheels over a distant planetary surface. They did all this even when they were speaking to their colleagues on a teleconference call with no one else in the room.

I came to recognize and codify these gestures as what I called "the Rover dance." Taken together with the visualizations, talk, and rituals that I observed on the mission team, this embodied approach to robotic experience cemented our connection with explorers on a distant world.

This connection had unusual social effects on Earth as well. When it was a difficult day on Mars, people shuffled around the office, hunched over under the weight of a dust storm on another planet. Soon people were telling me stories about how they hurt themselves working in their garden, going salsa dancing, or in a tae kwon do class, mirroring the stuck wheels or frozen shoulder joints that their robots suffered on Mars. When *Spirit* was

> When *Spirit* was trapped in the sand in the summer of 2011, people cried at their desks. They couldn't focus on their jobs. Relationships fell apart.

A shadow self-portrait of the Opportunity *Rover on its 180th Martian day of operation. (Courtesy NASA/JPL/Cornell)*

trapped in the sand in the summer of 2011, people cried at their desks. They couldn't focus on their jobs. Relationships fell apart.

As a sociologist studying the mission, these moments provided a fascinating opportunity to think about how we interact with technology in our daily lives. Certainly we develop strong relationships with and attachments to our machines, and the principles of anthropomorphism are well known. But going a step beyond this interpretation means thinking more seriously about the organizational context in which we encounter these devices. Here it's worth noting how the Mars Rover team works on Earth to understand why it is that they might perform

such dances or experience an emotional roller-coaster along with their robots' highs and lows.

I often describe working on a robotic spacecraft team as being on a bus with 150 other people, where everyone wants the steering wheel. The robot is not autonomous: a large group of scientists and engineers on Earth must look at the available data and make a decision. Where should we drive? Which images should we take? What will we do today on Mars, and what will we not have time for? All NASA mission teams face this problem, which means developing organizational tools and a culture of decision-making that is specific to that community and its robot.

On the Mars Rover mission, the team features a charismatic leader and a flattened hierarchy. Any scientist can use any instrument on the Rover to solve a scientific question. Decisions are made via unilateral consensus. This is unusual for NASA missions, which tend to look to bureaucratic engineering organizations for inspiration rather than the flat forms made famous in Silicon Valley in the 1990s. And now, after over 10 years working together, the Rover team's process is relatively seamless. Mission personnel exhibit an easy solidarity that sociologists since Durkheim would identify as mechanical or tribal.

Seen in organizational context, the visualizations, forms of talk, gestures, and even emotions on the mission help to make this consensus possible. The visual forms of seeing like a Rover accomplish the hard job of getting everyone on the same page, where they can more easily arrive at the tough decisions facing them each day as a unified team. Seeing Mars from the Rover's point of view (more specifically, the *team's version* of the Rover's point of view) cements this visual solidarity. Everyone begins and ends the day together, in the body of the robot on Mars. Just as it takes membership on the team to read and understand the visualizations that they produce, these visualizations make and reinforce membership on the team as well.

In his theory of interaction ritual chains, sociologist Randall Collins theorizes that a combination of mutual focus and shared rituals can give rise to emotional energy and an affective sense of belonging. In this case, we see that emotional attachment extended not only among members of the team, but to their robots as well. At a distance of millions of miles, the Rovers become something of a team totem: their success and well-being is both the purpose of the team's activities and the reflection of those activities.

Mars Rover team member uses her hands to embody the Rover's cameras as her "eyes." (Image drawn from ethnographic photo by author, courtesy C. Sylvester)

All this points to new avenues for thinking about the sociology of technology, robots in particular. We often examine people entranced by their mobile screens, their computers, or their wearable devices to make pronouncements about technology's role in our individual lives. Studies of human–robot interaction, too, tend to focus on whether or not the robot is humanlike enough for us to believe it has a life of its own. These studies of micro-level interactions are important for understanding human-machine communication, as ethnographer Lucy Suchman has shown, or for detecting the politics of platforms, as communications scholar Tarleton Gillespie has done.

But seeing robots and other technologies in organizational contexts exposes how these technologies are embedded in wider forms of social relations. In the case of the Rovers, doing sociology on a NASA mission means looking at how working with robots in space requires understanding important social work on Earth—in this case, the politics and practices of consensus management. It exposes the everyday technologies—the digital-image processing tools, the teleconference calls, even the PowerPoint slides—that assist in the production of consensus.

We can also look closer to Earth for how technologies participate in (or inadvertently subvert) such social contexts. Computers in the home are part and parcel of the hierarchies, emotions, and organizational context of a family. And as technologies move into health care, they will need to navigate the hospital hierarchies of surgeons, doctors, and nurses, too.

Doing robotic sociology is no longer a far-fetched enterprise. After all, as the Mars Exploration Rovers demonstrate, even robots millions of miles away hold an important place in our social world.

REVIEW QUESTIONS

1. This article raised issues regarding strong relationships and attachments to machines. What are some other examples of how humans interact and relate to technology in daily life?
2. What does the author mean when she says that the robots were "team totems"? How does this concept fit into Randall Collins's theory of interaction ritual chains, as described in this article?
3. The author says that the sociology of technology and robots should branch out beyond a micro-level focus on how people interact interpersonally with robots. What does she mean by this? What are some examples of what a researcher might study that goes beyond the micro level?

maria charles

what gender is science?

spring 2011

looking at science, technology, engineering, and mathematics (stem) fields across countries challenges the assumption that women in more economically and culturally modern societies enjoy greater equality. rather, freedom to choose a career may paradoxically cause women in affluent Western democracies to construct and replicate stereotypically gendered self-identities.

Gender equality crops up in surprising places. This is nowhere more evident than in science, technology, engineering, and mathematics (STEM) fields. The United States should be a world leader in the integration of prestigious male-dominated occupations and fields of study. After all, laws prohibiting discrimination on the basis of sex have been in place for more than half a century, and the idea that men and women should have equal rights and opportunities is practically uncontested (at least in public) in the United States today.

This egalitarian legal and cultural context has coincided with a long-standing shortage of STEM workers that has spurred countless initiatives by government agencies, activists, and industry to attract women to these fields. But far from leading the world, American universities and firms lag considerably behind those in many other countries with respect to women among STEM students and workers. Moreover, the countries where women are best represented in these fields aren't those typically viewed as modern or "gender-progressive." Far from it.

Sex segregation describes the uneven distributions of women and men across occupations, industries, or fields of study. While other types of gender inequality have declined dramatically since the 1960s (for example, in legal rights, labor force participation rates, and educational attainment), some forms of sex segregation are remarkably resilient in the industrial world.

In labor markets, one well-known cause of sex segregation is discrimination, which can occur openly and directly or through more subtle, systemic processes. Not so long ago, American employers' job advertisements and recruitment efforts were targeted explicitly toward either men or women depending on the job. Although these gender-specific ads were prohibited under Title VII of the 1964 Civil Rights Act, less blatant forms of discrimination persist. Even if employers base hiring and promotion solely on performance-based criteria, their taken-for-granted beliefs about average gender differences may bias their judgments of qualification and performance. Sociologists and economists have documented this cognitive bias and "statistical discrimination" through diverse experiments. It turns out that people's beliefs about men's and women's different natures lead them to assess task performance accordingly, even in the absence of any actual performance differences. Such biased assessments reinforce existing patterns of sex segregation because many occupational tasks are regarded as quintessentially "masculine" or "feminine." For example, beliefs about women's capacity for nurturing and men's technical and mechanical skills might lead an employer to perceive gender-conforming applicants (say, male pilots and female nannies) to be better qualified.

But discrimination isn't the whole story. It's well-established that girls and young women often avoid mathematically intensive fields in favor of pursuits regarded as more human centered. Analyses of gender-differentiated choices are controversial among scholars because this line of inquiry seems to divert attention away from structural and cultural causes of inequalities in pay and status. Acknowledging gender-differentiated educational and career preferences, though, doesn't "blame the victim" unless preferences and choices are considered in isolation from the social contexts in which they emerge. A sociological analysis of sex segregation considers how the economic, social, and cultural environments influence preferences, choices, and outcomes. Among other things, we may ask what types of social context are associated with larger or smaller gender differences in aspirations. Viewed through this lens, preferences become much more than just individuals' intrinsic qualities.

An excellent way to assess contextual effects is by investigating how career aspirations and patterns of sex segregation vary across countries. Recent studies show international differences in the gender composition of STEM fields, in beliefs about the masculinity of STEM, and in girls' and women's reported affinity for STEM-related activities. These differences follow unexpected patterns.

stem around the world

Many might assume women in more economically and culturally modern societies enjoy greater equality on all measures, since countries generally "evolve" in an egalitarian direction as they modernize. This isn't the case for scientific and technical fields, though.

Statistics on male and female college graduates and their fields of study are available from the United Nations Educational, Scientific, and Cultural Organization (UNESCO) for 84 countries covering the period between 2005 and 2008. Sixty-five of those countries have educational systems large enough to offer a full range of majors and programs (at least 10,000 graduates per year).

One way of ranking countries on the sex segregation of science education is to compare the (female-to-male) gender ratio among science graduates to the gender ratio among graduates in all other fields. By this measure, the rich and highly industrialized United States falls in about the middle of the distribution (in close proximity to Ecuador, Mongolia, Germany, and Ireland—a heterogeneous group on most conventional measures of "women's status"). Female representation in science programs is weakest in the Netherlands and strongest in Iran, Uzbekistan, Azerbaijan, Saudi Arabia, and Oman, where science is disproportionately female. Although the Netherlands has long been considered a gender-traditional society in the European context, most people would still be intrigued to learn that women's representation among science graduates is nearly 50 percentage points lower there than in many Muslim countries. As seen in figure 1, the most gender-integrated science programs are found in Malaysia, where women's 57 percent share of science-degree recipients precisely matches their share of all college and university graduates.

"Science" is a big, heterogeneous category, and life science, physical science, mathematics, and computing are fields with very different gender compositions. For example, women made up 60 percent of American biology graduates, but only about 19 percent of computing graduates,

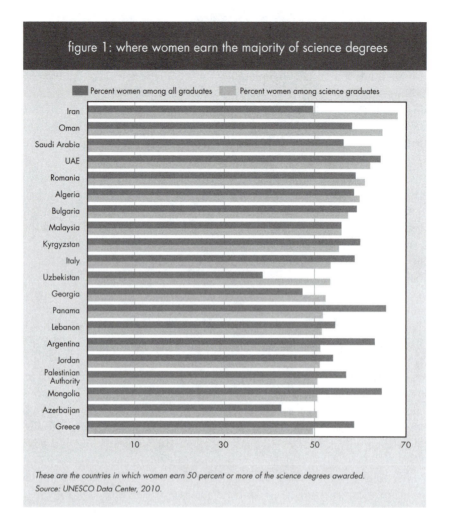

figure 1: where women earn the majority of science degrees

■ Percent women among all graduates   ■ Percent women among science graduates

Iran
Oman
Saudi Arabia
UAE
Romania
Algeria
Bulgaria
Malaysia
Kyrgyzstan
Italy
Uzbekistan
Georgia
Panama
Lebanon
Argentina
Jordan
Palestinian Authority
Mongolia
Azerbaijan
Greece

10   30   50   70

These are the countries in which women earn 50 percent or more of the science degrees awarded.
Source: UNESCO Data Center, 2010.

in 2008, according to the National Center for Educational Statistics.

But even when fields are defined more precisely, countries differ in some unexpected ways. A case in point is computer science in Malaysia and the United States. While American computer scientists are depicted as male hackers and geeks, computer science in Malaysia is deemed well-suited for women because it's seen as theoretical (not physical) and it takes place almost exclusively in offices (thought to be woman-friendly spaces). In interviews with sociologist Vivian Lagesen, female computer science students in Malaysia reported taking up computing because they like computers and because they and their parents think the field has good job prospects. The students also referenced government efforts to promote economic development by training workers, both male and female, for the expanding information technology field. About half of Malaysian computer science degrees go to women.

Engineering is the most strongly and consistently male-typed field of study worldwide, but its gender composition still varies widely across countries. Female representation is generally weaker in advanced industrial societies than in developing ones. In our 2009 article in the *American Journal of Sociology*, Karen Bradley and I found this pattern using international data from the mid-1990s; it was confirmed by more-recent statistics assembled by UNESCO. Between 2005 and 2008, countries with the most male-dominated engineering programs include the world's leading industrial democracies (Japan, Switzerland, Germany, and the United States) along with some of the same oil-rich Middle Eastern countries in which women are so well-represented among science graduates (Saudi Arabia, Jordan, and the United Arab Emirates). Although women do not reach the 50 percent mark in any country, they come very close in Indonesia, where 48 percent of engineering graduates are female (compared to a 49 percent share of all Indonesian college and university graduates). Women comprise about a third of recent engineering graduates in a diverse group of countries including Mongolia, Greece, Serbia, Panama, Denmark, Bulgaria, and Malaysia.

While engineering is uniformly male-typed in the West, Lagesen's interviews suggest Malaysians draw gender distinctions among engineering *subfields*. One female student reported, "In chemical engineering, most of the time you work in labs. . . . So I think it's quite suitable for females also. But for civil engineering . . . we have to go to the site and check out the constructions."

girl geeks in america

Women's relatively weak presence in STEM fields in the United States is partly attributable to some economic, institutional, and cultural features that are common to affluent Western democracies. One such feature is a great diversity of educational and occupational pathways. As school systems grew and democratized in the industrial West, educators, policy-makers, and nongovernmental activists sought to accommodate women's purportedly "human-centered" nature by developing educational programs that were seen to align functionally and culturally with female domestic and social roles. Among other things, this involved expansion of liberal arts programs and development of vocationally oriented programs in home economics, nursing, and early-childhood education. Subsequent efforts to incorporate women, *as women*, into higher education have contributed to expansion in humanities programs, and, more recently, the creation of new fields like women's studies and human development. These initiatives have been supported by a rapid expansion of service-sector jobs in these societies.

In countries with developing and transitional economies, though, policies have been driven more by concerns about advancing economic development than by interests in accommodating women's presumed affinities. Acute shortages of educated workers prompted early efforts by governments and development agencies to increase the supply of STEM workers. These efforts often commenced during these fields' initial growth periods—arguably before they had acquired strong masculine images in the local context.

Another reason for stronger sex segregation of STEM in affluent countries may be that more people (girls and women in particular) can afford to indulge tastes for less-lucrative care and social service work in these contexts. Because personal economic security and national development are such central concerns to young people and their parents in developing societies, there is less latitude and support for the realization of gender-specific preferences.

Again, the argument that women's preferences and choices are partly responsible for sex segregation doesn't require that preferences are innate. Career aspirations are influenced by beliefs about ourselves (What am I good at and what will I enjoy doing?), beliefs about others (What will they think of me and how will they respond to my choices?), and beliefs about the purpose of educational and occupational activities (How do I decide what field to pursue?). And these beliefs are part of our cultural heritage. Sex segregation is an especially resilient form of inequality because people so ardently believe in, enact, and celebrate cultural stereotypes about gender difference.

Sex segregation is especially resilient because people so ardently believe in, enact, and celebrate gender stereotypes.

believing stereotypes

Relationship counselor John Gray has produced a wildly successful series of self-help products in which he depicts men and women as so fundamentally different that they might as well come from different planets. While the vast majority of Americans today believe women should have equal social and legal rights, they also believe men and women are very different, and they believe innate differences cause them to *freely choose* distinctly masculine or feminine life paths. For instance, women and men are expected to choose careers that allow them to utilize their hardwired interests in working with people and things, respectively.

Believing in difference can actually produce difference. Recent sociological research provides strong evidence that cultural stereotypes about gender difference shape individuals' beliefs about their own competencies ("self-assessments") and influence behavior in stereotype-consistent directions. Ubiquitous cultural depictions of STEM as intrinsically male reduce girls' interest in technical fields by defining related tasks as beyond most women's competency and as generally unenjoyable for them. STEM avoidance is a likely outcome.

Shelley Correll's social psychological experiment demonstrates the self-fulfilling effects of gender beliefs on self-assessments and career preferences. Correll administered questions purported to test "contrast sensitivity" to undergraduates. Although the test had no objectively right or wrong answers, all participants were given identical personal "scores" of approximately 60 percent correct. Before the test, subjects were exposed to one of two beliefs: that men on average do better, or that men and women perform equally well. In the first group, male students rated their performance more highly than did female students, and male students were more likely to report aspiring to work in a job that requires contrast sensitivity. No gender differences were observed among subjects in the second group. Correll's findings suggest that *beliefs about difference* can produce gender gaps in mathematical self-confidence even in the absence of actual differences in ability or performance. If these beliefs lead girls to avoid math courses, a stereotype-confirming performance deficit may emerge.

Concern about such self-fulfilling prophesies was one reason for the public furor that erupted when Lawrence Summers, then president of Harvard, opined in 2005 that innate biological differences might help explain women's underrepresentation in high-level math and science. Summers's critics, who included many members of the Harvard faculty, reacted angrily, suggesting that such speculation by a prominent educational leader can itself reduce girls' confidence and interest in STEM careers by reinforcing cultural stereotypes.

enacting stereotypes

Whatever one believes about innate gender difference, it's difficult to deny that men and women often behave differently and make different choices. Partly, this reflects inculcation of gender-typed preferences and abilities during early childhood. This "gender socialization" occurs through direct observation of same-sex role models, through repeated positive or negative sanctioning of gender-conforming or nonconforming behavior, and through assimilation of diffuse cultural messages about what males and females like and are good at. During much of the twentieth century, math was one thing that girls have purportedly not liked or been good at. Even Barbie said so. Feminists and educators have long voiced concerns about the potentially damaging effects of such messages on the minds of impressionable young girls.

But even girls who don't believe STEM activities are inherently masculine realize others do. It's likely to influence their everyday interactions and may affect their life choices. For example, some may seek to affirm their femininity by avoiding math and science classes or by avowing a dislike for related activities. Sociologists who study the operation of gender in social interactions have argued that people expect to be judged according to prevailing standards of masculinity or femininity. This expectation often leads them to engage in behavior that reproduces the gender order. This "doing gender" framework goes beyond socialization because it doesn't require that gender-conforming dispositions are internalized at an early age, just that people know others will likely hold them accountable to conventional beliefs about hardwired gender differences.

The male-labeling of math and science in the industrial West means that girls and women may expect to incur social sanctions for pursuing these fields. Effects can be cumulative: taking fewer math classes will negatively affect achievement in math and attitudes toward math, creating a powerful positive feedback system.

celebrating stereotypes

Aspirations are also influenced by general societal beliefs about the nature and purpose of educational and occupational pursuits. Modern education does more than bestow knowledge; it's seen as a vehicle for individual self-expression and self-realization. Parents and educators exhort young people, perhaps girls in particular, to "follow their passions" and realize their "true selves." Because gender is such a central axis of individual identity, American girls who aim to "study what they love" are unlikely to consider male-labeled science, engineering, or technical fields, despite the material security provided by such degrees.

> Ironically, freedom of choice seems to help construct and give agency to stereotypically gendered "selves."

Although the so-called postmaterialist values of individualism and self-expression are spreading globally, they are most prominent in affluent late-modern societies. Curricular and career choices become more than practical economic decisions in these contexts; they also represent acts of identity construction and self-affirmation. Modern systems of higher education make the incursion of gender stereotypes even easier, by allowing wide latitude in course choices.

The ideological discordance between female gender identities and STEM pursuits may even generate attitudinal aversion among girls. Preferences can evolve to align with the gender composition of fields, rather than vice versa. Consistent with these arguments is new evidence showing that career-related aspirations are more gender-differentiated in advanced industrial than in developing and transitional societies. As can be seen in figure 2, the gender gap in eighth-graders' affinity for math, confidence in math abilities, and interest in a math-related career is significantly smaller in less affluent countries

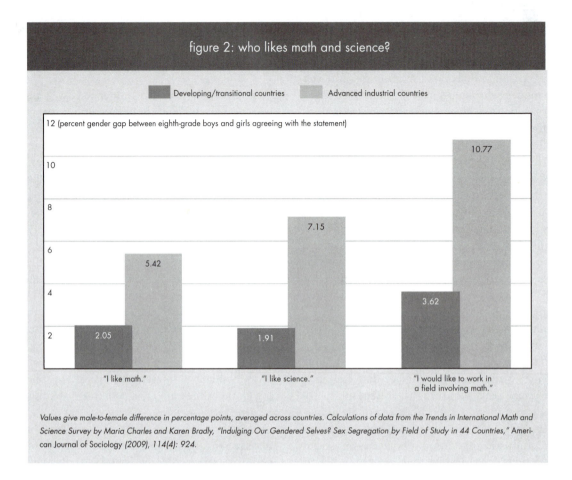

figure 2: who likes math and science?

Developing/transitional countries   Advanced industrial countries

12 (percent gender gap between eighth-grade boys and girls agreeing with the statement)

"I like math."   "I like science."   "I would like to work in a field involving math."

5.42
2.05
7.15
1.91
10.77
3.62

Values give male-to-female difference in percentage points, averaged across countries. Calculations of data from the Trends in International Math and Science Survey by Maria Charles and Karen Bradly, "Indulging Our Gendered Selves? Sex Segregation by Field of Study in 44 Countries," American Journal of Sociology (2009), 114(4): 924.

than in rich ("postmaterialist") ones. Clearly, there is more going on than intrinsic male and female preferences.

questioning stem's masculinity

Playing on stereotypes of science as the domain of socially awkward male geniuses, CBS's hit comedy *The Big Bang Theory* stars four nerdy male physicists and one sexy but academically challenged waitress. (Female physicists, when they do show up, are mostly caricatured as gender deviants: sexually unattractive and lacking basic competence in human interaction.) This depiction resonates with popular Western understandings of scientific and technical pursuits as intrinsically masculine.

But representations of scientific and technical fields as *by nature* masculine aren't well-supported by international data. They're also difficult to reconcile with historical evidence pointing to long-term historical shifts in the gender-labeling of some STEM fields. In *The Science Education of American Girls,* Kim Tolley reports that it was *girls* who were overrepresented among students of physics, astronomy, chemistry, and natural science in nineteenth-century American schools. Middle-class boys dominated the higher-status classical humanities programs thought to require top rational powers and required for university admission. Science education was regarded as excellent preparation for motherhood, social work, and teaching. Sociologist Katharine Donato tells a similar story about the dawn of American computer programming. Considered functionally analogous to clerical work, it was performed mostly by college-educated women with science or math backgrounds. This changed starting in the 1950s, when the occupation became attractive to men as a growing, intellectually demanding, and potentially lucrative field. The sex segregation of American STEM fields—especially engineering, computer science, and the physical sciences—has shown remarkable stability since about 1980.

The gender (and racial) composition of fields is strongly influenced by the economic and social circumstances that prevail at the time of their initial emergence or expansion. But subsequent transformative events, such as acute labor shortages, changing work conditions, and educational restructuring can effect significant shifts in fields' demographic profiles. Tolley, for example, links men's growing dominance of science education in the late nineteenth and early twentieth century to changing university admissions requirements, the rapid growth and professionalization of science and technology occupations, and recurrent ideological backlashes against female employment.

A field's designation as either "male" or "female" is often naturalized through cultural accounts that reference selected gender-conforming aspects of the work. Just as sex segregation across engineering subfields is attributed to physical location in Malaysia (inside work for women, outside work for men), American women's overrepresentation among typists and sewers has been attributed to these occupations' "feminine" task profiles, specifically their requirements for manual dexterity and attention to detail. While the same skills might be construed as essential to the work of surgeons and electricians, explanations for men's dominance of these

fields are easily generated with reference to other job requirements that are culturally masculine (technical and spatial skills, for example). Difference-based explanations for sex segregation are readily available because most jobs require diverse skills and aptitudes, some equated with masculinity, some with femininity.

looking forward

Should we be concerned about women's underrepresentation in STEM if this result follows from choices made in the absence of coercion or discrimination? I believe sex segregation should be of more than academic interest for at least three reasons. First, "separate but equal" principles often translate into "separate but unequal" outcomes, as is evident in the lower pay in female- than in male-dominated work. Second, sex segregation has feedback effects, reinforcing gender stereotypes and limiting perceived educational, family, and career options for subsequent generations. And third, women may represent an untapped labor pool in STEM fields where global shortages threaten to undermine national competiveness and economic development.

What then might be done to increase women's presence in STEM fields? One plausible strategy involves changes to the structure of secondary education. Some evidence suggests more girls and women complete degrees in math and science in educational systems where curricular choice is restricted or delayed; *all* students might take mathematics and science throughout their high school years or the school might use performance-based tracking and course placement. Although such policies are at odds with Western ideals of individual choice and self-expression, they may weaken penetration of gender stereotypes during the impressionable adolescent years.

Of course, the most obvious means of achieving greater integration of STEM is to avoid reinforcing stereotypes about what girls and boys like and what they are good at. Cultural shifts of this sort occur only gradually, but some change can be seen on the horizon. The rise of "geek chic" may be one sign. Aiming to liberate teenaged girls from the girls-can't-do-math and male-math-nerd stereotypes, television star and self-proclaimed math geek Danica McKellar has written three how-to math books, most recently *Hot X: Algebra Exposed*, presenting math as both feminine and fun. Even Barbie has been updated. In contrast to her math-fearing Teen Talk sister of the early 1990s, the new Computer Engineer Barbie, released in December 2010, comes decked out in a tight T-shirt printed in binary code and equipped with a smartphone and a pink laptop. Of course, one potential pitfall of this math-is-feminine strategy is that it risks swapping one set of stereotypes for another.

So, what gender is science? In short, it depends. When occupations or fields are segregated by sex, most people suspect it reflects fields' inherently masculine or feminine task content. But this presumption is belied by substantial cross-national variability in the gender composition of fields, STEM in particular. Moreover, this variability follows surprising patterns. Whereas most people would expect to find many more female engineers in the United States and Sweden than in Columbia and Bulgaria, new data suggest that precisely the opposite is true.

Ironically, the freedom of choice that's so celebrated in affluent Western democracies seems to help construct and give agency to stereotypically gendered "selves." Self-segregation of careers may occur because some believe they're naturally good at gender-conforming activities (attempting to build on their strengths), because they believe that certain fields will be seen as appropriate for people like them ("doing" gender), or because they believe they'll enjoy gender-conforming fields more than gender-nonconforming ones (realizing their "true selves"). It's just that, by encouraging individual self-expression in postmaterialist societies, we may also effectively promote the development and expression of culturally gendered selves.

RECOMMENDED RESOURCES

Shelly J. Correll. 2004. "Constraints into Preferences: Gender, Status, and Emerging Career Aspirations." *American Sociological Review* 69:93–113.

> Presents evidence from experiments on how beliefs about gender influence beliefs about our own competence and constrain career aspirations.

Paula England. 2010. "The Gender Revolution: Uneven and Stalled." *Gender & Society* 24:149–66.

> Offers reasons for the persistence of some forms of gender inequality in the United States.

Wendy Faulkner. 2000. "Dualisms, Hierarchies and Gender in Engineering." *Social Studies of Science* 30(5): 759–92.

> Explores the cultural linkage of masculinity and technology within the engineering profession.

Sarah Fenstermaker and Candace West, eds. 2002. *Doing Gender, Doing Difference: Inequality, Power, and Institutional Change.* New York: Routledge.

> Explores how and why people reproduce gender (and race and class) stereotypes in everyday interactions.

Cecilia L. Ridgeway. 2011. *Framed by Gender: How Gender Inequality Persists in the Modern World.* New York: Oxford University Press.

> Describes how cultural gender beliefs bias behavior and cognition in gendered directions and how this influence may vary by context.

Yu Xie and Kimberlee A. Shauman. 2003. *Women in Science: Career Processes and Outcomes.* Cambridge, MA: Harvard University Press.

> Uses data from middle school to midcareer to study the forces that lead fewer American women than men into science and engineering fields.

REVIEW QUESTIONS

1. What is cognitive bias?
2. How does cognitive bias contribute to the underrepresentation of women in STEM fields?
3. What is statistical discrimination?
4. Female representation in engineering fields is generally weaker in advanced industrial societies than in developing ones. What are some potential explanations for these differences?

part **10**

Politics

andy clarno

hiking the west bank

50

spring 2015

in palestine, hiking has become an act of resistance. the hills, valleys, and fields of palestinian villages are now the front lines of the struggle over Israeli colonization of the west bank.

In his award-winning 2008 memoir, *Palestinian Walks*, Palestinian lawyer and human rights activist Raja Shehadeh reflected on 25 years of hiking through the "vanishing landscape" of the West Bank: "As I stood in the ruins of one of my favorite places in the valley, this valley near where I was born and have always lived, I felt the hills were not mine any more. I am no longer free to come and walk." The hills, valleys, and fields of Palestinian villages are now the front lines of the struggle over Israeli colonization of the West Bank. Hiking has become an act of resistance.

For generations, trails have connected Palestinian villages and cities. Farmers use these trails to bring produce to regional markets; shepherds and Bedouins follow herds through the hills; well-worn paths enable visits to friends and relatives in neighboring villages. During the *nakba* (catastrophe) in 1948, hundreds of thousands of Palestinians walked these trails as they fled their villages. And after Israel occupied the West Bank and Gaza Strip, Palestinians formed hiking groups to encourage familiarity with the land and "voluntary work committees" to build ties among cities, villages, and refugee camps.

The Israeli occupation has transformed the landscape of the West Bank through the widespread confiscation of Palestinian land, the continual expansion of Israeli settlements, the construction of a network of settler highways, the proliferation of military checkpoints, the erection of an enormous separation wall, and the enforcement of military restrictions on Palestinian movement. Since the beginning of the Oslo "peace process" in the early 1990s, Israeli domination has deprived Palestinian communities of not only land but also connections. It has fragmented Palestinian society and isolated the villages.

The hills west of Bethlehem, for instance, are home to nine Palestinian villages. Thirteen Israeli settlements have been built on the land of these villages, separating them from one another as well as from Bethlehem and nearby Jerusalem. On a weekly basis, Israeli authorities confiscate small plots of land and prevent the villagers from working in their fields. In addition, the villagers confront daily forms of encroachment by Jewish settlers, who release sewage into cultivated fields, destroy olive trees and grape vines, expropriate property, and attack farmers trying to reach their own lands.

These settlements make up the Gush Etzion block, which Israeli officials insist will eventually be annexed to Israel. Four days after the ceasefire that brought an end to Israel's 2014 attack on Gaza, the Israeli government announced the

> In Palestine, hiking has become an act of resistance.

confiscation of 1,000 acres of land from four Palestinian villages for the expansion of these settlements.

In the face of intense pressure, Palestinians have developed numerous tactics to remain on their land, including court cases and collective mobilizations. Above all, they practice a culture of resistance known as *sumoud* (steadfastness)—a resilient will to remain present rather than succumb to dispossession and displacement. The village of Al-Araqib, for instance, has been demolished dozens of times since 2010 as the Israeli government tries to relocate Bedouin villages in the Naqab (Negev) desert. Each time it is demolished, Palestinians rebuild.

Similarly, millions of Palestinian refugees have remained in refugee camps in the occupied territories and neighboring countries for 65 years rather than give up on the goal of returning to their lands.

In the western villages of Bethlehem, farmers continue defiantly planting vegetables despite Israeli restrictions on access to land, water, and markets. A 70-year-old man explained, "I don't make any money from my vegetables. But I continue to farm in order to defend the land." Although the Palestinian Authority (PA) has little jurisdiction in the villages, a handful of nongovernmental organizations encourage *sumoud* by helping farmers rehabilitate land, plant trees, dig wells, and pave roads. "The primary form of resistance is land improvement. We have no other source of strength," said an organizer. In response, Israeli military authorities

New construction in the settlement of Betar Illit overlooks the fields of the Wadi Fukin village. (Andy Clarno)

routinely issue orders to destroy new wells, tear up new roads, or return freshly terraced land to its previous condition.

In recent years, Palestinians have reasserted their presence in the hills and valleys of the West Bank through a revival of hiking. Some villages have rehabilitated old trails and built new ones. In Battir, for instance, Palestinians have cleaned up old trails to Beit Jala and Bethlehem, placed trail markers and rest stops along the route, and built a guesthouse and an ecomuseum in the village.

In addition, organizations such as the Siraj Center promote hiking as a form of alternative or solidarity tourism. Hikers not only experience the dramatic beauty of the Palestinian landscape, they also visit sites of historical and religious significance, witness the occupation, and meet Palestinian families in villages along the trails. Local bookstores even sell a newly published guidebook to hiking trails in the West Bank (*Walking Palestine: 25 Journeys into the West Bank*).

And, for the first time in decades, Palestinian residents of cities and refugee camps have begun taking hikes through nearby villages. In the wake of the Second Intifada (uprising, from 2000–2005), Israel eased restrictions on Palestinian movement when the PA agreed to resume coordinated security operations. Alongside a growing number of hiking clubs, many Palestinians now go out as families or in small groups to visit friends, nearby springs, desert monasteries, or the tombs of local saints. Their hikes establish a Palestinian presence in contested territories, including sites identified as locations for future settlements. They also deepen popular knowledge of the land. A farmer from Al-Khader village, for instance, takes photographs during his walks of endangered plants that are no longer being cultivated.

Many hope that hiking can challenge the isolation of the villages and the fragmentation of the Palestinian population. An organizer in the Palestinian Farmers Union told me, "We have a monthly tour in a picnic style to see a lot of areas and villages. Maybe people volunteer, maybe they don't. But at least they come to know the places and one another. It is much like the voluntary work committees in the 1980s. They created connections so that when organizers went in to advocate, people knew each other and they worked together."

Hiking is also deeply rooted in Jewish Israeli culture, encouraged by religious, military, and political authorities. Israeli guidebooks advertise thousands of kilometers of hiking trails, many of which traverse the West Bank. Armed Israelis regularly venture into Palestinian villages on hikes to ancient Jewish landmarks and other sites of interest.

Villagers in Wadi Fukin, for instance, regularly encounter groups of settlers picnicking on their lands and swimming in the pools that feed their fields. A village leader described a recent encounter: "They were sitting in a farmer's hut. We didn't see how many, but there were groups of them and they were armed of course. When they saw us, they went in and got their guns and stopped us. We were walking toward them and they said, 'Stop. Where do you want to go? Give me your ID.' We said, 'How are you asking me where I want to go? We're going to our land. What are YOU doing here?'" As often occurs during such confrontations, Israeli soldiers were called in to diffuse tensions and ensure the safety of the trespassing settlers.

I had a similar encounter in 2013 when I accompanied two friends from Dheisheh refugee camp in Bethlehem on a visit to a spring in Al-Walaja village. It was the first time they had visited the area in more than 20 years.

> Armed Israelis regularly venture into Palestinian villages on hikes.

A family outing in Al-Walaja village. (Andy Clarno)

Enjoyment turned to anxiety when we arrived to find armed Israelis sitting by the beautiful pool. Feeling uncomfortable in their presence, we soon left. But two Palestinian boys from a nearby village remained undaunted. They swam in the pool, played in the springs, and refused to leave on account of the Israelis.

As Israel continues its steady colonization of the West Bank, Palestinian communities become smaller, more isolated, and more fragmented. The recent revival of hiking emerges from and contributes to the everyday culture of steadfastness, *sumoud*. Yet hiking is not necessarily a conscious political act—it is often simply a form of relaxation, exercise, meditation, or escape. Nevertheless, hiking in the West Bank must be understood within the context of resisting the occupation.

As Shehadeh reflects, "How unaware many trekkers around the world are of what a luxury it is to be able to walk in the land they love without anger, fear, or insecurity, just to be able to walk without political arguments running obsessively through their heads, without the fear of losing what they've come to love, without the anxiety that they will be deprived of the right to enjoy it. Simply to walk and savour what nature has to offer, as I was once able to do."

REVIEW QUESTIONS

1. Define the concept of *sumoud*.
2. According to the author, what are some of the political effects of hiking in the West Bank?
3. According to the author, what motivates people to hike in the West Bank?

silvia pasquetti

words burn lips

51

spring 2015

it is dangerous for palestinians who live in israel to be seen as political troublemakers in the west bank. individuals internalize this and learn not to speak out publicly, even to friends and neighbors as "words burn lips." they learn early on that it's better to be seen by the security forces as petty criminals than political activists.

When Sami (all names are pseudonyms) was a teenager in the Israeli city of Lod, he witnessed his older brother's arrest. He heard his parents say that his brother's "friend" had prompted him to speak against the Israeli state and then informed on him to the police.

For Sami, his brother's arrest was a valuable lesson. As he put it, "if every day you are served hot tea, you get used to blowing on the cup before drinking it." Talking freely is like gulping, and those freely spoken words can "burn lips." Like other poor Palestinians in Israel, Sami is reluctant to speak lest his words be seen as too political.

Sami's coping strategy of silence illustrates how Israel's security regime effectively produces feelings of fear, distrust, and entrapment among Israeli Palestinians who are treated as "suspicious" citizens. It is through their "Shabak education" (Shabak is the Hebrew acronym for the main Israeli internal security agency, also called Shin Bet) that poor Palestinians in Lod learn how to monitor their words and behaviors, how to distrust their friends and neighbors. In particular, they learn how to signal their lack of animosity toward Israel by avoiding political activism, nationalist feelings, and expressions of solidarity with Palestinians outside Israel. Their Shabak education teaches them that the consequences of unacceptable speech can be disastrous. Once charged with "security offenses," they can be interrogated for extended periods of time in total isolation and tortured (though illegal, the Shabak routinely uses torture). Security charges based on secret evidence or confession can lead to lengthy prison sentences.

As I learned in my 14 months of research between Lod and the adjacent West Bank, Shabak education also teaches Lod's Palestinians that acting as informants is also a way to seek various bureaucratic rewards. As Majid, an unemployed resident who failed to obtain a license for selling secondhand clothes, put it: "If I were to go to the police station right now, they would give me the license. I have to become a spy to obtain a [shop] license." Most Palestinians in Lod believe this, though the distribution of rewards by the security apparatus might be more erratic and less intentional than perceived. Still, the fact remains that the perception of the link between informing and access to scarce resources is conducive to a climate of distrust and recrimination.

> Like other civil and political rights, the freedom of speech of Palestinian citizens is effectively stifled by security practices. Social media activists, human rights activists, and journalists are primary targets.

Rami and Hassan took the author to visit the abandoned cemetery of an Arab village that was destroyed in 1948 before driving her to the ruins of Beit-Nabala. (Silvia Pasquetti)

Since the 1948 war, which led to the establishment of the Israeli state and turned hundreds of thousands of Palestinians into refugees, the security agencies have policed the political discourse and the national sense of belonging of Palestinians who managed to remain inside the newly established state, simultaneously granted citizenship and put under military rule. While Palestinians can vote, they are also heavily policed in a way that few Jewish Israelis will experience. The separate justice system for Jewish and Palestinian citizens is codified in law and practice. According to Adalah, a local NGO, there are 50 laws that discriminate against Palestinian citizens on issues such as state budget allocation, planning, and land ownership. Further, since the abolition of the military rule in 1966, Palestinian citizens have been under tight Shabak surveillance.

Like other civil and political rights, the freedom of speech of Palestinian citizens is effectively stifled by security practices. Social media activists, human rights activists, and journalists are primary targets. This was the case with Ameer Makhoul, an Israeli Palestinian human

While Rami and Hassan were highly tense when taking the author on a tour of Palestinian historical sites, they were more relaxed when driving inside the segregated districts where they live now. (Silvia Pasquetti)

rights activist who was sentenced to nine years in 2011 for "espionage" and "contact with enemy entities" after a visit to Lebanon where, according to the Shabak, he met with "an Hezbollah agent." Makhoul pleaded guilty to avoid the more serious charge of "assisting an enemy in war," which carries a life sentence. The conviction was partially based on a confession that Makhoul later argued he had given under the pressure of torture.

The history of displacement and destruction of Palestinian society—what Palestinians call Nakba (the catastrophe)—haunts the Israeli state and challenges the moral legitimacy of its actions. While the threat of terrorism is obviously a reality for Israel, the Israeli state is just as concerned, perhaps even more so, with systematically policing Israeli Palestinians' political ideas, nationalist feelings, and collective memories. Israel's decision to adopt a new law barring the commemoration of the Nakba by government-funded bodies such as schools (the initial version of the law considered the commemoration of the *Nakba* as a felony punishable with imprisonment) shows how Palestinians are seen as most dangerous by the state when they recount their history and attempt to gather and organize support from a global audience.

The Palestinian history of forced displacement is particularly visible in Lod. During the 1948 war, the Israeli army occupied the city (then known as Lydda) and expelled about 50,000 Palestinians, who are now reluctant to speak about it. For example, Sami knows that most *Ladadweh* (people originally from Lydda) now live in the refugee camps of the West Bank and the Gaza Strip. Reham, a neighbor of Sami, has listened many times to her grandmother's story of her nearly yearlong life as a refugee in the Gaza Strip after the 1948 war and of her clandestine return to the city. She knows where her grandmother lived before the 1948 war, how she was forced to leave Lydda on foot, how she returned, and where she hid after she returned. At the same time, Sami and Reham are restless when speaking about these events. Very experienced in the craft of what political scientist James Scott refers to as "seeing like the state," they are aware that speaking about Palestinian history in Lod is likely to be interpreted by Israeli authorities as a sign of hostility against the state.

Poor Palestinians' painful sense of danger highlights how the day-to-day activities of the security agencies effectively prevent Palestinians from developing their political voice and memory. For example, when I met Reham, I was interested in her grandmother's story, but Reham was preoccupied with a recent encounter with a man who had stopped her and told her that he worked "with the police." He asked her questions about drug addiction among the local youth. Reham doubted he was a police officer, but worried that he was with a security agency and had targeted her because one of her older children insisted on "speaking politics" though she repeatedly warned the kids that, in Lod, "you never know who is in front of you." With her energies already

It is safer for Lod's poor Palestinians to be seen as run-of-the-mill thieves than political troublemakers.

sapped by this encounter, Reham did not feel relaxed enough to speak about her grandmother's clandestine return to the city, which she is all too aware remains outside the boundaries of legitimate public discourse in Israel.

The policing of political voice is an experience shared by all Palestinian citizens of Israel. But it produces a particularly interesting situation for the Palestinian urban poor of Lod who live in districts where criminality and drug dealing are endemic and who are routinely labeled "petty criminals." While Israeli authorities attribute nationalist motivation to crimes committed by Palestinian citizens against their Jewish Israeli counterparts, this politicization of criminal activities remains much less comprehensive than that of political ideas and actions. In other words, in the eyes of the state, "petty criminals" are much less threatening than political activists. As a result, Lod's poor Palestinians sometimes cling to the label "petty criminals" to avoid unwanted attention from the security agencies.

This is what happened when Rami and Hassan, two middle-aged Palestinian residents of Lod—both of whom have criminal records for dealing drugs—drove me to Beit-Nabala, an Arab village destroyed during the 1948 war, to visit a building which used to be a school and is now an administrative office at the entrance of a new Israeli town. When we reached the entrance of the town, they were very tense. They wanted me to take a photo of the school, but they were afraid to stop the car because it might draw too much attention to them. They had no plausible explanation they could give the Israeli authorities to account for their presence there. If stopped, they said they would rather falsely confess a plan to steal something than mention that they had come show me the site of the destroyed village. In their experience, it was safer to be seen as run-of-the-mill thieves than as political troublemakers.

If Rami and Hassan were to openly claim historical and social ties to Palestinian sites of loss—like that school—it would make them likely targets for profiling, arrest, or harassment by the Israeli authorities. Rami was particularly afraid of the Shabak because he had already been interrogated, having been arrested at a local protest against house demolitions. Security officials had first told him that they had evidence that he had smuggled guns into the West Bank (a security charge equal to "assisting enemies"), then released him, ordering him to stay away from protests. Rami, who told me that the threatened charge was false, still had no desire to repeat the experience.

Rami commented, poignantly, "We had a history. Now we have cocaine."

It captures how Palestinians in Lod feel. They are trapped in a condition of marginality, where the Israeli state tolerates them as small-time criminals, but not living reminders of a Palestinian group or arc of history. Surrendering one identity—Palestinian—for another—petty thief—is a means of survival for many in Israel.

REVIEW QUESTIONS

1. According to the author, why does the Israeli state tolerate Palestinians as small-time criminals but not as people with a historic identity?
2. What are some of the security practices that limit Palestinians' civil and political rights?
3. Are there other places, in the United States or around the world, where the state polices political discourse? Briefly explain the circumstances of the places you identify.
4. Why do you think the author titled this piece "Words Burn Lips"?

viewpoints

it's high time

52

fall 2015

federal policy that regulates marijuana makes it difficult to access for medicinal purposes, and thousands are behind bars in the wake of the war on drugs. perhaps it's time for major policy change.

shehzad nadeem

Every month since the fall of 1982, Irvin Rosenfeld receives 300 joints, around nine ounces of pot, courtesy of the federal government. Packed tightly in a tin canister, they are delivered via FedEx to a local pharmacy. The Fort Lauderdale stockbroker, now 60, suffers from a degenerative bone disease—multiple congenital cartilaginous exostoses—that causes painful tumors, a condition he believes to be much relieved by smoking marijuana. What's more, he credits it with arresting the growth of the tumors and allowing him to live a relatively normal life. The pot itself is grown on a 12-acre federal farm at the University of Mississippi, the sole producer of federally legal marijuana since 1968. The plants are stored in a massive and securely guarded steel vault and then sent to Raleigh, North Carolina, where they are dried and prepared and rolled.

And yet, the government that provides Rosenfeld with the drug still classifies marijuana as a Schedule 1 substance. This puts it on par with heroin, LSD, and ecstasy, but renders it more dangerous than cocaine. It also makes research outside the narrow confines of the University of Mississippi's lab nigh on impossible. The federal government claims with unyielding certainty that cannabis has no "accepted medicinal use." Why then does it play the part of small-time dealer to people like Rosenfeld? The answer has to do with a narrowly defined "compassionate protocol" of the National Institute on Drug Abuse's Investigational New Drug Program (IND). The program was started in the late '70s when another Floridian, Robert Randall, successfully argued that pot was essential in treating the glaucoma he had suffered since his teens. First, however, Randall had to fend off cultivation charges after the pot he grew on his sunporch was discovered in a raid on his neighbor's house. Armed with cache of supporting research—including the results of exhaustive tests he had undergone—Randall argued that marijuana had kept him from going blind. The criminal charges against him were dismissed when D.C. Superior Court Judge James A. Washington determined with poetic succinctness that "the evil he sought to avert, blindness, is greater than that he performed." (One can still quibble with the implication of maleficence in cultivation and self-treatment.)

Later, in 1978, Randall sued the federal government to obtain legal access to federal pot

> The U.S. government classifies marijuana as a Schedule 1 substance. This puts it on par with heroin, LSD, and ecstasy, but renders it *more* dangerous than cocaine.

supplies. This resulted in an out-of-court settle-ment that provided him prescriptive access to pot and formed the legal basis for the Compas-sionate IND program. Randall was the first legal medical marijuana patient since cannabis prohibition began in 1937.

The government began supplying a handful of patients suffering from glaucoma and cancer with cannabis. The program was then expanded to include HIV-positive patients in the late 1980s. At its height, the program enrolled 30 patients. It stopped accepting new patients in 1992, and only four patients continue to receive cannabis from the federal government. Randall was also a prominent figure in a 1987 lawsuit that led the DEA's chief administrative law judge to conclude that marijuana is "one of the safest therapeuti-cally active substances known to man." The deci-sion was, of course, ignored by the DEA. Such frustrations led legalization activists to turn to the polls and state-ballot initiatives.

There are 23 states with laws allowing access to medical marijuana and 18 states that have decriminalized pot, including four states that have legalized the drug for recreational pur-poses. (It still actively prosecutes suppliers in those states—though the Obama administra-tion has shifted policy away from prosecuting medical marijuana dispensaries in states where its distribution is legal.) All told, around a mil-lion Americans use pot legally to treat an ailment.

As for Randall, he never did lose his sight, though he died of AIDS-related complications in 1991. Rosenfeld reckons he has smoked over 200 pounds of government pot—somehere north of 130,000 joints. What's rather interest-ing is that both Randall and Rosenfeld's love for cannabis is platonic: they claim not to get high from smoking; it's purely medicinal. As Jake Browne explains in his piece, they may be right: not all weed is the same. Strains can be grown

with varying levels of tetrahydrocannabinol, THC, the chemical responsible for "highs," as well as cannabidiol, a nonpsychoactive chemical that can purportedly suppress seizures. So you can make an effective medicine and you can make a pleasurable drug, or both at once.

Efforts to develop effective medication are severely curtailed by federal policy. The DEA, for example, has only issued a single license for the cultivation of marijuana for research, and that to the lab in Mississippi. But as frustrating as the situation is for research, the criminalization of marijuana has been even more disastrous in terms of lives wasted. According to the ACLU, there were over 8 million pot arrests in the United States between 2001 and 2010 and about $3.6 billion a year is spent on enforcing marijuana laws. Enforcement is deeply inflected by racial bias, as the brunt of failed war-on-drugs policies falls most heavily on communities of color. Mar-ijuana use is roughly equal among Blacks and Whites, yet the former are 3.73 times as likely to be arrested for marijuana possession.

In the meantime, the popularity of the war on drugs—with its mandatory minimum sentences for possession, its militarized policing, and its mighty contribution to the national trauma of mass incarceration—has plummeted. This dis-pleasure with the status quo, Craig Reinarman argues, is not just some inchoate sentiment. Rather, the hard work of sympathy-gathering, conscience-raising, and coalition-building has converted that outrage into something like a social movement pushing for policy reform. We might even take some grassroots pleasure in the fact that most of the gains have been at the state and local levels, and that federal mandates are increasingly seen as irrational. Change is in the air.

But as Wendy Chapkis reminds us, the same air is as suffocating as ever for drug war casu-alties behind bars. It is thus imperative that any reform efforts take their plight into consideration. The commuting of sentences for low-level offenders and the expunging of drug-related blemishes from criminal records, which hugely diminish one's employment and education prospects, are some ideas that come immediately to mind. Otherwise, any solution to the problem of prohibition will likely splinter along the familiarly depressing lines of race and class. Nonetheless the pressure for reform today is very real, and it suggests a future in which people mightn't suffer so needlessly under the draconian policies of the past.

craig reinarman

prohibition and its discontents

Opiate addiction is on a rampage, from Oxycontin to heroin. Overdoses have quadrupled since 2000 and are now the leading cause of injury-related death. "Synthetic marijuana" is putting people in the hospital, while HIV/AIDS is spreading rapidly among injection drug users in Indiana. The most notorious drug kingpin has escaped from Mexico's most secure prison. If asked to design headlines to fuel the war on drugs, one could hardly do better.

So, why is public support for the drug war at its lowest in decades? Punitive prohibition has come under increasing criticism as costly, inhumane, and ineffective. In July 2015, President Obama commuted the sentences of 46 nonviolent drug offenders and proclaimed to the NAACP that harsh drug laws and the imprisonment they spawned were bad policy: "Mass incarceration makes our entire country worse off, and we need to do something about it. . . . For nonviolent drug crimes, we need to lower long mandatory minimum sentences— or get rid of them entirely." The next day, former president Clinton criticized a draconian drug law he once boasted about: "I signed a bill that made the problem worse, and I want to admit it." Only recently, these sentiments would be blasphemous; now they only echo

shifts in public sentiment bubbling up from below.

In the Reagan years, hysteria about crack cocaine intensified the drug war, including the 1986 Anti-Drug Abuse Act, which helped lay the foundation for mass incarceration with mandatory minimum sentences of five years for possession of 5 grams of crack, often sold on inner-city street corners. (It took 100 times that amount of cocaine powder, used mostly by more-affluent Whites, to trigger the same sentence.) The new law eliminated parole and got whole families evicted from public housing. In a frenzy of bipartisanship, the House passed it 392–16 and the Senate 97–2.

The first Bush administration ratcheted up the drug war and the Clinton administration added more funding and police to it. Marijuana possession arrests nearly doubled to over 700,000 a year between 1992 and 2000. The drug czar's budget increased tenfold between 1980 and 2008—as did the number of drug offenders in prison, rising from roughly 50,000 to 500,000 over the same years. An Urban Institute study found that harsh drug laws led to less probation, more prison, and longer sentences, resulting in the most massive wave of imprisonment in U.S. history. The prison population quadrupled, giving the United States the world's highest incarceration rate.

According to FBI and Bureau of Prisons reports, all this hit people of color hardest—far out of proportion to their drug use, which is slightly lower than that of Whites. Discriminatory arrest patterns and the crippling holes left in families and communities by mass incarceration made drug laws the most potent form of racial oppression in America. Drug policy was transformed into a major civil rights issue. Today there is fierce new energy around drug-policy reform.

Over the last two decades a cornucopia of such reform efforts have solidified into a global social movement. Since 1996, 23 states and the District of Columbia have passed laws allowing marijuana for medical purposes. In 2012, movement activists waged successful campaigns in Colorado and Washington to legalize all marijuana use. In 2014, voters in Oregon and Alaska passed similar "tax and regulate" marijuana legalization measures. California reformers will put marijuana legalization on their state's November 2016 ballot.

In 2009, a coalition of activists pressured New York legislators to undo the harshest features of Rockefeller-era drug laws. Then Congress passed the Fair Sentencing Act of 2010, reducing the racialized 100-to-1 sentencing disparity between crack and powder cocaine offenses. In 2014, Senator Richard Durbin (D-IL) introduced the Smart Sentencing Act (still under debate, but cosponsored by members of both major parties), which would cut mandatory minimums for federal drug offenses in half.

The movement has also worked to keep drug offenders out of prison and to get them the help they need. Reformers in Seattle built an alliance of police, prosecutors, and politicians to pioneer the Law Enforcement Assisted Diversion Program (LEAD), explored in the Summer 2015 issue of *Contexts*, which allows police to redirect low-level drug offenders to community services before arrest. An independent evaluation by University of Washington scientists found a 58 percent reduction in recidivism among LEAD participants compared to a control group. Drug-policy reform can improve public safety. The LEAD model has been adopted by Gloucester, Massachusetts, a small fishing port. In an open letter, Gloucester's Police Chief Leonard Campanello wrote, "Any addict who asks for help will NOT be charged."

The drug-policy reform movement now has more organizations, members, and money than ever before, led by the Drug Policy Alliance in coalition with other nonprofits. The National Organization for the Reform of Marijuana Laws has 165 chapters in 46 states, 13,000 paid members, and a social media footprint of 1.2 million subscribers. Families Against Mandatory Minimums has been especially influential regarding the human costs of incarceration. Students for Sensible Drug Policy has grown to 100 chapters in 41 states. Americans for Safe Access, founded by medical marijuana patients in 2002, now has 30,000 members in 40 states. And Law Enforcement Against Prohibition (LEAP) was started by former narcotics officers whose frontline experience persuaded them that legalization was the only solution. Approximately 10,000 former police have joined LEAP across the United States and 90 other countries.

The movement has also attracted some unusual political bedfellows. The financial crisis of 2008 drew in some on the Right who, until recently, had never met a tough drug law they didn't like. Now, conservatives worried about the size and cost of the state have joined liberals focused on social justice in pushing drug-law reform. Who knew the Koch Brothers could find

> Punitive prohibition has come under increasing criticism as costly, inhumane, and ineffective.

common ground with the Center for American Progress, or Newt Gingrich with Van Jones?

Globally, a growing number of nations have made partial defections from UN drug-control treaties, fracturing the 50-year-old consensus around criminalization. Portugal decriminalized all drug use in 2001. Uruguay legalized the production of cannabis in 2014. Even traditional drug-war allies in Latin America are now in what journalist Alma Guillermopreito calls "open rebellion" against U.S.-style prohibition.

Underlying all this is the cultural force of a broad political constituency that sees drugs as technologies of the modern self. Illicit drug use is no longer the province of the marginal and deviant. Educated, employed, engaged citizens around the developed world see drug use as rather normal. They are harder to stigmatize and silence, and they are showing up in voting booths.

By exposing the full costs and consequences of punitive prohibition, the drug-policy reform movement has pushed drug policy to a historic inflection point. The drug-war consensus has collapsed. What is emerging to take its place are more harm-reduction programs like syringe exchange, treatment in lieu of prison, and further legalization. All legalization initiatives thus far, however, have been at the state level; marijuana possession remains a federal crime. The Obama administration has allowed these laws to stand. But if the next president is less sympathetic, we may be in for a constitutional confrontation.

wendy chapkis

terms of surrender

Marijuana prohibition can seem like a joke, especially to people like me—White, middle-class Americans living in politically progressive (and often cannabis-infused) communities such as coastal California, where I grew up, or southern Maine, where I now live. For many like us, "Reefer Madness" seems a ridiculous relic of a much less enlightened age. Stoners and dealers—from Cheech and Chong to Harold and Kumar and on to the *Pineapple Express*—are funny, not dangerous felons.

And then maybe someone we know gets arrested. For me, it was my friend Valerie, a member of that least-likely-to-be-arrested demographic: an economically secure White woman living in that most liberal of enclaves: Santa Cruz, California. Because she was growing five marijuana plants in her home garden, she was charged with felony cultivation. As I quickly learned, far from being a joke, marijuana prohibition is an ongoing horror show. It involves almost 700,000 arrests each year, 88 percent of them for possession. Huge numbers of Americans are being imprisoned, sometimes for decades, for marijuana offenses. In fact, according to the American Civil Liberties Union, at least 69 people are serving life sentences for nonviolent pot crimes.

Marijuana prohibition, moreover, has been absolutely central to the draconian war on drugs. According to the Pew Research Center, almost half of all Americans have tried marijuana; in contrast, according to the National Institute on Drug Abuse, less than 2 percent have ever used heroin. Marijuana is the only illicit drug used by large enough numbers of Americans to justify a massively expensive federal antidrug bureaucracy and a militarized police force.

Marijuana prohibition has made a significant contribution to mass incarceration, disproportionately of Black Americans, helping to make the United States "the world's most highly incarcerated society in history." Children have been removed from the custody of their marijuana-using parents; homes have been seized using asset forfeiture laws; students convicted of marijuana offenses have been denied federal scholarship aid; and patients have been punished for using a substance their physicians, research scientists, and now even CNN's Chief Medical Correspondent Sanjay Gupta believe would help.

But, finally, state by state, this prohibitionist approach to marijuana has begun to collapse. In 1996 California passed the nation's first medical marijuana law; there are now 23 states where authorized patients are allowed to legally access and use cannabis. In 2012, marijuana prohibition took another major hit when voters in Colorado and Washington legalized adult recreational use of marijuana. Two years later, in 2014, Oregon, Alaska, and the District of Columbia also voted for full legalization. It is likely that in 2016 additional states will vote to regulate and tax adult recreational sales and use of cannabis.

For the first time, more than half of all Americans now say that marijuana should be legalized. It increasingly appears to be true, as longtime marijuana activist Michael Corral argues, "the war against marijuana is over; now we are just negotiating the terms of surrender." But before we declare victory, it's important to remember that the devil is always in the details.

"Legalization" can mean radically different things. In the Netherlands, marijuana is currently available for legal purchase in small, independently owned "coffee shops" scattered throughout the country. Canada, on the other hand, has been attempting to centralize all legal (currently medical) marijuana cultivation in the hands of only a dozen industrial growers and distributors for the entire country.

In the United States, legalization looks very different in the states of Washington and Colorado. In Washington, voters surrendered the right to cultivate cannabis at home in exchange for legalized sales and use. In that state, marijuana consumers must purchase their cannabis through a small number of licensed distributors. In Colorado, individuals growing a few plants for themselves exist alongside small commercial cultivators and large industrial operations.

In other words, policy differences produce very different outcomes. It can seem trivial to debate competing legalization proposals in the face of the very real and very serious problems of prohibition. But it is also useful to remember that it can be difficult to undo, or redo, bad legislation. Take, for example, the end of alcohol prohibition. As Jon Walker notes in his book *After Legalization*, the Twenty-First Amendment ended federal prohibition, but states made very different decisions on how to regulate alcohol. Not only did a third of states continue to outlaw it entirely, even states that permitted the production and sale of alcohol generally didn't allow producers to sell directly to consumers. The result was the consolidation of production in the hands of a few very large companies. This, Walker reminds us, "was not some natural end state created by the invisible hand of the market. It was a policy choice. The government adopted regulations

Certainly marijuana legalization may represent a significant blow to the war-on-drugs apparatus. But it is equally possible it could be to the drug war what marriage equality is to the queer liberation movement: a celebrated step toward social justice, but not the only—or even the most important—one.

that disadvantaged small producers and made new startups almost impossible."

This is important to reflect on when we think of "regulating marijuana like alcohol." Which version of alcohol regulation are we referencing and what outcome do we desire? It wasn't until 1982, when California changed its liquor laws to allow small breweries to sell directly to consumers in "brew pubs" that the "microbrewery revolution" began. In 1983, there were only 80 breweries in the entire United States. By the late 1990s, hundreds of new breweries were founded every year.

So what terms of surrender should we demand in the failed war on cannabis? Should consumers be able to purchase pot directly from growers through a community supported agriculture (CSA) model of cultivation? Should local, small-scale growers be protected from competition with large corporate cultivators? Should we be allowed to grow for ourselves? And, even more importantly, how do we begin to undo the damage inflicted by the war on drugs, including the problem of prisoners of war?

Without a robust policy for releasing drug-war prisoners, there is a real risk that legalization of marijuana will mean that a few White men (in a still male-dominated industry) will make a lot of money on cannabis cultivation and sales, while many Black men (almost four times as likely as Whites to be arrested for marijuana possession despite similar rates of use) will remain behind bars or carry felony drug convictions forward. President Obama has recently begun a conversation about the need for the reduction or elimination of mandatory minimum sentences for nonviolent drug crimes, for an end to the practice of asking job applicants about their criminal histories ("ban the box"), and for the restoration of voting rights for felons who have completed their sentences. In July 2015, he even commuted the sentences of 46 low-level drug offenders. These are all important first steps. But there are tens of thousands more incarcerated people who need their marijuana sentences commuted and hundreds of thousands who need their records expunged.

Certainly marijuana legalization in itself is better than policies of prohibition and criminalization. It may even represent a significant blow to the war-on-drugs apparatus. But it is equally possible that marijuana legalization could be to the drug war what marriage equality is to the queer liberation movement: a celebrated step toward social justice but not the only—or even, arguably, the most important—one.

jake browne

please, think of the children

If someone had told you a decade ago that children would become the driving force behind the medical marijuana movement, you'd likely think they were high. Yet in 2015, we witnessed 15 states—including conservative bastions like Alabama and Texas—pass legislation designed primarily to give seriously ill minors access to cannabis. It has become one of the most fascinating developments as the concept of legalization becomes normalized, and it shows no signs of slowing down.

As marijuana moves into the mainstream, so too do growing techniques. For decades, underground black-market cultivators have bred for high amounts of tetrahydrocannabinol (THC) that provide the strongest high, whether that be a sedative body effect or a racing mental buzz. If something didn't get you "stoned," that would be the end of the line for that particular plant. Enter high-end testing laboratories with the onset of medical marijuana. Suddenly, scientists were finding cannabinoids (chemical compounds in weed) that were much more interesting than THC. The biggest cash cow in the industry was suddenly cannabidiol, or CBD, which showed a diverse range of medical applications as an antiemetic and anticonvulsant, among others. The only problem: it doesn't get you high. Growers had been axing the best medical marijuana plants for years.

What came next amounted to an arms race. With plants taking around four months from seed to smoke, finding CBD-rich strains of marijuana became paramount for those looking to jump into the emerging market. Some began tapping the industrial hemp market to find the compound, while others simply began testing their existing supply. One of the fastest to market, however, was Charlotte's Web, a type of marijuana named after the popular book as well as Charlotte Figi, a now 8-year-old girl who suffers from Dravet syndrome. It quickly became one of the most controversial.

In a nutshell, Dravet syndrome is characterized by a large number of epileptic seizures starting at about six months of age. Charlotte's parents heard of another child using medical marijuana to treat the symptoms and soon wound up working with Realm of Caring (ROC), a nonprofit based in Colorado that has a proprietary strain of high-CBD cannabis. They immediately noticed a dramatic decrease in the frequency of her seizures and improvement in her quality of life without the euphoria traditionally associated with weed. Soon, parents across the country were clamoring for similar strains to help their children. With limited supplies and communication issues at ROC, these recent transplants grew frustrated.

Other strains—with names like Cannatonic and Harlequin—began popping up, but few companies had the marketing resources and constant media attention to make them household names like Charlotte's Web. Families without access to or knowledge of these strains soon began lobbying for medical marijuana laws in their own state, but under a different guise than many: bills that would allow for CBD oil and not strains high in THC. The legislation, heralded by some, was decried by others as insufficient for many patients.

Dubbed "the entourage effect," advocates argue that we don't fully understand the interaction between various cannabinoids, including CBD and THC. Championed by Israeli researcher Raphael Mechoulam, this approach favors whole-plant medicine as opposed to isolated cannabinoids. Take, for instance, Marinol, the FDA-approved synthetic THC. While raw marijuana has never been directly attributed as a cause of death, Marinol has. Four times, in fact. Scientists believe there's a synergistic effect that isolated CBD alone cannot provide and CBD-only laws are a disservice to those who need medical cannabis.

That hasn't stopped the market from producing a wide variety of CBD products, many offering to ship across the nation because they claim to be derived from hemp. This remains a violation of the Controlled Substances Act, but patients with no other recourse are willing to take the risk, driving up prices for the limited supply. These companies are also in a bind as to

> Moving forward, whole-plant cannabis laws, including those around industrial hemp, are the only way to pave the road to the future. Otherwise, patients will continue to flock to legal states where they're left without a support system or resources. Will someone please think of the children?

how they can market their lines, with several receiving a February 2015 letter from the FDA warning about making claims of efficacy. "Consumers should beware purchasing and using any such products," the FDA noted. Of the product lines they tested, most came back with fractions of a percent of CBD. Patients were purchasing the equivalent of snake oil.

As with any nascent industry, there will be growing pains. New extraction methods, coupled with breeding projects, should help accelerate the process of finding medically appropriate strains for patients. For now, those in states with CBD-only legislation may find treatment insufficient and give up on marijuana altogether. Moving forward, whole-plant cannabis laws, including industrial hemp, are the only way to pave the road to the future. Otherwise, patients will continue to flock to legal states where they're left without a support system or resources. Will someone please think of the children?

REVIEW QUESTIONS

1. The authors make two arguments against the criminalization of marijuana. Summarize those arguments. Do you agree or disagree?
2. What are the long-term consequences of the war on drugs? Why do you think it has lost popularity in recent years?
3. What effect might legalization have on social inequality?

randy stoecker

community organizing and social change

winter 2009

community organizing became a lightning rod in the 2008 political campaign. its foundations in sociology are part of the reason why.

I t was 2008, early in the presidential campaign season. Everyone was talking about whether a woman or an African American would be the Democratic party nominee for president. And then they began talking about community organizing.

In the early days of the Democratic primary we learned that both Hillary Clinton and Barack Obama had connections to it. Clinton had written her undergraduate thesis on the famous community organizer Saul Alinsky. Obama had actually done it in Chicago through the Gamaliel Foundation, one of the national faith-based community organizing networks.

Obama's community organizing experience, described in his autobiography _Dreams from My Father_, became a lightning rod at the 2008 Republican National Convention where former New York City Mayor Rudolph Giuliani and Governor Sarah Palin mocked Obama and community organizing.

Community organizers responded—within days you could buy a T-shirt saying "Jesus was a community organizer. Pontius Pilate was a Governor." (Pontius Pilate, of course, was the public official said to have ordered the crucifixion of Jesus.) Networks grew across the country as community organizers and community organizing groups initiated a massive media strategy and registered voters by the hundreds of thousands. The Association of Community Organizations

for Reform Now (ACORN) alone registered more than 400,000 new voters and nearly 1 million others who had fallen off the rolls. Local community organizing groups in major cities each registered sometimes tens of thousands of voters.

Then came the Republican attacks on ACORN, one of the country's largest community organizing networks. ACORN's success at voter registration drives in swing states brought out the worst anti-democracy impulses from conservatives. In more than a dozen states right-wing politicians accused ACORN of voter registration fraud. Republican presidential candidate John McCain, in an impossibly bizarre attempt at misdirection, even charged ACORN with causing the global financial meltdown (ACORN had, in fact, identified predatory lending as a problem and began organizing against it more than a decade earlier).

ACORN fought back, and the GOP went down in defeat in virtually every battle, with their attempts to thwart voter registration turned back by courts, attorneys general and, increasingly, popular opinion.

And now, we have a president who is a community organizer. We could, perhaps, say "former" community organizer. But once you learn the craft of community organizing, and witness its ability to empower people, its spirit stays with you. It certainly has for Obama. Community organizing's democratic, and fundamentally sociological, impulses—understanding how power works and using that understanding to build the power of all the people—bring a sense of reward and satisfaction unmatched by other forms of political practice.

There's a great deal more to community organizing than Barack Obama and ACORN, however. At its root, community organizing isn't about big organizations or charismatic leaders, or even about specific political agendas or ideologies. Rather, it's about activating people at a local, neighborhood level to claim power and make change for themselves. It's the process by which grassroots organizations form and grow, their members develop leadership skills, and ordinary people learn to change social policy.

The belief is that poor and working-class people have been shut out from access to political and economic power because they haven't organized themselves in this way. Once they're organized, the theory goes, they'll have a voice in policy issues. Without community organizing, there are only fleeting demonstrations, isolated spokespeople, and top-down social policy.

the origins of organizing

Community organizing has been unique to the United States until recently when U.S.-style global capitalism downsized and eliminated government services in nation after nation and forced community-level responses. But in this country, Alexis de Tocqueville documented our foreparents' willingness to form voluntary organizations two centuries ago.

The founding of this country in opposition to central government and collective tax redistribution, by a relatively small group of people with exclusionary religious and cultural beliefs, in a very big space, provided fertile ground for a form of political action that focused on smaller community-based interest groups. The idea of bringing together like-minded neighbors to defend local space has remained ever since. And while the participatory impulses of community organizing now push it to be inclusive and democratic, its original populist underpinnings mean the craft is more anti-elitist than either conservative or progressive.

> Community organizing's democratic, and fundamentally sociological, impulses bring a sense of reward and satisfaction unmatched by other forms of political practice.

The power and presence of community organizing varies over time, as urban historian Robert Fisher explored in his book *Let the People Decide*. Working-class people forced to stand in bread lines during the Great Depression, African Americans responding to the ravages of segregation while their White neighbors enjoyed the expanding wealth of the late 1950s and 1960s, and urban neighborhood residents realizing that corporations and governments were disinvesting from their communities in the 1970s and 1980s were the source of the most powerful community organizing periods in the past century. But even during historical periods when not much appeared to be happening on the surface, community organizers were working behind the scenes in rural and urban communities across the nation.

The person most clearly associated with community organizing is Saul Alinsky, who helped build powerful neighborhood organizations, first in Chicago in 1939 and then across the nation into the 1970s. His influence extends to many of the community organizers working today, and he influenced the development of many of the community organizing networks—national organizations that support the development of thousands of neighborhood and community organizations across the country.

Those networks include Alinsky's own Industrial Areas Foundation (IAF), the Gamaliel Foundation, the PICO National Network, the Direct Action Research and Training Center (DART), the Midwest Academy, National People's Action (NPA), ACORN, and others. The list is split about evenly between those networks that are faith-based—relying on religious principles for their motivation and congregations for their participants—and secular networks such as ACORN, NPA, and the Midwest Academy.

In ACORN we see the other foundation of community organizing—the civil rights movement. While we best know the civil rights movement because of its large national events and its religious leaders, the movement was built by African-American community organizers such as Ella Baker in rural communities and urban neighborhoods across the southern United States. Myles Horton, the longtime leader and cofounder of the Highlander Folk School in Tennessee, was perhaps the crossing point between the Chicago influences that guided Alinsky and the southern civil rights movement.

Until today, the most successful recent community organizing period was in the 1970s when small neighborhood groups across the country began realizing banks weren't making loans in their communities. As they studied and fought against this practice of "redlining" they built a national movement that produced the federal Community Reinvestment Act. The result, by some estimates, was as much as $1 trillion of investment into poor and working-class communities across the country.

Today, there are community organizing groups in every state and every large city. Perhaps because of its local scale and methodological process, most scholars never judged community organizing interesting enough for serious study. So no one has counted all the groups, some of which come and go with the ebb and flow of issues and funding.

We know even less about the numbers of lives touched by those organizations. Many groups are part of one of the national community organizing networks, others operate independently. Many are informal groups composed of community members who have maybe never heard the term *community organizing*. We suspect the organizations number in the thousands and have hundreds of thousands, possibly millions, of members.

Despite these large numbers, community organizing didn't get the attention it deserved until the practice elected a community organizer as president of the United States. While nearly everyone knows something about the civil rights movement, and many have heard of Alinsky, few of us knew of any of the major community organizing networks until ACORN became so prominent this past election season.

Now we're finally understanding how powerful community organizing can be. Indeed, in many ways community organizing is the foundation of social change.

how it works

You may have encountered community organizers knocking on your door. They aren't the ones trying to convince you to adopt their religion, or give money and sign a petition, or vote for their candidate. They're the ones asking you about the most important issues in the community, and encouraging you to come to a meeting to talk about those issues. They want to know what you think and what issues you're willing to work on. They will definitely twist your arm—hard—to get you to contribute at least your time and maybe your money, too. But their main focus will be in getting you to work on issues you already care about. Of course, if you want to discriminate against gays and lesbians, oppose equal rights for all, or limit democracy to only the rich or educated, they won't work with you.

Their commitment, first and foremost, is to the expansion of democracy, and that's what leads those on the extreme right to fear them so much.

Consequently, individual community organizers are more likely to identify with the political left, because that's where they find the most sympathy for expanding democracy. But they also find themselves organizing in White working-class communities, where injecting progressive ideology into the process might get them booted from the neighborhood, and where community members often support discrimination. One of Alinsky's greatest disappointments was the racism practiced by his first, and most successful, community organizing effort in Chicago's Back of the Yards community. And community organizers today, such as Rinku Sen in her book *Stir It Up*, are asking whether some degree of ideology should help guide organizing.

But because community organizing groups focus on issues generated by their members from the ground up, they typically don't affiliate with political parties or strict ideological platforms that impose issues on them from the top down. Two slogans of community organizing show just how embedded the culture of populism is in the practice.

The first says "no permanent friends, no permanent enemies." In contrast to Giuliani's bluster at the Republican National Convention, in the documentary *The Democratic Promise* we see him promoting the efforts of East Brooklyn Congregations—a faith-based community organizing group—after the same film showed the previous Democratic mayor, Ed Koch, mocking them. The second slogan is "never do for anyone what they can do for themselves," which sounds as much like "pull yourselves up by your own bootstraps" as any conservative should want. The difference, of course, is that the organizer is there to help people develop their own strategy to demand and get boots.

In most cases, implementing these principles follows a common path. The community organizer enters the neighborhood and gets to know people. Some networks have a special name for this process—the one-to-one. In a one-to-one, the organizer talks with individuals in the community, learning how they feel about it, what issues they're passionate about, and what skills and resources they could contribute to an organizing effort. Sometimes the organizer also visits existing civic organizations and congregations.

You may have encountered community organizers knocking on your door. They're the ones asking you about the most important issues in the community.

At this point, they're organizing what historian Mary Beth Rogers described as cold anger in her book of the same name. This is the process of taking unfocused frustration and channeling it into social-change strategy. Hot anger is the anger of riots. Cold anger is rational anger, the anger of organizing.

Eventually, this process gives the organizer a sense of who the community leaders are—not the official leaders, but the actual leaders—and what the important issues are. Then they start organizing meetings in people's homes, church basements, or other places people gather. It's these places where most of the work of community organizing is actually done.

Those meetings lead to the selection of issues for the group to work on and the development of a strategy to work on them. In some communities that may be about trying to rid a park of gang violence, in others it may be about getting rid of an unwanted developer. The organizer's job is to help the group pick an issue they actually have some hope of winning, and then helping them develop a strategy for doing so. The group then initiates a campaign strategy around that issue, often involving some form of confrontation such as a large public meeting with a targeted corporate or public official. The group insists on a yes or no answer to very specific demands.

The goal is not just to win on the issue, but to build an organization that can win on other issues as well and become an institutionalized force in the political system. To this end, some community organizing groups hold large annual celebrations where they promote their past victories and prioritize their current issues.

organizing in action

Community organizing is guided by the principle "the people shall rule," and its task is to help the people not only gain power, but the skill to grow and use that power. Community organizers, with some exceptions, don't lead, they propel. The organizer is, in the best case, the expert who knows how to get people to a meeting, develop a strategy, and win a policy battle. But it's the people who come to that meeting who are supposed to choose the issue, develop a position on that issue, design a strategy, and lead the public effort.

An action training event led by Bertha Lewis, now ACORN's chief organizer, illustrates this process. Lewis and other ACORN organizers were part of a three-year project to build community organizing capacity in Toledo, Ohio, and they held monthly trainings the first year.

The day before this particular training she met with the leaders of two neighborhood organizations. Together they decided to focus the training around how to do a public action, and chose a local slumlord operating in both neighborhoods as the target.

The morning of the training Lewis brought together the neighborhood organizations' two dozen members to talk about the issue, come up with a position statement, and develop an action strategy—picketing the slumlord's suburban home. Then, everyone made signs and Lewis trained neighborhood people to lead all the important parts of the action. Someone would speak to the media, someone would lead the chants, someone would negotiate with the police if they came.

When the group left for the action, you could almost taste the tension and worry—it was the first time most of them had participated in a public action. Would they get arrested? Would they be slandered in the news? But they started picketing, negotiated the rules of peaceful protest with the police who arrived on the scene, were interviewed by the TV news, and they left with a new sense of power. It started out as just a training, but it launched a multiyear campaign that eventually helped shut down the slumlord's company.

In the early days of a community organizing effort like this one, the residents often don't know enough to sustain it without the organizer's help, just like they may not know enough to replace the shingles on their roof or repair their pipes without an expert to help. The organizer plays a much more prominent role in those early days. But unlike the roofer or plumber who does the work for you, the best organizers help you learn to do it yourself. In the best community organizing, it's the leaders—community residents—who give the news interviews, do the public speaking, and yell "Charge!" in the campaign.

building on the foundation

It's possible community organizing's new visibility will result in new resources, energy, and initiatives. There are now efforts through the National Organizers Alliance to channel former campaign organizers into community organizing. A newly revitalized community organizing practice may help turn the tide of a decaying polity and a corrupt economy, focusing especially on the poor and working class who lack access to the fundamentals of life itself—a living wage, an affordable mortgage, and health care.

These possibilities come with risks. Politicians don't necessarily have ideals and goals compatible with community organizing, and we don't know whether the office of president will influence Obama more than he can influence it.

Adding to this uncertainty, new initiatives have emerged posing as community organizing under labels such as consensus organizing, community building, or asset-based community development. Promoted by academics, foundation officials, and government officials, these models replace an understanding of oppressive social structures that divide the haves and have-nots with an assumption of common interests between them that will allow for conflict-free social change. Such an approach contains within it the threat of a renewed backlash against community organizing.

For community organizing to continue making meaningful contributions to broad-based empowerment and bottom-up social change, education about the realities of oppression and training in power-based community organizing strategies will be crucial. Most community organizing networks have to support their own organizer education programs, and in some cases that can mean only 10 days of training and an apprenticeship.

Our universities and colleges—and sociology departments—haven't been helpful in this regard. Community organizing courses don't exist on many college campuses, and the number of degree programs that focus on community organizing can be counted on two hands. This has long been the case. In fact, three main historical heroes of community organizing—Alinsky, Horton, and Jane Addams (who cofounded with Ellen Gates Starr the famous settlement house Hull House in Chicago)—studied with or were colleagues of the famous University of Chicago sociologists of their time. But none of them ever felt welcomed enough to make a career out of sociology or academia.

Perhaps now is the time to finally make that right. In the process, academics can begin to combine their efforts with community organizers and their grassroots leaders, replacing higher education's charity-based approach to service learning and civic engagement with a social justice approach that supports community organizing groups and helps secure the foundation for social change.

> A newly revitalized community organizing practice may help turn the tide of a decaying polity and a corrupt economy.

RECOMMENDED RESOURCES

COMM-ORG (Online Conference on Community Organizing). http://comm-org.wisc.edu.

> A website that assembles key works on community organizing from academics and practitioners, and offers a discussion list with more than 1,200 members.

Peter Dreier. 2008. "Shifting Gears: Transforming Obama's Campaign into a Movement for Change." *Huffington Post*, November 6.

> A sociological reflection on the role of community organizing in the Obama presidency by a prolific writer.

Robert Fisher. 1997. *Let the People Decide: Neighborhood Organizing in America.* Updated ed. New York: Twayne Publishers.

> A social history of community organizing in the United States.

Robert Kleidman. 2004. "Community Organizing and Regionalism." *City and Community* 3(4): 403–21.

> An analysis of the challenges of moving community organizing beyond local issues.

Aldon Morris. 1984. *The Origins of the Civil Rights Movement.* New York: Free Press.

> One of the few sociological studies of the civil rights movement from a community organizing point of view, focusing on the network of local organizations and strategies at the foundation of the movement.

Rinku Sen. 2003. *Stir It Up.* San Francisco: Jossey-Bass.

> Explores how to integrate racial–ethnic identity and ideology into community organizing, and move from local to larger issues.

REVIEW QUESTIONS

1. What is community organizing? How does it compare with other efforts to make social change in the world?
2. Several large companies and corporations have begun adopting the grassroots organizing tactics often seen in community organizing. Why do you think this is the case?
3. Activity: Understanding power—its uses and abuses—is essential to community organizing. Form small groups and discuss your opinions on the following statements:
   - Power corrupts.
   - Money is power.
   - Organizations that want to change things in their community should seek power.

richard alba

sacco and vanzetti and the immigrant threat   **54**

spring 2011

the anti-immigrant sentiment in america in the 1920s, exemplified by the case against sacco and vanzetti, provides a pertinent reminder of the power of nativism as an establishment faces threatening social changes.

ethal bombs exploding on American soil, suspicions about immigrant groups harboring terrorists, a drive to close the borders to unassimilable foreigners—this isn't just today, it's also the 1920s, a similar period of turmoil around immigration and the ethno-racial divisions that arise from it.

One case and two names symbolized the contradictions of the era for Americans in the '20s: Sacco and Vanzetti. Before two anarchist Italian immigrants were executed for their alleged involvement in a robbery and murder in South Braintree, Massachusetts (a suburb of Boston), their case became a cause célèbre among Americans, divided by their views of the men's guilt or innocence.

Nine decades on, we can look back at this case to recognize how easily justice is perverted by the intensifying perception of immigrants as "enemies" of American institutions. These perceptions are vulnerable to exploitation in uncertain times like the immediate post–World War I period. Then, as now, some immigrant groups were widely believed to be inferior to ordinary White Americans and unsuitable for assimilation into the mainstream.

nativism

By World War I, decades of mass immigration to the United States—the zenith was the first decade of the century—had produced a huge population of foreign origin. The twentieth-century high-water mark for immigrants in the population, 15 percent, was reached in 1910. In the largest American cities outside the South, immigrants and the second generation (those who'd grown up in immigrant homes) made up the majority of residents.

World War I triggered profound anxieties about the foreign born. Americans worried that immigrant communities from countries that were now enemy powers could shelter conspiratorial groups that would bring the war to the homeland through sabotage and propaganda. Just as is true today, native-born Americans thought language marked distance from the mainstream; a number of states passed laws to ban the teaching of foreign languages, particularly German.

The war ushered in a period of superpatriotism, when "100 percent Americanism" became the slogan of the day and the federal government passed laws to suppress and punish dissent. After the war ended, anxieties focused, during the Red Scare of 1919–20, on political radicals and labor organizers. Again, immigrant communities appeared in the crosshairs, and Attorney General A. Mitchell Palmer ordered raids on foreign-born radicals for the purpose of deportation. Anarchist groups, often anchored among Italian communities, responded with bombing campaigns, one of which reached the front steps of Palmer's Washington, D.C., residence.

Such events lent momentum to the long-term drive to limit immigration, especially for groups viewed as undesirable according to their race, religion, or national origin. Scientific racism, then widely accepted by even educated Americans, provided the theories and evidence (collected, in part, with the newly developed IQ test) to regard most of the recently immigrated groups as inherently inferior.

Asians had already been mostly eliminated from the immigrant stream (starting with the Chinese Exclusion Act of 1882), but now the targets became the heavily Catholic and Jewish immigrants from southern and eastern Europe. The Ku Klux Klan revived in the early 1920s, this time in northern cities, as Protestant Whites mobilized against the interlopers. In 1921 and 1924, Congress passed immigration laws that, "at long last" in the eyes of many native-born Americans, shut the golden door to the United States. These laws stipulated nationality quotas that discriminated against southern and eastern Europeans. The Italians, the most numerous of the immigrant groups, saw their annual limit for entrants set at less than 6,000, about 3 percent of the 200,000 newcomers they'd averaged in the early years of the century.

enter sacco and vanzetti

In April 1920, a gang pulled off a brazen robbery outside a South Braintree shoe factory. Two bandits gunned down the payroll master and his guard as they walked down the street, shooting the guard repeatedly from close range in an apparent execution. A car with three other men raced in to pick up the gunmen and their loot (almost $16,000) and sped away. The crime played out in full view of numerous witnesses.

The Sacco and Vanzetti case suggests how easily justice is perverted by the perception of immigrants as "enemies."

A few weeks later, two different plotlines intersected when police in a nearby town arrested Nicola Sacco and Bartolomeo Vanzetti, both carrying loaded revolvers on a streetcar. The men were part of a small contingent of Italian-born anarchists who were out that evening in an unsuccessful attempt to pick up and hide materials belonging to their group. Leaflets? Dynamite? No one knows for sure, but they were acting out of fear that the group had been fingered by two New York anarchists who'd been detained and interrogated for weeks by the Bureau of Investigation (the forerunner of the FBI). The police for their part had set a trap for anarchists they suspected of the South Braintree crime and of a failed Christmas Eve robbery in nearby Bridgewater.

Sacco and Vanzetti were exhibited to numerous witnesses of the crimes, most of whom failed to recognize them. Still believing they'd been arrested for their anarchism and wanting to protect their comrades, the men gave false and evasive answers to police questions. Later, this behavior was viewed in court as betraying "consciousness of guilt" and weighed heavily against them. In the event, the local police chief, Michael Stewart, a key player in the drama to come, was certain that he had his men and convinced the district attorney, Frederick Katzmann, to prosecute. Sacco and Vanzetti were trapped in a vise that would tighten relentlessly until they were dead.

Vanzetti went on trial first, for the Bridgewater robbery. (Sacco could not be tried for this crime because he could prove that he was at work when it occurred.) The trial foretold what was to come. Eyewitness testimony placing Vanzetti at the scene was thin, and his defense presented numerous Italian witnesses who said that he was elsewhere that day, selling eels, a customary Christmas Eve food in Italian families. But the alibi testimony, often requiring translation into English, counted for little, as the district attorney deployed courtroom tricks, asking the Italian witnesses to recall their experiences on randomly chosen dates to undermine their reliability. Vanzetti was convicted, and Judge Webster Thayer, who'd preside at the next trial as well, sentenced him to an exceptionally long period in prison—12 to 15 years—for the failed robbery.

The next trial, for the South Braintree robbery and murders, would make world history. Against Sacco, district attorney Katzmann presented a series of eyewitnesses who identified him as a gunman (the jury was not told about the more numerous witnesses who'd *not* recognized Sacco as one of the bandits). The courtroom testimony often deviated from what the witnesses had told investigators shortly after the crimes, and the defense tried its best to highlight the contradictions. Sacco's alibi, that he'd been in Boston attempting to secure an Italian passport to return home, was supported by defense witnesses and the affidavit of an Italian consular official. But his fate was sealed by ballistics tests that purported to show that a bullet from his gun had killed the guard.

Against Vanzetti, the evidence was much weaker. No witnesses placed him at the crime scene, though a few claimed to have seen him subsequently in the getaway car. The prosecution presented the theory that the gun in his possession when he was arrested had been taken from the dying guard. His alibi was that he was on the streets hawking fish that day, but the claim was hard to prove.

Though the evidence on which the trial turned has been analyzed and disputed ever since, the jury took just three hours to convict the two men of a capital crime. The verdict did not end the drama; it merely brought down the curtain on the first act. Between the close of the trial in July 1921 and the execution of the two

men in August 1927 lay six long years of appeals, controversy over their guilt and the fairness of the trial, and national and international mobilization on their behalf.

In those years, the defense filed multiple motions for new trials, which were heard and rejected by Judge Thayer and higher courts as well. In 1926, Herbert Ehrmann, a defense lawyer who would devote his life to the case, assembled evidence that a known Providence, Rhode Island, criminal gang, the Morellis, had carried out the crime. The possibility of a new trial was rejected again.

Appeals exhausted, Judge Thayer finally imposed the mandatory sentence of death in the spring of 1927. All hope was not yet extinguished, though: the governor could grant clemency. But, wary of acting on such a controversial case, he asked a three-man committee of luminaries, including the presidents of Harvard and MIT, to review it. Though they listened to extensive presentations from the defense, even evidence about the alternative theory of the crime, their report found the trial fair and the original verdict correct, thus paving the way for the executions.

closing ranks

The Sacco and Vanzetti case shows how an ethnically unified establishment can close ranks against outsiders, especially against those who are viewed as social and moral inferiors. In the process, those with power can pervert justice, acting in ways that they would probably condemn in others, but viewing their own actions as morally justified. One of the defenses frequently offered on behalf of those who sent Sacco and Vanzetti to their deaths is that they were "honorable" men, incapable of the perversions of justice that are apparent in retrospect (such as the subornation of perjury by the prosecution). Honorable they may have been, but when facing what they view as a crisis, those in power will generally do what they deem necessary to protect an established order in which they occupy positions of privilege.

None of the establishment actors from Sacco and Vanzetti's case escapes with honor intact. Not only did the prosecution put eyewitnesses on the stand who gave trial testimony that deviated considerably from what they'd previously told investigators, but some were explicitly coached to tailor their testimony to the prosecution's case. For instance, a shipping clerk appeared as a prosecution witness to tell about his observation of the getaway car loitering on a nearby street hours before the robbery, but he was urged to omit mention of a second car, whose driver appeared to be in communication with the other. Two cars might have suggested a more professional operation than immigrant anarchists were capable of mounting.

One of the most devastating misrepresentations involved Vanzetti. The theory presented to the jurors that the pistol in his possession had been taken from the dying guard was known by prosecutors to be false by the time of the trial. When the police records of the case were unsealed a half century later, the files of Michael Stewart, the police chief, revealed that his men had uncovered the original sales record for the guard's gun, which proved it wasn't the gun found on Vanzetti.

Prosecutor Katzmann's final remark had addressed the jurors as native-born Americans: "Stand together you men of Norfolk." And stand together they did. Interviewed many years later, they were unwavering in their views of the case and refused to consider the possibility that prejudice of any sort played a role in their deliberations. Yet they took remarkably little time to convict two men of a capital crime, even though the evidence was

contradictory and against Vanzetti, meager. (And sometimes ludicrous, as when one witness who claimed to have seen Vanzetti in the getaway car also stated that Vanzetti had yelled a warning in idiomatic, unaccented English. Vanzetti, like Sacco, spoke a stilted English with a strong accent.)

The role of Judge Thayer was controversial even at the time. Some observers recalled an icy courtroom atmosphere, where the hostility toward immigrants was almost palpable. The judge's contempt for the defense's lead lawyer, Fred Moore, was undisguised. Thayer had asked to preside at the South Braintree case, and he heard and rejected all of the appeals. His hostile attitudes burst through in private comments that were made public. At one of his clubs, he opined, "These two men are anarchists; they are guilty. . . . They are not getting a fair trial but I am working it so their counsel will think they are."

Then there's the governor's committee of advisors, who lent their prestige to a dubious verdict. Its three members, including Harvard's president, Abbott Lawrence Lowell, knew their review was the final step before execution, and seemed to take their responsibility seriously (they rebuked Judge Thayer for breaching the neutrality of his role with prejudiced outbursts, for instance). In the end, though they may have had reservations about the case, they stood with the establishment. Their hesitant conclusion about Vanzetti expresses the awkwardness of their position: "On the whole, we are of the opinion that Vanzetti also was guilty beyond reasonable doubt."

These indictments of establishment actors don't mean that Sacco and Vanzetti lacked for influential supporters. The case became a cause célèbre, both in the United States and abroad. Prominent among the supporters were radicals like Moore, who, as the lead defense lawyer

> Between the close of the trial and the execution lay six long years of appeals, controversy, and international mobilization.

during the trial, helped to raise the profile of the case to the international plane. Also flocking to their cause were intellectuals such as the novelist Upton Sinclair and the poet Edna St. Vincent Millay. In addition, members of minority groups, such as the Jewish future Supreme Court Justice, Felix Frankfurter, then a Harvard professor, made common cause with the two Italian immigrants. Upper-class Boston women, perhaps conscious of their recent suffrage struggle, supported the men with jail visits and English lessons.

Others saw the case as a test of the American system. After Moore left the case due to a dispute with Sacco, the two men were represented by the Brahmin lawyer William Thompson, who was convinced of the men's innocence. Harvard's president Lowell was harassed by alumni for linking the university's name to what they perceived as a miscarriage of justice. Many ordinary Americans were skeptical of the trial and the verdicts; on the night of the executions, men and women kept vigil throughout the world.

were they guilty anyway?

One hindsight defense of the Sacco and Vanzetti trial is that, though the judicial process may have been highly imperfect, it got the right men: Sacco and Vanzetti were guilty, or, in another version, only Sacco was. Some present-day conservatives, such as commentator Ann Coulter, deride the notion of Sacco and Vanzetti's innocence as yet another liberal delusion.

Without question, Sacco and Vanzetti *were* militant anarchists. They belonged to a group that preached violence against capitalism and the state, but the two men did not come to the United States as anarchists. Like thousands of other Italian immigrants at the time, they were radicalized by the harsh conditions under which they labored and lived and the discriminatory treatment they received at the hands of many native-born White Americans. They knew men who planted bombs, sometimes with lethal consequences. One of their friends, perhaps stumbling as he carried his bomb to Attorney General Palmer's house, blew himself up in front of it. Yet there is no indication that Sacco and Vanzetti participated in bombings.

The weight of the evidence speaks against the guilt of either man when it comes to the crimes for which they were convicted and executed. This evidence is negative in part, consisting of questions that, implausibly, have no answer. For one thing, no trace of the stolen money was ever found, though police went to great lengths, even asking Italian authorities to search the trunks of an immigrant anarchist who left the United States shortly after the robbery. Nor did the anarchist groups connected to Sacco and Vanzetti, which had been infiltrated by the authorities, show any sudden cash infusions. The failure to find the money strongly suggests the police were looking in the wrong place.

The accomplices in the robbery were never identified either. The anarchists in Sacco and Vanzetti's circle were investigated by the police, who initially believed they'd stumbled on a criminal band. However, no one else was ever tried for the South Braintree crime (and historians sifting the evidence have subsequently ruled out most of these men as potential participants). Moreover, the group involved in the crime was likely larger than the five bandits observed fleeing the scene (a second car was almost certainly involved in the getaway). This level of organization suggests a gang of professionals (as the Bureau of Investigation believed at the time), not an opportunistic handful of radicals.

There can be little doubt about Vanzetti's innocence. The evidence against him is so paltry

---

Nativism's powers are contingent, vulnerable to shifts in the social landscape.

---

that there's simply no reason to connect him to the South Braintree crime. Sacco remains the hard case, and his guilt or innocence can probably never be established in a way that will convince everyone. The ballistic evidence presented at trial has withstood the newer technologies that have been applied to it. That is, the bullet that was alleged to have mortally wounded the guard was fired, we can now be certain, by Sacco's gun.

However, the problems with the conclusion that he was guilty lie with everything else. Sacco was a family man with young children; by the time of the South Braintree robberies, he was a skilled worker earning good pay and with a considerable sum of money in the bank. He lived next door to his Irish-American employer, whose trust in him was not ended by the criminal charges. He had a credible alibi for the time of the crime, supported by an Italian consular official. Why would such a man engage in this sort of crime? Why would his anarchist comrades, some of whom were unmarried and had less to lose, bring him into the risky enterprise and give him the role of gunman?

If Sacco was innocent, then someone tampered with the ballistic evidence. There's a plausible case to be made here. A scrupulous analysis of the trial evidence by historians William Young and David Kaiser (in their book, *Postmortem*) found the bullets presented by the prosecution conflicted with eyewitness testimony—supposedly only one bullet came from Sacco's gun, though every witness reported the gunman firing several shots at the guard from close range. Even Young and Kaiser, though, can't explain convincingly how a bullet substitution could have been carried out.

past to present

Among other things, the Sacco and Vanzetti case illustrates the power of nativism in the hands of an establishment facing threatening social changes. One strategy its members pursue to protect position and privilege involves brightening the boundary between the mainstream and ethno-racial outsiders, highlighting that "they" are not "us." This is most effective when the boundary is already visible and legitimate to the broad majority population. The boundary that in the early twentieth century kept southern and eastern Europeans from easy access to the mainstream entailed social distinctions, including religious ones, with deep roots in American history and identity.

The nativism of today exhibits similar features. As was true a century ago, immigration is bringing about social changes that seem threatening to many majority Americans. The analogy is especially strong in terms of demographic shift: a hundred years ago, the changes threatened the position of Protestants of northern and western European ancestry; today, it's the position of a broader group of White Americans that is challenged. The tropes of criminality and threat to American institutions are as vital to nativism today as in the past. They're most potent when invoked in relation to already salient social distinctions, such as that between immigrant Latinos and native Anglos in the Southwest. The response of many majority Americans has been to support measures that place large portions of the immigrant population under suspicion and state surveillance, exemplified in the extreme by Arizona's 2010 law empowering local police to detain those they suspect are unauthorized immigrants.

Yet, in the midst of a period of intense nativism, it's easy to exaggerate the power of an establishment, and of the majority group more generally, and impose an enduring, inferior status on minorities. That view can lead to a mistaken emphasis on social reproduction at the expense of opportunities for change. In the case of the Italians, within three decades of the Sacco and Vanzetti case, they were well on their way to mass entry into the mainstream. That a minority group deemed inferior in the first half of a century could become part of the majority during the second half demonstrates that the exclusionary power of an establishment is not unlimited.

A repetition of mid-twentieth-century mass assimilation is not in the cards, at least for the foreseeable future, but the determinative power of today's nativism may also turn out to be limited. The most critical factor will be the demographically driven transition to a more diverse society that is already underway. It will likely offer opportunities to alter the balance of power in American society: that is, because of the shrinking number of White Americans in young age groups, the United States of the near future will almost certainly depend on young people from immigrant backgrounds to assume positions of leadership in the labor force and elsewhere. How this transition plays out, on the ground in everyday relationships as well as in the economy and the polity, will do much to determine the exclusionary—or inclusive—force of twenty-first-century ethno-racial boundaries.

The ultimate significance of the Sacco and Vanzetti case remains as paradoxical as some of the events themselves. While the men's fate demonstrates that nativism can even assume life-and-death powers, the subsequent integration of Italians reminds us that its powers are contingent, vulnerable to shifts in the social landscape and to the resistance of anti-nativists. This gives a new twist to the eloquent epitaph spoken by Vanzetti to a journalist a few months before the executions: "If it had not been for these thing, I might have live out of my life talking at street corners to scorning men. I might have die, unmarked, unknown, a failure. Now we are not a failure. This is our career and our triumph. Never in our full life can we hope to do such work for tolerance, for justice, for man's understanding of man as now we do by our dying."

RECOMMENDED RESOURCES

Paul Avrich. 1991. *Sacco and Vanzetti: The Anarchist Background.* Princeton: Princeton University Press.

> An in-depth portrait of radicalism among early-twentieth-century Italian immigrants.

Leo Chavez. 2008. *The Latino Threat.* Stanford: Stanford University Press.

> An analysis of the construction of American xenophobia toward Mexicans, the most numerous of today's immigrants.

Samuel P. Huntington. 2004. *Who Are We?* New York: Simon & Schuster.

> A demonstration that nativism has contemporary, establishment supporters.

Leo Lucassen. 2005. *The Immigrant Threat: The Integration of Old and New Migrants in Western Europe since 1850.* Urbana–Champaign: University of Illinois Press.

> A masterful analysis of the historical continuities of nativism in the European context.

Peter Schrag. 2010. *Not Fit for Our Society.* Berkeley: University of California Press.

> A narrative that convincingly links the nativism of earlier eras to the present.

Bruce Watson. 2007. *Sacco and Vanzetti.* New York: Viking.

> An excellent account of the Sacco and Vanzetti case, with useful references.

REVIEW QUESTIONS

1. Explain nativism.
2. How does nativity interact with race and ethnicity?
3. How were American institutions at play in the Sacco and Vanzetti case? Which institutions, and why?
4. What implications does the Sacco and Vanzetti case have for the United States today?

viewpoints

fifty years of "new" immigration   **55**

spring 2015

the articles in this forum discuss the legacy of the immigration and nationality act of 1965. readers can learn about (1) how the act led to expected and unexpected demographic shifts; (2) the effects of the act on the selectivity of asian immigrants; (3) the precarious status of the mexican-american middle class; (4) the unintended consequence of increasing undocumented mexican immigrants; and (5) the myths of feminization of immigrants.

shehzad nadeem

My father arrived in New York City in 1970 from Pakistan with only a few things: a suitcase, his green card in an officially sealed envelope, and a hand-woven rug he could sell if he needed some extra money. He had no immediate job prospects and slept in the alcove of his brother's Queens apartment. What he *did* have was a master's degree in physics and experience working in a bank, and it wasn't long before he got a $10,000 salary as a computer programmer for a marine insurance underwriter near Wall Street. Once settled, my mother came to join him. Some years and some jobs later, they had two kids, raising us in Virginia.

My parents arrived after the passage of the federal Immigration and Nationality Act of 1965, also known as the Hart-Cellar Act. The act replaced national-origin quotas, intended in large part to ensure a Euro-American majority, and aimed to attract skilled labor and reunite families. It opened the doors to immigrants from Asia, Africa, and Latin America and drastically altered the country's demographic complexion. In the case at hand, only 2,500 Pakistani immigrants entered the United States between 1947 and 1965. By 1990, there were about 100,000 Pakistani Americans. By 2005, their population had grown to 210,000.

The census did not have a category for Pakistanis. They were considered East Indians but counted as White. Pakistanis' particular ethnic threads had yet to be woven into the American fabric, and people struggled to make sense of us. In the South, my parents were greeted with surprise over their "good English" and education. After a history class on segregation in grade school, a blond, blue-eyed classmate mentioned that, if Jim Crow laws were still in place, I'd have to use a "colored bathroom." In junior high in the 1990s, a close friend's mother told me over supper that I was "mostly White" (her husband objected half-heartedly, noting that we had different foods and traditions). Dubious though her words may sound, the message acknowledged a demographic reality: the neighborhood, town, and county were mostly White. Apparently, so was I. In high school, I'd find even a guy who had become a Neo-Nazi still thought we could be friends (as did the White, hip-hop-loving bully who fended off the Neo-Nazi in exchange for me doing his art homework).

Since that time, successive immigration waves have further enhanced northern Virginia's ethnic and racial diversity. Where the presence of families like my own once seemed anomalous, now it is rather commonplace. Students from up to 200 countries now attend local schools. And more broadly, in three decades, non-Hispanic Whites are expected to be a minority in Virginia, and in the country as a whole. These shifts speak to the broader changes in American life that the 1965 act inaugurated.

The following articles discuss the legacy of the 1965 act. John Skrentny looks back at the passage of the act, and suggests that supporters must have had some inkling of the demographic revolution it would engender. In a very quiet way, it marked a shift toward democratic values in immigration policy.

Jennifer Lee punctures the myth of model minorities. She finds that Asian immigrants tend to be very well educated compared to those from other regions. This relative advantage—not unique cultural traits—she argues, are responsible for their relative prosperity.

Jody Vallejo writes about the impact of the act on Mexican migrants who now faced a restrictive hemispheric cap. This led to emergence of unauthorized Mexican migration due to the United States' increasing unmet demand for low-wage labor. It left migrants in a legal limbo. Likewise, Zulema Valdez writes that, while the act improved on the overtly racist policies of the past, it still carried nativist and illiberal traces evidenced in the increased surveillance, detentions, deportations, and maltreatment of guest workers.

Finally, Donna Gabaccia considers the moral panic that ensued upon discovery that more women than men were entering the United States. Fears of immigrant dependency circulated, suggesting that women would take more than they contributed (not least by having children).

john d. skrentny

did congress vote for whites to become a minority?

Many of the arguments we'll hear this year about the 50th anniversary of the Immigration Act of 1965 are likely to focus on demographics. Since the act ended national origin and race quotas Congress had established in the 1920s to favor northern and western Europeans, America's demographic shifts have been nothing short of remarkable: non-Latino Whites are already a minority in America's most populous state (California) and are headed for that status nationwide.

This leads to an obvious question: Did Congress *intend* for this result when it eliminated the quotas? The answer is "maybe." Members of Congress and President Lyndon Johnson expected change, though they hardly discussed the expected pace and magnitude. This lack of debate on the question of demographic transformation is fascinating—and puzzling—when considered from 2015.

In 1965, Latinos comprised around 5 percent of the U.S. population, Asian Americans less than 1 percent, and African Americans 11 percent. Whites (I refer to non-Latino Whites whenever I say "Whites") made up the rest: 83 percent of the people in the United States. By 2010, Latinos had overtaken African Americans as the largest minority group, at about 16 percent of the population. African Americans had increased their share to 13 percent, and Asian Americans had become the *fastest*-growing group at nearly 6 percent. Among young people, these percentages are considerably higher, and, of course, there is a rapidly growing percentage of Americans of mixed backgrounds. Whites' percentage of the population has fallen about 20 percent since the Immigration Act passed.

Is this what Congress and President Lyndon Johnson intended in 1965? Regarding Asian immigration, the conventional wisdom is that no one foresaw the rapid rise. However, archival and interview research by legal scholar Gabriel Chin has shown conclusively that the increase was no surprise to many supporters of the bill. In public statements and later reflections, they stated that more visas meant that more Asians would come to the United States. They knew that they were legislating a greater Asian presence in the American cultural mosaic.

The reason these statements are not more prominent in the historical memory is that supporters appeared to strategically downplay any effects on Asian immigration so as not to inflame the passions of immigration opponents. For example, Mike Masaoka of the Japanese Americans Citizens League noted that the law reserved the great majority of visas for relatives of current U.S. citizens. This was important because there were so few Asian Americans, so "the very arithmetic of past immigration now precludes any substantial gain in actual immigration opportunities for the Japanese, Chinese and other Asians." Yet Masaoka knew the end of racist quotas would still be a boon to Asian immigration, and he strongly supported the bill.

The story is different regarding Latino immigration. The 1965 law introduced a new *limit* on immigration from Latin America.

Supporters traded a western hemispheric quota of 120,000 to eliminate the discrimination against Asian and Eastern and Southern European migrants. An internal memo told Johnson that Michael Feighan (D-OH), chair of the House Immigration Subcommittee,

> appears to be looking for a way to justify a vote to abolish the national origins system. The justification has to make sense to the traditional supporters of the national origins system (veterans groups, patriotic societies, conservative nationality groups, etc.), whom Mr. Feighan regards as his constituency. He wants to be able to say that in return for scrapping the national origins system—which never really worked anyway—he has gotten a system that for the first time in our history puts a limit on *all* immigration, not just immigration from "quota" areas.

Supporters of the bill, including Johnson, went along.

Latino immigration increased after 1965 for a variety of reasons, many noted by Frank Bean and his colleagues. These include sinking White birth rates and economic restructuring that created great demand for both low- and high-skilled immigrant workers, including undocumented workers. Meanwhile, European immigration flows receded as European economies grew while European immigrant birth rates declined. These dynamics were unanticipated, yet the lack of debate around the demographic implications of the law at the time is striking from the perspective of the twenty-first century.

For example, in my research in the Johnson Library, I found no serious White House discussion of the law's impacts. The Johnson administration discussed it in terms of foreign policy or logrolling strategy in Congress. In

In President Johnson's discussion of the historic law in his memoirs—well, there isn't one. There isn't even an index entry for "immigration."

Johnson's discussion of the historic law in his memoirs—well, there isn't one. He says nothing about it at all. There isn't even an index entry for "immigration."

Gabriel Chin concludes that 1965 was truly a moment of egalitarian principles in politics. He writes, "Knowing that non-Whites would be likely to take advantage of the equalized opportunities, Congress passed the law anyway." Whether egalitarian principles will guide congressional majorities today remains to be seen as immigration continues to dominate debate.

jennifer lee

how hyper-selectivity drives asian americans' educational outcomes

The passage of the Immigration and Nationality Act in 1965 was a watershed moment for Asian immigration. By replacing national origins with a system that privileged family reunification and high-skilled applicants, the change ushered in a new stream of Asian immigrants with a markedly different profile. A century ago, Asians in the United States were poorly educated, low-skilled, low-wage laborers described as "undesirable immigrants" full of "filth and disease." Confined to crowded ethnic enclaves, they were denied the right to citizenship and even intermarriage with citizens. Today, Asian Americans are the most highly educated, least residentially segregated, and the group most likely to intermarry in the country. Driving the transformation was the change in selectivity of Asian immigration. Contemporary Asian immigrants who arrived after 1965 are, on average, highly selected, meaning that they are more highly educated than their ethnic counterparts who did not immigrate.

Not only did the 1965 act alter the selectivity of Asian immigrants, but it also fueled the rise in the Asian-American population. In 1970, Asians comprised only 0.7 percent of the U.S. population, but today they account for nearly 6 percent. Asians are the fastest-growing group in the country, and demographers project that, by 2050, Asians will make up close to 10 percent of the population.

Nationwide percentages pale in comparison to the percentage of Asian Americans in the country's most competitive magnet high schools and elite universities. Among the students offered admissions to New York City's famed Stuyvesant High School in the fall of 2014, more than 70 percent were Asian, 20 percent White, and less than 10 percent Other. Asian Americans typically comprise about one-fifth of the entering classes at Ivy League universities and, at the University of California's flagship campus, Berkeley, they make up more than 40 percent.

Vexed by Asian Americans' exceptional educational outcomes, some pundits have pointed to Asian culture: because Asian Americans possess the "right" cultural traits and value education, they outperform their non-Asian peers, including native-born Whites. However, it is worth remembering that Asian culture was not always hailed as exceptional; less than a century ago, Asians were described as "marginal members of the human race" and "unassimilable." Moreover, reducing educational outcomes to cultural traits and values is nothing more than reframing the "culture of poverty" thesis into a "culture of success" antithesis.

Missing from the cultural values argument are two key elements: "hyper-selectivity" and "starting points."

If we examine the three largest East Asian immigrant groups in the United States—Chinese, Vietnamese, and Koreans—we find that each is highly selected from its country of origin. More than half (56 percent) of Korean immigrants have a bachelor's degree or higher, compared to only 36 percent of adults in Korea. The degree of selectivity is even greater among Vietnamese immigrants; more than one-quarter (26 percent) have at least a bachelor's degree, while the comparable figure among adults in Vietnam is 5 percent. Chinese immigrants are the most highly selected: 51 percent have graduated from college, compared to only 4 percent of adults in China. U.S. Chinese immigrants are more than twelve times as likely to have graduated from college than Chinese adults who did not emigrate.

> Reducing educational outcomes to cultural traits and values is nothing more than reframing the "culture of poverty" thesis into a "culture of success" antithesis.

Furthermore, Chinese and Korean immigrants are more highly educated than the general U.S. population, 28 percent of whom have graduated from college. This dual positive immigrant selectivity is what Min Zhou and I refer to as "hyper-selectivity." The hyper-selectivity of Chinese and Korean immigrants in the United States means that their 1.5- and second-generation children begin their quest to get ahead from more favorable "starting points" than the children of other immigrant groups, like Mexicans, as well as native-born groups, including Whites.

Hyper-selectivity benefits all members of an immigrant group, because these groups are more likely to generate "ethnic capital," which manifests into ethnic institutions like after-school academies and SAT prep courses that support academic achievement. The courses range in price tags (some are freely available through ethnic churches), so they are often accessible to the children of working-class Chinese and Korean immigrant parents. Hence, the hyper-selectivity of an immigrant group can assuage a child's poor socioeconomic status (SES) and reduce class differences within an ethnic group. In turn, this produces stronger educational outcomes than would have been predicted based on parental SES alone.

While some pundits argue that there is something intrinsic about Asian cultural traits or values that explain their exceptional educational outcomes, this argument is as flawed and reductive as the "culture of poverty" argument sociologists debunked decades ago. Instead, the change in U.S. immigration law half a century ago, coupled with the resulting change in selectivity of Asian immigration, explain Asian Americans' educational outcomes.

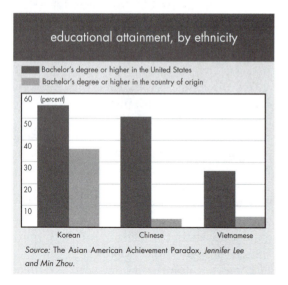

educational attainment, by ethnicity

■ Bachelor's degree or higher in the United States
■ Bachelor's degree or higher in the country of origin

Source: The Asian American Achievement Paradox, *Jennifer Lee and Min Zhou.*

jody agius vallejo

silva letters and the mexican-american middle class

Despite its liberalizing reputation, the 1965 Immigration Act was extremely restrictive for Mexicans. They now had to enter within narrow hemispheric quotas that did not adequately satiate our country's demand for low-wage labor, ushering in an era of large-scale, unauthorized Mexican migration. But there was one avenue by which unauthorized Mexican migrants could regularize their status: those with U.S.-born children could file for legal permanent residency under the family reunification clause.

This route emerged time and time again in my research on the Mexican-American middle class. A number of my respondents who had been raised in middle-class households insisted that their parents successfully attained legal residency, and eventually citizenship, after having children on U.S. soil. I eventually found Terry Feiertag, a Chicago immigration lawyer who, in the 1960s and 1970s, processed these "baby" cases. Feiertag relayed: "What happened is you gave birth, you sent the birth certificate to the U.S. Consulate, and that gave you your ticket in line to get an immigrant visa. Tons of undocumented people were living here, giving birth, registering."

This path to authorization helped hasten Mexican-American mobility into the middle class, allowing parents to obtain stable jobs or open businesses. Many purchased homes in middle-class neighborhoods; some found their higher economic status allowed them to send their children to private schools.

The "baby" provision was not unprecedented, as federal statutes provided similar avenues for legalization under the Alien Registration Act of 1940, but it was revoked in December 1976, when the 1965 act was revised. The Western Hemispheric quotas decreased from 120,000 a year to 20,000 per country per year. Those who had been on the list to legalize under their native-born children were immediately served deportation orders. Concurrently, Feiertag discovered that the State Department had wrongfully issued nearly 150,000 visas to Cuban refugees under the original Western Hemispheric quotas. Feiertag and his co-counsel filed a class-action lawsuit, _Silva v. Levi_, on behalf of those who had been in line for a visa prior to December 1976. They successfully argued for an injunction against the deportations.

As Feiertag recalls: "Part of the injunction was that anyone who had this ticket in line could go into a district office, present their letter of registration, and get a notice—what came to be known as the Silva Letters—saying you have the right to be here and to work. . . . My guess is that 500,000 people all over the country who had been chased by deportation officers were now given permission to remain. These letters allowed for mortgages and jobs and many, many once-undocumented immigrants, who now had this in-between status, were able to lead regular, middle-class lives."

This forgotten moment in our immigration history is particularly important considering Obama's recent executive order, Deferred Action for Parental Accountability (DAPA), which would provide deportation relief and work

> To grow the middle class, we need a comprehensive policy that will turn eligible immigrant parents—_and_ those who remain unconnected to native-born children—into American citizens.

permits to certain unauthorized parents of U.S. citizens and legal permanent residents. Like those before them, DAPA-eligible immigrant families will likely increase their economic status. But what will happen once their temporary protected status runs out after three years?

Protection under the Silva Letters lasted until December 1981. As Feiertag told me, "You had this built-in qualifying cohort. . . . What were you going to do with them when the injunction ran out? You said it was OK to set up your life . . . and now you were going to say, OK, go?" The Letters thus provided pressure for a pathway to legalization, eventually granted under the 1986 Immigration Reform and Control Act (IRCA). Under IRCA, unauthorized migrants who had been living in the United States since before January 1, 1982 (nearly the same date that the Silva injunction ran out) were able to legalize their status.

IRCA allowed more than 2 million immigrants to legalize their status, and the benefits of this legalization are significant. For example, research shows that the children of parents who remain unauthorized obtain lower levels of education than those whose are able to legalize.

It is ironic how history repeats itself. Like the Silva Letters, DAPA provides an in-between status that relieves the fear associated with deportation and will likely allow parents to obtain better jobs. DAPA does not go far enough, though. Parents will continue to lack the benefits associated with citizenship that might prompt a more direct path into the middle class. We stand at the precipice of another opportunity to create more American citizens who can make important social and economic contributions to our society. As we approach the fiftieth anniversary of the 1965 Immigration and Nationality Act, it is imperative that policy-makers reflect on this history. To grow the middle class, we need a comprehensive policy that will turn DAPA-eligible parents—*and* those who remain unconnected to native-born children—into American citizens.

zulema valdez

less than liberal

Coupled with civil rights legislation, the Immigration and Naturalization Act of 1965 has been characterized as representing a historical shift in America's race relations toward a more liberal racial democracy. The act abolished the 1924 Immigration Act's national origins quota system, a policy that was widely seen as racist. In particular, Jewish and Catholic migrants to the United States from southern and central Europe claimed that the 1924 system discriminated against them, favoring migration from northern europe. At the same time, larger geopolitical forces at the end of World War II had also motivated policy-makers to change the overtly discriminatory system that came to be seen as an embarrassment on a global scale.

Nevertheless, in the months leading up to the passage of the bill, most policy-makers and politicians tended to overlook the possibility for dramatic increases in migrants from non-White-sending countries. During the signing of the bill, President Johnson remarked, "The bill is not a revolutionary bill. It does not affect the lives of millions. It will not reshape the structure of our daily lives or add importantly to either our wealth or our power." At the same time, Johnson underscored the urgent need for the bill, which would abolish an "un-American" system that "will never again shadow the gate to the American Nation with the twin barriers of prejudice and privilege."

The 1965 act, which, for the most part, remains how U.S. immigration policy is conducted today, was based largely on a race-neutral system that sought to reunite American citizens and permanent legal residents with their families, grant refugees asylum, and prioritize the entry of highly skilled labor. Contrary to Johnson's claims, though, the shift markedly altered the ethnic and racial composition of the country. Following its passage, over 18 million legal immigrants entered the United States, triple the number that preceded the act, mostly from Latin America, Asia, Africa, and the Caribbean. However, the act failed to abolish racism and nativism from immigration policy.

Clearly, immigration policies that were overtly "racially restrictive," such as the Chinese Exclusion Act of 1882 or the National Origins Act of 1924, have given way to laws that are, in theory, race neutral. Yet, a restrictionist character remains. In particular, historian Erika Lee reminds us that "various gatekeeping systems of categorizing, processing, surveilling, detaining, and deporting immigrants that were first established during 1882 to 1924 continue to function—and have even been expanded—in the contemporary era."

One readily observed example underscoring the persistence of restrictionist policies in the post-1965 period is that of undocumented Mexican immigrants. As migration scholars Doug Massey and Karen Pren have shown, unauthorized immigration from Mexico was "near zero" before the passage of the 1965 act, due in part to the Bracero Program, which provided temporary migrants with guest-worker visas. This program, which allowed for a temporary and circular pattern of Mexican migration, was dismantled when the 1965 act's hemispheric cap took effect. Although unintended, the consequences of these immigration policy changes meant the displacement of approximately 500,000 guest-workers who could no longer receive visas. It left the door open to just 20,000 annual resident visa holders. Consequently, unauthorized immigration from Latin America, mostly from Mexico, increased to nearly 10 million by 2010.

> All told, the 1965 act did mark a significant shift away from *overtly* racist immigration policy.

The unprecedented rise in unauthorized immigration has been met with fierce societal and state resistance. We have seen increases in hate crimes; racial scapegoating; border enforcement and militarization; arrests, detentions, and deportations; and the creation of new policies, such as the Patriot Act and Arizona's Support Our Law Enforcement and Safe Neighborhoods Act (Arizona SB 1070). Together, these effectively place the entire Mexican-origin population in the United States under suspicion. Likewise, the hostile treatment of Middle Eastern immigrants after the 9/11 terrorist attacks, including the long-term detention of noncitizens under the Patriot Act, demonstrates the ways in which contemporary immigration policy continues to fall short of triumphal liberal goals.

All told, the 1965 act did mark a significant shift away from *overtly* racist immigration policy. However, such "race-neutral" or "color-blind" immigration policies do not do enough to rectify a disturbing legacy of policies to the contrary or to change the ways in which immigrant minorities and their descendants are incorporated into America's racially stratified economy and society.

donna r. gabaccia

the feminization of american immigration

In 1984, when statisticians at the U.S. Department of Labor first reported that women outnumbered men among immigrants, their announcement appeared amid growing fears that the immigration reforms of 1965 had precipitated a decline in the "quality" of America's immigrants. Critics claimed newer immigrants "took" more than they "gave." There was little evidence to support such fears, but the momentum increased and eventually Congress passed the Illegal Immigration Reform and Immigrant Responsibility Act of 1996, which ended most social services to America's foreign-born, whether or not they possessed green cards.

Scholars, politicians, and American citizens have long imagined immigrants as working-age men who built America through their hard labor. By contrast, immigrant women and children were long assumed to be economic dependents. The 1984 Department of Labor report showed, for example, that most immigrant women in the 1970s entered with visas facilitating family unification. Thus, the *New York Times*' decision to headline its article on the report "Men Only a Third of U.S. Immigrants" provocatively added fuel to the fire. It fed fears that adult immigrant women were no different from children: they all depended on men's support. The *Times* claimed the numbers upset "Conventional Wisdom" and suggested that the United States was unique in a world where other countries still attracted male workers.

In fact, the labor statisticians' report made none of these claims. On the contrary, it questioned the association of visa status with female dependency and showed that a third of women entering the United States to unify families listed an occupation. Other evidence showed that wage-earning rates among immigrant women since 1970 had been only slightly lower than rates among native-born women. What's more, many more adult women of both groups worked for wages both before and after marriage than in the past.

Family unification visas and female majorities also preceded the passage of the 1965 immigrant reforms by several decades. Restrictive immigration laws passed in 1921 and 1924 first provided for the entry of wives and dependent children of naturalized immigrant men. Already in the 1950s, the largest group of migrants entering the United States did so with visas for family unification.

Female majorities were equally long-standing. Women and girls had been only 34.9 percent of immigrants between 1910 and 1919. With immigration restriction, however, that percentage rose to 43.8 percent in the 1920s, 55.3 percent in the 1930s, and 61.2 percent in the 1940s. After the passage of the 1965 reforms—changes that undid many of the earlier restrictions—the percentage of female immigrants actually fell to 53 percent in the 1970s.

We now also know that the feminization of migration occurred globally; that is, it did not set the United States apart as either unique or uniquely disadvantaged in its labor force. Many

> Although many associate increased female migration with trafficking, scholarly studies all point toward family unification, the recruitment of female care-workers, and the admission of refugees as drivers of gendered dynamics of migration.

countries in Europe and Australia also had gender-balanced migrant populations before 1960, and it became more common among immigrants in parts of Asia, Africa, and Latin America after 1960. Today, women are 50 percent of refugees worldwide and migrant men outnumber women only as asylum-seekers and as undocumented or clandestine labor migrants. Although many associate increased female migration with trafficking, scholarly studies all point toward family unification, the recruitment of female care-workers, and the admission of refugees as drivers of gendered dynamics of migration.

Most significantly, no study has *ever* documented negative consequences of gender-balanced migrant populations. While the 1965 reforms of U.S. immigration policy certainly had unintended consequences and family unification provisions did encourage the multiplication of once-tiny Asian and Latin American migrations, the feminization of migration was not itself a consequence of immigration reform. Nor did women's use of visas for family unification render them economic dependents or "takers." Gender balance among immigrants—whether in the United States or elsewhere—is thus no cause for alarm and it provides no evidence to support either further restrictions or the stigmatization of recent migrants as undesirable.

REVIEW QUESTIONS

1. Describe the 1965 Hart-Cellar Act. What was the impact of the 1965 act on American immigration, particularly on Asian immigration and Latino immigration?
2. Explain the term *hyper-selectivity*. How can this concept help us better understand an immigrant group's assimilation pattern?
3. What are the expected consequences of the current Deferred Action for Parental Accountability? What do you think could be done to improve DAPA?
4. Can "race-neutral" or "color-blind" immigration policies help integrate racial minorities and their descendants into U.S. society?
5. What are the drivers of gender-balanced migration? What is the (counter) evidence that immigrant women are dependent on men?

brian k. obach

a fracking fracas demonstrates movement potential

fall 2015

56

a social movement against fracking is scoring victories in some states but not others. why are some groups finding more success?

Environmentalists in New York scored a major victory at the end of 2014 when Governor Andrew Cuomo banned fracking, the controversial method of extracting natural gas and oil from deposits embedded in shale rock deep underground. The governor's ban was the result of a massive anti-fracking campaign by New York environmental activists. In the previous years, they collected tens of thousands of petition signatures, convinced more than 200 local municipalities to pass resolutions opposing the practice, and held demonstrations across the state calling for a ban. In the end, they won, providing new protection for local watersheds and human health while putting the brakes on the development of another major greenhouse-gas contributor.

But victory was declared in New York as the use of this new technology continued to spread in several other states, from Texas to Pennsylvania to North Dakota, places where opponents failed to slow the tide. Fracking poses environmental and health risks wherever it is practiced. Why did significant mobilization fail to materialize in other states and why were activists successful in New York? There is no simple formula, but social-movement scholars have identified several factors that are important to movement success: resources, organization, a good message, and a little help from powerful people. Anti-frackers in New York had all of this going for them.

getting organized

One way New York differs from states like Texas and North Dakota is in the prevalence of environmental groups. Activist groups need resources like meeting space, funds, staff time, and expertise to mobilize successfully. Areas without such groups at the ready are vulnerable to the imposition of harmful environmental practices.

New York has many organizations capable of mobilizing against environmental threats. One online directory listed 159 environmental organizations in New York State. North Dakota had two. Even on a per capita basis, there are a third as many environmental groups in North Dakota as in New York. Under those circumstances, elected officials and policy makers primarily feel pressure from industry interests, which helps to explain why North Dakota has more than 8,000 fracking wells and New York has none.

> Fracking poses environmental and health risks wherever it is practiced.

Many environmental groups in New York State made opposition to fracking a priority, and at least one, Frack Action, was created specifically for this purpose. Several professional policy-oriented groups like Environmental Advocates have a significant membership base linked by e-mail and newsletters. These groups gathered signatures on petitions and sent out "action alerts" asking members to call or write their representatives at crucial junctures in the struggle.

Other groups, such as the New York Public Interest Research Group and the Sierra Club, have well-organized local and regional chapters with grassroots volunteers. This means they can get people on the street for demonstrations or turn out citizens for grassroots lobbying. All of this activity kept fracking in the media spotlight in New York and put pressure on elected officials fearful of alienating this mobilized constituency.

In addition to these formal organizations, many small informal groups, like the Climate Action Coalition (CAC) in my town of New Paltz, played an important part in the anti-fracking campaign. They helped to raise awareness among the public by distributing literature at community events, writing letters to the editor of local papers, and sponsoring educational forums. Given their strong local ties, such groups are also able to turn out participants at protests and other actions, of which the CAC organized many. In one action, 100 activists gathered at a nearby state environmental office, then called the governor and chanted their opposition to fracking into the phone. In another they lined up along Main Street behind a homemade, 50-foot pipeline drawing cheers and honks of support from passing motorists.

The CAC also mobilized people to testify at town board meetings where they helped to persuade officials to pass resolutions against fracking and to enact ordinances that would have inhibited gas industry development locally. This particular group has a key resource in that its members are primarily retirees and students, two populations that have flexible schedules, skills, and access to social networks, all of which are valuable for mobilization. Together, all of these groups and the resources at their disposal make up an infrastructure of resistance, an apparatus put into action when the threat of tracking was presented.

> North Dakota has more than 8,000 fracking wells and New York has none.

framing the issue

Aside from the organizational capacity and resources available to activists in New York, the messaging or "framing" of the issue was also crucial. Opponents needed to characterize the threat in a way that was attention-grabbing and persuasive. The use of the term "fracking" itself was part of that framing. Gas industry officials handed the ominous-sounding term to activists by using it informally within the industry. Had they been more careful they would have stuck to the more formal terminology, "horizontal hydraulic fracturing"—much more difficult to fit on a picket sign. Inevitably, the more militant fracking protesters adopted slogans like "No Fracking Way!" and "Frack Off!"

But framing is about more than just slogans. It is a broad battle of words and images between activists and their targets. Gas industry officials describe fracking as a safe, sophisticated means of extracting a clean-burning domestic fuel source. The American Petroleum Institute frequently touts it as a means to free America from "foreign oil," which they see as vital to national security. According to this logic, fracking is not only environmentally beneficial, it's patriotic, a message that likely played well in more conservative parts of the country like Texas.

In New York, economic appeals were the foundation of the industry's framing. Their core argument was that natural-gas development would create thousands of jobs and bolster the economy in a struggling region of rural upstate New York. This appeal worked well in neighboring Pennsylvania, which was quick to permit fracking based on the lure of economic development.

The promise of jobs and economic growth is part of a commonly used frame, especially in fights over natural-resource extraction in rural areas. Industry interests use this to dissuade working-class people from environmental advocacy, at the same time framing their adversaries as rich, big-city environmentalists who don't understand or care about rural communities.

Anti-fracking activists eventually won the war of words by highlighting not only the ecological issues, but also by putting personal health front and center. Opponents cited cases of water contamination, epidemiological studies on illness and birth defects in the vicinity of fracking wells, and ecological ramifications not captured by the "clean energy" message presented by natural-gas proponents.

However persuasive scientific studies may be, they cannot compare to a powerful image. And the anti-fracking movement had the ideal picture to present their message: a kitchen faucet with flames pouring out along with the flow of water. This disturbing iconic image was captured and popularized by documentary filmmaker Josh Fox. Fox proved himself to be a master of framing in his film *Gasland*, a moving and witty firsthand narrative of the effects of fracking in his native Pennsylvania. The film served as an important educational tool that was used by activists who drew audiences to free screenings.

Fox became something of a celebrity based on his award-winning film, and he would regularly speak at anti-fracking events across New York. But he was not the only famous figure to serve as a public voice for the movement. A number of celebrities, including actors Matt Damon and Mark Ruffalo, lent their star power to the cause by speaking at events and broadcasting recorded messages via the web. Several famous recording artists performed at a benefit concert that was filmed and distributed as a movie called "Dear Governor Cuomo," another vehicle for instilling the anti-fracking frame and linking it with admired figures.

powerful friends

Perhaps more important than celebrity endorsements, New York's anti-fracking movement also had the backing of some economic and political leaders whose interests diverged from the corporate powers vested in natural-gas extraction. Division among elites can often prove decisive for movement outcomes. Research shows that the poor and especially people of color most often bear the health and environmental consequences of ecologically damaging practices, a phenomenon referred to as environmental injustice. But in this instance, the potential victims of fracking's effects included a broad swath of people, including many economically and politically powerful actors.

The primary area suitable for natural-gas development in the region is known as the Marcellus Shale, a natural rock formation that stretches from West Virginia up through Pennsylvania to the southern and western parts of New York State, an area that also happens to be part of the New York City watershed. The downstate region of New York includes much of the state's population and New York City is home to some of the world's biggest corporations and wealthiest citizens. Given the potential threat to the watershed, many elected officials in the New York City region, including

New York City Mayor Bill de Blasio, voiced opposition to fracking. Over 1,000 businesses from across the state also called for a ban. Thus, in addition to the grassroots mobilization against fracking, there were also powerful interests allied with the movement that improved the likelihood of success.

Understanding movement outcomes also requires examining the interests and vulnerabilities of targeted decision-makers. In this case, it was up to the governor to decide whether fracking would be allowed. Although the state is majority-Democratic, a primary challenge by a little-known candidate successfully mobilized anti-fracking support, which helped push Cuomo to take a stand against fracking. A little over a month after the bruising primary, and following the release of a report indicating that fracking posed potential health and environmental hazards, the governor imposed the ban, a major victory for the movement.

Anti-fracking activists in New York State demonstrated how mobilized citizens can successfully challenge powerful actors. Despite a population that is more supportive of environmental protection than states such as Texas and North Dakota, New York activists still depended on good organization, access to resources, the right message, and support from at least some influential figures. With those resources, movements can overcome even the most powerful adversaries.

REVIEW QUESTIONS

1. What organizational and resource advantages does New York have over a state like North Dakota when it comes to successfully mobilizing an environmental movement such as the anti-fracking movement?
2. How is framing the issue important in the battle over an issue such as fracking? Explain how opposing sides use different angles and how they better connect with their intended audiences.
3. Explain how the backing of powerful economic and political leaders can help mobilize a movement such as the one to ban fracking.

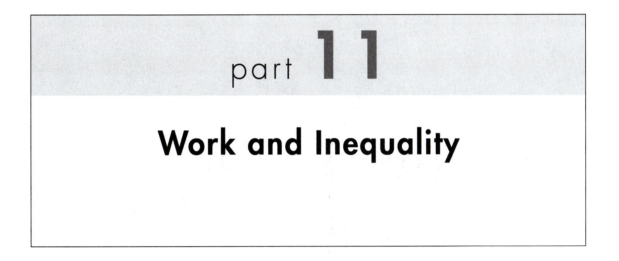

part **11**

Work and Inequality

margaret m. chin

asian americans, bamboo ceilings, and affirmative action

57

winter 2016

trusting in meritocratic processes is too simplistic, and elite cultural reproduction is too deterministic. intervening processes along the pipeline affect achievement outcomes for asian americans.

Asian Americans are popularly recognized as successful academic achievers, to the point of stereotype. Over half of Asian-American adults have a bachelor's degree or higher, compared to 37 percent of Whites, 27 percent of African Americans and 18 percent of Latinos. But they do as poorly as other minority groups in gaining management and executive suite jobs in major corporations. Why aren't there more Asian Americans in management and in the C-suites, given the significant numbers who are highly educated and skilled?

Getting a job, for the most part, is not a problem for the degree holder. Movement up the pipeline is. Asian Americans face barriers in all industries. The Bureau of Labor Statistics in 2013 estimated that over 35 percent of Asian-American workers were employed in professional industries, but their numbers in business executive positions and boardrooms were miniscule. And LEAP (Leadership Education for Asian Pacifics) found that Asian Americans comprise just 2 percent of executive officers and 2.6 percent of board members at *Fortune 500* companies. (Blacks and Latinos hold 7.4 percent and 3.3 percent of the *Fortune 500* corporate board seats, respectively.)

Even in Silicon Valley, Asian Americans encounter a glass ceiling. ASCEND, an Asian-American professional organization, using 2013 EEOC data from HP, Google, Intel, LinkedIn, and Yahoo, found that the higher you climb on the corporate ladder, the fewer minorities you will meet. Within these five companies, Asian Americans represent 27 percent of professionals, 19 percent of managers, and just 14 percent of executives. A similar phenomenon occurs with Blacks and Latinos. Whites are the only group whose proportion increases as they rise through the ranks.

Richard Zweigenhaft and G. William Domhoff, in their book *The New CEOs*, counted the non-White male CEOs of *Fortune 500* companies in 2010. They found only 25 White women, 15 Latinos, 14 African Americans, and 20 Asian Americans. Among the 20 Asian Americans, only 5 were U.S.-born, 11 were South Asian, and all were from upper-middle-class family backgrounds. In fact, all but the African Americans were from families in the upper one-third of the class structure, highly educated, and had a personal style that was similar to that of the "old" White male CEOs. Their analysis showed that the corporate elite is reproduced among a small set of elite women and non-White men.

Other researchers believe it is just a matter of time before U.S.-born and -raised Asian Americans will shatter the "bamboo ceiling" to enter the highest tiers of the workforce. In *Blurring the Color Line,* Richard Alba noted that, as White baby boomers retire, there should be more room at the top for Asian Americans to advance.

However, belief in such a meritocratic process is too simplistic and elite cultural reproduction by a few is too deterministic. Intervening processes along the pipeline affect achievement outcomes. For my forthcoming book on Asian Americans and corporate work, I interviewed over 80 second-generation Asian Americans between the ages of 29 and 57, U.S.-born or immigrated to the United States before age 13, who either felt trapped under the bamboo ceiling or had moved up the corporate ladders. What made the difference?

To get ahead today requires a combination of an ability to learn the requisite "soft" skills and businesses' investment in minority groups for management development. Diversity programs that look to race, gender, sexual identity, and/or the differently abled as factors for inclusion make a difference in who gets to the top.

Further, in reaching the managerial, directorship, or partnership levels, signaling to the organization that you are a cultural fit matters more than hard skills or "intelligence" alone. Building relationships with executives that provide visibility, learning how to brand yourself, and tooting your own horn are necessary. These soft skills, refined via presentations and interactions with peers, mentors, and sponsors, are key.

That proved frustrating for some of the people I spoke with. Alice said that a senior vice president at her company "sat me down in her office and started making some small talk, asking me 'How do you like the job?' Then she added, 'We know that you're doing a great job,

> Trusting in meritocratic processes is too simplistic, and elite cultural reproduction is too deterministic. Intervening processes along the pipeline affect achievement outcomes.

but you should make an effort to speak up more and make an effort to make people get to know you. Be more conversational.' " But Alice said that in her rank, those social skills had "no role. I can produce data and run models."

Discouraged workers like Alice told me that they had discovered too late that the techniques for school and college success—working hard, being smart, being the best at what you do, and not rocking the boat—were practically useless past the first few junior-level positions in the corporate world. Eric, who was able to adjust, had to "throw out the window" what he labeled "Asian stuff: kowtow to elders, defer to authority, don't ask questions." He used those methods early on to brand himself as a "trustworthy quant" to the point that "managing directors fought to have him on their team." After a number of years, though, his performance reviews started to suffer because of that reputation. Managers said Eric was "not commercial enough . . . not someone who can get the business." Eric changed his ways and his advancement up the pipeline was back in motion.

Compared with their White counterparts, Asian Americans also lacked sufficient social contacts—those individuals who would share information about important projects, initiatives, opportunities, and the hidden rules of the work world. While many parents were highly educated and worked as researchers, scientists, accountants, engineers, and ethnic entrepreneurs, they were not able to introduce their adult children to suitable mentors. The adult children were often the first ones in the corporate world. It was a rude awakening for the second gen to learn that their time could have been better spent at happy hour than in perfecting PowerPoint decks. Mike described his experience networking at a work function, "if you were used to this from a very young age, it would be easy. I observed people making small talk, discussing their families, vacations, sports, but not politics." He added that, "even me, having college-educated parents, did not do this."

The Asian Americans who rose to top levels possessed incredible people and leadership skills. They did not all come from the boarding schools and the Ivy League, although such credentials didn't hurt. They often spent time in high school, college, and graduate school learning and perfecting how to socialize, lead, and network. Some entered the work world with close friends who would later become executives and important contacts.

There was another factor that helped propel them into leadership positions. Quite a few who moved up the ladder in the late 1980s and 1990s credited affirmative action programs that had explicitly identified minorities for management development. Resources were invested in these programs because these corporations saw the value of diverse leadership. Significantly, affirmative action program participants learned what was required to be a leader and found themselves in a very supportive cohort. Periodically, they were assigned to work with executives and provided mentors. Among the skills one of my interviewees learned in his affirmation action program was effective networking: "I'm very conscious of speaking to executives. For every single person, I try to remember something about them, that I can relate to," he explained. "I need to find that fact, and figure out how it relates to me because I have a different background. It's one of the most important skills I learned."

More recently, diversity and talent management initiatives have replaced older affirmative action programs to hire, retain, and promote people from various racial, ethnic, gender, sexual orientation, and differently abled backgrounds. Once a potential candidate for management and executive titles self identifies, firms place them into leadership training, with mentors, sponsors, and coaches. They host conversations where employees can meet high-ranking executives and develop closer social contacts that they might not otherwise have. Their social skills are honed as they are exposed to a variety of people, especially when they are rotated through high-level positions.

> For the Asian Americans I interviewed, it was a rude awakening to learn that their time could have been better spent at happy hour than in perfecting PowerPoint decks.

Asian Americans, in particular, feel the stigma of diversity programs. Jim, a college graduate of the early 2000s, said he avoided referring to having been a part of a diversity program, if he could. He did not want to be associated with the negative impression that he might have gotten a leg up because of affirmative action or diversity initiatives. His comment reflects a wider sentiment that you might not be qualified if you had "that kind of help."

However, without these programs, there would be even fewer Asian Americans in high-ranked professional jobs. Diversity programs today are about inclusion, not attempts to proactively "fix" discrimination in the way past affirmative action programs were designed.

The second-generation adult workers I interviewed told stories that complicate the upward path that we assume most Asian-American children have. Their work narratives are relevant for women and all minority groups because they reveal how individual efforts and structural programs can help *all* those not yet equally represented in management positions and corner offices. If we are to fully understand what drives and limits social mobility, it is important to recognize and learn from the Asian-American experience.

REVIEW QUESTIONS

1. What does the term *bamboo ceiling* mean? What social problems does the term describe?
2. For Asian Americans and possibly other minorities to move up the corporate ladder, the author argues for both individual effort to learn interpersonal skills as well as the need for structural programs such as affirmative action. Do you agree? Do you have other suggestions?
3. What can or should be done to deal with the widespread negative sentiment toward affirmative action programs?

sarah halpern-meekin, laura tach, jennifer sykes, and kathryn edin

a hand up for lower-income families

58

spring 2016

cash welfare and snap benefits can come with stigma. what makes the earned income tax credit different?

Welfare queens driving Cadillacs. Food stamp kings buying filet mignon. The stereotypes are rife. What if there was a way to support lower-income families without the stigma? There is. And it comes from an unexpected source: the Internal Revenue Service.

First, listen to how Tracy Sherman, a 28-year-old medical coder and single mother of two, described her time on Temporary Assistance for Needy Families (TANF), which provides means-tested cash assistance (known colloquially as "welfare"). Right after her youngest daughter was born, the baby's father, an alcoholic, relapsed, and Tracy turned to TANF, feeling she had no other options. "I didn't feel good as a person. . . . They gave me [cash] plus they gave me food stamps for formula and everything like that. And every time I used it, I felt like crap." Now listen to Tracy's anticipation of her tax-refund check, made up largely of government transfers. "I think about [the refund] all year long. . . . It's like, 'Oh, I can't wait until I get my tax money!'" While Tracy said the $800 a month she received from TANF was not "really worth it," the $3,500 she received as a tax refund—a far smaller sum of money—fueled her dreams all year long.

Each year the Earned Income Tax Credit (EITC) and the Child Tax Credit (CTC) lift some 5 million children above the poverty line. The EITC has been credited with increasing employment, particularly among less-educated single mothers. And that's not all: the EITC has been tied to mothers receiving more prenatal care and being less likely to smoke and drink during pregnancy; in turn, their babies are less likely to be born low birth weight or preterm. The benefits for kids continue past infancy, with the children of EITC recipients being more likely to earn higher grades, graduate from high school, and enroll in college (Chuck Marr's research provides a review of the benefits associated with the EITC). All this without the humiliation and shame so many describe experiencing when receiving other means-tested cash and in-kind benefits.

Who qualifies for this program? The EITC is a refundable tax credit available to low-income workers, with its size determined by marital status, number of dependent children, amount of earnings and job status. For low-income workers without dependent children, only a small refund is available. The vast bulk of EITC payments go to parents who work but are still poor. As their incomes rise, so do benefits, with the maximum refund for a single parent of two—$5,548 delivered in one check at tax time—for those earning between $13,870 and $18,110 in 2015.

The average EITC for families with children is about $3,000. In addition, the Child Tax Credit offers up to $1,000 per child, depending on earnings, to those with kids under 17. Many EITC-recipient families also benefit from the refundable portion of the CTC, making for quite a substantial refund check at tax time. A single mother of two working full time at minimum wage can receive the equivalent of more than three months of earnings in her tax refund, pushing her annual income above the poverty line.

To learn more about what role the EITC plays in the lives of working families, we sat in the lobbies of H&R Block tax-prep offices and prepared taxes at Volunteer Income Tax Assistance sites in Boston, meeting parents like Tracy as they filed their taxes. After tax time ended, we visited Head Start centers across the metropolitan area to ensure we'd find those parents who filed taxes themselves or used the services of a tax-savvy uncle or friend. Through short surveys with over 300 parents, we learned how much they expected to get back as a tax refund and how they planned to use the money. We then drew a sample for in-depth interviews meant to capture a diversity of Black, White, and Hispanic families and married and unmarried parents; all were EITC recipients who had received at least $1,000 as a tax-time refund. While few were currently receiving TANF benefits, nearly half had done so at some point in the past, and the vast majority was currently receiving some form of government assistance, like SNAP (formerly known as food stamps) or subsidized housing. This allowed us to contrast the tax-refund experiences they described with their perceptions of other government assistance programs.

Six months after tax time, we sat down with 115 parents, typically in their homes, to learn about their finances and the role the tax-time windfall played in their lives. We solicited details on everything from how much they spent on groceries, to how much they earned braiding hair, to how much an ex handed over in child support each month. And, perhaps more importantly, we explored what this money meant to parents: the stress of living with debt, the disappointment of not being able to come through for the kids with presents at birthdays or Christmas, and the feelings of jubilation and hope that tax time elicits.

Immersed in research on the stigma recipients often experience when participating in TANF (and its predecessor, Aid to Families with Dependent Children [AFDC]), SNAP, and government housing programs, we were struck by what we heard from EITC-recipient parents. Government assistance could actually be means-tested and socially incorporating, rather than ostracizing. Decades of qualitative research, such as Kathryn Edin and Laura Lein's *Making Ends Meet*; and public opinion polls, such as those discussed by Martin Gilens in *Why Americans Hate Welfare*, have documented the shame associated with TANF/AFDC receipt, both on the part of recipients themselves and the public at large. Economist David Ellwood and political scientist Kent Weaver have explained that this is due, in part, to perceptions of such support as inconsistent with the widely shared American values of work, family, and self-reliance.

> A single mother of two working full time at minimum wage can receive the equivalent of more than three months of earnings in her tax refund, pushing her annual income above the poverty line.

And while politicians on both sides of the aisle have decried the nation's means-tested cash assistance programs, particularly prior to the 1996 welfare reform, both Republicans, like President Reagan and Speaker Ryan, and Democrats, like Presidents Clinton and Obama, have heartily endorsed the EITC. Michael Katz, historian of the American welfare state, noted that the EITC enjoys strong political and popular support because it serves working Americans, lifting up those who are seen as keeping up their end of the social contract; this contrasts with a program like TANF, which targets those who are marginally tied to the labor market. Further, research by political scientists finds that the American public prefers benefit programs that are administered via tax credits over direct spending. Unlike many other forms of government assistance to low-income families, the EITC is in line with these preferences. Although tax refunds do not meet all the needs of low-income workers—and they only assist those who are able to find and keep jobs—this method of delivering financial support offers a blueprint for how social assistance programs can provide a hand up without a perceived slap on the wrist.

> Unlike so many other government programs, then, assistance via the tax system does not make EITC beneficiaries feel they are marked as anything other than American.

In our study, the way parents talked about their tax refunds revealed the connection they saw between these benefits and their work effort. This is an intentional part of the law: When President Clinton oversaw the massive expansion of the EITC in the early 1990s, he noted that it had the power to "make work pay." Like most of us, EITC beneficiaries are fuzzy on the details of the tax code, but they know they get a large refund because they have kids, they work, and they don't earn a lot. The refund, therefore, affirms their core, positive identities as workers and parents. Parents told us their jobs often offered little by way of pay, status, or career mobility; the reward at tax time was, therefore, particularly welcome.

The way parents apply for and receive the EITC is distinct from the process for other means-tested benefits. The words "Overseers of the Public Welfare" are emblazoned above the now-empty home of East Boston's old AFDC office, implying that those making a claim to means-tested cash assistance require monitoring. In contrast, H&R Block's slogan is seen as a welcoming promise: "You've got people!" Unlike applying for TANF, the EITC and CTC application and delivery come through the tax system, which is universally used up and down the income ladder, making it less stigmatizing. Most Americans do not use an Electronic Benefit Transfer card at the supermarket; most Americans do not live in public housing; most Americans do not have to lay bare their lives to a caseworker to get cash welfare; but most Americans do file taxes each year, and most receive a refund check. In fact, Suzanne Mettler's research in *The Submerged State* shows that nearly half of EITC recipients in her survey reported not taking part in any government social programs; this illustrates the disconnect we saw in our qualitative study between EITC receipt and feeling like a proverbial "taker." Unlike so many other government programs, then, assistance via the tax system does not make EITC beneficiaries feel they are marked as anything other than American.

The arrival of the refund check at tax time gave families the opportunity to dig out of debt, pay ahead on bills, and stock up on food. While there are some myths or assumptions that low-income families will blow the lump sum on big-screen TVs or fancy sneakers, we saw that these stereotypes were far from the norm. Tracy explained, "You're thinking of all crazy things that you [could] spend it on. . . . But, I mean, realistically it comes at a good time, at that point where 'Okay, I need to pay bills,' and everything comes in perspective of what is a priority." Like Tracy, respondents in our study spent most tax-refund dollars on the mundane necessities of daily life—toilet paper, cleaning supplies, groceries—and getting caught up on bills and paying down debts—credit cards, utility bills, medical debts, student loans. Some saved a part of their refund, mostly to smooth income when the all-too-common "rainy day" arrives.

Much of the rest goes to durable goods like used cars, furniture, and appliances.

Meanwhile, in the weeks and months following receipt of the EITC, parents in our study described enjoying the small luxury of being able to put items in the shopping cart without an eye on the price comparison between name and store brand. They talked about the relief that came from making real progress digging out from under debt. Among those who put any refund dollars toward debt, the modal parent reduced her debt burden by about half. Some were able to save themselves from eviction, keep the lights from being shut off, get caught up on their student loans, start repairing their credit, and stop the harassing phone calls from creditors. Michelle and Jonah Tavares were a young couple with a baby son; both worked, but making ends meet remained a challenge. Michelle described their thinking when the refund check came: "We had to pay stuff that we knew would get shut off. I mean, you know you have other bills to pay, but you have to think of basic needs for your kid, you know. I have to think about his shelter and stuff. You go and pay your electricity because you want to have light." In short, tax time meant escaping some of the material hardship and easing some of the psychological pressure of living on the financial edge, even if such difficulties would return later in the year.

Parents only spent about one refund dollar in ten on treats, like meals at a sit-down restaurant, vacations, children's toys, and the like. But the chance to indulge in these items and experiences was more than a matter of dollars and cents. Spending on treats made them feel like they were able to fulfill their roles as parents as they wished they could all year round. Tamara Bishop, a 33-year-old assistant preschool teacher, described taking her kids to the movies and letting them buy movie-theater popcorn. What may be a routine rainy-day activity for wealthier families was a special treat for the Bishops. In a consumer culture such as ours, missing out on these little luxuries can make it feel like you're standing on the outside looking in. Extra money in your pocket means you can get off the sidelines and get in the game. Though this increased spending was small in absolute dollars and short-lived, it was symbolically meaningful to parents. As one mother put it, it makes you feel like "real Americans."

Yet another benefit of the refund check comes not in how it is spent, but in the hope it fuels. This massive infusion of cash made the parents we interviewed feel they could dream about a brighter future, one in which a refund check could be turned into a down payment on a home, a nest egg, or even a dream trip to Disney World. Though such dreams rarely come to pass, with more mundane concerns demanding attention, the hope offered by the refund is a benefit in and of itself. Recall Tracy, who enjoyed the flights of fancy anticipating the refund check allowed; while she ultimately spent her refund on necessities, she relished the chance to daydream about a life in which she could buy herself a new laptop. The laptop itself isn't the prize here; rather, the refund's existence buys Tracy a bit of middle-class fantasizing, a welcome break from the penny-pinching of her regular life. Or take, for example, parents' tendency to pay down debt with the refund. They explained that repairing their credit was one way they were moving toward their goal of becoming homeowners. A good credit score would put them in a better position to apply for a mortgage, they said; then, they could save next year's refund check as part of a future down payment. Pedro Rios and his wife Agustin were one

> Extra money in your pocket means you can get off the sidelines and get in the game.

such family. Pedro told us, "We're trying to save [next year's refund]. . . . In order to be a family, we want to get a house." Even if the home purchase never comes to pass, feeling as though you're on the path to owning a home of your own makes you feel like you're that much closer to securing your piece of the American dream.

Unlike TANF or SNAP, government assistance via refundable tax credits tends to fly under the public radar. Yet, while only some 1.8 million families receive TANF benefits, more than 27 million receive the EITC. Recipients perceive neither the social meanings of these tax refunds nor their method of delivery as stigmatizing. The programs' material, psychological, and social consequences are incorporating, making people feel a part of, rather than apart from, mainstream society. The refund fuels dreams of upward mobility and a more comfortable, middle-class life, providing hope for low-income working parents who are often scraping by day-to-day to cover necessities. There are, of course, drawbacks to refundable tax credits: they're of little help to those without jobs or dependent children, for example, nor do they fully address the financial needs of those they serve. Nonetheless, they offer a model for how government assistance can strengthen families financially, psychologically, and socially, with positive consequences for future generations.

RECOMMENDED RESOURCES

Nada Eissa and Hilary W. Hoynes. 2006. "Behavioral Responses to Taxes: Lessons from the EITC and Labor Supply." *Tax Policy and the Economy* 20: 73–110.

Studies the work-inducing nature of the EITC, finding that the program brings single mothers into the labor market but has limited effects on how much employees work.

Sarah Halpern-Meekin, Kathryn Edin, Laura Tach, and Jennifer Sykes. 2015. *It's Not Like I'm Poor: How Working Families Make Ends Meet in a Post-Welfare World.* Berkeley: University of California Press.

An in-depth portrait of EITC-recipient families that details family budgets, debts, and assets, exploring the role of the tax refund in parents' financial decisions and in the larger context of families' lives.

Chuck Marr, Chye-Ching Huang, Arloc Sherman, and Brandon DeBot. 2015. "EITC and Child Tax Credit Promote Work, Reduce Poverty, and Support Children's Development, Research Finds." Washington, DC: Center on Budget and Policy Priorities.

A brief overview of how the EITC and CTC work and their effects on beneficiaries.

Ruby Mendenhall, Kathryn Edin, Susan Crowley, Jennifer Sykes, Laura Tach, Katrin Križ, and Jeffrey R. Kling. 2012. "The Role of the Earned Income Tax Credit in the Budgets of Low-Income Households." *Social Service Review* 86: 367–400.

How parents spend their tax-refund dollars, including allocations to current consumption, asset accumulation, and debt repayment offers essential information about how the EITC functions as part of lower-income families' financial portfolios.

Jennifer Sykes, Katrin Križ, Kathryn Edin, and Sarah Halpern-Meekin. 2015. "Dignity and Dreams: What the Earned Income Tax Credit (EITC) Means to Low-Income Families." *American Sociological Review* 80: 243–67.

Explores the social inclusion created by the EITC, in contrast to the stigma engendered by welfare receipt.

Laura Tach and Sarah Halpern-Meekin. 2014. "Tax Code Knowledge and Behavioral Responses Among EITC Recipients: Policy Insights from Qualitative Data." *Journal of Policy Analysis and Management* 33: 413–39.

How and why EITC recipients do and do not respond to the incentive structures in the EITC, including whether they alter work behavior, marriage decisions, and childbearing.

REVIEW QUESTIONS

1. Briefly explain the differences between TANF, SNAP, and the EITC.

2. The authors describe the EITC as "socially incorporating, rather than ostracizing." Why do you think some public benefits carry more stigma than others?

3. Design a sample budget for a family with one parent and two children and an income of $16,000 per year, considering housing, transportation, food, personal care items, utilities, clothing, entertainment, and other spending categories. What changes would you make to the budget if you added $3,000 from the EITC?

dalton conley

falling upward   **59**

2011

economic inequality has increased since the great recession, and dalton conley aims to discover why this trend isn't slowing.

The top 1 percent of Americans reaped 70 percent of income growth during a period of economic expansion, average people became over-leveraged, and stocks soared.

At its most concentrated, that top 1 percent took in nearly a quarter of the national income. The economy got top heavy, the stock market crashed, and economic depression descended like a worldwide fog.

Sound familiar? Perhaps you're thinking Lehman Brothers, the Troubled Asset Relief Program (TARP), and the subprime crisis. But I'm talking about 1928–29. While the similarities in the lead up to the Great Depression echo eerily across the century, the aftermath of this crisis is anything but comparable. After the Great Depression, inequality leveled out until 1969; by contrast, since 2008, inequality has only continued its steady rise.

Tea Partiers and left-wingers who opposed TARP might say the reason for this difference is obvious: in 1929 there was no bail out of Wall Street (or the nascent auto industry, for that matter). There wasn't even deposit insurance. The free market was left to destroy fortunes—ill-gotten or not—"correcting" gross wealth inequalities in the process. No doubt, TARP (and even the FDIC) does play a role in explaining the differences between income inequality in the Great Depression and the Great Recession, but these days there are deeper social

forces that powerfully—though subtly—alter the economic landscape and may have made TARP and other pro–Wall Street policies inescapable.

First, the forces driving wage differentials don't show any signs of abating. Globalization combined with the rising skill premium of a knowledge economy means there are sure to be more Bill Gates in our future (and that work will continue to get outsourced by their inventions). But the real kicker is that while labor-market inequality will likely continue to rise, the interests of workers are increasingly yoked to those of their bosses.

Asset data are sketchy for the 1920s, but economic historians know that, while stock market participation did expand during those boom years, the overall rate was nothing like it is today. Thanks largely to the shift to defined contribution pension plans and the ease of Internet investing, half of Americans now have direct or indirect investments in the stock market. The catch is that while many of us are in for a penny, it's still the super-wealthy who are in for a pound. A study by the St. Louis Federal Reserve Bank found the richest 10 percent own upwards of 85 percent of stocks and other financial assets. So if the rest of us want to save our 401ks, we have to save the status quo for the super-rich, too. Thank heavens Social Security wasn't privatized (as George W. Bush proposed in 2005), or we'd be even more beholden to the financial industry.

Ditto for the housing market—home equity makes up a greater and greater share of household wealth as we drift down the income ladder. Back in 1930, fewer than half of Americans owned a home; by its peak in the 2000s, the home-ownership rate had hit 70 percent. So we're all invested in real estate values. A sluggish housing market used to at least mean falling rents for those at the bottom of the pyramid, but today, when most of us keep our life savings in the form of housing equity, price drops are devastating. Plus, home ownership reduces workers' ability to move for better job prospects; thus, limiting bargaining power.

Many scholars, including myself, have argued for the benefits of wider-spread asset ownership as a way to spread opportunity, good financial habits, a future orientation, and ultimately, a greater stake in capitalism and the rule of law. But we must be honest about the fact that an "ownership society" (to use Bush's term) also means a country in which the economic interests of the wealthy and the non-wealthy are increasingly tied to each other. Populist anger aside, letting robber barons sink would drown the rest of us, too.

Taken together, these trends suggest inequality is a quasi-permanent feature of the economic landscape. While research has yet to establish a causal link between inequality levels and human outcomes, it seems intuitive that there must be some effects of economic polarization. The problem is that while in absolute terms, everyone wants the same things—rising house and stock prices—in relative terms, those in the middle (and bottom) fall further and further behind. In other words, a rising tide lifts all boats, but that same tide causes more and bigger financial waves that risk swamping the dinghies while sparing the ocean liners and oil tankers.

Many on the left wonder why there isn't more of a backlash against rising inequality. But it's really not too bewildering—we're all implicated in the greatest Ponzi scheme ever. How to keep from swindling ourselves is the trick.

REVIEW QUESTIONS

1. What is Conley's main argument about the function and persistence of inequality? Do you buy it?
2. Can Conley's proposal of wider-spread asset ownership work to reduce income and wealth inequality?
3. What are some policies that you can think of that would be successful in reducing inequality in the way that Conley describes?

naomi gerstel and dan clawson

normal unpredictability and the chaos in our lives

60

fall 2015

dealing with disruptions to our daily routines seems to be becoming more commonplace in our lives. this creates strain on workers that spreads to the domestic, educational, and recreational spheres of their lives.

One of our students sent the following e-mail, pleading for an extension on her course paper:

I have more than half of my paper done, but I unexpectedly worked every night this weekend. I have documentation of everything, and I tried SO hard to get my shifts covered (I offered whoever took my shift $20, homemade cookies, and a shift cover) and no one would take any of my shifts and I've been stressing out and I may be able to finish my paper today, but in the event that I don't, is there a possibility of an extension?

Rosanna

Since we had just published a book, *Unequal Time*, about how people face increasing unpredictability in their work hours and schedules, we had a good deal of sympathy for her plight. Just as we heard from Rosanna, we saw in our research that what creates chaos and hardship in so many people's lives is not just the number of hours they work, but the unpredictability of those hours and the inability to control them. These play havoc with all our neatly laid plans.

Unpredictability implies events, from both work and home, that disrupt normal routines but that we have to find a way to deal with. It means having to stay at work late or arrive early, being sent home between shifts or upon arrival (without pay because there aren't enough customers/ patients), having much-needed shifts cancelled. Or it means having a sick child or relative whose needs throw our schedules into disarray. Such unpredictability is the new normal.

We studied employees and organizations in the medical system—hospitals, nursing homes, doctors' offices, ambulance dispatch centers. At one high-end nursing home we got the complete work records for a six-month period. These showed who was scheduled in advance to work and who, in fact, did work. The stunning finding was that one out of three shifts were not as planned in advance: someone was working when they had not been scheduled, or not working when they had been scheduled. This was a nursing home with very little turnover among patients/residents and much lower-than-normal rates of staff turnover. We found similar results in a random-sample survey of individuals who work in a wide array of organizations.

There is good reason to believe that such normal unpredictability—and the chaos in people's lives it causes—is happening more often now than in earlier decades. Much of it is created by an economic system in which employers increasingly squeeze workers and run on staffing margins so lean that *any* absence creates a problem. At the same time, a growing number of organizations hire temps, in effect outsourcing unpredictability to irregular workers whose livelihoods depend on unpredictability in their own schedules as well as in the schedules of regular workers. These broad economic trends all too often create stress, conflicts, and divisions. Add to these changes new technologies that increase the sway of unpredictability. Some comes from e-mails and cell phones that interrupt us and "require attention" day or night. Some comes from new scheduling software that allows and "requires" managers to send workers home when demand is slack or call them in when demand increases.

Life has also become more unpredictable because economic changes are situated in changing families. Lean staffing now characterizes not only the economy but also the family: More and more women—across race and class—are in the labor force as part of dual-earner couples. Husbands are less able to "outsource" unpredictability to stay-at-home wives. With high rates of divorce and the increase in babies born outside of an ongoing relationship, many more people are single parents (especially single mothers), increasing the impact of unpredictable events.

One unpredictable event cascades, creating others, in what we call a "web of time." For example, we observed a nurse calling in sick for a Friday evening shift. The scheduler explained that she needed coverage: "So I made a deal, I called one of the nurses that works down there regularly and asked her if she could work. She said no. I said listen—I'll give you whatever you want. I'll give you a weekend off. So she

did—she picked a weekend off." As a result, some other nurse had to rearrange her schedule to work the weekend. That nurse had to ask her grandmother to take care of her children over the weekend; the grandmother—who usually works on Sundays—cancelled work, which meant someone else needed to cover for her. Unpredictability expands to disrupt the lives of more and more people.

Unpredictability is pervasive, but the ability to deal with it depends on the degree of control someone has both at work and at home, and this control depends on class, gender, and race.

We analyzed professional and working-class occupations in which either men or women dominated, because the overall gender composition of the occupation shapes practices, cultural schemas, and policies. Consider two: a male doctor (68 percent of doctors are men) and a female nursing assistant (93 percent of nursing assistants are women).

Like other male professionals, male doctors work long hours and complain, often bitterly, about those hours. These doctors stay for what they see as unpredictable time to do paperwork or call a patient to explain that test results don't look so good. Though they grumble, doctors have significant control over this unpredictability. Why? First, they make a lot of money that they come to believe they need; so they decide to add patients, which adds hours and unpredictability. They could afford to decide otherwise. Second, they feel pressure to work more because they earn respect from their peers; as one said: "the ones who work the most are looked up to." Third, we rarely saw a male doctor respond to unpredictability coming from his family. When his own child was sick and needed to stay home, he could typically rely on

> Unpredictability is pervasive, but the ability to deal with it depends on the degree of control someone has at work and at home. This control depends on class, gender, and race.

someone else at home—his wife or a paid caregiver (often a low-wage woman with less control, whose life then becomes more unpredictable). Most male doctors, then, do gender in traditional ways, creating unpredictability for the women in their lives.

Women professionals also tend to do gender in conventional ways. Some women doctors worked similarly long and unpredictable hours, but many felt they must cut job hours to respond to family demands. As one woman doctor who worked part time and was married to a man doctor explained, "Just honestly, the vast majority of the burden of the household is on me, and if I were to work more it would just mean I work more and still have that burden."

Nursing assistants are at the other end of the spectrum in their control of unpredictability both at work and home. Like other low-level service workers, they are often hired for 24–32 hours per week; they must add time—often unexpected, additional shifts—to earn a living wage. At one nursing home we studied, most of the nursing assistants were White, and at the other, 88 percent of the nursing assistants were people of color. At the latter nursing home, although nursing assistants got six paid sick days a year, they were penalized each time they used a sick day. Penalties escalated from verbal to written warnings to dismissal. The nursing assistants, many of whom were single mothers, dealt with this by making use of a range of extended family members. In many cases, this works smoothly; in others, kids may be left alone or with a relative the mother doesn't fully trust.

For many years, a focus and aspiration of work–family activists and scholars has been flexible scheduling, allowing people to rearrange work hours to fit with family demands. What this research shows is that people who get such flexibility usually turn out to be women with professional or managerial positions; comparatively few men take advantage of this flexible scheduling and comparatively few working-class people are offered such flexibility. Now the meaning of flexibility is changing: as unpredictability has increased, employers are rebranding the term, demanding that *workers* show the "flexibility" to adjust to uncertain schedules and last-minute changes employers impose. The increasing deployment of the rhetoric of flexibility indicates a trend toward unpredictability but also masks a struggle to control it. A union official told us that "flexibility is the new word for control by management."

> A union official told us that "flexibility is the new word for control by management."

To say that "unpredictability is the new normal" is to say that most of the time people take it for granted, assume their lives will be chaotic, and often blame themselves. Many seek extra shifts (themselves unpredictable) so they can pay the bills, gain the admiration of peers, or avoid housework and tensions at home. Some resent the rules governing unpredictable schedules and fight back. Workers generally assume that if *they* unexpectedly need time off, they must talk to coworkers to arrange coverage themselves. As one said to her coworkers: "If this is gonna be the policy, we have to help each other out. Pretty much everyone's good with that; if you ask them, they'll work, cause they know they might need it." Management, they feel, creates unpredictability, but does not solve its problems. As one nursing assistant told us, "What are you going to do? You're not going to be able to really change it. They [employers] do what they want, basically. I've been here four years and I know that." Workers and their families solve the problems of unpredictability as best they can, providing flexibility rather than benefiting from it.

REVIEW QUESTIONS

1. What was the "stunning finding" in Gerstel and Clawson's nursing home study?
2. Why do Gerstel and Clawson believe that "normal unpredictability" is occurring more often now than it has in earlier decades?
3. What are the ways in which unpredictability is dealt with through "doing gender traditionally"?

viewpoints

on the sharing economy

winter 2015

in a world of airbnb and couchsurfer, the idea of letting a total stranger stay on the couch appears completely normal. nadeem and colleagues discuss the economic and social implications of a sharing economy. from misplaced trust to a possible economic revolution, the authors engage in conversation about the future of sharing space and resources.

shehzad nadeem

Sharing comes easily to us. We share particulars like names and lineages, ideas and experiences, kisses and embraces, as well as vital generalities like air and water, land and space. Sharing is a kindly and generous impulse and a critical aspect of what Marx would call our "species-being," our basic nature. Indigenous people even made sharing the basis of economic exchange through great gift-giving feasts called potlatches. Too little of this spirit stunts social relations, and we might wonder if culture could exist without it. But what happens when sharing is put to profit? Can it be the pivot on which economic activity turns?

Advocates of the "sharing economy" say yes. By privileging "access over ownership" and renting out underutilized assets—your apartment, your couch, your car, your appliances, your spare time—this new sector promises to deliver us of our possessiveness. The clearinghouse Shareable, for instance, claims "disownership" is "the new normal." Online profiles and accumulated user ratings mean that actual strangers become virtual friends you can eventually trust with your real stuff. All for a price, of course. The sharing economy is sharing made mercantile. It is goodwill with an instrumental purpose, occupying the rarest of places: where self-interest and public good happily coincide.

Or so we are led to believe. The truth of the matter is that the sharing economy is a floating signifier for a diverse range of activities. Some are genuinely collaborative and communal, while others are hotly competitive and profit-driven. A good many others are suspended somewhere in between. As such, studying the "industry" tells us much about a culture dominated by economic imperatives but yearning for more cooperative ways of doing things. The following essays help separate rhetoric from reality in an emerging economic sector.

Juliet Schor provides a neat précis of the industry as it stands, disaggregating the vague notion of the sharing economy into discrete components. She points to the growing power of industry giants crowding out the sector's more egalitarian and democratic experiments. Edward Walker looks beyond the sharing economy's progressive and participatory posturing, drawing attention to labor practices that have more in common with temporary and precarious work than with anything empowering. Caroline Lee considers the paradox of an industry that sees itself as a social movement, but has generated as much goodwill as resentment and created a risky business model by presuming trust. Finally, Paolo Parigi and Karen Cook look closely at the building of such trust. They argue that the "strangeness" of strangers is stamped out by technology—namely online profiles and ratings—that makes sharing less threatening, but also less surprising. Relationships multiply in such social networks, but they lack depth (consider, for instance, how many of your Facebook friends you could actually call on the phone).

Taken together, these four pieces describe a novel, evolving economic sector that makes use of what is best and worst in our social natures.

juliet b. schor

getting sharing right

The meteoric rise of the sharing economy has raised a compelling set of questions. Is it really about sharing? Is there anything new here? Does it represent a better model for organizing work and consumption? After more than three years of studying these initiatives, I can definitively say that the answers to these questions are: maybe, maybe, and maybe.

I define the new sharing economy as economic activity that is peer-to-peer, or person-to-person, facilitated by digital platforms. "P2P" is distinguished from models such as Zipcar, which is business-to-peer, in that the company owns the assets (cars) and rents them to consumers. The digital dimension is important for initiatives that aim for size, partly because it reduces transaction costs (the time involved in arranging exchanges), but also because it allows crowdsourcing of reputational information and ratings that mitigate the risks of intimate exchanges among people who don't know each other. While sharing has been around forever, this type of "stranger sharing" is new.

But is it really sharing? There's a class of platforms, typically nonprofits, where the answer is yes. Couchsurfers stay at each others' homes without payment. Gifting sites such as Freecycle and Yerdle enable people to offer free stuff to each other. Other true sharing sites include time banks, landsharing (which pairs would-be gardeners with people who have land), seed and tool libraries, and locally based, emerging forms of production and consumption like food swaps and pop-up repair collectives. Innovative practices of this type, based on social solidarity, ecological consciousness, and open access, are proliferating. Their Achilles' heel is that most haven't taken full advantage of the digital technologies or figured out the economic models that will yield robust and growing volumes of trades and reciprocal relations. In research with the MacArthur Foundation Connected Learning Research Network, my colleagues and I find that the time banks and food swaps generate only small numbers of exchanges.

The platforms that *are* growing are those where providers earn cash and consumers get a

> The platforms that *are* growing are those where providers earn cash and consumers get a good deal. But none of these is in the sharing business.

During World War II, even the U. S. government wanted to promote the sharing economy. (National Archives)

good deal. These are the large, well-funded, for-profits getting most of the attention—Uber, Lyft, and Airbnb. But none is in the sharing business. (An exception is the small slice of the market devoted to true ride sharing—strangers in a car together.) The ride-service companies are taking advantage of regulated barriers to entry and the resulting rents in the taxi industry in order to "disrupt" it. Uber has become notorious for predatory pricing and anticompetitive practices against other ride-sharing companies, bait-and-switch policies toward its drivers, invasion of privacy, and sexism. Airbnb is a rental site that allows people to monetize the housing assets they control or lease. These platforms are innovative, serve consumers well, and can be lucrative for certain providers. But increasingly, they're more about earning money (for providers) and managing labor and other costs cheaply (for the platforms) than the feel-good values of sociability, carbon footprint reduction, and efficiency many platforms emphasized when they started out.

Sharing is least evident in the labor platforms, particularly those that specialize in skills that are in ample supply: driving, running errands, housecleaning, or putting Ikea furniture together (a common ask on TaskRabbit, a low-end concierge site). Providers have no protections—not even minimum wage guarantees—when payment is by the job, rather than by time. The platforms are adamant that "gig" laborers are not employees, but "micro-entrepreneurs." We have found that people with specialized skills or high education can earn attractive sums of money, especially because they typically have other employment. It's much harder for those with run-of-the-mill competencies, because providers seem to be outstripping demand. Even if the economics were more favorable to providers, these sites are mainly taking advantage of collapsing labor markets rather than creating shared risk and reward.

Could it be different? Consumption sharing was originally conceived as the next stage in the peer production revolution. Peer production yields products that are not created for money and are freely available. Examples include open source software (Linux, Firefox), citizen science, shared cultural content, and crowd-sourced knowledge (Wikipedia). Peer production has emerged because information, ecological assets, and social relations are at the core of twenty-first-century economies. These resources are not well organized via private property and profit maximization, as a considerable body of economic theory shows. They are common resources, or "commons," better managed via fair allocations, collaboration, and democratic governance. Shared lodging, land, goods, and services could be the next steps in a new model

on the sharing economy **431**

that emphasizes cooperation and widely diffused value, rather than competition and concentration of wealth. Digital technology has made this path efficient. But to take advantage of these efficiencies at large scale, we're going to need platforms owned and controlled by their users (providers and consumers). That's technically feasible and democratic governance will mitigate against race-to-the-bottom dynamics and preserve value for consumers.

Whether we can get there before Uber, Airbnb, and other for-profits have achieved durable domination is now, the question. If we do, we'll have a shot at a true sharing economy.

edward t. walker

beyond the rhetoric of the "sharing economy"

Airbnb, the website through which users can rent out their home to overnight guests, is valued at $10 billion and has an estimated 800,000 rentals listed in 34,000 international cities. Uber, the ride-sharing service, also dominates its sector and has a valuation of no less than $40 billion.

Although these are the most successful, a variety of smaller start-up firms are revolutionizing industries: they are providing alternative, crowd-sourced services in areas ranging from meals (SupperShare), package shipment (PiggyBee), car or boat rental (respectively, RelayRides and Boatbound), home delivery of goods (Instacart), and even contracting with short-term laborers (TaskRabbit, Air-Tasker, Proprly). Their services build upon the well-established repertoires and rhetorics of local exchanges such as community-supported agriculture (CSA) programs, neighborhood tool-sharing, time banks, and the like, but are now using mobile technologies to facilitate their expansion.

These companies frame themselves as part of a broader "sharing economy," with the argument that these start-ups augur the onset of a more friendly, empowered, collaborative, and locally oriented capitalism. In some respects, this is accurate. Certainly, practitioners and advocates view these arrangements as a more progressive and participatory alternative to the power of multinational corporations and the entrenched problems of large bureaucracies.

But the reality isn't so simple. In terms of labels, labor, and lobbying, "sharing" doesn't quite capture what's taking place.

First, can each of these projects be accurately understood as part of the same "sharing economy"? Highly profitable, major companies like Airbnb and Uber are grouped alongside voluntary gift-giving exchanges like Freecycle or Couchsurfing. Calling them all part of the same "sharing economy" ignores vast differences.

> In terms of labels, labor, and lobbying, "sharing" doesn't quite capture what's taking place.

While, of course, it's true that a strength of all of these operations is their reliance upon decentralized networks of "producers" for their services, dominant firms extract substantial rents from the transactions on their sites, and the extent of these fees is not always clear: Uber, for instance, has been opaque about whether its drivers receive tips for their work.

The "sharing economy" label also misrepresents the labor issues involved, eliding the distinction between paid work and uncompensated volunteering. TaskRabbit, the odd-job household labor and cleaning service, goes so far as to suggest that they are little more than "an old school concept—neighbors helping neighbors—reimagined for today."

In many respects, though, such crowdsourced labor fits very well with the turn toward precarious employment and the privatization of risk documented by many sociologists. In fact, some have argued that the industry is more accurately understood as the "1099 economy," since their workers are not employees receiving IRS W-2 forms, but 1099-MISC forms. That is, they are temporary contractors. Some authors see this in an empowering, "be your own boss" light, but it's worth noting that contractors aren't offered the health and social safety-net benefits of conventional workers. Neither firms like TaskRabbit nor those who use their services pay benefits to workers.

Third, the "sharing economy" frame might also mislead one into thinking that such startups don't engage in lobbying, instead favoring softer, more collaborative political approaches.

There *is* some evidence from the transportation sector that incumbent taxi companies are outspending firms like Uber in campaign contributions. But it's also becoming clear that firms in the broader crowdsourcing sector are learning to flex their political muscles. This has recently been underscored by the scandal surrounding an Uber executive's comments that the company intends to "dig up dirt" through opposition research about the journalists writing negative stories about them.

Even more striking are the industry's "grassroots" efforts, both through Peers.org and Fair to Share and in other attempts to use grassroots lobbying strategies, which mobilize the public as pro-business citizen lobbyists. In these cases, the firms' workers, users, and supportive third parties are organized as frontline defenders of the industry.

In fact, these campaigns bear a notable resemblance to other industry-backed grassroots campaigns such as those I describe in my recent book. They trade on the power of everyday citizens to create an authentic voice for industry, they are often less than fully transparent about the role of the corporate funder, and they seek out individuals seen as local opinion leaders to most effectively make their case. Like other companies, they face the charge of "astroturfing," or simulating the appearance of independent, grassroots advocacy.

Peers.org, for instance, has leaders who have denied that it's a lobbying organization and claimed that it's a freestanding, independent, nonprofit organization. Nonetheless, Peers has been heavily funded and staffed by crowdsourcing firms and has served as a major political force for the industry. That isn't, of course, to deny that Peers helps bring together a variety of interests looking to improve crowdsourcing and provide social benefits, nor is it to suggest that self-styled sharing firms don't have a right to lobby. But greater transparency might help to alleviate the image that services like Peers are engaged in political ventriloquism on behalf of leading firms like Airbnb. And there's now evidence that this message might be getting through: Peers is currently rebranding itself as an association focused on problems facing vulnerable peer economy workers.

What we learn, then, is that the "sharing economy" would be much more accurately understood as the "crowdsourcing economy." The change in terms recognizes the sector's

> Crowdsourced labor fits well with the turn toward precarious employment and the privatization of risk documented by sociologists.

technology and approach without misleading by moralization.

So it's time to stop assuming that this sector plays by an entirely different set of rules. The technologies may be new and there are certain noteworthy social benefits, but let's not go so far as to mistake Silicon Valley's idealized self-image for reality.

caroline w. lee

the sharers' gently used clothes

The sharing economy busts a lot of the assumptions of our finance-obsessed, over-leveraged culture. It seems the perfect locally rooted, small-is-beautiful antidote to an economic crisis precipitated by reckless financial giants too big to fail. But it's not just tangible things like beds, bikes, and breast milk that are being shared. Equally important is the community *ethos* of sharing. The message of collective empowerment through human contact is its own viral product, touted by Harvard Business School professors and time-banking activists alike. Is the industry's egalitarian impulse real or a kind of window dressing? As I'll explain, it's a little of both.

For sociologists of democratic culture, the sharing economy is just the latest example of insurgent sentiment being used to sell the bona fides of profit-making corporations. Advertising agencies of the 1950s and '60s, for example, were quick to sell their products as countercultural and revolutionary. The same held for the "liberation marketing" of the '90s, which promised self-realization through consumption. By the turn of the century, large corporations were claiming to be regulation-oppressed little guys whose only interest was empowering stakeholders. In today's postcrash reality, sharing economy giants like Uber and Airbnb compete to be seen as leading the charge against "Big Taxi" and "Big Hotel."

On the surface, the idea that consumption can be collaborative seems radical indeed. Greed and growth are no longer the greatest goods. Shareable, an online news site, sees the "sharing transformation" as a "movement of movements" challenging "outmoded beliefs about how the world works—that ordinary people can't govern themselves directly; that nonstop economic growth leads to widespread prosperity; and that more stuff leads to more happiness." With its calls to fight old economy industries, the sharing economy seems to borrow from the "fuck the man" ethos of earlier generations of sharers, from hippies and activists sharing their lives in communes to punk rock kids distributing free 'zines at benefit shows to techies sharing music files on Napster.

The anti-establishment ideology sold by sharing-economy companies is hazier and cuddlier by comparison, and that's no mistake. Social change may be on offer, but it's more about self-realization through cooperation than it is about redistribution or mobilization. The companies seem to say, "A better world is within reach, once we tap into our own need for self-fulfillment and authentic connection, once we learn to trust our emotions and intuition."

> The rhetoric of peace, love, and understanding is more than clever marketing. There really is a new business model here; it depends on sharers believing the hype.

Testimonials from hosts on their website say that Airbnb sparked career-changing conversations about "life purpose and finding what is meaningful." Quotes like these let us believe hosts and guests don't just share herbal tea and towels, but "meaningful exchanges that further build community, foster cultural exchange, and strengthen understanding." Social change begins at home, over a bottle of wine with like-minded strangers.

This rhetoric of peace, love, and understanding is more than clever marketing. There really is a new business model here, and it depends on sharers believing the hype. The new sharing economy leverages value from strangers' tenuous social connections online—and for that to work, people need to have a significant amount of trust in their online communities, drivers, and new housemates. It's no wonder that companies like Lyft outfit drivers' cars with friendly pink mustaches and Airbnb takes a hard line on "bad actors" making big bucks off gullible tourists.

In the absence of regulation and clear guidelines, the industry relies, to a degree, on the moral policing of crowdsourced reputation scores and social network identity verification. Counting on the goodwill of others in an ongoing economic crisis is a risky gambit; however: assaults, thefts, prostitution rings, squatters, and other horror stories show the dark side of putting too much stock in strangers' online profiles. When an unhinged driver attacks a passenger with a hammer or an apartment is rented for what turns out to be a "XXX FREAK FEST," tamperproof surveillance cameras in licensed cabs and hotel lobbies start to seem sensible. As *New York* magazine puts it, "The Dumbest Person in Your Building Is Passing Out Keys to Your Front Door!" Despite promises of million-dollar insurance guarantees, sharing economy terms and conditions reveal that liability and risk are unclear and often unequally shared.

Global sharing hub OuiShare argues that "an economy based on community principles such as sharing, collaboration and openness can solve many of the complex challenges the world faces," from climate change to poverty. Far from warning sharers against opening their hearts and homes, I would caution them against investing too much faith in the idea that global problems can be solved by "peer-to-peer" conversations and self-governing communities of strangers.

As sociologists like Sandra Levitsky, who studies failures to mobilize among caregivers, show, the private politics of fellowship and mutual support don't easily translate into impact on the larger polity, despite backbreaking shared grievances. In fact, grander ambitions for challenging the status quo mean rude questions about ownership and rights and uncivil protests that don't look cooperative. Sharing may be caring, but so long as it builds upon existing inequalities in power and wealth, it may not add up to much.

paolo parigi and karen cook

trust and relationships in the sharing economy

The Internet has evolved rapidly as a new medium for human interaction, particularly as people generate online communities. While these communities typically have unifying objectives, they often attract individuals from different backgrounds. Facilitating contact and eventually the emergence of trust among strangers is an integral part of how the sites function. Such is the case, for example, with the community-based organizations springing up in the "sharing economy." These organizations ask members to share a good or service with strangers. Members of Lyft, for instance, trust car-owners to drive them to their destinations, while members of Airbnb stay in strangers' houses while traveling. Remarkably, what appears to be a very difficult act in the offline world—creating interpersonal trust—is a routine activity for organizations operating within this segment of the economy.

We have studied an extreme case of interpersonal trust in depth: Couchsurfing. A website created in 2003 to support international travel and cultural exchange, Couchsurfing built a community of members who both "host" others and "surf" to find a "couch" to sleep on as they travel the world, all without the exchange of funds. From its unassuming beginning, Couchsurfing has grown into a worldwide phenomenon with a distinctive culture. Members post detailed personal pages, recounting their experiences visiting other members or hosting them. Similar to Facebook pages, Couchsurfing pages list "friends," though the depth of information provided by Couchsurfers about their social lives greatly exceeds what most other social networking websites supply.

By studying this community, we discovered an interesting mechanism at the root of interpersonal trust, a mechanism that highlights the importance of technology. The accumulation of ratings about users (whether guests or hosts) had a double-edged effect on the emergence of trust and relationships: it made relationships easier to establish initially but it also weakened them after a certain threshold. That is, technology facilitated the emergence of interpersonal trust among Couchsurfers, but it also made establishing strong ties harder as users acquired more and more reviews.

For example, early on, social ties originated through a process of mutual discovery. As one Couchsurfer told researcher Paula Biasky: "He [the guest] would speak, and I would often listen. It was the first time I ever invited a stranger into my home, and the first time I ended up speaking to a stranger until the late hours of the night." Despite the perils of uncertainty, the psychological and emotional rewards of a successful interaction produced strong bonds and interpersonal trust. These interactions occurred in the context of an early rating system which provided little accumulated information about users. In contrast to early Couchsurfers' openness, the people we interviewed in 2010 were more calculating about the types of strangers they hoped to meet. Their experiences with other Couchsurfers were mediated by the organization's reputation system. While they welcomed the rating system, in part because it allayed some safety concerns, it also made relationships more predictable.

Technology thus operates as an assurance structure: it reduces overall uncertainty and promotes trust between strangers. At the same time, it strips away some of the serendipity involved in meeting new people. Interactions are more normalized, less open to chance. This is because trustworthiness is promoted not by interpersonal ties, but by the monitoring of one another in a network in which reputations are posted.

Does technology operate in the same way for other communities in the sharing economy? It is hard to know, as there is very little research so far on the mechanisms for building trust where it might not otherwise emerge. What our research suggests is that Internet-mediated interactions tend to become less open-ended

> Technology reduces overall uncertainty and promotes trust among strangers, but it strips away some of the serendipity. Interactions are more normalized, less open to chance.

and unexpected the more information the community accumulates about its members.

REVIEW QUESTIONS

1. Describe the sharing economy in your own words. Is this part of your daily life?
2. Using the arguments provided by the authors, what are the costs and benefits of a shared economy?
3. What kind of regulations would have to be set in place to get these shared economies to work? Is it possible?

esther sullivan and edna ledesma

same trailer, different park

winter 2015

62

mobile homes house 22 million americans, but as property values increase, mobile home dwellers who own their homes but rent the land face displacement. stories and photographs express the frustration and grief of residents facing eviction.

'm in my Florida room inside the Silver Sands Mobile Home Court. It is a linoleum-floored, screened-in porch that runs the length of my single-wide trailer. Fifteen feet away, in front of my neighbors' powder blue mobile home, a decorative sign reads: "Welcome to Paradise." I'm tending the orchids my neighbor across the street gave me when another of our neighbors left to move in with his children, abandoning an extensive orchid collection in his still-furnished mobile home. I mist my orphaned orchids to the sounds of an old radio. I hear country singer

Kacey Musgraves croon, "Same hurt in every heart. Same trailer, different park."

It resonates. All of us here in Silver Sands are being evicted. This 55-and-older mobile home park once housed about 130 residents. The few who had money saved or families willing to house them are already gone. The rest of us have six months to get our selves, our belongings, and our homes off the property.

Mobile homes are memorialized in country songs and in the iconography of middle America, but they are often ignored, stigmatized,

Walter: "I'm happy here. I'm happy as a bug in a rug right here. This is paradise in Florida. On a hot day, this is perfect and we have the view." (© Edna Ledesma)

restrictively zoned, or outright prohibited within urban policy and planning ordinances. Parks like Silver Sands are commonly sited on low-value land at the outer edges of cities and towns. Mobile home park owners create profitable uses for otherwise undesirable land by renting lots to residents who own their homes and pay low monthly lot rents. Together, these characteristics make mobile homes affordable sources of housing for 22 million Americans. In fact, mobile homes are the single largest source of unsubsidized affordable housing in the United States. They shelter large populations of poor, elderly, and immigrant homeowners.

These same characteristics make mobile home parks one of America's most precarious modes of housing. As cities expand around parks, the lands they occupy become more desirable, and selling them gets more attractive. Because residents own their homes but rent their lots, landlords can sell parks at any time and evict residents with only 30 days' notice in most states. In Florida, housing groups estimated that 1,500 parks were at risk of closing in 2010 alone. In 2011, I moved into one of these parks as part of two continuous years of ethnographic fieldwork living in and being evicted from closing mobile home parks in Texas and Florida, the two U.S. states with the largest numbers of mobile home parks.

These pictures were taken in Silver Sands (a pseudonym) where I lived for 11 months during the time before we received eviction notices and until the final date of our tenancy. Over this year and a year of return visits, I lived inside Silver Sands when it was still intact. I became part of residents' daily routines— gardening together, hanging out on patios, and talking in the communal laundry room. I was evicted alongside my neighbors and shared their experiences as our community was dismantled. I worked beside them as they attempted to manage the relocation process, hosting some in my trailer in the months it took to re-site their own homes. I kept up with them in the year after they were scattered from their homes to new parks, family homes, apartments, and homelessness.

Eviction at Silver Sands was experienced as both a sudden crisis and a prolonged and

(© Edna Ledesma)

confusing ordeal. Relocating a mobile home costs between $5,000 and $10,000, as much as a decade's worth of equity for mobile home owners and an out-of-reach cost for most in Silver Sands, who lived on meager or fixed incomes. The logistics of assessing, preparing, moving, and reinstalling a mobile home are complicated and involve the coordinated efforts of many different professionals. In their own words, residents of Silver Sands describe the park's closure and the community-wide

eviction as, more than anything, a brutal shock and a deeply felt loss. They also describe a second-order trauma, felt as a prolonged and disturbing dislocation in which nothing was certain and everything was "up in the air."

In these photographs, my colleague Edna Ledesma and I attempt to document life inside Silver Sands before, during, and after 130 residents were evicted from the park where many had lived for decades. These photographs and narratives capture the dismantling of a community.

Hilda cooks lunch with her friends in their trailer. (© Edna Ledesma)

Sam: "We are trailer trash to them. People say that people that live in trailer parks are trash, which means they're no good, is what that basically means. This here is a trailer park but it's not trailer trash because it's set up nice and it's good and there's good people." (© Edna Ledesma)

Christy: "You get to a point where you're like, 'God, Christy, I thought by the time you were 50, you would be a little more settled.' I never planned on leaving here."
Joan: "It's just miserable, you know. Everything familiar is gone. This is the first place I've ever lived in Florida. This is where I planned to die." (© Edna Ledesma)

Eddie (a licensed mobile home mover): "The builders figured out that they can buy these parks and get rid of the people cheaper than they can actually go and buy the land and pull buildings down and stuff. So I got in with the builders; I've actually been closing these parks for almost 25 years. . . . They'd call me and they'd say, 'Listen, we are going to go close this park,' two or three months before anybody would know. And I would go stake out these parks, and I would just ride around quietly and I would check everything out and see what was going on, and I would give them an idea of what it was going to cost. And then we'd set up a deal. . . . I have the contract, the builder is getting the thing emptied. Everybody is happy!" (© Esther Sullivan)

January 1, 2013, field notes: Today I'm talking over Walter's plans for Monday, when his home will be moved. I tell him that I want to be here to see him moved and to get his feelings recorded. Pulling my recorder close to his mouth he points out that he can answer that for me right now and says, simply, "Confused." (© Esther Sullivan)

Interior of Francis' home. Francis' home, like many others, was too old to move. Francis was blind, completely homebound, and unable to walk without assistance. She explained that her independence was the most important thing to her, and she was able to live alone comfortably because she was so familiar with the layout of her small mobile home. Now it is abandoned.

Anne: "I knew it was gonna come, but I am all by myself. It makes it harder that way, to be all by yourself. . . . You can't [imagine], unless you're my age and you go through the same thing. . . . I'll get through it. I'll get by. When you get to be my age, then you will see how hard it is." (© Esther Sullivan)

Harry: "These people are professionals. They're professionals. This is what they do. They close trailer parks." (© Edna Ledesma)

same trailer, different park   443

Kathleen, one year after moving and two years after receiving the first notice of the sale of Silver Sands: "It's been living hell for two years.... I'm not happy.... I don't know anybody. Down there," she sighs, "everybody knew everybody." (© Edna Ledesma)

Lee: "We drove through there last weekend, the place looked like a war zone.... I got upset. Don't get me wrong, this is my home you are taking away.... But I got over it. I said, 'It's time. You gotta do what you gotta do. It's either find a place or find a bridge.'" A pile of soil containing the remnants of residents' former homes sits at the former site of Silver Sands. A sign reads "Wash Out," indicating these remnants must be removed before the soil is reused. Silver Sands is now being redeveloped into 350 rental apartment units. (© Edna Ledesma)

Professional movers readied residents' homes for relocation, but many chose to carefully perform this work themselves. As Bob pointed out, "This is my home. This is my home you're taking away." (© Edna Ledesma)

REVIEW QUESTIONS

1. What is the difference between the value we place on trailer parks and the value we place on "tiny homes"?
2. What responsibility do cities and communities have when low-income housing is removed from an area?
3. Many trailer park residents are homeowners but live in areas removed from cities and towns. How is their experience of home ownership different from others?

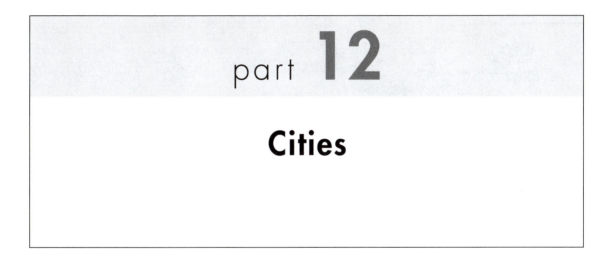

part **12**

Cities

dhruv dhawan

mumbai sleeping

fall 2015

each day, an average of 1,600 people flock from the farmlands to the pavements of mumbai in search of better prospects. many end up sleeping on the streets.

began photographing people sleeping in Mumbai in the summer of 2009 to explore the diversity of a universal human experience. I was in awe of my subjects' ability to use the urban landscape as a bed—most of the people I know cannot sleep with a light on, the sound of traffic, or on an uncomfortable mattress.

Mumbai is the largest and most affluent city in India. Yet 9 million Mumbaikars live in slums, and an estimated 1 million are homeless. Each

(© Dhruv Dhawan)

(© Dhruv Dhawan)

day, an average of 1,600 people flock from the farmlands to the pavements of Mumbai in search of better prospects. Many end up sleeping on the streets.

However, not all of the people photographed in these pictures are homeless. Mumbai has a year-round warm, humid, tropical climate, and many of the taxi drivers I photographed choose to sleep on top of their vehicles rather than in their shared accommodations so that they might find a fare-paying customer who wants to be taken to the suburbs where they reside or where they have to return their taxi.

Others have chosen to sleep outside as an alternative to stuffy and sometimes overcrowded homes, where large families share a space that is often less than 400 square feet.

While these images may appear sad to some of us, to those in the photographs, I doubt it is always sad. To many, if not most, this is normal. When I asked people who woke up while I was photographing them, most said that they managed to get a good sleep outdoors. Indeed, when I was 19, I spent a summer backpacking through India, sleeping on the streets with the poor. I do not remember anyone wallowing in self-pity or feeling sorry for their situation. Human beings have used the landscape of the earth as a bed for centuries and I think that we have fetishized a human necessity into a luxury.

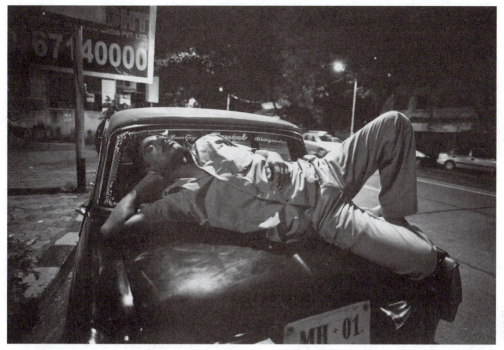

(© Dhruv Dhawan)

My inspiration for this project came from the romantic balance that Mumbai's taxi drivers sleep with their vehicles, having left the warmth of their homes and wives to make a living in India's city of dreams. (© Dhruv Dhawan)

(© Dhruv Dhawan)

(© Dhruv Dhawan)

This photograph was captured at 4 a.m., a few minutes after this boy went to sleep. I also captured video alongside my photographs. The scene of this boy going to sleep can be viewed at vimeo.com/129323596. (© Dhruv Dhawan)

Imposing a narrative on the lives of the poor ignores their perspective.

When I embarked on this project I had no intention to publicly exhibit these images—photography was just a hobby at the time. But after some of these photographs went public in the press and were displayed at exhibitions, I was forced to consider the ethical implications of photographing people without their consent.

In India, there is no social norm that requires consent before taking a photograph of someone. Most people are quite happy to be photographed and will often try to enter and pose in the frame of a street photographer. Over the course of three years, a handful of people did wake up while I was taking their picture, but no one ever opposed my actions after I told them what I was doing. Still, I cannot assume that everyone would give consent.

Due to the culture of modesty surrounding women in India, I generally chose not to publish any images of women sleeping. However, I have published this photograph of an elderly lady sleeping on the pavement, because we tend to perceive the elderly and women as fragile. This image dismantles the stereotype, revealing the strength and resilience of an Indian woman amid a harsh urban reality.

(© Dhruv Dhawan)

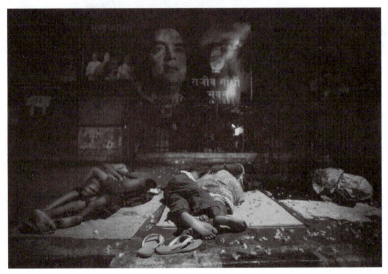

This photograph was captured in 2010, while the center-left Congress Party was still ruling India's democratic republic. The faces of the late Rajiv Gandhi and his Italian wife Sonia and son Rahul loom in the background. The family has held a dynastic grip over the country since Independence in 1967, though allegations of corruption and secret Swiss bank accounts have tainted the family's reputation. For me, this image epitomizes the state of our nation, with its corrupt leaders who emulate the parasitic practices of our former colonizers. (© Dhruv Dhawan)

Artists will always have to stop and question the ethical and moral boundaries we traverse in pursuit of expression. I am forever grateful to the people and visual culture of India whose hospitality toward photographers and reverence for the image allows us to capture real life without disrupting it with the politics of consent.

Over 2,000 images later, I still find myself compelled to document the phenomena of urbanization in which space has become so scarce that private acts are conducted in public. These photographs are a testament to the resilience of the urban lower class, who turn the wheels of the city by day and sleep on them at night.

REVIEW QUESTIONS

1. The author justifies his taking photos of sleeping people with the argument that Indian people like to be photographed and he never had anyone object when they woke up to find him photographing them. Do you agree with this position? What are the moral implications of the author publishing these photos? Would you take photos like these?

2. What does the author mean when he says that urbanization has caused private spaces to be moved into public?

3. What are your gut reactions to the photos? What feelings do they elicit? Do they represent a call to action for you in any way?

syed ali

permanent impermanence

spring 2010

dubai has been lauded by western statesmen and the media as a model for the rest of the muslim world to follow—a capitalist, consumerist paradise tolerant of alternative (read: western) lifestyles and undisturbed by terrorism. however, an in-depth look shows that laborers' lives are largely regulated by "sticks" while the middle class and professionals' lives are regulated mostly with "carrots" like high salaries, fast professional advancement, and luxury living.

was standing on the helipad of a new, swanky high-rise apartment building in the Dubai Marina with my friend Vishul in the summer of 2006. We took in the panoramic, nighttime view of skyscrapers in the making, each capped with cranes lit red and white like so many giant *Transformer* action figures. Vishul, who'd grown up in Dubai, turned 360 degrees and jokingly exclaimed, "*This* is the future!" And, until the global economic meltdown hit in late 2008, it probably was.

Dubai has been lauded by Western statesmen and the media as a model for the rest of the Muslim world to follow—a capitalist, consumerist paradise tolerant of alternative (read: Western) lifestyles and undisturbed by terrorism. This city of the future is ruled over by a benign autocrat, Sheikh Mohammed bin Rashid Al Maktoum, and is populated mainly by foreigners. These expatriates, who comprise over 90 percent of the population, account for 99 percent of the private-sector workforce and 90 percent of the public-sector workforce in jobs ranging from construction workers and maids to engineers, architects, and bankers. Because Dubai has been

a migrant-receiving city since the early 1900s, its massive foreign population is nothing new. In fact, even before the United Arab Emirates (of which Dubai is a semiautonomous member) received independence in 1971, Dubai's migrant population exceeded its native citizen population.

What's astounding, though, is that all expatriates are in Dubai on short-term visas. Unlike immigrant-receiving countries such as the United States, United Kingdom, France, and Germany, Dubai has no form of permanent immigrant incorporation. Even in countries as strict as Switzerland, migrants, including lower-skilled "guest workers," can find roads to permanent settlement and family reunification. So while guest workers and their children throughout Europe may find it varyingly difficult to acquire citizenship, they often have the legal right to stay permanently.

In Dubai, expatriates willingly give up political rights such as free speech and due process, and they live precariously on short-term visas that can be revoked at any time for any reason. In exchange, they earn tax-free wages as "economic mercenaries," fully aware that they are

> Dubai has been lauded as a model for the rest of the Muslim world—a capitalist, consumerist paradise tolerant of alternative lifestyles and undisturbed by terrorism.

there solely to work. For lower-level workers from developing countries, the trade-off includes the unstated promise that they will live and toil in harsh conditions in Dubai so they can send remittances and make a better life for themselves back home. The middle class, mainly South Asians and Arabs from outside the Arabian Gulf who fill the bulk of lower and middle white-collar positions, find better occupational possibilities, better schools, more comfortable family living, and a largely crime-free environment enticing. And for upper-class professionals (Westerners, but also South Asians, Arabs, and others) there is the lure of the "good life"— comprised of cheap household help (maids alone form 10 percent of the population), luxury accommodations, spas, clubs, bars, restaurants, outdoor sports, and prostitution—that has made Dubai so famous in the West.

> Even before the United Arab Emirates received independence, Dubai's migrant population exceeded its native citizen population.

On its surface, the case of Dubai and its permanently impermanent workforce seems singular. But, as many Western countries implement restrictive guest-worker programs that limit immigrants' ability to stay and circumscribe many of their rights, the case of Dubai's expatriates may actually be a harbinger of the future of global migration.

a mercenary life

All expatriates in Dubai, even those born in Dubai, are on short-term, renewable visas, regulated through the *kafala,* or sponsorship, system. Expatriates' residence visas are, as in the rest of the Arabian Gulf countries, tied to their sponsors, usually their employers. Changing jobs is virtually out of the question, and any expatriates who quit or are fired, with some exceptions for professionals, have to leave the country for a six-month period before they can return to take another job. So long as expatriates in Dubai hold on to their jobs and don't bring negative attention to themselves, though, they can stay until the retirement age of 60, at which point, unless they own a business or receive permission on a case-by-case basis, they must leave.

Not unexpectedly, laborers, the middle class, and professionals experience their temporariness differently. Laborers, including construction workers, maids, cab drivers, and lower-level service workers (who generally earn slightly better than third-world-level wages), constitute the vast majority of Dubai's population and are highly regulated in their working and social lives. Their passports are confiscated upon arrival (an illegal practice that even government ministries engage in), their wages are often withheld for months at a time to prevent them from quitting (a practice the government tolerates), and unions and strikes are illegal. Workers who have participated in strikes or protests have been immediately deported without a trial or due process of any kind. Many men (especially construction workers) are housed in remote, overcrowded, filthy labor camps, and most of the rest of the working class shares rooms in overcrowded, filthy, and dilapidated villas or apartment buildings. Socially, they fare no better: construction workers, for example, are often denied entry to the shopping malls they build.

Where laborers' lives are largely regulated by this series of "sticks," the middle class and professionals' lives are regulated mostly with "carrots" like high salaries, fast professional advancement, and luxury living. The government doesn't need to enforce discipline, as these expatriates essentially live in a "gilded cage," willingly trading political rights for economic possibilities. And the government is more than happy to allow these expatriates wide latitude in their social behaviors (they're free to worship as they like, drink, and openly visit prostitutes, for instance) so long as none of those behaviors looks remotely political.

While professionals, and to a lesser extent the middle class, find a great degree of social freedom, in the end they too, like laborers, are simply factors of production, there to create wealth for the ruler, the government, and the national citizen population. The *kafala* system essentially defines the bulk of the population as disposable and temporary. It is not incidental that the government insists expatriates are "guest workers."

> Laborers' lives are regulated by a series of "sticks," White middle class and professionals' lives are regulated mostly with "carrots."

The transience of expatriates is underscored by the fact that citizenship is basically unattainable and there is no such category as permanent residence. The most commonly stated reasons given by government officials for denying citizenship or permanent residence are the threats of cultural extinction and demographic imbalance posed by the possibility of absorbing so many expatriates into the pool of citizens. These twin arguments are repeated time and time again. However, there are two critical but unstated factors that are central to the management of expatriates in Dubai and the government's stance on naturalization. First, the government's legitimacy depends to a great degree on its ability to guarantee a high standard of living to national citizens. Allowing expatriates to naturalize might lead to the state having to spread its welfare largesse among a much larger pool of recipients. Second, the *kafala* system provides a simple and effective mechanism of social control. As expatriates are in Dubai primarily to work, the mere possibility of deportation is enough to stifle any kind of threat they may pose to the political-economic order.

Many scholars argue that formal, legal citizenship is becoming less important in an increasingly globalized world. As money, goods, ideas, and people move further and faster than ever before, legal and social barriers to movement have weakened. The idea of dual citizenship is more widely accepted than it ever has been, further eroding the historical notion that citizens should have loyalty to only one place. Even illegal migrants can often become legal by proving that they have conducted themselves like "good citizens" in their new land.

The literature on citizenship has expanded the concept to take into consideration how the boundaries of the nation-state have become, literally and figuratively, more permeable and, in some ways, less relevant over time. International treaties and institutions (especially those making human rights universal) and the free movement of people and capital greatly affect the sovereignty of states and how they relate to both citizens and noncitizens living within their borders. In the past 20 years, terms such as "flexible citizenship," "post-national citizenship," and "denationalized citizenship" have gained currency. And while there are major differences between these influential concepts and other ideas that expand upon the notion of what is and who is a citizen, taken together they announce that "citizen" is more than simply a legal category and that people can claim to "belong" to a place without legally belonging to that place.

But legal citizenship and the realistic possibility of obtaining it remains important—you simply cannot legally and securely live somewhere without a proper visa or citizenship. The nonlegal dimensions of citizenship, including the cultural, economic, consumer, and psychological angles, are largely meaningless without formal legal standing. Consider one of the most basic factors of citizenship: generally, you cannot be deported—and if you are deported, the other forms of citizenship become moot. For noncitizens, these other forms of citizenship can only be meaningful if the threat of deportation is minimal.

These are things that expatriates in Dubai, most of whom are from the developing world, understand all too well. While there are no publicly available data on the numbers of deportations, they occur frequently enough that stories of deportees serve as widely known cautionary tales that help keep laborers, the middle class, and professional expatriates in line. These nonnatives are careful to stay out of trouble with the police, they make certain not to engage in behavior that might look political, and they avoid criticizing the ruling family or national citizens in general. At any point and for practically any reason, the government or an employer may arbitrarily cancel a worker's visa and trigger immediate deportation.

The threat of deportation and the lack of any legal recourse is one reason why so many expatriates would welcome the possibility of naturalization or, at least, permanent residence. Without these possibilities, expatriates understand that their stay in Dubai, no matter how long-term, is by definition temporary. They plan accordingly: Westerners know they will return to the West. Laborers know they will also go back home. South Asian and Arab middle-class and professional expatriates must either go home (an undesirable outcome for many) or attempt to go to the West seeking new professional opportunities for themselves or education for their children.

Expatriates born in Dubai also understand that they are temporary residents. Of the 45 South Asian and Arab second-generation expatriates I interviewed, more than half had acquired permanent residence or citizenship in Western countries, and most of the rest were trying to do the same. Hardly anyone I interviewed intended to return to their legal home in their parents' third-world country of origin, but few had any illusions of calling Dubai home. I was stunned to hear one young, Indian corporate headhunter say bluntly, "Dubai is a pitstop, a place where you come, make a good amount of money and you get out." Why was this so shocking? The young man in question had been born and raised in this "pitstop." Until just before we met, he'd never even been outside the U.A.E.

In response to recent international pressure and spiraling unemployment among national citizens, some Arabian Gulf states have begun to rethink the *kafala* system. Bahrain was the first to initiate radical change, discarding the sponsorship system altogether in August 2009. Its expatriates will now be "sponsored" directly by the government, and their visas will no longer be tied to a particular job. Following Bahrain, Kuwait took a first step toward abolishing the *kafala* system when it announced that its expatriates would be able to change jobs after three years without sponsor approval or after one year if the sponsor doesn't object. Using language that Human Rights Watch would approve of, a Kuwaiti minister lauded the change and called the *kafala* system "modern-day slavery."

The abolition of the *kafala* system could lead to higher wages, especially at the middle and lower ends of the job market, where most workers are from the developing world and paid accordingly. Bahrain and Kuwait also hope that the current high unemployment rates among national citizens will be reduced, as the financial costs of hiring and training nationals become

Dubai's expatriates live in a "gilded cage," willingly trading political rights for economic possibilities.

more attractive to private-sector firms. Conspicuously though, officials in Dubai have remained mum on any similar changes. Their silence is deafening—and unsurprising, given that Dubai's government-owned companies in construction, hospitality, and other sectors employ tens of thousands of workers at all levels, and government coffers are enriched through those depressed wages.

These policy changes represent a monumental shift for the region. The basic premise of my research has been that the *kafala* system colors every aspect of life in Dubai. If similar, radical changes were undertaken in Dubai, the way of life for expatriates and national citizens alike would be drastically altered. Expatriates would have freedom of mobility in the labor market and would no longer have to fear deportation should they lose or quit their jobs. This is a particularly important issue today, as Dubai is in the middle of a recession, with megaprojects at a standstill and many completed high-rises standing empty. Workers are being laid off in such large numbers that some estimate Dubai's population may have shrunk by an incredible 17 percent in 2009.

Economist Paul Krugman writes that a guest-worker program could amount to a dangerous betrayal of the United States' democratic ideals.

the "dubai effect"

The story of Dubai's expatriate population feels, at first, like an outlier. But it may end up being replicated beyond Dubai and the Arabian Gulf countries. While Bahrain and Kuwait are in the process of abandoning the *kafala* system, Western countries are increasingly adopting labor policies similar to those of Dubai and the other Gulf countries. These policies mainly concern working-class laborers, but as in the Gulf, professionals may find themselves living under similar visa regimes. For example, more than half of skilled workers from non–European Union countries arrive in the United Kingdom on "intra-company" transfers. As of a 2008 overhaul, the United Kingdom's visa system is largely grounded through employers. While Tier 1 visas, issued for highly skilled professional migrants, do not require a sponsor, Tier 2 employees applying for permanent status must be sponsored or they'll be forced to leave. Further, in 2009, the government was considering banning transferred, "intra-company" workers from citizenship altogether, a move that could conceivably turn them into Dubai-like expatriates: legal, but impermanent.

Similarly, the United States has programs limiting the ability of professionals from overseas to stay, most notably the H-1B visa program. The H-1B program is mostly for IT professionals, whose visas are tied to their employers. They can stay up to six years, so long as they are employed, and they are allowed to apply for permanent residency. There is, however, no guarantee that it will be granted; my friend Vishul tried, but failed, to adjust his own H-1B status and had to leave the country. At its peak, the H-1B program covered roughly 200,000 people a year, but the number of these visas being issued yearly has since dropped to its original 1999 level of 65,000.

The United States has also toyed with the idea of a wide-ranging guest-worker program for lower-skilled workers. This would echo the Bracero Program, which brought temporary Mexican agricultural laborers to the United States from 1942 to 1964, but ended in part because of widespread abuse of workers. In 2006, Congress proposed a plan to create a permanent guest-worker program that would admit 400,000 more workers a year. While it was not enacted, many in Congress made it clear that when immigration reform is eventually addressed it must include some kind of temporary guest-worker program.

Recognizing aspects of the *kafala* system creeping into national policy debates, the Nobel Prize–winning economist Paul Krugman mused on what he called "the Dubai Effect" in the *New York Times*. Writing in 2006, Krugman said that a guest-worker program could amount to a dangerous betrayal of the United States' democratic ideals. It would, he wrote, basically form an entrenched caste system of temporary workers whose interests would largely be ignored and whose rights would be circumscribed. Further, their wages would undoubtedly be less than those of people with greater labor-market mobility, though the ripple effects of a glut of guest workers would be expected to lower wages for all workers in sectors where guest workers are "bonded" to their employers, Dubai-style.

Following Krugman, I wonder if Western states increasingly adopt policies like those in the Arabian Gulf countries, they will see situations of non-assimilation similar to those played out among expatriates in Dubai. Of course, unlike in Dubai, any children born in the United States acquire citizenship by birth, but there would still be a sizable community of adults who were essentially in the country, but not of it. If that's the case, Dubai and its permanently impermanent population would look less like a unique example and more like a prescient harbinger of the future experience of incorporation—or lack thereof.

RECOMMENDED RESOURCES

Human Rights Watch. 2006. "Building Towers, Cheating Workers: Exploitation of Migrant Construction Workers in the United Arab Emirates." www.hrw.org, November 11.

Examines government collusion in employers' exploitation of workers in the UAE.

Andrzej Kapiszewski. 2001. *Nationals and Expatriates: Population and Labour Dilemmas of the Gulf Cooperation Council States*. Reading, UK: Ithaca Press.

Explores how Arabian Gulf countries controlled their expatriate labor force and kept their citizens happy before the latest economic boom.

Aihwa Ong. 1999. *Flexible Citizenship: The Cultural Logics of Transnationality*. Durham, NC: Duke University Press.

Details how globalization and transnational behavior have changed the meaning of citizenship.

Yasemin Soysal. 1994. *Limits of Citizenship: Migrants and Postnational Membership in Europe*. Chicago: University of Chicago Press.

Shows how formal citizenship declines as states, influenced by the global discourse of human rights, increasingly grant rights and benefits to noncitizens.

REVIEW QUESTIONS

1. What are the strengths and weaknesses of Dubai's immigration policies? What are the intended and unintended consequences?
2. Who makes immigration policy in Dubai? Who benefits because of it? Who doesn't?
3. How is the situation of migrant workers in Dubai similar to the situation for U.S. migrant workers? How is it different?
4. Do you agree with the author's conclusion that Dubai's policy may be the future of global migration? Why or why not? Would this be desirable?

the king of compton

summer 2016

tick-a-lott is a dancer from compton who has dedicated his life to entertainment and "pop" dancing. author jooyoung lee illustrates the history of dance and its influence on the community of compton.

Straw Mann started the dance circle. As people backed up to clear space, Trenseta rhymed in the background. This was a typical night at Project Blowed, South Central Los Angeles' legendary hip-hop open mic workshop: rappers on stage, dancers hyping the crowd on the floor.

The crowd roared as Straw Mann cartwheeled across the room like a capoeira fighter. He popped up into a praying-mantis pose and staggered around like a Kung Fu master practicing "drunken style." There was a break in the action as he exited the circle. Nobody wanted to follow him. "Here's my chance," I thought, jumping into the middle. At first, I started "waving," a fluid style of "poppin'." Then I "floated" across the open space of the circle. I busted out all my best moves, hoping to win over the crowd.

But Tick-a-Lott—an old-school popper from Compton—wasn't impressed. He stood on the edge of the circle, hands on hips, and told everyone that I *wasn't* poppin'. He laughed while covering his mouth. "That's just tricks, man! You need to hit the beat!" he called out over the music.

Tick-a-Lott's critiques stung. I had learned how to "pop" years before I ever showed up to Project Blowed. My teacher was Tron, a street performer in Berkeley. I had practiced and trained with Tron for years when I was an undergraduate at UC Berkeley. He was like my Mr. Miyagi. I'd

show up at his house and he'd tell me to put my arms through a tree in his front yard. The tree had a dense web of intertwined branches. "Now take them out," he'd say. I'd scrape up my elbows extracting my limbs. "When you can do that without pain, you'll know how to 'wave'." I also became a member of "Boogie Knights," a mixed-styles dance crew comprised of poppers, lockers, B-boys, and house dancers from the East Bay. We battled crews from all over the Bay Area. And at the peak of my dancing days, I won an open-styles dance battle at "The Crackhouse," an abandoned warehouse near Oakland's Jack London Square.

But at Project Blowed, my moves and dance lineage were unimpressive. The poppin' (or "pop-locking," as it's sometimes called in L.A.) scene was different: in L.A., poppers evaluated each other by how hard they could *hit* or violently contract their muscles to the beat. I had no clue how to hit. I didn't fit into the local aesthetic.

Years later, Tick-a-Lott broke it down for me. He told me that hitting hard was an extension of local gang culture, in which young people work to present themselves as invulnerable on the streets. Once, watching me try to hit hard, he said, "We grew up in this gang shit. Even if you not into it, you gotta hit *hard*." I looked at my reflection in the glass doors outside the Vision Theatre, a performing arts venue in the historic Leimert Park area of South Central.

Tick-a-Lott demonstrates some moves outside Project Blowed.
(Jooyoung Lee)

Tick-a-Lott "tutting" and posing with the author. (Jooyoung Lee)

I wasn't hitting hard. I looked like I was having a seizure. My body convulsed awkwardly, moving too quickly or too slowly, almost always missing the beat.

I got to know Tick-a-Lott as I worked on my book, *Blowin' Up: Rap Dreams in South Central*. During those five years, he taught me how to pop. But more importantly, his story showed me the web of people that came together to support his pathway into poppin'. As Howard Becker describes in his study of art worlds, artists are often at the center of dense, supportive social networks. Tick-a-Lott's career was the result of support he received from peers at school, administrators, a marching band, and, perhaps most importantly, local gang members, who left him alone as he pursued dance. Dancing, like rapping or playing basketball, was a skill that young men like Tick-a-Lott could use to gain status and respect in their neighborhoods *outside* of gangs. It was another identity option in a world in which gangbanging was a familiar rite of passage.

> For Tick-a-Lott and others, dancing was another identity option in a world in which gangbanging was the more familiar rite of passage.

when poppin' blew up

In most art worlds, there are certain artists who launch the form into mainstream culture. Poppin' is usually linked to "Boogaloo Sam" from Fresno, California. During the 1970s, Sam invented the style while watching funk dancers on Soul Train. He modified their up-tempo "lockin' " into a slower, rhythmic dance that combined turns, poses, and freezes. He taught poppin' to others in Southern California when he moved to Long Beach in the late 1970s.

Years later, Michael Jackson would propel poppin' into the limelight. He "unveiled" it in 1983 during the televised 25th anniversary show for Motown Records. *Motown 25: Yesterday, Today, Forever* drew 34 million viewers and featured Stevie Wonder, Diana Ross & The Supremes, and the long-anticipated reunion of Smokey Robinson and The Miracles. But, in a night full of memorable performances, one stood out. When the beat dropped to "Billie Jean," Michael Jackson—rocking a black-sequined tuxedo—grabbed his crotch and thrust it to the beat. He spun, kicked his legs, and tossed his fedora offstage in one singular motion. The crowd was mesmerized for three-and-a-half minutes. And then, just as his performance reached a fever pitch, the "King of Pop" glided across the stage, as if on an invisible walkway. The moonwalk was born.

The public fell in love with the moonwalk, and many believed that the King of Pop had invented the move. But dance legend has it that, like Boogaloo Sam, he learned it from dancers on *Soul Train*. Michael Jackson was mesmerized by what he saw on TV and had his management get the names of dancers who could teach him how to do that move and others. Jackson would bring the moonwalk and poppin' to the masses.

Poppin', much like Bboyin' and Bgirlin' (breakdancing), soon saturated popular media. Hollywood studios rushed to hire street dancers for upcoming films, and funk dancers like Shabba Doo and Boogaloo Shrimp starred in movies like *Breakin'* and *Breakin' 2*, further popularizing these styles of street dance.

MJ's iconic performance and the popular attention it brought to poppin' and funk styles also changed how underground dancers thought about their craft. Tick-a-Lott and his crew, Mysterious Waves, tried to capitalize on the mainstream emergence of poppin' and got headshots taken. They auditioned for roles in films, TV shows, and commercials. They got rejected most of the time, but Mysterious Waves got what felt like a mini-break after a callback for *Breakin' 2: Electric Boogaloo*. Tick was excited, even if he and his crew weren't a featured act. He got to work with rapper Ice-T and other dancers performing at Radiotron, a community center in L.A.'s MacArthur Park. It felt momentous, like Tick-a-Lott and the other dancers were on the cusp of something big. Success felt within reach.

Poppin' continued to grow in popularity during the 1980s. Like Bboyin' and Bgirlin' before it, poppin' was eventually appropriated and commodified. In 1985, Mr. Rogers invited a 12-year-old street dancer named Jermaine Vaughn to teach him how to moonwalk and pop, right there in his neighborhood.

All of this was happening during a time of massive deindustrialization and job loss in Compton and other urban areas across the country. Poppin', to put it succinctly, was what Robin Kelley calls "play labor." When youth lack attractive work options in the formal labor market, they often turn to skills and talents that present them with opportunities—however fleeting—that don't appear possible in the given market. Much like hoop and rap dreams, poppin' (and hip-hop dance more broadly) seemed to offer youth from places like Compton a similar springboard to upward mobility. Dancers like Tick-a-Lott hoped their skills would propel them into the movies, music videos, and other popular media.

killer dance moves

But poppin' wasn't just a perceived way up in the world. Poppers like Ticka-Lott were also drawn to it for other, nonmaterial reasons.

Much like rappers, who enjoy being known for their songwriting and lyricism, poppers relish the status that comes with being known as a skilled dancer.

Tick-a-Lott was first drawn to poppin' in middle school. Back then, he was considered a locker or a "Campbell-locker." A 1970s dance, locking was created by Don Campbell and the Lockers in Los Angeles. Lockers pointed and froze their bodies, cocked their shoulders up and down, turned their hats, and jumped into the air, landing in the splits. They danced rhythmically to up-tempo funk and soul records like James Brown's "Get Up Offa That Thing."

Tick-a-Lott reminisced about the dramatic scene one night, telling me he had been at a school dance when some kids formed a huge dance circle. The circle was humming along until someone jumped into the circle and started poppin'. He said, "And then, this one kid he came out and starts hittin', like bam, bam, bam, bam!" He mimicked the other kids, wide-eyed and jaws dropped at the sight of this new dance style. Tick-a-Lott remembered, "I went right to the bathroom to practice what I seen."

> Michael Jackson's iconic "moonwalk" performance and the popular attention it brought to poppin' and funk styles changed how underground dancers thought about their craft. It felt momentous, like Tick-a-Lott and the other dancers were on the cusp of something big.

Tick-a-Lott was obsessed and practiced religiously. He often practiced in front of the bathroom mirror, while walking around the neighborhood, at school, or doing chores at home. He danced with a broomstick, pantomiming as he swept, and in front of the TV, watching the small reflection of his body move across the screen. The moves became second nature through repetition and practice.

Other people recognized and supported his talents. Classmates were impressed and his popularity grew: "Everybody knew that whenever I showed up, I was gonna shut it down. People wouldn't wanna dance after me!" Teachers and administrators took note and offered him a spot on the high school marching band. At first, Tick-a-Lott wasn't sure, but performing at parades, pep rallies, and football games would bring his moves to larger audiences. He was made a special drum major, left to improvise dance moves along with the band procession.

Tick-a-Lott also enjoyed attention from young women. Poppin' was a source of identity and status. Once, outside Project Blowed, Tick-a-Lott told us a story about a time when he danced at his high school football team's halftime show. He said a cheerleader from the visiting high school noticed his electric dance moves and started flirting: "Her boyfriend didn't like this! He was finna beat my ass!" Tick-a-Lott laughed as he recalled being chased by the girl's boyfriend and how he narrowly escaped, jumping over a fence to safety.

On another night, he showed us pictures from the many battles he won during his heyday. He fished around in his backpack and pulled out an old headshot. It was black-and-white and had veiny creases running through it. He was much younger in the photo and had a full head of glistening jheri curls. "All the ladies loved my hair!" he said. The next photo was from an "open styles" dance battle in Compton. He stood behind a four-foot trophy in a white tracksuit and Adidas Shell Toes. He had been one of the only poppers in that battle. After defeating a bunch of dancers in the early rounds, he went on to beat a Bboy in the finals. "That day, I *served* everybody. I was the King of Compton!"

I never doubted Tick-a-Lott, but a part of me always wondered if he was exaggerating his acclaim. These doubts were put to rest one afternoon at a Compton barbershop. When we walked in, a couple of the barbers—high school friends of Tick's—yelled, "Uh oh! Look who it is!" Tick-a-Lott started "tickin'," a style of rapid-fire stop motion that makes a dancer look like he's beneath a strobe light. His friends cracked up laughing, and they all exchanged handshakes. Tick-a-Lott introduced me, "This is J. He in school writing about me and my dancing." One of his friends beamed as he started telling his own tales of Tick-a-Lott's many battles and performances in Compton. Imitating Tick's dance moves, the barber told me, "He be out there getting down and people knew he would set it off. Everybody knew Tick." Tick-a-Lott said, "People used to go crazy when they saw me out there. They be like 'Do it again, do it again!'"

Gang members also recognized his talents, leaving him alone to "do his thing." Hanging out by the Martin Luther King Jr. statue in downtown Compton, Tick-a-Lott told me about his experience growing up around gangs. "They start buggin' out every time I come around," he said. "Did they ever ask you to join up?" "Nah. They knew what I was doing. Everybody knew I was poppin'."

There are probably many reasons for why Tick-a-Lott never got into the gang lifestyle. He may not have been drawn to it. Whenever the topic came up, he would shrug and laugh off the notion of being in a gang. Or, he'd say that being in a gang was for "little kids." Also, local gangs may not have seen him as a good recruit. There is a popular assumption that young people of color are drawn to gangs because they offer them a sense of family or belonging. While this rings true for some, it is not a universal explanation of what it is like to come of age in the shadows of gangs.

But, importantly, Tick-a-Lott was immersed in a social world that supported his passion for dancing. Poppin' gave him a respectable "pass" and an unimpeded path outside of gangs. In addition to friends who knew him as a killer on the dance floor, Tick-a-Lott was surrounded by peers, teachers, and administrators who endorsed his talents and provided him with support and a venue to show off his moves. All of this made a lifestyle and identity as a dancer attractive and, more importantly, possible.

Ultimately, our identities are a mix of how we see ourselves and how others see us. Self and social appraisals are complementary parts of a whole identity. For Tick-a-Lott, his identity as a dancer gave him an alternative way to become known and gain respect in his social world.

These days, you can find Tick-a-Lott performing out on Hollywood Boulevard, decked out in Locs, a Chinese Tuxedo, and a black porkpie hat. Sometimes he'll even set up shop along the Hollywood "Walk of Fame."

Even though he sometimes still entertains the possibility of a lucrative career as a dancer, he knows that this is probably a pipe dream. But Tick-a-Lott and other poppers aren't just motivated by a glimpse of fame or fortune. Poppin' is a fun, creative outlet that forms a core part of their identity. When social scientists write about art, music, and dance, we often lose sight of these nonmaterial attractions to creativity. Artists experience joy, camaraderie, and a sense of mastery while creating art. These experiences are intrinsically rewarding.

Poppin' also helped Tick-a-Lott avoid a path that swallows up so many other young people from his hometown, Compton. It was a creative intervention. In a recent interview for Noisey, mainstream Compton rapper Kendrick Lamar reflected on his own journey into hip-hop. He talked about his friends who had grown up in gangs and how his love for rhyming gave him a way out of that world. Tick-a-Lott's story was strikingly similar. Even though he never blew up like Kendrick Lamar, Tick still found a way to avoid a violent world that injures and ends the lives of so many of his peers.

Years after finishing my book, I met up with Tick-a-Lott on Hollywood Boulevard. He was there with old-school poppers like Scorpio and Midnight. They were performing along the Walk of Fame as crowds of people came and went between the restaurants, bars, and clubs outside Grauman's Chinese Theatre. Tick was dusting off a sweaty rubber mask he had spray-painted silver and black—Oakland Raiders colors. I asked about his upcoming performance, and he smiled. "When I'm pop-lockin', I feel like I'm in a zone. I'm just in it."

RECOMMENDED RESOURCES

Howard Becker. 1982. *Art Worlds*. Berkeley: University of California Press.

> How artists produce their work with the help of others.

Robin Kelley. 1997. *Yo' Mama's Disfunktional! Fighting the Culture Wars in Urban America*. Boston: Beacon Press.

> Explores hip-hop culture as a perceived pathway to upward mobility for urban African-American men.

Marcyliena Morgan. 2009. *The Real HipHop: Battling for Knowledge, Power, and Respect in the LA Underground*. Durham: Duke University Press.

> The early history of American emcees and Project Blowed.

Jorge "Popmaster Fabel" Pabon. 2006. "Physical Graffiti: The History of Hip-Hop Dance." In *Total Chaos*, ed. Jeff Chang. New York: Basic Civitas.

> Popper and hip-hop historian Pabon breaks down the origins of poppin' and locking.

Joseph Schloss. 2009. *Foundation: B-boys, B-girls, and Hip-hop Culture in New York*. New York: Oxford University Press.

An ethnographic look at how dancers compete for respect.

REVIEW QUESTIONS

1. Describe the term *play labor*.
2. How is the use of ethnographic research important for the author's analysis of Tick-a-Lott's story?
3. The author argues that poppin' kept Tick-a-Lott out of the violent gang life that took many lives of his peers in Compton. What kind of policy would you design that will give young people an "out"?

marcus anthony hunter

black philly after the philadelphia negro

66

winter 2014

black residents of philadelphia's seventh ward were not simply the passive witnesses of change, that actively helped reform housing policy. black residents have long been citymakers and a force for progressive change.

Along with Chicago's Bronzeville, Pittsburgh's Hill District, Washington, D.C.'s U-Street/Shaw area, Los Angeles's Watts, and New York City's Harlem, Philadelphia's Black Seventh Ward served as a major port-of-entry for southern Black migrants during the Great Migration.

At its height, the Black Seventh Ward contained close to 15,000 Black residents along with shops and myriad cultural institutions.

As W. E. B. Du Bois reported in his classic 1899 study *The Philadelphia Negro,* the Black Seventh Ward was "in the centre of the city, near places of employment for the mass of people and near the centre of social life," leading people to "crowd here in great numbers." Excited by the opportunity to research the neighborhood, he was struck by the diverse Black population, the extreme poverty and seemingly ever-present violence. "Murder sat at our doorsteps, police were our government, and philanthropy dropped in with periodic advice," he wrote.

Du Bois and his wife, Nina, arrived in Philadelphia in the autumn of 1896, amid "an atmosphere of dirt, drunkenness, poverty, and crime." Commissioned by local political leaders and scholars, Du Bois analyzed Black life in Philadelphia, demonstrating "how this class of people live; what occupations they follow; from what occupations they are excluded; how many of

their children will go to school; and to ascertain every fact which will throw light on this social problem."

Du Bois dove into his research, conducting demographic analyses, interviews, and participant-observation. Dressed in a well-fitted suit and bow tie, he spoke with more than 5,000 Black Seventh Warders, combing through archives. Du Bois found that the answers to key questions about urban inequality and the daily lives of Black city folk could be found by understanding their neighborhoods. The problems of African Americans in Philadelphia (and elsewhere) were the result of centuries of prejudice, enslavement, and discrimination.

Urban Black Americans, however, were not simply victims of the vast changes impacting American cities throughout the twentieth century—urban renewal, deindustrialization, the New Deal, the War on Poverty, and general urban disinvestment. Nor were they passive bystanders who watched the city change from the windows of their row homes. Black Philadelphians were and are agents of urban change—citymakers.

up south

What happened after W. E. B. Du Bois left Philadelphia? Did his research and policy recommendations impact the Seventh Ward? What was the fate of this historically Black neighborhood, and others like it? Curious about these questions, I looked at a pivotal period after Du Bois's study—the 1920s through the early 1940s. Looking at this period allows us to gauge the relationship of Philly's Black residents to the progressive politics that shaped urban New Deal policies and coalitions. This period also offers a historical window into the shifting allegiances of Black Americans and their retreat from the Republican Party and embrace of the Democratic Party.

Examining housing reform and the development of public housing in the city, I combed through public documents about local and national housing policies and changes, events in the Black Seventh Ward, voting results, and local and national political campaigns. I wanted to gain a better sense of the social, economic, and political conditions of the time, and the various stakeholders and players in reform efforts.

What I found is that three decades after Du Bois left Philadelphia, Black and White community organizations commissioned a study of "Negro migrants" in the Black Seventh Ward. They found insufficient water supply and toilet facilities, defective sanitary equipment, overcrowding, leaky roofs, plaster and paper falling off the walls, and windowless rooms. Du Bois had earlier documented similar deprivations: "Of the 2,441 families only 334 had access to bathroom and water-closets," he wrote. "Even these 334 families have poor accommodations. Many share the use of one bathroom with one or more families. Most of these houses have to get their water at a hydrant in the alley, and must store their fuel in the house."

Landlords responded to the increased Black population by refashioning apartments and rooming houses, dividing existing residences into several "new" rooms or apartments—many of which of lacked heating, bathrooms, or adequate plumbing. The persistence of poor housing decades after *The Philadelphia Negro* suggested a pattern of racial segregation and exploitation that has typically been associated with the South. The *Philadelphia Tribune*, a local Black newspaper, dubbed the Black Seventh Ward "Hell's Acre." Indeed, Philadelphia represented what historian Matthew Countryman refers to as "up south" racial oppression.

Black and White leaders attributed the neighborhood's deplorable conditions to the supposed "backwardness" of southern Black migrants, suggesting that housing conditions would improve once new arrivals were taught "how to live in a city." Because of this Republican opposition to intervention, the Democratic Party became more and more appealing to poor and working-class Black residents.

The Republican Mayor J. Hampton Moore declared that Philadelphia "was too proud to have slums" and that people were "merely living within their means." At the onset of the Great Depression, such a fiery statement would lead to a highly competitive mayoral race in 1935. Having witnessed the power of the Black voting bloc in the election of President Franklin Delano Roosevelt, Philadelphia's Democratic mayoral candidate John "Jack" Kelly used the deterioration of the Black Seventh Ward as a part of his 1934–1935 political platform. He assailed Republican leadership for continued inaction in the Black Seventh Ward, capitalizing on a political opportunity Du Bois had foretold in *The Philadelphia Negro*: "Any worthy cause of municipal reform can secure a respectable Negro vote in the city, showing that there is the germ of an intelligent independent vote which rises above even the blandishments of decent remunerative employment."

The *Philadelphia Tribune* supported Kelly's mayoral bid and focus on Black housing, running a series of investigative reports on the plight of the Black Seventh Ward. "Living conditions in [Hell's] Acre are not based on the house or apartment unit. Here the basis of any examination is the single room. . . . You find whole families living in ONE room, not two or three or four rooms," the *Tribune* reported. Black Philadelphians also embarked on a successful letter-writing campaign, which led to an allocation of $10 million from the secretary of the federal Public Works Administration for slum removal and new housing construction. But a tragic event would challenge this pattern of development.

an american tragedy

On the evening of December 19, 1936, Lucy Spease ate dinner with her three children—Bernice, age 13, Samuel, age 6, and Helen, age 5—in her small but homey second-floor apartment on South 15th Street. The Seventh Ward apartment was cold. Cracks along the walls gave way to the wintry air, and it was common practice for residents to sleep, eat, and cook in their winter coats. All of Spease's neighbors, including those in the apartment building next door, had repeatedly complained to the landlord, a White man by the name of Abraham Samson, about their poor living conditions.

That evening, a neighbor named Raymond Blackwell confronted the landlord, perhaps hoping to see repairs made before Christmas. In his plea to Samson, Blackwell exclaimed: "The walls on the second-floor front room are bulging at least a foot and a half and the paper in the kitchen is falling off and the walls have begun to crack." As the men spoke, Spease was busy tucking her children into bed. Soon after, she felt the walls shake. Plaster fell from the ceiling in huge chunks and, in a flash, the floor caved beneath her. Blackwell, believing his words might have finally pushed Samson to action, arrived home to find that the building had been reduced to rubble.

All that was left of the building was a stack of ruins more than a story high. Nearly 35 people were caught inside. Lucy Spease was found dead near the bodies of Bernice and Samuel. Helen, Spease's youngest daughter, died the following day. All told, seven people were killed, and more than two dozen were injured. The site took several days to clear.

The tragedy became the catalyst for an unprecedented period of housing reform and construction in Philadelphia, including several housing projects designed to supply affordable housing to the city's poor and working-class Black residents.

The day after the building collapse on South 15th Street, Crystal Bird Fauset, an emergent Democratic leader, led a committee of concerned Black residents and leaders through the site. Fauset took to the editorial pages of another Black newspaper, the *Philadelphia Independent,* after the visit: "Time after time, these housing needs have been pointed out to us," she wrote passionately. In spite of earlier reports and surveys "that reported that something needed to be done, and be done quickly," Fauset said. "The houses crashed and killed several women and little children."

"We women who make the homes of land, who revere the home, must act as well as merely observe or voice an opinion," she proclaimed. "Once sensing a situation, we must not wait on others to meet the need, whether they be officials or other [Black] people. . . . We must pitch in and compel action." Fauset tried to empower Black women, remind residents that these housing problems were both dangerous and nothing new, and broaden the scope of the tragedy, appealing to Black neighborhoods throughout the city.

unfit for habitation

Within a couple of weeks of the collapse, Mayor Wilson began razing dilapidated housing in the Black Seventh Ward. Using the $10 million acquired through the earlier letter-writing campaign, Wilson placed "Condemned, Unfit for Habitation" signs on many properties, with

Black Seventh Warders receiving his removal notices—which effectively left them homeless—as adding "insult to injury." A series of spontaneous protests broke out and later prompted the development of the Black-led Philadelphia affiliate of the National Negro Congress and Tenants League. Such activism halted Wilson's forced evictions and facilitated the development of the Philadelphia Housing Authority (PHA) in 1937.

Charged with new housing construction, the PHA received $20 million from the United States Housing Administration. It targeted two neighborhoods in North Philadelphia as the sites for what would become the James Weldon Johnson and Richard Allen Homes. Designated as Black housing, both projects would be built under what became known as the "racial composition rule." Employed in Atlanta, Chicago, and other cities, this rule required that housing projects be built in already heavily Black areas, and that their residents should reflect the existing racial composition of the surrounding neighborhood. Aware of the possibility that new housing would be located in North Philadelphia, some Black Seventh Warders migrated to North Philadelphia between 1937 and 1940, taking up residence with relatives and friends who already lived in the area.

This migration not only shrunk the population of the Black Seventh Ward but also led to the decline of its key Black institutions. Most notably, both the historic St. Thomas African Episcopal Church (founded 1793) and Frederick Douglass Memorial Hospital (founded in 1895) were forced to relocate to West Philadelphia. As the rector as St. Thomas intimated: "The church at 12th and Walnut streets was removed from its congregation and had no community in which it could effectively work." Without a robust Black community, neither institution could be widely effective in the Black Seventh Ward.

As Du Bois had observed in *The Philadelphia Negro*, churches such as St. Thomas were initially established as safe havens, providing protection from racial violence as well as spiritual guidance. The social and real protections of Black institutions wedded Black Philadelphians to the Seventh Ward: "The Negro [who] ventures away from the mass of his people and their organized life . . . finds himself alone, shunned and taunted, stared at and made uncomfortable." In this way, the decline of key institutions was a deep reflection of the dispersal of residents and the rising prominence of other Black enclaves in the city.

The fact that the Black Seventh Ward was not a central focus in housing construction was not lost on those who remained in the neighborhood. Reverend C. A. Roach, rector of St. Peter Claver Catholic Church, warned residents against the "political ballyhoo and political bluffs" of city leadership and argued: "We don't want Mayor Wilson going through the streets telling what he's going to do. Nothing has been done since these buildings collapsed, carrying to their deaths seven persons. Now we want some thing done." Such calls would go unaddressed, as the new housing efforts spurred by the deaths of the Spease family would be confined to a different neighborhood, providing incentives to leave the Black Seventh Ward.

By 1940, the Johnson and Allen Homes were slated to be fully occupied. Rejected families attempted to garner a spot in the newly proposed Tasker Homes, whose primary occupants were to be Whites. Their applications caused some short-term friction until Black leaders worked to quiet such dissent by reminding disgruntled families how the status quo actually favored Black Philadelphians.

black citymakers

Another short battle ensued when the PHA tried to sell the Allen Homes to the federal Defense Housing Administration. In response,

Black leaders wrote to President Roosevelt: "Sir, take immediate cognizance of the fact that the United States Housing Administration has diverted the use of these homes from their original purposes at the expense of the low-income group, who are least able to obtain decent housing even in normal times and not able at all in these times." They urged him to act "in the interest of these persons who cannot obtain decent housing within their capability to pay." He reversed the PHA's decision, and by 1942, the Allen Homes were fully occupied by Black families.

But the housing boom came to an abrupt end with the election of Republican Mayor Robert Lamberton in 1939. "Slums areas exist," said Lamberton, because "some people are so utterly shiftless that any place they live becomes a slum." And with that, progressive housing reform in New Deal–era Philadelphia was halted.

Today, over a century later, nearly all the churches, stores, and social clubs that lined blocks of Lombard and South Streets, in what was once the Black Seventh Ward, are gone. The site of the building that collapsed on South 15th Street nearly 90 years ago is now a parking lot. Replacing them are newly built residences and businesses catering mainly to White residents. The Black history of the neighborhood is recalled in myriad plaques commissioned by the Historical Society of Pennsylvania to mark the neighborhood's rich Black history. Indeed, this historically Black neighborhood is no longer.

And yet this history suggests that Black residents of Philadelphia's Seventh Ward were not simply the passive witnesses of change. They were actively involved in housing-reform efforts, shaping the ways local and federal officials addressed problems of housing and other urban issues. As Du Bois noted over a century ago, Black residents were keenly aware of their conditions, and they acted individually and *collectively* to ameliorate them. Black residents have long been citymakers, and a force for progressive change.

RECOMMENDED RESOURCES

W. E. B. Du Bois. 1899. *The Philadelphia Negro: A Social Study*. Philadelphia: University of Pennsylvania Press.

> Provides an in-depth analysis and portrait of Philadelphia's Black Seventh Ward from 1600 to 1897, the first monograph of its kind in American sociology.

Matthew Countryman. 2006. *Up South: Civil Rights and Black Power in Philadelphia*. Philadelphia: University of Pennsylvania Press.

> Provides an in-depth analysis and portrait of Black politics and protests in Philadelphia during the Civil Rights and Black Power eras.

Michael B. Katz and Thomas J. Sugrue. 1998. *W. E. B. Du Bois, Race, and the City: The Philadelphia Negro and Its Legacy*. Philadelphia: University of Pennsylvania Press.

> Provides an extensive interdisciplinary consideration of the various implications of *The Philadelphia Negro* for the study of race, history, and urban America.

REVIEW QUESTIONS

1. The author explained that residents of the Seventh Ward were relocated to housing projects built in North Philadelphia, leaving behind local social institutions. What roles can these social institutions play in a community, and specifically for this community, which had already relocated from the South?
2. How did activists in Philadelphia fight the relocation? What resources did they use?
3. What does the author mean when he uses the term *citymakers*?

syed ali

i gentrify bed-stuy

2014

an analytical, autobiographical essay on gentrification in one of the "hottest" neighborhoods in brooklyn.

If you have any young professional friends in Brooklyn, chances are they're gentrifiers who moved into a neighborhood that, until recently, was a ghetto. They'll probably get prickly if you probe too much, especially if they're White ("No, I'm not displacing poor African Americans!"), so go ahead and push that button. It's fun. But it's not their fault. They just want to rent or own a nicer place than they could afford in centrally located, White-majority neighborhoods

There are affordable middle-class neighborhoods they could live in at the edge of the city— far out in Queens and Staten Island. But the gentrifiers want to be in "the city." And today they want to live in Brooklyn because it's now the physical and metaphysical epicenter of the universe. That's not a value judgment, it's a fact. I know so because I read about it regularly in the *New York Times*. Every article on my almost-no-longer-ghetto neighborhood of Bed-Stuy (Bedford-Stuyvesant) signals its rising popularity and a rise in property values, even to the east of Malcolm X Boulevard—the poorer, more removed part of Bed-Stuy where I live.

The story of gentrification—the term was coined in reference to 1960s London by sociologist Ruth Glass—is pretty well known. Neighborhoods that are centrally located but industrial or poor (and in the United States, populated mostly by Blacks) have become attractive for their cheap rents for artists, queers, and college student "pioneers." Their arrival is followed by an influx of trendy bars, restaurants, cafes, and galleries, all of which make these neighborhoods attractive for young professionals who want to be where the excitement is.

In the 1980s and 1990s, when the gentrifiers were thinking of having kids, they grew more attentive to crime and bad schools and fled to suburbia. Eight years ago my wife and I moved to then-gentrifying Clinton Hill (bordering Bed-Stuy), off Myrtle Avenue— known as Murder Avenue back in the day. Murders are less common today, now the more common crime is joggers getting hit and robbed for their iPhones in Fort Greene Park. (Note: Do not jog with your iPhone in Brooklyn.) The other major crime is not getting an outdoor table at Madiba on a beautiful summer evening.

Partly because of lower crime rates today, the gentrifiers are staying put, especially those who are pregnant or have kids in tow. They are mainly White, or interethnic families, with a smattering of buppies (Black urban professionals). They love the city and want the "ethnic background ambience" gentrifying neighborhoods have to offer.

> We may all share the same neighborhood, but we're not neighbors in a Mr. Rogers or Jane Jacobs sense.

But what is our presence doing to the neighborhood? My Black neighbor likes my kind—young, upper-middle-class families buying brownstones—because we raise her property value. (And my White wife and half-breed kids are very sweet.) Does our moving to Bed-Stuy mean poor, Black residents will have to move? Many analysts think gentrification is like musical chairs, but where the last person is poor and Black, doesn't own their own home or have rent control, and so gets pushed out of the neighborhood as rents rise. However, Lance Freeman, an urban planning professor at Columbia University, says that gentrification is more complicated. In the 1990s at least, what appeared to be driving neighborhood change in Clinton Hill, Harlem, and elsewhere was the difference in who was moving into the neighborhood rather than how quickly people were moving out. Basically, the wealthier newcomers are not directly displacing poor, Black people. So if you gentrifiers were feeling guilty, you can relax and point to Freeman's research.

Then again, while we may all share the same neighborhood, we're not neighbors, in a Mr. Rogers or Jane Jacobs sense. The fancy new restaurants and stores cater to the gentrifiers, not to their poorer neighbors. And the gentrifiers' kids initially don't go to the local public or charter schools with the poorer neighbors' kids. At some point though, the yuppie offspring, usually out of necessity rather than choice, do end up at the local schools where they form a critical mass—and that's when you know for certain that the neighborhood can no longer be called a ghetto and that the prevailing cultural atmosphere will reflect the tastes of the gentrifiers.

If you're thinking, hey, I too would like to gentrify Bed-Stuy—you're out of luck. The bourgeois factor has reached the tipping point with the wine bars, organic groceries, and gourmet doughnuts. But you could try Staten Island.

REVIEW QUESTIONS

1. What does the term *gentrification* mean?
2. What are some of the explanations given for the gentrification of Bed-Stuy?
3. How is the increased presence of upper-income people changing the neighborhood?

editors and contributors

Syed Ali is in the sociology-anthropology department at Long Island University–Brooklyn. He is the author of *Dubai: Gilded Cage* and *Migration, Incorporation, and Change in an Interconnected World* (with Douglas Hartmann).

Philip N. Cohen is in the sociology department at University of Maryland, College Park. He is the author of *The Family: Diversity, Inequality, and Social Change* and *Enduring Bonds: Inequality, Marriage, Parenting, and Everything Else That Makes Families Great and Terrible*. He also writes the popular blog *Family Inequality*.

Richard Alba is in the sociology department at the Graduate Center of the City University of New York. He is the author most recently of *Strangers No More: Immigration and the Challenges of Integration in North America and Western Europe* (with Nancy Foner).

Sigal Alon is in the sociology department at Tel Aviv University. Her work focuses on class, gender, and racial–ethnic inequalities in higher education. She is the author of *Race, Class and Affirmative Action*.

Julie E. Artis is in the sociology department at DePaul University. She studies motherhood, family, and law.

Sutapa Basu is executive director of the women's center at the University of Washington. She studies women in developing economies and international development.

Katherine Beckett is in the department of sociology and the Law, Societies, and Justice Program at the University of Washington. She is the author, with Steve Herbert, of *Banished: The New Social Control in Urban America*.

Claudio E. Benzecry is in the department of communication studies at Northwestern University. He is the author of *From Head to Toe: Everyday Globalization in a Creative Industry*.

Joel Best is in the sociology and criminal justice department at the University of Delaware. He is the author of *Social Problems*.

Sarah Bowen is in the sociology and anthropology department at North Carolina State University. She is the author of *Divided Spirits: Tequila, Mezcal, and the Politics of Production*.

Denise Brennan is in the anthropology department at Georgetown University. She is the author of *Life Interrupted: Trafficking into Forced Labor in the United States*.

Joslyn Brenton is in the sociology department at Ithaca College. She does research on families, food, and health.

Tristan Bridges is in the sociology department at the University of California, Santa Barbara. He is the co-editor of *Exploring Masculinities: Identity, Inequality, Continuity and Change* with C. J. Pascoe.

Eliza Brown is in the sociology program at New York University. She studies family, marriage, and sexuality.

Jake Browne is a journalist, comic, and podcaster based in Denver, Colorado. He is the marijuana reviewer for *The Denver Post*.

Robert Brym is a sociologist at the University of Toronto. He is the author of *New Society: Sociology for the 21st Century*.

Carol Burke is in the English department and a faculty associate in the anthropology department at the University of California, Irvine. She is the author of *Camp All-American, Hanoi Jane, and the High-and-Tight: Gender, Folklore, and Changing Military Culture*.

Mónica L. Caudillo is a postdoctoral associate in the Maryland Population Research Center at the University of Maryland, College Park. She studies family demography, education, community violence, contraception, and sexual behavior.

Wendy Chapkis is in the departments of sociology and women and gender studies at the University of Southern Maine and coauthor, with Richard J. Webb, of *Dying to Get High: Marijuana as Medicine*.

Maria Charles is in the sociology department at the University of California, Santa Barbara. She is the co-editor (with David B. Grusky) of *Occupational Ghettos: The Worldwide Segregation of Women and Men*.

Andrew J. Cherlin is in the sociology department at Johns Hopkins University. He is the author of *Labor's Love Lost: The Rise and Fall of the Working-Class Family in America*.

Margaret M. Chin is in the sociology department at Hunter College and the City University of New York–Graduate Center. She is the author of *Sewing Women: Immigrants and the New York City Garment Industry*.

Bjorn Christianson is a photographer, designer, and developer in Minneapolis, Minnesota. An avid cyclist, Christianson helps create, document, and promote many kinds of bicycle events each year.

Susan Clampet-Lundquist is in the sociology department at St. Joseph's University. She is a coauthor of *Coming of Age in the Other America*.

Andy Clarno is in the department of sociology at the University of Illinois at Chicago. He is the author of *Neoliberal Apartheid: Palestine/Israel and South Africa after 1994*.

Dan Clawson is in the sociology department at the University of Massachusetts, Amherst. He is the coauthor, with Naomi Gerstel, of *Unequal Time* and, with Robert Zussman, coeditor of *Families at Work: Expanding the Boundaries*.

Simon A. Cole is in the department of criminology, law, and society at the University of California, Irvine. He is a member of the Human Factors Subcommittee of the National Commission on Forensic Science.

D'Lane R. Compton is in the sociology department at the University of New Orleans. She is the coauthor of *Legalizing LGBT Families: How the Law Shapes Parenthood* (with Amanda K. Baumle).

Dalton Conley is in the department of sociology at Princeton University. He is the author of *The Genome Factor: What the Social Genomics Revolution Reveals about Ourselves, Our History and the Future* (with Jason Fletcher).

Randol Contreras is in the department of sociology at the University of Toronto. He is the author of *The Stickup Kids: Race, Drugs, Violence, and the American Dream.*

Karen Cook is in the department of sociology at Stanford University. Cook studies social exchange, social networks, and trust.

James P. Curley is in the psychology department and the Columbia University Center for Integrative Animal Behavior at Columbia University. He has published research on molecular systems, organismal, and evolutionary levels of analysis in animals and humans.

Elliott Currie is in the department of criminology, law, and society at the University of California, Irvine. He is the coauthor of *Whitewashing Race: The Myth of a Color-blind Society.*

Gary C. David is in the department of sociology at Bentley University. He conducts research in the areas of medical records, ethnographies of work, and applied sociology.

Georgiann Davis is in the sociology department at the University of Nevada, Las Vegas. She is the author of *Contesting Intersex: The Dubious Diagnosis.*

Stefanie DeLuca is in the sociology department at Johns Hopkins University. She is the coauthor of *Coming of Age in the Other America.*

Amelia Seraphia Derr is in the social-work department at Seattle University. Her work focuses on social support and barriers to health and social services for immigrants.

Dhruv Dhawan is a documentary filmmaker and photographer in Vancouver and Dubai. The photographs in this text are from his recent book *Mumbai Sleeping*. His latest documentary film is *Why Knot: Breaking the Silence on Monogamy.*

Margaret Carlisle Duncan is in the human movement sciences department of the University of Wisconsin, Milwaukee. She is currently doing research on the meanings of obesity.

Troy Duster is at the Institute for the Study of Societal Issues at the University of California, Berkeley. He was, until recently, a member of the National Commission on Forensic Science.

Kathryn Edin is in the departments of sociology and population, family, and reproductive health at Johns Hopkins University. She is a coauthor of *Coming of Age in the Other America.*

Sinikka Elliott is in the department of sociology at the University of British Columbia. She is the author of *Not My Kid: What Parents Believe about the Sex Lives of Their Teenagers.*

Paula England is in the sociology department at New York University and president of the American Sociological Association. She studies changing family patterns; care work; sexual behavior; contraception; gender and labor markets; and interdisciplinary integration.

Dana R. Fisher is in the sociology department at the University of Maryland. She is the author of *Activism, Inc.: How the Outsourcing of Grassroots Campaigns Is Strangling Progressive Politics in America.*

Jessie Ford is in the sociology program at New York University. Her research interests include gender, sexuality, and sexual and reproductive health.

Hilary Levey Friedman is an affiliate at the Harvard Kennedy School of Government. She is the author of *Playing to Win: Raising Children in a Competitive Culture.*

Donna R. Gabaccia is in the history department at the University of Toronto–Scarborough. She is the coauthor (with Katherine Donato) of *Gender and Migration: From the Slave Trade Era to Our Own Global Times.*

Anne T. Gallagher is an advisor to the United Nations and author of *The International Law of Human Trafficking.*

Joshua Gamson is in the sociology department at the University of San Francisco. He is the author of *Modern Families: Stories of Extraordinary Journeys to Kinship.*

Amanda M. Gengler is in the sociology department at Wake Forest University. She studies illness, emotions, and the reproduction of inequalities.

Naomi Gerstel is in the sociology department at the University of Massachusetts, Amherst. She is a coauthor of *Unequal Time* and coeditor of *Families at Work: Expanding the Boundaries.*

Amin Ghaziani is in the sociology department at the University of British Columbia. He is author of *There Goes the Gayborhood?*

Sarah Halpern-Meekin is in the department of human development and family studies in the School of Human Ecology at the University of Wisconsin, Madison. She is the coauthor (with Kathryn Edin, Laura Tach, and Jennifer Sykes) of *It's Not Like I'm Poor: How Working Families Make Ends Meet in a Post-Welfare World.*

Joshua A. Hendrix is a research criminologist at RTI International. He studies policing and adolescent development, including why some adolescents abstain from delinquency.

Adam L. Horowitz is a postdoctoral fellow at the Edmond J. Safra Center for Ethics at Tel Aviv University. His scholarship examines how genetic technologies are changing the nature of how ethno-racial membership is evaluated.

Matthew W. Hughey is in the sociology department at the University of Connecticut. He is the author, most recently, of *The White Savior Film: Content, Critics, and Consumption.*

Marcus Anthony Hunter is in the sociology department at the University of California, Los Angeles. He is author of *Black Citymakers: How* The Philadelphia Negro *Changed Urban America.*

Lorien Jasny is in the department of politics at the University of Exeter.

Tania M. Jenkins is in the department of sociology and the Center for Health and Social Sciences (CHeSS) at the University of Chicago. She studies medical sociology and professional stratification.

Tomás R. Jiménez is in the department of sociology and the program on comparative studies in race and ethnicity at Stanford University. He is the author of *The Other Side of Assimilation: How Immigrants Are Changing American Life*.

Richard D. Kahlenberg is a senior fellow at the Century Foundation and the coauthor of *A Better Affirmative Action: State Universities that Created Alternatives to Racial Preferences*.

Sarah Esther Lageson is in the Rutgers University-Newark School of Justice. She is the coauthor of *Give Methods a Chance* (with Kyle Green).

Annette Lareau is in the sociology department at the University of Pennsylvania and is a former president of the American Sociological Association. The author of *Unequal Childhoods*, she is writing a practical guide for doing ethnographic research.

Edna Ledesma is a lecturer and research fellow at the University of Texas at Austin School of Architecture in the urban design program. She studies city design, planning, public spaces, housing and dwelling, hybrid space, incrementalism, and human geography.

Caroline W. Lee is in the anthropology and sociology department at Lafayette College. She is the author of *Do-It-Yourself Democracy: The Rise of the Public Engagement Industry*.

Jennifer Lee is in the sociology department at Columbia University. She is the author most recently of *The Asian American Achievement Paradox* (with Min Zhou).

Jooyoung Lee is in the department of sociology at the University of Toronto. He is a senior fellow in the Yale University Urban Ethnography Project and the author of *Blowin' Up: Rap Dreams in South Central*.

Michael J. Lovaglia is in the department of sociology at the University of Iowa. He is the author of *Knowing People: The Personal Use of Social Psychology*.

Janice McCabe is in the department of sociology at Dartmouth College. She is the author of *Connecting in College: How Friendship Networks Matter for Academic and Social Success*.

Mark McCormack is in the sociology department at Durham University, England. He is the author of *The Declining Significance of Homophobia: How Teenage Boys Are Redefining Masculinity and Heterosexuality*.

Michael A. Messner is a professor of sociology and gender studies at the University of Southern California. He is the author of *Some Men: Feminist Allies and the Movement to End Violence against Women* (with Max A. Greenberg and Tal Peretz).

Shehzad Nadeem is in the department of sociology at Lehman College and the Viewpoints editor at *Contexts*. He is the author of *Dead Ringers: How Outsourcing Is Changing the Way Indians Understand Themselves*.

Brian K. Obach is in the sociology department at the State University of New York at New Paltz. He is the author of *Organic Struggle: The Sustainable Agriculture Movement in the United States*.

Freeden Oeur is in the sociology department at Tufts University. He studies urban schools and the emotional lives of young men.

Paolo Parigi is in the department of sociology at Stanford University. Parigi is interested in social networks, trust, and cooperation.

Toby L. Parcel is in the sociology and anthropology department at North Carolina State University. Her current work focuses on families, schools and children. She is replicating the Wake survey in other cities.

C. J. Pascoe is in the sociology department at the University of Oregon. She is the author of *Dude, You're a Fag: Masculinity and Sexuality in High School*.

Silvia Pasquetti is in the department of sociology at Newcastle University. She studies displacement, refugees, and refugee camps.

Jennifer Pierce is in the department of American studies at the University of Minnesota. She is the author of *Racing for Innocence: Whiteness, Gender, and the Backlash Against Affirmative Action*.

Laurence Ralph is in African and African-American studies and anthropology at Harvard University. He is the author of *Renegade Dreams: Living through Injury in Gangland Chicago*.

Aliya Hamid Rao is a postdoctoral fellow at the Clayman Institute for Gender Research at Stanford University. Her areas of interest include gender work, family, emotions, qualitative methods, and religion.

Megan Reid is at the University of Wisconsin's Institute for Research on Poverty. She currently works on projects that examine and/or evaluate marriage and fatherhood programs, incarcerated parent reentry, racial disparities in social service delivery, and the relationship between housing family formation.

Craig Reinarman is a professor of sociology and legal studies at the University of California, Santa Cruz. His most recent book is *Expanding Addiction: Critical Essays*, edited with Robert Granfield.

Shalini Reddy is in the department of internal medicine at the University of Chicago. She is a hospitalist in the Section of Hospital Medicine.

Oliver Roeder is a senior writer at FiveThirtyEight, a blogger for *The Economist*, and a former fellow at the Brennan Center for Justice at NYU.

Amy Schalet is in the sociology department at the University of Massachusetts Amherst. She is the author of *Not Under My Roof: Parents, Teens, and the Culture of Sex*.

Kristen Schilt is in the department of sociology at the University of Chicago. She is the author of *Just One of the Guys? Transgender Men and the Persistence of Gender Inequality*.

Juliet B. Schor is a visiting professor at Harvard University's Radcliffe Institute. She is the author of *Plenitude: The New Economics of True Wealth*.

Howard Schuman is an emeritus professor of sociology at the University of Michigan. He is the author of *Meaning and Method in Polls and Surveys*.

Amy Scott is the education correspondent for American Public Media's *Marketplace* and the producer and director of the new documentary film *Oyler*. Learn more at oylerdocumentary.com.

Elena Shih is in the American studies department at Brown University. She studies the moral and political economies of human trafficking in China, Thailand, and the United States.

Jennifer M. Silva is in the sociology and anthropology department at Bucknell University. She is the author of *Coming Up Short: Working-Class Adulthood in an Age of Uncertainty*.

John D. Skrentny is codirector of the Center for Comparative Immigration Studies and in the sociology department at the University of California, San Diego. He is the author of *After Civil Rights: Racial Realism in the New American Workplace*.

R. Tyson Smith is in the sociology department at Muhlenberg College. He is the author of *Fighting for Recognition: Identity, Masculinity, and the Act of Violence in Professional Wrestling*.

Randy Stoecker is in the rural sociology department at the University of Wisconsin–Madison. He is the author of *Research Methods for Community Change*.

Jessi Streib is in the sociology department at Duke University. She is the author of *The Power of the Past: Understanding Cross-Class Marriages*.

Esther Sullivan is in the sociology department at the University of Colorado. She has an interest in urban sociology, poverty, and inequality.

Brian Sweeney is in the sociology department at Long Island University Post. His teaching and research focus on gender and sexuality among young adults.

Jennifer Sykes is in James Madison College, Department of Social Relations and Policy, at Michigan State University. She is the coauthor of *It's Not Like I'm Poor: How Working Families Make Ends Meet in a Post-Welfare World* (with Sarah Halpern-Meekin, Kathryn Edin, and Laura Tach).

Laura Tach is in the department of policy analysis and management in the College of Human Ecology at Cornell University. She is the coauthor of *It's Not Like I'm Poor: How Working Families Make Ends Meet in a Post-Welfare World* (with Sarah Halpern-Meekin, Kathryn Edin, and Jennifer Sykes).

Andrew J. Taylor is in the political science department in the school of public and international affairs at North Carolina State University. His current work focuses on Congress, elections, and political attitudes.

Steven W. Thrasher is in the American studies program at New York University and a weekly columnist for the *Guardian*. In 2012, he was named Journalist of the Year by the National Gay and Lesbian Journalists Association.

Donald Tomaskovic-Devey is in the sociology department at the University of Massachusetts, Amherst. He studies the sources, consequences, and challenges to racial and gender inequality.

Van C. Tran is in the department of sociology at Columbia University. He studies immigrant assimilation, neighborhood gentrification, and social inequality.

Zulema Valdez is in the sociology department at the University of California, Merced. She is the author of *The New Entrepreneurs: How Race, Class, and Gender Shape American Enterprise*.

Jody Agius Vallejo is in the sociology department at the University of Southern California. She is the author of *Barrios to Burbs: The Making of the Mexican-American Middle Class*.

Sudhir Venkatesh is in the sociology department at Columbia University. He is the author of *Gang Leader for a Day* and *Off the Books*.

Janet Vertesi is in the department of sociology at Princeton University. She is the author of *Seeing Like a Rover: How Robots, Teams, and Images Craft Knowledge of Mars*.

Lisa Wade is in the department of sociology at Occidental College. She is the author of *American Hookup* and, with Myra Marx Ferree, *Gender: Ideas, Interactions, Institutions*.

Joseph Waggle is in the sociology program at the University of Maryland and is in the program for society and the environment.

Edward T. Walker is in the department of sociology at the University of California, Los Angeles. He is the author of *Grassroots for Hire: Public Affairs Consultants in American Democracy*.

Patricia Warren is in the college of criminology and criminal justice at Florida State University. She studies racial disparity in crime and justice outcomes.

Niobe Way is in the applied psychology department at New York University. She is the past president of the Society for Research on Adolescence and the author of *Deep Secrets: Boys' Friendships and the Crisis of Connection*.

Ronald Weitzer is in the sociology department at George Washington University. He is the author of *Legalizing Prostitution: From Illicit Vice to Lawful Business*.

Laurel Westbrook is in the department of sociology at Grand Valley State University in Allendale, Michigan. Her multimethod studies revolve around the inner workings of the sex/gender/sexuality system.

Owen Whooley is in the sociology department and is a senior fellow at the Robert Wood Johnson Foundation Center for Health Policy at the University of New Mexico.

Simon J. Williams is in the department of sociology at the University of Warwick. He is the author of *Sleep and Society: Sociological Ventures into the (Un)Known*.

Nicole Willms is in the department of sociology at Gonzaga University. Her research focuses on the representation, performance, and negotiation of gender, race, and class in American sports.